### What readers are saying about Newcomer's Handbooks:

I recently got a copy of your *Newcomer's Handbook for Chicago,* and wanted to let you know how invaluable it was for my move. I must have consulted it a dozen times a day preparing for my move. It helped me find my way around town, find a place to live, and so many other things. Thanks.
– Mike L.
Chicago, Illinois

Excellent reading (*Newcomer's Handbook for San Francisco and the Bay Area*) ... balanced and trustworthy. One of the very best guides if you are considering moving/relocation. Way above the usual tourist crap.
– Gunnar E.
Stockholm, Sweden

I was very impressed with the latest edition of the *Newcomer's Handbook for Los Angeles*. It is well organized, concise and up-to-date. I would recommend this book to anyone considering a move to Los Angeles.
– Jannette L.
Attorney Recruiting Administrator for a large Los Angeles law firm

I recently moved to Atlanta from San Francisco, and LOVE the *Newcomer's Handbook for Atlanta*. It has been an invaluable resource—it's helped me find everything from a neighborhood in which to live to the local hardware store. I look something up in it everyday, and know I will continue to use it to find things long after I'm no longer a newcomer. And if I ever decide to move again, your book will be the first thing I buy for my next destination.
– Courtney R.
Atlanta, Georgia

In looking to move to the Boston area, a potential employer in that area gave me a copy of the *Newcomer's Handbook for Boston*. It's a great book that's very comprehensive, outlining good and bad points about each neighborhood in the Boston area. Very helpful in helping me decide where to move.
– no name given (online submit form)

# TABLE OF CONTENTS

1 **Introduction**
   *Chicago history, geography, reputation, local lingo; getting around*
   12   Map: Chicagoland
13 **Neighborhoods**
   15   **Chicago Street Address Locator**
   16   **County Basics**
   18   Map: North and West Side Neighborhoods
   20   **The City of Chicago**
      20   **North**
         20   Cityfront/Streeterville
         22   River North/River West
         24   Gold Coast
         26   Old Town
         27   Ranch Triangle/Clybourn Corridor
         29   Lincoln Park
         32   DePaul/Lincoln Park West
         34   Wrigleyville/Lakeview
         36   North Center/St. Ben's/Roscoe Village
         38   Ravenswood/Lincoln Square
         41   Edgewater
         44   Andersonville
         46   (East) Rogers Park
         47   West Rogers Park/West Ridge
      49   **West**
         49   Albany Park
         51   Logan Square (West Town)
         53   Wicker Park and Bucktown
         56   Ukrainian Village/East Village
         58   Taylor Street/University of Illinois–Chicago
         60   Pilsen/Little Village
      62   **South**
         62   South Loop
   63   Map: South Side
         66   Bronzeville/The Gap/Douglas
         69   Bridgeport/Chinatown
         71   Hyde Park/Kenwood
         74   Woodlawn
         76   South Shore
         78   Beverly/Morgan Park

v

*81* **North & Northwest Suburbs**
    81   Evanston
*82* *Map: North and Northwest Suburbs*
    86   Skokie
    88   Wilmette
    90   Kenilworth/Winnetka/Glencoe
    92   Highland Park
    93   Deerfield
    95   Northbrook
    97   Arlington Heights
    99   Schaumburg
    102  Des Plaines
    103  Rosemont
    105  Additional North/Northwest Suburbs

*106* **West Suburbs**
    106  Oak Park
    107  La Grange Park/Brookfield/Western Springs/La Grange
*108* *Map: West Suburbs*
    112  Downers Grove
    113  Wheaton
    115  Naperville
    117  Bolingbrook
    118  Additional Western Suburbs

*119* **South Suburbs**
    119  Blue Island
*120* *Map: South Suburbs*
    122  Burbank
    124  Evergreen Park
    125  Oak Lawn
    127  Oak Forest
    129  Orland Park
    130  Tinley Park
    132  Additional Southern Suburbs

**133** **Finding a Place to Live**
*Suggestions on renting or buying a home in Chicago and suburbs, including classifieds, online and other services, details about deposits and claims, landlord/tenant issues, insurance; houses, condos, and co-ops, real estate brokers, other resources*

**151 Moving and Storage**
*Truck rentals, movers, recommendations, storage, children, moving-related taxes*

**161 Money Matters**
*Banking, credit cards, federal, state, and local taxes, starting or moving a business*

**169 Getting Settled**
*Utilities, garbage and recycling; automobiles: licenses, registration, parking, emissions, insurance; parking: permits, tickets; voter registration; passports; library cards; broadcast and print media; finding a physician; pet laws and services; safety and crime*

**195 Helpful Services**
*Domestic services, mail, automobile repair, car winterizing, consumer protection, legal mediation/assistance, social security, services for the disabled, international newcomers, gay and lesbian life, police complaints*

**209 Childcare and Education**
*Childcare facilities and agencies, nanny and au pair services, child safety and resources; public and private schools, special education, homeschooling; higher education*

**237 Shopping**
*Shopping districts, malls, department stores, specialty stores, online shopping, second-hand shopping; food: grocery stores, farmers' markets, BYOB restaurants, ethnic districts*

**253 Cultural Life**
*Tickets, classical and contemporary music and dance, theater, film, comedy, clubs, museums and galleries; literary life: bookstores and libraries; culture for kids*

**277 Sports and Recreation**
*Professional and college sports; participant sports and recreational activities; health clubs*

**299 Greenspaces and Beaches**
*City parks, dog-friendly parks, park districts, fountains, nature centers, nature and wildlife gardens, cemeteries, forest preserves, beaches, state parks, national lakeshore*

**319 Weather and Climate**
*Seasons, weather statistics, insects*

**325 Getting Involved**
*Worship; volunteering; meeting people*

**345 Transportation**
*Getting around by car, by bike, by public transportation; trains and buses; airports and airlines*

**359 Temporary Lodgings**
*Hotels and motels, B&Bs, hostels/clubs, YMCAs, summer only, accessible accommodations*

**367 Quick Getaways**
*Day and weekend trips in Illinois and to Indiana, Michigan, and Wisconsin*

**375 A Chicago Year**
*Annual calendar of events*

**383 A Chicago Reading List**
*Fiction and nonfiction titles related to Chicago*

**389 Useful Phone Numbers & Websites**

**401 Index**

**417 About the Author**

# NEWCOMERS' HANDBOOK
# FOR MOVING TO AND LIVING IN CHICAGO

# INTRODUCTION

WELCOME TO CHICAGO—AND CONGRATULATIONS! YOU ARE NOW living in the best-kept secret in the United States. What's the secret about Chicago? Simply that it is one of the most livable big cities in America. With almost 600 parks, 29 miles of gorgeous lakefront, 24 beaches, six golf courses, and tennis courts throughout the city, you are sure to find some way to while away a summer day. Couple that with Chicago's cultural and ethnic diversity, officially celebrated in dozens of annual festivals, fairs and parades, and it's easy to see why many are happy to call Chicago home. And if the out-of-doors doesn't entice you, Chicago's shopping and cultural opportunities will. From its famous Magnificent Mile to its neighborhood boutiques, suburban malls and designer outlets, Chicago is a shopping addict's nirvana, with enough variety to please the pickiest fashionista. More interested in Italian opera than Italian shoes? Chicago is the theatrical and artistic Goliath of the Midwest, home to the world-renowned Lyric Opera of Chicago, the Chicago Symphony Orchestra, the Art Institute of Chicago, Ballet Chicago, the Steppenwolf and Goodman theater companies, the University of Chicago, Columbia College, Northwestern University, and hundreds of other art galleries, museums, dance and theater companies, arts organizations and schools, pop music venues, performance art spaces, comedy clubs…

Word is out, though: as the 2010 census reported, the Chicago metro area population weighed in at an all-time high of 9.8 million. Chicago's varied and deep economy, its cultural diversity, and its beautification and gentrification are even luring former residents who left decades ago. With their suburban nests empty, many ex-Chicagoans are now coming back to live where the action is.

So if you have already taken the first step and decided that Chicago is the place for you, many would agree that you have made a great choice. If you have bought this book hoping to find out more about the ins and outs of living in Chicago, read on. We offer you details about city living, descriptions of Chicago neighborhoods and suburbs, house- or apartment-hunting tips, information on signing leases or finding a real estate agent, and much more.

## CHICAGO'S HISTORY

Native Americans called the area around the mouth of the Chicago River "Checau-gou," possibly after the strong-smelling wild onions that grew there. In 1673, a Jesuit missionary, Fr. Jacques Marquette, and Louis Jolliet, a Canadian mapmaker and explorer, were the first Europeans known to come upon the future site of Chicago. Here they encountered three Native American villages with a combined estimated population of 6,500. The explorers were treated well by the natives: a peace pipe was extended, and when the Frenchmen left, six hundred natives escorted them on their way. Their journey took them down the Mississippi River to the mouth of the Arkansas River before they turned back due to reports of hostile natives and Spaniards farther south. Marquette and two companions spent the winter of 1674–75 in a shelter on the south branch of the Chicago River at what is now Damen Avenue. A cross at the bottom of the Damen Avenue Bridge marks the site.

Chicago's position near an easily portaged moraine, providing access to the Mississippi River on the west, made it a popular transit point with Native Americans and later with European explorers. The famed Chicago Portage National Historic Site marks the head of the I&M Canal National Heritage Corridor in a Cook County Forest Preserve, near 45th Street and Harlem Avenue.

By 1679, another French explorer, Robert de La Salle, had built a small outpost in the vicinity of the southwest suburb now known as Palos Hills. Little is known about the Chicago area between 1700 and 1763, when the region passed into the hands of the British after the French and Indian War. It wasn't until after the Revolutionary War, when the new country began to turn its attention westwards, that Chicago was really established. In 1779, Haitian trapper and fur trader Jean Baptiste Pointe du Sable and his Indian wife became the first permanent settlers here, establishing a fur-trading post on the left bank of the Chicago River near the present site of the Equitable Building. In 1804, the federal government completed Fort Dearborn at the intersection of present-day Wacker Drive and Michigan Avenue.

Illinois formally joined the Union in 1818. In 1830, the construction began on the Illinois-Michigan Canal, which connected the Chicago River with the Mississippi River. The canal, completed in 1848, the same year as the first locomotives arrived in the Chicago area, positioned Chicago to become the crossroads of the nation. Chicago was incorporated as a town in 1833 and as a city in 1837. In 1848, 82 merchants who recognized the need for a centralized marketplace and a way to ensure the timely execution of agricultural orders joined forces to create one of the world's great financial institutions, the Chicago Board of Trade. The Union Stockyards opened on Chicago's South Side in

1865, organizing the many small meat operations throughout the area. This, combined with the extensive rail network and the introduction of the refrigerated train car, put Chicago on the map as the nation's meatpacker for nearly 100 years.

Chicago's stupendous growth was temporarily cut short on October 8, 1871, when disaster struck. Starting on Chicago's West Side, the Great Fire destroyed most of the city. The fire seems to have begun in a West Side barn owned by Irish immigrant Mrs. Catherine O'Leary. The famous allegation that Mrs. O'Leary's cow started the conflagration by kicking over a lantern was invented by a creative reporter in 1893 but endures in the popular imagination. (Contemporary historians believe the real culprits may have been men, including Mrs. O'Leary's son, who were gambling in the barn.) In any case, the fire spread swiftly, and by midnight it had jumped to the south branch of the Chicago River. It raced through the downtown business district and the Near North sides before stopping three days later at Clark Street and Belden Avenue, a block south of Fullerton. As the fires dimmed, Chicagoans calculated the damage: 300 dead, 100,000 homeless, the entire central business district destroyed, and property losses of $200 million. Even the thickest safes and vaults could not escape the fire: over $1 million in currency was incinerated at the Custom House and Post Office alone.

Chicagoans dug in their heels and set to work to rebuild the more than two thousand acres known as the "Burnt District." Debris from the fire was pushed into the lake, making landfill for what is today much of Chicago's downtown lakefront. Shanties were quickly built on top of the town's ashes, and citizens vowed to rebuild their lost homes and businesses. One doughty businessman, Kerfoot Block, summed up hearty Chicagoans' post-fire attitude on a sign outside the shack that housed his newly opened real estate office: "All gone but wife, children and energy." The city's plight touched the hearts of many Americans: school children, civic organizations, and labor organizations from all over the country sent contributions totaling five million dollars.

Out of the rubble emerged one the country's finest architectural movements. The destruction of the old business district cleared the way for innovative East Coast architects, who rebuilt the city in a new design style that came to be known as the Chicago School. Daniel Burnham, Louis Sullivan, William Holabird, John Welborn Root, and a young Frank Lloyd Wright were instrumental in rebuilding the city in the decades following the Great Fire.

Following the Civil War, Chicago proved to be a popular destination for European immigrants and displaced Americans. Germans, Swedes, and Norwegians joined the Irish already present in Chicago. African-Americans, many of whom had abandoned Chicago in the years leading up to the Civil War due to its strict enforcement of the state's fugitive slave laws, returned to the city despite other residents' hostility toward their homecoming.

Between 1890 and 1910, waves of immigrants from across Europe contributed to the further growth of the city and added to its cacophony of tongues.

After World War I, in 1919, Prohibition went into effect. It was during this era, 1919–1933, that Chicago acquired its reputation as the gangster capital of the world. America's failed experiment with sobriety inspired most of the mob violence, sparked by turf wars over the lucrative trade in bootleg alcohol. The infamous 1929 St. Valentine's Day Massacre, which left seven dead in a North Clark Street garage, stemmed from a conflict between a North Side Irish gang led by Bugs Moran and a South Side Italian gang led by Al Capone. Though Moran himself was lucky enough not to be at the garage that morning, he retired from bootlegging shortly thereafter.

The first half of the 20th century saw the arrival of hundreds of thousands of African-Americans from the South, who, like newcomers from across the Atlantic, came north to escape political oppression and economic deprivation. The second half of the 20th century brought another wave of newcomers, primarily from Spanish-speaking countries, especially Mexico.

According to the 2010 census, 33% of Chicago's population is African-American, 29% is white, and 26% is Hispanic. In spite of the city's racial mix, there's no denying that Chicago remains highly segregated, notably by race and economics. Thus the North Side is primarily white and affluent, the West Side is more Hispanic, and the South Side is more African-American, and poorer. Unlike years past, however, the city is tolerant and cosmopolitan, with the many diverse communities that live here making one rich and dynamic human tapestry.

The suburbs remain a different, much whiter story, though census data and countless press reports have confirmed that many suburban areas, especially inner-ring suburbs like Berwyn, Evergreen Park, and Blue Island, have become increasingly popular with minorities and recent immigrants. Among the farther reaches of the suburbs, diversity has also made great strides in communities like Palatine, Schaumburg, Wheaton, and Naperville. Though few towns are all white any longer, people of similar ethnicities often tend to cluster together. Of Chicago's suburbs, for example, southwestern communities are most heavily African-American, Bridgeview is known for its large Middle Eastern population, and the north and northwest suburbs have seen especially significant rises in the number of Asian and Hispanic residents.

## CHICAGO'S GEOGRAPHY

While hills are virtually nonexistent in most of the city of Chicago (thanks to a series of glacial lakes that covered the area for several thousand years), its waterways offer a striking natural reminder of the days before concrete. Most of Chicago sits on marshy soil, only a few feet above the water level of Lake Michigan. Just a few miles west of the lake, parallel to what is now Harlem Avenue, is a natural subcontinental drainage divide. To the east of this divide, rivers drained into Lake Michigan and the St. Lawrence River; to the west of the divide, rivers—including the Des Plaines and Illinois—flowed to the Mississippi and onward to the Gulf of Mexico. When the water levels were high, the two water systems nearly became one, and boats could easily navigate between the two systems. But when the water levels were low, the area was a dense marshland full of leeches and mosquitoes. Portaging during late summer required dragging boats through waist-high muck. The solution was to dig a canal between the Chicago and Des Plaines rivers. In 1834, soldiers from Fort Dearborn, with the help of Chicago's new Irish and Norwegian immigrants, cut a canal in the sandbar that blocked the mouth of the Chicago River, giving traders direct access to the Chicago River. While the creation of a navigable harbor improved water traffic, an increasing Chicago population along the riverbanks caused major health problems.

As the turn of the century approached, Chicago's port was the busiest in the United States, and the population grew at an unprecedented rate. The city's many efforts to create a reliable sewage system continuously failed to meet the needs of its exploding population. The problem: sewage flowed from the Chicago River into Lake Michigan, which was the source of the city's drinking water. Epidemics of typhoid, cholera, and other diseases killed thousands. Eventually the mounting deaths from typhoid created a public health problem so serious that the Legislature was called upon to devise a permanent solution to Chicago's sanitation problems.

In 1892, Sanitary District engineers began to dig the Chicago Drainage Canal, later renamed the Sanitary and Ship Canal. This new canal would take waste away from the Lake and towards the Mississippi River via the Des Plaines and Illinois rivers. The Sanitary and Ship Canal, designed as a continuous waterway to carry 10,000 cubic feet of water per second, would run 28 miles from the tip of the south branch of the Chicago River to the town of Lockport. Upon completion, eight years later, the Sanitary and Ship Canal measured 25 feet deep and 306 feet wide, larger than the Suez Canal in Egypt, and it represented the largest earth-moving project in the world. The 8,500 laborers included many African-Americans as well as recently arrived Poles. This project had its critics, though, and at the end of 1899, the State of Missouri sought an injunction to opening the Canal, fearing its use would pollute St. Louis' drinking water. Thus in January 1900, Sanitary District engineers, concerned about the possible termination of their project, secretly detonated the temporary dam that separated the Chicago River from the new canal. The result was the permanent reversal of the Chicago River, the world's first river to flow away from its mouth—still considered one of the seven engineering feats of the world. Ongoing sewage projects in the years to come diverted all sewage and storm overflow into the Sanitary and Ship Canal, virtually eliminating any outflow into the lake. By 1908, these and other measures helped to reduce Chicago's typhoid rate by 91%.

As Chicago continued to expand into suburban areas after WWII, the sewage system began to show signs of strain, especially after rainstorms. By the 1970s, raw sewage was being dispersed directly into local rivers on the average of once every four days. Fearing a repeat of history, the City devised a new plan: the installation of an innovative new "Deep Tunnel System" that would divert and store all overflow storm water and sewage to storage reservoirs until treatment plants could process it. Today, Chicago continues to revise its sanitation techniques, upgrade its plants, and extend its reach. The Chicago Department of Sewers is responsible for more than 4,400 miles of sewer pipe, 230,000 catch basins and 340,000 catch basins and manholes. The Chicago River, once devoid of wildlife, now has more than 70 species of fish, and canoes, last seen on the river in 1850, now travel freely.

## CHICAGO'S REPUTATION

Although Chicago was for many years a Daley fiefdom under Richard M. Daley ("da Mayor"), the eldest son of the late machine strongman Mayor Richard J. Daley, Chicagoans moved into the post-Daley era by electing Rahm Emanuel, former chief of staff to President Obama, as mayor in 2011.

There are some things that the newcomer to Chicago needs to learn right away in order not to be recognized as an out-of-towner. First and foremost, Chicago's rapid transit system of elevated and subway trains is the 'L,' which is short for "elevated." Even the train lines that do go underground are referred to as part of the 'L.' An additional dead giveaway that you aren't from Chicago: calling "Belmont" "Belmont Avenue." Chicagoans mention roads only by their first names and will generally look confused if you ask, "Is that Halsted Street, Avenue, or Road?" No matter what the map says, the street is just "Halsted."

Next is "the Loop," which, strictly speaking, means the portion of Chicago's downtown business and retail district encircled by elevated train tracks that run along Wabash Avenue on the east, Lake Street on the north, Wells Street on the west, and Van Buren Street on the south. However, generally speaking, the Loop is any part of the downtown area south of the Chicago River. This area may also be referred to as "downtown," but beware: suburbanites often use the term "downtown" to refer to anything in Chicago. What you will find in the Loop are office towers, terrific modern architecture, and the bustling shopping district on State Street, anchored by the beloved, architecturally notable department store that, despite storms of local protest, was converted from the venerable local standby Marshall Field's into a Macy's.

"The Magnificent Mile," the stretch of North Michigan Avenue north of the Chicago River to Oak Street, is the city's premier shopping area. It boasts many international retail stores and shopping malls, including Water Tower Place and

# INTRODUCTION

Chicago Place. If you're a shopper (or just a people watcher), walking here is always a pleasure.

Although the Second City comedy troupe still performs at its Old Town location, Chicago is no longer the second city. Population-wise, it sits third, behind New York and Los Angeles. And O'Hare International Airport continues to come in second to Atlanta's Hartsfield Airport for the title of busiest airport in the country.

Chicago, home of the first skyscraper, has several of the world's tallest buildings, including The Willis Tower, located outside the southwest corner of the Loop; the Aon Center—a white neoclassical building at the north end of Grant Park on Randolph Street; the John Hancock Center, at the north end of Michigan Avenue, built in the late 1960s; and the most recent addition to the list, the Trump International Hotel and Tower, completed in 2009.

## LOCAL LINGO

So there's a sandwich called "Italian Beef" on the menu, and you decide to try it. "Wet or dry?" asks the kid behind the counter. "Sweet or hot?" What in the world is he talking about? Like most American cities, Chicago has its fair share of specialized lingo. If what you hear on radio traffic reports doesn't match up with the Interstate numbers on your map, or you don't know the difference between smelt and chads, read on.

**Alderman:** City council member, elected by ward

**The Bean:** Nickname for the popular, stainless steel, kidney-bean shaped Anish Kapoor sculpture in Millennium Park.

**Beef:** Italian beef sandwich. Thinly sliced beef piled between halves of an oblong Italian roll. When you order a "beef," you'll be asked "wet or dry?" A "wet" will be dipped in au jus and served dripping. You can also ask for some au jus—usually called "gravy" or "juice" here—on the side. If you're asked, "Sweet or hot?" they're talking about peppers.

**The Blues Brothers:** 1980 comedy, starring John Belushi and Dan Aykroyd, filmed in Chicago, and a great source of pride for many residents.

**Booted:** To get booted means that the Chicago parking police have locked one of your car's wheels in an immobilizing yellow metal device (called a Denver Boot)—punishment for those delinquent in paying previous parking violations.

**Boys Town:** The bar-lined section of Lakeview between Belmont and Addison on Halsted known as Chicago's center of gay culture.

**Brat:** Rhymes with "trot." Short for bratwurst.

**Brewski:** beer.

**The Cal-Sag:** The Calumet Saginaw Channel, a South Side waterway.

**Cheezborger, Cheezborger:** Phrase immortalized by John Belushi in a *Saturday Night Live* sketch about a burger place that serves only cheeseburgers,

Pepsi ("No Coke. Pepsi,") and "cheeps" (fries). Chicago-native Belushi based the sketch on the original downtown location of the Billy Goat Tavern, now a small local chain. The real Billy Goat serves only a few more menu items than the joint in the sketch—and brewskis, of course.

**Chicagoland:** Chicago and its suburbs. Synonym for "Greater Chicago."

**Chicago-style bungalow:** One-story single-family home of a design common to many of Chicago's older neighborhoods. Special tax breaks and other subsidies have been instituted to help preserve some of Chicago's heavily bungalowed districts.

**Chicago-style pizza:** Usually refers to deep-dish pizza such as that originated by Chicago's Pizzeria Uno. However, most Chicago pizza joints serve up a luscious thin-crust pizza as well as, or instead of, the deep-dish variety, and some natives will viciously argue that thin-crust is the *real* Chicago style.

**Chicago-style hot dog:** The best, most nutritionally complete incarnation of hot-dog-dom. In its purest form, with "everything," this means an all-beef "Vienna Beef" hot dog, nestled in a steamed poppy-seed bun, slathered with mustard and topped with diced tomatoes, onions, and cucumbers. This full-meal-in-a-bun is usually finished with a generous sprinkling of celery salt and a dill pickle spear tucked right into the bun. "Sport peppers" (known elsewhere as hot peppers), dark-green sweet relish, sauerkraut, and grilled onions are usual options. Beware asking for ketchup or fancy mustards: both are considered insults to the perfection of a good Chicago dog, and some traditionalist hot-dog-stand proprietors will proudly announce that, although ketchup is available for their French fries, customers themselves will have to go the extra mile of sullying their dogs with the syrupy red stuff.

**Chi-Town:** Chicago nickname.

**The City of Big Shoulders:** Chicago

**Collar counties:** The Chicagoland counties that surround Cook County.

**Crosstown classic:** The annual match-up between North Side baseball darlings the Cubs and their South Side rivals the White Sox.

**Cubbies:** Affectionate nickname for the perpetually losing North Side baseball team.

**Da:** The definite article "the" as pronounced by some Chicago oldtimers, primarily on the South Side. Popularized by a *Saturday Night Live* sketch that referred to Da Bears (the Chicago Bears), Da Bulls (the Chicago Bulls), and Da Coach (former Bears coach Mike Ditka). Also used by some to refer to "Da Mayor."

**The Dan Ryan:** The stretch of I-90/94 between south of downtown and north of the Chicago skyway.

**Dawg:** Hot dog.

**The Drive:** Lake Shore Drive, which runs along Lake Michigan on the city's eastern edge.

**The Edens:** I-94 between north Chicago and the Wisconsin border.

# INTRODUCTION

**The Eisenhower/The Ike:** The I-290 or Eisenhower Expressway.
**Flat:** An apartment unit or rental. Buildings with two units are called "two-flats," buildings with three are called "three-flats," and so on.
**Gapers' Delay:** Term used widely in Chicago media to describe traffic delays caused by other drivers slowly or stopping to "gape" at accidents.
**IDOT:** Pronounced "Eye-dot." Frequently used abbreviation for Illinois Department of Transportation, the fine folks whose construction efforts bring you months of traffic delays during the warm season.
**Inbound/outbound on the ...(name of highway or Lake Shore Drive):** Terms used to discuss traffic. Inbound means heading toward Chicago proper; outbound means heading from the city toward the suburbs in any direction.
**IPASS:** Pronounced "Eye-pass." A transponder system purchased to put in the car, which allows you to drive through "open road tollways" for half the price that it now costs to pay at tollbooths.
**Iron Mike:** Former Bears coach Mike Ditka.
**Juke:** To dance (used mainly on the South Side).
**The Junction:** Intersection of the Kennedy and Edens expressways north of the city. Commonly referred to in media traffic reports and on LCD highway signs announcing delays.
**The Kennedy:** The stretch of I-90/94 expressway north of downtown and south of the suburbs.
**Lake effect snow:** Snow caused by Chicago's proximity to Lake Michigan. (Sections of the city near the lake often get inches when outlying areas get mere flurries.)
**LSD:** Abbreviation for Lake Shore Drive, popularized by Chicago trio Aliotta-Haynes-Jeremiah in a 1970s pop song.
**The Mag Mile:** Shorthand for the Magnificent Mile, a portion of Michigan Avenue north of the Chicago River famous for upscale shopping.
**Maxwell Street:** Slang for Maxwell Street Market, a popular open-air Sunday market that is no longer located on Maxwell Street (now you'll find it on Canal Street, south of Roosevelt Road).
**North Side:** North of the Loop.
**Polish:** A Polish sausage—an alternative to the usual Vienna beef Chicago dawg.
**Pop:** Not soda. Not cola. Hereabouts, soft drinks are "pop."
**The Rock 'n' Roll McDonald's:** A tourist attraction known to all natives: one of the world's busiest McDonald's, located at 600 North Clark Street, famous for its rock 'n' roll–memorabilia theme.
**Sammich:** Translation: sandwich.
**Second City:** Nickname for Chicago. Also the comedy troupe/club/training ground which birthed both *SCTV* and legions of comedy legends including Joan Rivers, Bill Murray, Dan Aykroyd, Gilda Radner, John Candy, Shelley

Long, Mike Meyers, Chris Farley, Tina Fey, Steve Carell, Amy Sedaris, and, of course, the Belushi brothers.

**Six Corners:** Any of many Chicago spots where three avenues intersect, e.g., the North Center intersection of Ashland, Belmont, and Lincoln, or the Wicker Park intersection of North, Milwaukee, and Damen.

**Smelt:** Small, seasonally available fish, usually served whole, deep-fried, in a basket, accompanied by lemon and tartar sauce. Look for them in downtown restaurants in April.

**South Side:** South of the Loop.

**The Stevenson:** I-55 Expressway within Chicago.

**Streets and San:** The Department of Streets and Sanitation, responsible for garbage pick-up.

**The Taste:** The Taste of Chicago, an annual food-oriented Grant Park festival that takes place during the month of July.

**The Times:** The *Chicago Sun-Times*.

**The Trib:** The *Chicago Tribune*.

**UIC:** The University of Illinois at Chicago.

**UC:** The University of Chicago.

**Valpo:** The Northeast Indiana city of Valparaiso, or the University of the same name.

**The Windy City:** Yet another Chicago nickname. While many claim this refers to the weather, experts insist that Chicago's notoriously "windy" politicians were the real source of this old nickname.

## GETTING AROUND IN CHICAGO

Unlike some large cities in the United States, Chicago offers its residents a variety of transportation options, from bus to subway to commuter rail and automobile.

Our advice: *if possible, take public transportation*. Negotiating the Kennedy, or any of the other major expressways, especially at rush hour, can be a true exercise in patience. The Chicago Transportation Authority's (CTA's) rail transit system is safe, reliable, and fast. The only negative is that unlike, say, the New York City subway system, the 'L' is not comprehensive. Where the 'L' does not reach, buses will be an option, but service can vary depending on location. The 'L' will get you cheaply and quickly to both O'Hare and Midway airports. Whether you are taking the 'L' or the bus, expect a cramped ride during rush hours. Despite intermittent threats of fare hikes and schedule cuts, the CTA still beats driving for affordability and convenience when heading anywhere in the central city.

If you are doing a suburb-to-city (or reverse) commute, Metra, the commuter railroad, is the way to go. It's reliable, comfortable, and affordable. Note to bike riders: bicycles are allowed on Metra trains only in off-peak hours and on weekends, and even then with restrictions. (See the Metra website, www.metrarail.com, for more details.)

If you're wondering whether you'll need a car to live in Chicago, the answer is, not if you live within a few-mile radius of the Loop. By and large, train service is better on the far North Side than the far South Side. The suburbs, with a few exceptions such as Evanston and Oak Park, were created with the automobile in mind. While a car is certainly convenient for some excursions, trains, buses, and taxis are all easily accessible for daily commuting, or for the trip home after a night out. Regular use of Metra, the CTA's 'L' or bus lines, and taxis should cost far less than monthly car payments and auto insurance, not to mention the headache and expense of parking. For more details on getting around Chicago, see the **Chicago Address Locator** in the **Neighborhoods** chapter, as well as the **Transportation** chapter.

# NEIGHBORHOODS

CHICAGO IS DIVIDED, ROUGHLY, INTO THREE PARTS: THE NORTH SIDE, the West Side, and the South Side. Each of these geographical sections contains a mosaic of neighborhoods divided at times by ethnicity and at other times by income. (Due to its location on Lake Michigan, Chicago has no official East Side, although parts of southeast Chicago on the Indiana border may be referred to as the East Side.)

Do not be overwhelmed by Chicago's size. Take it slowly. There's no need to memorize the whole city. Each neighborhood has its own world to explore. Find your niche, your neighborhood grocery store, coffee shop, bar, 'L' stop, book or music store, and you will begin to have a sense of belonging. A good way to get acquainted with some of Chicago's more historical neighborhoods is to take a guided tour. Check with **Chicago Greeter** (free tours led by volunteers, 312-744-8000, www.chicagogreeter.com) for more information.

Like any other big city, Chicago has its share of crime, and no neighborhood is completely safe. But, according to the Chicago Police Department, since 1991 overall crime has continued to decline. If you keep your eyes open and use common sense, you should have no problem getting around safely. There are neighborhoods that would be best to avoid, and for that reason we have profiled only those neighborhoods that are most likely to attract newcomers. Up-and-coming communities, those in the process of revitalization/gentrification, such as Pilsen and Edgewater, have been included. Since the publication of previous editions of the *Newcomer's Handbook® for Chicago*, areas such as the Kenmore-Winthrop corridor of Edgewater, which were reported to be crime-ridden, have made tremendous improvements.

A word about police protection in Chicago. The city is divided into 25 police districts that serve as neighborhood headquarters for beat and tactical officers. The 25 districts are grouped into four areas. If you need police for an emergency, dial 911. For non-emergencies, dial 311—outside the city, 311 can be accessed by dialing 312-744-5000. The Chicago Police Department has a comprehensive website that can help you locate your local police station and provide other information about the city's neighborhoods, their crime rates, and other police hotline numbers: portal.chicagopolice.org.

Chicago has a large immigrant population, and there are neighborhoods where it is possible to imagine you are in a different country. Some of the most notable on the north and northwest sides include an Asian (mainly Vietnamese and Chinese) community centered at the intersection of Argyle, Broadway, and Sheridan roads; a primarily Indian neighborhood with a mix of Jewish, Assyrian, Pakistani, Thai, Russian, Croatian, Syrian, and Nepalese residents, located east of Kedzie and west of Ravenswood along Devon Avenue; and a Korean neighborhood west of the Chicago River and east of the Edens Expressway, between Foster and Montrose Avenues. Southwest of the Loop is Pilsen, a Hispanic community located around 18th Street and west of Halsted Street. Just south of the South Loop neighborhood, you will find Chicago's small but bustling Chinatown, in the neighborhood of Bridgeport. Chicago Greeter (see above) offers tours through these and other ethnically or historically noteworthy neighborhoods.

This edition of the *Newcomer's Handbook® for Chicago* covers many of Chicago's neighborhoods and outlying communities, with particular emphasis on the areas that are most likely to attract newcomers. In Chicago proper we begin with the downtown neighborhoods, work our way north along the lake, then head west for neighborhoods that are northwest of the Loop. Next, we begin exploring the South Side with the rapidly changing South Loop area, and finally the suburbs, beginning with Evanston and going north before heading off to investigate the west and south suburbs. Look after each neighborhood profile for pertinent information such as area codes, ZIP codes, the nearest post offices, district police stations, local hospitals, public libraries, public schools, community publications (check **Newspapers and Magazines** in the **Getting Settled** chapter for contact information), and community resources. Also listed are the nearest rapid-transit stations and the major bus routes running through the neighborhoods. To get a handle on what you can expect to pay for an apartment, scan the rental classifieds in the newspaper of your choice—many opt for the *Chicago Reader*—or search online to learn about the price ranges in some of Chicago's popular neighborhoods. Traditionally, the priciest neighborhoods are due north of the Loop: Streeterville, River North, Old Town, Gold Coast, and Lincoln Park. Recently, though, some popular northwestern neighborhoods such as North Center, Lincoln Square, Bucktown, and Wicker Park have almost caught up. Comparable space and convenient location for rentals can be found for somewhat less, at least for now, in the booming South Loop neighborhood; those looking to buy will find housing prices in the South Loop cheaper than what can be found north of the Loop. The university neighborhoods of Rogers Park, Edgewater, North Center, and Hyde Park continue to offer a good selection of affordable student rental accommodations. Not so true in the DePaul/Lincoln Park West neighborhood; just west of Lincoln

Park, this area is becoming less affordable for the student set. (For more see the **Finding a Place to Live** chapter.)

If you're looking for interesting pictures of Chicago neighborhoods, check Carla Surratt's engaging website: www.picturingchicago.com.

As far as neighborhood boundaries go, the boundaries used in this book are basic guidelines, designed to make learning the city easier for newcomers. Once you get to know Chicago, you can debate and gerrymander neighborhood boundaries at your leisure. Some Chicagoans hang the popular Chicago neighborhood maps in their homes; as well as displaying civic pride, these are a great tool for getting to know the city better. Dreamtown Realty offers a poster-sized version of such a map, free: www.dreamtown.com/poster.

## CHICAGO STREET ADDRESS LOCATOR

It is nearly impossible to get lost in Chicago. City surveyors designed much of Chicago on a grid system; just check street signs for area cross streets, and you'll know how far you are from downtown Chicago. The system is planned at eight city blocks to the mile with major streets every half mile. Addresses are divided north and south by Madison Street, and east and west by State Street. The intersection of State and Madison streets is at the heart of the Loop: all north/south running streets are indicated as being either east or west of State Street; east/west streets, running parallel to Madison, are indicated as being north or south of Madison. So, if you are standing on the corner of Belmont (3200 North) and Sheffield (1200 West), you are four miles north of Madison and a mile and a half west of State Street.

An exception to this eight-blocks-to-the-mile rule is on the South Side, due to this area being settled early in Chicago's history. Although Roosevelt Road is 1200 South by numbers, it is one mile south of Madison. Cermak Road, which is 2200 South, is a mile south of Roosevelt even though it's a 10-block count. The next mile comes at 31st Street, even though it's nine blocks south of Cermak.

A few diagonal streets cut through Chicago's neat grid. On the North Side, diagonals such as Clybourn Avenue, Milwaukee Avenue, Clark Avenue, Lincoln Avenue, and Ogden Avenue may confuse newcomers lulled into comfort by the usual ease of navigating Chicago's orderly streets. However, when you know where you want to go, these diagonal avenues can serve as handy timesavers when wishing to head, for example, due southeast or northwest. Diagonals Archer Avenue and Southwest Highway serve a similar purpose when driving on the city's South Side.

All north-south and east-west streets on the North Side have names. On the South Side, north-south streets have names, except in the southeast part of the city where a few have letters; most east-west streets are numbered, although some have both names and numbers, e.g., 22nd Street also is Cermak Road, and 39th Street is Pershing Road. The east-west streets are double-numbered, e.g.,

West 66th Street and West 66th Place, to represent half blocks. (See diagram below.)

The shaded area represents a full square city block. The distance between West 66th Street and West 66th Place and between Fremont and Bissell is considered a half city block. This is an esoteric point, but one that creates a lot of confusion when trying to give directions and tell people how many blocks away something is.

While the city's layout is well designed, it helps to have a good street map handy the first few months. Make sure, though, that the one you buy covers your neighborhood—many parts of the city are ignored by tourist-oriented maps. **The Savvy Traveller** (www.thesavvytraveller.com), and **www.firstbooks.com** are both good online locations to shop for newcomer-oriented maps.

*Quick note*: with some rare exceptions (State Street for example), Chicagoans do not refer to their streets and avenues by their complete names, e.g., Addison Street will be referred to only as "Addison." It may take some getting used to if you are from an area that uses the words "avenue," "boulevard," or "street" regularly.

See the **Transportation** chapter for details about area expressways.

## COUNTY BASICS

At one time, the Chicago area was made up of Cook, Lake, and DuPage Counties. But the explosive growth in neighboring counties has made Chicago rethink area counties that were once considered "too far" to be part of the Chicago area. Today, "Chicagoland," as it's often called, encompasses six counties:

- **Cook County**, www.cookcountygov.com, is home to Chicago proper as well as many north, northwest, west, and south suburbs. It is the largest county in the area.

# NEIGHBORHOODS

- **DuPage County,** www.co.dupage.il.us; within the DuPage County limits are the suburban communities of Schaumburg, Wheaton, Bensenville, Elmhurst, Lombard, Carol Stream, and West Chicago. DuPage County is a heavily developed county, with a strong retail base and a solid highway network. Traffic is heavy in this area with many residents commuting to Chicago on a daily basis.
- **Kane County,** www.co.kane.il.us; famous for its fairgrounds, Kane County is west of DuPage County, placing it among the communities that lie to the far west of Chicago. Within Kane County are Aurora, St. Charles, and Geneva.
- **Lake County,** www.co.lake.il.us, lies inland from Lake Michigan and runs up to the Wisconsin border. Lake County is experiencing tremendous housing development. Communities that lie within Lake County include Barrington, Antioch, Grayslake, Round Beach Lake, Zion, Waukegan, Winthrop Harbor, and North Chicago.
- **McHenry County,** www.co.mchenry.il.us; McHenry communities are far northwest of Chicago. McHenry County borders the western edge of Lake County. Its communities include Woodstock, Crystal Lake, Cary, and Lake in the Hills.
- **Will County,** www.willcountyillinois.com, is southwest of Chicago. It includes the towns of Joliet and Bolingbrook. There is a great deal of available land in this area. Also hosts a small airport (Lewis University Airport), and the Stateville and the Joliet correctional centers.

**Cook County Information**
- **Website:** www.cookcountygov.com
- **County Law Enforcement (Sheriff):** www.cookcountysheriff.org
- **City of Chicago Public School Districts:** www.cps.edu; this is the site for public schools that fall within the city limits.
- **County State Attorney:** www.statesattorney.org
- **County Information Center:** www.cookcountygov.com
- **Cook County Treasurer:** www.cookcountytreasurer.com
- **Emergency Hospitals:** Check www.ushospitalfinder.com to find the emergency hospital nearest you. A couple are John H. Stroger, Jr. Hospital of Cook County, 1969 West Ogden Ave, 312-864-6000 (in the city), and Oak Forest Hospital of Cook County, 15900 S Cicero Ave, Oak Forest, 708-687-7200 (in the suburbs).

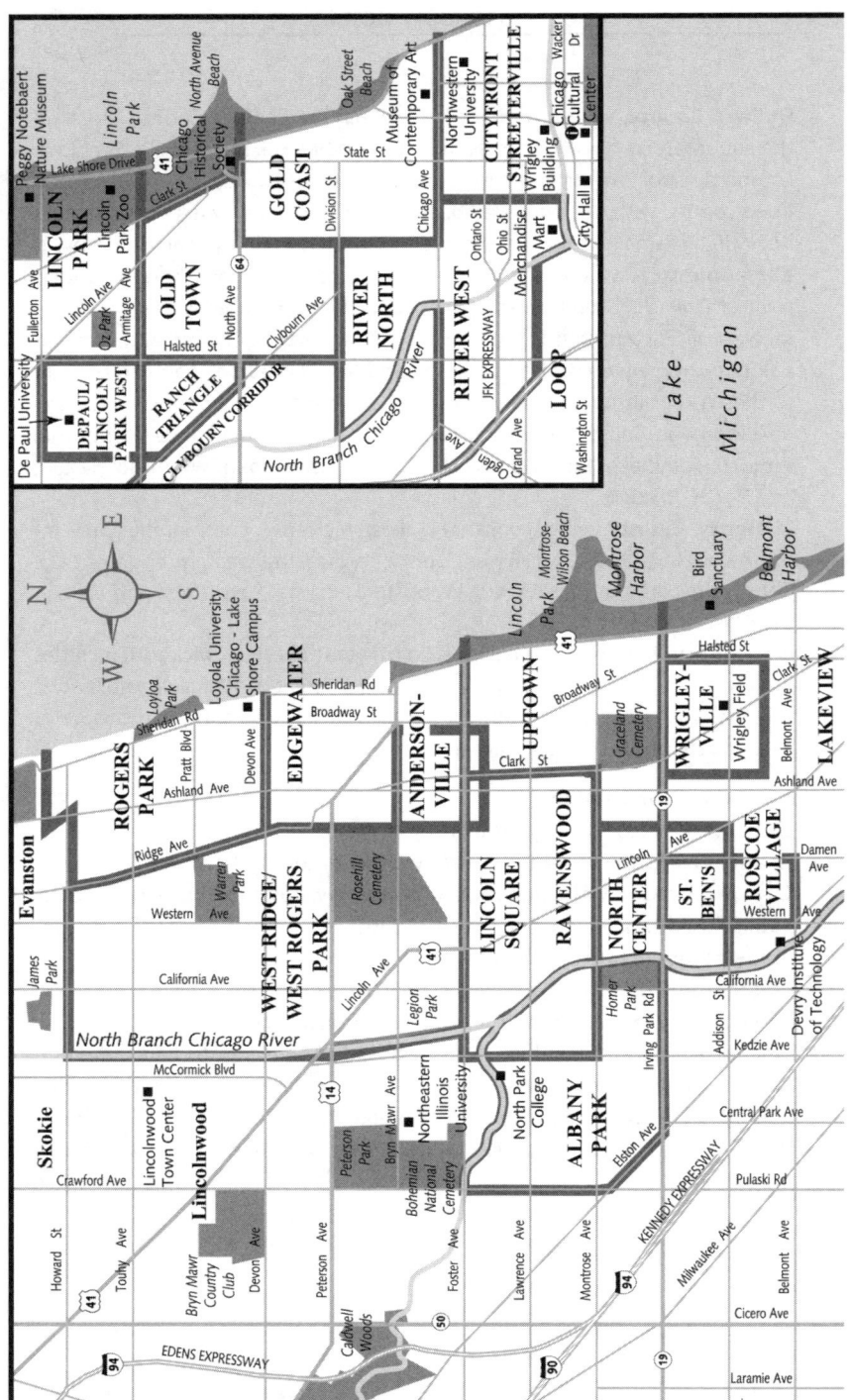

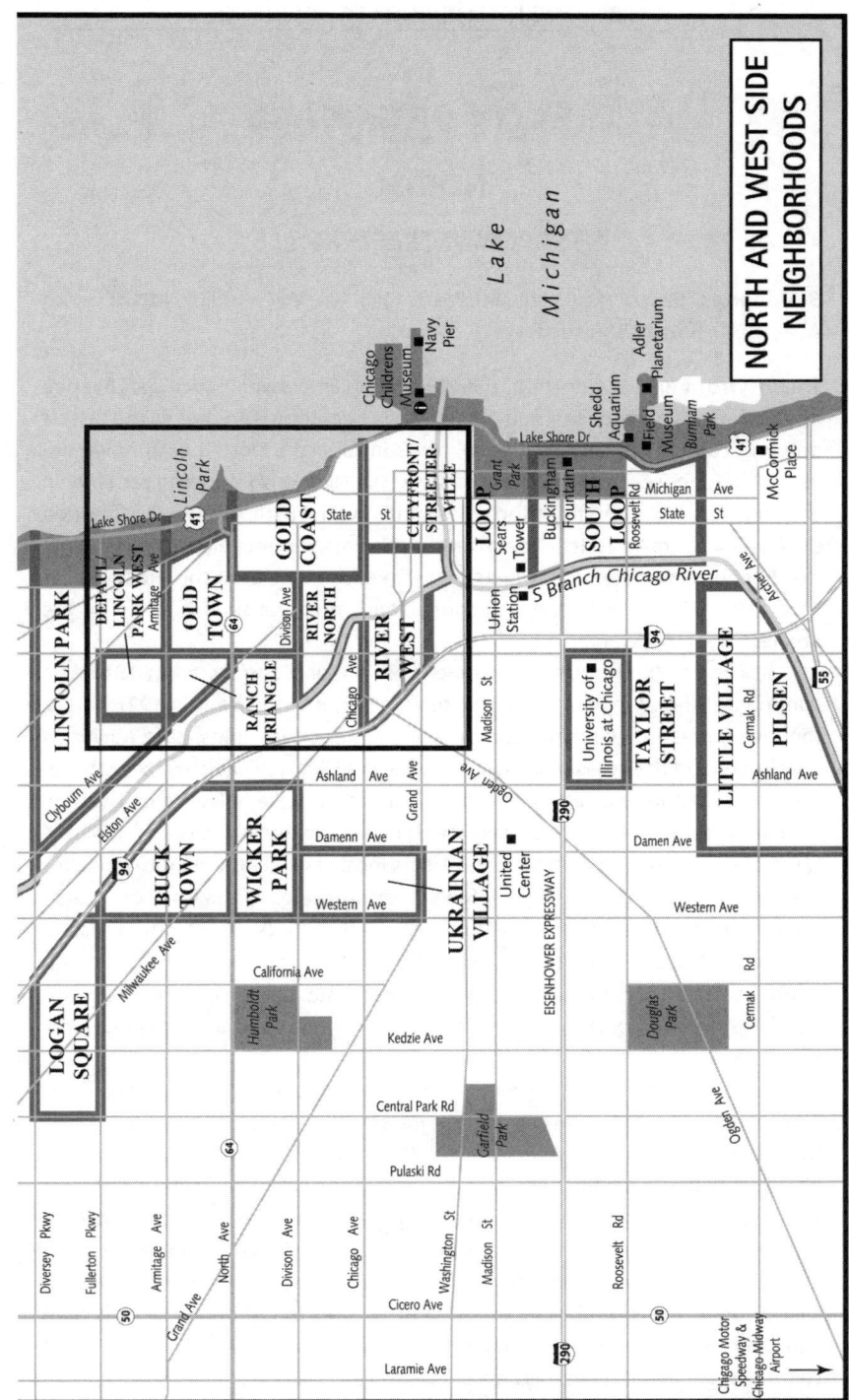

# THE CITY OF CHICAGO

## NORTH

### CITYFRONT/STREETERVILLE

**Boundaries: East:** Lake Michigan; **West:** Michigan Ave (100E); **North:** Grand Ave (500N); **South:** Chicago River

The **Cityfront** area lies north of the Chicago River, between Michigan Avenue and the lake, and since the mid 1990s, it has been home to one of the fastest growing commercial and residential areas in Chicago. Dotted with now converted warehouses built originally to serve the Nicholson shipping terminal in the 1920s and '30s, Cityfront today is popular with single and young, married professionals drawn to its expensive high-rise apartments, upscale shopping, and fine restaurants. You may hear some Chicagoans refer to this area as River East, North Pier, or even the Near North, and some consider it a part of the greater Streeterville area.

At the east end of Grand Avenue is Navy Pier. Constructed in 1916 as a commercial shipping pier, it was renamed in honor of the Navy in 1927. Today, the pier serves as a docking site for large dinner cruise ships, Lake Michigan tour boats, and the occasional naval vessel as well. Mayor Daley saw potential in this once-abandoned waterfront site and spearheaded a full-scale renovation, which was completed in 1995. Navy Pier is now a multi-use complex and one of Chicago's best attractions. The area attracts locals as well as out-of-towners for concerts at the 1,500-seat Skyline Stage, performances of the Chicago Shakespeare Theater, rides on the 15-story Ferris wheel, and visits to the Chicago Children's Museum. A winter ice rink, a summer outdoor beer garden, and an IMAX theater are additional draws. Navy Pier's Crystal Gardens, one of the country's largest indoor botanical parks, hosts a variety of public and private events year-round.

Just to the north of Navy Pier, right on Lake Michigan, is Milton Lee Olive Park, named for a local 18-year-old Congressional Medal of Honor winner from the Vietnam War. Don't let the Jardine Water Filtration plant nearby put you off. Olive Park is a small, quiet area, favored by bicyclists needing a rest, bird watchers, or picnickers looking for a great view. If you are heading to Olive Park from Navy Pier, you will pass charming Ohio Street Beach at 400 North Lake Shore Drive. Triathletes come here to train and area residents to relax. West of Lake Shore Drive is the Family Golf Center, 221 North Columbus Drive, where you can practice your drive or play a quick nine holes with a panoramic view of Lake Michigan. Renting in this area is expensive.

**Streeterville**, north of Cityfront, is named for Captain George Wellington "Cap" Streeter, one of Chicago's great eccentrics. This neighborhood was once

# THE CITY OF CHICAGO: NORTH

covered by Lake Michigan. In 1886, Streeter ran his schooner aground on a sandbar near Michigan Avenue. Unable to free his vessel, Streeter made his home on it. He encouraged contractors to deposit their debris there—for a fee. Gradually the landfill turned the lake into approximately 186 new acres and Streeter laid claim to 168 acres of it. After some scuffles with police and battles in court, Streeter eventually was evicted, though he pressed his claim until his death in 1921.

Streeterville is the heart of North Michigan Avenue, Chicago's blue-chip shopping district, which features Water Tower Place (Macy's, Lord & Taylor), 900 North Michigan Avenue (Bloomingdale's, Gucci), as well as Neiman Marcus, Saks Fifth Avenue, Crate & Barrel, and many more upscale retail shops. In addition to being home to fine restaurants, Rush Street bars, clubs, and movie theaters, Streeterville houses Northwestern University's Chicago campus, which includes its law and medical schools. Nearby are the University of Chicago's Graduate School of Business Evening Program and one of the area's premier hospitals—Northwestern Memorial Hospital. Indeed, you can probably find everything in this upscale neighborhood except a parking place. If you're moving here, and you have a car and intend to keep it, you'll want to find a building with parking or rent space in a lot.

*Streeterville*

**Neighborhood Website:** www.streetervillechamber.org
**Area Code:** 312
**ZIP Codes:** 60610, 60611
**Post Offices:** Fort Dearborn, 540 N Dearborn St; 355 E Ohio St
**Police District:** 18th/East Chicago District (Area 3), 1160 N Larrabee St, 312-742-5870
**Emergency Hospitals:** Northwestern Memorial Hospital, 251 E Huron St, 312-926-2000, www.nmh.org; Ann and Robert H. Lurie Children's Hospital of Chicago, 225 E Chicago Ave (between Fairbanks Ct & Mies Van der Rohe Way), 312-227-4000, www.luriechildrens.org
**Libraries:** Harold Washington Chicago Public Library, 400 S State, 312-747-4300, www.chipublib.org; Newberry Library, 60 W Walton St, has a first-rate

collection of rare books, manuscripts, and maps. Open to the public, research scholars and university students are its most frequent visitors; call first: 312-943-9090, www.newberry.org.

**Parks:** www.chicagoparkdistrict.com, 312-742-PLAY; among the dozen area parks included in the 60610 and 60611 ZIP codes are River Esplanade Park, 401 E River Dr, and Lake Shore Park, 808 N Lake Shore Dr

**Community Publications:** *Crain's Chicago Business, Chicago Daily Law Bulletin, Chicago Magazine, Chicago Reader, Chicago Reporter, N'DIGO, Newcity*

**Public Schools:** Chicago School District 299, 125 S Clark St, Chicago, IL 60603, 773-553-1000, www.cps.edu

**Transportation—Rapid Transit:** Red Line (stations: Grand, Chicago); Brown Line (stations: Chicago, Merchandise Mart)

**Transportation—Main Bus Routes:** #65 Grand, #66 Chicago, #125 Water Tower Express, #151 Sheridan, #156 LaSalle, #157 Streeterville

## RIVER NORTH/RIVER WEST

**Boundaries**: **North:** Chicago Ave/Chicago Ave; **East:** Clark St/Chicago River; **South:** Chicago River/Ohio St; **West:** Chicago River/ Kennedy Expy

What was once a neighborhood of factories and warehouses has blossomed into Chicago's answer to New York's SoHo. **River North** is a thriving neighborhood of art galleries, trendy restaurants, hotels, and nightclubs. Each Saturday from 11:00 a.m. until 12:30 p.m., local gallery owners conduct free tours. Meet at the Starbucks located at 750 North Franklin Street, no reservations needed. If you are ready for brunch after your tour, there are bistros, traditional diners, and cafés to suit every palate.

*River North*

# THE CITY OF CHICAGO: NORTH

The Merchandise Mart, 222 Merchandise Mart, between Wells and Orleans, is an unofficial landmark. Sitting on the north bank of the Chicago River, the Mart was built in 1931 by Marshall Field & Co. At 25 floors high and two city blocks long, it actually has its own ZIP code! Nowadays the attached West Mart Center and Apparel Center contain the Illinois Institute of Art as well as classrooms for Argosy University. Many of the warehouses in the neighborhood have been converted into loft space for offices and apartments. Rents have risen considerably here, because of River North's art and retail cachet as well as its proximity to Michigan Avenue.

**River West**, sometimes referred to as Illinois Center, is a former industrial/manufacturing zone located west of the Chicago River and east of the Kennedy Expressway. Far less scenic than River North, this neighborhood remains a maze of railroad tracks, under-and-over-passes, and truncated streets. Nonetheless, River West's felicitous location has led to rising rents for the apartments and condos located here. And, if you love chocolate, you may just *have* to live here: the Blommer Chocolate Company, the world's largest cocoa bean processor, is located at the corner of Kinzie and Des Plaines Streets. Despite a 2005 EPA pollution complaint (apparently, some residents grow weary of smelling chocolate all day every day), Blommer's continues to loft a heavenly aroma skyward, making River West one of the best-smelling neighborhoods in the city.

It wasn't always so. A hundred years ago the Chicago River was the largest open sewer in the Midwest and emptied, quite logically, into Lake Michigan, the city's source for drinking water. Nowadays the river actually supports aquatic life of the non-microbial sort. The sight of a turtle paddling along in the shadow of the Merchandise Mart is not the kind of urban scene you might expect this close to the Loop, but River North and River West are full of surprises.

**Neighborhood Websites:** www.rivernorthassociation.com
**Area Code:** 312
**ZIP Codes:** 60610, 60611, 60654, 60622
**Post Offices:** Fort Dearborn, 540 N Dearborn St; Merchandise Mart, 222 Merchandise Mart Plaza
**Police District:** 18th/East Chicago District (Area 3), 1160 N Larrabee St, 312-742-5870
**Emergency Hospitals:** Northwestern Memorial Hospital, 251 E Huron St, 312-926-2000, www.nmh.org; Ann and Robert H. Lurie Children's Hospital of Chicago, 225 E Chicago Ave (between Fairbanks Ct & Mies Van der Rohe Way), 312-227-4000, www.luriechildrens.org
**Library:** Harold Washington Chicago Public Library, 400 S State, 312-747-4300; www.chipublib.org
**Parks:** www.chicagoparkdistrict.com, 312-742-PLAY; Ward, A. Montgomery Park, 630 N Kingsbury St, 312-742-7895
**Community Publications:** *Crain's Chicago Business, Chicago Daily Law Bulletin, Chicago Magazine, Chicago Reader, Chicago Reporter, N'DIGO, Newcity*

**Public Schools:** Chicago School District 299, 125 S Clark St, Chicago, IL 60603, 773-553-1000, www.cps.edu

**Transportation—Rapid Transit:** Red Line (stations: Grand, Chicago); Brown Line (stations: Merchandise Mart, Chicago); Blue Line (stations: Grand, Chicago)

**Transportation—Main Bus Routes:** #8 Halsted, #11 Lincoln, #22 Clark, #36 Broadway, #56 Milwaukee, #65 Grand, #66 Chicago, #156 LaSalle

## GOLD COAST

**Boundaries: North:** North Ave (1660N); **South:** Chicago Ave; **East:** Lake Michigan; **West:** LaSalle Blvd

The Gold Coast was Chicago's second Millionaires' Row (the first was on the near South Side around 18th Street and Prairie Avenue, where a few old mansions still exist) and remains home to many well-to-do Chicagoans. Although the days when it was the heart of Chicago society have passed, this area retains much of its turn-of-the-20th-century charm and is still synonymous with living the high life. While there are a few single-family homes and apartments, most of the remaining brown-, red-, and graystone mansions in this two-square-mile neighborhood have been converted into expensive condominiums. Notably, Astor Street has landmark status and is now protected from further development.

Due to the wall of Lake Shore Drive high-rises, the Gold Coast sometimes feels like the bottom of a canyon. Despite this walled-in atmosphere, if you use your imagination, you can almost see the gaslights and hear the carriages and horse hooves on the cobblestones. If you happen to live in one of the Lake Shore Drive high-rises, you will enjoy a spectacular view of the lake. If you want a view that includes Lincoln Park, investigate some of the buildings bordering North Avenue.

*Gold Coast*

# THE CITY OF CHICAGO: NORTH

A landmark along the Clark Street boundary between the Gold Coast and Old Town is Carl Sandburg Village, a combination high-rise and low-rise condominium community constructed in the 1960s. One of the few remaining mansions, and the only one with real grounds, is home to the Archbishop of Chicago and can be found on North Boulevard at the base of Lincoln Park. While it's unlikely that you will find an apartment or condo with a lawn on the Gold Coast, you will find that Lincoln Park and the lakeshore are virtually at your doorstep.

The Gold Coast high-rises make for a high-density population, but that doesn't keep people from living and living well in this neighborhood; rentals are comparable to the upper end of Streeterville-area prices. Apartments here are mostly in high rises, and many have garage space available for their tenants. The shopper's paradise of North Michigan Avenue is a brisk walk away, and Division Street's nightlife is just around the corner. Oak Street Beach, dramatically situated at the bend in the lake where Michigan Avenue ends, is a favorite lunch spot and a great escape destination. Here, as in other downtown neighborhoods, on-the-street parking space is at a premium; owning a car is not recommended, unless you can find garage space.

**Neighborhood Website:** www.goldcoastneighbors.org
**Area Code:** 312
**ZIP Codes:** 60610, 60611
**Post Office:** Fort Dearborn, 540 N Dearborn St
**Police District:** 18th/East Chicago District (Area 3), 1160 N Larrabee St, 312-742-5870
**Emergency Hospitals:** Northwestern Memorial Hospital, 251 E Huron St, 312-926-2000, www.nmh.org; Ann and Robert H. Lurie Children's Hospital of Chicago, 225 E Chicago Ave (between Fairbanks Ct & Mies Van der Rohe Way), 312-227-4000, www.luriechildrens.org
**Libraries:** Harold Washington Chicago Public Library, 400 S State St, 312-747-4300; Lincoln Park Library, 1150 W Fullerton Ave, 312-744-1926, all at www.chipublib.org; Newberry Library, 60 W Walton, 312-943-9090; Near North Branch of the Chicago Public Library, 310 W Division St, 312-744-0991
**Community Resource:** every August the Gold Coast Art Fair attracts dozens of exhibitors from across the country.
**Parks:** www.chicagoparkdistrict.com, 312-742-PLAY: Seneca Playlot Park, 220 E Chicago Ave, 312-742-7891; Connors Park, 861 N. Wabash Ave, 312-742-7891; Lincoln Park, 2045 N Lincoln Park W, 312-742-7726; Lake Shore Park, 808 N Lake Shore Dr, 312-742-7891; Lake Front Trails, which lead to 15 miles of bathing beaches and 18 miles of bike paths along the Lakefront. Oak Street Beach is famous for its volleyball sand courts, beautiful sun worshipers, and inline skaters. Use one of the over/underpasses to cross Lake Shore Drive.
**Community Publications:** *Crain's Chicago Business, Chicago Daily Law Bulletin, Chicago Magazine, Chicago Reader, Chicago Reporter, N'DIGO, Newcity*

**Public Schools:** Chicago School District 299, 125 S Clark St, Chicago, IL 60603, 773-553-1000, www.cps.edu
**Transportation—Rapid Transit:** Red Line (stations: Clark/Division, Chicago)
**Transportation—Major Bus Routes:** #11 Lincoln, #22 Clark, #36 Broadway, #65 Grand, #66 Chicago, #70 Division, #72 North, #125 Water Tower Express, #135, #136, #145, #146, #147, #151 Sheridan, #156 LaSalle, #157 Streeterville

## OLD TOWN

**Boundaries**: **North:** Armitage Ave; **South:** Division; **East:** Clark St; **West:** Halsted St

Nestled between the Gold Coast and Lincoln Park is Old Town, a neighborhood once populated by German farmers who migrated here in the 1830s. The Great Fire of 1871 leveled the area from the lake to Larrabee Street, leaving only the smoldering shell of St. Michael's Church. Undaunted, Old Town residents rebuilt their neighborhood and church quickly. Many wooden structures were built in the workers' cottage style, which featured one-and-a-half-story homes set atop raised basements, until a city ordinance forbade further wooden structures. Today, the larger homes, row houses, and apartment buildings along these narrow tree-lined streets are made of brick, as are the Victorian single-family homes, and the two- and three-flats. The entire neighborhood was designated a landmark by the City of Chicago in 1977.

Old Town is the closest neighborhood to the Loop and North Michigan Avenue that truly has a neighborhood feel, with small front lawns, old architectural details, and balconies. Attractive and convenient, Old Town especially draws single professionals and many from the gay community.

*Old Town*

Wells Street, Old Town's main commercial drag, boasts many good eateries and interesting shops. You will also find a number of enjoyable restaurants on North Avenue. Many of Old Town's businesses are locally run and operated, adding to the feeling of neighborhood and community here. During the second weekend of June, Old Town hosts the Wells Street Art Festival, also known as the Old Town Art Fair. The festival, one of the largest neighborhood festivals in Chicago, attracts over 60,000 visitors and participants. Old Town is also the long-time home of the legendary improvisational comedy theater Second City (1616 North Wells Street), where aspiring John Belushis, Bill Murrays, and Tina Feys perform nightly for city dwellers and tourists alike. A theater district, including the renowned Steppenwolf Theatre, has taken root on Halsted, just north of North Avenue. Neighborhood bars are friendly and comfortable. Parking gets tougher closer to the lake.

**Neighborhood Website:** www.oldtowntriangle.com
**Area Codes:** 773, 312
**ZIP Codes:** 60614, 60610
**Post Office:** Lincoln Park, 2405 N Sheffield Ave
**Police District:** 18th/East Chicago District (Area 3), 1160 N Larrabee St, 312-742-5870
**Emergency Hospitals:** Ann and Robert H. Lurie Children's Hospital of Chicago, 225 E Chicago Ave (between Fairbanks Ct & Mies Van der Rohe Way), 312-227-4000, www.luriechildrens.org
**Libraries:** Public Library Branch facilities include Lincoln Park, 1150 W Fullerton Ave, 312-744-1926; Near North, 310 W. Division St, 312-744-0991; John Merlo, 644 W Belmont Ave, 312-744-1139; www.chipublib.org
**Community Resources:** Chicago History Museum, 1601 N Clark St, 312-642-4600, www.chicagohistory.org; Old Town Merchants & Residents Association, 1520 N Wells, 312-951-6106, www.oldtownchicago.org; (nonprofit) Chicago Artists' Coalition, www.caconline.org; Old Town Triangle Association, 1763 N Park Ave, 312-337-1938, www.oldtowntriangle.com
**Parks:** www.chicagoparkdistrict.com, 312-742-PLAY: Eugenie Triangle Park, 1701 N LaSalle St 312-742-7726; Stanton Park, 618 W Scott St, 312-742-7896; Bauler Playlot Park, 501 W Wisconsin St, 312-742-7898
**Community Publications:** *Crain's Chicago Business, Chicago Daily Law Bulletin, Chicago Magazine, Chicago Reader, Chicago Reporter, N'DIGO, Newcity*
**Public Schools:** Chicago School District 299, 125 S Clark St, Chicago, IL 60603, 773-553-1000, www.cps.edu
**Transportation— Rapid Transit:** Brown Line (stations: Sedgwick); Red Line (stations: Clark/Division, North/Clybourn—for the western edge of the neighborhood)
**Transportation—Major Bus Routes:** #11 Lincoln/Sedgwick, #22 Clark, #36 Broadway, #72 North, #73 Armitage, #135 Clarendon/La Salle Express, #151 Sheridan, #156 LaSalle

## *RANCH TRIANGLE/CLYBOURN CORRIDOR*

**Boundaries**: **North:** Armitage Ave; **East:** Halsted St; **South:** North Ave: **West:** Clybourn and Racine Aves

Heading west from Old Town you'll find both the community known as **RANCH** and a transformed section of Clybourn Avenue. RANCH is an acronym for the streets that form this neighborhood's boundaries: Racine, Armitage, North, Clybourn, and Halsted. The residential area is located east of Clybourn toward the western fringes of Old Town (the spire of St. Michael's Church is just a few blocks away). Here you'll find single-family homes, three-flat and larger apartment buildings. Because it's not as close to the lake as some other near north neighborhoods (about a mile away), the RANCH neighborhood was a relative late bloomer in the North Side gentrification tsunami, going through its upscale makeover in the 1990s. During this time, many Victorian-era buildings were either torn down or remodeled beyond recognition. However, in an attempt to slow down the mass modernization of building facades, the RANCH Conservation Association has been working hard to get official recognition for some buildings they consider significant to the community. While they still have a long way to go, the group has managed to get some buildings listed as architecturally significant on the Illinois State Historic Resources Survey. As the desirability of the area (i.e., its proximity to shopping, public transportation, and the lake) is increasingly recognized, housing prices in the area are rising.

As recently as the 1980s, Clybourn Avenue was the main artery through an industrial work zone. At night and on weekends, when the laborers went home and the trucks and freight cars stopped rolling, it was a no-man's land of railroad crossings, hulking factories, and blowing trash. These days just try to find a parking space on Saturday morning: heavy industry has given way to consumer frenzy. The name **Clybourn Corridor** refers to the area that stretches from Clybourn to the Chicago River, and from North Avenue (1600N) to Wrightwood (2600N). Clybourn is home to strip malls, megastores, and loft apartments in buildings that once were factories. Some small retail developments have also been added between North and Webster Avenues. Highlights at the south end of the Clybourn Corridor include a Best Buy and Sam's Wine and Spirits, which many North Siders consider the best liquor store in the city—it's certainly one of the biggest. A cluster of outlet stores for major retailers contains a Bed Bath & Beyond, a gourmet supermarket, and several furniture stores. Farther north are the Goose Island Brewery, a microbrewery and restaurant, and the Webster Place cinemas. In short,

*Clybourn Corridor*

THE CITY OF CHICAGO: NORTH

you could spend your whole weekend shopping this mile-long stretch. While parking lots are provided at many of the stores, road congestion is a big topic of conversation, and a sore point, in this neighborhood.

A few factories remain in the neighborhood, and the community is working to keep them from leaving. If you're tired of shopping but feeling adventurous, you may want to check out the Finkl Steel Company (where Cortland Street crosses the river) for a firsthand glimpse of this neighborhood's industrial heritage. Though there are no official tours, you can check out a photo tour on the company's website: www.finkl.com. Because the bay doors on Cortland open into the factory and are frequently left open in the summer to help cool the place down, you may see molten steel being poured as you walk or drive by.

**Neighborhood Website:** www.ranchtriangle.org
**Area Codes:** 773, 312
**ZIP Code:** 60614, 60622
**Post Office:** Lincoln Park, 2643 N Clark St
**Police District:** 18th/East Chicago District (Area 3), 1160 N Larrabee Ave, 312-742-5870
**Emergency Hospitals:** Ann and Robert H. Lurie Children's Hospital of Chicago, 225 E Chicago Ave (between Fairbanks Ct & Mies Van der Rohe Way), 312-227-4000, www.luriechildrens.org
**Library:** Lincoln Park, 1150 W Fullerton Ave, 312-744-1926; www.chipublib.org
**Community Resource:** Ranch Triangle Conservation Community Association, www.ranchtriangle.org
**Parks:** www.chicagoparkdistrict.com, 312-742-PLAY: Clybourn Park, 1755 N Clybourn, 312-742-7787; Adams Playground Park, 1919 N Seminary Ave, 312-742-7787; Privet Playlot Park, 1844 N Sheffield Ave, 312-742-7787;
**Community Publications:** *Crain's Chicago Business, Chicago Daily Law Bulletin, Chicago Magazine, Chicago Reader, Chicago Reporter, N'DIGO, Newcity*
**Public Schools:** Chicago School District 299, 125 S Clark St, Chicago, IL 60603, 773-553-1000, www.cps.edu
**Transportation—Rapid Transit:** Red Line (stations: North/Clybourn); Brown Line (stations: Armitage)
**Transportation—Major Bus Routes:** #8 Halsted, #73 Armitage, #72 North

## *LINCOLN PARK*

**Boundaries**: **North:** Diversey Pkwy (1800N); **South:** North Ave (1600N); **East:** Lake Michigan; **West:** Clybourn Ave

Lincoln Park is at the heart of Chicago's North Side. For many it is a quintessential city neighborhood with everything you could possibly want—except readily available parking and affordable rents. Housing ranges from high rises

*Lincoln Park*

to two- and three-flat brownstones to cottages. Unfortunately, after more than 30 years of gentrification, there are no real-estate bargains left.

Lincoln Park is lively and serves as host to many young Chicago families and singles alike; the median age here is 31. You'll find restaurants galore to match any taste and budget; bars and dance clubs run the gamut; and there's little you won't find shopping-wise on either Clark or Halsted. Warm weather makes for a vibrant outdoor scene, with nearly every restaurant offering seating on back patios, rooftop decks, at tables spilling out onto the narrow sidewalks, or at seen-and-be-seen windows open to the streets. The area's most obvious asset is Lincoln Park itself. Designed by Frederick Law Olmsted, designer of New York City's Central Park, this rolling 1,200-plus-acre park is the largest of Chicago's 550 parks and features bike paths, picnic areas, the lovely Lincoln Park Zoo (with free admission), a seasonal restaurant in the middle of the park, and 20 free tennis courts. The south end of the park has extensive playing fields for soccer and football, and barbecues. In the spring, bird lovers lead walks around the North Pond, seeking out the migratory birds that gather around the lily pond at Fullerton and North Cannon Drive. In the summer, the zoo hosts a summer series concert. Or you might investigate the nine-week series of plays at Theatre on the Lake (Fullerton & Lake Shore Drive). For up-to-date information about family programs, plays, and live performances available in the park year-round, call the hotline: 312-742-7994.

Lincoln Park is steeped in history. A lone, fenced-off mausoleum on LaSalle Drive behind the Historical Society stands as a reminder that the park first served as a city cemetery, holding many victims of the smallpox and cholera plagues. (The bodies have long been relocated.) The park's old name, Lake Park, was changed in 1886 to honor the assassinated president. A boulder near Clark and Wisconsin Streets marks the grave of the last survivor of the Boston Tea Party. The Great Fire of 1871 reached its northernmost extent at roughly Clark and

# THE CITY OF CHICAGO: NORTH

Belden. Two blocks south at 2221 North Clark Street, on a site that is now a lawn, stood the garage where the infamous St. Valentine's Day Massacre took place.

You will find single-family homes, condos, and rentals in this area. Its popularity is reflected in its prices, but you may find some discounted real estate as you search closer to one of the three elevated train stops in this neighborhood. The train service is another top draw to this neighborhood. With an average three- to six-minute wait between trains during rush hour, Lincoln Park is an ideal location for Loop-area commuters. Drawbacks are cost and congestion—both symptoms of its enduring popularity. There isn't a lot of street parking available either. Still, it remains the preferred address for many Chicagoans.

**Neighborhood Websites:** Lincoln Central Association, 312-409-2783, www.lincolncentral.org; Mid-North Association, 773-296-1721, www.mid-northassociation.org

**Area Codes:** 773, 312

**ZIP Code:** 60614

**Post Offices:** Lincoln Park, 2643 N Clark St; Lincoln Park Postal Store, 2405 N Sheffield Ave

**Police Districts:** South of Fullerton: 18th/East Chicago District (Area 3), 1160 N Larrabee St, 312-742-5870; North of Fullerton: 19th/Town Hall Chicago District (Area 3), 850 W Addison St, 312-744-8320

**Emergency Hospitals:** Ann and Robert H. Lurie Children's Hospital of Chicago, 225 E Chicago Ave (between Fairbanks Ct & Mies Van der Rohe Way), 312-227-4000, www.luriechildrens.org; Saint Joseph Hospital, 2900 N Lake Shore Dr, 773-665-3000, www.saintjosephhospital.reshealth.org

**Libraries:** Lincoln Park, 1150 W Fullerton Ave, 312-744-1926; John Merlo/Lake View, 644 W Belmont Ave, 312-744-1139; Lincoln Belmont, 1659 W Melrose St, 312-744-0166; www.chipublib.org

**Community Resources:** Lincoln Park Chamber of Commerce, 1925 N Clybourn Ave, Suite 301, 773-880-5200, www.lincolnparkchamber.com; Lincoln Park Conservancy, 2000 N Racine, Suite 2080, 773-883-7275, www.lincolnparkconservancy.org; Chicago Ornithological Society, 28 East Jackson Building, 10th Floor, http:// chicagobirder.org; Peggy Notebaert Nature Museum, 2430 N Cannon Dr, 773-755-5100, www.chias.org; Florence G. Heller JCC, 524 W Melrose, 773-871-6780, www.gojcc.org/content/view/36/65.

**Parks:** www.chicagoparkdistrict.com, 312-742-PLAY: Lincoln Park, 2045 N Lincoln Park West, 312-742-7726; Lincoln Park Conservatory, 2391 N Stockton Dr, 312-742-7736; Oz Park, 2021 N Burling St, 312-742-7898

**Community Publications:** *Crain's Chicago Business, Chicago Daily Law Bulletin, Chicago Magazine, Chicago Parent, Chicago Reader, Chicago Reporter, N'DIGO, Newcity, Windy City Times*

**Public Schools:** Chicago School District 299, 125 S Clark St, Chicago, IL 60603, 773-553-1000, www.cps.edu

**Transportation—Rapid Transit:** Red Line (stations: Fullerton); Brown Line (stations: Armitage, Fullerton, Diversey)
**Transportation—Major Bus Routes:** #8 Halsted, #11 Lincoln/Sedgwick, #22 Clark, #36 Broadway, #73 Armitage, #74 Fullerton, #76 Diversey, #151 Sheridan, #156 LaSalle

## DEPAUL/LINCOLN PARK WEST

**Boundaries**: **North:** Fullerton Pkwy (2400N); **South:** Armitage (2000N) to Fullerton; **East:** Halsted St (800W); **West:** Racine Ave (1200W)

DePaul University anchors this affluent neighborhood located just to the west of Lincoln Park proper. Founded in 1898 by the Catholic Vincentian Fathers, DePaul University has expanded over the years to accommodate over 20,000 students. The twin towers of St. Vincent's Church, where the school got its start, remain neighborhood landmarks. DePaul's Lincoln Park Campus, which lies south of Fullerton Avenue between Halsted Street and Racine Ave, offers a quiet refuge from the buzz of the main thoroughfares. The showpiece of the campus is the $25 million John T. Richardson Library, built in 1992, on Kenmore Avenue.

The eastern edge of **DePaul** blends seamlessly into the upscale verve of Lincoln Park, offering a strip of high-end boutiques—a mix of independent local businesses and small outposts of national upscale chains—stretching to the north and west at the intersection of Halsted and Armitage Avenues. As you move westward, though, the neighborhood's character changes. Immediately adjacent to the university the younger population makes for a lively nightlife. Popular options include the nightclubs, restaurants, movie theaters, and bars along Lincoln Avenue. On weekend nights those without a parking permit will find it impossible to park in the vicinity. In response, many restaurants now offer valet parking.

*Lincoln Park West*

# THE CITY OF CHICAGO: NORTH

West of DePaul, in an area called **Lincoln Park West**, the neighborhood was once firmly working class, home to the blue-collar laborers who worked in the factories along Southport Avenue and the Clybourn Corridor. In recent years, those old factories have been converted into residential lofts while new luxury homes have sprung up on formerly abandoned industrial lots. Plenty of older and smaller single-family homes have been torn down to make way for larger apartment buildings and condos. It's quieter in the area west of DePaul but by no means dead; there are many excellent restaurants and friendly corner bars, especially along Webster and Wrightwood Avenues.

At its western edge, Lincoln Park West is bounded by Clybourn Avenue, and the pace picks up considerably. The great shopping along Clybourn (see the RANCH Triangle/Clybourn Corridor profile in this chapter) is best experienced on foot. Even formerly grimy Ashland is catching the gentrification bug, with new apartment buildings and factory makeovers. Some light industry still exists here. Nevertheless, it seems only a matter of time before the whole neighborhood becomes exclusively residential and service-oriented.

**Area Code:** 773
**ZIP Code:** 60614
**Post Offices:** Lincoln Park, 2643 N Clark St; Lincoln Park Postal Store, 2405 N Sheffield Ave
**Police Districts:** South of Fullerton: 18th/East Chicago District (Area 3), 1160 N Larrabee St, 312-742-5870; North of Fullerton: 19th/Town Hall Chicago District (Area 3), 850 W Addison St, 312-744-8320
**Emergency Hospitals:** Ann and Robert H. Lurie Children's Hospital of Chicago, 225 E Chicago Ave (between Fairbanks Ct & Mies Van der Rohe Way), 312-227-4000, www.luriechildrens.org; Advocate Illinois Masonic Medical Center, 836 W Wellington Ave, 773-975-1600, www.advocatehealth.com/immc/
**Library:** Lincoln Park, 1150 W Fullerton Ave, 312-744-1926; www.chipublib.org
**Community Resources:** DePaul Community Music, 773-325-7262, http://music.depaul.edu/cmd/; DePaul University School of Music Concert Hall, 800 W Belden Ave, 773-325-7260
**Parks:** www.chicagoparkdistrict.com, 312-742-PLAY: Trebes Park, 2250 N Clifton Ave, 312-742-7769
**Community Publications:** *Crain's Chicago Business, Chicago Daily Law Bulletin, Chicago Magazine, Chicago Parent, Chicago Reader, Chicago Reporter, N'DIGO, Newcity, Windy City Times*
**Public Schools:** Chicago School District 299, 125 S Clark St, Chicago, IL 60603, 773-553-1000, www.cps.edu
**Transportation—Rapid Transit:** Red Line (stations: Fullerton); Brown Line (stations: Armitage, Fullerton, Diversey)
**Transportation—Major Bus Routes:** #8 Halsted, #9 Ashland, #11 Lincoln/Sedgwick, #73 Armitage, #74 Fullerton, #76 Diversey

## WRIGLEYVILLE/LAKEVIEW

**Boundaries:** *Wrigleyville:* **North:** Irving Park Rd (4000N); **South:** Roscoe St; **East:** Halsted St (800W); **West:** Southport Ave; *Lakeview:* **North:** Irving Park Rd (4000N); **South:** Diversey Pkwy (2800N); **East:** Lake Michigan; **West:** Chicago River (includes Lakeview East, Lakeview Central, and West Lakeview)

**Wrigleyville**, so named for its most famous landmark, Wrigley Field, is located directly north of the DePaul–Lincoln Park West area. Its proximity to the lake, its relative affordability, and its lively social scene make it the neighborhood of choice for many recent college grads. In fact, Wrigleyville has all of the amenities of Lincoln Park—not to mention its own baseball team!—without the higher prices of its well-to-do neighbor to the south.

A dynamic part of town, Wrigleyville/Lakeview includes a large gay population along Broadway, between Diversey and Addison. Chicago's Annual Pride Parade takes place here the last Sunday in June. The exuberant and colorful celebration starts at the corner of Broadway and Montrose, parties south on Broadway, south on Halsted, and then east into Lincoln Park. (Check www.chicagopridecalendar.org for more details.)

Antique shops, florists, furniture stores, and coffeehouses also dot the retail areas along Broadway and Halsted Street. The majority of the buildings here are two- and three-story brick or graystone flats, and several buildings in the neighborhood are listed in the National Register of Historic Places. Parking for visitors can be a problem closer to the lake, particularly on weekends and on game days for the Cubs. Parking without a neighborhood permit is tough and is enforced especially strictly on game days. Selling parking spaces during Cubs games has become a cottage industry for some residents, who will rent their garages to fans not wanting to get blocked into the official neighborhood parking lots. Year-round, you're most likely to nab a parking space early in the morning and early in the evening—when residents are either headed to work

*Wrigleyville/Lakeview*

or out for the night. Residents can easily obtain permits at the 44th Ward police office on Belmont.

During baseball season, Wrigley Field's demands rule the neighborhood. In 2002, the Cubs owners sued the owners of several tall Wrigleyville buildings, all of which had created big-money businesses based on renting out rooftops to Cubs spectators. (Some charged up to $60 admission, built their own bleachers, and served beer and snacks.) In 2004, the building owners agreed to share profits with team owners, so the rooftop audiences still enjoy their view. In addition to the cottage industries of Cubs parking and the rooftop viewing decks, the area's large number of sports bars and restaurants, full to overflowing on game days, can be an issue not only on weekends but on most nights throughout the year. Those seeking quiet and solitude will not find it in Wrigleyville.

Although some single-family homes exist in the Wrigleyville/Lakeview neighborhood, most housing is a mixture of new and turn-of-the-20th-century buildings that were designed for apartment living. Depending on the current market, it may take some effort to find lower-priced rental apartments in the Wrigley area. Still, rents in Wrigleyville generally skew lower than in the rest of **Lakeview**.

For a slightly quieter scene, check out the area around Southport Avenue on Lakeview's western edge, where you may be able to find some single-family homes on the market. While Southport has seen an explosion of trendy restaurants and bars in recent years, the pedestrian-friendly avenue lacks the party-hearty atmosphere of Clark and Halsted. It is also home to one of Chicago's few remaining old-style movie palaces, the Music Box Theater (3733 North Southport, 773-871-6607). Foreign and independent films are usually featured in a beautifully restored interior that only adds to the feeling of escapism. Walking south on Southport you'll spot the narrow green spire of St. Alphonsus Redemptorist Church. Look up and you may catch a glimpse of the only residents of West Lakeview who actually get a lake view—the pigeons.

**Neighborhood Websites:** Southport Neighbors Association, www.southport-neighbors.com; Lake View Citizens' Council, www.lakeviewcitizens.org
**Area Code:** 773
**ZIP Codes:** 60613, 60657
**Post Offices:** Lake View, 1343 W Irving Park Rd; 3026 N Ashland
**Police Districts:** 19th/Town Hall Chicago District (Area 3), 850 W Addison St, 312-744-8320
**Emergency Hospitals:** St. Joseph Hospital and Health Care Center, 2900 N Lake Shore Dr, 773-665-3000, www.saintjosephhospital.reshealth.org; Advocate Illinois Masonic Medical Center, 836 W Wellington Ave, 773 975-1600, www.advocatehealth.com/immc; Thorek Memorial Hospital & Medical Center, 850 W Irving Park Rd, 773-525-6780, www.thorek.org

**Libraries:** John Merlo/Lake View, 644 W Belmont Ave, 312-744-1139; Uptown Branch, 929 W Buena Ave, 312-744-8400; Lincoln Belmont, 1659 W Melrose St, 312-744-0166; www.chipublib.org

**Community Resource:** Lakeview Chamber of Commerce, 1409 W Addison St, 773-472-7171, www.lakeviewchamber.com

**Parks:** www.chicagoparkdistrict.com, 312-742-PLAY: Gill Park, 825 W Sheridan Rd, 312-742-7802; and many more parks

**Community Publication:** Chicago Magazine, Chicago Parent, Chicago Reader, Chicago Reporter, N'DIGO, Newcity, Windy City Times

**Public Schools:** Chicago School District 299, 125 S Clark St, Chicago, IL 60603, 773-553-1000, www.cps.edu

**Transportation—Rapid Transit:** Red Line (stations: Belmont, Addison, Sheridan); Brown Line (stations: Wellington, Belmont, Southport, Paulina)

**Transportation—Major Bus Routes:** #8 Halsted, #9 Ashland, #11 Lincoln/Sedgwick, #22 Clark, #36 Broadway, #76 Diversey, #77 Belmont, #80 Irving Park, #151 Sheridan, #152 Addison, #156 LaSalle

## NORTH CENTER/ST. BEN'S/ROSCOE VILLAGE

**Boundaries:** *North Center:* **North:** Montrose Ave (4400N); **South:** Addison St (3600N); **East:** Ravenswood (1800W); **West:** Chicago River; *St. Ben's:* **North:** Irving Park Rd (4000N); **South:** Addison St (3600N); **East:** Damen Ave (2000W); **West:** Western Ave (2400W); *Roscoe Village:* **North:** Addison St (3600N); **South:** Belmont Ave (3200N); **East:** Damen Ave (2000W); **West:** Western Ave (2400W)

One hundred years ago **North Center** was primarily a German/Swedish neighborhood, but with time, the delis, social clubs, and beer halls with singing waiters have all but faded from memory. In the last ten years the eastern edge of North Center, and the Belmont/Lincoln/Ashland intersection in particular, has seen explosive growth. Former department stores, movie palaces, and factories have been tastefully transformed (with original facades intact) into lofts and condos; delightfully, the diners and bowling alleys also remain. This gentrification, though slow in coming, was inevitable once the development in North Center's tonier neighbor, Lakeview/Wrigleyville, peaked. North Center has made up for lost time quickly: according to the *Chicago Tribune*, the median price of home sales in North Center has exceeded even that of upscale Lincoln Park since 2005.

This tri-neighborhood area has more breathing space than the heavily populated Lakeview area; this, along with its convenience to public transportation, makes it very attractive to young families and young professionals. Both Roscoe Village and St. Ben's are distinct neighborhoods within the North Center boundaries. (Officially, Roscoe Village, sitting south of North Center, is the western

# THE CITY OF CHICAGO: NORTH

*Roscoe Village*

edge of West Lakeview, bound by Addison, Ravenswood, Belmont, and the Chicago River.) **Roscoe Village** is predominantly made up of single-family homes and converted condos. On Roscoe Street, the main thoroughfare, you will find several restaurants, small shops, and antique stores. Wander over to Belmont for Roscoe Village's own little antique row, with several shops tucked between Ravenswood and Western. Just north of Roscoe Village lies the neighborhood of **St. Ben's**, named for St. Benedict's, a Catholic Church that started over one hundred years ago to serve and educate what was then a primarily German community. The St. Ben's area has developed rapidly over the last decade, with a lot of rehabbing of single-family homes, two-flats, and apartment buildings, all of which are nestled on clean, tree-lined streets. Homeowners tend to be young professionals, though some long-time residents of German ancestry can still be found here.

While North Center is not as trendy as Wrigleyville to the east, it is considerably quieter, and you can even park your car on the street at night without a permit. The 'L' Brown Line runs along the eastern edge of the neighborhood and is the commute of choice for those who work downtown. Lincoln Avenue, North Center's main shopping drag, is a collage of old-world and new-age businesses where chic blends into kitsch and comes out…unique. Newer developments along the avenue include a Trader Joe's and a CB2, Crate and Barrel's lower-priced subsidiary. And, last but not least, for an authentic Chicago experience—driving way too fast, radio blaring, straight as an arrow down a pot-holed, neon-drenched street—check out Western Avenue, which marks the western edge of Roscoe Village. Lined with used-car lots, large commercial developments, strip malls, and fast food joints, this is one of the longest, continuous city streets in the country. Western Avenue runs straight north to the border of Evanston and all the way south through the city and into the southern suburbs.

**Neighborhood Websites:** www.northcenterchamber.com; www.roscoevillage.org
**Area Code:** 773
**ZIP Codes:** 60613, 60618, 60657
**Post Offices:** Graceland, 3024 N Ashland Ave; Finance Station T, 2011 W Montrose Ave; Lakeview, 1343 W Irving Park Rd
**Police District:** 19th/Town Hall Chicago District (Area 3), 850 W Addison St, 312-744-8320
**Emergency Hospital:** Illinois Masonic Medical Center, 836 W Wellington Ave, 773-975-1600, www.advocatehealth.com/immc
**Libraries:** Lincoln Belmont, 1659 W Melrose St, 312-744-0166; Sulzer Regional, 4455 N Lincoln Ave, 312-744-7616; Uptown Branch, 929 W Buena Ave, 312-744-8400; www.chipublib.org
**Community Resource:** Roscoe Village Chamber of Commerce, 3201 N Wolcott Ave, 773-327-5123, www.rvcc.biz
**Parks:** www.chicagoparkdistrict.com, 312-742-PLAY: Revere Park, 2509 W Irving Park Rd, 773-478-1220; Filbert Park, 1822 W Larchmont, 312-742-7826; Fellger Playlot Park, 2000 W Belmont, 312-742-7785
**Community Publications:** *Chicago Magazine, Chicago Parent, Chicago Reader, Chicago Reporter, N'DIGO, Newcity, Windy City Times*
**Public Schools:** Chicago School District 299, 125 S Clark St, Chicago, IL 60603, 773-553-1000, www.cps.edu
**Transportation—Rapid Transit:** Brown Line (stations: Paulina, Addison, Irving Park, Montrose)
**Transportation—Major Bus Routes:** #9 Ashland, #11 Lincoln/Sedgwick, #49 Western, #50 Damen, #76 Diversey, #77 Belmont, #78 Montrose, #80 Irving Park, #152 Addison

## *RAVENSWOOD/LINCOLN SQUARE*

**Boundaries**: **North:** Foster Ave (5200N); **South:** Montrose Ave (4400N); **East:** Clark St; **West:** Chicago River

The **Ravenswood** neighborhood, located directly north of North Center, was named for Ravenswood Avenue, which runs alongside the Chicago and North Western Railway (C&NW). The neighborhood first became popular in the 1860s when the C&NW opened a station at Wilson Avenue, and grew quickly during the 1880s and '90s when streetcar lines reached the area. While the official maps refer to this community as Lincoln Square, and that is how most realtors and city officials will refer to this area, most Chicago residents think of Ravenswood as the larger community, and Lincoln Square as a neighborhood in the western part of the Ravenswood area.

Renovation and rehabilitation have taken precedence over raze and ruin in family-oriented Ravenswood, which is filled with wonderful vintage buildings and multi-unit apartment complexes. The East Ravenswood Historic District (bounded by Lawrence Avenue/Irving Park Road/Ravenswood Street), one of Chicago's first planned communities, has been placed on the National Register of Historic Places. Today you'll find carefully rehabbed Victorian homes and two- and three-flat brick buildings. Many apartments in Ravenswood have been converted into condos, and many older homes, prized for their oversized lots, have been sold as tear-downs. Unsurprisingly, young professionals have discovered the leafy area and are thought to be the driving force behind the real estate boom here.

Right across the street from the Ravenswood neighborhood's southwest corner is one of Chicago's best-known funerary landmarks, Graceland Cemetery. Here you can marvel (or wince) at the sumptuous sepulchers of former captains of industry, such as Pullman, Potter, and Getty. Ravenswood's calm, tree-lined streets are family-friendly, and while the neighborhood lacks the restaurants and nightlife of nearby Wrigleyville and Andersonville, it's conveniently close to them.

**Lincoln Square** (boundaries: Ainslie Street, Eastwood Avenue, Bell Avenue, Rockwell Street), an old German neighborhood that developed during the late 19th century, still retains its European flair. In the newly renovated two-block-long Lincoln Square Mall, a brick-paved stretch just south of Lawrence Avenue, you will find plenty of Old World–style restaurants, outdoor cafés, and shops, which lend authenticity to its theme of "A Touch of Europe." To experience the neighborhood's historic German flavor, head to Merz Apothecary, to the Chicago Brauhaus—which provides an authentic German experience, right down to the lederhosen-clad oompah band—or just across the street to the Huettenbar, a friendly neighborhood pub that serves a variety of German brews on tap. Despite its German roots, today's Lincoln Square is not by any means

*Lincoln Square*

homogeneous. The portions of Western and Damen Avenues near Lawrence, which boast a concentration of Asian eateries, and neighborhood groceries that stock Baltic, Mediterranean, Slavic, and Mexican specialties on shelves and at deli counters, reflect this neighborhood's truly international make-up. Come to the mall on Tuesday mornings for the open-air farmers' market. In the summer it's the Auto Show, the Sidewalk Arts & Crafts Show, the Folk & Roots Festival, the German-American Fest, and the Lincoln Square Applefest. The number of community activities and local merchants—there are approximately 1,000 small and medium-sized local businesses in the Lincoln Square neighborhood—is a testament to the community's diversity and vitality.

Gentrification has sped up in the last several years, with more upscale retail shops opening along Lincoln Avenue. Five-star restaurants have arrived, rents and housing prices have risen, and the face of the neighborhood, especially east of Rockwell Avenue, has gotten much whiter. You can't blame affluent families and young professionals for being attracted to Lincoln Square. In addition to great bars and restaurants, the neighborhood also offers a collection of tasteful public art that includes murals, copper fountains, German maypoles, and a statue of Lincoln at the corner of Lawrence and Western Avenues. The tree-lined streets are peppered with wonderful examples of Chicago-Style architecture, as featured in the wood-frame Victorians, graystone mansions, and single-family bungalows. One of the most beautiful and best examples of 1920s architecture is the Museum of Decorative Arts, located at 4611 North Lincoln Avenue. Once the home and music store of William Krause, this building is the last work of Louis Sullivan, the same architect who was responsible for many Chicago landmarks including the Carson Pirie Scott Building on State Street. The Museum sells a wide variety of decorative art and objects from the Victorian, Art Deco, Art Nouveau, and Arts and Crafts movement eras. Directly across the street is the flickering marquee of the bargain basement Davis Theater, which shows second-run Hollywood movies and occasional independent films. South of the Davis are the digs of the popular and long-lived Old Town School of Folk Music, which offers concerts, a music store, and its own publications and recordings, as well as music lessons.

Conrad Sulzer Regional Library, located on the corner of Lincoln and Sunnyside, is another example of the area's outstanding architecture. One of the largest neighborhood library branches in the city, Sulzer houses more than 250,000 books. It was designed by Hammond, Beeby, and Babka, the architects who designed the Harold Washington Library in the Loop.

**Neighborhood Websites:** www.lincolnsquare.org
**Area Code:** 773
**ZIP Codes:** 60625, 60640
**Post Offices:** Ravenswood, 2522 W Lawrence Ave; Lakeview, 1343 W Irving Park Rd; Uptown, 4850 N Broadway

**Police District:** 19th/Town Hall District (Area 3), 850 W Addison St, 312-744-8320
**Emergency Hospitals:** Methodist Hospital, 5025 N Paulina St, 773-271-9040, www.methodistchicago.org; Swedish Covenant Hospital, 5145 N California Ave, 773-878-8200, swedishcovenant.org
**Library:** Sulzer Regional, 4455 N Lincoln Ave, 312-744-7616; www.chipublib.org
**Community Resources:** Old Town School of Folk Music, 4544 N Lincoln Ave, 773-728-6000, www.oldtownschool.org; Jane Addams Resource Corp., 4432 N Ravenswood Ave, 773-728-9769, www.jane-addams.org; Lincoln Square Chamber of Commerce, 773-728-3890, www.lincolnsquare.org
**Parks:** www.chicagoparkdistrict.com, 312-742-PLAY: Clarendon Community Center, 4501 N Clarendon Ave, 312-742-7512; Welles Park, 2333 W Sunnyside Ave, 312-742-7511; Winnemac Park, 5001 N Leavitt Ave, 312-742-5101
**Community Publications:** *Chicago Magazine, Chicago Parent, Chicago Reader, Chicago Reporter, N'DIGO, Newcity, Windy City Times*
**Public Schools:** Chicago School District 299, 125 S Clark St, Chicago, IL 60603, 773-553-1000, www.cps.edu
**Transportation—Rapid Transit:** Brown Line (stations: Montrose, Damen, Western); Metra/Union Pacific North Line (station: Ravenswood)
**Transportation—Major Bus Routes:** #11 Lincoln/Sedgwick, #22 Clark, #49 Western, #50 Damen, #78 Montrose, #80 Irving Park, #81 Lawrence, #92 Foster

## EDGEWATER

**Boundaries: North:** Devon Ave; **South:** Foster Ave; **East:** Lake Michigan; **West:** Ravenswood Ave

Located diagonally east from Ravenswood is the Edgewater neighborhood. Between World War I and World War II, Edgewater was synonymous with elegance and the Edgewater Beach Hotel was *the* north shore spot for fine dining and dancing. But as times changed, this once-elite community fell into decline. The Edgewater Hotel was torn down in 1969, along with many of the other fine, lakeshore mansions that surrounded it. One survivor is the 19-story, flamingo-pink cooperative that houses the Edgewater Beach Apartments. While the majority of housing in Edgewater—especially along the lakefront—is in the form of apartments and condos, if you walk inland a few blocks you can still find large houses, now being rehabbed by a new generation of homeowners.

Edgewater's more recent history is a wonderful example of community spirit. The area has experienced a remarkable turnaround over the past two decades. At one time, sixteen boarded-up buildings marred the Winthrop-Kenmore corridor, and the commercial strip along Bryn Mawr Avenue contained grimy storefronts, rundown residential hotels, and abandoned buildings. Gang infestation was driving the neighborhood into rapid decay. But the community

*Edgewater*

was given a second chance in 1995, when a section of Bryn Mawr Avenue, from Broadway to Lake Michigan, was declared a historic district. That led the way for tax breaks and a renewed interest in the area by commercial developers. Ridge Avenue was another blighted area in the 1990s; buildings owned by absentee landlords attracted criminal activity and threatened the core of the neighborhood. The Edgewater Community Council led the way for several of those buildings to transfer ownership and for another 72-unit building to be renovated. Just recently, another section of Edgewater was added to the National Register of Historic Places: Lakewood Balmoral, a 12-square-block area stretching from Broadway to Glenwood, and Foster to Bryn Mawr. The community's efforts have paid off with the crime rate in Edgewater consistently decreasing over the past several years. Today, Edgewater is a multicultural mix of Chicagoans, who have brought with them a variety of restaurants—from Ethiopian to Asian to Bosnian. Numerous large supermarkets and strip malls provide good shopping, and several community theaters lend a touch of culture.

Loyola University lies at Edgewater's northern edge, attracting many students to live in the area. Also here: home-based business owners, retirees, and a large number of families of Hispanic, Asian, and Russian descent. And, according to the 2000 Census, Edgewater has the largest community of gay couples in Chicago, many of whom live in Andersonville, the little Scandinavian enclave in Edgewater's southwest corner (see next profile). With its convenient location, easy access to Lake Shore Drive, major bus routes running through it, and an active community council, Edgewater has long been poised to become the next great neighborhood in north Chicago. While prices for houses, brick flats, and condos are rising slowly and steadily, one can still get a condo for about $50,000 to $100,000 less than its equivalent in Lakeview. (Single-family homes rarely come onto the market.)

The vast park and the accompanying bike path that follows the beach side of Lake Shore Drive come to an end at Edgewater's southeast corner. The family-friendly beaches here at Hollywood, Ardmore, and Foster Avenues are

# THE CITY OF CHICAGO: NORTH

beautiful and offer excellent views of the shoreline to the north. On clear days you can make out the lakeshore campus of Northwestern University in Evanston. Looking eastward, out across the lake, you will spot a squat, cylindrical shape that hovers about two miles off the shoreline. Don't be misled by locals who may try to convince you that it is (1) a giant floating storage tank for industrial waste, (2) a casino, or (3) the new Bears stadium. It's actually a water intake crib, one of three (if you look south you can see the others) that provides the city with its fresh water.

**Neighborhood Websites:** Edgewater Triangle Neighbors Association, www.etnabc.org; www.andersonville.org

**Area Code:** 773

**ZIP Codes:** 60640, 60660

**Post Offices:** Rogers Park, 1723 W Devon Ave; Uptown, 4850 N Broadway

**Police Districts:** South of Peterson Avenue: 20th/Foster Avenue District (Area 3), 5400 N Lincoln Ave, 312-742-8714, 312-742-8715; north of Peterson Avenue: 24th/Rogers Park District (Area 3), 6464 N Clark St, 312-744-5907

**Emergency Hospital:** Weiss Memorial Hospital, 4646 N Marine Dr, 773-878-8700

**Library:** Edgewater, 5917 N Broadway Street, 312-744-0718; www.chipublib.org

**Community Resources:** Edgewater Chamber of Commerce, 1210 N Thorndale, 773-561-6000, www.edgewater.org; Edgewater Triangle Neighborhood Association, www.etnabc.org; Storycatchers Theatre, 920 N Franklin St, Suite 302, 312-280-4772; Organization of the North East, www.onechicago.org, 773-769-3232, 773-381-1490; Edgewater Development Corporation, www.edgewaterdev.org, 773-506-4016; Edgewater Historical Society, www.edgewaterhistory.org, 773-506-4849

**Parks:** www.chicagoparkdistrict.com, 312-742-PLAY: Berger Park, 6205-47 N Sheridan Rd, 773-761-0376; Broadway Armory Park, 5917 N Broadway St, 312-742-7502; Foster Avenue Beach, Foster Ave and Lake Michigan, 312-742-5121; Lane Beach Park, 5915 N Sheridan Rd (Loyola), 773-761-0376

**Community Publications:** *Chicago Magazine, Chicago Parent, Chicago Reader, Chicago Reporter, N'DIGO, Newcity, Windy City Times*

**Public Schools:** Chicago School District 299, 125 S Clark St, Chicago, IL 60603, 773-553-1000, www.cps.edu

**Transportation—Rapid Transit:** Red Line (stations: Berwyn, Bryn Mawr, Thorndale, Granville)

**Transportation—Major Bus Routes:** #22 Clark, #36 Broadway, #50 Damen, #84 Peterson, #92 Foster, #136 Sheridan/LaSalle Express, #147 Outer Drive Express, #151 Sheridan, #155 Devon

## ANDERSONVILLE

**Boundaries: North:** Bryn Mawr (5600N); **South:** Foster (5200N); **East:** Clark St; **West:** Ravenswood Ave (1800W)

Who needs Wisconsin or Minnesota? If you're looking for Scandinavian history and heritage, you can find it here. Located in a half square mile in the southwest corner of Edgewater, Andersonville is an old Swedish neighborhood, first settled in the mid-19th century with cherry orchards. Although most of the Swedes are long gone, Andersonville retains some of its ethnic flavor in a few neighborhood bakeries, gift shops, and, of course, the Swedish American Museum at 5211 North Clark Street (773-728-8111). The neighborhood's contemporary ethnic mosaic can be glimpsed in the variety of restaurants, bakeries, and produce stands along Clark Street, which range from Swedish to Persian, Asian to Mexican and beyond.

Housing in this neighborhood consists primarily of attractive, large single-family homes and stylish three-flats. While it is less expensive than the better-known areas to the south, Andersonville is no longer the delightful bargain it once was. For those without a car, there is one drawback to living here: no easy access to the 'L.' Yet somehow, the convergence of shops and eateries along Clark Street near Foster Avenue is always bustling and, each June, nearly 40,000 people find their way to Andersonville's Midsommarfest for two days of eating, dancing, and music.

Clark Street, Andersonville's commercial strip, hosts spots where one can buy antiques, books, jewelry, toys, and chocolates, as well as a pleasing array of restaurants and unique bars with a neighborhood feel. Several of the stores and restaurants are owned and operated by local residents, many of them women.

*Andersonville*

# THE CITY OF CHICAGO: NORTH

Chicago's largest gay and lesbian population thrives in Andersonville, and many businesses, such as video rental stores, bookstores, and restaurants, are owned by and cater to this crowd. One of the better-known bookstores, Women & Children First, has a large collection of feminist/lesbian material, and is known for its author readings and signings. North of Catalpa Avenue, you will find a large commercial area catering to the neighborhood's Hispanic community. Two of the city's best bakeries are located in Andersonville. For freshly baked pita bread and scrumptious spinach pies, among other delicacies, check out the Middle East Bakery on Foster Avenue between Clark and Ashland. Finally, for your own sake, do not buy a coffeecake from the Swedish Bakery at 5348 North Clark Street (773-561-8919)! You will devour the whole thing and wind up guilt-ridden, covered with crumbs, and completely satisfied. On second thought...

**Neighborhood Websites:** Edgewater Triangle Neighborhood Association, www.etnabc.org; www.andersonville.org
**Area Code:** 773
**ZIP Code:** 60640
**Post Office:** Uptown, 4850 N Broadway
**Police District:** 20th/Foster Avenue District (Area 3), 5400 N Lincoln Ave, 312-742-8714, 312-742-8715
**Emergency Hospitals:** Methodist Hospital, 5025 N Paulina St, 773-271-9040, www.methodistchicago.org; Vanguard Weiss Memorial Hospital, 4646 N Marine Dr, 773-878-8700, www.weisshospital.com
**Library:** Edgewater, 5917 N Broadway St; Bezazian, 1226 W Ainslie St, 312-744-0019 www.chipublib.org
**Community Resources:** Andersonville Chamber of Commerce, 5356 N Clark St, 2nd Fl, 773-728-2995, www.andersonville.org; Edgewater Development Corporation, 1106-08 W Bryn Mawr Ave, 773-506-4016, www.edgewaterdev.org; Edgewater Historical Society, 773-506-4849, www.edgewaterhistory.org; East Andersonville Residents' Council, earc@yahoo.com
**Parks:** www.chicagoparkdistrict.com, 312-742-PLAY: Andersonville Playlot Park, 5233 N Ashland Ave, 312-742-5101
**Community Publications:** *Chicago Magazine, Chicago Parent, Chicago Reader, Chicago Reporter, N'DIGO, Newcity, Windy City Times*
**Public Schools:** Chicago School District 299, 125 S Clark St, Chicago, IL 60603, 773-553-1000, www.cps.edu
**Transportation—Rapid Transit:** Red Line (station: Berwyn)
**Transportation—Major Bus Routes:** #22 Clark, #50 Damen, #92 Foster, #36 Broadway

## (EAST) ROGERS PARK

**Boundaries: North:** city limits with Evanston; **South:** Devon Ave; **East:** Lake Michigan; **West:** Ridge Ave

Tucked between Edgewater and Evanston, Chicago's northernmost community offers a history of affordable living and close proximity to a long stretch of Lake Michigan coastline. Referred to variously as Rogers Park or East Rogers Park, this area is home to one of Chicago's most diverse populations. People of European, Mexican, Asian, Hispanic, African, and Middle Eastern descent live in Rogers Park along with large contingents of Caribbean Americans and Orthodox Jews. According to 2010 Census figures, Rogers Park residents speak about 40 languages and come from over 80 countries.

The neighborhood's name came from Philip Rogers, a pioneer and trader who saw development potential in the area where two Native American trails—now Ridge Boulevard and Rogers Avenue—intersected. After purchasing the land from tribes he traded with, Rogers opened the area for settlement by the European farmers who poured in between 1830 and 1850. The original village of Rogers Park, centered on the old post road (now Clark Street) leading to Green Bay, Wisconsin, was annexed by the City of Chicago in 1893.

In the early twentieth century, many Chicagoans wishing to "summer" up north built homes near Lake Michigan in Rogers Park. In 1952, an alliance of civic-minded residents organized to prevent private developers from building high-rise apartments along the beachfront, ushering in an era of proactive community involvement that continues to this day. Rogers Park's traditionally affordable housing has attracted a mix of immigrants, artists, and students, especially from Loyola University, which anchors the neighborhood's southern edge, and nearby Evanston's Northwestern University. Unfortunately, the area's affordability has often attracted negligent landlords, transients, and crime as

*(East) Rogers Park*

well. Active community groups continue to work with local officials to remove the remaining slumlords, criminals, and prostitutes.

While vigilant residents have helped reduce the crime rate, gentrification has also been changing the neighborhood. Leafy streets lined with low-rise brick apartment complexes and two- and three-story Victorian homes create a suburban feeling despite Rogers Park's convenience to both Chicago and Evanston. Spacious vintage apartments, beckoning beaches, and good connections to both the Chicago 'L' system and the suburban Metra train system have made Rogers Park "hot" for real estate development for much of the last decade. By November 2005, scores of recent condominium conversions meant that almost 50% of Rogers Park's housing stock was owner-occupied. Since an estimated 90% of the buyers for condo conversions since 2000 have been white, neighborhood demographics continue to change.

Compared to many of Chicago's lakefront neighborhoods, Rogers Park is still an affordable place to live and play. You'll find a string of mostly independently owned Asian, Mexican, and Caribbean restaurants along Howard Avenue and a number of relaxed, friendly coffeehouses and bars on Sheridan, Clark, and Broadway Avenues. The 16-acre Gateway Center includes a Dominick's supermarket and other retail shopping. In the summer, residents relax in the lovely green environs of Loyola Park or enjoy barbecues, swimming, and 4th of July fireworks displays at any of eight beaches that extend south from Evanston like pearls on a string. The Heartland Café, located at 7000 North Glenwood, has been a popular meeting place since its establishment in 1976. In addition to a "wholesome food" restaurant, the Heartland enterprise includes a gallery that exhibits local artwork, a General Store, a studio theater, and the Red Line Tap bar, which offers live music and open mike poetry readings. Its newspaper, *The Heartland Journal*, focuses on community issues and progressive action. Such establishments, combined with large artist and student populations, continue the neighborhood's vibrant counter-cultural legacy. Late spring, when college students from nearby Loyola and Northwestern University (in Evanston) head home for the summer, is the best time to find an apartment.

## *WEST ROGERS PARK/WEST RIDGE*

**Boundaries**: **North:** Howard St; **South:** Bryn Mawr Ave & Peterson Ave; **East:** Ridge Blvd; **West:** Kedzie Ave

Though its formal name is West Ridge, the neighborhood that borders Rogers Park to the west is often referred to as West Rogers Park. Quieter and less densely populated than its neighbor to the east, with a more suburban feel and higher home prices, West Ridge attracts more families than singles to its mix of well-kept bungalows and low-rise apartment buildings.

*West Rogers Park*

Devon Avenue, which runs along the southern edge of West Ridge, reflects the neighborhood's rich mix of ethnicities. The strip of shops and restaurants between Western and Kedzie Avenues is the undisputed center of Indo-Pakistani culture in the Chicago area. Here are stores selling every conceivable foodstuff—Indian, Syrian, Pakistani, and Kosher—and restaurants to please every palate. If you're looking for a truly diverse, family-friendly neighborhood, or just looking for a great, inexpensive meal, West Rogers Park is the place to go.

**Neighborhood Websites:** Northside Community Resources, www.rogerspark.org
**Area Code:** 773
**ZIP Codes:** 60626, 60645, 60659, 60660
**Post Office:** Rogers Park, 1723 W Devon Ave
**Police District:** 24th/Rogers Park District (Area 3), 6464 N Clark St, 312-744-5907
**Emergency Hospital:** St. Francis Hospital of Evanston, 355 Ridge Ave, Evanston, 847-316-4000, saintfrancishospital.reshealth.org
**Library:** Rogers Park, 6907 N Clark Street, 312-744-0156; Northtown, 6435 N California Ave, 312-744-2292; www.chipublib.org
**Community Resources:** Rogers Park Community Council/Rogers Park Community Development Corporation 773-338-7722, www.rogerspark.org/ www.rogersparkcdc.org; Seniors Initiative Program, 773-338-7722; Organization of the North East, www.onechicago.org, 773-769-3232; Loyola University Crown Center Gallery, 1001 W Loyola Ave, 773-508-3811; North Lakeside Cultural Center, 6219 N Sheridan Rd, 773-743-4477
**Parks & Beaches:** www.chicagoparkdistrict.com; 312-742-PLAY (see the **Greenspaces and Beaches** chapter for a list of Rogers Park's street-end beaches)
**Public Schools:** Chicago School District 299, 125 S Clark St, Chicago, IL 60603, 773-553-1000, www.cps.edu
**Community Publications:** *Chicago Magazine, Chicago Parent, Chicago Reader, Chicago Reporter, The Heartland Journal, N'DIGO, Newcity, Windy City Times*
**Transportation—Rapid Transit:** Red Line (stations: Loyola, Morse, Jarvis, Howard); Metra/Union Pacific North Line (station: Rogers Park)
**Transportation—Major Bus Routes:** #22 Clark, #49B North Western, #93 California/Dodge, #96 Lunt, #147 Outer Drive Express, #151 Sheridan, #155 Devon

# WEST

## ALBANY PARK

**Boundaries**: **North:** Chicago River; **South:** Irving Park Rd and Elston Ave; **East:** Chicago River; **West:** Elston Ave and Pulaski Rd

Albany Park, directly west of Ravenswood, is another example of Chicago's amazing diversity. With a foreign-born population of nearly 50%, and with more than 70 languages spoken in this community, it's easy to walk down the streets here on a hot summer night and feel certain that you're in another country. But which one? When it comes to food, the questions can get overwhelming, especially on an empty stomach. Kimchee? Falafel? Fajita? Pad Thai? Happily, the answers are all equally delicious.

Once a large Jewish middle-class community, now Albany Park is sometimes referred to as Koreatown, for the concentration of Korean restaurants, retail shops, and grocery stores along Lawrence Avenue. The mile-long section of Lawrence between the river and Pulaski Road has been given the honorary name of Seoul Drive. While nearly 40% of the stores here are Korean owned, if you veer off towards Kedzie, between Lawrence and Wilson Avenues, you'll find another of the neighborhood's identities, displayed in Middle Eastern bakeries, bookstores, and restaurants. There are large Hispanic and Caucasian communities in Albany Park as well.

The Lawrence Avenue strip is so busy that traffic frequently slows to a crawl, especially on weekends. But don't let the hustle and bustle of the avenues mislead you; veer down a side street and you will understand the practical reasons why many people choose to live here: two- and three-story brick flats and single-family homes on quiet tree-lined streets, friendly neighbors, and easy access to markets and local eating establishments. Public transportation

*Albany Park*

is good. The northbound 'L' Brown Line meets land in Albany Park after crossing the Chicago River. The resulting street-level crossings, with flashing red lights, warning bells, and barriers, give the southeast corner of the neighborhood the feel of a small town.

This area is also bounded, and very much defined, by the river; along it you will find quiet streets, abundant greenery, and plenty of attractive single-family homes and apartments. Westward, the neighborhood recovers its big city edge but remains quiet and residential. Easy access to the Kennedy and Edens expressways are additional perks. It should be noted that Albany Park is poorer than neighboring Lincoln Square and parts of it can still be rough, particularly the area north of Lawrence and east of Kedzie Avenues. Many of the apartment buildings here were built in the 1920s, and though rents are rising and more and more buildings have been converted into condominiums, prices remain relatively affordable.

Albany Park's ethnic diversity is not surprising. It has always been known as a stepping-stone neighborhood, a place where generations of immigrants have cut their teeth on the New World before moving on to the suburbs. As an increasing number of natives discover this neighborhood's charms, it is gradually experiencing more of the gentrification seen in nearby Lincoln Square.

**Neighborhood Websites:** Albany Park Community Center, www.apcc-chgo.org
**Area Code:** 773, 312
**ZIP Codes:** 60618, 60625, 60630, 60641
**Post Offices:** Finance Station Q, 4749 N Bernard St; Ravenswood, 2522 W Lawrence Ave
**Police District:** 17th/Albany Park District (Area 5), 4461 N Pulaski Rd, 312-742-4410
**Emergency Hospitals:** Methodist Hospital, 5025 N Paulina St, 773-271-9040, www.methodistchicago.org; Swedish Covenant Hospital, 5145 N California Ave, 773-878-8200, swedishcovenant.org
**Libraries:** Mayfair, 4400 W Lawrence Ave, 312-744-1254; Independence, 3548 W Irving Park Rd, 312-744-0900; www.chipublib.org
**Community Publications:** *Chicago Magazine, Chicago Parent, Chicago Reader, Chicago Reporter, N'DIGO, Newcity, Windy City Times*
**Community Resources:** Albany Park Theatre Project, 773-866-0875, aptpchicago.org; Albany Park Community Center, 3403 W Lawrence, 773-583-5111, www.apcc-chgo.org
**Parks:** www.chicagoparkdistrict.com, 312-742-PLAY: Buffalo Park, 4501 N California Ave, 773-478-3499; Ravenswood Manor Park, 4604-46 N Manor Ave, 773-478-3499; Jensen Park, 4650 N Lawndale Ave, 312-742-7054; Ronan Park, 3000 W Argyle St, 312-742-7516
**Public Schools:** Chicago School District 299, 125 S Clark St, Chicago, IL 60603, 773-553-1000, www.cps.edu

**Transportation—Rapid Transit:** Brown Line (stations: Francisco, Kedzie, Kimball)
**Transportation—Major Bus Routes:** #53 Pulaski, #78 Montrose, #81 Lawrence, #82 Kimball/Homan, #93 California/Dodge

## LOGAN SQUARE (WEST TOWN)

**Boundaries**: **North:** Diversey Pkwy (2800N); **South**; Armitage Ave (2000N); **East:** Western Ave (2400W)/Kennedy Expy; **West:** Central Park Ave (3600W)

South of Albany Park but still counted among the northern neighborhoods of Chicago is West Town, or as it is more commonly known, Logan Square. The city's fifth largest neighborhood is known for its European-style, tree-lined boulevards, its central square, and its attractive architectural variety. Also here are a substantial number of multi-family dwellings, including two-flats and apartment buildings. In the center of Logan Square stands a 68-foot-tall pink marble column topped with an eagle, which commemorates the 100th anniversary of Illinois' entry into the Union. Architecturally speaking, the Logan Square stretches of Palmer Boulevard, Kedzie Avenue, and Logan Boulevard make a delightful centerpiece for the neighborhood; a walk along these leafy thoroughfares will reveal stately multi-family and single-family homes, many now restored, of Art Nouveau, Prairie, Renaissance Revival, and Gothic styles of architecture. Purists beware, however; many homes are a compilation of styles—architecturally inspired creations rather than formally designed. Because most of the mansions in the Logan Square area were never converted into rooming houses or low-rent apartments as in many other Chicago neighborhoods, you'll find that many unique characteristics such as original stained glass and carved woodwork remain intact. In 1985, the boulevards of Logan Square were included on the National Register of Historic Places. For a closer

*Logan Square*

look at these beautiful homes, take a neighborhood tour through the Chicago Architecture Foundation (www.architecture.org).

The Logan Square community is both economically and ethnically mixed; many residents are of Hispanic and Eastern European—particularly Polish—descent. In fact, a recent *Wall Street Journal* article reported that there are 800,000 people of Polish descent in Chicago—many of whom can be found in and around the Logan Square community. The housing here is close to 70% multi-family, much of it in the form of two-flat brick buildings. Crime has been a concern here; however, an active community alliance has been instrumental in reducing the crime rate. Community groups are vocal and cooperate with the police to actively decrease criminal activity, including loitering and littering. But there are still problems and you may be better off avoiding some areas such as Armitage Avenue west of Western Avenue. In the past decade, more affluent Chicagoans have snapped up townhouses around Logan Boulevard, Palmer Square, and Fullerton and Kedzie Avenues, and bargain hunters have found spacious treasures among the many single-family homes and apartment buildings converted to condos. (Few such bargains are available today.) Many of those coming here to make their homes were raised in this neighborhood, then moved to the suburbs, and are now returning to their roots. As is often the case, area crime lessens as the economic mix continues to improve.

Over the past decade, a restaurant and retail scene has slowly developed in Logan Square, especially near the Kedzie Avenue and California Avenue intersections with Logan Boulevard. Coffee shops, fine cuisine, and ethnic eateries have arrived to serve the more gentrified population now strolling the neighborhood's pleasant streets. Rents may still be lower than those in the neighborhoods directly to the east. And the location is commuter-friendly: the Kennedy Expressway cuts through Logan Square's northeastern corner, and the 'L' Blue Line runs parallel to Milwaukee Avenue, with stops on California and Kedzie Avenues. Elston and Milwaukee Avenues are Logan Square's two traditional commercial streets, lined with thrift stores, fruit markets, and Mexican and Polish restaurants. The Logan Theater screens second-run Hollywood films. For a real time warp, don't miss the local landmark: Margie's Candies (at the southwest corner of Western and Armitage Avenues). An honest-to-goodness ice cream parlor, Margie's has been dishing out homemade ice cream and fudge sauce for over seventy-five years.

**Website:** Logan Square Neighborhood Association, www.lsna.net
**Area Code:** 773
**ZIP Code:** 60647
**Post Office:** Roberto Clemente, 2339 N California Ave
**Police District:** 14th/Shakespeare District (Area 5), 2150 N California Ave, 312-744-8290

THE CITY OF CHICAGO: WEST 53

**Emergency Hospitals:** Saints Mary and Elizabeth Medical Center, 2233 W Division St/1431 N Claremont Ave, 312-770-2000/773-278-2000, http://www.reshealth.org/sub_smemc/default.cfm; Norwegian American Hospital, 1044 N Francisco Ave, 773-292-8200, www.nahospital.org
**Libraries:** Logan Square, 3030 W Fullerton Ave, 312-744-5295; Bucktown–Wicker Park, 1701 N Milwaukee Ave, 312-744-6022; www.chipublib.org
**Community Resources:** Logan Square Chamber of Commerce, 3147 W Logan Blvd, Suite 12, 773-489-3222, www.loganchamber.org; Near Northwest Arts Council, 773-278-7677, www.nnwac.org; Logan Square Neighborhood Association, 2840 N Milwaukee Ave, 773-384-4370, www.lsna.net; Logan Square Boys & Girls Club, 3228 W Palmer Ave, 773-342-8800, logansquare.bgcc.org; Logan Square Preservation, www.logansquarepreservation.org
**Parks:** www.chicagoparkdistrict.com, 312-742-PLAY: Holstein Park, 2200 N Oakley, 312-742-7554; Senior Citizens Memorial Playlot Park, 2228 N Oakley Ave, 312-742-7554; Erhler Park, 2230 W Cortland St, 312-742-7769; Haas Park, 2402 N Washtenaw Ave, 312-742-7552
**Public Schools:** Chicago School District 299, 125 S Clark St, Chicago, IL 60603, 773-553-1000, www.cps.edu
**Community Publications:** *Chicago Magazine, Chicago Parent, Chicago Reader, Chicago Reporter, N'DIGO, Newcity*
**Transportation—Rapid Transit:** Blue Line (stations: Western, California, Logan Square)
**Transportation—Major Bus Routes:** #49 Western, #52 Kedzie/California, #56 Milwaukee, #73 Armitage, #74 Fullerton, #76 Diversey, #82 Kimball/Homan

## WICKER PARK AND BUCKTOWN

**Boundaries:** *Bucktown:* **North:** Fullerton Ave (2400N); **South:** North Ave (1600N); **East:** Kennedy Expy/Ashland Ave (1600W); **West:** Western Ave (2400W); *Wicker Park:* **North:** North Ave (1600N); **South:** Division Ave (1200N); **East:** Ashland Ave (1600W); **West:** Western Ave (2400W)

Southeast of Logan Square is the Wicker Park/Bucktown community, which is blessed with gorgeous and once-forgotten Queen Anne and Italianate mansions. In the late 1980s and 1990s, Wicker Park's cheap rents and proximity to the city helped it become a "slacker haven" and music hub. Currently considered one of the hippest neighborhoods in Chicago, Wicker Park and Bucktown have seen rapid gentrification, meteoric rises in housing costs, and an influx of new clubs, retail establishments, and restaurants catering to the now well-heeled residents. Long-time residents attracted to the area for its bohemian atmosphere, inexpensive rents, and racial mix have lately reconsidered their living options.

*Wicker Park*

Historically, **Wicker Park** and **Bucktown** were bastions of European immigration, with Germans holding sway in Wicker Park and Poles in Bucktown. Wicker Park is named for the small park in the middle of the neighborhood; Bucktown got its name because its poorer immigrants kept goats in their backyards. Median incomes have jumped substantially in both neighborhoods, particularly in Bucktown, which now boasts some of the highest rents in Chicago. Still, the community retains an edgy feel that distinguishes it from other costly areas like Lincoln Park and the Gold Coast. A casual glance at the pedestrian traffic around the six-corners intersection of Milwaukee, Damen, and North Avenues (where *The Real World: Chicago* was filmed) still reveals more tattoos per exposed inch of skin than in any other Chicago neighborhood. The neighborhood remains very proud of its artistic residents: Wicker Park claims it is the largest working-artist community in the nation and Bucktown promotes the creative elements of its neighborhood by hosting the annual Bucktown ArtFest. This 20-year-old neighborhood tradition draws over 30,000 art lovers to the area each August.

The boundary between Wicker Park and Bucktown is the elevated Soo line railroad track, with Bucktown to the north and Wicker Park to the south. Beyond that, it's difficult to distinguish one neighborhood from the other. But you may notice that Wicker Park has more period homes, including turn-of-the-century mansions, while Bucktown is characterized by its cottage-style homes and coach houses. Both Wicker Park and Bucktown fell on hard times during the flight to the suburbs after World War II. Latinos filled the post-war void and today remain the area's largest ethnic group—although that has been changing as gentrification creeps north and west. As throughout Chicago, new construction here, including condos and townhomes built on the sites of tear-downs and a few pricey single-family homes, is being targeted to empty nesters, upscale families, and single professionals. The introduction of these new residents often re-energizes communities and galvanizes efforts to improve the neighborhoods' living conditions. In Bucktown, for example, cooperation between the community and the local police department contributed to over 600 prostitution arrests in one year.

Over the past decade, Wicker Park/Bucktown has become a favorite destination for chic diners and shoppers; the perennially clogged traffic at the intersection of Damen, Milwaukee, and North Avenues signals your arrival at the area's gastronomical and entertainment hub: restaurants, lounges, clubs, and hipster boutiques fill every available storefront. Division Street and the Wicker Park stretch of Milwaukee Avenue have developed into additional concentrations of restaurants and boutiques—though the odd reminder of the neighborhood's former identity pops up in the form of the occasional taqueria or Mexican bakery. Among the cuisines available are French, Mexican, Costa Rican, Cajun, Asian, Chilean, Italian, Japanese (sushi), and vegan. Valet and permit parking have also arrived and vehicular mayhem reigns, especially on the weekends. But take care, a short walk northwest of the main Six-Corners intersection, and the area turns grittier.

**Websites:** Bucktown Community Organization, www.bucktown.org; West Town Chamber of Commerce, www.westtownchamber.org
**Area Codes:** 312, 773
**ZIP Codes:** 60614, 60622, 60647
**Post Offices:** Wicker Park Retail Store, 1300 N Ashland Ave; Roberto Clemente, 2339 N California Ave
**Police District:** 14th/Shakespeare District (Area 5), 2150 N California Ave, 312-744-8290
**Emergency Hospitals:** Saints Mary and Elizabeth Medical Center, 2233 W Division St/1431 N Claremont Ave, 312-770-2000/773-278-2000, http://www.reshealth.org/sub_smemc/default.cfm
**Libraries:** Logan Square, 3030 W Fullerton Ave, 312-744-5295; Bucktown–Wicker Park, 1701 N Milwaukee Ave, 312-744-6022; www.chipublib.org
**Community Resources:** Wicker Park & Bucktown Chamber of Commerce, 1414 N Ashland Ave, 773-384-2672, www.wickerparkbucktown.com; Wicker Park Garden Club, 773-278-9075, www.wpgarden.org; Wicker Park Advisory Council, 1425 N Damen, 312-742-7553, wickerpark.org; Bucktown Community Organization, www.bucktown.org; Polish Museum of America, 984 N Milwaukee Ave, 773-384-3352, www.polishmuseumofamerica.org
**Parks:** www.chicagoparkdistrict.com, 312-742-PLAY: Clemente Park, 2334 W Division St, 312-742-7538; Commercial Club Playground, 1845 W Rice St, 312-742-7558; Eckhart Park, 1330 W Chicago, 312-746-5490; Pulaski Park, 1419 W Blackhawk St, 312-742-7559; Wicker Park, 1425 N Damen Ave; Holstein Park, 2200 N Oakley Ave, 312-742-7554; Walsh Playground Park, 1722 N Ashland, 312-742-7769
**Public Schools:** Chicago School District 299, 125 S Clark St, Chicago, IL 60603, 773-553-1000, www.cps.edu

**Community Publications:** *Chicago Magazine, Chicago Parent, Chicago Reader, Chicago Reporter, N'DIGO, Newcity, Windy City Times*
**Transportation—Rapid Transit:** Blue Line (stations: Division, Damen, Western)
**Transportation—Major Bus Routes:** #9 Ashland, #49 Western, #50 Damen, #56 Milwaukee, #70 Division, #72 North, #73 Armitage, #74 Fullerton

## UKRAINIAN VILLAGE/EAST VILLAGE

**Boundaries:** *Ukrainian Village:* **North:** Division St (1200N); **South:** Grand Ave (500N); **East:** Damen Ave (2000W); **West:** Western Ave (2400W); *East Village:* same North and South boundaries; **West:** Damen Ave (2000W); **East:** Ashland Ave (1600W)

The name says it all: mostly Ukrainian immigrants who came to Chicago at the turn of the 20th century settled this west side neighborhood, located southwest of Wicker Park. Unlike many of Chicago's former ethnic enclaves, the Ukrainian stamp remains on this quiet neighborhood with its onion-domed churches and signs lettered in Cyrillic. The Holy Trinity Orthodox Cathedral, 1121 North Leavitt Street, designed by famed Chicago architect Louis Sullivan, was granted landmark status in 1979, and is well worth a visit. Also check the Ukrainian National Museum, 2249 West Superior Street. The area bordered by Haddon Avenue on the north, Cortez Street on the south, Damen Avenue on the east, and Leavitt Avenue on the west was granted preliminary landmark status in 2002. Approximately one-third of the brick flats in this area were completed by 1906 and were built by William de Kerfoot's construction company. De Kerfoot was also instrumental in rebuilding Chicago after the Great Fire of 1871.

Architecturally, the neighborhood has everything, from mansions on Hoyne, to graystone flats, to workers' cottages. Many of these buildings retain

*Ukrainian Village*

original, ornate designs and details that attract rehabbers and do-it-yourselfers. Housing prices are generally lower here than in Wicker Park, though interest in this community caused a rise in prices during the 1990s and early 2000s.; in fact, median home values here increased 176% during the 1990s, the steepest increase in the city. While home values have declined in recent years nationally, the average sale price for a two-bedroom condo in Ukrainian Village is still above $275,000. Local community groups continue to press for more affordable housing, and some builders have responded with two-flats that are affordable to working-class families. One drawback to living in Ukrainian Village: because the area lacks an 'L' stop, commuters must rely on buses or at least take a bus north to the 'L' stop on Damen Avenue or north or east to the 'L' stop on Division Street.

The rapidly growing eastern section of the neighborhood (from Damen to Ashland) has attracted large numbers of Hispanic families as well as artists and students seeking bargains. Less attractive housing stock than in the western part of Ukrainian Village has led to many teardowns and, subsequently, a large array of two- to four-flat condo developments. However, some descendants of the Eastern Europeans who founded the area still live around the neighborhood. Live here and you may find yourself next door to the adult children and grandchildren of a building's original inhabitants.

Division Street forms the border between Wicker Park and the Ukrainian Village; along this section of Division, you will find Greek, Italian, and Japanese cuisine, as well as boutiques and newer restaurants with valet parking. The stretch of Damen Avenue leading from Ukrainian Village to Wicker Park is dotted with funky boutiques, cafés, and bars. On Western and Chicago Avenues, you will find Polish restaurants and bakeries, Italian delis, French cafés—even a vegetarian place. All told, you will find that Ukrainian Village is a rich mix of old-world traditions and modern sensibilities.

**Website:** Ukrainian Village Neighborhood Association, www.uvna.org
**Area Code:** 312, 773
**ZIP Codes:** 60612, 60622
**Post Offices:** Wicker Park Retail Store, 1300 N Ashland Ave
**Police District:** 13th/Wood District (Area 4), 937 N Wood St, 312-746-8357
**Emergency Hospitals:** Saints Mary and Elizabeth Medical Center, 2233 W Division St/1431 N Claremont Ave, 312-770-2000/773-278-2000, http://www.reshealth.org/sub_smemc/default.cfm; Rush University Medical Center, 1620 W Harrison St, 312-942-5000, www.rush.edu
**Libraries:** West Town, 1625 W Chicago Ave, 312-743-0450; Bucktown-Wicker Park, 1701 N Milwaukee Ave, 312-744-6022
**Community Resources:** West Town Chamber of Commerce, 1819 W Chicago Ave, 312-850-9390, www.westtownchamber.org; Ukrainian Village Neigh-

borhood Association, www.uvna.org; Ukrainian National Museum, 2249 W Superior St, 312-421-8020
**Community Publications:** *Chicago Magazine, Chicago Parent, Chicago Reader, Chicago Reporter, N'DIGO, Newcity*
**Parks:** www.chicagoparkdistrict.com, 312-742-PLAY: Clemente Park, 2334 W Division St, 312-742-7538; Commercial Club Playground, 1845 W Rice St, 312-742-7558; Snowberry Playlot Park, 1851 W Huron St, 312-742-7558; Superior Playlot Park, 2101 W Superior St, 312-742-7558; Western Park, 907 N Western Ave, 312-742-7538; Wicker Park, 1425 N Damen
**Public Schools:** Chicago School District 299, 125 S Clark St, Chicago, IL 60603, 773-553-1000, www.cps.edu
**Transportation—Rapid Transit:** Blue Line (stations: Damen, Division)
**Transportation—Major Bus Routes:** #9 Ashland, #49 Western, #50 Damen, #65 Grand, #66 Chicago, #70 Division

## TAYLOR STREET/UNIVERSITY OF ILLINOIS-CHICAGO

**Boundaries**: **North:** Harrison St (600S); **South:** Roosevelt Rd (1200S); **East:** Halsted St (800W); **West:** Ashland Ave (1600W)

Heading south from Ukrainian Village is the area generally referred to as the Near West Side. It includes several neighborhoods, such as **Little Italy**, **University Village**, and the **Jackson Boulevard Historic District**. The Little Italy area is the oldest continuously Italian neighborhood in Chicago. Now only a small enclave, this neighborhood has suffered severe demolition of its pre–World War II row houses and brick flats. The original demolition made way for the 560-acre University of Illinois Medical District, and a 305-acre West Side Medical Center, now one of the world's largest concentrations of medical facilities. The old neighborhood was reduced again to make room for the Eisenhower Expressway, and then again, for the university's Circle Campus. These demolitions dispersed the tight-knit Italian community to neighborhoods as far west as Harlem Avenue, and on into the suburbs of Melrose Park, Chicago Heights, and Blue Island. While these areas went on to form strong Italian communities, in Chicago, **Taylor Street** remains synonymous with "Little Italy."

As the university continues to grow (what once was a commuter college now has dormitories), the neighborhood loses a little more of its ethnic color. The strip of Italian restaurants on Taylor Street and Vernon Park Place is a fine example of what the entire area once looked like. Recently there has been a revived interest in the area, and building renovation is taking place in the Taylor Street neighborhood; takers for the newly constructed townhomes once consisted mainly of medical personnel wanting to live close to the cluster of large

# THE CITY OF CHICAGO: WEST

*Taylor Street*

hospitals in the area. With new housing have come new amenities; Taylor Street now offers a handful of trendy retail shops as well as Thai, sushi, and French bistros along with its Italian mainstays. As the neighborhood has grown more residential and amenities have improved, a wider variety of residents have been attracted to its environs.

**UIC** is in the midst of a large southward expansion of its campus, which is good news for construction companies and students—but neighbors to the south are wary. Given the college's track record of swallowing up low-income neighborhoods, they have good reason. But in building the new University Village, it seems community interests have been given some consideration, especially in the area of preserving the old Maxwell Street Market. Though the popular open-air attraction has been moved a few blocks from its former location (to the vicinity of Canal and Roosevelt), the huge outdoor flea market still thrives every Sunday during the warmer seasons, offering everything from snacks and kitchen wares to socks. At the former site of the market a new community has been built; comprising over 900 townhomes and condominiums with a wide range of pricing, the planned community includes 12 new buildings as well as the eight old rehabbed buildings on Halsted and Maxwell Streets. Retail shops, restaurants, and offices, as well as a system of public parks, are among University Village's amenities.

**Area Code:** 312
**ZIP Code:** 60607
**Post Office:** Pilsen, 1859 S Ashland Ave
**Police District:** 12th/Monroe District (Area 4), 100 S Racine Ave, 312-746-8309

**Emergency Hospitals:** John H. Stroger, Jr. Hospital of Cook County, 1900 W Polk St, 312-864-6000; Rush University Medical Center, 1620 W Harrison St, 312-942-5000, www.rush.edu; University of Illinois Hospital and Health Sciences System, 1740 W Taylor St, 866-600-2273, hospital.uillinois.edu
**Library:** Roosevelt, 1101 W Taylor St, 312-746-5656
**Parks:** www.chicagoparkdistrict.com, 312-742-PLAY, Arrigo Park, 801 S Loomis St, 312-746-5369; Garibaldi Park, 1520 W Polk St, 312-746-5369; Miller Playlot Park, 848 S Miller St, 312-746-5369; Sheridan Park, 910 S Aberdeen St, 312-746-5369
**Public Schools:** Chicago School District 299, 125 S Clark St, Chicago, IL 60603, 773-553-1000, www.cps.edu
**Community Publications:** *Chicago Magazine, Chicago Parent, Chicago Reader, Chicago Reporter, N'DIGO, Newcity*
**Transportation—Rapid Transit:** Blue Line (stations: UIC-Halsted, Racine, Illinois Medical District), Pink Line (stations: Polk)
**Transportation—Major Bus Routes:** #8 Halsted, #9 Ashland, #12 Roosevelt, #50 Damen, #60 Blue Island/26th

## PILSEN/LITTLE VILLAGE

**Boundaries: North:** 16th St; **South:** South Branch of Chicago River; **East:** Canal St; **West:** Damen Ave

In recent decades it's been a familiar story: a poor neighborhood with attractive but run-down housing stock is "discovered" by budding creative types, who gradually rehab the area and who are then in turn replaced by well-heeled newcomers with higher economic means. For better or for worse, Pilsen is the latest of these discoveries. Conveniently located south of the University of Illinois Chicago campus and in close proximity to the Loop, public transit, and three expressways, its turn-around was inevitable, though this is scarce comfort to many families who now find themselves unable to afford living here.

Czechs, Poles, Germans, Bohemians, and Lithuanians originally settled this area, also known as the **Lower West Side.** In the 1920s, immigrant Czechs dubbed the neighborhood Pilsen after the city of the same name in the former Czechoslovakia. For many years it was an industrial neighborhood whose inhabitants worked in the factories, lumberyards, and docks along the Chicago River and the Sanitary & Ship Canal. Beginning in the 1950s, Mexicans and Puerto Ricans began arriving—and by 2000 it had the highest percentage of Latino residents (close to 90%) of any Chicago neighborhood, down to about 82% by 2010. It is still, however, one of the largest Mexican communities in the United States. The median age of a Pilsen resident is 25.

*Pilsen*

While many area residents are poor, several positive developments are brewing in Pilsen. Eighteenth Street, the main east-west artery through the neighborhood, is hopping at all hours with restaurants, bars, ice cream shops, and bakeries galore. Blue Island and Ashland Avenues cut across 18th Street; here you'll find small grocery stores and taquerias. Among the sights of the contemporary neighborhood are advertisements for luxury condos: symptoms of the shift in Pilsen's fortunes. The creative types head to the area called **Pilsen East**, the unofficial artists' community clustered mainly around 18th, 19th, and Halsted Streets. A one-time commercial district where stores and factories have become artists' studios, streets here are sprinkled with storefront galleries and finding live/work space is still possible, though by no means as cheap as it was before the neighborhood was "discovered." (Note: tenants here are usually responsible for gas and electric bills.) During fall, the artists who live in the buildings along 18th and 19th Streets open up their studios to the public. Don't overlook the courtyards between buildings—there are exhibits set up there too. Also in the neighborhood: the National Museum of Mexican Art at 1852 West 19th Street is the largest Latino or Mexican art institute in the nation and has an excellent gift shop. Pilsen leads the way in public art. You will be hard pressed to find another Chicago community that has so many examples of artistic expression displayed throughout its streets. Mexican-themed murals signal Pilsen's ethnic pride to anyone debarking from the 18th Street station of the Blue Line 'L,' and vibrant murals cover scores of public spaces from 16th Street to the Chicago River east and south, then west to Western Avenue.

Given the background of most area residents it's no surprise that many local celebrations revolve around Mexican culture. On the last weekend of July, make plans to attend the Fiesta del Sol for live music, games, rides, and food. Each spring the National Museum of Mexican Art hosts the Del Corazon Performing Arts Festival and the Sor Juana Festival in the fall. Then through October and early November, experience the Dia de los Muertos/Day of the

Dead festival. If you enjoy parades you won't want to miss the Cinco de Mayo parade on the first Sunday in May. The parade travels up Cermak Road and ends with a festival in Douglas Park.

While Pilsen has its charms, it is like many other poor areas in the nation—the crime rate is high, with property crime particularly prevalent, and there is gang violence. Caution should be exercised when considering living in this neighborhood. Visit and see for yourself.

**Website:** pilsenneighbors.org
**Area Code:** 312
**ZIP Codes:** 60608, 60616
**Post Offices:** Pilsen, 1859 S Ashland Ave; Twenty-second, 2035 S State St
**Police District:** 12th/Monroe District (Area 4), 100 S Racine Ave, 312-746-8309
**Emergency Hospitals:** John H. Stroger, Jr. Hospital of Cook County, 1900 W Polk St, 312-
864-6000; Rush University Medical Center, 1620 W Harrison St, 312-942-5000, www.rush.edu;
University of Illinois Hospital and Health Sciences System, 1740 W Taylor St, 866-600-2273, hospital.uillinois.edu
**Library:** Lozano, 1805 S Loomis St, 312-746-4329
**Community Resources:** Early Outreach Hispanic Math/Science Initiative, 1101 W Taylor St, 3rd Fl, 312-996-2549; WRTE 90.5 FM Radio (youth-operated community radio station), 312-455-9455; National Museum of Mexican Art, 1852 W 19th St, 312-738-1503, www.nationalmuseumofmexicanart.org
**Community Publications:** *Chicago Magazine, Chicago Parent, Chicago Reader, Chicago Reporter, N'DIGO, Newcity*
**Public Schools:** Chicago School District 299, 125 S Clark St, Chicago, IL 60603, 773-553-1000, www.cps.edu
**Transportation—Rapid Transit:** Blue Line (stations: 18th, Damen)
**Transportation—Major Bus Routes:** #8 Halsted, #9 Ashland, #18 16th/18th, #21 Cermak, #50 Damen, #60 Blue Island/26th

# SOUTH

## SOUTH LOOP

**Boundaries**: **North:** Jackson Blvd; **South:** 24th St; **East:** Lake Shore Dr; **West:** Chicago River

The South Loop has been developing steadily since the early 1980s and continues to enjoy a construction boom. Most recently, and most exciting, is the Lake Shore Drive Improvement Project. In 1997, the city moved Lake Shore Drive's northbound lanes west of Soldier Field and the Field Museum. That

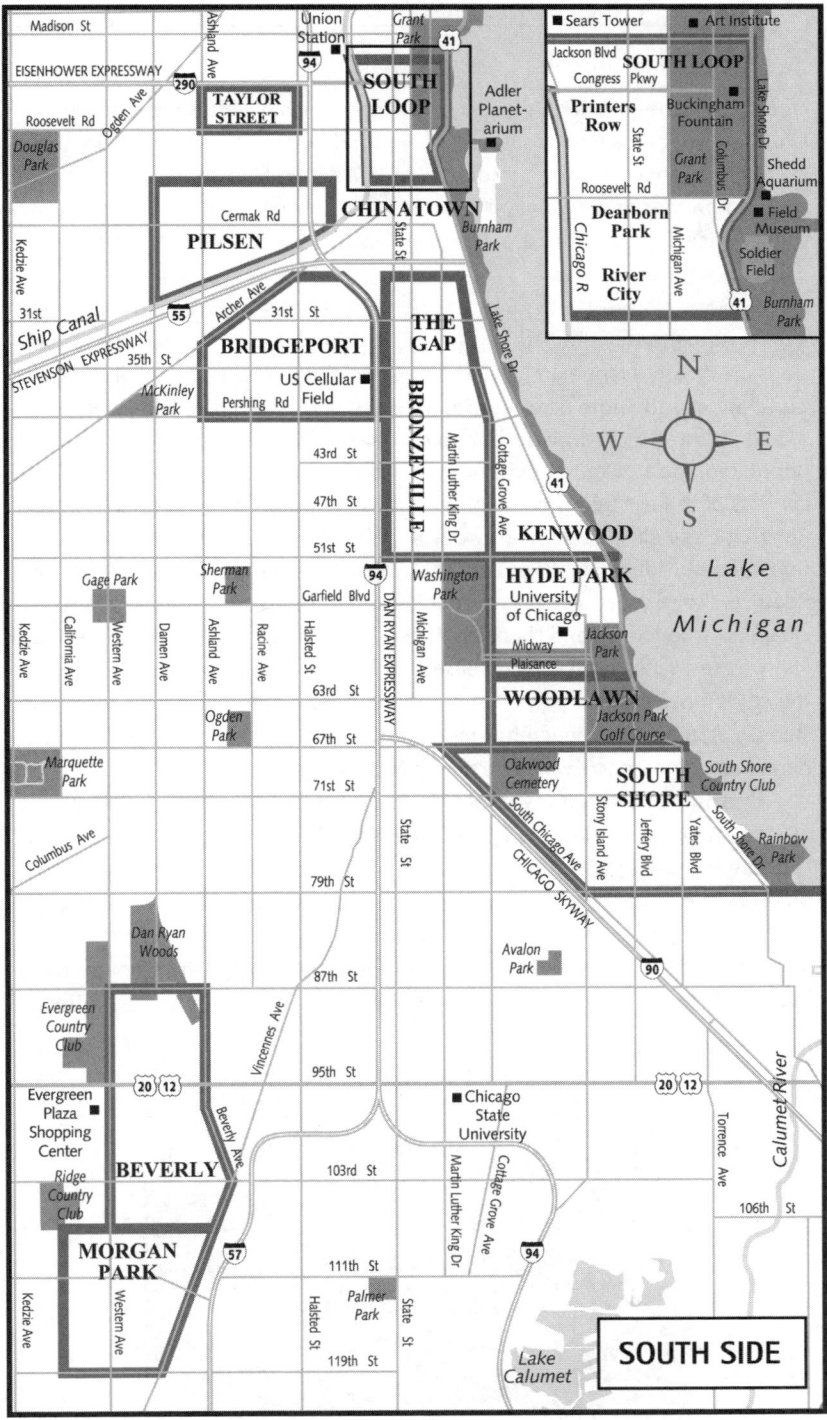

created ten acres of parkland along the shore, which was finished with elegant landscaping and bike and footpaths. Neighborhoods to the west of Lake Shore Drive are connected to the park and to CTA's Blue Line stop by newly constructed bridges and walkways. If you work in the Loop and want to live close to the office, few locations are as convenient or as architecturally attractive as those in the South Loop.

Renewed interest in the South Loop is great news for an area once labeled a slum. At the turn of the 20th century, the wealthy left behind their grand mansions on Prairie Avenue and headed north to the newer environs of the Gold Coast and North Shore neighborhoods. Eventually, the Illinois Central Railroad too abandoned its nearby tracks and rail yard. Desolate, unsafe, and minimally populated, the area remained a no-man's land for years. Today the South Loop consists of three established neighborhoods: Dearborn Park, Printers Row, and River City, as well as other nearby developments, such as the large Central Station neighborhood, which lies east of Michigan Avenue and south of Roosevelt Road. As the support services most neighborhoods enjoy—grocery stores, dry cleaners, drug stores, and the like—have slowly filtered in, the neighborhood feel of the South Loop has increased and the location has become among the city's most desirable. Alas, home prices in the South Loop have increased steadily along with the neighborhood's reputation. Nowadays, the home prices here are beginning to rival those on the Near North Side.

**Dearborn Park** is a townhouse/rentals/condominium development that was over 20 years in the making. The dream of Dearborn Park survived through the administrations of six mayors and innumerable political stalemates before finally becoming a reality. Built on land formerly owned by several railroads, it now lies directly south of the Loop between State and Clark Streets, south of Polk Street to 15th Street. New, beautiful, and expensive single-family homes have been built to the south of Dearborn Park's original high-rise and townhouse

*South Loop*

development. Dearborn Park II, as it is called, at 14th and State Streets, contains single-family homes, row houses, and townhomes.

**Printers Row**, a condominium and rental area housed in buildings that once held printing firms, is located just south of the Loop, steps away from the Chicago Board of Trade, and centrally located to several colleges, including Columbia College, Roosevelt University, and John Marshall Law School. Despite its urban surrounds, the area has a definite neighborhood feel. The intimate Printers Row is a friendly place, with bike paths, leafy trees, and young families enjoying the amenities. Restaurants, bars, and bookstores abound, and every June the neighborhood hosts one of the largest outdoor book fairs in the country. Five blocks, in the 500 to 700 blocks of South Dearborn, are tented to accommodate the fair's 70,000 yearly visitors (see **Literary Life** in the **Cultural Life** chapter for more information).

A little farther south, **River City**, an apartments-only complex, boasts outstanding views of the Loop and has docking facilities for 70 boats on the south branch of the Chicago River. Developed in the mid-1980s, River City is a city within a city, containing a health club, restaurants, and other amenities.

The largest of the planned communities downtown, **Central Station** (www.centralstationsouthloop.com) sits west of Soldier Field, near the location of Chicago's one-time Central Station terminal. Among some of the first residents of the 80-acre mixed-use project were former Mayor Richard M. Daley and his family, who moved here from their long-time South Side home in the Bridgeport neighborhood. This development, with its proximity to the lovely Museum Campus—the greenspaces, trails, and parks surrounding Shedd Aquarium, the Field Museum, and the Adler Planetarium—is popular with area residents and tourists alike. Among the many residential developments in Central Station, Burnham Station at 15th and Clark Streets (www.burnhamstation.com) has condominiums and row houses. Prairie District Homes at 18th Street and Prairie Avenue offers townhomes, tower residences, and a new pedestrian bridge to Soldier Field; and Museum Park (www.museumpark.com) is a posh development, complete with a clubhouse, swimming pool, and fitness center.

Area amenities include two chain supermarkets, a Dominick's at Canal and Roosevelt, and a Jewel at Roosevelt and State, chic new restaurants, and art galleries.

**Neighborhood Websites:** Friends of Downtown, www.friendsofdowntown.org; South Loop Neighbors, www.southloopneighbors.org
**Area Code:** 312
**ZIP Codes:** 60604, 60605, 60606, 60607, 60616
**Post Offices:** Cardiss Collins Postal Store, 433 W Harrison St; Loop Station, 211 S Clark St; 22nd Street, 2035 S State St
**Police District:** 1st/Central District (Area 1), 1718 S State St, 312-745-4290
**Emergency Hospitals:** University of Illinois Hospital and Health Sciences System, 1740 W Taylor St, 866-600-2273, hospital.uillinois.edu; Mercy Hospital

and Medical Center, 2525 S Michigan Ave, 312-567-2000, www.mercy-chicago.org

**Library:** Harold Washington Library, 400 S State St, 312-747-4300; www.chipublib.org

**Community Resources:** South Loop Neighbors, 47 W Polk St, Suite 100-218, 312-409-1700, www.southloopneighbors.org; Near South Planning Board, 2600 South Michigan Ave, 312-987-1980, www.thenearsouthplanningboard.org; Sherwood Conservatory of Music, 1312 S Michigan Ave, 312-427-6267, www.sherwoodmusic.org

**Parks:** www.chicagoparkdistrict.com, 312-742-PLAY: Dearborn Park, 865 S Park Terrace, 312-747-7649; Coliseum Park, 1466 S Wabash Ave, 312-328-0821; Roosevelt Park, 62 W Roosevelt Rd, 312-742-7649

**Community Publications:** *Columbia Chronicle*, 312-369-8999; *Chicago Defender*, *Chicago Daily Law Bulletin*, *Chicago Journal*, *Chicago Magazine*, *Chicago Parent*, *Chicago Reader*, *Chicago Reporter*, *Crain's Chicago Business*, *N'DIGO*, *Newcity*

**Public Schools:** Chicago School District 299, 125 S Clark St, Chicago, IL 60603, 773-553-1000, www.cps.edu

**Transportation—Rapid Transit:** Red Line (stations: Jackson, Harrison, Roosevelt); Brown Line (stations: LaSalle/Van Buren); Green Line (stations: Roosevelt, Adams/Wabash); Blue Line (stations: Jackson, LaSalle); Orange Line (stations: Roosevelt, Library)

**Transportation—Main Bus Routes:** #3 King Drive, #4 Cottage Grove, #11 Lincoln/Sedgwick, #12 Roosevelt, #22 Clark, #24 Wentworth, #29 State, #36 Broadway, #62 Archer

## BRONZEVILLE/THE GAP/DOUGLAS

**Boundaries: North:** 26th St; **South:** 47th St; **East:** Cottage Grove; **West:** Federal St

This South Side neighborhood, which includes the adjoining Gap and Douglas, has been enjoying a renaissance since the late '90s. The near South Side neighborhood called **The Gap** is a mixture of high-rise developments, including the South Commons located at 2845 South Indiana Avenue, and original Victorian graystone and brownstone flats. This area, between 25th and 36th Streets, earned its name years ago when it literally was the gap between Chinatown to the north and De LaSalle High School to the south. (Some residents have adopted a new moniker, "South Gap," for the area south to Pershing Road, between Giles and Prairie streets, which is undergoing extensive development.)

Today there is renewed interest in **Bronzeville's** residential properties, with large-scale rehabbing of landmark homes as well as the creation of new luxury townhomes. This is good news in an area long known mainly for its subsidized

*Bronzeville*

housing complexes, criminal activity, and high jobless rates. While many of the earlier Victorian and graystone homes are gone, some highly altered versions of the first buildings still exist facing Groveland Park. Groveland Park, which lies between 33rd and 35th Streets near Lake Michigan, is a remnant of Senator Stephen A. Douglas' landholdings in the area. (Douglas ran against Abraham Lincoln for president in 1860.)

In the 1870s, the Bronzeville area was an upper-class neighborhood of mostly white residents. After the Great Fire of 1871, many German Jews who lost their homes in the fire relocated to Bronzeville. These immigrants, along with the previously established residents, created the historic landmarks you see today: street after street of Victorian row houses, some designed by Louis Sullivan and, later, by Frank Lloyd Wright. Between the 1870s and the early 1900s, Bronzeville continued to thrive as a wealthy commercial and residential area. In 1891, one of the country's first African-American surgeons, Daniel Hale Williams, established Provident Hospital, one of only a handful of interracial institutions.

In the first half of the 20th century, the neighborhood saw a lot of change: by the 1900s, apartment buildings had been built, and the area transformed from a wealthy enclave into a working-class residential area with some light industry. The western portion of **Douglas** was settled by Italian immigrants and southern Blacks, both looking for work and a better life. Racial tensions in the area exploded in 1919 with a race riot on 29th Street Beach. This signaled the beginning of the exodus of white residents; by 1924, the Douglas neighborhood was predominantly black. The '20s saw a flourishing of African-American business, culture, and music. For a while, Chicago was the undisputed jazz center of the world: Louis Armstrong, Billie Holiday, and Duke Ellington were among the luminaries who spent stretches of the 1920s in Bronzeville. The appellation "Bronzeville," coined in the 1930s, celebrated the complexion of most area residents.

By the 1940s, Bronzeville was the heart and soul of Chicago's African-American community, and the area surrounding 47th Street was known as the "Harlem of Chicago." As Bronzeville's popularity increased, so did demand for housing. Single-family homes were altered to create apartments, and by 1950, many houses were being torn down to clear space for the much-publicized and even then much-criticized public housing developments, which included the Robert Taylor Homes, Stateway Gardens, and the Ida B. Wells projects. What followed was the steep decline of any remaining community vitality: crime rose dramatically, industry moved out, and buildings were left vacant. Between 1950 and 1990, the area lost nearly two-thirds of its population.

Today, Bronzeville is making a strong comeback as professionals, many of them African-American, have picked up the run-down graystones at bargain-basement prices and rehabbed them to their former glory. By 2007, the public housing developments had nearly vanished, with the last building of the Robert Taylor Homes facing demolition in March 2007. Thousands of displaced public housing residents were relocated or received Section 8 vouchers to subsidize their rent in private apartments; five mixed-income, low-rise developments are planned to replace 7,300 of the homes Bronzeville lost when the old projects were demolished. The attractive new buildings already completed have proved popular.

In 2001, Chicago instituted the African-American Showcase of Homes to encourage residents to rebuild Bronzeville. The city donated land and the African-American Home Builders Association donated two million dollars to assist local builders in creating market-rate homes on South St. Lawrence Avenue. As one drives south on Dr. Martin Luther King Jr. Drive, the contrast between old and new is remarkable. From 26th Street to 35th Street, the new developments tower overhead, but they are surrounded by large open spaces. South of 35th, you feel like you've stepped back a hundred years. The houses are spectacular, with intricate stonework and wrought-iron fences, a perfect complement to this wide, tree-lined boulevard. Bronzeville remains primarily, and proudly, an African-American neighborhood, with historical awareness continuing to increase along with property values. However, word is spreading, and improvements are bringing demographic changes to the community. The *Chicago Reporter* found that, in 2003, 34% of those buying homes near the sites of the former Robert Taylor and Stateway Garden projects were white, while another 6% were Latino or Asian.

A word of caution: this neighborhood is still edgy in terms of safety and is best suited for those comfortable with urban environs.

**Neighborhood Website:** Bronzeville Visitor Information Center, www.bviconline.info
**Area Codes:** 312, 773
**ZIP Codes:** 60616, 60653, 60609

**Post Offices:** Henry W McGee, 4601 S Cottage Grove Ave; Chinatown, 2345 S Wentworth Ave, Suite A

**Police Districts:** North of 31st St: 1st/Central District (Area 1), 1718 S State St, 312-745-4290; south of 35st St: 2nd/Wentworth District (Area 1), 5101 S Wentworth Ave, 312-747-8366

**Emergency Hospitals:** Mercy Hospital and Medical Center, 2525 S Michigan Ave, 312-567-2000, www.mercy-chicago.org

**Libraries:** King, 3436 S King Dr, 312-747-7543; Chicago Bee, 3647 S State St, 312-747-6872; www.chipublib.org

**Community Resources:** Chicago Urban League Development Corp., 4510 S Michigan Ave, 773-285-5800, www.thechicagourbanleague.org; Wabash Avenue YMCA, 3763 S Wabash Ave, 773-285-0020, www.ymcachicago.org/wabash/

**Parks:** www.chicagoparkdistrict.com, 312-742-PLAY: Dunbar Park, 300 E 31st St, 312-747-6287; Stateway Park, 3658 S State St, 312-747-6707; Lake Meadows Park, 3117 S Rhodes Ave, 312-747-6287

**Public Schools:** Chicago School District 299, 125 S Clark St, Chicago, IL 60603, 773-553-1000, www.cps.edu

**Community Publications:** *Chicago Defender, Chicago Daily Law Bulletin, Chicago Journal, Chicago Magazine, Chicago Parent, Chicago Reader, Chicago Reporter, Hyde Park Herald, N'DIGO*

**Transportation—Rapid Transit:** Green Line (stations: 35th/Bronzeville/IIT, Indiana, 43rd); Metra Electric District (stations: 27th St)

**Transportation—Major Bus Routes:** #1 Indiana/Hyde Park, #3 King Dr, #4 Cottage Grove, #35 35th, #39 Pershing

## BRIDGEPORT/CHINATOWN

**Boundaries**: **North:** Archer Ave; **South:** Pershing Rd (3900S); **East:** Dan Ryan Expy; **West:** Ashland Ave (1600W)

West of The Gap is **Bridgeport**, a fine old Chicago neighborhood that encompasses the area around the new US Cellular Field (formerly Comiskey Park), home of the Chicago White Sox. Bridgeport is filled with bungalows, two- and three-flats, and a few churches built in the 1800s. Over the past decade, real estate prices have risen dramatically in this middle-income neighborhood well away from the lake. The average price for a single-family home in Bridgeport is now $330,000—more affordable than high-cost Near North communities but nearly on par with far North Side neighborhoods.

Bridgeport has been an established community for over 160 years. The area's scrappy past can be glimpsed from the names that preceded its current moniker: the neighborhood was called first Hardscrabble, then Cabbage Patch, before "Bridgeport" finally stuck. The first residents here were Lithuanian, Italian,

Polish, and Irish immigrants who moved in to work on the Illinois & Michigan Canal. Bridgeport has since served as the breeding ground for five Chicago mayors, including both Mayor Daleys.

Bridgeport is a world unto itself, a residential island surrounded by factories, railroad tracks, and the Stevenson Expressway. The world-famous Chicago stockyards, which inspired Upton Sinclair's classic exposé of the meat-packing industry, *The Jungle*, lie just south of here. (A large industrial park occupies the former stockyards' site today.) These days, although Bridgeport remains a bit insular—it's not unusual for residents to live within a few doors of the house where they grew up—names on neighborhood mailboxes have been changing as a new wave of immigrants makes this family-friendly neighborhood their own. In addition to the established Chinese population, Bridgeport's newest immigrant residents, those of Mexican descent, are pumping new life into the once-declining retail strip on Halsted Street. Move here and, along with the remaining Lithuanian and Italian restaurants, you will also find Asian grocery stores, myriad discount variety stores, Mexican restaurants, and other businesses catering to the local ethnic enclaves. While most street parking is zoned residential (meaning you must have a sticker in order to be legally parked), there is metered parking available along Halsted, 31st, and 35th Streets.

New housing has risen in the vicinity of the ball park, and developers have also targeted areas such as the Old Glue section of Bridgeport, where new, bungalow-style housing developments and one- and two-story buildings blend in with the existing styles. Improvements in the quality of the Chicago River have made it an attractive feature to homeowners along its banks. More housing developments, in various stages of completion, have popped up along the west bank of the river, and along Bubble Creek, a tributary of the river's south branch.

Bridgeport includes Chicago's eight-block **Chinatown**, bounded by Cermak Road, Wentworth, and 26th Street. The area offers a plethora of eating

*Chinatown*

THE CITY OF CHICAGO: SOUTH

choices—some of the small neighborhood's more-than-40 restaurants dish up Thai and Japanese, as well as Chinese fare—and a handful of authentic Asian groceries. Parades are held every Chinese New Year, and the Chinatown Summer Fair has been taking place every July for a quarter of a century. According to the *Chicago Tribune*, revitalization is finally taking hold in this often-overlooked part of the city. Development geared toward residential life, including a new community center and the building of single-family homes, townhomes, and condominiums, is trying to lure would-be homeowners, especially young Chinese-American professionals and families. Though available housing so far remains limited, Chinatown's location and relatively low prices make it a good prospect for many.

**Area Codes:** 312, 773
**ZIP Codes:** 60608, 60609, 60616
**Post Office:** Stockyards, 4101 S Halsted St, Suite 1
**Police District:** 9th/Deering District (Area 1), 3120 S Halsted St, 312-747-8227
**Emergency Hospitals:** Mercy Hospital and Medical Center, 2525 S Michigan Ave, 312-567-2000, www.mercy-chicago.org
**Library:** Daley, Richard J. - Bridgeport, 3400 S Halsted St, 312-747-8990; www.chipublib.org
**Community Resource:** Chicago Chinatown Chamber of Commerce, 2169B S China Pl, 312-326-5320, www.chicagochinatown.org
**Parks:** www.chicagoparkdistrict.com, 312-742-PLAY, Armour Square Park, 3309 S Shields Ave, 312-747-6012; Donovan Playground Park, 3620 S Lituanica Ave, 312-747-6111; McKeon Playlot Park, 3548 S Wallace St, 312-747-6111
**Public Schools:** Chicago School District 299, 125 S Clark St, Chicago, IL 60603, 773-553-1000, www.cps.edu
**Community Publications:** *Chicago Defender, Chicago Daily Law Bulletin, Chicago Journal, Chicago Magazine, Chicago Parent, Chicago Reader, Chicago Reporter, Hyde Park Herald, N'DIGO*
**Transportation—Rapid Transit:** Red Line (stations: Sox/35th, Cermak/Chinatown); Orange Line (stations: Halsted, Ashland)
**Transportation—Major Bus Routes:** #8 Halsted, #35 35th, #39 Pershing, #44 Wallace/Racine, #62 Archer

## HYDE PARK/KENWOOD

**Boundaries**: **North:** 47th St; **South:** 60th St; **East:** Lake Michigan; **West:** Cottage Grove Ave

Hyde Park is something of an anomaly on the otherwise unpolished South Side. The University of Chicago, established in 1925 when this area was one of wealth and prestige, has made Hyde Park a bastion of cosmopolitan culture

*Hyde Park*

in the midst of a Southside environment known for its racial tensions and impoverished, crime-ridden neighborhoods. Still surrounded by poorer areas, Hyde Park prides itself on being one of the few truly racially integrated neighborhoods in Chicago, and it seems to be helping to create safer surrounding neighborhoods. Slowly but surely, neighborhoods to the north, south, and west are improving. To ensure the safety of Hyde Park proper, both the Chicago Police and the large University of Chicago Police Force patrol the neighborhood. With such diligence, it is no wonder that Hyde Park enjoys a relatively low statistical crime rate; however, it is never wise to wander late at night alone. (Hyde Park residents should check the University's website, safety-security.uchicago.edu/transportation/transportation/, for the wide range of transportation services available around the campus grounds and housing facilities. There is even an on-call, late-night van service.)

In 1893, Hyde Park was the site of the World's Columbian Exposition, celebrating the 400th anniversary of the discovery of America. The reconstructed Museum of Science and Industry, 5700 South Lake Shore Drive, is the only surviving building from that enormous event. If you stop by the Museum, don't forget to visit the lovely Osaka Gardens, between the east and west lagoons; it's a Chicago designated landmark. In addition, the neighborhood is filled with architectural jewels, including Frank Lloyd Wright's famous Robie House at 5757 South Woodlawn Avenue, the Rockefeller Memorial Chapel, located at 5850 South Woodlawn Avenue, and the University's Oriental Institute, 1155 East 58th Street—home to a vast collection of Egyptian, Persian, and Sumerian antiquities. If you decide to make Hyde Park your home, you will quickly become acquainted with yet another landmark area, the large expanse right on Lake Michigan, called Promontory Point (5491 South Shore Drive), which is popular with area residents, university students, and faculty alike.

# THE CITY OF CHICAGO: SOUTH

Grand old high-rise apartment buildings line the lakefront, and away from the lake the neighborhood is chock-a-block with low-rise apartments, many of which have become condominiums. While single-family homes in Hyde Park are expensive (rivaling the Gold Coast and Lincoln Park areas), townhouses and condominiums are more in line with the price of new construction in other middle-class areas of the South Side. As befits an area with one of the country's leading universities, there are several first-rate bookstores on South Hyde Park Boulevard, and between 53rd and 59th Streets, particularly Seminary Co-op Bookstore (5751 South Woodlawn Avenue), and Powell's Bookstore (1501 East 57th Street).

With all of the university activity going on in Hyde Park, it is easy to overlook the quiet elegance of Hyde Park's northerly neighbor, **Kenwood**. The last ten years have seen the development of new townhouses that are well below the price of the Hyde Park homes. New businesses have also been developing on 47th Street. Kenwood is worth looking into if you like quiet shaded streets and easy university access. More than half of the university's faculty live between Hyde Park and Kenwood, in what locals call **South Kenwood**: between 51st and 47th Streets, running east to Lake Michigan, and west to Cottage Grove Avenue. It's a small, pricey neighborhood with old estates on large lots.

As mentioned earlier, violent crime is not overly common in the Hyde Park–South Kenwood community, but it does happen. (See the **Getting Settled** chapter for more on personal safety issues.)

**Neighborhood Websites:** www.uchicago.edu, www.hydepark.org
**Area Code:** 773
**ZIP Codes:** 60615, 60637
**Post Offices:** Finance Station U, 956 E 58th St; Jackson Park Post Office, 700 E 61st St; Lake Park Station, 1510 E 55th St
**Police District:** 2nd/Wentworth District (Area 1), 5101 S Wentworth Ave, 312-747-8366
**Emergency Hospital:** The University of Chicago Medical Center, 5841 S Maryland Ave, 773-702-1000, www.uchospitals.edu
**Library:** Blackstone, 4904 S Lake Park Ave, 312-747-0511, wwwchipublib.org
**Community Resources:** Hyde Park Art Center, 5020 S Cornell Ave, 773-324-5520, www.hydeparkart.org; Southeast Chicago Commission, 1511 E 53rd St, 2nd Fl, 773-324-6926, secc-chicago.org/secc_chicago; Oriental Institute, 1155 E 58th St, 773-702-9514, oi.uchicago.edu; Museum of Science & Industry, 57th St and Lake Shore Dr, 773-684-1414, www.msichicago.org; DuSable Museum of African American History, 740 E 56th Pl, 773-947-0600, www.dusablemuseum.org
**Parks:** www.chicagoparkdistrict.com, 312-742-PLAY: Bixler Playlot Park, 5641 S Kenwood Ave, 312-747-2469; Butternut Playlot Park, 5324 S Woodlawn Ave, 312-747-2703; Elm Park, 5215 S Woodlawn Ave, 312-747-2703; Nichols

Park, 1355 E 53rd St, 312-747-2703; Promontory Point, 5491 South Shore Dr; Spruce Playlot Park, 5337 S Blackstone Ave, 312-745-2476; Stout Park, 5446 S Greenwood Ave, 312-747-2703

**Public Schools:** Chicago School District 299, 125 S Clark St, Chicago, IL 60603, 773-553-1000, www.cps.edu

**Community Publications:** *Chicago Defender, Chicago Daily Law Bulletin, Chicago Journal, Chicago Magazine, The Chicago Maroon, Chicago Parent, Chicago Reader, Chicago Reporter, Hyde Park Herald, N'DIGO*

**Transportation—Rapid Transit:** Red Line (stations: 47th, 51st, Garfield); Metra Electric District [stations: 47th St (Kenwood), 51st/53rd St (Hyde Park), 55th/56th/57th St, 59th St (Univ. of Chicago)]

**Transportation—Major Bus Routes:** #1 Indiana/Hyde Park, #2 Hyde Park Express, #4 Cottage Grove, #6 Jackson Park Express, #28 Stony Island, #47 47th, #51 51st, #55 Garfield, #170 U of Chicago/Midway, #171 U of Chicago/Hyde Park, #172 U of Chicago/Kenwood

**Note**: U of C students can ride CTA bus routes #170, 171, and 172 for free when they present their student IDs.

## WOODLAWN

**Boundaries**: **North:** 60th St; **South:** 67th St; **East:** Lake Michigan; **West:** Cottage Grove Ave

Woodlawn is a largely African-American neighborhood just south of Hyde Park. The revitalization of this neighborhood has been slow, but bit by bit the neighborhood has become an established community of choice. Revitalization here has been made possible by independent initiatives led by several organizations including The Woodlawn Organization (TWO), which was established in the 1960s, the University of Chicago, private investors, and groups like WECAN (Woodlawn East Community and Neighbors) and Woodlawn Preservation Investment Corporation (WPIC). WECAN works to renovate the area's low-income flats, rebuilding them into affordable, attractive apartments for families or singles. Columbia Pointe, a joint effort of Woodlawn's community revitalization organizations, has completed dozens of single-family homes valued around $275,000. Other developments in the area include new upscale homes on 63rd Street, from Ingleside to Kimbark Avenues. These developments, along with dozens of lovely old buildings finally seeing quality renovation and condo conversion, are welcome news in a community that was once plagued with gangs and deteriorating housing.

As a result of these efforts, professionals, working-class families, staff, and students from the University of Chicago have begun to relocate here, attracted by the convenient location and lower rents and home prices. Additionally, the

# THE CITY OF CHICAGO: SOUTH

*Woodlawn*

openings of two banks within the past few years (branches of the Cole Taylor Bank and First Chicago banks) have helped to attract businesses, and several areas of the neighborhood have been voted "dry" to curb the illegal sale of liquor to minors, and to help remove loitering and other illegal activities.

Woodlawn is within walking distance of the lakefront Jackson Park, a neighborhood favorite with its beach, harbor, and lagoons. Washington Park is to the west, and the colossal Museum of Science and Industry is nearby as well. Woodlawn residents also enjoy proximity to Hyde Park's retail district, although several small grocery stores have served the neighborhood for over 50 years.

While the area has improved, poverty remains an issue, and safety is definitely a concern in Woodlawn, especially in the west end. Be sure to visit at different times during the day to ascertain your comfort level before deciding to move here.

**Neighborhood Websites:** www.ncp-woodlawn.org
**Area Code:** 773
**ZIP Code:** 60637
**Post Office:** Jackson Park, 700 E 61st St
**Police District:** 3rd/Grand Crossing District (Area 1), 7040 S Cottage Grove Ave, 312-747-8201
**Emergency Hospital:** The University of Chicago Medical Center, 5841 S Maryland Ave, 773-702-1000, www.uchospitals.edu
**Library:** Coleman, 731 E 63rd St, 312-747-7760; www.chipublib.org
**Community Resources:** DuSable Museum of African American History, 740 E 56th Pl, 773-947-0600, www.dusablemuseum.org
**Parks:** www.chicagoparkdistrict.com, 312-742-PLAY: Harris Park, 6200 S Drexel Ave, 312-747-2706; Flying Squirrel Playlot Park, 6600 S Woodlawn Ave, 312-747-7661; Beehive Park, 6156, S Dorchester Ave, 312-747-6545

**Public Schools:** Chicago School District 299, 125 S Clark St, Chicago, IL 60603, 773-553-1000, www.cps.edu

**Community Publications:** *Chicago Defender, Chicago Daily Law Bulletin, Chicago Journal, Chicago Magazine, Chicago Maroon, Chicago Parent, Chicago Reader, Chicago Reporter, Hyde Park Herald, N'DIGO*

**Transportation—Rapid Transit:** Green Line (stations: King Drive, Cottage Grove); Metra Electric District (stations: 59th St, Univ. of Chicago, 63rd St)

**Transportation—Major Bus Routes:** #4 Cottage Grove, #6 Jackson Park Express, #15 Jeffery Local, #28 Stony Island, #59 59th/61st, #63 63rd, #67 67th/69th/71st

## SOUTH SHORE

**Boundaries: North:** 67th St; **South:** 79th St; **East:** Lake Michigan; **West:** S Chicago Ave

Southeast of Woodlawn, along the lakefront, is the South Shore neighborhood. Extending from the base of Jackson Park to 79th Street, South Shore is a study in contrasts. Many working professionals live along the park, attracted by the ease of the commute downtown via South Shore and Lake Shore Drives (20 minutes to the Loop) and affordable housing. Recently, the revitalization of neighborhoods just to the north has helped increase awareness of South Shore's assets as well as its proximity to both the Loop and Museum Campus. In the last few years, many stately old buildings have been renovated and converted into condos, while less valuable properties have been razed and replaced with new construction. For the time being, anyway, the still-inexpensive rents also attract artists to the area.

In this predominantly African-American neighborhood, the divisions are based on economics rather than race. While South Shore has the most subsidized housing units in the city, immediately south of Jackson Park, and all along the lakefront, the apartments and high rises are well maintained. Head farther south along South Shore Drive and the buildings tend to be more run down. Away from the lake there are blighted areas, but, again, these are balanced by immaculate middle- and upper-middle-class residential streets.

Jackson Park, at the neighborhood's northern edge, is a beautiful lakeshore park with inland lagoons and a golf course. There is an extensive lakefront bike path that starts at Soldier Field and ends at 71st Street. To the south of the park is the landmark South Shore Cultural Center. Built as an elite country club in 1906, it was acquired by the Chicago Park District in the 1970s. It offers daily classes in the performing arts, as well as a full schedule of concerts, lectures, and plays. The South Shore Cultural Center is home to the annual JazzFest Heritage Music Weekend (not to be confused with the much larger Chicago Jazz

*South Shore*

Fest). This relaxed musical event welcomes individuals and families to the lakefront the first weekend in August. (Although Friday night each year is a ticketed event, admission on Saturday and Sunday is free.) Go to www.chicagoparkdistrict.com for more information. If you are interested in historical architecture, then take a walk through the Jackson Park Highlands, an area bounded by Jeffrey Boulevard, Cregier Avenue, and 67th to 71st Streets, where you will find no less than 278 historically significant homes, some of which are listed in the National Register of Historic Places.

A Dominick's supermarket anchors a retail area consisting of both chain and locally owned businesses near the intersection of 71st and Jeffrey. At the south end of the neighborhood, and at the lakefront, you will find restaurants and entertainment. The New Regal Theatre, a striking Moorish-style landmark at 1645 East 79th Street, was originally built in the 1920s and called the Avalon Theater. After closing in the '70s, it was remodeled in the 1980s when the local community raised $4.5 million to restore the exotic, Middle Eastern interior, which includes mosaic murals, a huge stage watched over by gargoyles, and a mammoth oriental rug suspended from the lobby ceiling. The theater closed again in 2003, the building has been foreclosed upon, and it may be demolished.

On the extreme east end of 79th Street, you'll find the entrance to the lakefront Rainbow Beach and the adjacent park with its fieldhouse and sports fields. The attractive beach bustles in the summer, when the park is full of athletes, children, and families taking advantage of the amenities. Many community events are held here as well.

**Neighborhood Website:** http://www.southshorechamberinc.org
**Area Code:** 773
**ZIP Code:** 60649
**Post Office:** Grand Crossing, 7715 S Cottage Grove Ave

**Police District:** 3rd/Grand Crossing District (Area 1), 7040 S Cottage Grove Ave, 312-747-8201

**Emergency Hospitals:** Jackson Park Hospital and Medical Center, 7531 S Stony Island Ave, 773-947-7500, www.jacksonparkhospital.org; St. Bernard Hospital and Health Care Center, 326 W 64th St, 773-962-3900, www.stbh.org; South Shore Hospital, 8012 S Crandon Ave, 773-356-5000, www.southshorehospital.com

**Library:** South Shore, 2505 E 73rd St, 312-747-5281

**Community Resources:** South Central Community Services, 773-483-0900, www.sccsinc.org; South Shore Cultural Center, 7059 S South Shore Dr, 773-256-0149, www.chicagoparkdistrict.com; DuSable Museum of African American History, 740 E 56th Pl, 773-947-0600, www.dusablemuseum.org

**Parks:** www.chicagoparkdistrict.com, 312-742-PLAY: Woodhull Playground Park, 7340 S East End Ave, 773-256-1903; Chestnut Playlot Park, 7001 S Dante Ave, 773-256-1903

**Public Schools:** Chicago School District 299, 125 S Clark St, Chicago, IL 60603, 773-553-1000, www.cps.edu

**Community Publications:** *Chicago Defender, Chicago Daily Law Bulletin, Chicago Journal, Chicago Magazine, Chicago Maroon, Chicago Parent, Chicago Reader, Chicago Reporter, Hyde Park Herald, N'DIGO*

**Transportation—Rapid Transit:** Metra Electric District, South Chicago Branch Line (stations: 75th St (Grand Crossing), Stony Island, Bryn Mawr, South Shore, Windsor Park, 79th St (Cheltenham); since there is no CTA station servicing South Shore directly, commuters can take a bus to the 63rd St/Red Line station (6300S/200W), where they can board a CTA train to the Loop.

**Transportation—Major Bus Routes:** #6 Jackson Park Express, #22 Clark, #26 South Shore Express, #28 Stony Island, #67 67th/69th/71st, #71 71st/South Shore, #75 74th/75th, #79 79th

## BEVERLY/MORGAN PARK

**Boundaries:** *Beverly:* **North:** 87th St; **South:** 107th St; **East:** Beverly Ave; **West:** Western Ave; *Morgan Park:* **North:** 107th St; **South:** 119th St; **East:** Vincennes Ave; **West:** California Ave

The Gold Coast of the South Side, **Beverly** is one of the most affluent neighborhoods in Chicago. Huge old mansions, including a Frank Lloyd Wright, line the western slope of Longwood Drive south of 100th Street, as well as the maze of twists and turns farther north. Longwood Drive's ridge, one of the highest geographical points in Chicago, formed the edge of Lake Michigan about 10,000 years ago. Though the proper name of this community is Beverly Hills, most locals call this southwest neighborhood Beverly. The most exclusive section,

# THE CITY OF CHICAGO: SOUTH

North Beverly, between 89th Street and 94th Street, features large, Revival-style houses built in the 1920s and '30s on hilly lots. In fact, Beverly has one of the largest historic districts in the country, with more than 3,000 buildings registered. The first homes in the area date from the mid-19th century, before Beverly was incorporated into Chicago. Once predominantly Irish-Catholic, the neighborhood has integrated successfully and remains a stable and desirable place to live. The average homeowners are young to middle-aged professionals, many with children, seeking an alternative to life in downtown Chicago. There is very little turnover in the single-family housing market, but homes here can still seem like bargains compared to similar properties in the upscale neighborhoods on Chicago's North Side. Apartment seekers should note that Beverly is primarily a neighborhood of single-family residences, though there are a handful of apartment buildings and recently converted condos.

Beverly's Irish-Catholic heritage can be seen in the wealth of Irish-themed pubs sprinkled throughout the neighborhood, and is celebrated every March, when the stretch of Western Avenue from 103rd to 115th Streets serves as the parade route for the raucous, party-hearty Southside Irish Parade. Though many Beverly residents head to the malls and superstores of nearby Evergreen Park for heavy-duty shopping, both chain and independently owned businesses line 95th Street; another small, charming commercial strip, tucked away along 103rd Street near the Metra stop, offers a coffee shop, Italian deli and café, a gourmet cooking store, and a music shop. Joggers and families also enjoy the Dan Ryan Woods, a large wilderness area that is part of the Cook County Forest Preserves.

**Morgan Park**, nestled in the southeast corner of Beverly Hills, is a predominantly African-American community. Here too, the neighborhood is comprised of young, professional families and there is a similar variety of architecture

*Beverly/Morgan Park*

along well-kept streets. Home prices are a bit lower than in Beverly but still maintain a strong market value. More apartments are available than in Morgan Park's neighbor to the north, and offerings include some vintage Tudor buildings that have been converted into studios and condominiums. Morgan Park High School is rated among the top five public high schools in Chicago, and the private Morgan Park Academy, a prestigious and historic K–12 academy, claims an impressive 100% graduation rate.

The commercial district of town, 111th to 115th Streets and Western Avenue, was targeted as a Chicago redevelopment area for the two communities. The investment has resulted in attracting new businesses to the area. Through various agencies and organizations, the Beverly Arts Center was able to raise the $10 million it needed to build a new and larger center, replacing its 30+-year-old facility. In September 2002, the 40,000-square-foot Arts Center re-opened to the public, featuring a 420-seat theater, performance and rehearsal space, classrooms, a gift shop and gourmet café, and a landscaped courtyard for seasonal performances. The Arts Center is open year-round and offers a wide range of programs, such as concerts, workshops, arts-and-crafts classes for adults and children, community outreach programs, weekly showings of art films, and artist-in-residence programs.

**Neighborhood Websites:** www.ridgehistoricalsociety.org
**Area Code:** 773
**ZIP Codes:** 60643, 60655, 60620
**Post Office:** Morgan Park, 1805 W Monterey Ave
**Police District:** 22nd/Morgan Park District (Area 2), 1900 W Monterey Ave, 312-745-0710
**Emergency Hospitals:** Little Company of Mary Hospital and Health Centers, 2800 W 95th St, Evergreen Park, 708-422-6200, www.lcmh.org; Roseland Community Hospital, 45 W 111th St, 773-995-3000, www.roselandhospital.org
**Libraries:** Beverly, 1962 W 95th St, 312-747-9673; Walker, 11071 S Hoyne Ave, 312-747-1920; Woodson Regional, 9525 S Halsted St, 312-747-6900; Mount Greenwood, 11010 S Kedzie Ave, 312-747-2805; www.chipublib.org
**Community Resources:** Edna White Community Garden, 1830 W Monterey; Ridge Historical Society, 10621 S Seeley Ave, 773-881-1675, www.ridgehistoricalsociety.org; Beverly Area Planning Association, 11107 S Longwood Dr, 773-233-3100, www.bapa.org; Beverly Arts Center, 2407 W 111th St, 773-445-3838, www.beverlyartcenter.org
**Parks:** www.chicagoparkdistrict.com, 312-742-PLAY, Ridge Park, 9625 S Longwood Dr, 312-747-6640; Ridge Park Wetlands Park, 9512 S Wood St, 312-747-6639; Beverly Park, 2460 W 102nd St, 312-747-6024; Kennedy Park, 11320 S Western Ave, 312-747-6198; Blackwelder Park, 11500 S Homewood Ave, 312-747-6198

**Public Schools:** Chicago School District 299, 125 S Clark St, Chicago, IL 60603, 773-553-1000, www.cps.edu
**Community Publications:** *The Beverly Review, Southtown Star, Chicago Defender, Chicago Daily Law Bulletin, Chicago Journal, Chicago Magazine, Chicago Maroon, Chicago Parent, Chicago Reporter, N'DIGO, Ridge Historical Society Newsletter, Suburban Family Magazine, The Villager*
**Transportation— Rapid Transit:** Metra Rock Island District (Beverly Hills 91st St, Beverly Hills 95th St, Beverly Hills 99th St, Beverly Hills 103rd St, Beverly Hills107th St, Morgan Park 111th St, Morgan Park 115th St, 119th St)
**Transportation—Major Bus Routes:** #49A South Western, #49 Western, #87 87th, #95W West 95th, #103 West 103rd, #111 Pullman/111th/115th, #112 Vincennes/111th, #119 Michigan/119th

# NORTH & NORTHWEST SUBURBS

## EVANSTON

If city life is where it's at, why would anyone move to the suburbs? Well if the 'burb is Evanston, it's not hard to understand. Evanston's environs, its physical beauty—both manmade and natural—leaves a lasting impression. Here you can live on a wide, tree-lined street, walk to the lakeshore at dusk for an evening stroll, or easily pop over to a café in Evanston's thriving downtown. All this only 14 miles from downtown Chicago. With its history, culture, natural beauty, academic offerings, wide range of ethnic dining, and lively entertainment, Evanston is the perfect suburb.

Census 2010 results reported an Evanston population of 74,486, and the population is slowly and steadily increasing. Area residents come from all walks of life—from high-tech developers to home-based entrepreneurs, from medical researchers to graduate students, and university professors to stay-at-home moms. While predominantly white, many nationalities are represented here, including a substantial African-American population and a growing Hispanic community. Evanston is thriving, with a well-developed shopping district, lakefront parks, and the renowned Northwestern University. The extensive network of biking paths, running trails, 65 public parks, and beaches along the shoreline are additional assets. Lovely, turn-of-the-20th-century mansions, lining either side of Sheridan Road, will take your breath away. In fact, Evanston has three neighborhood districts listed on the National Register of Historic Places. Although the lakeshore area is often the only part of Evanston that many people see, it should be noted that not all of the neighborhoods are as spectacular, and some are more affordable, comparable to much of Chicago's north side. Still, the value of homes has increased so rapidly in recent years that many long-time

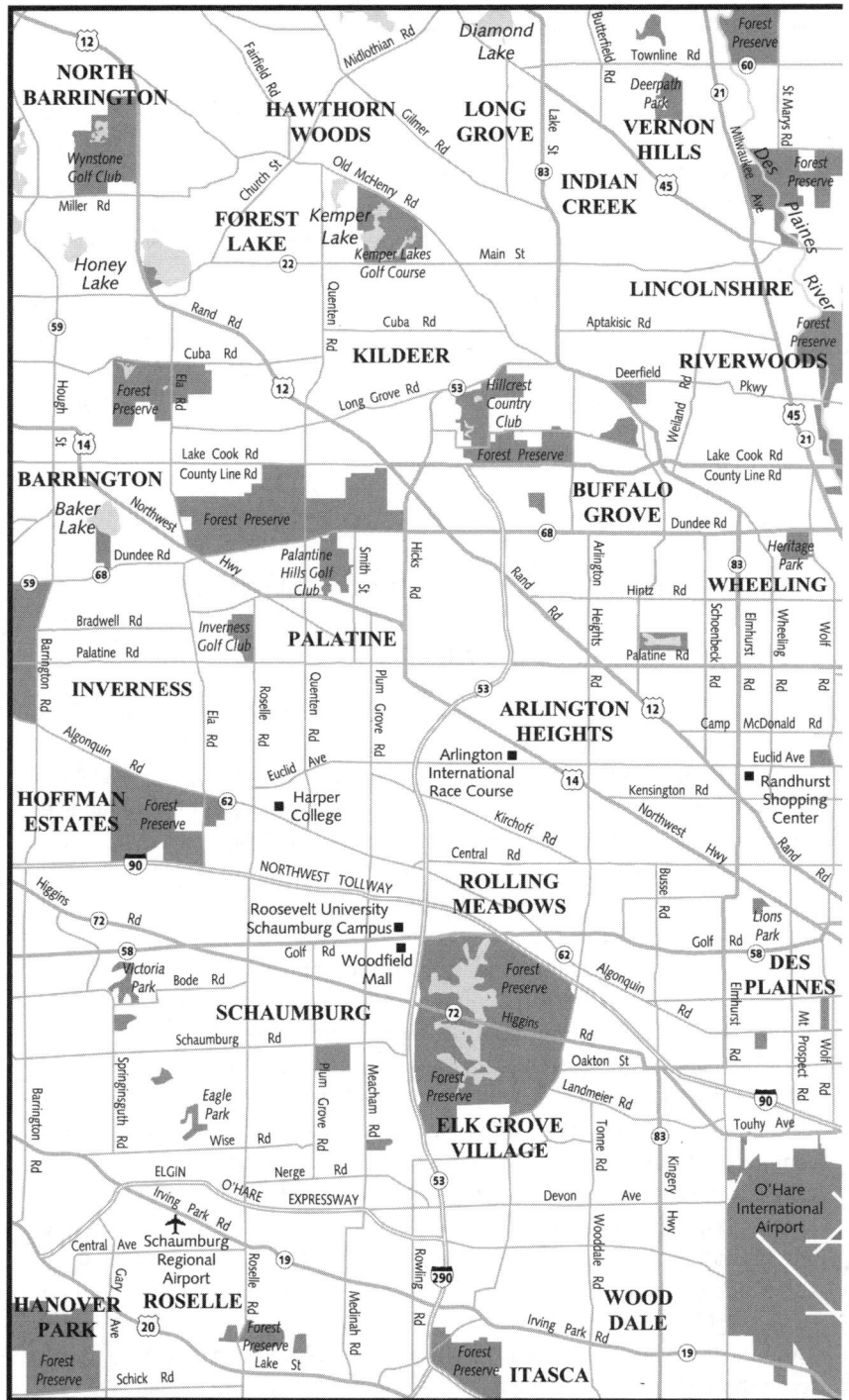

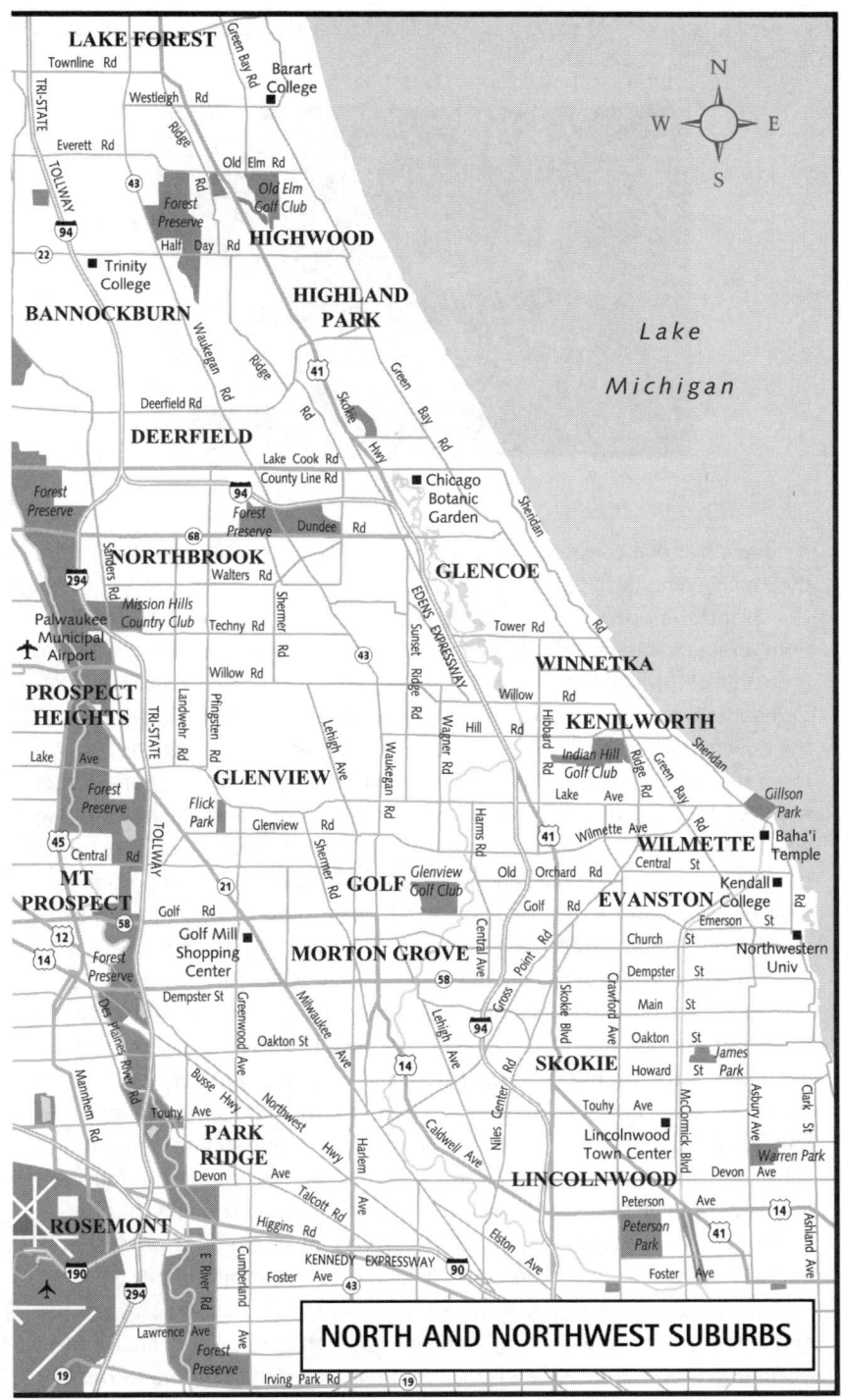

*Evanston*

residents fear that correspondingly rising property taxes may force them from their beloved homes.

Evanston's downtown Church Street/Davis/Sherman area has benefited from a remarkable revitalization effort, producing a great deal of excitement in an area of town once bypassed by developers. Church Street has been transformed from a no-man's land near the train tracks, to a trendy, upbeat part of the downtown scene, with an 18-screen movie theater, luxury condos, a 175-room Hilton Inn, and a Wolfgang Puck restaurant. The stretch of Church Street from Oak to Chicago Avenue has become a walkway of ethnic eateries, offering everything from Nepalese to Irish to gourmet Mexican. In 2007, a luxury condo development opened in the downtown Fountain Square area, offering high-end retail on the ground floor. Though the condos have proved popular, controversy is still raging among Evanston residents, who are not all sure that they want to add more population density to the quaint downtown environment.

A bustling office park near Northwestern University has brought still more business to the community and the quick Purple Line Express commuter train offers direct transportation to and from the Loop during rush hours. Board the Purple Line Express at any of the following 'L' stations: Central Street, Davis Street, and Main Street. The Metra commuter train (same stations as for the 'L') will make a trip to downtown Chicago in 25 minutes. Near the Metra stop you'll find a mix of chain stores, cafés, modest ethnic restaurants, and small businesses with ample, inexpensive parking. Most streets are biker-friendly, and if you work in Evanston you can easily commute via bicycle to and from your office.

As home to one of the nation's most prestigious universities, Evanston enjoys the benefits that hosting such an institution brings. There are a variety of cultural events, festivals, and fairs, most featured during the warm weather months. The public schools enjoy a solid reputation and childcare options are numerous. Students looking for housing should contact the Northwestern

# NORTH & NORTHWEST SUBURBS

University Student Housing Office at 847-491-7564; 312-503-8514 (Chicago campus), or go online to www.northwestern.edu/housing for more information.

**Websites:** www.evanstonillinois.net, www.cityofevanston.org

**Area Code:** 847

**ZIP Codes:** 60201, 60202, 60203, 60204, 60208, 60209

**Post Offices:** Evanston, 1101 Davis St; Evanston South, 701 Main St; Evanston North, 1929 Central St

**Police:** Evanston Police Department, 1454 Elmwood Ave, 847-866-5000

**Hospitals:** North Shore Evanston Hospital, 2650 Ridge Ave, 847-570-2000, http://www.northshore.org/locations/evanston-hospital/; St. Francis Hospital of Evanston, 355 Ridge Ave, 847-316-4000, www.reshealth.org/sub_sfh/default.cfm

**Libraries:** Evanston Public Library (www.epl.org): Main Branch, 1703 Orrington (entrance on Church St), 847-448-8600; North Branch, 2026 Central St, 847-866-0330

**Community Resources:** Civic Center, 2100 Ridge Ave, 847-866-2900; Evanston Chamber of Commerce, LM 110, 1840 Oak Ave, 847-328-1500, www.evchamber.com; Evanston Community Foundation, 1007 Church St, Suite 108, 847-492-0990, www.evanstonforever.org; Evanston History Center, 225 Greenwood, 847-475-3410; Evanston Art Center, 2603 Sheridan Rd, 847-475-5330, www.evanstonartcenter.org

**Parks:** 847-448-4311, www.cityofevanston.org: Beck Park, east of the Canal/from Lyons to Emerson St; Burnham Shores, lakefront between Dempster and Hamilton St; Butler Park, east of Canal/from Emerson to Bridge St; Centennial, lakefront/between Church St and University Pl; Dawes, lakefront/between Dempster and Church St; Elliot, lakefront/between Hamilton and Lee St; Garden, lakefront/north of Sheridan Sq; Ladd Arboretum, southeast of McCormick/from Emerson to Grant St; Lighthouse Landing, 2603 Sheridan Rd; **Beaches**: Lighthouse Beach, Central St/Sheridan Rd; Clark Street Beach, Clark St/Sheridan Rd; Greenwood Street Beach, Greenwood St/lakefront; Lee Street Beach, Lee St/Lake Shore Blvd; South Boulevard Beach, S Blvd/lakefront

**Community Publications:** *Courier News*, *Daily Herald* (Chicago suburban edition), *Evanston Review*, *North Shore Magazine*, *Evanston RoundTable*, *Evanston Now*

**Public Schools: Evanston School District 65** (elementary), 1500 McDaniel Ave, 847-859-8000, www.district65.net; **High School**: Evanston Township High School, 1600 Dodge Ave, 847-424-7000, www.eths.k12.il.us

**Transportation—Rapid Transit:** Purple Line (stations: South Blvd, Main, Dempster, Davis, Foster, Noyes, Central); Metra Union Pacific/North Line (stations: Main Street, Davis Street, and Central Street)

**Transportation—Major CTA Bus Routes:** #97: Skokie (Evanston & Skokie), #201 Central/Ridge, #N201 Central/Sherman, #205 Chicago/Golf, #206 Evanston Circulator; **Major Pace Bus Routes:** #208 Golf Road, #213 Green Bay Road, #215 Crawford-Howard, #250 Dempster Street, #290 Touhy Avenue. Evanston has several dozen buses traveling throughout the Chicagoland area, including shuttle buses to shopping malls and Metra train stations. To find the bus service you need, please check www.pacebus.com.

## SKOKIE

Three miles west of the lake is Skokie, Evanston's western neighbor. A village of 63,000, it was incorporated more than 100 years ago. In 1940, the name was changed from Niles Center to Skokie, which is a Potawatomis word for swamp. An agricultural and greenhouse center for years, its early settlers emigrated here from Germany, Switzerland, and Luxembourg in the 1830s. Known as a western settlement in the early part of the 20th century, film studios once used the village's unpretentious main street to film cowboy movies. After World War II, large numbers of Jewish refugees settled in Skokie, and to this day there is a substantial Orthodox/Hasidic Jewish population. More recently, immigrants from Korea, Malaysia, India, and Russia have been calling Skokie home.

Much of the village consists of single-family homes, most of which are owner occupied, although there are some condominiums and apartment buildings scattered throughout. Rentals make up about 25% of the housing market. Typical family homes here are brick bungalows from the 1940s, which, as in Evanston, can be pricey. The community has done a good job of combining family programs and an interest in the arts. Skokie's North Shore Center for the Performing Arts is home to the Northlight Theatre, Centre East Theatre, an active youth theater, and The Skokie Valley Symphony Orchestra. The park

*Skokie*

district boasts a nine-hole golf course, an ice-skating rink, and almost 200 acres of parkland and swimming pools. The Skokie Historical Society organizes tours and publishes a chronicle of the village's early days. Topics include the history of the circa-1887 fire station (now a museum) and other buildings included on the National Registry. The Chamber of Commerce is active in community celebrations, sponsoring the widely regarded North Shore Arts Festival, sidewalk sales, the Festival of Cultures, Fourth of July parade, and many others. Skokie's industrial base is mainly light industry, with firms such as Bell & Howell, Rand McNally, and G.D. Searle in the area.

Skokie has established itself as a suburban shopper's paradise. There are small malls, such as Village Crossing Center, and Fashion Square, strip malls in downtown Skokie, and shops, ethnic grocery stores, and bakeries along Dempster Street. The recently revamped outdoor Old Orchard Mall makes the community the eleventh largest retail center in the state.

**Websites:** www.skokienet.org, www.skokiechamber.org, www.skokie.org
**Area Code:** 847
**ZIP Codes:** 60076, 60077
**Post Office:** 4950 Madison St
**Police:** Skokie Police Department, 7300 Niles Center Rd, 847-982-5900
**Hospitals:** North Shore Skokie Hospital, 9600 Gross Point Rd, 847-677-9600, http://www.northshore.org/locations/skokie-hospital/; Advocate Lutheran General Hospital, 1775 Dempster St, Park Ridge, 847-723-2210, http://www.advocatehealth.com/luth/
**Library:** Skokie Public Library, 5215 Oakton St, 847-673-7774, www.skokielibrary.info
**Community Resources:** Chamber of Commerce, 5002–5006 Oakton St, 847-673-0240, www.skokiechamber.org; Village of Skokie, 847-673-0500, www.skokie.org; North Shore Center for the Performing Arts in Skokie/Centre East, 847-673-6300, www.centreeast.org; Skokie Historical Society and Skokie Heritage Museum, 847-674-1500 ex 3000
**Parks:** www.skokieparkdistrict.org: indoor ice rink, water playground, 49 parks, 40 tennis courts
**Community Publications:** *Courier News*, *Daily Herald* (Chicago suburban edition), *Northshore Magazine*, *Skokie Review*
**Public Schools:** Skokie School District 68, 9440 Kenton Ave, Skokie, 847-676-9000, www.sd68.k12.il.us; Skokie–Morton Grove School District 69, 5050 Madison St, 847-675-7666, www.skokie69.k12.il.us; Skokie School District 73-5, 8000 E Prairie Rd, 847-324-0509, http://www.sd735.org/education/school/school.php?sectionid=74
**Transportation—Rapid Transit:** Metra (Park Ridge Station); CTA Transit: Yellow Line (Skokie Station)

**Transportation—Major CTA Bus Routes:** #97 Skokie; **Major Pace Bus Routes:** #210 Lincoln Avenue, #250 Dempster Street, #290 Touhy Avenue, #422 Linden CTA/Glenview/Northbrook Court, #626 Skokie Valley Limited
**By Car:** I-90, I-94; local main roads: Dempster, Skokie, Touhy

# WILMETTE

The lakeshore Village of Wilmette, just north of Evanston, is a relatively affluent suburb of approximately 28,000. According to *Money* magazine, which recently listed Wilmette among its "100 Best Places to Live," Wilmette residents enjoy a median family income of $146,328 a year. The lakefront community is best known for its tree-lined streets; large, expensive homes; and one of the finest school districts in the country. Besides the expansive, impeccably manicured lawns and homes, and the lack of racial diversity (Wilmette is estimated at 90% white), one way to tell that you have passed from Evanston into Wilmette is by the brick streets, which Wilmette residents have fought to keep over the years. The village is run by a president and board of trustees, employing 210 full-time employees (including a village nurse). They can be reached at 847-251-2700.

Wilmette's crime rate is less than half that of many of Chicago's North Side communities. Located only 16 miles north of the Loop, residents have an easy weekday commute by Metra. Known as the place where many Evanston residents move when they have outgrown a first home, Wilmette's real estate prices reflect both the size of its homes and its exclusivity; according to the *Chicago Tribune,* Wilmette boasted a median home price twice that of its suburban neighbor to the south in 2006. The suburbs north of Wilmette, including Kenilworth, Winnetka, and Glencoe (see next profile), are even more well-to-do. In addition to the lovely homes, Wilmette offers a wide range of amenities: two public and two private golf courses, an extensive park system, one of the

*Wilmette*

longest beach fronts in the area, beautiful Wilmette Harbor (from which residents can launch their sailboats), as well as a public outdoor pool, the indoor arena for performing arts, and two indoor ice skate rinks.

Wilmette is the home of Bahá'í Temple, a gleaming, nine-sided, white-domed building that is situated on Sheridan Road across from Lake Michigan. This beautiful sight, both incongruous and striking, rising from the banks of the suburban North Shore, is well worth stopping for, even if you're just passing through. (See "Places of Worship" in the **Getting Involved** chapter for more information.)

**Websites:** www.wilmette.com, www.wilmettechamber.org
**Area Code:** 847
**ZIP Code:** 60091
**Post Office:** 1241 Central Ave
**Police:** Wilmette Police Department, 710 Ridge Rd, 847-256-1200
**Hospitals:** North Shore Evanston Hospital, 2650 Ridge Ave, Evanston, 847-570-2000, http://www.northshore.org/locations/evanston-hospital/; North Shore Skokie Hospital, 9600 Gross Point Rd, Skokie, 847-677-9600, http://www.northshore.org/locations/skokie-hospital/; North Shore Glenbrook Hospital, 2100 Pfingsten Rd, Glenview, 847-657-5800, http://www.northshore.org/locations/glenbrook-hospital/; St. Francis Hospital, 355 Ridge Ave, Evanston, 847-316-4000, www.reshealth.org/sub_sfh/default.cfm
**Library:** Wilmette Public Library, 1242 Wilmette Ave, 847-256-5025, www.wilmette.lib.il.us
**Community Resources:** Village of Wilmette, 1200 Wilmette Ave, 847-251-2700, www.wilmette.com; The Wilmette Golf Club, 3900 Fairway Dr, 847-256-9777; Lakeview Center (Gillson Park), 847-256-9656; Chamber of Commerce, 1515 Sheridan Road, 847-251-3800
**Parks:** www.wilmettepark.org, 847-256-6100; Centennial Recreation Complex, 2300 Old Glenview Rd, 847-256-9670; Gillson Park, Sheridan Rd and Michigan Ave, 847-256-9656; Avoca Park, 2929 Illinois Rd; Green Bay Bike Trail, From Shorewood Park to Wilmette/Kenilworth border
**Community Publications:** *Courier News*, *Daily Herald* (Chicago suburban edition), *Northshore Magazine*, *Wilmette Life*, *Winnetka Talk*
**Public Schools:** Wilmette School District 39, 615 Locust Rd, Wilmette, 847-256-2450; Avoca School District 37, 2921 Illinois Rd, 847-251-3587, http://avoca37.org/; New Trier Township High School District 203, 385 Winnetka Ave, 847-446-7000, www.newtrier.k12.il.us/
**Transportation—Rapid Transit:** Purple Line (stations: Linden); Metra - Union Pacific/North Line (Wilmette Station)
**Transportation—Major Pace Bus Routes:** #421 Wilmette Avenue, #422 Linden CTA/Glenview/Northbrook Court, #423 Linden CTA-The Glen-Harlem CTA
**By Car:** I-94 (30 minutes to the Loop)

## KENILWORTH/WINNETKA/GLENCOE

Some might label **Kenilworth**, a small community 17 miles north of Chicago's Loop, a hamlet. Its borders barely comprise a square mile, containing a population of a mere 2,500. Slightly older than its neighbors, Kenilworth regularly ranks as one of the wealthiest communities in the country. Unlike many other suburbs, Kenilworth was a planned community. Streets run at northeast and southwest angles, so that sunlight reaches every window in every house at some point in the day. The homes are understated mansions in a mix of styles that appear to blend seamlessly: English Tudor, Classical Revival, Contemporary, and Georgian. There is a feeling of old money about this town, similar perhaps to Newport, Rhode Island. There is little turnover among the huge single-family homes here, with few homes costing less than a cool million. For top dollar, residents enjoy amenities within walking distance, convenience to commuter trains, and a high-end shopping area along Green Bay Road. Unsurprisingly, Kenilworth boasts a good school district, and it shares the nationally renowned New Trier Township High School with Evanston.

Head a bit north to get to **Winnetka**, another hamlet-like town with large homes priced in the same range as Kenilworth's. An upscale, young to middle-aged family community (average resident age 39), Winnetka offers more homes for sale than Kenilworth and some similar perks: excellent schools and a comprehensive park district that offers residents golfing, ice skating, sailing, and boating lessons. It has four beaches (including a dog-friendly beach), tennis courts, and despite its small size, Winnetka offers one of the largest hockey club programs in the state.

Last in the trio is **Glencoe**, 21 miles north of the Loop and home to about 8,400. The northernmost of the three communities, Glencoe boasts similarly steep housing prices. Built on the bluffs of Lake Michigan, it's a bit roomier than Winnetka and Kenilworth at 3.8 square miles—room enough for the nine Frank

*Kenilworth*

Lloyd Wright homes, and the nearly 100 homes that are listed as architecturally significant with the town's Historic Preservation Commission. Homes on the lakeside of town are especially expensive. Despite all appearances, this is not just another wealthy suburb. Call it the Berkeley of Chicago's North Shore: Glencoe has no police or fire department, instead, public safety officers carry out those functions, and it was the first community in Illinois to establish a council-manager form of government.

Glencoe's location makes it accessible to several of Chicago's outdoor delights: the Chicago Botanic Garden is just outside its borders, and three golf courses (one public, two private) are close by. On the western boundary of Glencoe lies Skokie Lagoons, with bike paths that meander past 300 acres of woods and water ending at the Botanic Garden. All this, if you can afford it, lies just a 36-minute (non–rush hour) drive from the Loop.

**Websites:** www.villageofglencoe.org, www.villageofwinnetka.net, www.villageofkenilworth.org
**Area Codes:** 847
**ZIP Codes:** 60043, 60022, 60093
**Post Office:** 336 Hazel Ave, Glencoe; 512 Chestnut St, Winnetka; 408 Green Bay Rd, Kenilworth
**Police:** Glencoe Public Safety, 675 Village Court, 847-835-4114; Winnetka Police, 410 Green Bay Rd, 847-501-6034; Kenilworth Police Department, 419 Richmond Rd, 847-251-2141
**Hospitals:** North Shore Evanston Hospital, 2650 Ridge Ave, Evanston, 847-570-2000, http://www.northshore.org/locations/evanston-hospital/; North Shore Skokie Hospital, 9600 Gross Point Rd, Skokie, 847-677-9600, http://www.northshore.org/locations/skokie-hospital/; North Shore Glenbrook Hospital, 2100 Pfingsten Rd, Glenview, 847-657-5800, http://www.northshore.org/locations/glenbrook-hospital/; North Shore Highland Park Hospital, 777 Park Ave West, Highland Park, 847-432-8000, www.enh.org/locations/highlandpark/
**Libraries:** Glencoe Public Library, 320 Park Ave, 847-835-5056, www.glencoepubliclibrary.org; Winnetka Public Library, 768 Oak St, 847-446-7220, www.winnetkalibrary.org
**Community Resources:** Writer's Theatre/Glencoe, 664 Vernon Ave (venue), 376 Park Ave (box office), 847-242-6000, www.writerstheatre.org; Chicago Botanic Garden, 847-835-5440, www.chicagobotanic.org
**Parks:** Glencoe Park District, 999 Green Bay Rd, 847-835-3030, www.glencoeparkdistrict.com; Winnetka Park District, 540 Hibbard Rd, 847-501-2040, www.winpark.org
**Community Publications:** *Courier News*, *Daily Herald* (Chicago suburban edition), *Glencoe News*, *Northshore Magazine*, *Winnetka Talk*

**Public Schools:** Kenilworth School District 38, 542 Abbotsford Rd, 847-256-5006, www.kenilworth38.org; Glencoe School District 35, 620 Greenwood Ave, 847-835-7800, glencoeschools.org; Winnetka Public School District 36, 1235 Oak St, 847-446-9400, www.winnetka36.org
**Transportation—Rapid Transit:** Metra: Union/Pacific North Line (stations: Glencoe, Hubbard Woods, Winnetka, Indian Hill, Kenilworth)
**Transportation—Pace Bus:** www.pacebus.com

## HIGHLAND PARK

North of Glencoe on Lake Michigan, 26 miles north of downtown Chicago, lies Highland Park. As one of Chicago's fringe suburbs, it is unique in that it offers residents a variety of single- and multi-family housing. Styles range from the Chicago Bungalow–style to Frank Lloyd Wright designs. Thirty-two homes and sites in Highland Park are listed on the National Register of Historic Places. Located in Lake County, this is a well-to-do community. Though housing prices here continue to increase, and average home prices exceed those in any Chicago city neighborhood, the median home price here still represents a bargain compared to the lakefront communities to its south.

Much to the delight of area residents and Chicagoans alike, Highland Park is home to the Ravinia Festival, which plays summer host to the Chicago Symphony Orchestra. Ravinia offers a summer-long series of open-air concerts (ranging from classical to folk and jazz) with much of the seating on the lawn. People bring blankets and elaborate picnics and dine al fresco to the music of Bach or Broadway—it's all very refined and very fun. The community has an active and rich repertoire of its own for creative outlets. Some of these include the Highland Park String Orchestra, Pilgrim Chamber Players, opera, theater, and an annual arts journal called *East on Central*. Though the trip to downtown

*Highland Park*

Chicago is approximately 30 minutes long via the commuter train, Highland Park's 32,000 residents find plenty to do in town. The 44 parks here cover 600 acres and offer fishing, boating, ice skating, hockey, water sports, an 18-hole golf course, and an extensive park district program.

**Websites:** www.cityhpil.com, www.highlandpark.org
**Area Code:** 847
**ZIP Code:** 60035
**Post Office:** 833 Central Ave; 582 Roger Williams Ave
**Police:** 1677 Old Deerfield Rd, 847-432-7730
**Hospital:** North Shore Highland Park Hospital, 777 Park Ave W, Highland Park, 847-432-8000, www.enh.org/locations/highlandpark
**Library:** Highland Park Library, 494 Laurel Ave, 847-432-0216, www.hplibrary.org
**Community Resources:** Chamber of Commerce, 508 Central Ave, 847-432-0284, chamberhp.com; City of Highland Park, 1707 St. Johns Ave, 847-432-0800, www.cityhpil.com; The Art Center, 1957 Sheridan Rd, 847-432-1888, www.theartcenterhp.org; Sunset Valley Golf Course, 1390 Sunset Rd, 847-432-7140; North Shore Yacht Club, 847-432-9800, www.northshoreyachtclub.com; Ravinia Festival, 200 Ravinia Park Rd (north of Lake Cook Rd, right off of Greenbay Rd), 847-266-5100, www.ravinia.org
**Parks:** Highland Park Park District, 636 Ridge Rd, 847-831-3810, www.pdhp.org: Hidden Creek Aqua Park, 1220 Frederickson Pl, 847-433-3170; Centennial Ice Arena, 3100 Trail Way, 847-432-4790; **Beaches**: Park Ave Beach, Park Ave/Lake Michigan; Moraine Beach (dog-friendly with permit), 2501 Sheridan Rd, 847-579-3130; Rosewood Beach, 883 Sheridan Rd
**Community Publications:** *Courier News*, *Highland Park News*, *The Highlander* (www.cityhpil.com), *Highland Park Conservation Society Newsletter* (www.highlandpark.org), *East on Central*
**Public Schools:** Township High School District 113, 1040 Park Ave W, 224-765-1000, www.dist113.org; North Shore School District 112, 1936 Green Bay Rd, 224-765-3000, www.nssd112.org; Northern Suburban Special Education District, 760 Red Oak Ln, 847-831-5100, www.nssed.org
**Transportation—Rapid Transit:** Metra: Union Pacific/North Line (stations: Highland Park, Ravinia, Ravinia Park, Braeside)
**Transportation: Major Pace Bus Routes:** #471 Highland Park-Northbrook Court, #472 Highland Park-Highwood
**By Car:** I-94, US-41

## DEERFIELD

Southwest of Highland Park, next to the Tri-State Tollway in Lake County, is the Village of Deerfield (population 19,000). By 2006, average home prices almost

*Deerfield*

cracked the $500,000 mark. Deerfield offers plenty of family-friendly features including an extensive system of parks and recreational facilities, and an excellent public school system. The majority of the residents are homeowners. While Deerfield offers commuters easy access by car or train—it is only 21 miles north of downtown Chicago—a number of large companies that call Deerfield home, including Baxter International, Dade Behring, and Walgreens, provide employment to many residents.

Deerfield enjoys a close proximity to the Chicago Botanic Garden, the North Branch Bicycle Trail (see **Greenspaces and Beaches** for more information on both), and the famous Ravinia Park, which is located in the neighboring suburb of Highland Park (see above). With three malls within the town limits and an easy drive to five others—including Gurnee Mills and Hawthorne Center—shopping here is a breeze. The Deerfield Park District manages over 21 parks and playgrounds, as well as two swimming pools, and every type of playing field or sports facility you can imagine.

**Website:** www.deerfield-il.org
**Area Codes:** 847, 224
**ZIP Code:** 60015
**Post Office:** 707 Osterman Ave
**Police:** 850 N Waukegan Rd, 847-945-8636
**Emergency Hospital:** North Shore Highland Park Hospital, 777 Park Ave West, Highland Park, 847-432-8000, www.enh.org/locations/highlandpark
**Library:** Deerfield Public Library, 920 N Waukegan Rd, 847-945-3311, www.deerfieldlibrary.org
**Community Resources:** Village of Deerfield, 850 Waukegan Rd, 847-945-5000, www.deerfield-il.org; Deerfield Chamber of Commerce, 601 Deerfield Rd, Suite 200, 847-945-4660; Historical Society, 517 Deerfield Rd, 847-948-0680, www.deerfieldhistoricalsociety.org; **Shopping**: Deerfield Square, south-

west corner Waukegan/Deerfield Rd; Cadwell's Corners, northeast corner Lake Cook Rd/Waukegan Rd
**Community Publications:** *Courier News*, *Daily Herald* (Chicago Suburban edition), *Deerfield Review*, *Northshore Magazine*
**Public Schools:** Deerfield School District 109, 517 Deerfield Rd, 847-945-1844, www.dps109.org
**Transportation—Rapid Transit:** Metra: Milwaukee District/North Line (stations: Lake Cook Road, Deerfield)
**Transportation: Major Pace Bus Routes:** #471 Highland Park-Northbrook Court, #576 Deerfield Metra to Buffalo Grove/Lincolnshire, #626 Skokie Valley Limited
**By Car:** US-41, I-94, I-294; major roads are Deerfield and Waukegan roads

## NORTHBROOK

The Village of Northbrook, with a population just over 33,000 and a median age of about 50, is a much sought-after address. Incorporated in 1901 as Shermerville, it is located 25 miles northwest of downtown Chicago. Commuter-friendly, it offers a 40-minute Metra ride to downtown Chicago and instant access to both the Edens Expressway (I-94) and the Tri-State Tollway (I-294). The quiet neighborhoods are popular with families, who enjoy the Northbrook Park District's tennis courts, two swimming pools, a golf course, indoor ice arenas, and even a velodrome. The local schools have a reputation for excellence. Single-family homes account for more than 75% of the housing stock.

Northbrook's most prominent architectural landmark is probably Northbrook Court, the first of Chicago's luxury malls, and home to Lord & Taylor, Neiman Marcus, and I. Magnin, among other blue-chip retailers. For more

*Northbrook*

down-to-earth shopping, the area's retail base includes Home Depot, Barnes & Noble, and a string of smaller shops and chain stores.

Northbrook offers a lot to its residents. The good news is that, even if you can't afford to live here, you can shop here.

**Websites:** www.northbrook.il.us, www.northbrookchamber.org
**Area Codes:** 847, 224
**ZIP Codes:** 60065, 60062
**Post Offices:** Main Post Office, 2460 Dundee Rd; Downtown Northbrook, 1157 Church St
**Police:** 1401 Landwehr Rd, 847-564-2060
**Hospitals:** North Shore Highland Park Hospital, 777 Park Ave West, Highland Park, 847-432-8000, www.enh.org/locations/highlandpark; North Shore Glenbrook Hospital, 2100 Pfingsten Rd, Glenview, 847-657-5800, www.enh.org/locations/glenbrook; North Shore Evanston Hospital, 2650 Ridge Ave, Evanston, 847-570-2000, http://www.northshore.org/locations/evanston-hospital/
**Library:** Northbrook Public Library, 1201 Cedar Lane, 847-272-6224, www.northbrook.info
**Community Resources:** Northbrook Theatre, 3323 Walters Ave, 847-291-2367; North Suburban YMCA, 2705 Techny Rd, 847-272-7250; Chicago Botanical Gardens, www.chicagobotanic.org, 847-835-5440
**Parks:** Northbrook Park District, 1810 Walters Ave, 847-291-2980, www.nbparks.org; Countryside Park, Walnut Circle/Oakwood Rd; Indian Ridge Park, 3323 Walters Ave; Oaklane Park, 636 Berglund Pl; Village Green, Shermer Rd/Meadow Rd; West Park, 1730 Pfingsten Rd; Wescott Park, 1820 Western Ave; Williamsburg Square Park, 200 Lee Rd
**Community Publications:** *Daily Herald* (Chicago suburban edition), *Northshore Magazine*, *Northbrook Star*
**Public Schools:** Northbrook School District 27, 1250 Sanders Rd, 847-498-2610, www.northbrook27.k12.il.us; Northbrook School District 28, 1475 Maple Ave, 847-498-7970, northbrook28.net; Northbrook-Glenview School District 30, 2374 Shermer Rd, 847-498-4190, www.district30.k12.il.us; high school: Glenbrook North, 2300 Shermer Rd, 847-272-6400, www.glenbrook225.org/gbn/home
**Transportation—Rapid Transit:** Metra: Milwaukee District/North Line (Northbrook station)
**Transportation: Major Pace Bus Routes:** #471 Highland Park-Northbrook Court, #213 Green Bay Road, #422 Linden CTA/Glenview/Northbrook Court, #623 Glen of N. Glenview Station-Willow Road Corridor, #626 Skokie Valley Limited, #619 Des Plaines Station-Willow Road Corridor
**By Car:** I-94, I-294. Major local roads: Dundee Rd, Milwaukee Ave, and Waukegan Rd

## ARLINGTON HEIGHTS

One of the most successful mergers of cozy small town comforts with big city amenities can be found in Arlington Heights. Located 27 miles northwest of downtown Chicago, this vibrant community has a long history. Established as Dunton in 1850, the town was incorporated and renamed Arlington Heights in 1887. Today it is home to about 76,000 and is unique among Chicago's suburban communities in providing approximately 50,000 local jobs. Its busy mixed-use downtown area offers apartment living, townhouses, and single-family homes. A walker's delight of small shops and thriving, locally owned cafés, professional services, and boutiques, the downtown area boasts free parking as well. The city's central business district includes 7,000 square feet of restaurant space, 22,000 square feet of retail space, and 35,000 square feet of office space. Obviously area residents need not commute to Chicago to make a living, but for those who head to the city daily, the Metra train takes just 45 minutes from the newly renovated train platforms centrally located in downtown Arlington Heights. Light industry is located on the north and south sides of town.

Two area attractions dominate Arlington Heights: the 325-acre Arlington Park Racetrack (see **Sports and Recreation**) and the 300-seat Metropolis Performing Arts Centre. The Centre is located in the central business district. In addition to theatre arts workshops, children's theatre, and professional live theatre, the Arts Centre provides a home-away-from-home to the Second City comedy troupe and the Boiler Room, an 88-seat basement jazz supper club.

Arlington Heights is a carefully planned city and, unlike many rural-styled suburban towns, it features sidewalks and streetlights. A recently completed 10-year city plan included the upgrade of the storm sewer system, the five-acre manmade Lake Arlington, and surrounding amenities such as a boathouse, boat rentals, a small sandy beach, and a bike/walk path around the lake's perimeter. A former landfill was transformed into the much more attractive nine-hole

*Arlington Heights*

Nickol Knoll Golf Course. Arlington Heights also boasts its own cable network station and a state-of-the-art library facility—weekend used-book sales, which are held several times a year, are well attended. Housing options are varied, with median home costs actually declining between 2010 and 2012. Three federally subsidized housing complexes offer seniors and low-income families affordable housing. A shared housing program matches the elderly with low-income families, providing seniors with a viable alternative to living alone. The Single Family Rehabilitation Loan program offers zero percent loans to low-to-moderate income homeowners. Empty nesters and commuting couples are attracted to the chic new townhouses and loft-style apartments located near the Arts Centre, as well as the larger-scaled apartment houses located within walking distance of the train station. In addition to the variety of housing and stable business community, area residents benefit greatly from the local park system. Several of Arlington Heights' 58 parks include indoor or outdoor swimming pools. Residents and neighboring folks alike enjoy a wealth of year-round activities and special events sponsored by the park district.

**Website:** www.vah.com
**Area Code:** 847
**ZIP Codes:** 60004, 60005, and 60006
**Post Office:** 909 W Euclid Ave
**Police:** 200 E Sigwalt St, 847-368-5300
**Hospitals:** Northwest Community Healthcare, 800 W Central Rd, 847-618-1000, www.nch.org; Holy Family Medical Center, 100 N River Rd, Des Plaines, 847-297-1800, www.reshealth.org/sub_hfmc/default.cfm
**Library:** Arlington Heights Memorial Library, 500 N Dunton Ave, 847-392-0100, ahml.info/
**Community Resources:** Arlington Heights Teen Center, 112 N Belmont Ave, 847-577-5394; Chamber of Commerce, 311 S Arlington Heights Rd, 847-253-1703, www.arlingtonhtschamber.com; Village of Arlington Heights, 33 S Arlington Heights Rd, 847-368-5000, www.vah.com; Metropolis Performing Arts Center, 111 W Campbell St, 847-577-2121 (box office), 847-577-5982 ext. 221 (education office), www.metropolisarts.com
**Parks:** Arlington Heights Park District, 410 N Arlington Heights Rd, 847-577-3000, www.ahpd.org
**Community Publications:** *Arlington Heights Post, Courier News, Daily Herald* (Chicago Suburban edition), *Suburban Family Magazine*
**Public Schools:** Arlington Heights School District 25, 1200 S Dunton Ave, 847-758-4900, www.sd25.org
**Transportation—Rapid Transit:** Metra: Union Pacific/Northwest Line (stations: Arlington Heights, Arlington Park/Race Track; 45 minutes to downtown on express train)

**Transportation—Major Pace Bus Routes:** #606 Northwest Limited, #616 The Chancellory Connection, #696 Randhurst/Woodfield/Harper College
**By Car:** I-290, I-90; local major roads: US-12/Rand Rd, US-14/Northwest Hwy, US-58/Golf Rd

## SCHAUMBURG

The Village of Schaumburg, one of seven municipalities in Schaumburg Township, lies 29 miles northwest of Chicago's downtown. Many of the area's earliest settlers were German, and the Township was named in 1850 for Schaumburg-Lippe, the region of Germany from which several influential settlers hailed. By 1886, the land here was owned almost entirely by German immigrants and those of German descent. By then, the settlement consisted of a school, a church, a couple of stores, and just a dozen homes. Though the Great Depression changed the area's ethnic make-up by forcing the sale of many properties to non-Germans, Schaumburg's German heritage is still evident in many street names and in traditions such as the annual Christkindlesmarkt. Without a railroad depot to connect it with Chicago, Schaumburg grew slowly for over one hundred years; in the early 1950s, the sleepy rural village still had only 130 residents.

Three major mid-1950s developments—O'Hare Airport's expansion, the construction of the nearby Northwest Tollway, and the incorporation of the Village of Schaumburg—led to a rapid population boom. The population had swelled to 19,000 by 1970 and doubled again by 1976. Today there are over 75,000 residents in Schaumburg. While some commute daily to Chicago, this is not primarily a bedroom community. Along with the headquarters of Motorola, the Schaumburg offices of Advantis, IBM, Zurich-American Insurance, and Cellular One bring commuters from across the Northwest Chicago region to Schaumburg. Area centers of light industry and warehousing add to the diversity and health of the local economy. In July 2006, the Renaissance Schaumburg Hotel and Convention Center opened just off the Northwest Tollway. Sleek and contemporary in design, the $224,000,000 facility has brought hundreds of new jobs and millions of dollars of additional revenue to the Schaumburg area.

Today Schaumburg suffers the traffic congestion and high real estate prices of a bustling city—but it offers the conveniences and attractions of a prosperous city as well. As the second largest center of retail development in Illinois, Schaumburg is home to the enormous Woodfield Shopping Mall as well as the popular Streets of Woodfield development and one of just two IKEA stores in Illinois. The Schaumburg Woodfield Trolley, connecting 12 Woodfield-area shopping destinations with the Renaissance Center as well as with one another, provides a free low-stress alternative to the hassles of traffic and parking. In 1978, a district containing many historic structures from the

*Schaumburg*

pre-boom settlements was designated as "Olde Schaumburg Centre." Careful planning, grants for property owners willing to renovate, and stringent building and design requirements have ensured that not only historic properties but also newer constructions are compatible with the architectural flavor of the district's existing historic buildings. The recently developed Town Square, located at the heart of Olde Schaumburg Centre (the intersection of Roselle and Schaumburg roads), offers shopping, dining, and entertainment in an indoor/outdoor atmosphere. In addition, scores of chain retail establishments and restaurants offer Schaumburg locations. Among the most interesting and popular is the only Midwestern location of Medieval Times Dinner and Tournament (1-866-543-9637).

Schaumburg is especially popular with families, which enjoy not only the pleasant neighborhoods but also the village's many family-friendly amenities. The 166,550-square-foot Schaumburg Township District Library (847-985-4000) opened in Town Square in 1998. The Schaumburg Parks Department offers recreation centers, an aquatic center, the Volkening Farm, and two golf courses. The farmers' market, held in the Town Square on the south side of the Athenaeum, offers fruits, vegetables, baked goods, specialty items, and entertainment; it runs from mid-June to mid-October, Fridays, 7 a.m. to 1 p.m. (call 847-923-3855 for more information). Just east of Town Square across Roselle Road, the Schaumburg Prairie Center for the Arts (www.prairiecenter.org, 847-895-3600) provides performance space for local and visiting theater productions, professional musical acts, and comedy and dance troupes; highlights include an annual Christmas season production of the Nutcracker and a ballet recital every spring. For nature lovers, the Oak Hollow Conservation Area, south of Schaumburg Road between Cedarcrest and Samoset Drives, (847-985-2115), offers hiking and glimpses of wildlife among restored woodlands and meadows.

Outside of its historic district, most of Schaumburg's architecture dates from the 1960s-1970s boom or after. The village's housing stock combines a very few scattered farmhouses with 1960s tract homes, 1970s split-levels and ranches, and contemporary homes in newer developments. While new development has recently slowed due to a lack of available land, building continues to the west of town, and older homes are still being torn down to make way for new housing. Upscale townhomes in the $400,000 range can be found near Town Square. More affordable multi-family housing is also available, particularly in the northwest corner of Schaumburg, off Roselle and Golf roads.

Until 2009, there was no municipal property tax in Schaumburg. Since its institution at that time, however, its rate has been reduced each year. Interstates 90 and 290 intersect at Schaumburg's northeast corner, allowing easy access to nearby communities including Hoffman Estates, Palatine, Rolling Meadows, and Arlington Heights to the north. Drive time to O'Hare Airport is about 20 minutes, while driving to the Loop takes about 45 minutes, considerably longer during rush hours. Train fare from the Metra station at 2000 South Springsguth Road to Chicago's downtown Union Station costs just over $5 each way; the ride takes about an hour.

**Websites:** www.ci.schaumburg.il.us, www.schaumburgtownship.org
**Area Code:** 847
**ZIP Codes:** 60159, 60168, 60173, 60179, 60192–60196
**Post Office:** Schaumburg, 450 W Schaumburg Rd
**Police:** 1000 W Schaumburg Rd, 847-882-3586
**Emergency Hospital:** Northwest Community Hospital, 800 W Central Rd, Arlington Heights, 847-618-1000, www.nch.org; St. Alexius Medical Center, 1555 N Barrington Rd, Hoffman Estates, 847-843-2000, www.stalexius.org; Alexian Brothers Medical Center, 800 W Biesterfield Rd, Elk Grove Village, 847-437-5500, www.alexian.org
**Library:** Schaumburg Township District Library, 130 S Roselle Rd, Schaumburg, 847-985-4000, www.stdl.org
**Community Resources:** Village of Schaumburg, 101 Schaumburg Ct, 847-895-4500, www.ci.schaumburg.il.us; Township of Schaumburg, 1 Illinois Blvd, Hoffman Estates, 847-884-0030, TTY 847-884-1560; Schaumburg Prairie Center for the Arts, 847-895-3600, www.prairiecenter.org; Roosevelt University, Schaumburg Campus, 1400 N Roosevelt Blvd, 847-619-7300, www.roosevelt.edu/schaumburg; Schaumburg Regional Airport, 905 W Irving Park Rd, 847-895-0315; Septemberfest, www.septemberfest.org; Alfred Campanelli YMCA, 300 W Wise Rd, 847-891-9622, campanelliymca.org
**Parks:** Schaumburg Parks Department, 847-985-2115, 847-490-7020 (programs), www.parkfun.com; Schaumburg Water Works (aquatic center), 505 N Springsguth Rd, 847-490-2505; Walnut Greens Golf Course (nine holes), 1150 N Walnut, 847-490-7878; Schaumburg Golf Club (27 holes), 401 N Roselle Rd, 847-885-9000
**Community Publications:** *Daily Herald* (Chicago Suburban edition)

**Public Schools:** Schaumburg School District 54, 524 E Schaumburg Rd, 847-357-5152, sd54.org; Township High School District 211, 1750 Roselle Rd, Palatine, 847-755-6600, www.d211.org

**Transportation—Rapid Transit:** Metra: Milwaukee District/West Line (stations: Schaumburg)

**Transportation: Major Pace Bus Routes:** #208 Gold Road, #554 Elgin-Woodfield, #602 Higgins-Salem-Cedarcrest, #606 Northwest Limited, #696 Randhurst/Woodfield/Harper College, #757 Northwest Conection, #905 Schaumburg Trolley, #237 Schaumburg-Soldier Field Express, #282 Schaumburg Wrigley Field Express, #284 Schaumburg-Great America Gurnee Express

**By Car:** I-90 (45 minutes to the Loop)

## DES PLAINES

East of Schaumburg and about 17 miles northwest of the city is the Village of Des Plaines (pronounced with the "s" sounds), maybe best known as the birthplace of McDonald's. In fact, one of the village's biggest attractions is the McDonald's Original Restaurant and Museum. Founded in 1835, the Village of Des Plaines was named for its location along the river of the same name. Before the construction of O'Hare International Airport it consisted mostly of truck farms and factories. Today Des Plaines is a thriving middle-class town. Most of its nearly 59,000-plus residents make a daily commute into the city via the Metra/Union Pacific Rail (about a 45-minute trip to the Loop) or by the Tri-State Tollway. Des Plaines has 37 parks, including the expansive 73-acre Lake Park, which offers boating, a golf course, and spacious picnic spots. Other facilities include bike trails and a large family aquatic center. Teeming shopping centers and malls, the world's largest non-residential YMCA, and excellent schools are among the assets of this very suburban community. Home to several Fortune

*Des Plaines*

500 companies, the village's industrial and commercial base allows the residents to enjoy a variety of services with a low property tax base. Although rental properties are somewhat limited, apartments are affordable.

In 2000, the town began a revitalization project for the downtown area. Along with a new state-of-the-art library, and several new retail shops and condos, local business took part in a Façade Rehabilitation Program that included replacement of signage, lighting, and restoration of original architectural features. In addition, major construction is now complete on the Metropolitan Square project, which aims for a Main Street atmosphere, including automobile lanes, pedestrian lanes, and walkways; the huge project offers 56,000 square feet of retail space, anchored by a huge grocery store, and 22,000 square feet of office space.

**Website:** www.desplaines.org
**Area Code:** 847
**ZIP Codes:** 60016, 60017, 60018, 60019
**Post Office:** Des Plaines, 1000 E Oakton St; Downtown Des Plaines, 684 Lee St
**Police:** Des Plaines Police Department, 1418 Miner St, 847-391-5400
**Emergency Hospitals:** Holy Family Medical Center, 100 N River Rd, Des Plaines, 847-297-1800, www.reshealth.org/sub_hfmc/default.cfm; Advocate Lutheran General Hospital, 1775 W Dempster St, Park Ridge, 847-723-2210, www.advocatehealth.com/luth/
**Library:** Des Plaines Public Library, 1501 Ellinwood St, 847-827-5551, dppl.org/
**Community Resources:** Des Plaines Chamber of Commerce, 1401 Oakton St, 847-824-4200, www.dpchamber.com; City of Des Plaines, 1420 Miner St, 847-391-5300, www.desplaines.org; YMCA (Lattof Y), 300 E Northwest Hwy, 847-296-3376, www.lattofymca.org
**Parks:** Des Plaines Park District, 847-391-5700, www.desplainesparks.org: Prairie Lakes Community Center, 515 E Thacker St, Des Plaines, 847-391-5711
**Community Publications:** *Journal Online*
**Public Schools:** Des Plaines School District 62, 777 East Algonquin Rd, 847-824-1136, www.d62.org
**Transportation—Rapid Transit:** Metra: Union Pacific/Northwest Line (stations: Des Plaines, Cumberland)
**Transportation—Major Pace Bus Routes:** #290 Busse Highway, #234 Wheeling-Des Plaines, #208 Golf Road, #221 Wolf Road, #226 Oakton Street, #230 South Des Plaines, #250 Dempster Street, #305 Cicero-River Forest, #619 Des Plaines Station-Willow Rd Corridor

## ROSEMONT

South of Des Plaines, and only five minutes from O'Hare International Airport, the small (population 4,200) Village of Rosemont was initially established as an

*Rosemont*

industrial park, offering support to the airport and nearby office parks. While only 25% of the village is zoned for residential housing, there are a variety of townhouses and apartments to choose from, including a senior citizen housing complex.

A single mayor, Donald E. Stephens, remained in office from the village's incorporation in 1956 until his death in 2007. Upon Stephens' passing, his son Bradley A. Stephens, a long-time member of Rosemont's board of trustees, was elected as new mayor, continuing his father's legacy.

When the elder mayor Stephens took the helm, the place consisted of little more than truck farms (where vegetables were grown and then driven into the city) and several sparsely populated subdivisions. When O'Hare International Airport was built, both the Northwest Tollway and the Tri-State Tollway soon followed, making the village a convenient stop-off and eventually a convention destination. In 1976, a former factory was converted into the then–Rosemont Convention Center, the tenth-largest meeting space in the country. Today, the newly rechristened Donald E. Stephens Convention Center is a major area employer. Many other residents work in nearby office parks, in restaurants, in the many area hotels, or in retail shops—all supported by Rosemont's proximity to the airport. Advance Transformer and Galileo International are also major area employers. In addition, the Allstate Arena regularly hosts the Ringling Brothers and Barnum & Bailey Circus, DePaul University basketball, and the Chicago Wolves, an International Hockey League team. The plush, modern Rosemont Theatre proudly hosts Broadway musicals, the Chicagoland Pops Orchestras, and other events capable of filling its 4400 seats.

**Websites:** www.rosemontchamber.com; www.rosemont.com
**Area Code:** 847
**ZIP Codes:** 60018, 60019
**Post Office:** Rosemont Post Office, 6153 Gage St (drop-off only, no phone)

**Police:** Rosemont Public Safety, 9501 E Devon Ave, 847-823-1134
**Emergency Hospitals:** Holy Family Medical Center, 100 N River Rd, Des Plaines, 847-297-1800, www.reshealth.org/sub_hfmc/default.cfm; North Shore Skokie Hospital, 9600 Gross Point Rd, Skokie, 847-677-9600, www.northshore.org/locations/skokie-hospital/; Advocate Lutheran General Hospital, 1775 W Dempster St, Park Ridge, 847-723-2210, www.advocatehealth.com/luth/
**Library:** Des Plaines Public Library, 1501 Ellinwood St, 847-827-5551, dppl.org
**Parks:** Rosemont Park District, 6140 N Scott St, 847-823-6685
**Community Publications:** *Daily Herald* (Chicago suburban edition), *Journal Online*
**Public Schools:** Rosemont School District 78, 6101 N Ruby St, 847-825-0144
**Transportation—Rapid Transit:** Blue Line (stations: Rosemont); Metra: North Central Service (stations: Rosemont, O'Hare Transfer Station)
**Transportation—Major Pace Bus Routes:** #221 Wolf Road, #223 Elk Grove-Rosemont CTA Station, #303 Forest Park-Rosemont, #332 River Road-York Road
**By Car:** I-90, I-294; major local roads: Route 72/Higgins Rd, US 45/Manheim Ave, and Touhy Ave

## ADDITIONAL NORTH/NORTHWEST SUBURBS

- **Bannockburn:** www.bannockburn.org
- **Barrington:** www.barrington-il.gov/
- **Buffalo Grove:** www.vbg.org
- **Elk Grove Village:** www.elkgrove.org
- **Glenview:** www.glenview.il.us
- **Hoffman Estates:** www.hoffmanestates.com
- **Morton Grove:** www.mortongroveil.org
- **Mount Prospect:** www.mountprospect.org
- **Palatine:** www.palatine.il.us
- **Park Ridge:** www.parkridge.us/
- **Prospect Heights:** www.prospect-heights.il.us/
- **Rolling Meadows:** www.ci.rolling-meadows.il.us
- **Roselle:** www.roselle.il.us
- **Wheeling:** www.vi.wheeling.il.us

# WEST SUBURBS

## OAK PARK

One of Oak Park's famous sons, Ernest Hemingway, is said to have described this western suburb as a community of wide lawns and narrow minds. The wide lawns (and avenues) remain, but the narrow minds do not. Oak Park today is a vibrant community whose progressive policies in the mid-20th century provided for controlled integration rather than the white flight that plagued other suburbs. It was also the first municipality in Illinois to offer same-sex domestic partner benefits to city employees. The village is filled with architectural landmarks, including Frank Lloyd Wright's long-time home and studio at 951 Chicago Avenue, as well as his Unity Temple (875 Lake St), and many residences designed by the master.

Located directly west of Chicago proper, Oak Park is divided by the Eisenhower Expressway. (You'll notice that the ramps at Austin and Harlem enter and exit on the left; residents didn't want Oak Park cut up any more than necessary.) Generally, the area south of the expressway is more affordable. If you want to live close to Chicago, but not in it, Oak Park is a good choice. It's convenient for those needing to commute to Chicago: two CTA train lines run through the community, Metra's Oak Park station is at Harlem/Marion Streets, and the Eisenhower Expressway is immediately accessible. The downtown still enjoys a quaint small-town aura, and there are several additional shopping areas throughout the village. Many of the streets are beautiful, lined with huge oak and maple trees and large rambling brick dwellings. Overall, the housing stock is very attractive and well-kept, as well as reasonably priced.

If you decide to live here, note that parking can be a problem, especially if you have guests. Even residents may not park on the streets between 2:30

*Oak Park*

a.m. and 6 a.m. Visitors are allowed to park on the street, but only if a resident notifies the Oak Park Police and gives them the car's license plate number. As a new resident, you will receive a 30-day pass from the parking office to park on the street. After that, you'll need to buy a sticker and park overnight in village lots. For more information, call the Oak Park Village parking department at 708-358-5750.

**Website:** http: www.oak-park.us
**Area Code:** 708
**ZIP Codes:** 60301, 60302, 60303, 60304
**Post Offices:** Main Station, 901 Lake St; 1116 Garfield St
**Police:** Oak Park Police Department, 123 Madison St (Lower Level), 708-386-3800
**Emergency Hospitals:** Rush Oak Park Hospital, 520 S Maple Ave, 708-383-9300, www.roph.org; West Suburban Medical Center, 3 Erie Ct, 708-383-6200, www.westsuburban.reshealth.org
**Libraries:** Oak Park Main Library, 834 Lake St, 708-383-8200; Dole Branch, 255 Augusta St, 708-386-9032; Maze Branch, 845 S Gunderson Ave, 708-386-4751, www.oppl.org
**Community Resources:** Village of Oak Park, 123 Madison St, 708-383-6400, www.oak-park.us; Frank Lloyd Wright Home & Studio, 951 Chicago Ave, 312-994-4000, www.wrightplus.org; Unity Temple Restoration Foundation, 875 Lake St, 708-383-8873; Unity Temple Unitarian Universalist Congregation, 708-848-6225, www.unitytemple.org; Historical Society of Oak Park and River Forest, 217 Home Ave, 708-848-6755, www.oprfhistory.org; West Cook YMCA, 255 S Marion St, Oak Park, 708-383-5200, www.westcookymca.org/
**Parks:** Park District of Oak Park, 218 W Madison St, 708-383-0002, www.oakparkparks.com
**Community Publications:** *Oak Park Journal*, *Oak Leaves*
**Public Schools:** School District 97 (elementary), 970 W Madison St, 708-524-3000, www.op97.org; Oak Park & River Forest School District 200 (high school), 201 N Scoville Ave, Oak Park, 708-383-0700, http://oprfhs.org
**Public Transportation—Rapid Transit:** Green Line (Austin, Ridgeland, Oak Park, Harlem/Lake); Blue Line (Austin, Oak Park, Harlem, Forest Park); Metra: Union Pacific/West Line (Oak Park Station)

## LA GRANGE PARK/BROOKFIELD/ WESTERN SPRINGS/LA GRANGE

Follow Ogden Avenue about thirteen miles west of the Loop to the adjoining communities of Brookfield (west of La Grange Road), La Grange Park, Western Springs, and La Grange (all on the other side of La Grange Road). The four interdependent communities appeal to families at a variety of economic levels. All enjoy easy access to both the East-West and Tri-State tollways as well as Metra

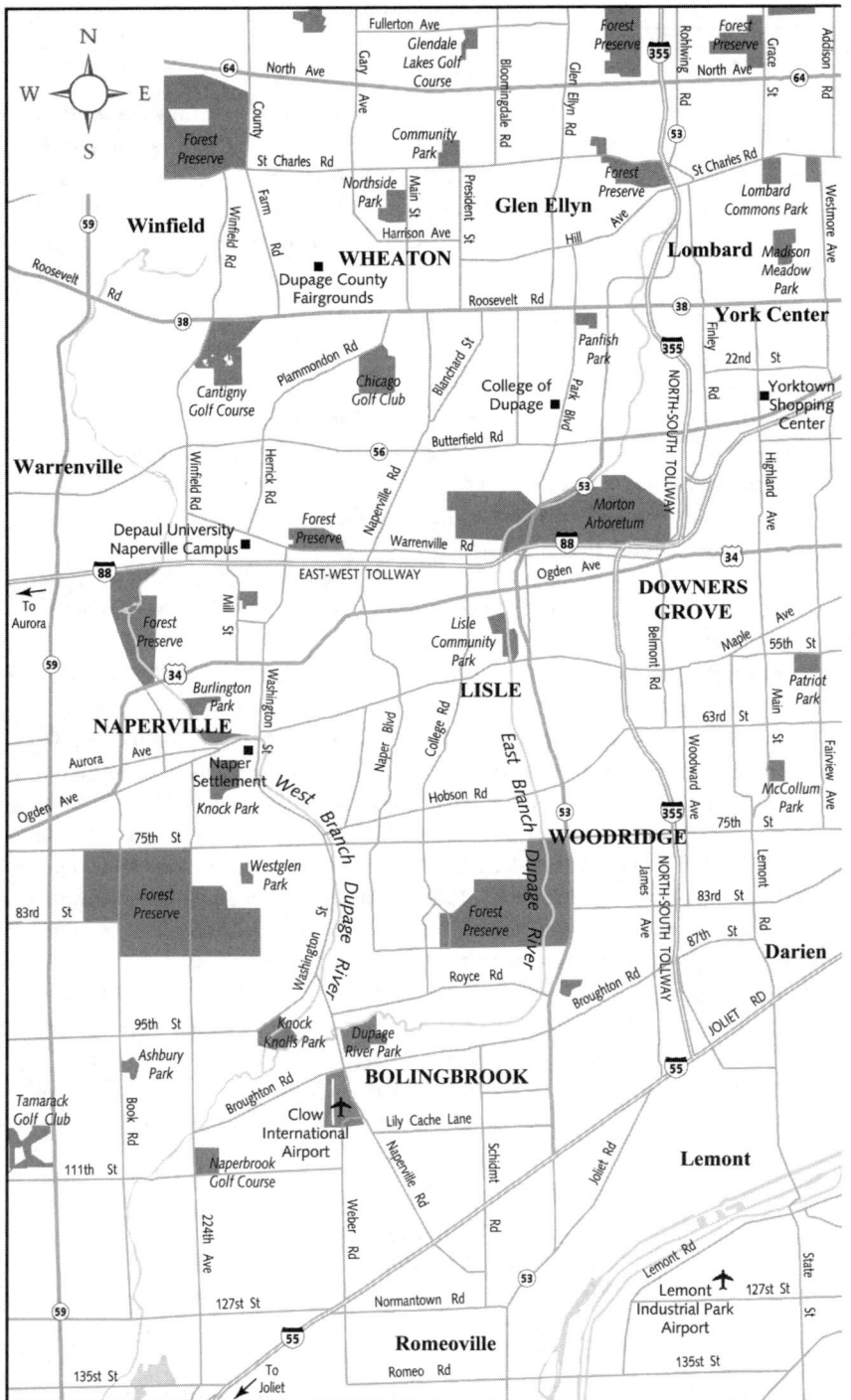

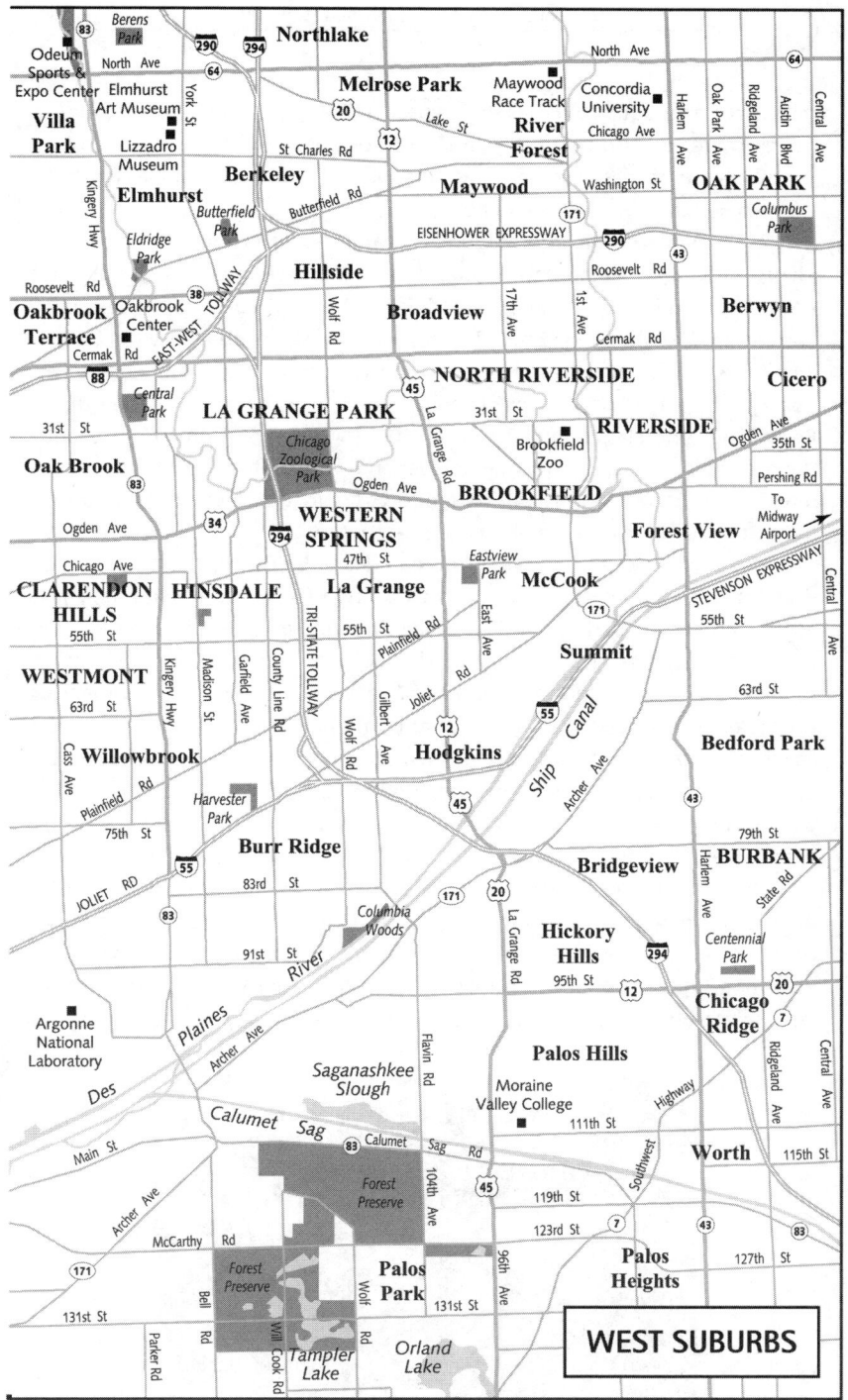

train times of about 30 minutes to downtown Chicago during peak commuting hours. There are also more than a dozen Fortune 1000 companies within a 10-mile radius of these communities, creating plenty of opportunities for those who would rather work closer to home.

**Brookfield** was incorporated in 1893 and has approximately 19,000 residents. Although median home values in this solidly middle-class community hovered around $255,000 in 2009, following the housing crash, values stabilized in 2012 at about $172,000. The community enjoys quiet environs, a low crime rate, a network of solid schools, and easy access to the amenities and quality shopping of the higher-priced suburbs on the other side of La Grange Road. The world-class Brookfield Zoo (3300 Golf Road, 708-485-0263) is both the community's major in-town employer and its claim to fame. This large and outstanding zoo organizes a wide range of family activities on its premises, from travel lectures to celebrating National Pig Day.

The adjoining, more upscale communities of **La Grange** (farthest north), **Western Springs** (in the middle), and **La Grange Park** (farthest south) lie just across La Grange Road (also called Highway 12/45) from Brookfield. Together, the three villages serve as the comfortable home to about 50,000. The housing stock here consists largely of well-maintained and stately older homes, many of the Victorian era, nestled along leafy, family-friendly streets. (There are even a few Frank Lloyd Wright homes sprinkled around the area.) Of the three communities, Western Springs has the highest median home value ($420,000 in 2012), with prices lower in La Grange Park (244,000) and La Grange (344,000). All three enjoy excellent public schools.

The area along La Grange Road between Hillgrove and Cossitt Avenues offers a combination of small-town charm and big-town variety. The attractive commercial district, which branches off to both sides of shop-lined La Grange Road, offers quaint boutiques, cafés with sidewalk seating in the summer, ethnic restaurants, beer gardens, and national chain stores ranging from Walgreens to

*La Grange*

## WEST SUBURBS

Trader Joe's. A lovely historical residential district surrounds the retail amenities; parking is reasonably easy here, even on weekends, and the Metra train tracks that run nearby lend to the bustling sense of vitality in this pleasant area.

**Websites:** www.villageofbrookfield.com, www.lagrangepark.org, www.villageoflagrange.com; www.wsprings.com

**Area Code:** 708

**ZIP Codes:** 60513, 60525, 60526, 60558

**Post Offices:** 3731 Prairie Ave, Brookfield; 121 W Hillgrove Ave, La Grange; 701 E 31st St, La Grange Park; 4479 Lawn Ave, Western Springs

**Police:** 8820 Brookfield Ave, Brookfield, 708-485-8131; 304 W Burlington Ave, La Grange, 708-579-2333; 447 N Catherine Ave, La Grange Park, 708-352-2151; 740 Hillgrove Ave, Western Springs, 708-246-1800

**Emergency Hospitals:** Adventist La Grange Memorial Hospital, 5101 S Willow Springs Rd, La Grange, 708-245-9000, www.keepingyouwell.com; Vanguard MacNeal Hospital, 3249 S Oak Park Ave, Berwyn, 708-783-9100, www.macneal.com

**Library:** Brookfield Public Library, 3609 Grand Blvd, 708-485-6917, brookfieldlibrary.info; La Grange Park Public Library, 555 N La Grange Rd, 708-352-0100, http://www.lplibrary.org/; La Grange Public Library, 10 W Cossitt Ave, 708-352-0576; Thomas Ford Memorial Library, 800 Chestnut, Western Springs, 708-246-0520, www.fordlibrary.org

**Community Resources:** Brookfield Chamber of Commerce, 708-268-8080, www.brookfieldchamber.net; West Suburban Chamber of Commerce, 9440 Joliet Rd, Ste B, Hodgkins, 708-387-7550, www.westsuburbanchamber.org; Western Springs Business Association, www.westernspringsbusiness.com/

**Parks:** Brookfield Park District, 708-485-7344; Park District of La Grange, 536 East Ave, La Grange, 708-352-1762 www.pdlg.org; Western Springs Park District, 708-246-4225, www.wsparks.org

**Community Publications:** *Daily Herald* (Chicago suburban edition), *My Suburban Life*

**Public Schools:** Brookfield School District 95, 3524 Maple Ave, Brookfield, 708-485-0606, www.d95.w-cook.k12.il.us; Riverside Brookfield High School, 160 Ridgewood Rd, Riverside, 708-442-7500, www.rbhs208.net; La Grange District 102, 333 N Park Rd, La Grange, 708-482-2400, www.dist102.k12.il.us; La Grange District 105, 701 S Seventh Ave, La Grange 708-482-2727, d105.net; La Grange District 106, 1750 Plainfield Rd, La Grange, 708-246-3085, www.district106.net/; Lyons Township High School, District 204, 100 S Brainard Ave, 708-579-6300, www.lths.net

**Transportation—Rapid Transit:** Metra: BNSF (Western Springs, La Grange Stone Avenue, La Grange Road, Congress Park, Brookfield, Hollywood)

**Transportation—Major Pace Bus Routes:** #302 Ogden-Stanley, #304 North Riverside-La Grange, #330 Mannheim-La Grange Roads, #669 Western Springs-Indian Head Park, #331 Cumberland-5th Avenue
**By Car:** I-80, I-55, I-290, I-294

## DOWNERS GROVE

Continue west past La Grange Park on Ogden, past Hinsdale and Clarendon, and you come to Downers Grove. Incorporated in 1873, Downers Grove is one of DuPage County's more vibrant communities. Only 23 miles west of Chicago's Loop, Downers Grove is experiencing an economic boom, due in part to its carefully planned expansion projects. Over the past several years, this community of 51,000 spent $12 million to upgrade its downtown infrastructure to encourage more retail investments and downtown living. In addition to landscape and streetscape enhancements, a 40-unit condo development and additional parking spaces have been added to improve the downtown's appearance and livability. These efforts quickly paid off, generating new sales tax revenues and helping to keep property taxes among the lowest in the county.

With FTD, Spiegel, Butterball, and Service Master all headquartered here, Downers Grove's job growth rate has been above average, due, as well, to the city's 12 business districts, which host 3,000 businesses. While the residents here tend to be on the younger side, the local economy is supported by incomes above the national average and much of the housing is dedicated to family living, with homes ranging from first-time buyer's price tags to custom-built luxury homes. The median home value in 2012 was around $270,000. One curious feature of Downers Grove's housing stock: among the older homes are over 20 Sears Catalog homes, all built (from Sears mail-order kits) between 1908 and 1940. Maps for a self-guided tour are available by phoning 630-729-0380.

*Downers Grove*

Residents also enjoy quality schools and plenty of greenspace. The Downers Grove Parks District maintains 48 public parks located on 600 acres of land, 17 tennis courts, several community pools, walking trails, and baseball fields.

**Websites:** www.downersgrove.org, www.downers.us
**Area Code:** 630
**ZIP Code:** 60515, 60516, 60517
**Post Office:** 920 Curtiss St
**Police:** Downers Grove Police Station, 825 Burlington Ave, 630-434-5600
**Emergency Hospital:** Advocate Good Samaritan Hospital, 3815 Highland Ave, 630-275-5900
**Library:** Downers Grove Library, 1050 Curtiss St, 630-960-1200, www.downersgrovelibrary.org
**Community Resources:** Village Hall, 801 Burlington Ave, 630-434-5500; Illinois Prairie Path, www.ipp.org; Indian Boundary (YMCA), 711 59th St, 630-968-8400; Downers Grove Chamber of Commerce, 2001 E Butterfield Rd, 630-968-4050, www.downersgrove.org; Lyman Woods and Interpretive Center, 901 31st St, www.dgparks.org
**Parks:** Downers Grove Park District, 2455 Warrenville Ave, 630-963-1304, www.dgparks.org
**Community Publications:** *Downers Grove Reporter*
**Public Schools:** Downers Grove School District 58 (elementary and middle school), 1860 63rd St, 630-719-5800, www.dg58.org; Community High School District 99, 6301 Springside Ave, 630-795-7100, www.csd99.org
**Transportation—Rapid Transit:** Metra: BNSF (stations: Downers Grove Main Street, Fairview Avenue, Belmont)
**Transportation—Major Pace Bus Routes:** #313 St. Charles Road, #461 North Downers Grove, #462 Southwest Downers Grove, #463 Southeast Downers Grove, #821 IL 53/83rd St-Belmont Metra Station, #834 Joliet-Downers Grove, #464 West Downers Grove
**By Car:** I-294, I-355, I-88, I-55 (approximately 45 minutes to downtown Chicago)

## WHEATON

Northwest of Downers Grove lies Wheaton. In the mid-1830s, two brothers, Jesse and Warren Wheaton, with Erastus Gary, settled in what was to become the City of Wheaton. In 1890, the village was officially incorporated as a city, which grew steadily until it became the DuPage County seat, a position it still holds today. Wheaton is located five miles northeast of Naperville and 23 miles west of Chicago. With a population of 53,000 and a median home price in 2012 at $267,000, Wheaton is a family-focused middle- to upper-income community that appeals to many professionals. The community is home to close to 40

*Wheaton*

churches, 20 public schools, and generous park facilities, featuring 40 public tennis courts and four public golf courses.

In an effort to attract and retain local business, the city has given the downtown area a face lift, refurbishing historic storefronts and cobblestone streets, installing new traffic systems, and replacing awnings. The results were so successful that *Midwest Living Magazine* featured the downtown area in its March/April 2002 issue. There are dozens of small boutiques, cafés, wine shops, and day spas to visit. The Downtown Wheaton Association is very active in organizing community events.

Wheaton is home to the highly respected Wheaton College, which also houses the Billy Graham Museum, documenting evangelism in the US. The Cantigny Gardens, the 500+ acres of wooded lands and gardens that were once home to Colonel McCormick, publisher of the *Chicago Tribune*, is now a public garden. Outdoor concerts are performed here during the summer months.

While there are several large employers in Wheaton, including NICOR, Tellabs, Molex, and the Hub Group, the two biggest employers are county government and the local school districts. Commuters can choose from two Metra train stops, with about a 40-minute ride to downtown Chicago.

**Website:** www.wheaton.il.us
**Area Code:** 630
**ZIP Codes:** 60187, 60188, 60189
**Post Office:** 122 N Wheaton Ave, 46 Danada Square West
**Police:** 900 W Liberty Dr, 630-260-2161
**Hospitals:** Central DuPage Hospital, 25 N Winfield Rd, Winfield, 630-933-1600, www.cdh.org; Elmhurst Memorial Healthcare, 155 E Brush Hill Rd, Elmhurst, 331-221-1000, www.emhc.org
**Library:** Wheaton Public Library, 225 N Cross St, 630-668-1374, www.wheatonlibrary.org

**Community Resources:** City Office: 630-260-2000, www.wheaton.il.us; Wheaton Chamber of Commerce, 108 E Wesley St, 630-668-6464; Illinois Prairie Path, www.ipp.org; Cantigny Park, 151 1 S Winfield Rd, 630-668-5161, www.cantigny.org; Arrowhead Golf Club, 630-510-5070, www.arrowheadgolfclub.org
**Parks:** Wheaton Park District, 102 E Wesley St, 630-665-4710, www.wheatonparkdistrict.com
**Community Publications:** Beacon News, Wheaton City Newsletter (www.wheaton.il.us)
**Public Schools:** Wheaton/Warrenville Community School District 200, 130 W Park Ave, Wheaton, 630-682-2000; Community School District 89, 22 W 600 Butterfield Rd, Glen Ellyn, 630-469-8900, www.ccsd89.org
**Transportation—Rapid Transit:** Metra: College Avenue, Wheaton
**Transportation—Major Pace Bus Routes:** #301 Roosevelt Rd, #709 Carol Stream-North Wheaton, #711 Wheaton-Addison, #714 College of DuPage-Naperville-Wheaton Connector, # 591 Wheaton-Winfield Call-n-Ride
**By Car:** I-290, I-294, I-355, I-88. Major local roads: Roosevelt Rd, Routes 56, 64, 53

## NAPERVILLE

Located south of Wheaton, Naperville has over 140,000 residents and is the fourth largest city in Illinois. Known as a main stop on the Illinois High Tech Corridor, Naperville's corporate residents include many companies specializing in high technology, internet systems, program development, and the like. Naperville has consistently ranked high in the nation as a good place to start a business, raise a family, or retire. In addition to a low crime rate, a solid educational system (there are 40 public schools currently), and one of the finest libraries in the country, Naperville provides its residents with a wealth

*Naperville*

of services. As the oldest city in DuPage County, Naperville has carefully preserved many of its historical sites. The Naperville Settlement, located at 523 South Webster Street, is a museum village, complete with costumed workers who demonstrate what life was like during the 1800s. The many historically and architecturally significant private homes in Naperville include some Frank Lloyd Wright creations, and more than 150 Naperville sites dating from 1830 to 1920 are listed on the National Register of Historic Places.

While there are many features of interest in Naperville, two stand out in particular. The 72-bell Millennium Carillon, located in the Bell Tower, one quarter mile west of Washington Street on Aurora Avenue, is one of only four in the world spanning six full octaves. The bronze bells sound automatically several times daily, and in the summer visiting musicians are invited to play the bells. The community's award-winning Riverwalk, created by Naperville residents in celebration of its 150th birthday, consists of a brick-paved path that winds along the DuPage River and through downtown Naperville. It features fountains, covered bridges, a sled hill, a gazebo, amphitheater, shaded seating areas, and paddleboat rides. Maintained by the park district, it's open year-round, from dawn until midnight. For a Riverwalk map, call the Naperville Park District at 630-848-5000.

Residents enjoy plenty of shopping options. The downtown area offers boutiques, antique stores and a variety of small shops and restaurants. For more serious shopping, residents take to the road and head for the Fox Valley Mall on Route 59 and Aurora Avenue. All along Route 59 from 111th Street to Diehl Road, shoppers will find a number of outdoor malls and stores.

**Websites:** www.naperville.il.us, www.naperville.net
**Area Code:** 630
**ZIP Codes:** 60540, 60563, 60564, 60565, 60566, 60567
**Post Offices:** 5 S Washington St, Suite 105 (downtown); main office, 1750 W Ogden Ave
**Police:** Naperville Police Department, 1350 Aurora Ave, 630-420-6666
**Emergency Hospital:** Edward Hospital, 801 S Washington St, 630-527-3000, www.edward.org
**Libraries:** 200 W Jefferson Ave; 2035 S Naper Blvd; 3015 Cedar Glade Rd, 630-961-4100, www.naperville-lib.org
**Community Resources:** City of Naperville, 400 S Eagle St, 630-420-6111, www.naperville.il.us; Chamber of Commerce, 55 S Main St, 630-355-4141, www.naperville.net; DuPage Children's Museum, 301 N Washington St, 630-637-8000, www.dupagechildrensmuseum.org; Kroehler Family YMCA, 630-420-6270
**Parks:** Naperville Park District, 320 W Jackson Ave, 630-848-5000, www.napervilleparks.org; Centennial Beach; DuPage River Trails, Burr Oak Park to 115th

St; Fox Valley Park District, www.foxvalleyparkdistrict.org; Morton Arboretum, 4100 IL Route 53, Lisle, 630-968-0074; Riverwalk, 630-848-5000
**Community Publications:** *Naperville Sun*
**Public Schools:** Naperville C.U. School District 203, 203 W Hillside Rd, 630-420-6300, www.naperville203.org; Indian Prairie School District 204, 780 Shoreline Dr, Aurora, 630-375-3000, www.ipsd.org
**Transportation:** Metra: BNSF (stations: Naperville); Amtrak for points west of Aurora (www.amtrak.com, 800-USA-RAIL)
**Transportation—Major Pace Bus Routes:** #676 Cress Creek, #677 Naperville-West Glens, #680 Naperville-Knoch Knolls, #681 Naperville-Saybrook, #682 Naperville-Brookdale, #683 Naperville-Ashbury
**By Car:** I-88, I-355. Local main roads: Naper Blvd, Washington St, Ogden Ave

## BOLINGBROOK

South of Naperville and 30 miles southwest of Chicago's downtown area lies Bolingbrook (population 63,000). Once made up of farm fields of Will and DuPage Counties, it wasn't incorporated until 1965. Accordingly, almost all the housing and development in the community has been built since the mid-'60s, and median home prices have stabilized around $163,000. Three-quarters of village residents are homeowners, but there is a good market for multi-family units and apartments here as well. Increasing sales tax revenues from new businesses are helping to keep property taxes down. According to local realtors, Bolingbrook is a growing, middle-income, racially integrated community.

The community, popular with young families, offers a variety of sports and recreation facilities, including two fitness centers, an indoor and outdoor aquatic center, and more than 30 neighborhood parks. Area shopping is good too. The Michigan grocery-giant Meijer selected Bolingbrook for its first Chicagoland

*Bolingbrook*

stores: 755 E Boughton Road, 630-783-5300, and 225 North Weber Road, 630-679-6500. In 2005, the newer of Chicagoland's two IKEA stores opened at 750 East Boughton Road. In spring 2007, The Promenade Bolingbrook opened on Boughton Road just off I-355. The pedestrian-friendly, open-air shopping mall features dozens of stores and restaurants, including anchors such as Macy's and Barnes & Noble. Bolingbrook Clow International Airport, a small general aviation facility owned by the village and located 29 miles from downtown Chicago, offers hangar space, tie downs, aircraft rental, and flying lessons.

**Website:** www.bolingbrook.com
**Area Code:** 630
**ZIP Code:** 60440, 60490
**Post Office:** 105 Canterbury Lane
**Police:** 375 W Briarcliff Rd, 630-226-8600
**Hospitals:** Adventist Bolingbrook Hospital, 500 Remington Blvd, 630-312-5000, www.keepingyouwell.com; Edward Healthcare Center, 130 N Weber Rd, Bolingbrook, 630-646-5770, www.fountaindale.org
**Library:** 300 W Briarcliff Rd, 630-759-2102, http://fountaindale.lib.il.us/
**Community Resources:** Village of Bolingbrook, 375 W Briarcliff Rd, 630-226-8400, www.bolingbrook.com; Bolingbrook Performing Arts Center, 375 W Briarcliff Rd, 630-226-8400; Bolingbrook Chamber of Commerce, 201-B Canterbury Ln, 630-226-8420, bolingbrook.org; Bolingbrook Golf Course, 2001 Rodeo Dr, 630-771-9400; Bolingbrook Community Television, 375 W Briarcliff Rd, 630-226-8425; Bolingbrook Clow International Airport, 130 S Clow International Pkwy, 630-378-0479, www.clowairport.com
**Parks:** Bolingbrook Park District, 201 Recreation Dr, 630-739-0272, www.bolingbrookparks.org
**Community Publications:** *Beacon News*, *Bolingbrook Reporter*
**Public Schools:** Valley View School District, 755 Dalhart Ave, Romeoville, 815-886-2700, www.vvsd.org
**Transportation—Rapid Transit:** Amtrak information: 800-USA-RAIL.
**Transportation—Major Pace Bus Routes:** #824 East Bolingbrook Lisle, #825 Central Bolingbrook-Lisle, #834 Joliet-Downers Grove, #855 Plainfield-East Loop Express, #768 Bolingbrook/Burr Ridge-Soldier Field Express, #775 Bolingbrook/Burr Ridge-US Cellular Field Express, #755 Plainfield-IMD-West Loop Express
**By Car:** I-355, I-80, I-55, I-294

## ADDITIONAL WESTERN SUBURBS

- **Clarendon Hills:** Village Hall, 630-286-5400, www.clarendonhills.us
- **Hinsdale:** Village Hall, 630-789-7000, www.villageofhinsdale.org
- **Lisle:** Village Hall, 630-271-4100, www.vil.lisle.il.us

- **North Riverside:** Village Hall, 708-447-4211, www.northriverside-il.org
- **Oak Brook:** Village Hall, 630-368-5000, www.oak-brook.org
- **Riverside:** Village Hall, 708-447-2700, www.riverside-illinois.com
- **Westmont:** Village Hall, 630-981-6200, www.westmont.illinois.gov
- **Woodridge:** Village Hall, 630-852-7000, www.vil.woodridge.il.us

# SOUTH SUBURBS

## BLUE ISLAND

Located just across the Chicago border from the Beverly/Morgan Park neighborhood, the small city of Blue Island got its curious name because it was built on the high ground of a glacial ridge. Early travelers said that, from a distance, the thickly wooded ridge seemed enveloped in a bluish haze, like a blue island rising above the flat surrounding prairie. Established in 1835, Blue Island at first served as a way station for travelers heading to or from Chicago on the historic Vincennes trail. The town really took off in the 1860s, when the Rock Island Railroad constructed tracks and a station; in following decades the railroad added a roundhouse and freight yards, and Blue Island became known as a transportation hub and the home of heavy industry.

Today, most of the industry has been replaced by retail and service. After a gradual mid-century decline, Blue Island has sprung back in the past couple decades. Residents are proud of Blue Island's assets, such as the quaint retail strip of Western Avenue between 127th and Vermont Street, which looks like Main Street America and offers Illinois' largest concentration of antique stores, as well as several bakeries, restaurants, cafés, pubs, an authentic Italian deli, and two full-service Hispanic supermarkets. An additional retail strip, even quainter, lies

*Blue Island*

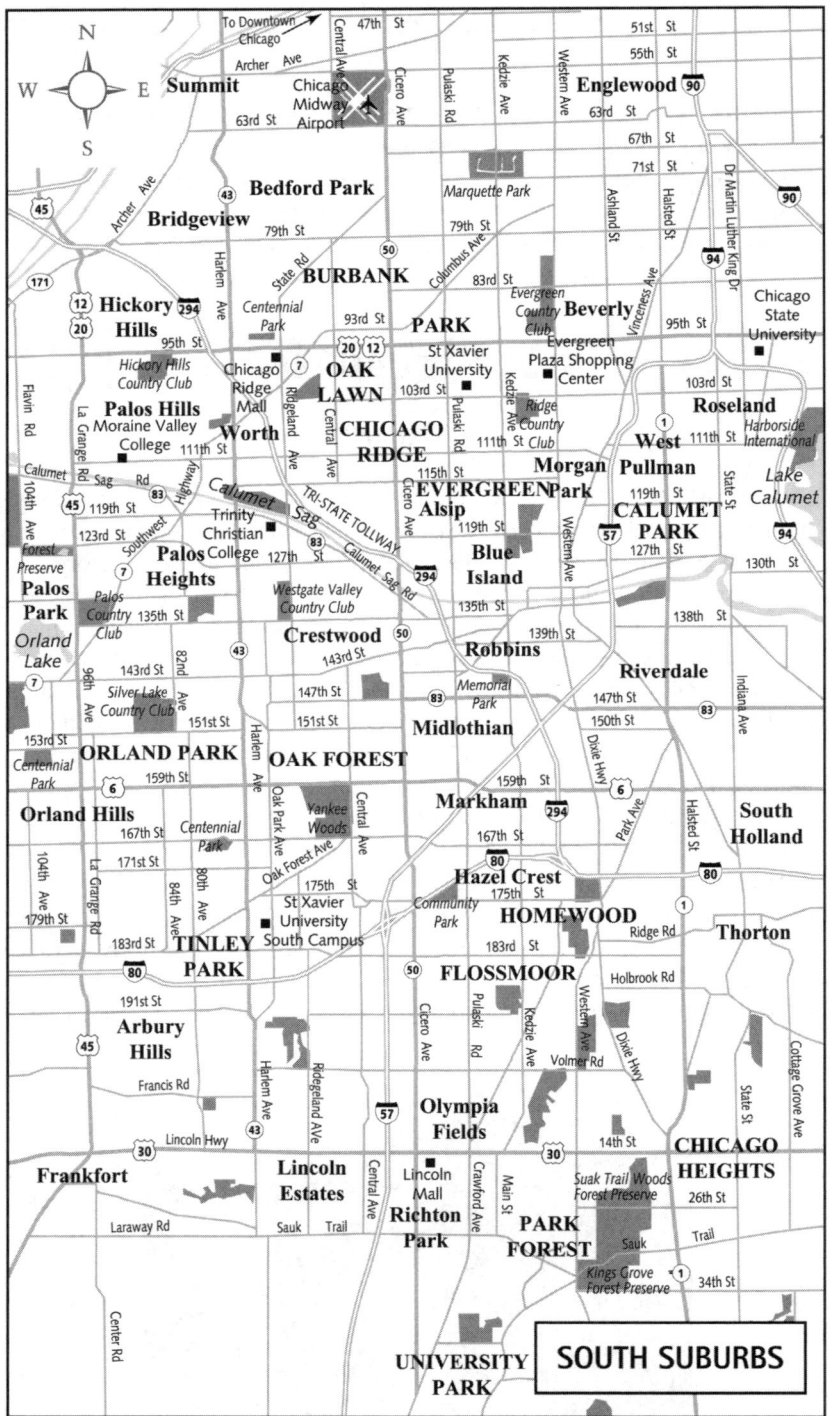

on Old Western Avenue just south of the Cal-Sag Channel; this two-block stretch hosts hardware stores, taverns, and much-loved Mexican and Cajun eateries. In recent years, the old-fashioned charm of these commercial areas, in addition to the homes and avenues of the historic residential district, has attracted several Hollywood productions to film in Blue Island. Moraine Valley Community College, based in nearby Palos Hills, opened its satellite Blue Island Education Center on Western Avenue in 2004. The successful state-of-the-art facility offers several certificate and degree programs, as well as a full menu of general courses.

So far, Blue Island's growth remains steady and gradual, with an increasing number of young couples and families lured from Chicago by Blue Island's peaceful atmosphere, quick commute to the Loop, and affordable vintage housing stock. (Median single-family home prices are still under $90,000.) Especially desirable is the "Silk Stocking District," the concentration of well-kept single-family homes just west of Western Avenue and south of 127th Street, which boasts many homes from the 1870s, '80s, and '90s, as well as stately brick mansions that date a few decades later. This district is located within minutes' walking distance from the library, post office, shopping, and both of Blue Island's two commuter train lines. During peak commuting hours, trains arrive at least every twenty minutes, and express trains to the Loop take less than half an hour.

Residents say that Blue Island combines small town attributes—friendly neighbors, tree-lined streets, involved homeowners, a quaint downtown strip, and walkable amenities—with attributes more common to Chicago proper, such as ethnic diversity, smaller-sized lots, and easy access to trains. Hometown pride shows in frequent civic celebrations, including an annual Fourth of July parade and festival and a New Year's Eve celebration on Western Avenue, and in the popularity of events such as weekly summer TGIF picnics, and a yearly house walk that shows off some of Blue Island's lovingly preserved architectural treasures. In 2005, the city adopted an ambitious development plan to make the area between the commuter train stations and main strip more attractive and pedestrian-friendly. Fay's Point, a planned community, was recently built at the town's southeastern edge, on a peninsula where the Cal-Sag Channel and Little Calumet River meet; the development includes condos, townhomes, 84 boat slips, a marina club, and wilderness trails through restored wetlands.

**Websites:** www.blueislandbiz.com, www.blueisland.org
**Area Code:** 708
**ZIP Code:** 60406, 60827
**Post Office:** 2441 Vermont St
**Police:** Blue Island Police Department, 13031 S Greenwood Ave, 708-597-8601
**Emergency Hospitals:** Little Company of Mary Hospital, 2800 W 95th St, Evergreen Park, 708-422-6200, www.lcmh.org; MetroSouth Medical Center, 12935 S Gregory St, Blue Island, 708-597-2000, www.metrosouthmedicalcenter.com

**Library:** Blue Island Public Library, 2433 York St, 708-388-1078, www.blueislandlibrary.org

**Schools:** Cook County School District 130, 12300 S Greenwood Ave, 708-385-6800; Scool District 218, Dwight D. Eisenhower High School, 12700 Sacramento, 708-597-6300

**Community Resources:** Blue Island Chamber of Commerce, 2434 Vermont St, 708-388-1000, www.blueislandchamber.org; Meadows Golf Club, 2802 W 123rd St, 708-385-1994, www.meadowsgc.com; Moraine Valley Community College Blue Island Education Center, 12940 S Western Ave, 708-974-5300, www.morainevalley.edu/blueIsland

**Parks:** Blue Island Park District, 12804 S Highland Ave, 708-385-3304; Memorial Park, 12804 S Highland Ave; Centennial Park, 1732 Vermont St; Bark Park, 2601 W 119th St; Hart Park, 123rd and Western Ave

**Community Publications:** *Southtown Star*, *Southwest News Herald*, *The Star*, *Blue Island Forum*

**Transportation—Rapid Transit:** Metra: Rock Island District (stations: Blue Island-Vermont St, Prairie St, 123rd St, 119th St); Metra Electric Line (stations: Blue Island, Burr Oak)

**Transportation—Major CTA Bus Routes:** bus #49A South Western; **Major Pace Bus Routes:** #359 Robbins/South Kedzie Avenue, #349 South Western, #877 South Suburban Oakbrook Limited, #385 87th/111th/127th, #348 Harvey-Riverdale-Blue Island

**By Car:** I-294, I-57

## BURBANK

North and west of Chicago's Beverly Hills neighborhood and 15 miles southwest of the Loop in Cook County is the town of Burbank. This relatively new community was incorporated in 1970 and today has nearly 28,000 residents. In this safe, middle-class neighborhood, new housing construction is the rule rather than the exception, and the 2012 median home price was $137,000. While there are some rental apartments, single-family homes in residential developments predominate. Burbank's tax base remains one of the lowest in the southwest Chicagoland area, making it a good deal for many first-time homebuyers. The town supports a dozen parks, a community pool and waterpark, and two volunteer fire departments. Burbank is home to some large-scale employers, including offices of several of *Fortune Magazine's* Top 1000, including McDonald's, Sara Lee, Abbott Laboratories, Baxter International, Walgreens, and the Aon Corporation. Burbank is just a few miles from several of Chicago's major universities and colleges, including Saint Xavier University and Trinity Christian College. A straight shot up Cicero Avenue to Midway Airport offers easy access for those needing to fly. Travel time to downtown Chicago via the Metra train is approximately 35 minutes.

# SOUTH SUBURBS

*Burbank*

**Website:** www.burbankil.gov
**Area Code:** 708
**ZIP Code:** 60459
**Post Office:** 6801 W 73rd St, Bedford Park
Police Department: 5650 W 75th Pl, Burbank, 708-924-7300
**Emergency Hospitals:** Little Company of Mary Hospital, 2800 W 95th St, Evergreen Park, 708-422-6200, www.lcmh.org; MetroSouth Medical Center, 12935 S Gregory St, Blue Island, 708-597-2000, www.metrosouthmedicalcenter.com
**Library:** Prairie Trails Public Library, 8449 S Moody Ave, 708-430-3688, www.prairietrailslibrary.org
**Schools:** Elementary: Burbank School District 111, 7600 S Central Ave, 708-496-0500, www.burbank.k12.il.us; high school: Reavis/District 220, 6034 W 77th St, Burbank, 708-599-7200, www.reavisd220.org
**Community Resources:** City of Burbank, 708-599-5500, 6530 W 79th St; Stickney Township, 5635 State Rd, Burbank, 708-424-9200, www.townshipofstickney.org; Senior Center, 7745 S Leamington, 708-636-8850, www.townshipofstickney.org/Stickneysenior.html
**Parks:** Burbank Park District, 8050 S Newcastle, 708-599-2070, www.burbankparkdistrict.org; Stevenson Park (water park), 6100 W 85th St, 708-598-9945
**Community Publications:** *Southtown Star, Southwest News Herald, The Star*
**Transportation—Rapid Transit:** Amtrak (www.amtrak.com) (stations: Summit); CTA Orange Line (Midway)
**Transportation—Major Pace Bus Routes:** #379 Midway-Orland Square, #382 Central/Clearing, #383 South Cicero, #384 Narragansett-Ridgeland, #386 South Harlem, #390 Midway CTA-UPS Hodgkins, #385 87th/111th/127th
**By Car:** I-294, I-57

## EVERGREEN PARK

Surrounded on three sides by neighborhoods long ago absorbed into Chicago, the middle-income community of Evergreen Park has resisted annexation since 1893. Located 17 miles southwest of the Loop, this town of over 21,000 continues to grow at a leisurely pace. Like the adjoining Chicago neighborhoods of Beverly and Mount Greenwood, Evergreen Park historically has had an Irish-American flavor. Of its white inhabitants today, almost 40% are estimated to be of Irish background. This heritage can also be seen in the town's thirteen churches and in the Irish Catholic origins of Saint Xavier University, a mid-sized university that, though technically located in Chicago's Mount Greenwood neighborhood, snuggles up against Evergreen Park's southwest side. With no industry to speak of, the suburb's main employers are the numerous health centers and hospitals—Little Company of Mary Hospital is the town's largest employer—as well as a variety of service-oriented businesses. Evergreen Park is perhaps best known for the Evergreen Shopping Plaza, one of the first regional malls in the country. The area surrounding the mall, west of the intersection of 95th Street and Western Avenue, comprises Evergreen Park's main shopping district. Many chain retailers have large stores here, though smaller local businesses continue to thrive as well. One of Chicagoland's first Walmarts opened in January 2006 just on the Evergreen Park side of the 95th Street Chicago border.

The majority of the residents are homeowners, and Evergreen's wide range of housing prices attracts both first-time buyers and those further up the corporate ladder. (The median home price in 2012 was $140,000.) Single-family homes predominate and come in a variety of styles: Victorians, bungalows, Cape Cods, and Georgians. Some condos and apartment units are available as well. Other amenities include an 18-hole public golf course, a private and family-oriented racquet club, and pleasant parks. Evergreen Park is a well-kept community with tree-lined streets, a variety of restaurants, quality schools, and good services.

*Evergreen Park*

**Websites:** www.evergreenpark-ill.com
**Area Code:** 708
**ZIP Code:** 60805
**Post Office:** Evergreen Post Office, 9359 S Kedzie Ave
**Police:** Evergreen Park Police Department, 9420 S Kedzie Ave, 708-422-2144
**Emergency Hospitals:** Advocate Christ Medical Center and Hope Children's Hospital, 4440 W 95th St, Oak Lawn, 708-684-8000, www.advocatehealth.com/cmc; Little Company of Mary Hospital, 2800 W 95th St, Evergreen Park, 708-422-6200, www.lcmh.org; Palos Community Hospital, 12251 S 80th Ave, Palos Heights, 708-923-4000; MetroSouth Medical Center, 12935 S Gregory St, Blue Island, 708-597-2000, www.metrosouthmedicalcenter.com
**Library:** Evergreen Park Public Library, 9400 S Troy, 708-422-8522, www.evergreenparklibrary.org
**Community Resources:** Village Hall, 708-422-1551, www.evergreenpark-ill.com; Office of Citizens Services, 708-422-8776
**Parks:** Evergreen Park and Recreation District, 708-229-3374; Evergreen Park Recreation Department, 3450 W 97th St, 708-229-3373; Youth Center, 3450 W 97th St, 708-229-3377; Ice Rink, 8900 S Kedzie
**Schools:** Evergreen Park School District 124 (elementary), 708-423-0950, www.d124.org; Evergreen Park Community High School District 231, 708-424-7400, www.evergreenpark.org
**Community Publications:** *Southtown Star, Southwest News Herald, The Star, The Reporter*
**Transportation—Rapid Transit:** Metra: Rock Island District (Beverly Hills stations: 91st St, 95th St, 99th St, 103rd St, 107th St)
**Transportation—Major Pace Bus Routes:** #349 South Western, #381 95th St, #395 CTA 95th St Station-UPS Hodgkins; CTA buses also run along Evergreen Park's three borders with Chicago
**By Car:** I-294, I-94, I-57

## *OAK LAWN*

Directly west of Evergreen Park is Oak Lawn, a middle-income community and home to about 57,000. Its earliest known settlers, arriving in 1842, established a modest farming community. Amenities like a high school (1948) and hospital (1960) came much later, along with a growing population that migrated from Chicago's South Side after World War II. Despite its small size, it provides a wide range of services to its residents: public parks, recreational sites, 24 tennis courts, nature trails, three outdoor swimming pools, and a golf course, all spread throughout a 300-acre area. Oak Lawn's large and well-stocked public library is one of the best in Chicago's south suburbs. Oak Lawn has no industrial center; the source of its commercial viability is its service sector. The Oak Lawn Hilton

*Oak Lawn*

Hotel & Conference Center (9333 South Cicero), located just 15 miles southwest of the Loop, attracts business conferences throughout the year. The community also offers quick access to the Tri-State Tollway and a 40-minute Metra ride to Chicago's Loop.

In 1967, Oak Lawn (as well as the nearby communities of Palos Hills, Hometown, and Evergreen Park) was struck by a devastating tornado. The destruction included dozens of homes, a roller rink, a trailer park, and a rectory. For years, Oak Lawn had no attractive development in its downtown area, but a huge downtown renovation project began in 2002. Several blocks along the north and south sides of 95th Street were cleared to make way for multi-story luxury condominiums with ground-floor retail space, a multi-level parking garage, an expanded and beautifully renovated Metra train station, and a new children's museum. On Wednesdays from June to October, a farmers' market occupies the parking lot north of Village Hall.

Housing styles here range from Colonials to ranch-style homes, with many in the first-home-buyer price range. If you are looking for a newly built home, Oak Lawn has at least 13 newer developments to choose from and enjoys median home prices similar to those in adjoining Evergreen Park. Throughout the community, however, older homes are being torn down to make way for newer, more palatial residences. While Oak Lawn has a solid school system and is family-friendly, some observers claim the town seems increasingly oriented towards older residents as younger families and singles often choose to live either in Chicago proper or in suburban communities farther south.

**Website:** www.oaklawn-il.gov
**Area Code:** 708
**ZIP Codes:** 60453, 60454
**Post Office:** 9249 S Cicero Ave
**Police:** 9446 S Raymond Ave, Oak Lawn, 708-422-8292

**Emergency Hospital:** Advocate Christ Medical Center and Hope Children's Hospital, 4440 W 95th St, Oak Lawn, 708-684-8000, www.advocatehealth.com/cmc
**Library:** Oak Lawn Library, 9427 S Raymond Ave, 708-422-4990, www.lib.oaklawn.il.us
**Community Resources:** Oak Lawn Chamber of Commerce, 708-424-8300, www.oaklawnchamber.com; Village Hall, 9446 S Raymond Ave, 708-636-4400, www.oaklawn-il.gov; Farmers' market, Village Hall north parking lot, June through October; Summer concerts on the Village Green.
**Parks:** Oak Lawn Park District, 708-857-2222, www.olparks.com
**Schools:** Oak Lawn–Hometown School District 123, 4201 W 93rd St, 708-423-0150, www.d123.org; Oak Lawn Community High School District 229, 9400 Southwest Hwy, Oak Lawn, 708-424-5200, www.olchs.org
**Community Publications:** *Southtown Star, Suburban Life, Southwest News Herald, The Star*
**Transportation—Rapid Transit:** Metra: Southwest Service (stations: Oak Lawn)
**Transportation—Major CTA Bus Routes:** #53A South Pulaski; **Major Pace Bus Routes:** #395 CTA 95th St Station-UPS Hodgkins, #769 Palos Heights/Oak Lawn-Soldier Field Express, #774 Palos Heights/Oak Lawn-US Cellular Field Express
**By Car:** I-80, I-90, I-94, I-295, I-55, I-57

## OAK FOREST

Farther south of Oak Lawn is Oak Forest, a small (population: 28,000) community nearly surrounded by forest preserves and tucked in the southwest corner of Cook County, 24 miles from Chicago's Loop. The overwhelming majority of residents are homeowners (about 80%), many with families. Area homes are priced similarly to those in other south suburban communities like Oak Lawn. Taxes are also low. With big employers such as Corn Products International, Tellabs, The ServiceMaster Company, and Molex right here in their own back yard, Oak Forest residents don't have to commute to the Loop for employment. In addition, two areas in town have been set aside for industrial development, the Harlem Avenue Business Center, and the Corporate Center of Oak Forest. Those who do need to head north to Chicago will find that either a typical Kennedy/Dan Ryan expressway trip or a Metra train ride will take about 40 minutes.

There are 19 public parks located in Oak Forest, and the park district runs a health and fitness center. For the serious golfer, there's the George W. Dunne National Golf Course, one of the best public courses in the country; for the less serious player, there's a public mini-golf course as well. Those seeking higher education will appreciate the South Suburban College University and College Center, which houses branches of DePaul University, The College of Saint Francis, Chicago State University, Governors State University, and South Suburban College.

*Oak Forest*

Those with a taste for the supernatural may be interested in Bachelor's Grove, an abandoned, mostly desecrated cemetery within Oak Forest's Rubio Forest Preserve, which is alleged to be among the world's most haunted places (www.bachelorsgrove.com).

**Website:** www.oak-forest.org
**Area Code:** 708
**ZIP Code:** 60452
**Post Office:** 15811 Central Ave
**Police:** 15440 S Central Ave, 708-687-1376
**Emergency Hospital:** Oak Forest Hospital of Cook County/John H. Stroger, Jr. Hospital, 15900 S Cicero Ave, 708-687-7200, www.cchil.org/dom/oak.html
**Library:** Acorn Public Library, 15624 S Central Ave, 708-687-3700, www.acornlibrary.org
**Community Resources:** City Hall, 15440 S Central Ave, 708-687-4050; Oak Forest Chamber of Commerce, 708-687-4600; South Suburban College University and College Center, 16333 S Kilbourn Ave, 708-596-2000, www.southsuburbancollege.edu
**Parks:** Oak Forest Park District, 15601 S Central Ave, 708-687-7270
**Schools:** Arbor Park School District 145, 708-687-8040 (elementary), www.arbor145.org; Bremen High School District 228, 708-389-1175, www.bhsd228.com; also check Tinley Park below.
**Community Publications:** *Southtown Star, Suburban Life, Southwest News Herald, The Star, The Reporter*
**Transportation—Rapid Transit:** Metra: Rock Island District (stations: Oak Forest)
**Transportation—Major Bus Pace Routes:** #354 Harvey-Oak Forest Loop, #364 159th Street, #383 South Cicero
**By Car:** I-57, I-80, I-294

## ORLAND PARK

Family-focused Orland Park, located west of Oak Forest, was incorporated in 1892. Orland Park has been growing quickly. In 2006, *Money* magazine listed Orland Park as number 45 on its Top 100 Best Places to Live. With its low crime rate, attractive amenities—21 public golf courses, 25 tennis courts, 36 parks, and loads of shopping—Orland Park has property values well above those in most of the south suburbs (around $270,000 in 2012). The community is popular with high-end blue-collar workers as well as white-collar professionals. While condos are available, most housing consists of spacious single-family homes, and some area residents complain that "McMansions" are starting to dominate newer residential developments. In contrast to many area communities, Orland Park is overwhelmingly white (90% in the 2010 Census) and comparatively Republican.

Across Chicago's south suburbs, Orland Park is acknowledged as the most important retail center of the region. A large upscale shopping complex, Orland Square Mall, many huge outposts of major national chains, and dozens of smaller specialty stores help fill the community's over-five-million-square-feet of retail space. Though all this commercial activity has led to traffic congestion, road improvements are under way, and the government of Orland Park is still actively seeking to encourage more businesses, especially upscale retail, light industrial, and high-tech and research facilities, to locate within its borders. The village also has a 10,000-square-foot civic center available for conferences, weddings, and other events. A new, 3200-square-foot commuter train station opened in spring 2007. The town's largest employer is the telecommunications firm, Andrews Corporation, followed by School District 135. With several institutions offering coursework in Orland Park locations, it's not surprising that statistics indicate that a majority of Orland Park residents have completed at

*Orland Park*

least "some college." Institutions with Orland Park campuses include Saint Xavier University, ITT Technical Institute, and Robert Morris College.

**Website:** www.orland-park.il.us
**Area Code:** 708
**ZIP Codes:** 60462, 60467
**Post Office:** 9500 W 144th Pl; Orland Park Retail Branch, 15128 S La Grange Rd
**Police:** 15100 S Ravinia Ave, 708-349-4111
**Emergency Hospitals:** Palos Community Hospital, 12251 S 80th Ave, Palos Heights, 708-923-4000, www.paloscommunityhospital.org
**Library:** Orland Park Library, 14921 Ravinia Ave, 708-428-5100, www.orlandparklibrary.org
**Community Resources:** Village Hall, 708-403-6100, www.orland-park.il.us; Orland Park Chamber of Commerce, 708-349-2972; Saint Xavier University–Orland Park Campus, 18230 Orland Pkwy, 708-802-6200, sxu.edu/campuslife/orland/
**Parks:** Orland Park Recreation & Park District, 708-403-7275, www.orland-park.il.us
**Public Schools:** Orland Park School District 135, 15100 S 94th Ave, 708-364-3300, www.orland135.org
**Community Publications:** *Southtown Star*, *Suburban Life*, *Southwest News Herald*, *The Star*
**Transportation—Rapid Transit:** Metra: Southwest Service (stations: Orland Park 143rd Street, Orland Park 153rd Street, Orland Park 179th Street)
**Transportation—Major Pace Bus Routes:** #832 Joliet-Orland Square
**By Car:** I-80, I-57, I-294, I-355

## TINLEY PARK

It's the tale of two counties—Cook and Will. Tinley Park, divided by the I-80 Development Corridor, sits mostly in the southwest corner of Cook County, but it is Tinley Park's section of Will County that is a blessing to this community. The lower tax base of Will County is very attractive to local businesses, and is one of the features that the local government uses to bring more business to the community. And a solid foundation for area businesses creates a low tax base for residents. Tinley Park is experiencing a steady growth rate, much like Orland Park, its neighbor to the north.

Young and growing families are especially attracted to Tinley Park, but since Tinley Park issues as many multi-family building permits as it does single-family homes, Tinley Park has many condos and townhouses available as well. This is unusual in a Chicago fringe community, where the overwhelming choice is only single-family homes, and good news for empty nesters, young singles, childless couples, and seniors who are looking for affordable living space.

# SOUTH SUBURBS

*Tinley Park*

Tinley Park is a safe, close-knit community with quality city services, attractive playgrounds and parks, and an active recreational department that offers free summer concerts held in the parking lot of the gorgeous and newly renovated Metra station. The station also boasts a café and clock tower and can be rented out for special events. Recently, Tinley Park has instituted an ambitious downtown revitalization project, which includes construction of new businesses and condominiums arranged along attractive brick-paved streets.

The community's assets include hiking trails, a water park, an 18-hole public golf course, easy access to Orland Park's extensive shopping, and the First Midwest Bank Amphitheatre, the largest outdoor performance facility in North America.

**Website:** www.tinleypark.org
**Area Code:** 708
**ZIP Code:** 60477, 60487
**Post Office:** 7230 W 171st St
**Police:** 7850 W 183rd St, Tinley Park, 708-532-9111
**Emergency Hospitals:** Franciscan St. James Health, Olympia Fields Campus, 20201 S Crawford Ave, Olympia Fields, 708-747-4000, www.franciscanalliance.org/hospitals/olympiafields; Advocate South Suburban Hospital, 17800 S Kedzie Ave, Hazel Crest, 708-799-8000, www.advocatehealth.com/ssub
**Library:** 7851 Timber Dr, 708-532-0160, www.tplibrary.org
**Community Resource:** Village of Tinley Park, 16250 S Oak Park Ave, 708-444-5000; Tinley Park Chamber of Commerce, 708-532-5700, www.tinleychamber.org; First Midwest Bank Amphitheatre, 19100 S Ridgeland Ave, 708-614-1616, http://www.firstmidwest.com/FMBA/
**Parks:** Park District, 8125 W 171st St, 708-342-4200

**Public Schools:** C.C. School District 146 (elementary), 708-614-4500, www.ccsd146.k12.il.us; Kirby School District 140 (elementary), 708-532-6462, www.ksd140.org; Bremen High School District 228, 708-389-1175, www.bhsd228.com (also see Oak Forest and Orland Park)
**Community Publications:** *Southtown Star, Suburban Life, Southwest News Herald*
**Transportation—Rapid Transit:** Metra: Rock Island District (stations: Tinley Park-80th Ave, Tinley Park)
**Transportation—Major Pace Bus Routes:** #386 South Harlem, #773 Markham/Tinley Park-US Cellular Field Express, #356 Harvey-Homewood-Tinley Park
**By Car:** I-80, US 43, US 45

## ADDITIONAL SOUTHERN SUBURBS

- **Bridgeview:** www.villageofbridgeview.com
- **Calumet Park:** www.calumetparkvillage.org
- **Chicago Ridge:** www.chicagoridge.org
- **Homewood Village:** village.homewood.il.us
- **Palos Heights:** www.palosheights.org
- **Palos Park:** www.palospark.org
- **Park Forest:** www.villageofparkforest.com
- **University Park:** www.university-park-il.com

# FINDING A PLACE TO LIVE

FINDING A PLACE TO LIVE IN CHICAGO MAY FEEL OVERWHELMING IF you're moving here from a smaller town, but those from another large metropolis may find Chicago's housing market comparatively easy to maneuver. Where's the ideal place to live in the Chicago area? Though that depends on personal preference, for many, the perfect place is attractive, clean, spacious, affordable, and located in a safe area convenient to work and public transportation. Some also want a place close to the lake, with spectacular views, central air, ample on-street parking, and permission to keep pets. Nothing is impossible…if you have enough money. For most people, though, having clear priorities before beginning to search will save time and reduce stress.

In Illinois, there is no upper limit on how much rent a landlord can charge for a rental property. That, combined with the area's high incomes, the transformation of Chicago into a cultural powerhouse, and the continued gentrification and beautification of the downtown, means that many formerly affordable neighborhoods are now filled with the wealthier than average. In popular, upscale neighborhoods such as the Gold Coast, brace yourself for sticker shock. But don't despair! Chicago is a large and varied city, and the rental market in particular is softer, and more renter-friendly, now, than it was in the 1990s. You *can* find a great, affordable apartment if you are willing to do a bit of digging, particularly outside the most popular neighborhoods. It will require some research and exploring—which can be interesting, and is important if you want to get to know your new city.

Unless you're fabulously wealthy, cost will probably be a major consideration. Try the following websites for average rental prices in various neighborhoods (note: many Chicago neighborhoods go by a variety of names, so names and boundaries may not always correspond with the names and boundaries in this book): **www.apartmentpeople.com** or **chicago.apartments.com**.

Whether you are looking for an apartment to rent or a place to buy, here are some issues to keep in mind when exploring your targeted neighborhood:

**Airport noise:** If you are considering living in the suburbs, you will want to know if your potential new home is in a landing or takeoff route of one of the major airlines. Here's where an experienced real estate broker may be of assistance. Airport noise is no small matter; it can make a big difference in the quality of your television/cell phone reception, outdoor entertaining, the resale value of your home, and the likelihood of getting a good night's sleep. The good news is that, overall, airport noise complaints have dropped significantly since 1998 with the introduction of quieter aircraft and permanent noise monitoring. But with a major O'Hare expansion recently finished and a proposed third airport in the south suburbs, it will remain an important issue for years to come. Contact the O'Hare Noise Compatibility Commission at 773-686-3198 or www.oharenoise.org for more information. The noise of Midway Airport can be a factor in south suburban Burbank as well as nearby South Chicago neighborhoods. For more information, contact the Midway Community Noise Resource Center: www.ohare.com/cnrc/midway/midway-noise.shtm.

- **Flooding:** Much of the Chicago area was once swamp and some suburbs are situated on flood plains, so a big thunderstorm may mean a mini-lake in your backyard or, worse, your basement. This can also affect your insurance coverage. Try to stay away from flood-prone areas, no matter how much of a bargain the house may seem. If you're considering a "garden" apartment, be aware that if the storm sewers back up—and they do in the heaviest downpours—you may find yourself bailing to save yourself from a rush of brown water. These types of mini-floods can occur very quickly, often at night in tandem with a thunderstorm; fortunately, they seem to disappear almost as fast as they come.
- **Bugs:** Termites, carpenter ants, long-horned beetles, cockroaches—find out the specifics on such pests in your neighborhood and in your building, and whether they have been or can be eradicated from the place you are considering. (See **Helpful Services** for more on area pests.) Roaches, for example, sometimes infest one building while another, right next door, may be roach-free.
- **Turnover:** Are you considering a neighborhood where residents move out regularly after a few years, or is it a stable community? If you have school-aged children, this may be of particular interest to you.
- Can you get a **sense of community** in the neighborhood or building you are visiting? Neighborhood types vary greatly but some are specifically bedroom-commuter suburbs, young singles areas, retiree havens, or neighborhoods made up of mostly young families. Which is right for you?
- **Traffic:** During rush-hour commutes, when major thoroughfares are crowded, many drivers use residential streets as shortcuts. Although some

neighborhoods have speed bumps, frequent stop signs, and one-way streets to discourage speeding commuters, many streets that are tranquil on weekends still turn into speedways come Monday morning.
- **Highway noise** can also be a problem depending on how close you are to the road. The best way to find out about noise problems in a prospective neighborhood is to visit several times, at different times of day. Also, if you are moving within the city limits, be aware that if you live right next to the 'L,' vibrations from the train can be a nuisance—a lot depends on the building, however. Remember, being close to an 'L' stop makes getting around the city much easier!
- **Crime**: How safe is your prospective neighborhood? Visit both during the day and at night to get a feel. Also check chicago.everyblock.com/crime for statistics about the area.

## APARTMENT HUNTING

Take a breath and tell yourself you don't expect to find a new pad in one day; otherwise, you may end up with something that isn't right for you. Ideally, you should give yourself at least a week to find your first apartment here. Also note that many desirable places may become available only on the 1st or the 15th of the month, when the previous tenants' lease expires.

### DIRECT ACTION

If you're the do-it-yourself kind of person, the **classifieds**, either print or online, are still probably the best way to find a place to live in Chicago. **Word-of-mouth referrals** and **pavement pounding** are among the next-best direct methods to finding a future pad in the Windy City. Old school and hometown connections can be helpful in choosing a neighborhood and a home. As soon as you know you're moving to Chicago, you may want to contact friends or family who have moved here, or who know someone here, and ask them to keep their eyes and ears open. Also, check with your **college alumni office** for help with finding housing here. If you know of a building you'd like to live in, call the rental office, management company, or condo association and simply ask about upcoming vacancies. Other tactics include looking for posted rental notices on coffee shop, grocery store, and laundromat bulletin boards, and on vacant apartment windows in the neighborhoods that attract you. If you are a university student, contact your **student services office** for tips about where to look and which areas of town to avoid. For example, Loyola University Chicago has useful housing information on its website (www.luc.edu/judicial/pdfs/off_campus_living.pdf), as does Chicago Kent College of Law (www.kentlaw.edu/adm/housing)—and you don't need to be a student to read their web pages.

If you are enrolled at the University of Chicago as a graduate student, you can take advantage of their student housing program. You can view vacancies at http://reo.uchicago.edu. The U of C student government also lists Hyde Park rental information at http://apartments.uchicago.edu/realtors, and you can find even more (Hyde Park mostly) housing possibilities at the U of C "marketplace" website: http://marketplace.uchicago.edu. Northwestern University has a similar program for graduate students and a program for students who will be living on campus with spouses or families: contact the Northwestern University Student Housing Office at 847-491-8430, or go online to www.northwestern.edu/offcampus for more information.

Is your job bringing you to the Chicago area? If so, be sure to ask about any **relocation assistance** your employer might provide. Benefits vary but many organizations provide temporary housing and assistance finding permanent housing.

If perusing classifieds and pavement pounding is too much work for you, or if your time is limited, you may do better to go to a **Rental Agent** (see below).

## CLASSIFIED ADVERTISEMENTS

Reading the newspaper classifieds, either online or in print, is not only the most common way to begin searching for an apartment but will also give you a good sense of the market. Most rental ads are placed in the Sunday newspapers, which are available on Saturday at convenience stores, some of the larger supermarkets, and newsstands. If you weren't able to buy a copy of the Sunday paper, you can always go to the local library. Also, many newspaper classifieds are online; see listings below for sites:

- *Chicago Reader*: This free weekly paper has a good rentals and real estate section. The online version's housing section is updated every Tuesday by about 7 p.m., http://www.chicagoreader.com/.
- *Chicago SunTimes*: Available at newsstands, drugstores, and convenience stores throughout Chicago, the *Sun-Times* contains rental and real estate classifieds. The online section is a bit more cumbersome to navigate than the *Tribune's*, but there are tons of listings—go to http://www.suntimes.com/marketplace.
- *Chicago Tribune*: The Sunday edition has the most comprehensive rental and real estate listings for Chicago and surrounding communities. Rentals are divided into apartments and houses in the rental section, and then further subdivided by location. Houses for sale are listed in the "Home/Real Estate" section, also organized by location. Online, homes for sale appear in the www.chicagotribune.com/classified/realestate section; apartment listings appear in the www.chicagotribune.com/classified/realestate/renting section. You can also use the *Tribune's* links to find a roommate, obtain a free

credit report, learn more about renter's insurance, read their neighborhood profiles, and many other moving-related topics.
- To find housing in Chicago's **surrounding communities**, check out the classified ads in these major newspapers:
  - **Naperville Sun**, **Beacon News**, and **Courier News** can all be accessed online at www.suburbanchicagonews.com
  - **Daily Herald**, homes.dailyherald.com; a good resource for the five-county area.
  - **Southtown Star**, http://southtownstar.suntimes.com/marketplace/index.html; good for the south and southwestern suburbs

## RENTAL AGENTS/APARTMENT SEARCH FIRMS/ONLINE RESOURCES

One way to find an apartment, particularly if your time is limited, is to use an apartment search firm. When speaking to an apartment search firm agent, be specific about your needs and budget. Also, find out if there is a fee. Some services charge to view their listings, others get their revenue from the property owners. Here are a few to get you started. The local ones tend to favor the North side, where most of them are located. For more, check the Yellow Pages or go online and look for "Apartments & Home Rentals," or "Apartment Agency Referral Services." Note: rental agents typically favor units in larger buildings and this is especially true with the national services. You'll probably have to find that charming abode in a two-flat on your own.

### LOCAL APARTMENT SEARCH FIRMS
- **The Apartment Connection,** www.theaptconnection.com, 1000 W Diversey, 773-525-3888 or 877 525-3888 (Chicago only)
- **Apartments and Homeseekers,** 5503 N Broadway, 773-784-9100, www.aptandhomeseekers.com
- **Chicago Apartments and Condos,** 867 W Buckingham Place, 773-857-7368, www.homes-condos.com
- **Chicago Apartment Finders,** 906 W Belmont Ave, 1-888-346-3377, www.chicagoapartmentfinders.com

### NATIONAL APARTMENT SEARCH FIRMS
- **www.apartments.com;** national online apartment search service and guide based in Chicago
- **www.apartments-in-chicago.com**
- **www.move.com**
- **www.apartmentsearch.com**; a national agency with a Chicago area office
- **www.rent.com**
- **www.rentwave.com**

Locally, **The Habitat Company** (www.habitat.com) is worth investigating. One of the largest residential property managers in Chicago, it manages big buildings like Cityfront Place and Huron Plaza as well as over 3,000 condos in the Chicago area. Call 312-527-5400, or visit their headquarters at 350 West Hubbard Street. Another website worth looking into is http://www.apartmentratings.com/rate/IL-Chicago.html, which offers qualitative and quantitative reviews of (mostly large) apartment buildings and complexes, rated by actual tenants.

Pet owners should ask potential landlords about their pet policies before bothering to view properties. Additionally, the Anti-Cruelty Society (SPCA of Illinois) maintains information on **pet-friendly apartments**. Call 312-644-8338 or visit their website at www.anticruelty.org and click on "Programs and Services," then "Pet Friendly Housing."

## ROOMMATES AND SUBLETS

If you're single and moving here on your own, perhaps you'd like to share an apartment—it's more economical, and renting a room in a house can be a great way to meet people. Sometimes a group will get together and find a home, though more often one or two people will rent a house and then seek roommates through advertising, word-of-mouth referrals, or a roommate-referral service. There is a brisk market for summer sublets, particularly near colleges and universities. With luck and connections, you might even find a house-sitting position.

Others find roommates through the bulletin boards in colleges and universities, in cafés and in bookstores. You can find listings in the major newspapers above, as well as on their websites, under "Housing to Share" and "Rooms for Rent."

If you don't want to do the work yourself, contact **Chicago Apartment Finders** (906 W. Belmont Avenue, 1-888-346-3377), or go online to www.roommates.com.

The following websites appear to offer roommate finding/matching:

- www.chicagoroommate.com
- www.easyroommate.com
- www.metroroommates.com

Keep in mind that with roommates come issues. Cleaning duties, guests, smoking/drinking/drugs, the kitchen, pets, and rent should all be the objects of frank discussion before you agree to join forces in rental real estate. It's also wise to ask for (and check) references—personal and professional—and you should have your references ready too.

**Sublets** are another option. University neighborhoods, such as Evanston, Hyde Park, the area around DePaul University, and the area around Northwestern University's downtown campus are good bets for summer vacancies.

Check with the university or walk around the neighborhood and look for sublet postings on bulletin boards in coffee shops, supermarkets, and bookstores.

On the web, you may find listings at the following sites:

- www.collegesublease.com
- www.sublet.com

## CHECKING IT OUT

It's two months into your lease and, suddenly, the cozy budget bachelor pad you found is feeling a little claustrophobic; to make matters worse, the neighbors argue all night long, the water pressure is dismal, and there's a smell coming from under the floor that you can't (and don't want to) put your finger on. To avoid this scenario, we suggest you view prospective apartments knowing what's crucial for you, and that you inspect to make sure the apartment's beauty is not just skin-deep. A little forethought and advance scrutiny may save you a huge headache later on. Specifically, you may want to look for the following:

- Are the kitchen appliances clean and in working order? Do the stove's burners work? How about the oven? Is there enough counter and shelf space?
- Do the windows open, close, and lock? Do the bedroom windows open onto a noisy or potentially dangerous area? Is there an air-conditioning unit or central air?
- Are there enough closets and is there enough storage space? Any basement storage for renters?
- Are there enough electrical outlets for your needs? Do the outlets work?
- Does the toilet flush properly?
- What about laundry facilities? Are they in the building or nearby? Is the laundry area well lit?
- Do you feel comfortable outside the building? Will you feel safe here at night? Is there secured parking? (Some two-flats offer garage spaces.) Is there an extra fee for parking? How far is public transportation and shopping?
- Are you responsible for paying gas, water, heat, and/or electricity? (This varies from the tenant paying any combination or none at all.)
- If you are looking at a ground-floor apartment, are there bars on the windows? Any signs of water damage or flooding?
- Does the unit smell as if it has just been sprayed for bugs? (This may be a sign that the building has a problem.)
- Is there a smoke detector in the apartment?
- How is the water pressure? Turn on every faucet, as well as the shower, to check. Water pressure throughout Chicago is low; if the building is old, you might only get a trickle. Can you imagine washing your hair? If you love baths or long showers, consider asking how much hot water is available.

Ed Sacks' *Savvy Renter's Kit* contains a thorough renter's checklist for those interested in augmenting theirs.

If it passes all the items that you can muster, be prepared to stake your claim without delay!

## STAKING A CLAIM

While the market is softer now than it has been in years past, it's still true that the early bird gets the worm. This is particularly true for the most desirable apartments. Take along your checkbook, photo ID, a cell phone, and references (personal and professional) so you can be ready. Generally, a landlord will do a credit check and possibly contact your references. Once the landlord is satisfied that you are good tenant material, you can expect to sign a lease and provide a security deposit. Normally, the security deposit is equal to one or two months' rent—renters with pets often pay an additional deposit.

## LANDLORD/TENANT RIGHTS AND RESPONSIBILITIES

A lease is a legally binding contract that outlines the landlord's responsibilities as well as your obligations as a tenant. It goes without saying that you should read your lease carefully before signing it.

The lease should state your name and address as well as the name and address of the landlord. It should state the first and last dates of your contracted occupancy, the monthly rent figure, and when and where it is to be paid. Look for language that may be added to the contract concerning pets or guests or other matters. Remember that you don't have to sign the lease immediately. You have the right to examine it and return it at a mutually agreed-upon time. Illinois law doesn't require that you have a written lease, but it is in your best interest to have one. Without a written lease, the landlord can evict you without cause or raise your rent at any time.

Quite often, you will be moving into your new apartment on the heels of the previous tenant, leaving no time for a proper inspection of the unit accompanied by your landlord. If you notice problems such as beat-up cabinets, chipped tiles, or a damaged floor, make note of them and have the landlord write these conditions into your lease so you are not held liable when moving out. It's a good idea to have your landlord visit and verify the damage as soon as possible or you can provide photographs to be attached to the lease. (Be sure to provide the landlord with copies of the photos as soon as possible.)

Landlords typically ask for one to two months' rent as security deposit to protect them from damages after a tenant moves out. If you leave your apartment in good condition, you are entitled to a refund of your security deposit within 45 days. If your landlord dawdles in returning your security deposit you can file a claim in pro se court (where you don't need a lawyer to represent you) for up to double the amount of your deposit. If you live in a building with more than six units, Illinois requires the landlord to pay interest on your security deposit.

Chicago's **Residential Landlord and Tenant Ordinance**, which was enacted in 1986 and amended in 1991, applies to tenants who live in all-rental units with written or oral leases, and to tenants of single-family residences and condominiums. It does not apply to tenants living in owner-occupied buildings containing six units or fewer. The ordinance spells out the contractual obligations between landlord and tenant. You can pick up a copy of the ordinance at the **Chicago Department of Housing**, 121 North LaSalle Street, 10th floor, or view it online via http://www.cityofchicago.org/city/en/depts/dcd/supp_info/rents_right.html. For more information about your rights, contact the **Chicago Rents Right Hotline** at 312-742-7368.

Among their obligations, landlords must supply adequate heat from September 15 to June 1 (68° during the day and 63° at night), hot water, plumbing, security, extermination of pests, and general maintenance. Your landlord may keep a key to your apartment but can enter only after giving you proper notice, if there is a specific need for the entry, or in the event of an emergency. If your landlord is not meeting these contractual requirements, your first recourse is to call and discuss the problem with him or her. If your request about heat or hot water is not met within a reasonable amount of time, you can call the city's **Non-Emergency Hotline** at 311 or 312-744-5000. If that doesn't resolve the problem, you have the option of reducing your rent as outlined under the Tenant Ordinance (see above). If a repair is at issue, you can have the repair made yourself, and deduct those costs from future rental payments. Before you bring in a handyman to work on your apartment, you may want to consult a lawyer or a tenant's rights organization. While your complaint may be valid and your understanding of the Tenant Ordinance clear, having repairs done on your own can be an expensive decision. If licensed repairmen do not make the repairs, and your repairman inadvertently causes structural damage in an attempt to make your repairs...well you can see how sticky this situation can get. In addition, the Illinois Tenant's Union warns tenants that while there is a legal way to reduce your rent for failure to make repairs, if you don't follow proper procedure, your landlord can start eviction proceedings against you for failure to pay the rent.

Organizations that may be helpful in disputes with a landlord or provide more detailed information about your rights as a tenant include:

- **Chicago Department of Housing**, 121 North LaSalle Street, 10th floor, www.cityofchicago.org/housing
- **Chicago Urban League**, 4510 S Michigan Ave, 773-285-3000
- **Housing Resource Center**, 4429 N Clifton, 773-769-1555 (low income and senior housing)

- **Illinois Tenants Union**, 4616 N Drake Ave, 773-478-1133, www.tenant.org
- **Lawyers Committee for Better Housing**, 100 W Monroe St, Ste 1800, 312-347-7600
- **Legal Assistance Foundation of Chicago**, 312-341-1070
- **Metropolitan Tenants Organization**, 773-292-4988, www.tenants-rights.org
- **Landlord and Tenant Fact Sheet** from the Office of the Attorney General, www.ag.state.il.us
- **Rogers Park Community Action Network** (RPCAN), 1545 W Morse, 773-973-7888

If your lease is set to expire and you plan on moving out, you should inform your landlord of your plans. In the event that you must **break your lease**, you are required to give your landlord one month's written notice of your intent to vacate. Close to moving day, take pictures of your apartment to verify its condition and ask your landlord to meet you to examine the apartment together. The ideal scenario is to have your landlord sign a statement indicating that you have left the apartment in good condition, that you returned the keys directly to her and on time, and that you notified her of your plans to move in a timely fashion. Short of that, mail her the keys prior to the last day of your lease, keeping a copy of the attached letter which states you are leaving the apartment at the appointed time, and in good condition. If you break your lease, your landlord can charge a subletting fee to cover the cost of finding a new tenant for the apartment. If a new tenant cannot be found who will rent the apartment at the same rate you were charged, you will be liable for the extra amount for the remainder of the lease. It might be a good idea to find a new tenant on your own to save on these expenses—although the new tenant will need to be approved by the landlord. If your landlord does find a new tenant to take your place, it is illegal for her to charge you for the remainder of your lease.

A landlord may not refuse to rent or lease an apartment or house to potential tenants or have different rental terms on the basis of race, skin color, religion, national origin, ancestry, sex and marital status, or disability. Under the Federal Fair Housing Act, it is illegal to discriminate against families with children when leasing a rental unit. Complaints about discrimination may be filed with the **Illinois Department of Human Rights**, 312-814-6200.

To complain of discrimination in the suburbs, call, the **HUD Fair Housing Complaint Hotline** at 800-669-9777 or **South Suburban Housing Center**, 708-957-4674. In Chicago, contact the **Leadership Council for Metropolitan Open Communities**, http://www.luc.edu/curl/lcmoc/

## RENT CONTROL

Neither the City of Chicago nor the State of Illinois imposes rent control. That means your landlord can charge whatever the market will bear. If you are renting on a month-to-month basis, your landlord can legally raise your rent by any amount, as long as you are given 30 days' notice. If you have a fixed-term lease, your rent can only be raised when the lease expires.

## RENTER'S/HOMEOWNER'S INSURANCE

You've moved into your new apartment, and the last boxes have been cleared away. Look around and ask yourself, "How much would it cost to start over if everything I see was destroyed by fire?" Probably more than you think. Imagine having to replace your clothing, furniture, computer, and other accumulations of a lifetime. The bill might be enormous.

With renter's insurance, you typically are protected against fire, hail, lightning, explosion, aircraft, smoke, vandalism, theft, building collapse, frozen plumbing, defective appliances, and sudden electrical damage. Renter's insurance also may cover personal liability as well as damage done (by you) to the property of others. Be sure to shop around as insurance rates vary considerably and, when deciding on a policy, consider replacement cost coverage rather than a cash value policy. It's worth the (usually) modest extra premium.

Before looking in the phone book or contacting your own insurance company, you might want to call the **Illinois Department of Insurance** at 312-814-2427, insurance.illinois.gov/. They keep track of all major insurance companies' "complaint ratios" (number of complaints filed per year to dollars paid out each year). Tell them that you're interested in the ratios for renter's insurance, though ratios for other types of insurance are also available. If the company that insures your car has a clean record, you might want to consult with them about renter's insurance. Many companies offer a discount if you purchase more than one type of coverage with them.

You can purchase renter's insurance through almost any insurance agency or company. Try the Yellow Pages for an agency near you. Websites worth investigating as you search for renter's insurance are www.insure.com/, which offers quotes from over 300 insurance companies and an extensive Q&A section about insurance in general. www.insweb.com also offers online insurance hunting. Insurance Finder at www.insurancefinder.com can help you find insurance companies in the Chicago area.

## HOUSE, CONDO AND CO-OP HUNTING/BUYING

Ah, yes, the American dream of a white picket fence, grassy front lawn, and a wide front porch on which to while away the day. As you would expect, Chicago didn't escape the residential real estate craze that struck the country in the last decade. With a seemingly insatiable demand for owner-occupied housing, housing starts and sales of existing properties here skyrocketed, only to come back to earth with the housing crash in 2008–2011.

According to *Chicago Magazine*, top neighborhoods for real estate appreciation in the 1990s included the usual suspects: Lincoln Park, DePaul, Lakeview, Wicker Park, Bucktown, and Wrigleyville. The condo conversion tide has swept across ever more of the North Side and West Loop to include Ravenswood, Lincoln Square, North Central, and Andersonville. More recently, near south neighborhoods such as the South Loop, Bridgeport, and Pilsen have seen substantial gentrification. Many of the city neighborhoods profiled in this book led the charge, with annual 8 to 12% increases in appreciation, pre-housing crash. But, with lower prices and relatively low interest rates, lenders are still eager to finance to those with steady income and respectable credit. You don't need a huge income or a large sum of cash to join the American dream club.

That said, buying a house or condo is no small undertaking. With time and effort, though, you will be rewarded. To get a sense of the market, read the "Real Estate" section of Sunday's *Chicago Tribune*. Most weeks, the *Tribune* features a chart showing the number of homes sold by ZIP code, the median price of home sales in the past year, and the current mortgage rates at area lenders, as well as a weekly profile of a Chicago neighborhood.

When figuring how much money you'll need, be aware that in addition to the purchase price there is title insurance, the inspection, land survey, recording tax, mortgage origination, and usually some real estate transfer tax ("stamp tax"); in Chicago the buyer is responsible for this levy and it's set at $3.75 for every $500 of the home's purchase price. So, for a $300,000 townhouse, you'll owe the city an additional $2,250. Then there's the property tax payment and homeowner's insurance premiums, which you'll be required to place in an escrow account. In all, expect to pay 5 to 8% more than the purchase price. Assuming you are not paying cash but seeking a mortgage, you can usually borrow up to three or four times your annual income. Be prepared for a thorough examination of your credit history, finances, and employment status. The required down payment varies with the loan program for which you are eligible. Lenders are required to give you a good-faith estimate of closing costs.

**Fannie Mae** (www.fanniemae.com, 202-752-7111) and the **US Department of Housing and Urban Development** (www.hud.gov) are terrific resources for information on home buying and government assistance.

Most people wanting to buy a house (or condo or co-op) enlist the services of a real estate broker—a buyer's agent who knows the market and the neighborhood. You might also want a real estate lawyer to make sure the sales contract is in order, to guide you through the latest available tax credits, and perhaps help you with any special hurdles involved in buying a home that is, or could be, declared historic. And you might benefit from the services of a mortgage broker—a financial specialist who is supposed to help you get the best possible mortgage (see the end of the chapter for mortgage resources). Lenders suggest that you "pre-qualify" for a loan so that when you do find a place you like, you can make a swift, credible offer. Before talking to a lender, contact one or more of the three major credit bureaus listed below to make sure your credit history is accurate and up to date. You will need to provide your name, address, previous address, and social security number with your request. Contact each company for specific instructions, or visit www.icreditreport.com, for online access to all three. You can obtain a free report if you've been denied credit within the last 30 days; otherwise, you may be charged up to $8. By law you are entitled to one free "credit file disclosure" (credit report) each year from all three major credit bureaus (see below). To obtain your free yearly disclosure, go to www.annualcreditreport.com. More information about your credit report rights can be found through the **Federal Trade Commission,** online at www.ftc.gov or at 1-877-FTC-HELP.

The major **credit bureaus** are:

- **Experian** (formerly TRW), P.O. Box 2104, Allen, TX 75002-2104, 888-397-3742
- **TransUnion**, P.O. Box 390, Springfield, PA 19064-0390, 800-916-8800
- **Equifax**, P.O. Box 105873, Atlanta, GA 30348, 800-685-1111

Before a home sale can be completed, a termite inspection is mandatory, and most prospective homeowners will hire a building engineer to make a thorough inspection of the structure, heating and cooling systems, plumbing, roof, and major appliances, if any. Should an inspector's report find that major repairs will be likely within a few years, you may be able to negotiate a reduction in the purchase price—or you might decide to keep looking.

If you're **purchasing a condo**, you are buying one unit in a multi-unit building. Each one is the owner's to live in, rent, or sell. Annual or monthly condo fees, in excess of the purchase price, cover the expenses of a condo association, which takes care of the building and grounds, laundry room, parking lots or garages, swimming pool, and any other shared amenities. Condo fees can be steep, and when looking at prospective units, it's not enough to have the annual fee quoted. Check past records to find out how often and by how much the fees have been raised, and if there have been any special assessments. You will also want a lawyer, or a real estate agent specializing in condos, to examine the condominium's prospectus and financial statement, so you don't buy into a financially unstable property.

If you're in the market for a condominium, and you think you might want to rent out your unit in the future, keep in mind that your condominium association might have restrictions in place on renting out units. The association even has the power to limit renting out a unit *without* a specific ban on it in the association bylaws. As the *Sun-Times* reported, "renters have become such a problem that the associations are starting to declare them persona non grata." More broadly, if you're the kind of person who likes to be left alone or has trouble getting along in a group with strict rules, a condominium or co-op could be a nightmare. If such possible limitations are not an issue, then take the plunge.

Questions to ask about a **co-op or condo**:

- What percentage of the units are owner-occupied?
- How much are the association dues and projected assessments?
- What are the rules and regulations?
- Who manages the property?
- Have there been any lawsuits involving the association in the past five years?

These and many other issues are covered in the complimentary "Condominium/Townhome Guide," published by Re/Max Real Estate, 800-525-7452. The guide provides information about different styles of housing, associations, and comprehensive checklists to use to evaluate developments.

Upon signing a standard purchase agreement, the seller is required to disclose only certain problems and environmental hazards like lead paint. It is wise to protect yourself by having a professional roof/mechanical systems inspection before purchase. Professional residential inspectors can be found in the Yellow Pages under "Home and Building Inspection," or ask your realtor for a recommendation. There is a free pamphlet available from the **American Society of Home Inspectors** (847-759-2820 or www.ashi.com); ask for document #1029.

Chicago is one of the few places in the country where you will find housing cooperatives for sale. **Co-ops,** as they are commonly known, are most popular in New York City, and in Chicago are found mainly in the tonier downtown and lakefront neighborhoods. They can sell from $50,000 to over $2 million for a 1920s-era co-op building facing Oak Street Beach near Michigan Avenue. Affordable cooperative units can be found in communities like Hyde Park and South Shore on the south side or on the north side in Lakeview, Uptown, Edgewater, and Rogers Park.

The cooperative structure is fairly simple, with co-ops consisting of membership shares in a corporation that owns a residential building. While condominiums offer outright ownership of a particular unit plus a share of the common area, buying into a housing cooperative entitles you to a share of the value of the building, not a particular unit. However, just as in a condominium development, the cooperative's members elect a board of directors, and they typically have financial responsibility for the cooperative corporation. Housing cooperatives function best through a form of participatory democracy that encourages owners to get involved by serving on the board and committees; this reduces the costs of operating the cooperative. Those who wish to sell their cooperative share earn interest and equity on their initial investment and can also pass along improvements that they have made to their cooperative unit to the future buyer. You can also deduct your pro-rata share of your mortgage interest on your taxes, just like a single-family home or condominium. Moreover, these are no longer the days when prospective buyers had to self-finance their cooperative unit, with banks in Chicago (such as the National Cooperative Bank at 202-336-7700) willing to offer financing.

For more information, contact the **National Association of Housing Cooperatives**, www.coophousing.org.

## BUYING STRATEGIES

If you're ready to jump on the owner bandwagon, you might want to consider the following strategies. As with apartment hunting, perhaps the simplest way to look for a place to buy is to walk or drive around the neighborhood you're interested in and look for "For Sale" signs. At the same time, start scanning the classifieds. Both the *Chicago Tribune* and the *Sun-Times* have extensive real estate sections. The *Tribune* also offers an online database of residential properties for sale at its website, as well as a weekly "Your Place" section in Friday's paper. Then there's the tried-and-true method: enlist the services of a real estate agent or broker. Ask around for a recommendation or look in the Yellow Pages under "Real Estate." If you are computer-savvy and want to narrow down the search on your own, most real estate companies now have websites, often great ones. Here you can check out the available homes through photos, floor plans, and community information, and organize your search along whatever line suits you.

## REAL ESTATE BROKERS

There is no substitute for the advice of an experienced, local real estate broker. Brokers are highly trained, tested, licensed professionals who keep a close eye on the neighborhoods they serve. A good broker knows the average SAT scores at the local high school, the crime rate in the local police precinct, how many minutes it takes to drive to the highway, and—most important—the trends in property values right down to a given block. A good broker will interview you in detail about your needs and desires as they relate to buying a place to live. Are you planning to have more children? Do you like to garden? Do you hate to drive to work? The more of such information you share with your broker, the better he or she can match you with a home.

So how do you find a broker who knows the neighborhood where you want to live? Most real estate agencies claim to serve the entire Chicago area, and indeed, most agencies can offer some assistance with any home on the market. However, an agency is best qualified to show you homes in the neighborhood where it is located—where their geographic expertise is greatest. In the absence of a personal recommendation, try the Yellow Pages or go online to www.realtor.com for real estate brokers serving the neighborhoods or cities you select.

## FOR SALE BY OWNER

If you are familiar with your targeted neighborhood, are an experienced home-owner, and/or would like to eliminate the not-insignificant cost of the middleman (the real estate broker), you can look for For Sale By Owner ("fsbo") properties. Even if you have a real estate broker, you may consider such properties, especially since your realtor may not. Websites specializing in home listings by owners include:

- www.buyowner.com
- www.HomesByOwner.com
- www.owners.com

## ADDITIONAL ONLINE RESOURCES

Another good resource if you are looking in the northernmost Illinois counties is the National Association of Realtors' **Multiple Listing Service of Northern Illinois**. They claim to list over half of the houses for sale in the northern counties. Try them at www.realtor.com/chicago.

The following websites offer a variety of services including providing listings of homes nationwide, and providing information about moving, mortgages, real estate agents, neighborhoods, home improvement, and more:

- **Bankrate.com**, www.bankrate.com; as its name suggests, everything about mortgages and interest rates.
- **Freddie Mac**, www.freddiemac.com, provides information on low-cost loans, a home inspection kit, and tips to help avoid unfair lending practices.
- **www.zillow.com** gives pricing information about individual homes, including former sales prices, estimated current value, and comparable homes in the neighborhood.
- **The Mortgage Professor**, www.mtgprofessor.com, demystifies and clarifies the confusing and often-expensive world of mortgage brokers, helpfully written by an emeritus Wharton professor who answers questions; useful calculators.
- **www.quickenmortgage.com**; from the people who brought you Quicken.
- **www.scorecard.org**; learn about pollution and toxic waste in a prospective neighborhood *before* you buy there; includes useful and eye-opening ZIP code searchable database.
- **Family Watchdog**, www.familywatchdog.us; search by city, street, or ZIP code to see a map of sex offenders' homes or workplaces in your area.

- **National Center for Education Statistics**, http://nces.ed.gov/; a great resource for school information and statistics.
- **School Matters,** www.schoolmatters.com; a Standard and Poor's service rife with helpful information about school systems, school spending, school demographics, and school performance anywhere in the US.

## PRINTED RESOURCES—BUYING A HOME

Five books that we found useful:

- *100 Questions Every First Time Homebuyer Should Ask: With Answers from Top Brokers From Around the Country*, 2nd edition (Times Books) by Ilyce R.Glink
- *The 106 Common Mistakes Homebuyers Make (And How to Avoid Them)*, 3rd edition (Wiley) by Gary W. Eldred
- *The Co-Op Bible: Everything You Need to Know About Co-Ops and Condos: Getting In, Staying In, Surviving, Thriving* (Griffin) by Sylvia Shapiro
- *Opening the Door to a Home of Your Own*, a free pamphlet by the Fannie Mae Foundation, 800-834-3377
- *Your New House: the Alert Consumer's Guide to Buying and Building a Quality New Home* (Windsor Peak) by Alan and Denise Fields

## MOVING AND STORAGE

BEFORE YOU CAN START YOUR NEW LIFE IN CHICAGO, YOU AND YOUR worldly possessions have to get here. How difficult that will be depends on how much stuff you've accumulated, how much money you're willing or able to spend on the move, and from where you are coming. A word of advice to packrats: the less stuff you move, the easier and cheaper your move will be!

Most leases in Chicago start either May 1 or October 1, which makes the last weekends in April and September a time of chaos in certain neighborhoods. Those **moving within the city** should be aware that during these busy times Chicago truck-rental companies rent trucks in three four-hour shifts—from 8 a.m. to noon; noon to 4 p.m., and 4 p.m. to 8 p.m. If you're moving locally, be sure to reserve a truck early (at least four weeks in advance) to ensure availability.

### TRUCK RENTALS

The first question you need to answer: Am I going to move myself or will I have someone else do it for me? If you're used to doing everything yourself, you can rent a vehicle, load it up, and head for the open road. Look in the Yellow Pages under "Truck Rental" and call around and compare; also ask about any specials. Below we list four national truck rental firms and their toll-free numbers and websites. For the best information, you should call a local office. Note: most truck rental companies now offer "one-way" rentals (don't forget to ask whether they have a drop-off/return location in or near your destination) as well as packing accessories and storage facilities. Of course, these extras are not free and if you're cost conscious you may want to scavenge boxes in advance of your move and make sure you have a place to store your belongings upon arrival (see **Storage** below). Also, if you're planning on moving during the peak moving months (May through September), call at least one month in advance of when you think you'll need the vehicle.

Once you're on the road, keep in mind that your rental truck may be a tempting target for thieves. If you must park it overnight or for an extended period (more than a couple of hours), try to find a safe place—preferably somewhere well-lit and easily observable by you—and do your best not to leave anything of particular value in the cab.

- **Budget**, 800-527-0700, www.budget.com
- **Penske**, 888-996-5415, www.penske.com
- **Ryder**, 800-297-9337, www.ryder.com (now a Budget company, still operating under the Ryder name)
- **U-Haul**, 800-468-4285, www.uhaul.com

## COMMERCIAL FREIGHT CARRIERS AND CONTAINER-BASED MOVERS

Not sure if you want to drive the truck yourself? Commercial freight carriers, such as **ABF U-Pack Moving** (800-240-7422, www.upack.com), offer an in-between service: they deliver a 28-foot trailer to your home, you pack and load as much of it as you need, and they drive the vehicle to your destination (often with some other shipper's freight filling up the empty space). Unlike with most self-move truck rental companies, you can't rent dollies, ramps, etc., from U-Pack. Keep in mind, also, if you have to share truck space with another customer, you may arrive far in advance of your boxes—or bed. Try to estimate your needs beforehand and ask for a date when you can expect your boxes to arrive. You can get an on-line estimate from some shippers so you can compare rates. If you aren't moving an entire house and can't estimate how much truck space you will need, keep in mind this general guideline: two to three furnished rooms equals a 15-foot truck. Four to five rooms, a 20-foot truck.

ABF, **PODS** (877-770-PODS, www.pods.com), **Door-to-Door Storage and Moving** (888-366-7222, www.doortodoor.com), and several other companies offer container-based moves. In this type of move, the carrier delivers plywood, metal, or fiberglass cubes or other containers to your home. You can generally take a few days to load the containers; when you're done loading, the company picks up the containers, transfers them to flatbed trucks, moves them to your destination city, and delivers them to your new home. You generally only pay to transport the containers you actually use, and, unlike a truck, the containers can be placed in storage at either end of the journey. However, a set of containers has a smaller storage capacity than a large truck, so this option may not work for people with large houses full of furniture. In addition, some large pieces of furniture—grandfather clocks, for example—may not fit inside the containers; if you have to move items that are very long or tall, ask the company for its containers' *interior* dimensions before you commit.

# MOVERS

## INTERSTATE

First, the good news: moving can be both affordable and problem-free. The bad news: if you're hiring a mover, the chances of either are far slimmer.

Probably the best way to find a mover is through a **personal recommendation**. Absent a friend or relative who can point you to a trusted moving company, you can turn to what surveys show is the most popular method of finding a mover: the **Yellow Pages**. Then there's the **internet**; just type in "movers" on a search engine and you'll be directed to hundreds of more or less helpful moving-related sites.

In the past, ***Consumer Reports*** (www.consumerreports.org) has published useful information on moving. You might ask a local realtor, who may be able to steer you towards a good mover, or at least tell you which ones to avoid. Members of the **AAA** can call their local office and receive discounted rates and service through their Consumer Relocation Service.

*But beware!* Since 1995, when the Interstate Commerce Commission was eliminated by the federal government, the interstate moving business has degenerated into a wild and virtually unregulated industry with thousands of unhappy, ripped-off customers annually. (There are so many reports of unscrupulous carriers that we no longer list movers in this book; same for the US Postal Service in its *Movers Guide*.) Since states do not have the authority to regulate interstate movers, and since the federal government won't, you are pretty much on your own when it comes to finding an honest, hassle-free interstate mover. That's why we can't emphasize enough the importance of carefully researching and choosing who will move you.

To aid you in your search for an honest and hassle-free **interstate** mover, we offer a few general recommendations.

First, get the names of a half-dozen movers and check to make sure they are licensed by the US Department of Transportation's Federal Motor Carrier Safety Administration (FMCSA). Call 800-832-5660 or go online to www.fmcsa.dot.gov. If the companies you're considering are federally licensed, your next step should be to check with the Better Business Bureau (www.bbb.org) in the state where the moving company is licensed, as well as with that state's Attorney General and Consumer Protection office. Assuming there is no negative information, you can move on to the next step: asking for references. Particularly important are references from customers who did moves similar to yours. If a moving company is unable or unwilling to provide references or tells you that they can't give out names because their customers are all in the federal Witness Protection Program, eliminate them from your list. Unscrupulous movers have even been known to give phony references who will falsely sing the mover's praises—so talk to more than one reference and ask questions. If something feels fishy, it probably is. One way to learn more about a prospective mover: ask them if they have a local office (they should) and then walk in and check it out.

For an informative—but terror-inducing—read, check out the **MovingScam** website (www.movingscam.com). MovingScam.com provides sound, unbiased consumer education and is committed to bettering consumer protections in the moving industry. The site features a host of useful articles and recent moving news, and maintains a "Blacklist." Its message boards are tended by dedicated volunteers who respond promptly and knowledgeably to moving-related queries, free of charge. The FMCSA operates a similar website (www.protectyourmove.gov). This website provides one-click checking to make sure that an interstate mover is properly registered and insured. (You can also get this information by phone, at 888-368-7238 or 202-358-7028.) It also includes news of recent criminal investigations and convictions, and offers links to local Better Business Bureaus, consumer protection agencies, state attorneys general, and state moving associations.

Once you have at least three movers you feel reasonably comfortable with, it's time to ask for price quotes (always free). Best is a binding "not-to-exceed" quote—of course, in writing. This will require an on-site visual inspection of what you are shipping. If you have *any* doubts about a prospective mover, drop them from your list before you invite a stranger into your home to catalog your belongings.

**Angie's List** (www.angieslist.com) is another resource for information about which moving companies are reliable and responsible. The membership-based service charges a $14.40 start-up/one month fee (or $39 per year) for access to member ratings of local contractors—including housekeeping services, home builders, and all types of tradesmen and craftsmen as well as movers. Compared to the price of replacing or repairing damaged belongings, joining Angie's List might seem like a bargain.

## ADDITIONAL RECOMMENDATIONS

- If someone recommends a mover to you, get names (the salesperson or estimator, the drivers, the loaders). To paraphrase the NRA, moving companies don't move people, people do. Likewise, if someone tells you they had a bad moving experience, note the name of the company and try to avoid it.
- Remember that price, while important, isn't everything, especially when you're entrusting all of your worldly possessions to strangers.
- Ask about the other end—subcontracting increases the chances that something could go wrong.
- In general, ask questions, and if you're concerned about something, ask for an explanation in writing. If you change your mind about a mover after you've signed on the dotted line, write them a letter explaining that you've changed your mind and that you won't be using their services. Better safe than sorry.

- Ask about insurance; the "basic" 60-cents-per-pound industry standard coverage is not enough. If you have homeowner's or renter's insurance, check to see if it will cover your belongings during transit. If not, ask your insurer if you can add that coverage for your move. Otherwise, consider purchasing "full replacement" or "full value" coverage from the carrier for the estimated value of your shipment. Though it's the most expensive type of coverage offered, it's probably worth it—trucks get into accidents, they catch fire, they get stolen…If such insurance seems pricey to you, ask about a $250 or $500 deductible. This can reduce your cost substantially while still giving you much better protection in case of a catastrophic loss.
- Before a move takes place, ask your mover to give you a copy of "Your Rights and Responsibilities When You Move," which provides detailed information about your rights and what you can expect from your moving company. Ask for it as soon as you decide on a mover.
- Whatever you do, *do not* mislead a salesperson/estimator about how much and what you are moving. And make sure you tell a prospective mover about how far they'll have to transport your stuff to and from the truck as well as any stairs, driveways, obstacles or difficult vegetation, long paths or sidewalks, etc. The clearer you are with your mover, the better he or she will be able to serve you.
- Think about packing. If you plan to pack yourself, you can save some money, but if something is damaged because of your packing, you may not be able to file a claim for it. On the other hand, if you hire the mover to do the packing, they may not treat your belongings as well as you will. They will certainly do it faster. Depending on the size of your move and whether or not you are packing yourself, you may need a lot of boxes, tape, and packing material. Mover boxes, while not cheap, are usually sturdy and the right size. Sometimes a mover will give a customer free used boxes—it doesn't hurt to ask. Also, *don't* wait to pack until the last minute. If you're doing the packing, give yourself at least a week to do the job, two or more is better.
- You should personally transport all irreplaceable items such as jewelry, photographs or key work documents. Do not put them in the moving van! For less precious items that you do not want to put in the moving truck, consider sending them via the US Postal Service or by UPS.
- Ask your mover what is not permitted in the truck: usually anything flammable or combustible, as well as certain types of valuables.
- Although movers will put numbered labels on your possessions, you should make a numbered list of every box and item that is going in the truck. Detail box contents and photograph anything of particular value. Once the truck arrives on the other end, you can check off every piece and know for sure what did (or did not) make it. In case of claims, this list can be invaluable. Even after the move, keep the list; it can be surprisingly useful, especially if you have to file a claim for damages.

- Movers are required to issue you a "bill of lading"; do not hire a mover who does not use them.
- Consider keeping a log of every expense you incur for your move, i.e., phone calls, trips to Chicago, etc. In many instances, the IRS allows you to claim these types of expenses on your income taxes. (See **Taxes** below.)
- Be aware that during the busy season (May through September), demand can exceed supply and moving may be more difficult and more expensive than during the rest of the year. If you must relocate during the peak moving months, call and book service at least a month in advance of your move. If you can reserve service way in advance, say four to six months early, you may be able to lock in a lower winter rate for your summer move.
- Listen to what the movers say; they are professionals and can give you expert advice about packing and preparing. Also, be ready for the truck on both ends—don't make them wait. Not only will it irritate your movers, but it may cost you. Understand, too, that things can happen on the road that are beyond a carrier's control (weather, accidents, etc.) and your belongings may not get to you at the time or on the day promised.
- Treat your movers well, especially the ones loading your stuff on and off the truck. Offer to buy them lunch, and tip them if they do a good job.
- Before moving pets, attach a tag to your pet's collar with your new address and phone number in case your furry friend accidentally wanders off in the confusion of moving. Of course, never plan on moving a pet inside a moving van.
- Be prepared to pay the full moving bill upon delivery. Cash or bank/cashier's check may be required. Some carriers will take VISA and MasterCard but it is a good idea to get it in writing that you will be permitted to pay with a credit card since the delivering driver may not be aware of this and may demand cash. Unless you routinely keep thousands of dollars' worth of greenbacks on you, you could have a problem getting your stuff off the truck.

## INTRASTATE AND LOCAL MOVES

All moves within Illinois are regulated by the Illinois Commerce Commission (ICC), and all movers operating within the state of Illinois are required to have an active license issued by the ICC. Contact them at 217-782-4654, www.icc.illinois.gov, for information on a prospective mover.

For moves within Illinois, ones that are less than 35 miles are designated **local moves**, ones greater than 35 miles are designated **intrastate moves**. In Illinois, local moves are charged on an hourly basis; intrastate move prices are regulated by the state and are calculated based on weight of the shipment, distance and additional services, if any.

To find a local or intrastate mover, follow many of the same guidelines (above) as with an interstate move. After you've verified that a prospective mover is currently licensed to operate in Illinois (www.icc.illinois.gov/consumer/

default.aspx#householdgoods), you can call the **Illinois Attorney General Consumer Fraud Bureau** at 800-386-5438 to find out if the company you're considering has a complaint history. Another good idea is to contact the **Illinois Movers' and Warehousemen's Association (IMAWA)**, to see if a mover is a member. The IMAWA is a professional organization whose members must be licensed movers, hold the appropriate insurance minimums, and work with the government agencies that oversee this industry. You can reach the IMAWA for a membership list or other information by calling 217-585-2470 or by visiting their website at www.imawa.com. Another industry group that you can check with: the **American Moving and Storage Association**, 888-849-2672, www.moving.org.

## STORAGE

If your new pad is too small for all of your belongings or if you need a temporary place to store your stuff while you find a new home, self-storage may be the answer. Most units are clean, secure, insured, and inexpensive, and you can rent anything from a locker to your own mini-warehouse. You may need to bring your own padlock, and be prepared to pay first and last month's rent up front. Many will offer special deals to entice you, such as the second month free. Probably the easiest way to find storage is to look in the Yellow Pages under "Storage—Self Service," "Storage—Household & Commercial," or "Movers & Full Service Storage." Online, go to a search engine and type in "Storage, Household." Your mover may also offer storage and, while this may be easier than moving it into storage yourself, it may also be much more expensive.

A recent wrinkle in the self-storage business: "containerized storage." This means the storage company will drop off a (large) storage bin at your house, you fill it up, and they return with a truck and cart it off to their storage facility.

Keep in mind that demand for storage surges in the prime moving months (May through September), so try not to wait till the last minute to rent storage. Also, if you don't care about convenience, your cheapest storage options may be out in the boonies. You just have to figure out how to get your stuff there and back. Things to keep in mind when considering a storage facility:

- When do I have access?
- Do my belongings need heat and/or AC? If so, ask if the facility is "climate controlled."
- What about security and insurance?
- Will I feel safe visiting the facility?
- Are there carts or hand trucks for moving in and out?
- What are the payment options?

Finally, a word of warning: unless you no longer want your stored belongings, pay your storage bill and pay it on time. Storage companies may auction the contents of delinquent customers' lockers.

## STORAGE FACILITIES

Listing here does *not* imply endorsement by First Books. For more options check the Yellow Pages.

- **The Cache**, 1000 W. Grace St, 773-248-5005
- **Chicago Lock Stock & Storage**, 2001 N Elston Ave, 773-227-2448
- **East Bank Storage,** 429 W Ohio St, 312-644-2000
- **Public Storage** has more than 50 storage facilities in the Chicago metropolitan area. Check the Yellow Pages or call 800-688-8057.
- **Strongbox** has two Chicago locations: 1516 N Orleans St, 312-787-2800; 1650 W Irving Park Rd, 773-248-6800.
- **U-Haul Self-Storage** has storage facilities throughout the Chicago area. In Chicago, check 1200 W Fullerton Ave, 773-935-0620 or 4055 N Broadway, 773-871-7155.

# CHILDREN

Studies show that moving, especially frequent moving, can be hard on children. According to an American Medical Association study, children who move often are more likely to suffer from such problems as depression, worthlessness, and aggression. Often their academic performance suffers as well. Aside from not moving more than is necessary, there are a few things you can do to help your children through this stressful time:

- Talk about the move with your kids. Be honest but positive. Listen to their concerns. To the extent possible, involve them in the process.
- Make sure the child has his or her favorite possessions with them on the trip; *don't* pack "blanky" in the moving van.
- Make sure you have some social life planned on the other end. Your child may feel lonely in your new home and such activities can ease the transition.
- Keep in touch with family and loved ones as much as possible. Photos and phone calls are important ways of maintaining links to the important people you have left behind.
- If your children are school age, take the time to introduce them to their new school as soon as possible, preferably before they start the new school year. In this way, they can dispel any unfounded fears and apprehensions they have about the next school. And finally, try to involve yourself in their new school and in their academic life.

For younger children, there are dozens of good books designed to help explain, or at least help ease the transition of, moving. These books include *Max's Moving Adventure: A Coloring Book for Kids on the Move* by Danelle Till, illustrated by Joe Spooner; *Alexander, Who's Not (Do You Hear Me? I Mean It!) Going to Move* by Judith Viorst; *Goodbye/Hello* by Barbara Hazen; *The Leaving Morning* by Angela Johnson; *Little Monster's Moving Day* by Mercer Mayer; *Who Will Be My Friends?* (Easy I Can Read Series) by Syd Hoff; *I'm Not Moving, Mama* by Nancy White Carlstrom, illustrated by Thor Wickstrom; and *The Berenstain Bears' Moving Day* by Jan and Stan Berenstain.

For older children, try *The Moving Book: A Kid's Survival Guide* by Gabriel Davis; *Amber Brown is Not a Crayon* by Paula Danziger; *The Kid in the Red Jacket* by Barbara Park; *Hold Fast to Dreams* by Andrea Davis Pinkney; *Flip Flop Girl* by Katherine Paterson; and *My Fabulous New Life* by Sheila Greenwald.

For general guidance, read *Smart Moves: Your Guide through the Emotional Maze of Relocation* by Nadia Jensen, Audrey McCollum and Stuart Copans (Smith & Krauss).

## TAXES

If your move is work-related, some or all of your moving expenses may be tax-deductible—so you may want to keep those receipts. Though eligibility varies, depending, for example, on whether you have a job or are self-employed, generally the cost of moving yourself, your family and your belongings is tax deductible, even if you don't itemize. The criteria: in order to take the deduction your move must be employment-related, your new job must be more than 50 miles away from your current residence, and you must be here for at least 39 weeks during the first 12 months after your arrival. If you take the deduction and then fail to meet the requirements, you will have to pay the IRS back, unless you were laid off through no fault of your own or transferred again by your employer. It's probably a good idea to consult a tax expert regarding IRS rules related to moving. However, if you're a confident soul, get a copy of IRS Form 3903 (www.irs.gov) and do it yourself!

## ADDITIONAL RELOCATION AND MOVING INFORMATION

- **www.erc.org**; the Employee Relocation Council, a professional organization, offers members specialized reports on the relocation and moving industries.
- **www.firstbooks.com**; relocation resources and information on moving to Atlanta, Boston, Chicago, Los Angeles, Minneapolis–St. Paul, New York City, Portland, San Francisco, Seattle, Texas, and Washington, D.C., as well as London, England, and a handbook for foreigners moving to the U.S.A., plus *the Furniture Placement and Room Planning Guide,* a functional and practical

solution to space planning and furniture placement needs featuring an innovative grid and "static" reusable adhesive sticker format.
- **www.move.com**; realty listings, moving tips, and more.
- ***How to Move Handbook*** by Clyde and Shari Steiner; an excellent resource.
- **www.usps.com**; relocation information from the United States Postal Service.

# MONEY MATTERS

TO EASE YOUR FINANCIAL TRANSITION TO YOUR NEW CITY, HERE IS some information about personal savings and checking accounts, credit cards, and taxes.

## BANK ACCOUNTS & SERVICES

As soon as you find a place to hang your hat, you will want to find a home for your money. For major deposits, shop around for the best interest rates; for routine checking and savings, you'll probably be more interested in ATM fees, fees for visits to the teller, check-guard options, online banking options, and direct-deposit services. Check with your employer to find out if your firm offers direct deposit.

Also consider a **credit union**, which may be your best banking option. Credit unions generally offer affordable banking/financial service packages to their members, and higher interest rates on savings and checking accounts. Look into whether your place of business or professional organization offers a credit union membership. Some credit unions will accept applicants beyond their original membership base; that is, you may not have to be an employee of a specific organization or labor union in order to join. **Credit Union National Association** can help you find a credit union in your area. Visit their website at www.cuna.org.

In the 1990s, regional and national giants acquired dozens of local banks, so it's possible that your old bank has a branch in your new neighborhood. All major banks offer a variety of checking accounts to fit a variety of personal banking habits. Most also offer Internet access with options to check your balance, transfer money from different accounts, and pay bills. If you write a lot of checks and keep a low average balance, you will want to pay attention to per-check fees and service charges that kick in when your balance drops below a certain minimum. If you only use your checking account to pay your monthly bills, you might want an interest-bearing checking account with some fees instead of a non-interest-bearing free checking account. Be sure to ask about ATM fees—at your own bank's automated teller machines and at network ATMs owned by other banks. Also, inquire about the average and maximum time between a deposit and the availability of funds.

All major banks also offer money market accounts and certificates of deposit, with terms and interest rates displayed in the lobby or the window, as well as regular passbook savings accounts.

Many prefer the service of a small community bank, of which there are many in the Chicagoland area. Others prefer a large institution, which will have many branches throughout the city or the nation. Here are some of the largest banks in the Chicago area:

- **Citibank**, 800-627-3999, www.citibank.com
- **Cole Taylor Bank**, www.ctbnk.com
- **First American Bank**, 847-952-3700, www.firstambank.com
- **Harris Bank,** www.harrisbank.com
- **Bank of America**, www.bankofamerica.com

## CHECKING/SAVINGS ACCOUNTS

Call around before opening an account; some banks offer special promotions and perks like fee waivers or rewards programs for new customers. Most banks require a minimum deposit, so take some cash, a money order, or a paycheck with you. When you apply for a new account, two references are often required—usually the name of your current or previous bank, and that of your employer—together with two signed pieces of identification: a driver's license, state ID card, credit card, or student ID with photo are all acceptable. It's also a good idea to bring checks along from your previous checking account. If your checking account was in good standing at your previous institution, the new bank will often begin your new checks at a higher number. Your account can be opened immediately. You will be given some temporary checks, but checks printed with your name and address won't be issued until your signature is verified. Some firms arrange for employees to open accounts at their own banks, which facilitates the process and may be fee-free; check with your benefits officer.

The best advice when choosing a bank is to shop around and compare services and fees. You might be able to do some of that online before you move. If you are relocating to Chicago for your job, your human resource representative might be able to give you some suggestions for banks within your work neighborhood. Some banks allow you 15 checks per month before they begin charging a per-check fee; others allow unlimited checking and charge only a monthly service fee. Area banks lure customers with special offers, such as a special window for business clients, or fee-free checking accounts (read the fine print: some banks may require only a $500 minimum balance, others much more, and many charge fees for other things). "Free" checking is also being offered to customers. With such an account, you can generally expect no monthly fees, no minimum balance, internet access to your account, and unlimited use of your checking account. However, these accounts often do not earn interest. The more traditional interest-bearing accounts will often eliminate service charges as long as a minimum daily balance is maintained or if you link your account to a money market account, certificate of deposit, or savings account.

Whichever bank you finally select, nearly all come with an ATM/Debit card. Be sure to ask if the bank will charge you to use an ATM other than theirs or to use a teller. If their fee structure doesn't make sense with your usual banking habits, look elsewhere.

## ONLINE BANKING

Nowadays, virtually every bank offers online banking. If you prefer to bank from the comfort of your own home, you'll find you can track your account activity, pay your bills automatically, and even apply for some loans, all online. If you plan to do most of your banking online, check on fees for automatic bill-paying and other important services before opening your checking account. Contact information for local banks is listed above in **Bank Accounts & Services**. You might also consider an internet-only bank, such as **www.netbank.com**, which may offer higher interest rates than "brick and mortar" competitors.

## CREDIT CARDS

It is said that the average American owns seven credit cards! If you would like to join the masses, contact the following credit and charge card companies, or just look in your mailbox…an offer is bound to show up soon.

- **American Express**, 800-528-4800, www.americanexpress.com; once famous for issuing charge cards that must be paid off every month, American Express now offers nearly two dozen different cards, including credit cards and airline affinity cards that accumulate frequent-flyer miles. With the exception of a student card, all Amex cards have minimum income requirements, and all but the Optima True Grace Card charge annual fees.
- **Diner's Club**, 800-234-6377, www.dinersclub.com; with annual fees and income requirements, the Diner's Club card is accepted mainly in travel and hospitality circles; cardholders have access to special amenities at most major airports.
- **Discover/Novus**, 800-347-2683, www.discovercard.com; Discover cards and affiliated Novus/Private Issue cards offer an annual rebate based on the

amount you charge, and some plans let you accumulate credit at various hotels or retail chains.
- **VISA**, www.visa.com, **MasterCard**, www.mastercard.com; almost all banks issue VISA and MasterCard credit cards, but so do airlines, long distance companies, magazines, car manufacturers, professional associations, charities, and retailers. Competition is fierce not just for interest rates or low fees, but for fringe benefits—from airline mileage to shopper's discounts—so it pays to shop around, especially if you don't pay off your balance every month. Many will offer low or zero six-month introductory rates, no annual fees, and no transfer balance fees. And like American Express, these credit card companies offer more than one kind of card. Check their websites to find out the particulars. Most purchases made with these cards are automatically insured against loss or damage.
- **Department stores**: most department stores and other major retail chains issue charge cards, sometimes with lines of credit. Usually these accounts are issued automatically and instantly if you already have a VISA or MasterCard account. While the perks may include advance notice of sales, access to special services, and cardholder discounts, be aware that credit cards in this category are usually offered with some of the highest rates around.

For a handy way to compare rates and to learn more about credit cards, visit **bankrate.com**. **Card Track** provides an online directory of credit cards; search or browse by interest rates, fees, special offers, or affinity features such as frequent-flyer miles or charity donations based on the amount you charge. And finally, you can visit the personal finance section of **epinions.com** for customer reviews of specific institutions' credit cards.

## BANKING & CREDIT RESOURCES

To look up current interest rates on deposits, go to www.bankrate.com.

If you're buying a car or boat, renovating your new fixer-upper, or sending the kids to college, you can still shop for loans the old-fashioned way, using the Yellow Pages and the financial section of the newspaper, but the Internet can make the job a lot easier. Online loan calculators let you experiment with different payment plans. There are several loan calculators on **bankrate.com** but you can look at other sites as well:

- **www.myfico.com**
- **Eloan**, www.eloan.com
- **Financial Power Tools**, http://financialpowertools.com
- **The Motley Fool**, www.fool.com (an excellent place to learn about money, investing and banking. They offer online seminars, well-written articles, and an active discussion board.)

- **Women's Financial Network**, www.wfn.com

Obtain copies of your credit report from the three major credit bureaus at **www.annualcreditreport.com** or **www.freecreditreport.com**. Avoid ordering your credit report more than once a year, though—too-frequent requests could adversely affect your credit rating.

## TAXES

### FEDERAL

Federal (and state) **Income Tax** forms are available at many libraries or post offices, but don't wait until April 14—indeed, such places may run out of the more common forms by early March, and may not have any of the more esoteric forms at all. You can also **download tax forms** at www.irs.gov or order them by mail at 800-829-3676.

Federal forms may also be obtained in the lobby of the Federal Building, 230 South Dearborn Street, 17th floor. Call 800-829-1040, TDD 800-829-4059, to obtain literature as well as answers to specific questions. The local Internal Revenue Service office, 230 South Dearborn, 312-292-4912, is open from 8:30 a.m. to 4:30 p.m., and provides assistance and answers to specific questions regarding the mysteries of calculating your federal income tax, but they will not do it for you.

Finally, don't be afraid to call the IRS and ask for help. You may be placed on hold for a long time, but you will get your questions answered by a real person. A variety of recordings regarding general tax questions is available at the **IRS Tele Tax Information Line**, 800-829-4477. Of course, there are plenty of accountants listed in the Yellow Pages. Go to "Tax Return Preparation," for dozens of firms, including the giants: H&R Block (www.hrblock.com) and Jackson Hewitt (www.jacksonhewitt.com).

### STATE OF ILLINOIS

As with federal tax forms, most of the filing materials you'll need are available at your local library or government office: the **State of Illinois Building**, 100 West Randolph Street, in the lobby or at the Federal Building (see above). You can also download a number of tax forms from the state's website, www.iltax.com, or you can file your state taxes electronically. For information about state income taxes, state forms, or filing online, contact the Illinois Department of Revenue toll free at 800-732-8866 or visit their website. The basic form is the IL-1040—the Illinois Individual Income Tax Return. For individuals, the state income tax rate is 3% of your federal taxable income.

## ONLINE FILING AND ASSISTANCE

Filing your taxes online can save you time, especially if you already keep your personal financial records using compatible software such as Turbot, Quicken, or Quickbooks.

If your taxable income is below a certain amount and you are not self-employed, you may be eligible to file your federal taxes by touch-tone phone—visit www.irs.gov or call 800-829-1040 for more details. If you have filed, and have been waiting more than four weeks for your return, contact the IRS at 800-829-4477, for an update on your status. If you need help with a tax problem or are suffering some hardship due to the tax law, you can contact the **Taxpayer Advocate Service**, an independent agency within the IRS designed to help taxpayers resolve tax problems. You can contact them at www.irs.gov/advocate.

If you enjoy researching taxes or tax legislation, the **Arkansas Society of Public Accountants** has developed an excellent portal on their website to a variety of state, federal, and independent agencies having to do with tax revenue. Visit www.arcpa.org for more information. For a peek at the extensive online database of IRS revenue rulings since 1954, visit www.taxlinks.com, and for questions regarding individual taxes, go to www.irs.gov/individuals.

## CITY OF CHICAGO

For questions about Chicago taxes, contact the **Chicago's WebTax Customer Service**, 312-747-4747, or check the links online at www.cityofchicago.org. The City of Chicago **Comptroller's Office** can be reached at 312-744-7100.

### PROPERTY AND SALES TAX
Chicago's high taxes may come as a shock to newcomers (car owners especially). For instance, in Chicago the sales tax rate is 9.5%. Sales tax in Chicagoland suburbs varies from 6.75% to 9%. (Taxes may also vary by the product purchased.) The current sales tax rate in the state of Illinois is 6.25%.

### LUXURY TAX
Historically, according to the AAA–Chicago Motor Club, Chicago area gasoline prices range 20 to 30 cents higher than the national average. Here's why: in addition to the national 18.3-cent motor fuel tax, the State of Illinois charges a 6.25-cent-per-gallon gasoline sales tax, a 1.1-cent Illinois leaking underground fuel storage tax, and a 19-cent Illinois motor fuel tax. Between the federal, state, county, and city charges, taxes currently add about 80 cents to the price of every gallon pumped in the city of Chicago. DuPage County collects a 4-cent-per-gallon motor fuel tax and a .25% sales tax. Kane County levies

a 2-cent-per-gallon motor fuel tax. No wonder that Chicagoans venturing to nearby Indiana or Wisconsin tend to fill their tanks before heading back home!

In Chicago, beer and wine purchases have a city, county, and excise tax applied to them. The state applies a tax to cigarettes—18% of the wholesale price. Surcharges on luxury items, liquor, cigarettes, and gasoline, vary from community to community. Again, many savvy Chicago dwellers take advantage of out-of-state trips to stock up on cigarettes, booze, and other "sin" items taxed heavily at home.

## STARTING OR MOVING A BUSINESS

Starting a new business is exciting, and the City of Chicago is rooting for your success. Resources to consider include the **Business Affairs and Consumer Protection Department**, http://www.cityofchicago.org/city/en/depts/bacp/supp_info/bacpbusinesses.html, the city's liaison to the business community. Check here for loan programs, job training, infrastructure specifics, and a host of other solutions to issues faced by business owners. When you contact this office, you will be assigned an account manager. Be sure to ask about the *Business Resource Guide*, which discusses how to do business with the city, the bid process, permits, city services and more. It also provides a listing of other agencies that assist business owners in Chicago. Chicago's Department of Housing and Economic Development is located at 121 North LaSalle Street, 10th floor. The Illinois State agency, **Illinois Department of Commerce and Economic Opportunity** (DCEO; 312-814-7179, www.illinoisbiz.biz/dceo), is a referral agency that can direct you to the organizations you will need to contact for forms, licenses, funding, etc. It's a good first step for learning about what you need to do as an Illinois business owner. The State of Illinois also has a page with additional information, http://www2.illinois.gov/Business/Pages/run.aspx. Your business may be required to register with the Illinois Department of Revenue; for general information call 800-732-8866 or visit www.revenue.state.il.us, where you can register with the state and receive a provisional Federal Employer Identification Number (FEIN) in one online session. Finally, you can also check the **US Small Business Administration Home Page** at www.sba.gov.

# GETTING SETTLED

Now that you've found your place, signed all the paperwork, and are ready to move in, it's time to get settled. Setting up your utilities and telephone service, registering to vote, getting a library card and driver's license, registering your vehicle, finding a doctor…it's all here, and more.

## UTILITIES

### NATURAL GAS

If you have an all-electric apartment, skip this section. If you live in the City of Chicago and use gas to heat or cook, call **Peoples Gas** (a subsidiary of **Peoples Energy**) at 866-556-6001 to request service, or sign up at www.peoplesenergy.com. Customer service representatives are available 24 hours for emergencies; Monday–Friday, 7 a.m. to 7 p.m.; Saturday, 7 a.m. to 3 p.m. Peoples Gas offers several billing options: automatic withdrawal from your checking account, budget billing, credit card options, or payment via the internet. If you have gas heat, you will be paying a considerably larger bill in winter than in summer. This may seem only logical, but the winter bills can be staggering, especially if you live in an older and/or drafty apartment or house. (In the summer, it's the electric bill that will send you reeling, if you own an air conditioner.) For gas emergencies, call 866-556-6002. **North Shore Gas**, also a subsidiary utility of Peoples Energy Service, serves residents in northern Cook and Lake County. You can reach them by dialing 866-556-6004, or go to www.peoplesenergy.com; for emergencies dial 866-556-6005. To choose a natural gas supplier other than Peoples Gas or North Shore, go to www.peoplesenergy.com or call Peoples Energy and ask about their "Choices for You" program.

Outside the Chicago city limits, **NICOR** (888-642-6748, http://nicorgas.aglr.com/) serves most of the northern third of Illinois, and is one of the nation's largest gas distributors. It offers a monthly budget billing plan, which varies depending on the size of your apartment. (During the warmer months, your payments build up credit for the more expensive winter months. At the end of a year's service, you will pay the balance of what you owe or receive credit for your next year or next apartment if there are excess funds remaining. If you are leaving town, NICOR will reimburse you for the amount.) Some of the south suburbs, such as Olympia Fields, are also serviced by **Northern Illinois Gas** (http://nicorgas.aglr.com/), a NICOR subsidiary headquartered in Naperville.

If you are looking for ways to reduce your gas bill, the Energy Information Administration suggests the following:

- Request a home energy audit before the heating season begins; your utility company can send a representative to ensure that all your appliances and space-heating equipment are operating efficiently.
- Make sure your home and water heaters are properly insulated.
- Reduce the temperature settings on your thermostat when you are not at home.

## ELECTRICITY

After years of looking to ComEd as the sole supplier of electricity in Chicago, the city has moved forward in recent years to utilize a variety of suppliers. At the end of 2012, Chicago chose **Integrys Energy Services**, a sister company to Peoples Gas, to supply electricity to about 1 million Chicagoans in 2013. It's the largest such deal negotiated by a city on behalf of its residents and locks in a rate of 5.42 cents per kilowatt hour until May 2014. More information about Integrys Energy Service can be found at www.integrysenergy.com or by calling 877-377-7297.

## TELEPHONE SERVICE

Whether you are calling across town or around the world, in Chicago your connection still starts with **AT&T** (formerly SBC and Ameritech, www.att.com). To order service, call 800-288-2020. Most apartments in Chicago have phone jacks; just call AT&T to request service and then plug in your phones. The installation fee is about $45 for home customers. If your apartment does not have phone jacks, AT&T will install them but it will cost you. AT&T offers other services that may be of interest. For $4/month, *Phone Protect* will cover up to $400 worth of phone replacements and repairs charges on every phone in your home. For a $4 set-up fee and $4/month, *Line-Backer Maintenance Service* will cover you against unexpected telephone wire and jack repairs. (If you are a tenant, check with

# GETTING SETTLED

your landlord first to determine if the building is responsible for maintaining the inside telephone wires.) In addition, AT&T offers various phone usage options such as Call Waiting, Voice Mail Plus, Speed Calling, Call Forwarding/Screening, and Voice Mail. Your service representative will explain these options to you when you establish service; they are also detailed in the front of the White Pages phone book. When you call AT&T, you will need to name your preferred long-distance carrier. The biggies are:

- **AT&T**, 800-288-2020, www.att.com
- **GTC Telecom**, www.gtctelecom.com
- **IDT**, 800-CALL-IDT, www.idt.com
- **MCI-WorldCom**, 800-444-3333, www.mci.com
- **Sprint**, 866-866-7509, www.sprint.com
- **Verizon**, www.verizon.com
- **Credo Mobile**, 877-762-7336, www.credomobile.com

If you want to compare long distance pricing, go to SmartPrice at www.smartprice.com. You will be asked questions regarding your phone usage, your area code, and the first three digits of your phone number; they will then provide a free instant analysis of the carriers available in your area.

When you leave your home, call AT&T, 800-244-4444, to disconnect service and re-establish it at your new place. There is no charge to disconnect service.

**Bundled telecommunications**: digital phone, cable, and computer service is available from RCN, Comcast, and Wide Open West as well as AT&T. See below under **Cable Television** for contact information.

**Phone solicitations** can be curbed by going to the government's **Do Not Call Registry**, www.donotcall.gov, and registering your phone number—or call 888-382-1222, TTY 866-290-4236.

## AREA CODES

With the ever-increasing number of cell phones, pagers, phone and fax lines, Chicago, like the rest of the country, is grappling with the issue of area codes. In the late 1990s, the city was divided into two area codes (the old 312 and the new 773), which created confusion for natives and newcomers alike. The borders of the 312 (central Chicago) area code were North Avenue, Western Avenue, and 35th Street. If you lived south, east, and north of these streets your area code was 312; if you didn't, yours was 773. If only life were so simple. The truth is, the border between the two zones has never been very clear and is getting fuzzier all the time. If you live near the border, you could be in either one. An area code overlay may confuse this even more. In Chicago, it has been proposed that area code 872 will overlay the existing 312 and 773 area codes; 464 will overlay the existing 708 area code; and 331 will overlay area code 630. What this means for you is, depending on where you live, in addition to the older 708, 312, 630, and

773 area codes, newly assigned phones, cell phones, or pager numbers may receive one of three new codes: 464, 872, or 331. The overlay area code 224 has already been added to the 847 region (Chicago's north and northwest suburbs). Where an overlay is in place, callers must dial 11 digits (1 + area code + 7-digit phone number), no matter which area code is being dialed. You may still dial 911 for emergencies.

Finally, if you feel frustrated with AT&T, a company that serves a major portion of the nation, know you are not alone. Contact the **Illinois Commerce Commission Consumer Services Division** (www.icc.illinois.gov, 800-524-0795, TTY 800-858-9277) or your Congress representative with complaints, and join the **Citizens Utility Board** (CUB; www.citizensutilityboard.com, 800-669-5556) in their effort to open and improve local telephone service.

### DIRECTORY ASSISTANCE

In today's web-oriented world, directory assistance does not have to cost a lot of money. An online Yellow Pages is available from **Dex** (www.dexknows.com), and numerous sites are dedicated to providing telephone listings and websites. A few include:

- **www.anywho.com**; AT&T's service, which includes searches for toll-free numbers
- **www.bigbook.com**, Big Book
- **www.switchboard.com**
- **www.yellowbook.com**
- **www.infospace.com**

If you are feeling lazy and decide to call directory assistance, 411, keep in mind each call costs 75 cents for local assistance, more if you are asking for nationwide directory help.

### CELL PHONES

Here are some of the city's **major** cellular service providers. Check the Yellow Pages for a provider in your neighborhood.

- **AT&T Wireless Service**, 888-333-6651; several authorized dealers in Chicagoland area.
- **T-Mobile**, 312-944-9221 or 800-866-2453; several locations in Chicago as well as neighboring areas.
- **US Cellular One**, 888-944-9400 or 312-630-9365; several locations within Chicago and neighboring area.
- **Verizon Wireless**, 312-464-1390; several locations within Chicago and neighboring area.

# GETTING SETTLED

If you are considering a cell phone purchase, find out as much as possible before signing a contract. Better yet, try to find a service that does not require a long-term contract. And be sure to determine whether the cell phone you want to purchase is only operable if you subscribe to a particular service plan. If your phone has a simlock—which prevents you from using your phone with another service provider—go elsewhere. The Better Business Bureau (www.bbb.org) has a page on their website dedicated to cell phone service provider complaints.

## NATIONAL ONLINE SERVICE PROVIDERS

Here is a listing of the major local online service providers. Non-national providers are often less expensive, sometimes costing less than half of what the biggies charge—good for those wanting e-mail and internet access sans bells and whistles.

- **America Online,** 800-827-6364, www.aol.com
- **AT&T,** 800-222-0300, www.consumer.att.com
- **Comcast,** www.comcast.com
- **Earthlink,** www.earthlink.net, 800-511-2041
- **MSN8,** 800-386-5550, www.msn.com
- **NetZero One,** www.netzero.net
- **Verizon Online,** 888-649-9500, www22.verizon.com

## WATER

Unless you're a homeowner, you won't be paying for water. If you are living in an older home, you may not have a water meter, in which case Chicago's **Department of Water Management** will send you a bill semi-annually, based on standard assessments of your property and the home's interior fixtures. If you want to set up service or have questions about your water bill, visit the city's website at www.cityofchicago.org/city/en/depts/water.html.

Whether you're paying for it or not, the water here may surprise you, especially if you're moving from an area where the water source is less compromised. In Chicago and many suburbs, tap water comes from Lake Michigan, and while it ends up perfectly safe to drink (after extensive filtering and treatment), the taste can take some getting used to. The water is considered moderately hard, but you will be the best judge of that, and the water is fluoridated.

If you live in a community that depends on well water for its drinking supply, you may notice sediments, a rusty color, or other hard minerals. Some will change the color of your white enamel bathtubs and washing machines. Most authorities will tell you there is no cause for alarm; simply run your water until the color and sediments are gone. But if you want harder facts, contact your Illinois **Source Water and Assessment and Protection Program (SWAP)** coordinator at 217-785-4787 or go to www.epa.state.il.us. As part of the state's EPA, SWAP monitors and assesses well water.

Whether you drink lake or well water, you will notice a whitish film on some of your glasses and pots after filling them with water or while they are drying. That is calcium carbonate, courtesy of Mother Nature. It's harmless, if not attractive, and can be removed with ordinary white vinegar. For drinking water, many opt for bottled water, but over time it's more expensive than even the priciest filters. The water filter pitchers and faucet attachments available at most hardware and department stores will remove the most offensive element—the chlorine taste—but have only a modest impact on other pollutants. If you're concerned, you can buy more expensive filters, which attach directly to the water line. Or you can have bottled water delivered to your home from suppliers like Culligan. Some of the larger supermarkets, such as Jewel, offer drinking water from a coin machine; you supply your own jug. It should be stressed that Chicago water meets or exceeds both the EPA's and the Illinois Pollution Control Board's standards for water purity and is better than much of the groundwater in the area. And interestingly, 40% of the water that is pumped out of the lake is sold to neighboring suburbs. For more, go to the EPA's site, www.epa.gov, and read their guidelines on microbiological contaminants. Or call the **Safe Drinking Water Hotline**, 800-426-4791.

## CONSUMER COMPLAINTS—UTILITIES

If you have problems with any utility company (gas, electric, water, phone, or cable TV) and the service provider does not handle it to your satisfaction, don't hesitate to call the Consumer Services Division of the **Illinois Commerce Commission** at 800-524-0795, TTY 800-858-9277 or go to www.icc.illinois.gov. However, while they are required to take your complaint, they may not be as helpful as you'd like.

Another group that looks out for consumers' interests in Chicago is the **Citizens Utility Board** (CUB; 309 West Washington Street, Suite 800, Chicago, IL 60606, 800-669-5556, www.citizensutilityboard.org). CUB is a consumer watchdog organization, constantly on the alert for excessive utility rate hikes. Over the years, they have successfully lobbied for lower rate increases, and even rate reductions and refunds.

## GARBAGE & RECYCLING

In Chicago, the Department of Streets & Sanitation is in charge of all residential garbage pick-up and disposal. The city defines residential garbage as waste from a single-family home or a unit with four or fewer separate units. No need to call to set up service, just use the alleyway dumpster or city-provided cans.

Each ward in Chicago has a superintendent responsible for coordinating local area garbage pickups, snow removal, and other services. Visit the Department of Streets and Sanitation's web page to locate your ward and its superintendent: www.cityofchicago.org/StreetsAndSan/. If you do not have a trashcan, call the Department of Environment at 311 (312-744-5000) to request one.

In the suburbs, sanitation service varies by community. Ask your neighbors or call your city hall for details. Trash haulers can be found in the Yellow Pages under "Garbage & Rubbish Removal." **Waste Management** serves a large number of outlying communities. Check their website, www.wastemanagement.com.

Recycling for City of Chicago citizens is basically defined by the kind of building in which you live. If you live in a building that has four or fewer units, or a single-family building, you are served by the Blue Cart Program, administered by the Department of Streets and Sanitation. Until the 2010 city budget was passed, the city had promised to have blue carts delivered to the approximately 600,000 buildings covered by this program by the end of 2011. However, no money was allocated to Streets and Sanitation for 2010, which means that the roll-out of blue carts was frozen at about 240,000 buildings. Chicagoans in single-family buildings who do not have blue carts can take recyclables to one of 37 drop-off locations provided by the city.

If you live in a building with more than five units, you are served by a private waste hauler that has been hired by your building owner or manager or association.This hauler also handles your recycling. By Chicago law, your building is required to offer its tenants an effective recycling plan. If your multi-unit building doesn't have a recycling system in place, use one of the drop-off locations. If your building doesn't have a recycling plan, or you have questions about the one in place now for the City of Chicago, go to www.cityofchicago.org/city/en/depts/streets/supp_info/blue_cart_recyclinginchicagoasofoctober2009.html.

Never dispose of motor oil or hazardous liquids via your storm drains.

## DRIVER'S LICENSES, AUTOMOBILE REGISTRATION, AND ILLINOIS STATE IDS

### CHICAGO VEHICLE STICKERS—CITY STICKERS

Chicago residents with vehicles must have **Chicago vehicle stickers** (usually called "city stickers") attached to the inside windshield of their cars. Think of it as a yearly usage fee for the "privilege" of parking on city streets. Not everyone living in the suburbs will escape this little urban pocket squeezer, as many of the 'burbs require them too. Rates in the suburbs vary, and the suburban city halls usually offer a discount if you purchase your sticker more than 30 days before the due date. Check with your municipality for details. In Chicago, the cost is $85 (expect to pay an additional $3 to $5 service charge if you use a non-city outlet). Purchase vehicle stickers from the City Clerk at City Hall, 121 North LaSalle, 312-744-6774, at most currency exchange offices, or one of the Department of Revenue Payment Centers: 2550 West Addison Street, 4770 South Kedzie, 2006 East 95th Street. You can also purchase your vehicle sticker at the City Clerk's North Side or South Side Satellite Offices, 5430 West Gale Street and 5674 South Archer Avenue, Unit A; at the James R. Thompson Center, 100 West Randolph Street, lower level; and at the DMV building at 5401 North Elston Avenue. To do it online, go to www.chicityclerk.com. Stickers are valid from July 1st to June 30th of the following year. If you buy your vehicle sticker more than 30 days after the renewal date, an additional $60 fee will be assessed. The ticket price for not having a sticker is $200. Since the city has access to the Illinois Secretary of State's records, it's easy for a meter reader to enter a plate number on a computer and see if you should have a sticker. **Note:** if you are new to Chicago, you do not need to wait for your new Illinois license plates in order to purchase a vehicle sticker. Simply bring proof of your new Chicago address to any city clerk facility and purchase your vehicle sticker. For more information call 312-744-6774 or go to www.chicityclerk.com.

## DRIVER'S LICENSE AND STATE IDENTIFICATION CARD

Residents of Illinois who own and operate a vehicle must have an Illinois driver's license and Illinois license plates. The grace period to obtain an Illinois license is 90 days. Until then, you are allowed to drive in the state under the driver's license of your former home state. **Illinois driver's licenses** are obtained through the **Illinois Secretary of State**, www.cyberdriveillinois.com. There are 130 facilities located in the Chicagoland area. Contact the Secretary of State's Chicago Information Office at 312-793-1010. They can assist you in finding the closest DMV office to you, or you can do it yourself at www.cyberdriveillinois.com.

If you have never held an Illinois state driver's license, you'll need your current, out-of-state driver's license, a social security card, proof of birth—a valid passport, alien registration card, or a military ID card—and proof of your new address: a utility bill or voter's registration card will do. Several other forms of ID are acceptable; visit the DMV website (www.cyberdriveillinois.com) to view all your options. You will be asked to take a written test based on Illinois *Rules of the Road,* and an eye test. If you need to brush up on your rules you can contact the Illinois Secretary of State's Chicago Information Office at 312-793-1010 for a helpful driver's rule book, or download it from www.cyberdriveillinois.com (it's big, 102 pages). The fee for an Illinois driver's license is $30, and it is valid for five years. You may also be asked to take a road test. There is no fee for the road test. If you don't drive but need a **photo identification**, you can get an Illinois identification card through the Illinois Secretary of State offices, and at many of the Motor Vehicle offices. The fee for the state ID is $20 and is valid for five years.

## FINES AND TICKETS

Should you be so unfortunate as to receive a ticket for a moving violation or illegal parking in Chicago, you'll need to become acquainted with Chicago's **Traffic Court**. The downtown court is at 50 West Washington. To determine which court office will handle your case, call the Traffic Court's automated information line for Cook County: 312-603-2000. (If you are ticketed outside of Cook County, check with that municipality for court information.) If you receive a ticket for a moving violation, you must either pay the ticket or contest it within seven days. If you contest the ticket, you will be assigned a court date. Be aware that in Illinois you must post bond when you receive a moving violation citation. If you do not have a spare $75 in cash or a bail bond card (available through many automobile clubs such as AAA or Allstate), the officer will take your license until you post bond or pay your fine. This can be a huge inconvenience, but you will get a receipt that can be used as a temporary substitute, so it's not the end of the world. If you decide to pay your ticket, you can do so by mail, online (www.cityofchicago.org), or at one of the city's payment facilities; call 312-603-2000 for payment center addresses. You can also pay at City Hall, 121 North LaSalle. If you have any questions about a parking violation, contact the city's **Ticket Helpline** at 312-744-PARK (7275).

Go to the Chicago Bar Association's website, www.chicagobar.org, for more information about traffic citations in Cook County or if you need to hire an attorney. Their lawyer referral service line is 312-554-2001.

## LICENSE PLATES & VEHICLE REGISTRATION

New residents have 30 days after bringing the vehicle to Illinois in which to apply for an Illinois title and to register their vehicles. Bring proof of identification, address, the odometer reading, name and address of any party that has a lien on the vehicle, date your vehicle was purchased, make, model, year, body type, vehicle identification number (VIN), and either the copy of the out-of-state title, or bill of sale. (If you have recently purchased a vehicle and it is not registered yet in any state, you will need to fill out the proper tax forms, applicable taxes, and attach them to your application when you mail it to the Secretary of State's office. Contact the Department of Revenue for more information, 800-732-8866.) If you have a **disability** and need special plates, you will need to bring in proof of disability or military disability proof. You will also need to provide liability insurance records, and if the car is more than three years old, proof of vehicle inspection certification (see above).

Illinois license plates can be purchased at any office of the Illinois Secretary of State or at neighborhood currency exchanges. The price of plates varies, ranging from $78 to $118, depending on your car ($39 for a motorcycle). Vanity plates cost more. Title fees are $95 for an automobile and $65 for an all-terrain vehicle or motorcycle. If you have any questions concerning the registration process, call the Secretary of State's Public Information Line at 217-782-6306.

You can bring your car registration application in to any Secretary of State Driver Service facility. Go to www.cyberdriveillinois.com for a list of facility addresses. Call the Secretary of State's Chicago Information Office, 312-793-1010, with any questions (none of the following Illinois Secretary of State offices accept incoming phone calls):

- **James R. Thompson Center**, 100 W Randolph St
- **North**, 5401 N Elston Ave
- **South**, 9901 S Martin Luther King Jr. Dr

For those moving to Illinois with a **leased vehicle**, there's a bit more work involved to register it with the state. Bring your car's lease, power of attorney from the leasing company, and registration information to the Secretary of State's office (see above), where you will not only pay for normal registration, but will also file an RUT25 form for use tax on the vehicle. If you paid tax on the vehicle in another state you must bring proof of this as well. Call the **Illinois Department of Revenue** at 800-732-8866 with any questions.

## EMISSIONS TEST

The State of Illinois requires all gasoline-powered cars and light trucks (diesel-powered vehicles are exempt) to undergo a biannual (once every two years) **auto emissions test** starting in the fourth model year. If you have purchased a vehicle that has an expired emissions test, you will be required to have it retested as soon as you receive your new registration. Drivers will receive notification in the mail. The testing takes about 10 minutes, tops—but you may need to wait in a line. Your notice will provide a list of the nearest emission test centers, but you can take your vehicle to any authorized facility. Look for signs around town or check for emissions testing locations in the "Services for Motorists" section of www.cyberdriveillinois.com. An official notification of the test results will come in the mail in a few weeks. If you have any questions regarding the testing, you can contact the **Emissions Hotline** at 847-758-3400.

## AUTOMOBILE INSURANCE REQUIREMENTS

If you own a registered car in the state of Illinois, the law states you must have auto insurance. Liability insurance of $20,000 per person, $40,000 per accident for bodily injury, and $15,000 for property damage is the minimum coverage required. However, the Insurance Information Institute, www.iii.org, recommends that you carry $100,000 for bodily injury per person and $300,000 per accident. Typically this additional coverage will cost you about $200 to $300 more per year. You must also carry uninsured/underinsured motorists insurance, which protects you in the event you are hit by a driver who has no insurance or who is carrying less insurance than what will be needed to pay for the damages. For more information visit their website or contact their offices at 212-346-5500.

A few notes on **state driving laws**: Illinois has a mandatory seat belt law, and an officer can legally stop your car for non-compliance. The fine for not using a seat belt in the front seat is $25. Under the Child Passenger Protection Act, children over four and under sixteen years of age must use a safety belt. The fine for a first violation can be up to $75; thereafter the fine can be as high as $200. Children under four need to be seated in a child safety seat. (If you need some tips on how to properly install a child safety belt, visit www.safekids.org.) In Illinois, the legal definition of **driving while intoxicated** (**DWI**) is a blood alcohol limit of 0.08. If you are stopped for suspected intoxication and you are found to have a blood alcohol level above the legal limit, or if you refuse to take the blood alcohol content (BAC) test, it is grounds for on-the-spot revocation or suspension of your driving license. You are also forbidden to have any unsealed containers of alcohol in the passenger compartments.

## CONSUMER PROTECTION—AUTOMOBILES

Just bought a nice shiny lemon? Depending on the severity of the problem, you may not be stuck with it. In order to be covered by the Illinois Lemon Law, a vehicle must have a nonconformity that both substantially impairs the use, market value, or safety of the vehicle and is not repairable by the dealer or manufacturer in at least four attempts for the same repair, or be out of service for a total of 30 or more business days. **The lemon law covers** new cars (purchased or leased), light trucks and vans under 8,000 pounds, recreational vehicles (excluding trailers), vehicles in their first 12 months or 12,000 miles, whichever occurs first, and only vehicles purchased in Illinois. **The lemon law *does not* cover** used cars, altered or modified vehicles, motorcycles, or boats.

To initiate action under the Lemon Law, contact the manufacturer's representative for your car. This representative will forward the required information and forms to you. Manufacturers have established an Industry Third Party Dispute Resolution Program to evaluate your claim. (Check your vehicle ownership manual for more about this program.)

Lemon law claims *cannot* be initiated directly through the dealer, and *you* must initiate any claims with your manufacturer's representative *within 12 months of the purchase date*. If the Dispute Board rules in your favor, you can expect one of the following compensations: you will receive a replacement vehicle of like or similar value, or the manufacturer will buy your vehicle back from you, less the value for miles driven.

If you are dissatisfied with the decision of the dispute board, you may bring a civil action to enforce your rights under the Lemon Law Act. The manufacturer, however, may not dispute the board's decision.

There are also other federal and Illinois laws that deal with contracts and warranties for new products. Before deciding on a particular course of action, consult a private attorney to discuss the various alternatives and determine the best course of action for your situation.

Remember, keep good records and *all* receipts and correspondence concerning repairs to your vehicle. Note the purpose and date of all repairs along with the length of time your vehicle is in the shop. The records you keep will be important in winning your claim. Contact the State of Illinois Attorney General's Office at 800-386-5438, www.ag.state.il.us.

## PARKING

### PARKING GARAGES AND LOTS

Parking downtown on a daily basis is prohibitively expensive. A "bargain" day rate can run about $22—and you usually have to get to the lot by 7 a.m. to enjoy that deal. But if you find that you must bring your car downtown occasionally, here are a few tips to keep the cost down. As a general rule, the farther away from State Street, the kinder the fee. If you try the parking lots east of the Ogilvie Transportation Center, where the Metra trains turn in for their final stop from the suburbs, you can find very reasonable parking for $8 to $12—a good deal even if you need to pay a few extra bucks to catch an 'L' train to your destination.

If you plan to spend an evening downtown, say at the opera or theater, consider taking public transportation. Depending on how far you're traveling, even taking a cab may be cheaper or equivalent in price to paying for parking. Alternatively, you can simply drive around and spot signs that offer "deals" for customers pulling in after 6 p.m. If you are dining along Michigan Avenue, consider parking in the 900 North building, where for a minimum purchase in one of the stores within the building you can have your parking ticket validated.

If you plan on being downtown on a daily basis, your best bet is a monthly pass with CTA or Metra. See the **Transportation** chapter for more details.

### RESIDENTIAL PARKING PERMITS

In most neighborhoods, residential parking permits are not valid without a current Chicago Vehicle Sticker. Streets designated R1–R5 are zoned for residential parking permits. The zoning status signifies that more than 33% of the cars parked on a given block do not belong to residents of the area. This type of zoning is usually bestowed in neighborhoods where not enough parking is an issue, such as Wrigleyville, where Chicago Cubs night games turn the neighborhood into a parking nightmare, and parts of Wicker Park/Ukrainian Village, where the hopping nightlife means residents are otherwise unable to find parking within blocks of their homes. If you're not sure whether your neighborhood requires a parking permit, you can call your ward office or, easier still, walk down the block and look for parking regulation signs. You can't miss them. If your neighborhood is zoned for residential parking permits, you can obtain an application from the **City Clerk's Office**, 312-744-6774, or go to http://chicityclerk.com/vehicle-stickers/parking-for-guests.html. Bring your proof of residence (lease, mortgage book, utility bill) and proof of Chicago Vehicle Sticker (receipt from sticker). At this time you can also purchase packs of single-day guest-permit parking stickers—$3 for a pack of 15. Purchase a residential parking permit at several locations:

- **City Clerk's Satellite Offices**, 5430 W Gale St, 5674 South Archer Ave, Unit A
- **City Clerk's Office** (Room 107) in City Hall, 121 N LaSalle St
- **Secretary of State Office**, 5401 N Elston Ave
- **Secretary of State Office**, 9901 S Martin Luther King Jr. Dr

Residential Parking Permits can also be obtained by mail; go to www.chicityclerk.com to download the application. Mail the application to City Clerk, 121 North La Salle, Room 107, Chicago, 60602. The fee is $25 and the permit expires each year on June 30th.

## PARKING TICKETS

Parking fines start at $25 and soar to $120 depending on the offense. If you want to fight the parking ticket, it's the same procedure as a moving violation: mail back the envelope after marking an "X" in the box requesting a hearing. The city will send a card telling you when and where to go for your hearing. Or you can contest the ticket by mail, writing your reasons why you feel the ticket was unwarranted. The city will respond, informing you whether or not you will have to pay the ticket. (Go to www.cityofchicago.org to pay the ticket online or see **Fines and Tickets**, above, for a list of payment centers.) For a list of outstanding violations, call the **Ticket Helpline** at 312-744-7275 or go to www.cityofchicago.org.

Parking enforcement in Chicago varies depending upon location. In order to save on-street parking places for residents, permit parking is the rage in many popular neighborhoods. Lincoln Park, DePaul/Lincoln Park West, Wrigleyville/Lakeview, and sections of Wicker Park and Bucktown are particularly hard places to find a space without a permit. Tow trucks cruise through these areas with cruel regularity.

If you find your car has been towed (be careful, many a person has come out convinced his or her car has been towed, only to find out later he/she was mistaken as to where it was parked), call the **Police Department Auto Pound HQ**, 312-744-4444, to find out where your vehicle was taken. To retrieve your wheels, you must pay a $150 towing fee (for cars up to 8,000 pounds), plus a $10-per-day holding fee for the first five days—$35 daily after five days. Cars weighing over 8,000 pounds pay $60 for the first 5 days, $100 daily thereafter. You must pay cash or use VISA or MasterCard; personal checks are not allowed.

If your car was **booted** for unpaid parking violations, you must pay a $60 booting fee and the balance of any unpaid parking tickets within 24 hours after the booting. The city is serious about collecting fines—three unpaid tickets can get your car booted, and if you fail to appear to resolve the issue within 24 hours, your car will be towed. Then you will be required to pay not only the $60 booting fee, but also the $150 towing fee, plus $10 per day for storage for the first five days, $35 thereafter.

Also, be aware that Illinois requires a license plate on both the front and back end of your car. Failure to comply can result in a $25 fine. A broken windshield will get you the same. Both fines can be issued at the same time your expired parking meter citation is being written.

## STOLEN CARS

If it turns out your car has been stolen rather than towed, the police will need your license and city vehicle sticker numbers, the car's year, make, model and color as well as the vehicle identification number. You also should mark your sound system, radar detector, car phone, and other accessories with your driver's license number. You can borrow an engraving pen through your local police district's Operation Identification program. Locations of Chicago auto pound locations can be found by going to www.cityofchicago.org.

## VOTER REGISTRATION

The old Chicago Election Day slogan, "Vote early and often," is a reminder of days gone by when the city played fast and loose with election results. Today, Chicago elections are honest.

To be eligible to vote in Chicago, you must be a resident of the precinct for 30 days, be 18 years of age by Election Day, and be a US citizen. You can register to vote anytime during the year, up until 28 days before an election. Register when applying for services at driver's license facilities, the Departments of Public Aid, Public Health, Mental Health & Developmental Disabilities, or Rehabilitation Services; or go to the Board of Elections office, 69 West Washington, #600 and #800, 312-269-7900, your county clerk's office, city hall, or village or township offices. You need two pieces of identification; one must have your current address. If you register at the Board of Elections office, you can also request an absentee ballot or change your voter's registration there.

Close to election time, voter registration drives are held throughout the city. In many cases, you will be able to register with a volunteer in less than five minutes. If you are moving to any of the nearby counties, you can call your county for more information or go to www.voterinfonet.com to find your polling place and to read about the candidates:

- **Suburban Cook County**, 312-603-0906, TDD 312-603-0902
- **DuPage County**, 630-407-5600
- **Kane County**, 630-232-5990
- **Lake County**, 352-343-9734
- **McHenry County**, 815-334-4242

Political campaigns make for exciting times in Chicago. Here are some places for those who want to take a more active role:

- **Chicago Board of Elections**, 312-269-7900, www.chicagoelections.com
- **Democratic Party of Cook County**, 134 N LaSalle St, 312-263-0575, www.cookcountydems.com.
- **Republican Party of Cook County**, 205 W Randolph, Ste 1245, 847-496-7871, www.cookrepublicanparty.com
- **Reform Party**, 1255 N Sandburg Terrace, 312-266-7431, www.rpil-ilrp.com/index.html
- **League of Women Voters**, 332 S Michigan Ave, Ste 525, 312-939-5949, lwvchicago.org
- **Illinois Green Party** (HQ in Urbana, IL), www.ilgp.org
- **Illinois State Board of Elections**, 312-814-6440, www.elections.state.il.us
- **Libertarian Party**, 312-841-7760, www.il.lp.org

## PASSPORTS

You can apply for a passport at the **US State Department** office in the Federal Building, 230 South Dearborn Street, 18th floor, or at any suburban satellite location. To make a quick search for the passport facility nearest you, go to http://iafdb.travel.state.gov. The Bureau of Consular Affairs, the agency that oversees the issuing of passports, no longer accepts calls with routine passport questions. You can call the **National Passport Information Center** at 888-362-8668 or 900-225-5674 (you will be charged $4.95 per call to the 888 number; the 900 number is 35 cents per minute for recorded information and $1.05 per minute for operator assistance). Or go to www.travel.state.gov for free. Bring two standard passport photos taken within the last six months, a picture ID, and proof of US citizenship, such as a previous US passport, certified birth certificate, naturalization certificate or certificate of citizenship. The cost is $135 for a new passport ($80 for those under 16) and $110 to renew a passport less than 15 years old. The standard turnaround time for a new passport is 25 days, but it can take longer; an expedited three-day passport can be requested for an additional $60 fee. You can download an application (form DSP-11) with instructions from the Bureau of Consular Affairs website at www.travel.state.gov and download the application from there.

Passports are valid for 10 years for those 16 and older; five years for children 15 and under.

## LIBRARIES

If you are a resident of the city of Chicago, you can apply for a Chicago Public Library card at any **Chicago Public Library**, www.chipublib.org. It's simple, fast and free. In addition to the Chicago Public Library's Harold Washington Library, the city's main central library at 400 South State Street, 312-747-4300, there are many neighborhood branches throughout the city (check the **Neighborhood Profiles**), as well as university and independent libraries, many of which are open to the public. (See **Literary Life** in the **Cultural Life** chapter for more details.)

## BROADCAST AND PRINT MEDIA

### TELEVISION STATIONS

Provided you have a good antenna and you don't live in a basement or a highrise, you should be able to receive the following network and local independent stations without cable service:

- Channel 2 WBBM (CBS)
- Channel 5 WMAQ (NBC)
- Channel 7 WLS (ABC)
- Channel 9 WGN (Tribune)
- Channel 11 WTTW (Public Broadcasting System)
- Channels 19, 21, 27, 36, 42 CAN TV (Chicago Access Network)
- Channel 20 WYCC (Public Broadcasting System affiliated with Chicago City Colleges)
- Channel 23 WWME-CA (Independent)
- Channel 26 WCIU (Independent)
- Channel 32 WFLD (Fox)
- Channel 35 WWTO (TBN)
- Channel 38 WCPX (Ion)

- Channel 40 WESV-LD (Estrella TV)
- Channel 44 WSNS (Tel)
- Channel 50 WPWR (My Network TV)
- Channel 56 WYIN (PBS)
- Channel 62 WJYS (Independent)
- Channel 66 WGBO (Uni)

Daily program listings are printed in both the *Chicago Sun-Times* and the *Chicago Tribune* and their weekly TV magazines, as well as in *TV Guide*.

## CABLE TELEVISION

Chicago is divided into five areas for cable service from three cable television companies: **Comcast** (866-594-1234, wwwb.comcast.com); **RCN** (800-746-4726, www.rcn.com); and **Wide Open West** (866-496-9669, www.wowway.com). Each company offers basic cable service with the premium channels available for an extra fee; there are slight differences in channels and programming.

To find out which cable area you are in, call the **City of Chicago Cable Communications Administration, Information and Complaints**, 312-744-4052, or visit the Department of Business Affairs and Consumer Protection section of www.cityofchicago.org and click the "Cable" link.

## RADIO STATIONS

If you can't make it through the day without morning talk radio, National Public Radio, your favorite shock jock, or your own personal musical soundtrack, you're in luck in Chicago, where radio stations offer everything from indie rock and regional Mexican to progressive to Christian/Catholic talk. Note that many stations—especially those affiliated with universities—can only be heard in certain parts of the Chicago area. Here are Chicago's radio stations and their programming:

### FM

- 87.7 (WKQX-LP) alternative
- 88.1 WCRX Columbia College Radio
- 88.5 WHPK University of Chicago Radio
- 88.7 WLUW Loyola University Radio
- 89.3 WNUR Northwestern University Radio
- 90.1 WMBI Christian
- 90.9 WDCB Jazz and Blues
- 91.5 WBEZ National Public Radio by day (NPR); jazz at night
- 93.1 WXRT rock
- 93.9 WLIT adult contemporary

- 94.7 WLS oldies
- 95.5 WNUA Mexican Spanish radio
- 95.9 WERV classic rock
- 96.3 WBBM top 40, hip hop, and R & B
- 96.7 WSSR adult contemporary
- 97.1 WDRV classic rock/hits
- 97.9 WLUP mainstream/classic rock
- 98.3 WCCQ country
- 98.7 WFMT classical
- 99.5 WUSN country
- 100.3 WNND hits of the 80s and 90s
- 101.1 WKQX adult contemporary
- 101.9 WTMX adult, urban contemporary
- 102.3 WYCA gospel
- 102.7 WVAZ R & B
- 103.5 WKSC top 40
- 104.3 WJMK variety hits
- 105.1 WOJO regional Mexican
- 105.9 WCFS adult contemporary
- 106.3 WSRB soul
- 106.7 WPPN adult contemporary/Espanol
- 107.5 WGCI hip hop, R & B
- 107.9 WLEY regional Mexican

## AM
- 560 WIND talk
- 670 WSCR news, White Sox, Bulls games
- 720 WGN talk, Cubs games
- 780 WBBM News
- 820 WCPT progressive talk
- 890 WLS talk radio
- 950 WNTD Catholic talk
- 1110 WMBI Spanish Christian
- 1160 WYLL Christian talk
- 1390 WGRB gospel
- 1450 WVON ethnic, religious
- 1530 WJJG talk, adult standards, classic hits
- 1690 WVON talk

## NEWSPAPERS AND MAGAZINES

Whether your interest is in theater, poetry readings, or trendy restaurants, there is probably a local (and often free) publication to suit you. And since Chicago

# GETTING SETTLED

is one of the few remaining cities with competing daily newspapers—the *Chicago Sun-Times*, *Daily Herald*, *Southtown Star*, and the *Chicago Tribune*—news coverage is sharp, ground-breaking (the local television news stations regularly pick up stories from the dailies), and thorough. For in-depth regional news and business, *Crain's Chicago Business* is regarded as one of the best weeklies in the country. Alternative papers such as the *Reader* and *Newcity* are feature-driven, as is the monthly *Chicago Magazine*. Other publications dedicated to business, legal matters, entertainment or other are *Chicago Daily Law Bulletin*, *Chicago Reporter*, *Chicago Parent*, and the *Utne Reader*. There are also various student and independent magazines available in area coffeehouses and record stores, although the *Reader* or *Newcity* offer the most dependable movie, club, or theater listings. Two local papers that cover news and events with an emphasis on Chicago's African-American community are *N'DIGO*, a free weekly paper with listings, reviews, editorials, and feature articles; and the *Chicago Defender*, which covers local and national news. In addition, there are over 45 community newspapers—not including suburban communities—that cover neighborhood happenings. They are generally weeklies. Check at your local convenience store or drugstore for a copy.

Corner newsstands are scattered throughout the city and offer a good selection of some of the most popular newspapers and magazines. For the ultimate selection, try **Chicago City Newsstand**, 4018 North Cicero, 773-545-7377 in Chicago, and 860 Chicago Avenue/Main Street in Evanston, 847-425-8900, www.citynewsstand.com.

- **Chicago Defender**, 4445 South King Drive, 60653, 312-225-2400, www.chicagodefender.com
- **Chicago Daily Law Bulletin**, oldest daily courts newspaper in the country, 312-644-7800, www.chicagolawbulletin.com.
- **Chicago Journal**, weekly news publication covering south, near, and west Loop, 141 S Oak Park Ave, Oak Park, 312-243-2696, www.chicagojournal.com.
- **Chicago Magazine**, 435 N Michigan Ave, Ste 1100, 60611, 312-222-8999, www.chicagomag.com
- **Chicago Parent**, 141 S Oak Park, Oak Park, 708-386-5555, www.chicagoparent.com; award-winning free monthly, found in many libraries.
- **Chicago Reader**, 350 N Orleans St, 312-828-0350, www.chicagoreader.com; free weekly, comes out on Thursdays. Available in shops, restaurants, and clubs all over the North Side and selected South Side areas.
- **Chicago Reporter**, 332 S Michigan Ave, 312-427-4830, www.chicagoreporter.com; publication devoted to the issues of race and poverty.
- **Chicago Sun-Times**, 350 N Orleans St, 60654, 312-321-3000 or 888-848-4637, www.suntimes.com

- **Chicago Tribune**, 435 N Michigan Ave, 60611, 312-222-3348 or 800-TRIBUNE; electronic edition, www.chicagotribune.com; the *Red Eye*, www.redeyechicago.com.
- **Crain's Chicago Business**, 150 N Michigan Ave, 16th Floor, 60601, 312-649-5200, www.chicagobusiness.com; daily local business news.
- **Hyde Park Herald**, Chicago's oldest community newspaper, serving Hyde Park, Oakland, and Kenwood, 1435 East Hyde Park Blvd, Chicago, 773-643-8533, www.hpherald.com.
- **Inside Publications**, 6221 N Clark St, 773-465-9700, www.insideonline.com, www.yournews.com, weekly news coverage of Chicago's North Side: Loop, Lincoln Park, Gold Coast, Lakeview, Lincoln Square, Uptown, Andersonville.
- **N'DIGO**, 1006 S Michigan Ave, Ste 200, 60605, 312-822-0202, www.ndigo.com; free African-American weekly, available in shops and restaurants throughout Chicago.
- **Newcity**, 770 N Halsted St, Ste 303, 60642, 312-243-8786, www.newcitychicago.com; free entertainment weekly, comes out on Thursday. Available in Chicago shops, restaurants, and clubs.
- **Utne Reader**, 800-736-UTNE, www.utne.com; alternative news magazine.
- **Windy City Times**, 5315 N Clark St, #192, Chicago, 773-871-7610, www.windycitymediagroup.com; gay and lesbian focus.

**Suburban publications** include:

- **Chicago Suburban Newspapers**, www.mysuburbanlife.com: *Beacon News*, 630-978-8880, western suburbs; *Bolingbrook Reporter*, 630-368-1100; *Courier News*, 630-978-8880, north and northwest suburbs; *News Sun*: Bolingbrook, Naperville, Wheaton, Glen Ellyn, 847-249-7223, west suburbs; *Herald News*, 815-773-7152, Will and Grundy Counties; *Naperville Reporter*, 630-368-1100; *Suburban Life*, 630-368-1100, DuPage County and central and east Cook County; *Downers Grove Reporter*, 630-368-1100.
- **Daily Herald**, 155 E Algonquin Rd, Arlington Heights, 847-427-4333, www.dailyherald.com.
- **Southtown Star**, 6901 W 159th St, Tinley Park, 708-633-5999, southtownstar.suntimes.com; covers Chicago's south suburbs.
- **Journal Online**, 622 Graceland Ave, Des Plaines, 847-299-5511, http://www.journaltopics.com/.
- **Lakeland Newspapers**, 1100 Washington St, Ste 101, Grayslake; serving 11 Lake County communities, www.lakecountyjournals.com, 800-589-9363.
- **Lombardian/Villa Park Review**, 116 S Main St, Lombard, 630-627-7010, www.lombardian.info.
- **Oak Park Journal Newspaper**, www.oakparkjournal.com.
- **Pioneer Press**, www.pioneerlocal.com: *Evanston Review*, 847-486-7481; *Skokie Review*, 847-486-7481; *Lincolnwood Review*, 847-486-7481; *Highland*

*Park News*, 847-599-6944; ***Deerfield Review***, 847-486-7342; ***Glencoe News***, 847-486-7256; ***Northbrook Star***, 847-486-7256; ***Wilmette Life***, 847-486-7256; ***Winnetka Talk***, 847-486-7256; ***Oak Leaves***, Oak Park, 708-524-4412.
- *Rosemont Journal*, www.journal-topics.com/news/rosemont/.
- *Southwest News Herald*, 773-476-4800, www.swnewsherald.com; south and southwest suburbs including Burbank and Oak Lawn.
- *Suburban Focus Magazine*, 630-863-7183, www.chicagosuburbanfamily.com; free monthly publication. A leisure magazine covering the west and southwest suburbs of Chicago.

## FINDING A PHYSICIAN

Some of the country's best hospitals are in the Chicago area, and include many university-affiliated teaching hospitals as well as first-rate specialty clinics. Treatment plans here are often cutting edge, with many innovations in a variety of fields coming out of this area—certainly good news for those needing a specialist. If you just need a family health care provider, you should have no trouble finding a good doctor. Usually recommendations from a co-worker or friend are the best way to go when looking for a doctor, although you should check with your medical plan's list of preferred providers. For those less fortunate, area clinics are available. County Health boards are good sources of information about area health clinics for low income/uninsured patients. Here are a few of the **Chicagoland area county health boards**: Lake County Board of Health, 847-377-8000; Chicago Department of Public Health, 312-747-9884; Kane County Health Department, 630-897-1124; DuPage County Health Department, 630-682-7400.

Nearly all of the university hospitals have a physician referral line. The American Medical Association (www.ama-assn.org) also has a doctor locator service. Following is a list of some **physician referral services** for the Chicagoland area:

- www.alsa.org; for those with Lou Gehrig's disease
- www.thebody.com; for those with HIV
- www.uchospitals.edu; for the University of Chicago Hospital's referral service

For general health questions, the Mayo Clinic, www.mayohealth.org, and the federal government's www.healthfinder.gov, are good resources. To determine if a doctor is board-certified in a specialty area you can go to the American Board of Medical Specialties at www.certifacts.org, 800-733-2267, or to HealthGrades, www.healthgrades.com. HealthGrades rates 600,000 physicians and 5,000 hospitals. If you have a complaint about a local physician, contact the Illinois Department of Professional Regulation at 312-814-4500 or 888-473-4858.

## PET LAWS & SERVICES

If you're going to keep a dog in Chicago, he or she will need a rabies vaccination and a license. The former is available from any vet; they will also give you a vaccination tag to put on your dog's collar. Dog licenses are available at the **City Clerk's Office**, 121 North La Salle Street, 312-744-5375, but you will need proof of a rabies vaccination to get one. Dog licenses cost $5 if your dog is neutered, $50 otherwise; for senior citizens: $2.50 for a neutered dog, $5 for an unneutered pet. The licenses are valid for one year. Birds and snakes do not require a license—but horses do! Check with the City Clerk's office for pricing. The City Clerk's office also has two **satellite offices**, located at 5430 West Gale St, 312-742-5318 and 5674 South Archer Ave, 312-745-1100. If Fido is lost and captured by Animal Control, it will cost you $20 to redeem him—if he is licensed; it's $35 for an impounded unlicensed stray. (The cat redemption fee is $20, plus rabies shots if you cannot prove the animal has been properly vaccinated.) Chicago has a leash law and a waste removal (scoop the poop) law, so bring a bag or some newspaper when you are out for your daily stroll. Violating any of the above ordinances can bring fines of up to $200.

Dogs are not allowed on Chicago's beaches. Despite this, you will find a multitude of frolicking, slap-happy, water-loving dogs on the beach in the early mornings. During the day, check out Belmont Harbor just north of Belmont Avenue; there's a small spit of fenced-in beach there called Doggie Beach. Because this is not officially classified as a "beach," it is more dog than beach most weekends. Be warned: if you let your dog off leash here, you may be ticketed. The only official dog beach on Chicago's lakefront is the fenced-off area at the north end of Montrose Beach—just follow the sounds of joyous barking. Be careful to keep your dog within the fenced-in area, and do not let the dog off leash until you have entered this area.

If you don't live near the lake and want companionship for your pup, just wake up early and walk on over to the nearest neighborhood park. All over the city, parks are transformed into early morning doggie play groups. Just remember to pick up the poop! A recent law requires all dogs at "dog-friendly areas" in the city of Chicago to have permits. These can be purchased for $5 from many veterinarians (www.chicagoparkdistrict.com/facilities/dog-friendly-areas/permits-and-tags/). Check **Chicago Canine** at www.chicagocanine.com/beach.htm for a list of participating veterinarians. **Chicagoland Tails** (www.tailsinc.com), an online magazine, is another good resource. Check "Animal Resources" on their site for a list of dog parks in the Chicago area as well as the **Greenspaces and Beaches** chapter for more on dog-friendly parks. And if you don't have the time to walk your dog every day, there are plenty of dog-walking services. Just look in the Yellow Pages under "Pet Exercising Services."

In the suburbs, many of the larger pet store chains offer low-cost veterinary services several times a year, including inexpensive vaccinations for dogs, cats, and ferrets. Call your local chain and ask about their clinic services. If you lose your cat or dog, first contact your local police district; then make sure you talk to neighbors, postal carriers or sanitation workers for leads. Also check out the Lost/Found ads in your local newspaper and put up signs with photos in the neighborhood. In Chicago, pets are impounded in three main locations:

- **Animal Welfare League**, 773-667-0088, 6224 S Wabash; in the suburbs, 708-636-8586, 10305 Southwest Hwy, Chicago Ridge; www.animalwelfareleague.com
- **The Anti-Cruelty Society**, 510 N LaSalle, 312-644-8338, www.anticruelty.org; private, non-profit humane society. Their website offers a host of information about owning pets in Chicago and the suburbs, from downloading license application forms to municipal regulations for pet owners to checking fees.
- **Tree House** (cats only), 773-784-5488, 1212 W Carmen Ave, www.treehouse-animals.org

You can also log on to www.chicagolostpets.org for an extensive list of animal rescue organizations in the Chicagoland area. In the suburbs, check with your local animal control for information on animal impounds.

Looking to adopt a pet? You can do the initial research in the comfort of your own home through a handy online catalogue that is updated daily—www.petfinder.com. This site lets you browse photos and details for adoptable animals; you can search by age, size, gender, and breed as well as species. Listed pets include some of those housed at Chicago animal care facilities, organizations like the Anti-Cruelty Society and Animal Welfare League, and numerous smaller local shelters, many breed-specific. Some who want to adopt a pet head straight to the **City of Chicago Animal Care and Control**, 2741 South Western Avenue, 312-744-5000. A dog, or cat, spayed or neutered, with license and all necessary shots, and an AVID Microchip for identification, will cost you $65. You will even get a pet carrier in which to take your new pet home. All rabbits are spayed or neutered and the $25 fee includes some educational tips on care and a rabbit carrier. The **Anti-Cruelty Society** (510 North LaSalle Street, 312-644-8338, www.anticruelty.org) also offers an adoption service for abandoned pets. The fee is a flat $60 for cats and $95 for dogs and includes the necessary shots, a free collar, an ID chip, and spaying or neutering. Pets can also be adopted at the **Animal Welfare League**, www.animalwelfareleague.com: in the city at 6224 South Wabash, 773-667-0088, or in the south suburbs at 10305 Southwest Highway, Chicago Ridge, 708-636-8586. The adoption fees here include spay/neuter surgery as well as all the necessary shots, a microchip, a collar, and a leash (for dogs) or carrier (for cats). Dogs cost $135 to adopt; cats are $73 for one or two.

## FINDING A VETERINARIAN/PET INSURANCE

If you are moving to Chicago with a pet, you'll want to track down a vet fairly soon. Find one by asking fellow pet owners in your neighborhood or checking with your local pet store for a referral.

If you are looking for pet insurance, two national organizations offer medical coverage for pets: Veterinary Pet Insurance, 888-899-4874 and Pet Assure, a Pet HMO, 888-789-7387. Also, most PetSmart stores are affiliated with a clinic that offers pet health insurance. Contact the store nearest you for details.

Finally, be an advocate of the humane treatment of dogs by reporting any incident of dog fighting. It's illegal in all 50 states and is a felony in Illinois. If you suspect there is a dog-fighting event being staged in your area, dial 311. To report one in progress, call 911.

## SAFETY AND CRIME

Like all big American cities, Chicago has its share of crime. However, it has seen its crime rate drop in recent years (since 1991, most types of violent crime in Chicago are down nearly a third). According to the Chicago Police Report, Chicago's 2010 crime rates were down 1.8 percent from 2009. During that time, however, crime has increased in almost half of the towns that make up suburban Cook County. The remaining communities reported stable rates, decreases, or, in a few rare cases, no violent crime at all. Despite the recent rise in violent crime in some suburban communities, the average crime rate in Cook County is still just about half of the crime rate reported in Chicago, and rates continue to fluctuate; for example, in 2006, suburban Cook County reported a 4% drop in murder, theft, and auto theft. That said, there are a few common-sense tips that a newcomer to the Windy City—especially a newcomer to urban life—should keep in mind:

- Trust your intuition. If something doesn't feel right, act accordingly. Healthy survival instincts are a good thing.
- When outside, keep your eyes and ears open. Remaining constantly alert and aware of your surroundings is key to personal safety.
- Never let a stranger get in your car and never get in a car with a stranger. Studies show that once you are in a vehicle with a would-be criminal, your chances of survival decrease dramatically.
- Don't move into a neighborhood that makes you uncomfortable. Before you take an apartment, walk around the neighborhood at different times of the day and evening to see what the area is like.
- Make sure your apartment or home is safe from potential intruders. That means, for example, that if you are on a ground floor or in a garden apart-

ment, you should probably have sturdy bars on your windows. Err on the side of caution when assessing your risk.
- On the 'L,' try to sit in a car with other people.
- Resist the temptation to travel alone or at night through a neighborhood with which you are unfamiliar. Also resist taking shortcuts through alleyways or on streets that are unfamiliar.
- If something does happen to you, whether you are in your home or car or on the street, remember that most incidences of crime do not result in loss of life. However, if you feel your life may be in danger, run, scream, fight—whatever it takes to save your life. In life-threatening situations, being passive may not be the best response.
- Report crime immediately. Whether it's happening to you or not, call 911 when you know of any crime in progress. For non-emergency police questions, call 311, Chicago's other help line. They can tell you the location of your nearest District or Area police headquarters.

If you are interested in finding out more specifics about a particular neighborhood, go to **chicago.everyblock.com/crime**. There you will find the latest statistics of reported crimes divided into districts. It is a good source of information because it tells you what kind of crime—vandalism, burglary, rape, murder, etc.—may be going on in different areas. As mentioned earlier in the book, you should also try to become acquainted with your neighborhood CAPS (Chicago Alternative Policing Strategy) organization. Also check the Chicago Police Department's website, www.cityofchicago.org/police, to learn more about citizen policing (CAPS), neighborhood crime maps, and to view a list of scheduled neighborhood meetings.

# HELPFUL SERVICES

So you've made your way down your relocation checklist: find place to live (check); establish utility accounts (check); set up bank accounts (check). Now it's time to fine-tune that list. What about housecleaning services, a place to repair the car, pest control, and mail service? Information regarding all these helpful services, and more, follows. (Inclusion of a company or organization does not imply endorsement by First Books. Be sure you check references of a company or service before hiring, particularly if they will be coming into your home.)

## DOMESTIC SERVICES

### HOUSECLEANING SERVICES

You may be a star at your office and whiz in the kitchen, but if you lead a busy life, you may not have time to tidy all the messes that come your way. If you are looking for a housecleaning service, check with your neighbors or co-workers, peruse the Yellow Pages (under "House Cleaning") or contact one of the following:

- **Chicago Maid Pro**, 773-292-0520, www.maidpro.com
- **Maid to Order**, 312-951-8100, www.maid-to-orderinc.com
- **Merry Maids**, toll-free, 866-212-5846, www.merrymaids.com
- **The Maids (Chicago and North/Northwestern Suburbs)**, toll-free, 866-857-7401, www.maids.com
- **The Maids of Oak Lawn**, 708-667-5092, www.maids.com

## DIAPER SERVICES

If you're hoping for an old-fashioned cloth diaper service, be warned that they're scarce in the Chicago area. Try the Yellow Pages and/or call **Bottoms Up Wash Diaper Service** in Waukegan, 847-336-0040.

## DRY CLEANING DELIVERY

You will be hard pressed to find a suburban dry cleaner that picks up and delivers your laundry and dry cleaning to your door, but it is possible in central Chicago. If you are afraid you are going to get caught with no clean shirts in the closet, another option is to check at the office. Many large corporations, especially those located in the suburbs, have dry cleaners on site. You can drop your dry cleaning off in the morning before getting into the elevator and pick it up on your way home.

- **Drive Cleaning**, 312-321-0033
- **Press This Cleaners & Laundry**, 312-664-3212

## PEST CONTROL

Chicago gained nationwide attention in 1998 with the arrival of the Chinese long-horned beetle. Arriving as stowaways in wooden packing crates, these voracious insects spread through neighborhood maple trees so quickly that the City of Chicago was forced to cut down 1,400 trees in order to contain them. All crates from China now must either be made from chemically treated wood or else be heated before arrival to the United States to kill any infestation. While the Department of Agriculture has diligently and quickly worked to control the problem, beetles were still sighted occasionally as late as July 2002. The infestation was declared eradicated in 2008.

When the first cases of West Nile virus hit Chicago in 2001, the city sprang into action. Still, by 2002, 100 of the state's 102 counties reported infected birds, horses, and mosquitoes. By the end of that year, Illinois led the nation with more than 800 human cases of this mosquito-borne illness and 64 deaths. Cases have declined since then, largely due to the activities of the Public Health Department, which strives to eliminate mosquito breeding grounds in and around the Chicagoland area through spraying insecticides, surveillance, and testing of mosquitoes and animals indicating infection. Mild cases of West Nile virus cause slight fever and headache. More acute cases include other symptoms such as high fever, body aches, convulsions, tremors, and in the most severe cases, paralysis and death. If you find a dead animal you suspect has been infected with West Nile virus, contact the Cook County Health Department at 708-232-4500.

# HELPFUL SERVICES

If your space is being infringed upon—whether by bugs, weeds, invading deer, or Canada geese—you may need some outside help. You can search the Yellow Pages under "Exterminators" or try one of the following websites for more information about pest control:

- **www.doityourself.com**; information on controlling pests in lawns, homes, and garden, including a section on Japanese beetles and deer.
- **www.epa.gov**; the EPA's Pesticide Program has suggestions on how to control pests without the use of chemical pesticides.
- **www.victorpest.com**, the website of Woodstream Corporation's Victor brand of "least toxic" pest controls. Offers poison-free products as well as useful information about the habits of roaches, fleas, flies, ants, mosquitoes, rats, and mice.

## MAIL

### JUNK MAIL

Junk mail will surely follow you to your new locale. In order to curtail this kind of unwanted mail we suggest you send a written note, including name and address, asking to be purged from the **Direct Marketing Association's** list (Direct Marketing Association's Mail Preference Service, P.O. Box 9008, Farmingdale, NY 11735). Some catalogue companies will need to be contacted directly with a purge request. For **junk e-mail**, you may also go to the Direct Marketing Association's website, www.dmaconsumers.org, and request an opt-out service for your e-mail address. The service will accept three non-business e-mail addresses at a time. This should reduce the amount of e-mail you receive from national e-mail lists. Another option is to call the "opt-out" line at 888-567-8688, and request that the main credit bureaus not release your name and address to interested marketing companies. (**Curb phone solicitations** by going to the government's Do Not Call registry, www.donotcall.gov, and registering your phone number—or call 888-382-1222, TTY 866-290-4236.)

### MAIL DELIVERY/SERVICE

Maybe you've heard the nasty rumors: Chicago has a terrible reputation when it comes to delivering mail. In the past, thousands of undelivered pieces of mail were discovered in the apartments and houses of carriers and in garbage dumpsters. While reform has been glacial, a federal task force resulted in important management changes, and consequently, service has improved (though cynics point out it hardly could have gotten worse). At times, you may find that letters mailed in the city take longer to arrive in a neighboring town than to travel to the East Coast! If you experience a problem with your postal service, we suggest you contact the **USPS Office of Consumer Affairs** by calling 800-275-8777. Also use this number for postal rates, services, and ZIP codes, or check the website at www.usps.com. If a chat with the Consumer Affairs Office at USPS doesn't resolve your problem, contact your congressperson; he or she may be able to help.

If you're in between addresses but still need a place to get your mail, there are dozens of businesses that will rent you a mailbox, have your mail forwarded, and accept packages for you. You can use the ones listed below, or check with your local post office.

- **C & L One Stop Postal Service**, 1448 E 52nd St, 773-667-9088
- **Mail Center of Chicago**, 28 E Jackson Blvd, 312-922-1788
- **Mailbox Plus**, 2248 W Belmont Ave, 773-477-5600
- **UPS Stores** (formerly Mail Boxes, Etc.): 910 W Van Buren St, 312-226-3333; 4064 N Lincoln Ave, 773-871-1400; 47 W Division, 312-943-6260. Check the Yellow Pages or www.ups.com for addresses of more of their dozens of Chicagoland locations.

For walk-in post office customers, the old USPS "central facility" downtown has been replaced by the **Cardiss Collins Postal Store** (433 West Harrison Street, 312-983-8182), open 24/7 except for postal holidays and every third Saturday p.m./Sunday a.m. for an audit. Check www.usps.com for the post office nearest you. A few of the central US postal facilities include:

- **Haymarket**, 168 N Clinton St, 312-906-8557; open weekdays, 9 a.m. to 6 p.m.
- **Nancy B. Jefferson**, Midwest Station, 116 S Western Ave, 312-243-2560; open weekdays, 9 a.m. to 5 p.m., Saturdays, 9 a.m. to 12:30 p.m.
- **Pilsen**, 1859 S Ashland Ave, 312-733-4750; open weekdays, 9 a.m. to 5:30 p.m., Saturdays, 9:30 a.m. to 2:30 p.m.
- **Wacker Drive**, Willis Tower, 233 S Wacker Dr, lower level one, 312-876-1024; open weekdays, 9 a.m. to 5 p.m.

For ZIP code information, go to www.usps.com.

## SHIPPING SERVICES

For conventional packages, the nationwide parcel services are all familiar names:

- **FedEx**, 800-463-3339, www.fedex.com (for ground, express or air freight information)
- **Mail-Sort**, Deerfield, 847-291-4900, www.mail-sort.com
- **Pitney Bowes**, 800-811-1920, www.pb.com
- **United Parcel Service**, 800-742-5877, www.ups.com
- **US Postal Service Express Mail**, www.usps.com

## AUTOMOBILES

### REPAIR

Finding a mechanic you can trust can be difficult. Ask around for a referral from co-workers, neighbors, or friends. Short of a personal endorsement, you can try a dealer. Though dealers are generally reliable and have the right equipment to fix your type of car, they are usually far more expensive than a general repair shop. Contact the Better Business Bureau of Chicago and Northern Illinois, 312-832-0500, about a prospective shop to see if any complaints have been filed against it.

### POTHOLES AND WINTERIZING YOUR CAR

Freezing winters followed by spring thaws, as well as continual heavy truck traffic, wreak havoc on Chicagoland's streets. While you will frequently spot repair crews, the process of patching potholes is an ongoing battle. If your car has sustained damage due to the potholes on Chicago's city streets, you may be eligible for some reimbursement from the city for repairs. If you think you have a case, take photographs, get at least two estimates for the repair work, and file a report with the City Clerk's office. Download the report form from www.chicityclerk.com/programs/claims.html.

In general, you should make sure your car's suspension and tires are in good shape, and around Halloween you should also "winterize" your vehicle: this involves checking and replacing all fluids including antifreeze and making sure the car's heater is in good condition. Most car owner's manuals will provide several steps for winterizing.

If you plan to purchase a new car, many residents advise waiting until after the cruel winter, which can put excessive wear and tear on even the sturdiest vehicle. Many opt to never buy new while driving the streets of Chicago. If potholes and salt from the winter streets don't catch up to your car, a grocery cart or a carelessly opened car door in a supermarket parking lot surely will.

It's always a good idea to investigate the local automobile club that offers its members emergency road service. Some insurance plans automatically include roadside assistance. Ask your friends and co-workers for the organization they use or call **AAA Chicago Motor Club**, www.aaa.com, 312-372-1824.

## CONSUMER PROTECTION—RIP-OFF RECOURSE

Got a beef with a merchant or company? A number of agencies monitor consumer-related businesses and will take action when necessary. The best defense against fraud and consumer victimization is to read the fine print—including all the terms and exclusions—in every contract you sign. Also, save all receipts and canceled checks; get the name of any telephone sales and service people with whom you deal; and check your contractor's license number with the Department of Consumer Affairs (see below) for complaints. At times, despite your best efforts, you still may fall victim to unfair practices: A dry cleaner returns your blue suit, but now it's purple, and he merely shrugs. A shop refuses to provide a refund, as promised, on an expensive gift, which didn't suit your mother. Your landlord fails to return your security deposit when you move. After $898 in repairs to your automobile's engine, the car now vibrates wildly, and the mechanic claims innocence. Negotiations, documents in hand, fail. You're angry and embarrassed because you've been had. There *is* something you can do.

- **Better Business Bureau of Chicago and Northern Illinois**: 312-832-0500; files complaints by consumers about area businesses.
- **Chicago Bar Association**, Consumer Law Program, 312-554-2000, www.chicagobar.org
- **City of Chicago, Department of Consumer Services**, search for "Business Affairs and Consumer Protection" at www.cityofchicago.org
- **The Consumer Action Website:** www.consumer-action.org; provides a listing of the government agencies dealing with consumer complaints.
- **Illinois Attorney General**, **Consumer Fraud Division**, 800-386-5438, www.ag.state.il.us/consumers/index.html; maintains a public inquiry unit that reviews and mediates consumer complaints.
- **Illinois Attorney General, Consumer Protection Division**, 800-243-0618, TTY 877-844-5461; Chicago Office, 312-814-3000, TTY 800-964-3013; mediation services between businesses and consumers.
- **Illinois Department of Professional Regulation**, 312-814-4500, www.idfpr.com; the place to go when your beef is with a professional licensed by the state of Illinois (architects, barbers, chiropractors, cosmetologists, dentists, nurses, security companies, veterinarians, etc.).
- **State of Illinois/Department of Insurance**, 312-814-2427, is a state agency that investigates insurance complaints.
- **www.consumeraffairs.com**

For consumer protection information regarding utilities see **Consumer Complaints—Utilities** in the **Getting Settled** chapter.

## LEGAL MEDIATION/REFERRAL PROGRAMS

### LOW COST/FREE
- **AIDS Legal Council of Chicago**, 180 N Michigan Ave, 312-427-8990
- **Chicago Kent College of Law Legal Clinic**, 565 W Adams, Ste 600, 312-906-5050; employment, criminal, tax, and health law only

# HELPFUL SERVICES

- **Center for Conflict Resolution**, 11 E Adams St, Ste 500, 312-922-6464; mediation only
- **Chicago Lawyers Committee for Civil Rights Under the Law**, 100 N LaSalle, Ste 600, 312-630-9744; class actions, civil rights, employment, housing and lending
- **Chicago Legal Clinic**: 2938 E 91st St (South), 773-731-1762; 1914 S Ashland (Pilsen), 312-226-2669; 118 N Central St (Austin), 773-854-1610; 211 W Wacker Dr, Ste 750, 312-726-2938
- **Chicago Volunteer Legal Services Foundation, Inc.**, 100 N LaSalle, Ste 900, 312-332-1624; all issues except criminal, civil rights, and environmental
- **The Law Project**, 100 N LaSalle St, Ste 600, 312-939-3638; contract, employment, tax, real estate, and environmental only
- **DePaul Legal Law Clinic**, 25 E Jackson Blvd., Ste 950, 312-362-8294; only Family Law and domestic violence
- **Evanston Community Defender**, 1123 Emerson St, Evanston, 847-492-1410; criminal, juvenile, probate, and public aid only
- **Lawyers Committee for Better Housing**, 100 W Monroe St, Ste 1800, 312-347-7600; eviction, sexual harassment/discrimination regarding housing, landlord retaliation only
- **Metropolitan Family Services**, 1 N Dearborn, Ste 1000, 312-986-4200, TDD 312-986-4237; family law only
- **Legal Assistance Foundation of Metropolitan Chicago**; all issues except class action, criminal, environmental, real estate, probate and tax. **General Intake Offices**: 120 S LaSalle St, 312-341-1070,TDD 312-431-1206; 828 Davis St (Evanston), Ste 201, 847-475-3703, TDD 847-475-5580
- **The Domestic Violence Legal Clinic**, 555 W Harrison St, Ste 1900, 312-325-9155; orders of protection for domestic violence cases

## LEGAL ASSISTANCE FOR THE ELDERLY

- **City of Chicago**, Department on Aging, 312-744-4016; investigates elder abuse and nursing home problems
- **Illinois Attorney General**, advocacy division/consumer protection, 217-782-1090, 800-243-0618, TTY 217-785-2771 www.ag.state.il.us; Chicago office: 312-814-3000, TTY 312-814-3374
- **Illinois Department on Aging**, 800-252-8966 (senior help line), www.state.il.us/aging

## SOCIAL SECURITY

If you are a US citizen, you probably already have a social security card and can skip this section. But for the rest of you, this might be new information. Non-citizens who are working or studying here need a Social Security Number. This can be done through the mail by first calling 800-772-1213 for the necessary forms, or going online to www.ssa.gov. You can also visit the nearest Social Security office, no appointment necessary, making sure to bring along the following items:

- A certified birth certificate (with its raised stamp, not a copy)
- A translation of your birth certificate if it was not originally printed in English.
- Two other pieces of identification, which can be: a passport; driver's license; school or government ID; health insurance card; military records; or an insurance policy with your name on it.

A Social Security employee will complete the application, and you should receive a card with your number within several weeks. Non-citizens will need a birth certificate and/or a passport and a green card or student documentation. It will most likely take more than a month to receive a card. If you already have a number but have lost your card, call the number above to apply for a new card.

## SERVICES FOR THE DISABLED

The City of Chicago would like all its new residents, physically challenged or not, to experience the best Chicago has to offer. Below is a mix of services that you may want to investigate, sign up for, or just know about, in order to make your transition to Chicago easier.

- The **Mayor's Office for People with Disabilities** (**MOPD**), 312-744-7050, TTY 312-744-4964, is an excellent resource offering services and programs to Chicagoans with disabilities. MOPD provides case management services, employment services, skills training, information on how to find accessible housing, emergency home-delivered meals, and a host of other services for the disabled. They even have a pamphlet for business owners, which details the tax incentives available for making facilities accessible to people with disabilities. For a complete list of services, call, or write them at City Hall, 121 N LaSalle St, Rm 104, 60602.
- **Chicago Lighthouse**, 1850 W Roosevelt Rd, 312-666-1331, TTY 312-666-8874, as well as the **Guild for the Blind**, 65 E Wacker Pl, #1010, 312-236-8569, provides employment and independent-living services for the blind and visually impaired. Check the Yellow Pages under "Disabled Persons" for more resources.
- Free or low-cost legal services for the disabled include:
- **Center for Disability & Elder Law**, 79 W Monroe St, Ste 919, 312-376-1880; all issues for disabled clients except criminal, domestic relations, environmental, immigration, and tax.
- **City of Chicago Mayor's Office for People With Disabilities**, 312-744-7050, TTY 312-744-4964

- **Illinois Attorney General's Office**, Veterans Hotline: 800-382-3000, www.ag.state.il.us
- **Equip for Equality, Inc.**, 20 N Michigan Ave, Ste 300, 312-341-0022, 800-537-2632, TTY 800-610-2779, www.equipforequality.org; this non-profit organization operates the federally mandated Protection & Advocacy System for Illinois and offers information on disability resources, services, rights, and advocacy.
- **Guardianship and Advocacy Commission**, 160 N LaSalle, 312-793-5900, TDD 312-866-333-3362

## GETTING AROUND

**CTA Customer Service**: many CTA 'L' stations are equipped with elevators. Call the Regional Transportation Authority (RTA) customer service center at 312-913-3110 for a list of handicap-accessible train stations. All buses are equipped to handle wheelchairs. For more information about special services, contact the CTA at 888-968-7282, TTY 888-282-8891/888-CTA-TTY-1.

## COMMUNICATION

- **Illinois Telecommunications Access Corp. (ITAC,** www.illinoisrelay711.com) provides Illinois Relay Service, and conducts a free TTY program (a teletypewriter that allows those who cannot communicate through a conventional telephone the ability to do so with ease) for Illinois residents who are hard of hearing, deaf, blind, or speech-impaired. ITAC is governed by the Consumer Advisory Council and monitored by the Illinois Commerce Commission. Other agencies (see below) also provide free TTY equipment. In order to be eligible for a free TTY you must be an Illinois resident, your disability must be certified by a licensed audiologist, physician, or speech pathologist, or by a certified DHS/ORS counselor. The last requirement: you must have working telephone service at the address you provide on your application. Write to ITAC, 3001 Montvale Drive, Suite D, Springfield, IL 62704, call 800-841-6167 (voice/TTY), or request an application through the ITAC website: www.itactty.org. To learn how to communicate with a person using TTY while you are using a conventional telephone, log on to www.illinoisrelay711.com.
- **Illinois Relay Center** enables hearing/speech-impaired TTY callers to call individuals or businesses who do not have TTY equipment. Service is 24/7. Calls are confidential and billed at regular phone rates. Call TTY: 800-526-0844 or voice: 800-526-0857.
- **Illinois Assistive Technology Program** is a state-funded project whose mandate is to help the physically challenged obtain the proper devices (communication, daily living, etc.), and funding to pay for them. Contact the

program at 800-852-5110 (voice/TTY); Illinois only: 217-522-7985 (voice); 217-522-9966 (TTY), for more information. Or visit www.iltech.org.
- **Chicago Public Library** provides services for the hard of hearing and visually impaired. If you need a sign interpreter for a special event hosted by the library, please provide the library with 10 business days' notice. Contact the CPL at 312-747-4252, TTY 312-747-4066, or check the website at www.chipublib.org/howto/lib_disability.php. Headphones for special events, programs in the auditorium, or Video Theater are available by contacting the Library's Marketing Department at 312-747-4130 or the TTY Administrative Telephone service: 312-747-4066. A talking book center, computers with enlarged monitors, and power Braille catalogs are available on the 5th floor of the Harold Washington Library.
- **Chicago Hearing Society**, 2001 N Clybourn, teaches young children sign language, offers assistance in obtaining hearing aids, and assists in establishing an in-home TTY: 773-248-9121, TTY 773-248-9174

## ADDITIONAL RESOURCES

Following is a variety of resources, both governmental and non-profit, that may be of use to those with special needs. Their services include advocacy, referrals, training, assistance towards independent living, family resources, housing assistance, and information. Those using TTY phones may receive operator and directory assistance by calling 800-855-1155. For a copy of the *US Government TTY Directory*, visit www.gsa.gov/frs, or write to: Federal Citizen Information Center, Department TTY, Pueblo, CO 81009, or phone: 877-387-2001.

- **DuPage County Center for Independent Living**, 739 Roosevelt Rd, Bldg 8, Ste 109, Glen Ellyn, 630-469-2300 (voice and TTY)
- **Family Resource Center on Disabilities**, 20 E Jackson Blvd, Room 300, 312-939-3513, TTY 312-939-3519, www.frcd.org
- **Federal Citizen Information Center**, 800-FED-INFO, TTY 800-326-2996, www.usa.gov; for questions about federal agencies, programs, benefits, or services. Staff will answer your question or get you to someone who can, 8 a.m. to 8 p.m., Monday–Friday. Recordings of frequently requested information are available around the clock.
- **National Library Service for the Blind and Physically Handicapped**, 202-707-5100, TTY 202-707-0744, www.loc.gov/nls/

## INTERNATIONAL NEWCOMERS

Chicago, the "City of Big Shoulders," has been a haven for immigrants since it was first settled in the 1800s. According to the 2010 US Census, over 17% of the Chicago area's current population is still foreign-born.

A variety of helpful information can be found online at the **US Citizen and Immigration Services** website: http://uscis.gov. If you have specific questions, you can also contact the USCIS national customer service center, 800-375-5283, TTY 800-767-1833. Once you know what you need to do, you'll undoubtedly have to fill out paperwork. To get the proper forms, call 800-870-3676 or look on the USCIS website, above.

For further assistance, you can schedule an appointment with US Citizen and Immigration Services by calling 800-375-5283. The Chicago field office for the USCIS is located at 101 West Congress Parkway. Register for an appointment there using **INFOPASS**, http://infopass.uscis.gov/.

## PUBLICATIONS

You can download a useful guide, "Welcome to the United States: A Guide for New Immigrants," free, by choosing the "Resources for New Immigrants" link in the "Education and Resources" section of the USCIS website. The guide booklet is available in a variety of languages and includes information on your rights and responsibilities as well as the steps to take to become a US citizen.

International newcomers experiencing culture shock can get a quick overview of American culture, etiquette, expectations, and quirks in the *Newcomer's Handbook for Moving to and Living in the USA*, by Mike Livingston, published by First Books (www.firstbooks.com).

## LOCAL CONSULATES

Many countries have consulates in Chicago. Search online for the address and phone number of your home country's consulate or delegation.

## MOVING PETS TO THE USA

- *The Pet-Moving Handbook* (First Books) covers domestic and international moves, via car, airplane, ferry, etc. Primary focus is on cats and dogs.
- **Cosmopolitan Canine Carriers,** out of Connecticut, 800-243-9105, www.caninecarriers.com, has been shipping dogs and cats all over the world for 30 years. Contact them with questions or concerns regarding air transportation arrangements, vaccinations, and quarantine times. You can submit a "pet relocation estimate" form online.

## GAY AND LESBIAN LIFE

Chicago is a good place to live if you're gay or lesbian. It's determinedly tolerant, from inclusive governmental policies, to friendly gay and/or lesbian neighborhood enclaves, to the annual gay pride celebration in June. In Cook County, anti-bias statutes protect gays and lesbians from housing and workplace discrimination. Progressive suburb Oak Park was the first municipality in Illinois to offer domestic partner benefits to city employees; Chicago followed suit in 1996. In June 2011, Illinois passed a law that legalized same or opposite sex civil unions. The civil union grants health insurance for the partner, hospital visitation/health care decision rights, and rights to sue over a partner's death. The application for the civil union license costs $60 and requires valid identification with proof of age. For more information, check with the Office of County Clerk at www.cookcountyclerk.com or call 312-603-5656.

If you're looking for gay nightlife, look no further than Boystown (male) or Andersonville (female). While it may not have the reputation of New York's Greenwich Village or San Francisco's Castro, the stretch of Wrigleyville/Lakeview known as Boystown is out and proud. Easily identified by rainbow-hued street banners, the neighborhood near Halsted Street between Belmont Avenue and Irving Park Road is the backbone of gay Chicago. Of course, boys don't have all the fun. Andersonville, just two miles to the north along Clark Street, is a preferred nesting ground for the city's lesbian community.

The weekly **Windy City Times** (5315 N Clark St, #192, 773-871-7610, www.windycitymediagroup.com) is an excellent free resource for finding out what is happening in the gay, lesbian, bisexual, and transgender (GLBT) community. It's available at coffeehouses, bookstores, and music stores throughout Chicago. Also look online for **Gay Cities**, a travel guide that lists gay-friendly clubs, hotels, and restaurants: www.gaycities.com

The **Gerber/Hart Library** (1127 West Granville Avenue, phone 773-381-8030) is a private, community-supported library and archive, open to the public and devoted exclusively to gay and lesbian publications and concerns. It offers discussion groups, photography and archival displays, a visiting author series and "a free cup of coffee." Closed Mondays and Tuesdays. (See **Literary Life** in the **Cultural Life** chapter for more information.)

Join hordes of Chicagoans and visitors—gay, straight, and everything in between—for the **Gay & Lesbian Pride Parade**, which usually takes place the last Sunday of June. It starts at the corner of Montrose and Broadway. Everyone dresses: up, down, in drag, in leather, chests bared, in costume—and a great time is had by those on the floats, in the march, on the sidelines, and at the often-raucous after-parties. Public transportation is highly recommended, as parking spots in the area are scarce on normal days, and much less when you're competing for parking with the *other* 400,000 or so folks heading to the Pride Parade. Check the *Windy City Times* or http://chicagopride.gopride.com for the exact day, times, and route.

Other resources geared toward gay life include:

# HELPFUL SERVICES

- **Area hospitals and medical centers** in Chicago's gay and lesbian communities (Wrigleyville and Edgewater) include NorthStar Medical Center, 2835 N Sheffield Ave, 773-296-2400; Northwestern Memorial Physicians Group, 3245 N Halsted St, 312-926-3627, www.nmpg.com; Brasch Medical Center, 2360 N Clark St, 800-979-7100; Weiss Memorial Hospital, 4646 N Marine Dr, 773-878-8700; St. Joseph Hospital and Health Care Center, 2900 N Lake Shore Dr, 773-665-3000; Illinois Masonic Medical Center, 836 W Wellington Ave, 773 975-1600; Thorek Memorial Hospital, 850 W Irving Park Rd, 773-525-6780.
- **Windy City Queercast** has programs geared towards the GLBT community, go to www.WindyCityQueercast.com.
- **Chicago Metropolitan Sports Association**, 773-830-1492, www.chicagomsa.com, is the largest non-profit gay and lesbian sports organization in the Midwest.
- **Chi-Town Squares**, www.iagsdc.com/chitownsquares, a gay and lesbian square dance club that holds open lessons, workshops, and over a dozen special dances per year; membership costs $35, but many lessons are open to the public.
- **Fairy Gardeners' Guild**, 312-485-9338; lesbigay gardening group, citywide and in the suburbs.
- **Gay and Lesbian Chamber of Commerce**, 773-303-0167.
- **www.glyp.com**, an online alternative Yellow Pages
- **Windy City Gay Chorus/Unison: Windy City Lesbian & Gay Singers**, www.windycitysings.org

## POLICE COMPLAINTS

If you feel you were abused or mistreated by a Chicago police officer, and you want justice, your first response should probably be to file a complaint with the city. Try the Mayor's office by dialing 311 or go online to www.cityofchicago.org. You can also call the Chicago Police Department directly at 312-744-4000, the Police Superintendent's "hotline" at 773-533-6272, or the office of the Inspector General at 773-478-7799, established to "detect and prevent misconduct." Don't hold your breath, though. According to one report, few of the complaints and allegations of police misconduct filed with the city result in any disciplinary action, and you'll find cynicism about police corruption common among Chicago residents.

Fortunately, you can seek redress in other ways. First of all, consider contacting the media (see **Broadcast and Print Media** in the **Getting Settled** chapter for a list in this book). *The Chicago Reporter*, in particular, has a long history of reporting on abuse by the Chicago Police Department. They can be found at 332 South Michigan Avenue, Suite 500, and on the web at www.chicagoreporter.com.

Other organizations to try:

- **American Civil Liberties Union**, www.aclu-il.org
- **Chicago Bar Association**, 312-554-2000, www.chicagobar.org
- **Cook County State's Attorney**, 312-325-9200, www.statesattorney.org
- **State of Illinois, Attorney General**, 312-814-3000, www.ag.state.il.us
- **US Department of Justice**, 202-353-1555, www.justice.gov

Law school clinics might be interested to know about what happened to you. See the **Higher Education** section of the **Childcare and Education** chapter of this book for a list of institutions of higher learning.

If all else fails, and you have the stomach, you can hire an attorney and seek justice the American way: file a lawsuit.

# CHILDCARE AND EDUCATION

WHETHER YOU'RE LOOKING FOR THE PERFECT SCHOOL FOR YOUR child or considering earning a degree for yourself, Chicago presents a dizzying array of educational choices. While this chapter provides basic information about childcare, as well as schools (public and private) and institutions of higher learning, the listings here cannot possibly cover all the educational options available in the greater Chicago area. Please note: listings in this book are merely informational and are not endorsements.

## CHILDCARE

When moving to a new area, one of the most important tasks parents face is finding good childcare and/or schools for their children. The results of this search can be a deciding factor in, among other things, choosing a community in which to purchase a home. Key factors to consider when looking for a daycare center or school are affordability, convenience, safety, and, most importantly, the quality of care and instruction.

### DAYCARE

In Illinois, childcare centers are arranged in the following types:

- **Childcare Homes** are small facilities (in Illinois, eight or fewer children) which are run out of the house of the provider. The care here is more individualized and the setting more familiar than the larger centers, and the prices tend to be lower. Though some may advertise in neighborhood papers, many get their business through word of mouth; ask around your neighborhood or at work, or call your area childcare resource and referral agency. Childcare

resource and referral agencies typically recruit potential daycare home providers, and provide technical support and assistance to them (both in terms of start-up, and in maintaining a quality program).
- **Group Childcare Homes** are also run out of the house of the provider, but the number of children allowed is greater (up to twelve). These homes usually employ one or more assistants, along with the operator, to care for the children.
- **Childcare Centers** are what most people think of when they think "daycare." These are larger, more school-like facilities, which tend to be around much longer, though the staff may change. Because of the number of employees and the higher overhead required to operate a separate building, the prices are higher than daycare homes. Frequently there are waiting lists to get in, especially for the infant and toddler age groups. Many centers have a capacity in the range of 50 children, although some are larger, with space for around 100—or, in a few instances, 200—children.
- **License-Exempt Childcare** facilities are either too small (three children or fewer) to be regulated or are operated by non-profit organizations such as churches.
- **Non-Traditional Options,** such as religious institutions, and neighborhood churches and synagogues, often provide good care at a reasonable price, and you do not necessarily have to be a member. Universities, too, may offer quality preschool with fees on a sliding scale for the children of parents who are attending classes. Chicago Public Schools now offer some fee-based, all-day preschool programs in several neighborhood schools. Contact CPS for more information (see below under **Schools**). Parent Networks, which work like co-ops, offer great options for those in need of part-time childcare. Or, along the same lines, trading childcare time with friends can be a great, economical way to be a part-time caregiver while still working. Finally, of course, some parents use the informal option of care from relatives, most often a grandparent.

In Illinois, the state agency responsible for licensing and regulation of childcare centers and daycare family homes is the **Department of Children and Family Services (DCFS)**, a state agency whose primary function is investigating possible child abuse, child abuse prevention through parenting classes, family counseling, foster care, and adoption services. The Department of Children and Family Services also publishes two useful pamphlets: "A Message to Parents of Children in Day Care Centers," and "Child Care Choices." Both outline DCFS regulations regarding child-staff ratio, group size, and caregiver qualifications, as well as checklists of quality factors to look for in childcare programs, and the phone number of the Child Abuse Hotline. The "Child Care Choices" pamphlet also provides a list of Child Care Resource and Referral Agencies statewide (see below), and information on subsidized day care: eligibility standards, application procedures, and availability. For more about services in your area call one of the **Greater Chicago Area DCFS Offices**: City of Chicago, 312-814-8783; Aurora Region, 630-801-3400; Glen Ellyn, 630-790-6800; Joliet, 815-730-4000; Elgin, 847-888-7620; Round Lake, 847-546-0772; Woodstock, 815-338-1068; Tinley Park, 708-633-5300. Or call their daycare information hotline at 877-746-0829.

Child Care Resource and Referral Agencies offer a phone referral service to parents, usually for a small fee, where they discuss their childcare needs with them and send them a list of facilities meeting their criteria, along with helpful information on choosing childcare. Some companies, particularly large employers, may have a contract with their local Child Care Resource and Referral Agency to provide referrals to employees in need of this service. Childcare Resource and Referral Agencies, and county offices, include:

- Cook County, 312-823-1100
- DuPage and Kane Counties, 630-790-8137
- Lake County, 847-662-4247
- McHenry County, 815-344-5510
- Will County, 815-741-1163
- YWCA of Metro Chicago, 312-372-6600, www.ywcachicago.org; phone numbers vary by site
- United Way of Will County, 815-723-2500
- Child Care Aware, 800-424-2246, childcareaware.org

State licensing standards are as follows:

- **Staff/Child Ratios** for childcare centers: 4:1 (infants to 15 months); 5:1 (toddlers to 2 years); 8:1 (2 years); 10:1 (3–4 years); 20:1 (5 years and up).
- **Maximum Group Size** for childcare centers: 12 (infants to 15 months); 15 (toddlers to 2 years); 16 (2 years); 20 (3–4 years, 5 years and kindergarten); 30 (school-age).
- **Teacher Qualifications** for childcare centers: directors must be at least 21 years of age with 2 years of college including 18 semester hours of child development or equivalent experience and credentials. **Childcare workers** (**lead teachers**) must be at least 19 years of age with two years of college including six hours of child development or equivalent experience and credentials. **Teacher assistants** or **aides** must have a high school diploma, or equivalent, and work under the direct supervision of a teacher.
- **Training requirements:** beyond the above-mentioned qualifications, 15 hours of in-service training each year for each staff member is required. A staff member trained in first aid, CPR, and the Heimlich maneuver must be on the premises at all times.

## ONLINE RESOURCES—DAYCARE

Several helpful online agencies and organizations can assist with the details of finding quality childcare, a good school, etc., in communities across the United States. Care Guide (https://careguide.com) offers assistance to those needing childcare or eldercare. This free service provides pertinent care-related news articles and advice. The Office of Child Care (www.childcare.gov) provides links to other childcare sites on the web. Child Care Aware (800-424-2246) provides free referrals to childcare agencies in your community. ParentLink Information Services (www.metroprofiles.com) features capsule profiles of Chicagoland communities, giving names and contact information for childcare providers in each one.

## NANNIES

Probably the most expensive daycare option, with a monthly cost of $1,400 to $2,000+, is a full-time or live-in nanny, but if the right person is found this can be a rewarding experience for everyone involved. A number of nanny agencies exist in the Chicago area (some of which also provide other domestic services such as eldercare and housekeeping). An agency is also likely to investigate criminal and driving records and credit information. Be sure the nanny agency you use is licensed and bonded. Also, there are several childcare consultants locally who can assist families with background checks, tax issues, and other matters related to employing a nanny. If you prefer to have private screenings done of prospective nannies, Infotrack Information Services, Inc. (111 Deerlake Rd, Ste 105, Deerfield, IL 60015, 888-606-2010, www.infotrackinc.com) is a private investigative company that conducts background investigations for pre-employment screening. Their "nanny screening" includes checks of driving record, criminal record, and social security.

Nanny services around Chicago include:

- A+ Domestic, 6308 N Milwaukee Ave, 773-957-0500, www.apluschildcare.com
- American Registry for Nurses & Sitters, Inc., 866-964-0866 or 312-475-1515, www.americanregistry.com
- Childminders Inc., 4350 Oakton St, Ste 204, Skokie, IL 60076, 847-673-8998, www.childmindersinc.com
- Family Perfect Care, Inc., 773-545-5352, www.familyperfectcare.com
- Gold Coast Domestic Employment Agency, 3257 N Sheffield Ave, 773-525-4273, www.goldcoastagency.com
- Lakeview Domestic Agency, Inc., 3166 N Lincoln Ave, Ste 214, 773-404-8452
- Margaret's Employment Agency, 8632 W 145th St, Orland Park, 60462, 708-403-8707, http://margaretsagency.com (childcare and eldercare)

# CHILDCARE AND EDUCATION

- Midwest Nannies, LTD, 1358 Draper Rd, McHenry, 60050, 815-344-5899, www.midwestnanny.com
- Nanny Sitters, 200 W Higgins Rd, Ste 233, Schaumburg, IL 60195, 847-885-1700, www.nannysittersinc.com
- TeacherCare, 888-TEACH-07, 312-214-6411, www.teachercare.com
- Traycee Nannies, 448 Sheridan Rd, Highwood, IL 60040, 877-872-9233, www.traycee.com
- Village Nannies (Wilmette), 847-256-6162, www.villagenannies.com

The Northside Parents Network (1218 West Addison, Chicago, IL 60613, 312-476-9351, www.npnparents.org) offers a "nanny-share" program. This program is predominantly for member families who have hired a nanny independently (not through an agency), for, perhaps, three days a week, and will "share" the nanny with another family for the other two days. There are no fees involved.

Eisenberg Associates (800-777-5765, www.eisenbergassociates.com) offers health insurance and other fringe benefits for nannies.

## NANNY TAXES

For those hiring a nanny direct (not using a nanny agency) there are certain taxes that will need to be paid, specifically social security and Medicare, and possibly unemployment. For help with such issues, check with 4NannyTaxes (www.4nannytaxes.com, 800-NANITAX,) provider of household payroll and employment tax preparation services, or The Nanny Tax Company (www.nannytaxprep.com, 847-696-7260 or 800-747-9524). Or check the IRS's household employer page (www.irs.gov, topic 756), which discusses taxes for household employees.

## AU PAIRS

The US Information Agency oversees and approves the organizations which offer this service. Younger women (between 18 to 25) provide a year of in-home childcare and light housekeeping in exchange for airfare, room and board, and a small stipend ($150 to $225 per week). The program is certainly valuable for the cultural exchange that goes on between the host family and the (usually European) au pair. The downside is that the program only lasts one year and the au pairs don't have the life or work experience of a career nanny. Any of the following national agencies will connect you with a local coordinator who will match up your family with the right au pair.

- Au Pair in America, 800-928-7247 www.aupairinamerica.com
- Au Pair International, 888-649-2876, www.aupairint.com
- Au Pair USA, 212-924-0446, www.interexchange.org

- Cultural Care Au Pair, 800-333-6056, www.culturalcare.com
- EurAuPair, 1-800-333-3804, Ext 2, www.euraupair.com

## BABYSITTING

References from co-workers or friends are usually the best way to go when looking for a competent and reliable babysitter. The average range for babysitters is $8 to $10/hour. Many Park Districts offer babysitting classes to children ages 12 and up, and may be a source of referrals. Other organizations that will assist with locating a babysitter are nanny services and college job referral services, sometimes called the campus employment office. The Parent and Child Education and Support Society (PACES; headquartered at 1920 S Highland Ave, Lombard, IL 60148, 630-916-3190, www.pacesinfo.org, and with chapters across the Chicago area) includes babysitting co-ops among its programs and services. The Northside Parents Network (see above; 312-476-9351) also runs a babysitting co-op.

## CHILD SAFETY

National as well as local resources are available for parents looking to make their child's new environment safer. The Board of Health (312-747-9428) provides safety pamphlets, especially with regard to lead paint in older homes. The local SAFE KIDS chapter, a national organization dedicated solely to preventing accidental injuries to children, is SAFE KIDS Chicago (www.safekids.org). The Children's Memorial Hospital is the coalition leader for the Chicago area. It teaches children and caregivers about bicycle helmets, child safety seats and seat belts, fire and burn prevention, and other ways to keep children safe from injury. Other local hospitals host emergency training classes (infant and child CPR). Local companies offering home safety inspections and products include A & H Child Proofers in Northbrook, IL (847-650-2519, www.ahchildproofers.com) and Safety Matters (444 Lake Cook Rd, Ste 14, Deerfield, IL 60015, 800-9SAFE06, www.safetymatters.com). A list of Chicago-area child-safety-seat inspection sites is available at www.nhtsa.gov (National Highway Traffic Safety Administration).

## GENERAL RESOURCES

- **Child Care Connections** offers a 280-page spiral-bound book with detailed listings of nearly 1,000 child care centers and preschool programs in the Greater Chicago Area. Available for $24.95 from ParentLink Information Services, 1674 Cumberland, Aurora, IL 60504, 630-499-5810, www.metroprofiles.com. If you provide an e-mail address, you will also receive the book electronically (as Word files) at no extra cost.

# CHILDCARE AND EDUCATION

- The **Northside Parents Network**, 1218 W Addison, Chicago, IL 60613, 312-476-9351, www.npnparents.org, is a group of around 650 parents that offers babysitting co-ops, playgroups, a new moms group, a "nanny-share" program (see above), and parenting advice. They put out a newsletter as well as an excellent information booklet that profiles local schools (both public and private).
- **Parent and Child Education and Support Society (PACES)**, PACES; headquartered at 1920 S Highland Ave, Lombard, IL 60148, 630-916-3190, www.pacesinfo.org, has chapters throughout the Chicago area, offering a variety of programs, seminars, publications, and services such as babysitting co-ops. Memberships are available, though their meetings and many of their events and programs are open to the public.
- *Chicago Parent* magazine (and *Valley Kids*, its counterpart in the far-west suburbs along the Fox River); published monthly, the magazine contains articles on child- and family-related issues, a directory of events across the area, and special sections or separate publications (published annually at various times of the year) including *Chicago Baby*, *Going Places*, *Healthy Child*, *Healthy Woman*, *Camp Guide*, and *School Guide*. *Chicago Parent* is available free of charge at libraries, park districts, and some childcare centers, retail stores, and doctor's offices throughout the area. Subscriptions are also available, call 708-386-5555. *Chicago Parent* is online at www.chicagoparent.com.

## SCHOOLS

There are approximately 2,000 public and private schools in the greater Chicago area. To check out the range of religious and secular private schools, you will need a guidebook or plenty of time to surf the web, but even enrolling your children in public school might warrant some scouting beyond your neighborhood school. The public school systems in the City of Chicago, and in a few suburban districts, offer a growing range of choices, with the proliferation of magnet programs and public charter schools.

## SCHOOL RESOURCES

Before you begin your search, you might want to first collect as much printed information as possible. Begin with the following resources:

- "**School District Reports**" (school district information including curriculum, programs and test score data), and "**School's In—Chicago**" (a 160-page book with detailed listings of private and parochial schools in the Greater Chicago Area, price $16.55); both are available from ParentLink Information Services,

1674 Cumberland, Aurora, IL 60504, 630-499-5810, www.metroprofiles.com/SICInfo.htm.
- **A Guide to Chicago-area Independent Schools**: online guide, www.independentschools.net, containing descriptions of about 30 member schools, including application deadlines and the availability or type of financial aid, transportation, summer school and before- and after-school programs. Their website has a brief overview of member schools in a chart form. Each listing has a link to a page with a more detailed description, as well as links to school websites and/or e-mail addresses when available.
- **The Northside Parents Network**, 1218 W Addison, Chicago IL 60613, 312-476-9351, www.npnparents.org, is a group of around 650 parents that offers babysitting co-ops, playgroups, a new moms group, and parenting advice. They put out a newsletter as well as an annual "School Information Booklet" that profiles local schools (both public and private), and offers guidelines for choosing a school for your child. The cost is $25 for members and $45 for non-members. You can also choose to get just the pre-school volume or the elementary school volume for $15 (members) or $25 (non-members) per volume.
- **School Match**, 614-890-1573, www.schoolmatch.com, offers a variety of school information. The website offers basic information including the name/address/phone of the school system, along with the grade range, enrollment, and number of full-time teachers and schools in a district at no charge. Prices for their school reports range from $10 to $97.50, according to the comprehensiveness of the report and whether it's ordered online or by phone or fax. Sample snapshots and school report cards are provided on the website.

## STATE OF ILLINOIS GUIDELINES AND FEES

Illinois schools are primarily funded through property and sales taxes. Reliance on local property taxes creates wide disparities in the amounts spent per pupil across the Chicago area. School districts that lack a substantial amount of commercial or industrial development, particularly in areas where property values are lower, can have high residential property tax rates, but still struggle to fund their schools adequately. Currently, many school districts are struggling financially. According to former Illinois State Board of Education Chairman Ron Gidwitz, "Most of our districts are faced with staggering financial problems and we must provide greater state support or they will continue to run deficits and be forced to cut vital programs necessary to help students achieve state standards as required by federal law." (See the Illinois State Board of Education's website for more, www.isbe.state.il.us.)

Some districts are having a hard time keeping up with the local growth and subsequent overcrowding. Districts across the region have cut programs and services (in areas often regarded as "peripheral," such as extracurricular activities, art, music, gifted education, etc.) in response to budgetary problems. In some cases, staffs have been reduced, resulting in larger class sizes.

Public schools in Illinois can, and do, charge an instructional fee (usually in the $50 to $100 range at the elementary school level, and somewhat higher for high schools). Extracurricular activities, particularly sports, often carry a "user fee," and high schools require the purchase of many of the textbooks (with a few exceptions the textbook loan program ends after 8th grade). Fees can be waived or reduced for families whose children qualify for the free or reduced rate lunch program (contact your local school district for specifics). Funding for special programs or equipment (field trips, computers, etc.) often comes through school-related organizations such as the Parent Teacher Association (PTA), and a district's Educational Foundation, both of which obtain money from dues, donations, and fundraising efforts.

All Illinois public schools use the Illinois School Achievement Test (ISAT) for grades K–8, and the Prairie State Assessment Exam (PSAE), which now includes the ACT, for grade 11. Students are assessed in the areas of reading, math, writing, science, and social studies. Student performance is grouped into four categories: Exceeds Standards, Meets Standards, Below Standards, and Academic Warning. The percentage of students in each category is included for individual schools, school districts, and for the entire state. Scores are recorded for all students in a school, as well as for subcategories such as race, ethnic background, limited English proficient, low-income, and students with disabilities. The "School Report Card" with the test scores and other school data, is available online at the Illinois State Board of Education's website, www.isbe.state.il.us. All school districts that have a website are required to post their district's information on their website (though this may take weeks or months beyond the state release of the scores in November). The school reports are also published as paper copies, available from school districts upon request (some districts charge a small fee to recover their printing costs).

For the City of Chicago Schools, check their website, www.cps.edu, for test score data as well as other information about the Chicago Public Schools. You can also call their main number, 773-553-1000.

## CHICAGO PUBLIC SCHOOLS

Chicago public schools have long suffered from a number of problems, including the poor physical condition of many schools, low educational achievement of students, as evidenced by poor test scores, and high drop-out rates at the high school level. In the mid-1990s, former Mayor Richard M. Daley and then-school chief Paul Vallas took direct control of the schools, and addressed chronic financial problems, repaired the worst physical conditions, and implemented and revised a number of initiatives designed to increase student achievement. Though problems persist, some schools have made considerable progress at increasing student academic achievement, in spite of the larger social and economic factors such as poverty and crime that impact the schools. To contact the Chicago Public Schools, write to Chicago School District 299, 125 South Clark Street, Chicago, IL 60603, call 773-553-1000, or access their website at www.cps.edu.

One of Chicago Public Schools' initiatives to enhance its educational program (which is also, not coincidentally, an attempt to keep students in the system that would likely enroll in private schools or leave the area all together), is the magnet school program. About three-quarters of Chicago's high schools offer magnet programs, as do just over half of the elementary and middle schools.

At the high school level, Whitney Young Magnet High School (773-534-7500, www.wyoung.org) provides a well-regarded six-year program, offering gifted and talented students a chance to move through course material at their own pace.

The Northside College Prep High School (773-534-3954, www.northside-prep.org) is a multi-million dollar facility that has attracted many applicants. Facilities include a swimming pool, outdoor stadium, science labs, computer labs, library, and art and music rooms. It's a college preparatory school and all core courses are offered at the honors and advanced placement level. The school offers a number of student services, including tutoring, health/wellness education, counseling, and service learning. Special Education services are available for students with diagnosed learning disabilities (LD), speech/language impairments (SPL), emotional/behavioral disorders (EBD), health impairments (OHI), and severe/profound cognitive delays (SPH). Northside College Prep has selective enrollment.

About 15 elementary schools are magnet schools, drawing pupils from throughout the City of Chicago. Elementary school magnet programs are arranged into "magnet clusters." Each magnet cluster consists of two to five neighborhood schools that together offer enhanced instruction in areas such as math/science, fine/performing arts, world language, and the International CPS Scholars and International Baccalaureate Middle School programs. Because these magnet programs are in place in neighborhood schools, children have a greater chance of taking advantage of these programs in schools close to where they live.

Magnet program information is available online at cpsmagnet.org or by calling 773-553-2060 and requesting a copy of the "Options for Knowledge" booklet. A computerized lottery system of selection is used for all magnet programs/schools, except for Classical Schools (magnet schools designed to provide a challenging liberal arts course of instruction for students with high academic potential), 7th/8th grade programs for academically talented students, International Baccalaureate Programs, and regional gifted centers, which have specific academic criteria for entrance. Schools for 7th/8th grade academically talented students, International Baccalaureate Programs, and Regional Gifted Centers provide full transportation; all others provide only restricted transportation (for residents living from 1.5 to 6 miles of the school). No transportation is provided for high school students. Applications are not required for admission to Advanced Placement, Education to Careers, and/or Bilingual Education Programs.

Another program initiative by the Chicago Public Schools is "Small Schools," which is either a "school within a school" or a freestanding building of no more than 350 students (elementary level) or 500 students (high school level). The aim is to provide a more personal, theme-based educational program that will improve the attendance, behavior, and achievement levels (grades) of enrolled students, particularly at the high school level. The school system is also addressing poor reading skills in the primary grades with a system-wide intensive reading program, focusing primarily on grades K–3.

The Chicago Public School System instituted local school councils some years ago as a way to provide the community, parents, and school personnel input into governing the local schools. While many local school councils operate successfully, others suffer from lack of participation, and, in a few instances, financial mismanagement.

## SCHOOL REGISTRATION

Public school enrollment/registration in Illinois is fairly simple, at least for neighborhood schools; policies vary for magnet school programs. You will need a proof of residency (such as a lease or closing papers on a house, and a recent utility bill in your name), and your child's birth certificate and immunization records. Medical and dental exams are required before entry into kindergarten, and again before high school. Immunizations (MMR, DPT, HIB, Hepatitis B, and now the chicken pox vaccine) are required prior to kindergarten entry, and a D/T booster before entering high school. Waivers to the requirement are possible for parents who object on religious grounds or whose child has a health condition putting him/her at risk from the immunization. To obtain a waiver, parents should check with the school district.

## SUBURBAN SCHOOLS

Suburban schools, in general, have a better reputation for educational quality than do the Chicago Public schools. Some districts, particularly in the southern Cook County region, are plagued by the same problems related to lower income levels that affect the city schools. Despite the day-to-day difficulties of funding, suburban schools in most areas offer consistent quality schooling.

## SCHOOL CONTACTS

### SUBURBAN COOK COUNTY

- **Arlington Heights School District 25,** 1200 S Dunton Ave, Arlington Heights, IL 60005, 847-758-4900, www.sd25.org
- **Arlington Township High School District 214,** 2121 S Goebbert Rd, Arlington Heights, IL 60005, 847-718-7600, www.d24.org
- **Avoca School District 37,** 2921 Illinois Rd, Wilmette, IL 60091, 847-251-3587, www.avoca37.org
- **Bannockburn School District 106,** 2165 Telegraph Rd, Bannockburn, IL 60015, 847-945-5909, www.bannockburnschool.org
- **Brookfield School District 95,** 3524 Maple Ave, Brookfield, IL 60513, 708-485-0606, www.district95.org
- **Blue Island/Alsip/Crestwood/Robbins: Cook County School District 130,** 12300 S Greenwood Ave, Blue Island, IL 60406, 708-385-6800, www.district130.org
- **Burbank School District 111 (elementary),** 7600 S Central Ave, Burbank, IL 60459, 708-496-0500; high school: Reavis/District 220, 6034 W 77th St, Burbank 708-599-7200; www.burbank.k12.il.us
- **Cook County School District 59,** 2123 S Arlington Heights Rd, Arlington Heights, IL 60005, 847-593-4300, www.ccsd59.org
- **Community High School District 218,** 10701 S Kilpatrick Ave, Oak Lawn, IL 60453, 708-424-2000, www.chsd218.org
- **Consolidated High School District 230,** 15100 S 94th Ave, Orland Park, IL 60462, 708-745-5203, www.d230.org
- **Des Plaines C.C. School District 62,** 777 E Algonquin Rd, Des Plaines, IL 60016, 847-824-1136, www.d62.org
- **East Prairie School District 73,** 3907 W Dobson St, Skokie, IL 60076, 847-673-1141, www.eps.n-cook.k12.il.us
- **Evanston/Skokie School District 65 (elementary),** 1500 McDaniel Ave, Evanston, IL 60201, 847-859-8000, www.district65.net
- **Evanston Township High School District 202,** 1600 Dodge Ave, Evanston, IL 60201, 847-424-7000, www.eths.k12.il.us
- **Evergreen Park School District 124 (elementary),** 9400 S Sawyer, 708-423-0950, www.d124.org; **Evergreen Park Community High School District 231,** 9901 S Kedzie Ave, Evergreen Park, IL 60805, 708-424-7400, www.evergreenpark.org
- **Flossmoor School District 161,** 41 E Elmwood Dr, Chicago Heights, IL 60411, 708-647-7000, www.sd161.org
- **Glenbrook High Schools District 225,** 3801 W Lake Ave, Glenview, IL 60026, 847-998-6100, www.glenbrook225.org
- **Glencoe School District 35,** 620 Greenwood Ave, Glencoe, IL 60022, 847-835-7800, www.glencoeschools.org

- **Glenview C.C. School District 34,** 1401 Greenwood Rd, Glenview, IL 60026, 847-998-5000, www.glenview34.org; also see Northbrook School District
- **Golf School District 67,** 9401 Waukegan Rd, Morton Grove, IL 60053, 847-966-8200, www.golf67.net
- **Highland Park District 113,** 1040 Park Ave West, Highland Park, IL 60035, 224-765-1000, www.dist113.org; **North Shore School District 112,** 1936 Green Bay Rd, Highland Park, 224-765-3000, www.nssd112.org; **Northern Suburban Special Education District,** 760 Red Oak Ln, Highland Park, 847-831-5100
- **Homewood School District 153,** 18205 Aberdeen St, Homewood, IL 60430, 708-799-8721, www.homewoodsd153.org
- **Homewood-Flossmoor High School District 233,** 999 Kedzie Ave, Flossmoor, IL 60422, 708-799-3000, www.hfhighschool.org
- **Indian Prairie School District 204,** 780 Shoreline Dr, Aurora, 630-375-3000, ipsdweb.ipsd.org
- **Kenilworth Elementary District 38 – Sears School,** 542 Abbotsford Rd, Kenilworth, IL 60043, 847-256-5006, www.kenilworth38.org
- **La Grange Highlands School District 106,** 1750 W Plainfield Rd, La Grange, IL 60525, 708-246-3085, www.district106.net
- **La Grange School District 102,** 333 N Park Rd, La Grange Park, IL 60526, 708-482-2400, www.dist102.k12.il.us
- **La Grange School District 105 (South),** 701 S Seventh Ave, La Grange, IL 60525, 708-482-2700, www.d105.w-cook.k12.il.us
- **Leyden High School District 212,** 3400 Rose St, Franklin Park, IL 60131, 708-451-3000, www.leyden212.org
- **Lyons Township District 204,** 100 S Brainard Ave, La Grange, IL 60525, 708-579-6300, www.lths.net
- **Maine Township District 207,** 1131 S Dee Rd, Park Ridge, IL 60068, 847-696-3600, www.maine207.org
- **Morton Grove School District 70,** 6200 Lake St, Morton Grove, IL 60053, 847-965-6200, www.mgsd70.org
- **New Trier High School District 203,** 7 Happ Rd (Administration, grade 9), Northfield IL 60093; 385 Winnetka Ave (grades 10–12), Winnetka, IL 60093, 847-446-7000 (both campuses), www.newtrier.k12.il.us
- **Niles School District 71,** 6921 W Oakton St, Niles, IL 60714, 847-966-9280, www.culver71.net
- **Niles Township School District 219,** 7700 Gross Point Rd, Skokie, IL 60077, 847-626-3000, www.niles-hs.k12.il.us
- **North Palos School District 117,** 7825 W 103rd St, Palos Hills, IL 60465, 708-598-5500, www.npd117.net
- **Northbrook School District 27,** 1250 Sanders Rd, Northbrook, IL 60062, 847-498-2610, www.northbrook27.k12.il.us

- **Northbrook School District 28,** 1475 Maple Ave, Northbrook, IL 60062, 847-498-7900, northbrook28.net
- **Northbrook-Glenview School District 30,** 2374 Shermer Rd, Northbrook, IL 60062, 847-498-4190, www.district30.k12.il.us
- **Oak Forest, Arbor Park District 145,** 17301 Central Ave, Oak Forest, IL 60452, 708-687-8040 (elementary), www.arbor145.org; Bremen High School District 228, 15233 S Pulaski Rd, Midlothian, IL 60445, 708-389-1775, www.bhsd228.com; also check Tinley Park High School.
- **Oak Lawn Community High School District 229,** 9400 SW Hwy, Oak Lawn, IL 60453, 708-424-5200, www.olchs.org
- **Oak Lawn–Hometown District 123,** 4201 W 93rd St, Oak Lawn, IL 60453, 708-423-0150, www.d123.org
- **Oak Park and River Forest School District 200,** 201 N Scoville Ave, Oak Park, IL 60302, 708-383-0700, www.oprfhs.org
- **Oak Park Elementary School District 97,** 970 W Madison St, Oak Park, IL 60302, 708-524-3000, www.op97.org
- **Orland Park School District 135,** 15100 S 94th Ave, Orland Park, IL 60462, 708-364-3300, www.orland135.org
- **Palos Heights School District 128,** 12809 S McVickers Ave, Palos Heights, IL 60463, 708-597-9040, www.d128.k12.il.us
- **Palos School District 118,** 8800 W 119th St, Palos Park, IL 60464, 708-448-4800, www.palos118.org
- **Park Ridge–Niles School District 64,** 164 S Prospect Ave, Park Ridge, IL 60068, 847-318-4300, www.d64.org
- **River Forest School District 90,** 7776 W Lake St, River Forest, IL 60305, 708-771-8282, www.district90.org
- **Riverside-Brookfield Township High School District 208,** 160 Ridgewood Rd, Riverside, IL 60546, 708-442-7500, www.rbhs208.net
- **Rosemont School District 78,** 6101 N Ruby St, Rosemont, IL 60018, 847-825-0144, www.rosemont78.org
- **Schaumburg School District 54,** 524 E Schaumburg Rd, Schaumburg, IL 60194, 847-357-5000, sd54.org; Township High School District 211, 1750 Roselle Rd, Palatine, 847-755-6600, www.d211.org
- **Skokie Fairview School District 72,** 7040 Laramie Ave, Skokie, IL 60077, 847-929-1048, www.fairview.k12.il.us
- **Skokie School District 68,** 9440 Kenton Ave, Skokie, IL 60076, 847-676-9000, www.skokie68.org
- **Skokie–Morton Grove School District 69,** 5050 Madison St, Skokie, IL 60077, 847-675-7666, www.skokie69.k12.il.us
- **Skokie School District 73½,** 8000 E Prairie Rd, Skokie, IL 60076, 847-324-0509, www.sd73½.org
- **Sunset Ridge School District 29,** 525 Sunset Ridge Rd, Northfield, IL 60093, 847-881-9400, www.sunsetridge29.net

# CHILDCARE AND EDUCATION

- **Tinley Park: C.C. School District 146 (elementary),** 6611 W 171st St, Tinley Park, IL 60477, 708-614-4500, www.ccsd146.k12.il.us; **Kirby School District 140 (elementary),** 16931 S Grissom Dr, Tinley Park, 708-532-6462, www.ksd140.org; **Bremen High School District 228,** 708-389-1175, www.bhsd228.com (also see Oak Forest and Orland Park information)
- **Township High School District 211,** 1750 S Roselle Rd, Palatine, IL 60067, 847-755-6600, www.d211.org
- **West Northfield School District 31,** 3131 Techny Rd, Northbrook, IL 60062, 847-272-6880, www.dist31.k12.il.us
- **Wilmette School District 39,** 615 Locust Rd, Wilmette, IL 60091, 847-256-2450, www.wilmette39.org (elementary), www.newtrier.k12.il.us (high school)
- **Winnetka School District 36,** 1235 Oak St, Winnetka, IL 60093, 847-446-9400, www.winnetka36.org

## LAKE COUNTY

- **Deerfield School District 109,** 517 Deerfield Rd, Deerfield, IL 60015, 847-945-1844, www.dps109.org
- **Highland Park Township High School District 113,** 1040 W Park Ave, Highland Park, IL 60035, 224-765-1000, www.dist113.org
- **North Shore School District 112,** 1936 Green Bay Rd, Highland Park, IL 60035, 224-765-3000, www.nssd112.org

## DUPAGE COUNTY

- **Bolingbrook (Will and DuPage Counties), Valley View School District,** 755 Dalhart Ave, Romeoville, IL 60446, 815-886-2700 (administration) www.vvsd.org
- **Butler School District 53,** 2801 York Rd, Oak Brook, IL 60523, 630-573-2887, www.butler53.com
- **Community High School District 99,** 6301 Springside Ave, Downers Grove, IL 60516, 630-795-7100, www.csd99.org
- **Downers Grove School District 58 (elementary and middle school),** 1860 63rd St, 630-719-5800, www.dg58.org; Community High School District 99, 6301 Springside Ave, 630-795-7100, www.csd99.org
- **Glen Ellyn Community School District 89,** 22W600 Butterfield Rd, Glen Ellyn, 630-469-8900, www.ccsd89.org
- **Hinsdale School/Community Consolidated School District 181,** 6010 S Elm St, Burr Ridge, IL 60527, 630-887-1070, www.d181.org
- **Hinsdale Township High School District 86,** 5500 S Grant St, Hinsdale, IL 60521, 630-655-6100, www.hinsdale86.org
- **Indian Prairie School District 204,** 780 Shoreline Dr, Aurora, IL 60504, 630-375-3000, ipsdweb.ipsd.org
- **Lisle C.U. School District 202,** 5211 Center Ave, Lisle, IL 60532, 630-493-8000, www.lisle.dupage.k12.il.us

- **Lombard School District 44,** 150 W Madison St, Lombard, IL 60148, 630-827-4400, www.sd44.org
- **Naperville C.U. School District 203,** 203 W Hillside, Naperville, IL 60540, 630-420-6300, www.naperville203.org
- **Westmont C.U. District 201,** 133 S Grant St, Westmont, IL 60559, 630-468-8000, www.cusd201.org
- **Wheaton/Warrenville Community School District 200,** 130 W Park Ave, Wheaton, 630-682-2000, www.cusd200.org; Community School District 89, 22W600 Butterfield Rd, Glen Ellyn, 630-469-8900, www.ccsd89.org

KANE COUNTY
- **Aurora East Unit School District 131,** 441 N Farnsworth Ave, Aurora, IL 60506, 630-299-5900, www.d131.org
- **Aurora West Unit School District 129,** 80 S River St, Aurora, IL 60506, 630-301-5000, www.sd129.org

## SPECIAL EDUCATION

All public schools provide special education and related support services (speech, physical and occupational therapy, counseling) to children ages 3–21 who have special needs. The core of the special education system is the Individual Education Plan (IEP), which determines where the child will be placed (regular education classroom, special education class in the regular school, special school, etc.) and what services he or she will receive (for babies and toddlers, this is called the Individual Family Service Plan or IFSP). Parents can request testing of their child, or school personnel can recommend it and then proceed only with parental permission. Parents who disagree with the type of placement and/or level of services proposed can obtain private testing of their child (at the parents' expense), and have outside professionals (such as a therapist) accompany them to the IEP conference.

    Virtually all school districts provide screenings of preschoolers for developmental delay, annually and/or by appointment. Many districts band together into special education co-ops to provide services to children with less common ("low-incidence") conditions such as Autism, Blindness, Deafness, Multiple Handicaps, etc., for which a small district may have too few children to operate an entire classroom, or employ full-time therapists, independently. Participating districts in each co-op provide classroom space and other support for the special education students in their districts. Early intervention services for children, birth to three years, are now available through some of the special education co-ops and through some private therapy agencies, such as Easter Seals.

# CHILDCARE AND EDUCATION

- **Aero Special Education Co-op,** 7600 S Mason Ave, Burbank, IL, 708-496-3330, www.aerosped.org
- **Cooperative Association for Special Education (CASE),** 22W600 Butterfield Rd, Glen Ellyn, IL 60137, 630-942-5600, www.casedupage.com; serves: DuPage County School Districts 15, 16, 41, 44, 87, 89, and 93 (Glen Ellyn, Glendale Heights, Lombard, Carol Stream)
- **DuPage West Cook Low Incidence Programs,** 6 S 331 Cornwall Rd, Naperville, IL 60540, 630-778-4500, www.sased.org; serves: DuPage and Western Cook Counties. Services for children with vision, hearing, and physical disabilities (SASED Highland Hills School program); testing for children birth to three
- **East DuPage Special Education District (EDSED),** 1110 S Villa Ave, Villa Park, IL 60181, 630-279-4726 or 630-617-2647; serves school districts 4, 45, 88, and 205 (Addison, Villa Park, Elmhurst)
- **La Grange Area Department of Special Education (LADSE),** 1301 W Cossitt Ave, La Grange, IL, 708-354-5730, www.ladse.org; serves DuPage County School Districts 53, 61, 62, 86, 181 (Hinsdale, Oakbrook, Burr Ridge, Darien, Clarendon Hills); Western Cook County School Districts 94, 95, 96, 101, 102, 103, 105, 106, 107, 204, 208 (La Grange, Riverside, North Riverside, Brookfield, Lyons)
- **Niles Township Department of Special Education (NTDSE),** 8701 Menard Ave, Morton Grove, IL, 847-965-9040, www.ntdse.org; includes school district 68 and 69 in Skokie
- **North DuPage Special Education Cooperative (NDSEC),** 255 E Lake St, Bloomingdale, IL, 630-894-0490, www.ndsec.org; serves school districts 2, 7, 10, 11, 12, 13, 100, 108 (Roselle, Itasca, Bensenville, Medinah, Wood Dale, Bloomingdale)
- **Northern Suburban Special Education District (NSSED),** 760 Red Oak Ln, Highland Park, IL, 847-831-5100, www.nssed.org; serves school districts 27, 28, 29, 30, 31, 34, 35, 36, 37, 38, 39, 65, 67, 106, 109, 112, 113, 203, 225 (Deerfield, Glenview, Glencoe, Highland Park, Kenilworth, Lake Forest, Lake Bluff, Northbrook, Northfield, Wilmette, Winnetka). Programs and services for children, birth to 21. Early childhood (birth to three) services provided in collaboration with Glenkirk (3504 Commercial Ave in Northbrook, 847-272-5111)
- **Proviso Area for Exceptional Children (PAEC),** 1000 Van Buren St, Maywood, IL, 708-450-2100, paec803.org
- **School Association for Special Education in DuPage County (SASED),** 6 S 331 Cornwall Rd, Naperville, IL, 630-778-4500, www.sased.org; serves School Districts 20, 25, 33, 34, 58, 60, 63, 66, 68, 69, 94, 99, 180, 201, 202 (Lisle, Westmont, West Chicago, Winfield, Downers Grove, Darien, Clarendon Hills)
- **Southwest Cook Cooperative,** 6020 W 151st St, Oak Forest, IL, 708-687-0900, www.swcccase.org
- **Special Education District of Lake County (SEDOL),** 18160 Gages Lake Rd, Gages Lake, IL, 60030, 847-548-8470, www.sedol.k12.il.us; 37 member school districts in Lake County

- **Special Education District of McHenry County (SEDOM),** 1200 Claussen Dr, Woodstock, IL, 815-338-3622, www.sedom.org; school districts: 3, 11, 12, 13, 15, 18, 26. 36. 46, 47, 50, 154, 155, 156, 157, 158, 165, 200 (Fox River Grove, Spring Grove, Richmond, Johnsburg, McHenry, Alden-Hebron, Cary, Harrison, Crystal Lake, Harvard, Marengo, Union, Huntley, Woodstock). Classes in districts in Cary, Crystal Lake, Huntley, Johnsburg, McHenry, Union, and Woodstock
- **SPEED Coop (Special Education Joint Agreement #802),** 1125 Division St, Chicago Heights, IL, 708-481-6100, www.speed820.org; programs for children and families from birth to 21; school districts: 144, 153, 161, 162, 163, 167, 168, 169, 170, 172, 194, 201U, 206, 207, 233 (South Suburbs including Markham, Homewood, Flossmoor, Park Forest, Glenwood, Sauk Village, Ford Heights, Chicago Heights, Park Ridge, Harvey, Steger, Crete, Olympia Fields, Hazel Crest, Matteson)

## SPECIAL EDUCATION SCHOOLS

Special education schools serve children with a variety of special needs, including learning disabilities, hearing impairment, mental retardation, autism, and emotional/behavioral problems. In some instances, such as when a child is placed at the school as mandated by his or her Individual Education Plan (IEP) as the only program that can meet his/her needs, the referring district picks up the costs. Some Special Education Schools in the Greater Chicago Area:

- **Acacia Academy,** 6425 S Willow Springs Rd, La Grange, IL 60525, 708-579-9040, www.acaciaacademy.com
- **Alexander Graham Bell Montessori School,** 9300 Capitol Dr, Wheeling, IL 60090, 847-850-5490, www.agbms.org
- **The Bridge High School,** 2318 Wisconsin Ave, Downers Grove, IL 60515, 630-964-1722, www.littlefriendsinc.com
- **Cove School,** 350 Lee Rd, Northbrook, IL 60062, 847-562-2100, www.coveschool.org
- **Chicago City Day School,** 541 W Hawthorne Pl, Chicago, IL 60657, 773-327-0900, www.chicagocitydayschool.org
- **Elim Christian School,** 13020 S Central Ave, Palos Heights, IL 60463, 708-389-0555, www.elimcs.org
- **Gateway to Learning School,** 4825 N Lincoln Ave, Chicago, IL 60625, 773-784-3200, www.gtlchicago.com
- **Krejci Academy,** 619 E Franklin Ave, Naperville, IL 60540, 630-355-6870, www.littlefriendsinc.com/programs_krejci.cfm
- **Shore Lois Lloyd Center,** 2525 Church St, Evanston, IL 60076, 847-869-6610

## PAROCHIAL SCHOOLS

Many parents, out of concern for the quality of the public schools, or other reasons, consider alternative schooling for their children. For them, there are several options, including parochial schools, Montessori and Waldorf schools, and college-prep programs.

## CATHOLIC SCHOOLS

The Catholic school system is the largest non-public system in the Chicago area. While, due to low enrollment, the Archdiocese of Chicago has closed some schools, mostly on the south and west sides of Chicago, Catholic schools remain a viable alternative to the public schools for many parents. Average tuition at the grade school level is in the range of $2,500 for one child, while high school tuition and fees run around $3,500 to $4,000, on average. The Archdiocese of Chicago is currently looking into the financial feasibility of opening a new co-ed Catholic high school in the Southwest Cook County suburb of Orland Park. The Office of Catholic Education, Archdiocese of Chicago, which serves Catholic schools in the City of Chicago, and suburban Cook and Lake Counties, provides an online Catholic School Directory, which can be searched by area, ZIP code, or city, at http://schools.archdiocese-chgo.org. The **Archdiocese of Joliet School Directory**, 815-838-2181, www.dioceseofjoliet.org/cso serves the Catholic schools in DuPage, Will, and Kankakee Counties.

Sampling of **Catholic schools in Chicago**:

- **Brother Rice High School,** 10001 S Pulaski Rd, Chicago, IL 60655, 773-429-4300, www.brotherrice.org
- **Cristo Rey Jesuit High School,** 1852 W 22nd Pl, Chicago, IL 60608, 773-890-6800, www.cristorey.net
- **Marist High School,** 4200 W 115th St, Chicago, IL 60655, 773-881-5300, www.marist.net
- **Mother McAuley Liberal Arts High School,** 3737 W 99th St, Chicago, IL 60655, 773-881-6500, www.mothermcauley.org
- **Mt. Carmel High School,** 6410 S Dante Ave, Chicago, IL 60637, 773-324-1020, www.mchs.org
- **St. Ignatius College Prep,** 1076 W Roosevelt Rd, Chicago, IL 60608, 312-421-5900, www.ignatius.org
- **St. Juliana School,** 7400 W Touhy Ave, Chicago, IL 60631, 773-631-2256, www.stjuliana.org
- **St. Patrick High School,** 5900 W Belmont Ave, Chicago, IL 60634, 773-282-8844, www.stpatrick.org
- **St. Rita of Cascia High School,** 7740 S Western Ave, Chicago, IL 60620, 773-925-6600, http://stritahs.com

## OTHER RELIGIOUS SCHOOLS

To find a private school in your area, check the Yellow Pages, under "Schools," for listings. For Jewish schools you might first contact the Community Foundation for Jewish Education (CFJE) of Metropolitan Chicago, www.cfje.org. Those interested in Lutheran schooling should go to www.goodnewsfund.org/pages/schoollist.asp or www.lcms.org (for Missouri Synod). There are several Islamic schools operating in the Chicago area, including the Islamic Foundation School in Villa Park (300 West Highridge Road, 630-941-8800, www.islamicfoundation.org), and in Bridgeview, the Universal School (7350 West 93rd Street, 708-599-4100, www.universalschool.org), and AQSA (7361 West 92nd Street, 708-598-2700, www.aqsa.edu).

## PRIVATE SCHOOLS

Private schools in the Chicago area are mostly non-sectarian, and provide what most people think of as a good, "well-rounded" education. Some programs have a special emphasis on a particular area of the curriculum, such as foreign language or fine arts. The independent schools tend to be expensive, with tuition in some cases around $10,000 or more annually, especially at the high school level. Two such private programs include The Latin School of Chicago and Francis Parker School in Lincoln Park. The Latin School of Chicago (59 West North Boulevard, Chicago, IL 60610, 312-582-6000, www.latinschool.org) was founded in 1888, and serves grades K–12. The school emphasizes an interdisciplinary curriculum at all levels, and features foreign language instruction starting in junior kindergarten. The Upper School (high school) provides a college preparatory curriculum, and features an interdisciplinary humanities class for ninth-graders. Facilities at the Middle/Upper School include a middle school center, two gymnasiums, a performing arts center, and a 19,000-volume, online library complex. The Lower School features an early childhood learning center, gymnasium and play/performance space, a rooftop playground, and a library. Francis Parker School (330 West Webster Avenue, Chicago, IL 60614, 773-353-3000, www.fwparker.org) was founded in 1901, and serves grades K–12 with a lower school for grades K–5, a middle school for grades 6–8, and a high school for grades 9–12. Located on 5.2 acres on the near North Side of Chicago, the school features three gymnasiums, a science center, a large auditorium, a conference center, an outdoor playground, an athletic field, and a new library. The school seeks diversity among its student body in terms of students' economic, cultural, and social backgrounds, and requires student involvement in social service activities. An after-school program (Parker PM) is available for grades K–5. Those looking for a private fine arts school in Chicago should check the Chicago Academy for the Arts, located at 1010 West Chicago Avenue, 312-421-0202.

Additional **private independent schools in Greater Chicago** include:

# CHILDCARE AND EDUCATION

- **Baker Demonstration School,** 201 Sheridan Rd, Wilmette, IL 60091, 847-425-5800, www.bakerdemschool.org
- **The Catherine Cook School,** 226 W Schiller St, Chicago, IL 60610, 312-266-3381, www.catherinecookschool.org
- **The Chicago City Day School,** 541 W Hawthorne Pl, Chicago, IL 60657, 773-327-0900, www.chicagocitydayschool.org
- **Hinsdale Adventist Academy,** 631 E Hickory St, Hinsdale, IL 60521, 630-323-9211, www.haa.org
- **Lake Forest Academy,** 1500 W Kennedy Rd, Lake Forest, IL 60045, 847-234-3210, www.lfanet.org
- **Lake Forest Country Day School,** 145 S Green Bay Rd, Lake Forest, IL 60045, 847-234-2350, www.lfcds.org
- **Lake Shore Schools,** 6759 N Greenview, Chicago, IL 60626, 773-561-6707,
- www.lake-shore-schools.com
- **Lycee Francais de Chicago,** 613 W Bittersweet Pl, Chicago, IL 6013, 773-665-0066, www.lyceechicago.org
- **Morgan Park Academy,** 2153 W 111th St, Chicago, IL 60643, 773-881-6700, www.morganparkacademy.org
- **North Park Elementary School,** 2017 W Montrose, Chicago, IL 60618, 773-327-3144, www.npeschool.org
- **North Shore Country Day School,** 310 Green Bay Rd, Winnetka, IL 60093, 847-446-0674, www.nscds.org
- **Plato Academy,** 733 Lee St, Des Plaines, IL 60016, 857-768-7188, www.platoacademy.org
- **Roycemore School,** 1200 Davis St, Evanston, IL 60201, 847-866-6055, www.roycemoreschool.org
- **The Willows Academy,** 1012 E Thacker St, Des Plaines, IL 60016, 847-824-6900, www.willowsacademy.org

## PRIVATE GIFTED SCHOOLS

- **Avery Coonley School,** 1400 Maple Ave, Downers Grove, IL 60515, 630-969-0800, www.averycoonley.org
- **Quest Academy,** 500 N Benton St, Palatine, IL 60067, 847-202-8035, www.questacademy.org
- **Science & Arts Academy,** 1825 Miner St, Des Plaines, IL 60016, 847-827-7880, www.scienceandartsacademy.org

## MONTESSORI

Montessori schools follow the hands-on educational philosophy of Maria Montessori, and use specified Montessori materials in their schools. Most Montessori schools in the United States are members of the American Montessori Society and are accredited by, or affiliated with them. All teachers in accredited Montessori schools are Montessori-trained and certified. For a complete list of over a dozen Montessori Schools in the greater Chicago area—including locations in Rogers Park (www.rpmschool.org) and Beverly (www.beverlymontessori.org)—visit the American Montessori Society's website at www.amshq.org, or check the Yellow Pages under "Schools" for listings.

## WALDORF

Waldorf schools are based on the educational philosophy and instructional methods of Rudolph Steiner, which emphasize the importance of the arts in the curriculum. The website of the Association of Waldorf Schools in America (www.awsna.org) goes into detail about the Waldorf philosophy and curriculum, and has links to other Waldorf-related websites. Waldorf schools in the Greater Chicago Area include Chicago Waldorf School (grades pre-K–12; 1300 West Loyola Avenue, Chicago, IL 60626, 773-465-2662, www.chicagowaldorf.org) and Four Winds Waldorf School (pre-K–8; 30 West 160 Calumet Avenue, Warrensville, IL 60555, 630-836-9400, www.fourwindswaldorf.org).

## HOMESCHOOLING

Some parents prefer to educate their children at home. In Illinois, homeschools are considered to be private schools, and the only state requirements are that children are taught, in English, the same broad subjects as are taught in the public school curriculum. Curriculum and other resources for homeschoolers are available online on websites such as Homeschool World (www.homeschool.com), which provides news articles, information, resources and notices of events related to homeschooling. Chicago area homeschooling organizations include:

- **A.K. Nuni-Hudson, Interfaith Home Education,** 986 Grand Ave, Aurora, IL 60506, lurningathome@aol.com
- **CHESS of Illinois,** 129 Webb St, Calumet City, IL 60409
- **Christian Home Educators Coalition (CHEC) of Illinois,** P.O. Box 34885, Chicago, IL 60634, 773-278-0673
- **Christian Home-Oriented Individualized Curriculum Experience (CHOICE),** P.O. Box 425, Wheaton, IL 60189
- **Grassroots Homeschoolers,** www.grassrootshomeschoolers.com
- **Illinois Christian Home Educators,** PO Box 307, Russell, IL 60075, 847-603-1259, www.iche.org

# CHILDCARE AND EDUCATION

- **Islamic Homeschool Education Network,** 241 Meadowbrook Dr, Bolingbrook, IL 60440
- **Kane County Christian Home Schoolers,** P.O. Box 48, Sugar Grove, IL 60554, jjmew4@yahoo.com
- **Northside Unschoolers Group,** 5051 W Belle Plaine, Chicago, IL 60641, 708-524-1262, www.northsideunschoolers.org
- **Restore Our Catholic Kids (ROCK),** 630-213-9167
- **Teaching Homes for Christ,** P.O. Box 113, W Chicago, IL 60186, info@teachinghomes.org, www.teachinghomes.org
- **Tri-County Christian Home Educators,** 40 W Timbercreek Dr, Yorkville, IL 60560, karlrpfizenmaierjr@prodigy.net
- www.homeschoolnewslink.com
- **Homeschool Resource Center,** www.fofchomeschool.org

This group is not Chicago-based, but may also be useful: **Muslim Home School Network & Resource** (**MHSNR**), P.O. Box 803, Attleboro MA, 02703

## HIGHER EDUCATION

Whether you are just getting started on your college degree, contemplating a second degree, or simply interested in taking continuing education courses, the colleges and universities in and around Chicago offer a wide range of options. Whether it's a doctorate in medieval history or a weekend pottery class, you can find it here. In addition, concerts, plays, lecture series, and many other cultural opportunities await you at these institutions of higher learning.

The following list of larger and better-known institutions is far from comprehensive. Please note that many area institutions have multiple campuses; institutions are listed under the location of their largest or most prominent Chicagoland campuses. Look in the Yellow Pages under "Schools—Universities and Colleges" for those in or close to your neighborhood.

### CHICAGO
- **City Colleges of Chicago,** 312-553-2500, www.ccc.edu; has seven campuses and twelve satellite locations throughout the city. A variety of two-year associate degrees are offered.
- **Chicago State University,** 773-995-2000, www.csu.edu; this far south side university offers 36 degree and certificate programs as well as 29 advanced degree and advanced study certificates.
- **Columbia College,** 312-663-1600, www.colum.edu; an art school that is highly regarded for its dance, film, writing, and photography programs.

- **DePaul University,** 312-362-8000, www.depaul.edu; Lincoln Park, Loop, and O'Hare Airport–area campuses. The largest Catholic university in the country, well known for its business and theater departments.
- **DeVry Institute of Technology,** 773-929-8500, www.devry.edu; Addison, Chicago, and Tinley Park campuses. Offers career-oriented programs such as business, information/computer technology, and engineering degrees.
- **Illinois Institute of Art,** 800-351-3450, www.artinstitutes.edu/chicago or www.artinstitutes.edu/schaumburg; courses in the visual arts, including game art and fashion merchandising; Chicago and Schaumburg campuses.
- **Illinois Institute of Technology,** 312-567-3000, www.iit.edu; Chicago, Wheaton, and Summit campuses. Wide range of technology-based academic certificate and degreed programs.
- **Loyola University,** 773-274-3000, www.luc.edu, is Chicago's other major Catholic university. Founded in 1870, it is located on the lake in East Rogers Park. If you live on the far North Side, this is a convenient place to take classes.
- **National Louis University,** 888-658-8632, www.nl.edu; Loop, Elgin, Skokie, and Lisle campus. Offers undergraduate through doctoral degrees—especially respected for its education programs.
- **Northeastern Illinois University,** 773-583-4050, www.neiu.edu; located in the city's far northwest corner, offers very reasonable tuition rates and a full complement of undergraduate degrees, as well as 38 graduate programs and schedules tailored to suit the schedules of nontraditional and working students, with many evening classes.
- **North Park University,** Chicago, 773-244-6200, www.northpark.edu; evangelical Christian university and seminary. Colleges include schools of nursing, business, education, and music.
- **Robert Morris College,** 1-800-762-5960, www.robertmorris.edu; Chicago, DuPage County, Orland Park, Bensenville, Lake County campuses. Career-designed programs and certificates.
- **Roosevelt University,** 847-619-7300, www.roosevelt.edu; Chicago Loop and Schaumburg campuses. Private, liberal arts college.
- **Saint Xavier University,** 773-298-3000, www.sxu.edu; Chicago and Orland Park campuses. Midsize liberal arts university offering undergraduate and graduate degrees, including well-respected programs in nursing and education.
- **School of the Art Institute of Chicago,** 312-629-6100, www.saic.edu; one of the nation's most highly regarded art schools. Though affiliated with the famous Art Institute museum, which is located just across Michigan Avenue, the school's course offerings aren't limited to painting and sculpture. Performance art, video, and poetry are just some of the fine arts options.
- **The University of Chicago (UofC),** 773-702-1234, www.uchicago.edu; the area's premier institution of higher learning. Founded in 1890 by John D. Rockefeller and located in Hyde Park, seven miles south of the Loop, its stern,

gothic campus is home to more Nobel Prize winners than any other educational institution in the world.
- **The University of Illinois at Chicago (UIC),** 312-996-7000, www.uic.edu; just west of downtown, UIC offers a variety of degree programs. It has a large, modern, and growing campus and is convenient to public transit and all major expressways.

### NORTH AND NORTHWEST SUBURBS
- **College of Lake County,** 847-543-2000, www.clcillinois.edu; offers 40 career-preparation programs in which students earn an associate degree or career certificates. Well known for its BA program for transfer students.
- **Harper College,** Palatine, 847-925-6707, www.harpercollege.edu; community college with branch campus in Prospect Heights. Strong IT and career-oriented certificate programs and degrees.
- **ITT Technical Institute,** 847-375-8800, www.itt-tech.edu; Burr Ridge, Mount Prospect, and Matteson campuses. Associate and bachelor degrees in such fields as IT, industrial design, electronics.
- **Kendall College,** Evanston, 888-905-3632, www.kendall.edu; offers career-oriented programs: hospitality management, human services, business and technology, culinary school, criminal justice management, and early childhood education.
- **Knowledge Systems Institute,** Skokie, 847-679-3135, www.ksi.edu; graduate school for computer information and sciences.
- **Lake Forest College,** Lake Forest, 847-234-3100, www.lfc.edu; private liberal arts college.
- **Northwestern University,** 847-491-3741, www.northwestern.edu, is a well-regarded private university whose main campus is in leafy Evanston. The downtown Chicago campus is home to its law, medical, and dental schools.
- **Oakton Community College,** Des Plaines, 847-635-1600, www.oakton.edu; career programs resulting in an AAS or certificate, and BA-oriented college transfer programs.
- **Shimer College,** Waukegan, 312-235-3500, www.shimer.edu; well-regarded, small liberal arts and science college with a "great books" curriculum.
- **Trinity International University,** Deerfield, 847-945-8800, www.tiu.edu; four-year college also offering master's degrees and doctorates in divinity and law.
- **Westwood College of Technology,** www.westwood.edu; River Oaks, DuPage, O'Hare, and Loop campuses. Computer-based technology and design programs, CAD, and engineering.

## WEST SUBURBS
- **Aurora University,** Aurora and Lake Geneva campuses, 630-892-6431, www.aurora.edu; undergraduate, graduate and doctoral programs.
- **Elmhurst College,** Elmhurst, 630-617-3500, public.elmhurst.edu; private, four-year college affiliated with the United Church of Christ.
- **Northern Illinois University,** 815-753-1000, www.niu.edu, is primarily a commuter school located in DeKalb. Part of the state university system, nearly 25,000 students attend this affordable institution best known for its teacher-training program.
- **Wheaton College,** Wheaton, 630-752-5000, www.wheaton.edu; well-regarded interdenominational Christian college. Strong music, theology, education, and psychology departments.

## SOUTH AND SOUTHWEST SUBURBS
- **Benedictine University,** Lisle, 630-829-6000, www.ben.edu. Catholic liberal arts college that prides itself on its campus diversity.
- **College of DuPage,** Glen Ellyn, 630-942-2800, www.cod.edu; the largest single-campus community college in the Midwest.
- **Concordia University,** River Forest, 708-771-8300, www.cuchicago.edu; Lutheran liberal arts college.
- **Dominican University,** River Forest, 708-366-2490, www.dom.edu; Catholic liberal arts college and university. Student-faculty ratio of 13:1, with an average undergraduate class size of 15.
- **Fox College,** Oak Lawn, 708-444-4500, www.foxcollege.com; offers ten sixteen-month certificate programs in business and health care fields.
- **Governors State University,** University Park, 708-534-5000, www.govst.edu; undergraduate and graduate degrees, specializing in business, education, and health professions.
- **Midwestern University,** Downers Grove, 630-969-4400, www.midwestern.edu; university for osteopathic studies, pharmacology, and health sciences.
- **Moraine Valley Community College,** Palos Hills, 708-974-4300, TTY 708-974-9556, www.morainevalley.edu; four types of associate degrees, a wide variety of occupational certificates, and a satellite location in Blue Island.
- **National University of Health Sciences,** Lombard, 800-826-6285, www.nuhs.edu; programs in alternative healing practices.
- **North Central College,** Naperville, 630-637-5100, www.noctrl.edu; independent college of liberal arts and sciences affiliated with the United Methodist Church, emphasizes academics, leadership, ethics and values. Also offers graduate degree programs.
- **Prairie State College,** Chicago Heights, 708-709-3500, www.prairiestate.edu; associates degrees and career certificates.

- **South Suburban College,** South Holland, 708-596-2000, www.southsuburbancollege.edu; associate degrees in arts, sciences, fine arts, applied science, and engineering, as well as career certificates.
- **Trinity Christian College,** Palos Heights, 866-874-6463, www.trnty.edu; four-year liberal arts college "in the Reformed tradition"; offers a variety of majors as well as professional programs.
- **University of Saint Francis,** Joliet, 800-735-7500, www.stfrancis.edu; sixty undergraduate programs including nursing and education. Ten graduate programs. Strong athletic division.

# SHOPPING

When shopping in Chicago, don't forget about the **State Street** shopping area. In the late 1990s, the city routed car traffic back down State Street—it had been a buses-only route for years—hoping that more traffic to the area would naturally revitalize this once-hopping shopping district. The city was right. With its turn-of-the-century gaslight lampposts, the grand architecture of the original Marshall Field's department store (now a Macy's), independent local stores, and outposts of modern chain stores such as Old Navy, it's once again a popular and pleasant destination for shoppers at a variety of income levels. For shopping of a more exclusive nature, head a little north and toward the lake to **North Michigan Avenue**, the "Magnificent Mile." Up and down the avenue are dozens of boutiques, vertical malls, restaurants, and retail stores of every kind. The **Gold Coast**, west of Michigan Avenue, offers boutiques selling luxury goods and jewelry, beauty services, and designer clothing. But you don't have to head to the heart of the city for good shopping. Nearly every neighborhood and surrounding community has its own little retail area, and there are many fine shopping malls in the city and suburbs. Indulge yourself and explore them all.

Unless otherwise noted, all listings are in Chicago.

## SHOPPING MALLS

### CHICAGO

- **900 North Michigan Shops,** 312-915-3916, www.shop900.com
- **The Atrium,** 100 W Randolph St, 312-346-0777, www.atriummallchicago.com
- **The Century,** 2828 N Clark St, 773-929-8100
- **Ford City,** 7601 S Cicero Ave, 773-767-6400, www.shopfordcitymall.com

- **Harlem/Irving Plaza,** 4104 N Harlem, 708-453-7800, 773-625-3036, www.shopthehip.com
- **North Bridge,** 520 N Michigan Ave, 312-222-1622, www.theshopsatnorthbridge.com
- **Piper's Alley Mall,** 210 W North Ave, 312-337-0436
- **Water Tower Place,** 835 N Michigan Ave, 312-440-3166, www.shopwatertower.com

## SUBURBS

- **Chicago Ridge Mall,** 444 Chicago Ridge Mall Dr, Chicago Ridge, 708-499-0840, www.ShoppingChicagoRidgeMall.com
- **Deer Park Town Center,** 20530 N Rand Rd, Deer Park, 847-726-7755, www.shopdeerparktowncenter.com
- **Edens Plaza,** 3200 Lake Ave, Wilmette, 312-675-5446, www.shopedensplaza.com
- **Evergreen Plaza,** 9500 S Western Ave, Evergreen Park, www.theplazamall.org
- **Fox Valley Mall,** 195 Fox Valley Center, Aurora, 630-851-7200, www.westfield.com/foxvalley/
- **Golf Mill Shopping Center,** 239 Golf Mill Center, Golf & Milwaukee Rds, Niles, 847-699-1070, www.golfmill.com
- **Gurnee Mills Mall,** 6170 W Grand Ave, Gurnee, 847-263-7500, www.gurneemillsmall.com
- **Hawthorn Center,** 122 Hawthorn Center, Vernon Hills, 847-362-2600, www.westfield.com/hawthorn
- **Lincoln Mall,** Route 30/Lincoln Hwy, Matteson, 708-747-5600, www.lincoln-mall.com
- **Northbrook Court,** 2171 Northbrook Ct, Northbrook, 847-498-8161, www.northbrookcourt.com
- **Oak Brook Center,** 100 Oakbrook Center, Rte 83 and Cermak Rd, Oak Brook, 630-573-0700, www.oakbrookcenter.com
- **Old Orchard,** 4999 Old Orchard Center, Skokie Blvd & Old Orchard Rd, Skokie, 847-673-6800, www.westfield.com/oldorchard
- **Orland Square Mall,** 288 Orland Sq Dr, Orland Park, 708-349-1647, www.shoporlandsquare.com
- **Plaza del Lago,** 1515 Sheridan Rd, Wilmette, 847-251-0362, www.plazadelago.com
- **Randhurst Village,** 55 E Euclid Ave, Mt. Prospect, 847-259-0500, www.randhurstmall.com
- **River Oaks Center,** 96 River Oaks Center Dr, Calumet City, 708-868-0600, www.shopriveroakscenter.com

# SHOPPING

- **Stratford Square,** 152 Stratford Sq, Army Trail Rd & Gary, Bloomingdale, 630-539-1000, www.stratfordmall.com
- **Woodfield Mall,** 5 Woodfield Shopping Center, Golf Rd at Route 53, Schaumburg, 847-330-1537, www.shopwoodfield.com
- **Yorktown Shopping Center,** Butterfield Rd & Highland Ave, Lombard, 630-629-7330, www.yorktowncenter.com

## OUTLET MALLS

Outlet shopping malls are not conveniently located in Chicago, but their discounts may make a trip worthwhile.

- **Lighthouse Place,** 601 Wabash St, Michigan City, IN, 219-879-6506, www.premiumoutlets.com/lighthouseplace/; if you are willing to travel out of your way (consider taking the Skyway, a bit scary if you are afraid of heights, but there will be less traffic because it's a toll road), come spend the day at the Michigan City malls. Many find them to be worth the hour's drive from Chicago. Over twenty upscale outlets and trendy boutiques.
- **Huntley Outlet Center,** 11800 Factory Shops Blvd, Huntley, 847-669-9100, www.premiumoutlets.com/outlets/outlet.asp?id=98; Jeffersonian architecture, food court, playground and over 40 brand-name stores. Fifty miles west of Chicago along the Interstate 90 corridor.
- **Pleasant Prairie Premium Outlets,** 11211 120th Ave, Pleasant Prarie, WI, 262-857-2101, www.premiumoutlets.com/pleasantprairie/; 65 upscale name-brand stores, halfway between Chicago and Milwaukee.
- Department Stores
- **Bloomingdale's,** 900 N Michigan Ave, 312-440-4460, www.bloomingdales.com; home furnishings available at 600 N Wabash Ave, 312-324-7500.
- **Carson Pirie Scott & Company,** www.carsons.com; offers everything from clothing and furniture to bridal wear to stamps and coins to jewelry. Although the flagship store on South State Street closed in 2007, Carson's still has stores throughout Chicago and the suburbs, including a city location at Gateway Shops, 120 S Riverside Plaza, 312-744-5380.
- **Lord & Taylor,** www.lordandtaylor.com; located at Woodfield, Old Orchard, Northbrook Court, and other suburban malls.
- **Macy's,** www.macys.com; in 2006 Macy's took over Marshall Field's, a venerable Chicago institution and—despite much local protest—changed the name of all Chicagoland Marshall Field's stores to Macy's. The stores still offer everything from designer clothing to gourmet food and home furnishings. During the Christmas season, visitors come from around the country to see the window displays at the beautifully renovated and historic State Street store. Chicago locations include the flagship stores in the loop, 111 N State St, 312-781-1000, and the Water Tower Place at 835 N Michigan Ave, 312-335-

7700. Many suburban locations, which include: Northbrook, 1555 Northbrook Court, 847-509-5100; Oak Brook, 1 Oak Brook Center Mall, 630-684-2400; and Skokie, 1 Old Orchard Shopping Center, 847-329-2700.
- **Neiman-Marcus,** 737 N Michigan Ave, 800-642-4480 or 312-642-5900, www.neimanmarcus.com; the opulent Texan retailer carries expensive non-necessities that many with cash and/or room on their credit cards find they absolutely must have. Nice restaurants and a good gourmet food department.
- **Nordstrom,** 24 N State St, 312-377-5500, and 55 E Grand Ave, 312-464-1515 (as well as many suburban locations), shop.nordstrom.com; employees at this Seattle-based retailer have a reputation for being "motivated" and enthusiastic. The merchandise ranges from shoes and clothing for the entire family to jewelry and cosmetics and more. Perhaps most popular here are the women's shoe sales. Their online service is also top-notch.
- **Saks Fifth Avenue,** 700 N Michigan Ave, 312-944-6500, www.saksfifthavenue.com
- **Sears,** www.sears.com; Sears stores are located in malls in the suburbs, or as stand-alone stores, including one at 2 N State St, 312-373-6000, which contains a Land's End boutique. Check their website for the closest store to your area.

## DISCOUNT DEPARTMENT STORES

- **Kmart,** www.kmart.com; many local Kmart stores have been liquidated; the remaining metro stores are located at 1360 N Ashland Ave, 773-292-9400; 5033 N Elston Ave, 773-685-1121; 5050 S Kedzie Ave, 773-476-7887, and 7050 S Pulaski Ave, 773-767-2800. In the suburbs, check 1155 Oakton St, Des Plaines, 847-296-6136 and 4101 W 95th St, Oak Lawn, 708-422-5872.
- **Marshalls,** www.marshallsonline.com (five metro locations, many in the suburbs): 600 N Michigan Ave, 312-280-7506, 1834 W Fullerton, 773-296-4494.
- **T.J. Maxx,** www.tjmaxx.com (many in suburbs too): 11 N State St, 312-553-0515; 1745 W Fullerton, 773-327-1124; 2840 N Broadway, 773-975-2347; 6456 W Irving Park Rd, 773-725-9400.
- **Target,** www.target.com; an excellent choice for stylish but reasonably priced lighting, smaller furniture, kitchen wares, clothing, simple electronics, and, of course, the irresistibly priced package of 200 rolls of toilet paper. Now if you can only figure out how to get it into the car. The Chicago stores are located at 1 S State St, 312-279-2133; 1154 S Clark St, 312-212-6300; 2656 N Elston Ave, 773-252-1994; 7100 S Cicero Ave, Bedford Park, 708-563-9050; and 2901 S Cicero Ave, Cicero, 708-863-6830. Suburban locations include: 2209 W Howard St, Evanston, 847-733-1144; 6150 W Touhy Ave, Niles, 847-588-2800; 1700 E Rand Rd, Arlington Heights, 847-222-0925. Others are located in Chicago Ridge, Chicago Heights, Evergreen Park, Park Ridge, Skokie, River Forest, and Lincolnwood.
- **Walmart,** www.walmart.com; city locations at 4650 W North Ave, 773-252-7465; 3636 N Broadway St, 773-281-3321; 570 W Monroe St, 312-470-1460;

many suburban locations including Bridgeview, Crestwood, Evergreen Park, Niles, Bedford Park, Forest Park, Northlake, Villa Park.

## SPECIALTY STORES

### APPLIANCES, ELECTRONICS, CAMERAS

- **Best Buy,** www.bestbuy.com, has a large selection and good prices. Salespeople definitely won't pester you here; in fact, it may be hard to find them. The Chicago stores are located at 1000 W North Ave, 312-988-4067; 875 N Michigan Ave, 312-397-2146; 2650 N Clark St, 773-388-2920; 2100 N Elston Ave, 773-486-0142; suburban sites include Evanston, 2301 Howard St, 847-570-0450; Skokie, 5425 Touhy Ave, 847-933-9170; and North Riverside, 2358 Harlem Ave, 708-447-2757.
- **Central Camera,** 230 S Wabash Ave, 312-427-5580, www.centralcamera.com
- **Helix Camera & Video,** www.helixphoto.com, has three suburban locations, as well as two city locations: main store (the largest camera store in the United States), 310 S Racine Ave, 312-421-6000

### BEDS AND BEDDING

- **Bed, Bath and Beyond,** www.bedbathandbeyond.com, has four locations: 530 N State St, 312-755-9890; 1800 N Clybourn Ave, 312-642-6596; 2838 N Broadway, 773-528-5055; 555 W Roosevelt Rd, 312-850-4657; also located in Bolingbrook, Calumet City, Chicago Ridge, Deerfield, Forest Park, Homewood, Kildeer, Mount Prospect, Naperville, Norridge, Schaumburg, Orland Park, Downers Grove, Wilmette, Skokie, and Vernon Hills

### CARPETS AND RUGS

- **Caspian Oriental Rugs,** 700 N LaSalle St, 312-664-7576, www.caspianorientalrug.com
- **Home Carpet & Linoleum Center,** 3071 N Lincoln Ave, 773-528-3355
- **Peerless Imported Rugs,** www.peerlessrugs.com, 3033 N Lincoln Ave, 773-525-0296
- **Rexx Rug & Linoleum Co.,** www.rexxrug.com, 3312 N Lincoln Ave, 773-281-8800, has a large discounted inventory of carpeting for immediate installation

### COMPUTER EQUIPMENT

The listings for computer sales and support go on and on. Check the Yellow Pages under "Computers."

- **CDW Business Technology Center,** 120 S Riverside, 312-705-9700
- **Chicago Computer Supply,** www.chicagocomputersupply.com, 27 N Wacker Dr, #110, toll-free 877-474-7774
- **Micro Center,** www.microcenter.com, 2645 N Elston Ave, 773-292-1700; Westmont, 80 E Ogden Ave, 630-371-5500

## FURNITURE/HOUSEHOLD GOODS

Chicago has stores to accommodate every taste and pocketbook.

- **Affordable Portables,** www.affordableportables.net, located at 2608 N Clark St, 773-935-6160, and Evanston, 924 Davis St, 847-866-8124
- **At Home Furniture,** 1330 S Milwaukee, Libertyville, 847-367-0009
- **Bloomingdale's,** 600 N Wabash Ave, 312-324-7500; home furnishings, luggage, bridal registry.
- **The Container Store,** www.containerstore.com, 908 W North Ave, 312-654-8450, offers Chicagoans that most precious of urban commodities: more efficient (and stylish) use of scarce living space. Also in Northbrook, Schaumburg, and Oak Brook.
- **Crate & Barrel,** www.crateandbarrel.com; a notable company that offers contemporary furniture and household accessories. Crate & Barrel stores are located at 646 N Michigan Ave, 312-787-5900; 850 W North Ave, 312-573-9800; 35 Oak Brook Center Mall, Oak Brook, 630-572-1300; and in Deer Park, Northbrook, Oak Brook, Wilmette, Schaumburg, Vernon Hills, Michigan City and Skokie. There's also a CB2 at 800 W North Ave, 312-787-8329. Outlet stores are at 1864 N Clybourn Ave, 312-487-4775, and in Naperville.
- **Ethan Allen Home Interiors,** www.ethanallen.com, in the suburbs including, Naperville, Schaumburg, Orland Park, Gurnee, Lombard, Skokie, and Wheaton
- **European Furniture Warehouse,** www.eurofurniture.com, 2145 W Grand Ave, 800-243-1955
- **Ikea,** www.ikea-usa.com; two locations in the Chicagoland area, a gigantic store filled with stylish, well-made and affordable Scandinavian furniture and home items, at 1800 E McConnor Pkwy, Schaumburg, 847-969-9700, and Bolingbrook at 750 E Broughton Rd, 630-972-7900.
- **Pier 1 Imports, Inc.,** www.pier1.com, has many locations, including 1350 N Wells St, 312-787-4320; 2112 N Clybourn Ave, 773-871-6610; 2532 N Narragansett Ave, 773-622-2512; and 2862 N Ashland Ave, 773-975-1033, as well as many suburban locations.
- **Pottery Barn,** www.potterybarn.com; several metro and suburban locations: 1000 W North Ave, 312-944-0467; 4999 Old Orchard Center, Skokie, 847-673-8416; 21 Oak Brook Center, Oak Brook, 630-572-3307; 1850 Second St, Highland Park, 847-681-9873; 288 Orland Square Dr, Orland Park, 708-349-4118; also in Naperville and Geneva

# SHOPPING

- **Walter E. Smithe Custom Furniture,** www.smithe.com, in the city at 2009 N Clybourn Ave, 773-528-7787; many suburban locations including Arlington Heights, Crystal Lake, Lincolnshire, Naperville, Oak Brook, Skokie, Schaumburg, Vernon Hills
- **Williams-Sonoma,** www.williams-sonoma.com, has several locations within Chicago and suburbs including 900 N Michigan Ave, 312-587-8080; 4999 Old Orchard Center, Skokie, 847-933-9803; 142 Oak Brook Center, Oak Brook, 630-571-2702; 9 W Jackson Ave, Naperville, 630-369-4167; also in Lake Forest, Deer Park, Orland Park, and Highland Park

## HARDWARE, PAINTS, AND WALLPAPER

Hardware stores can be found in every neighborhood. Chicago's biggest chains are ACE and True Value. Home Depots are also increasingly prevalent; in the suburbs, multiple locations of the massive Home Depot, Menards, and Lowe's compete with the smaller chains and a few remaining locally owned businesses.

- **ACE Hardware:** many more locations are listed at www.acehardware.com: 4654 N Broadway, 773-334-7146; Ashland Paint & Hardware, 1013 N Ashland Ave, 773-486-1271; Lakeview ACE Hardware, 3921 N Sheridan Rd, 773-525-1700; Meyer's ACE Hardware, 315 E 35th St, 312-225-5687
- **Lowe's,** www.lowes.com, 2630 N Narragansett Ave, 773-413-5120, and eight suburban locations.
- **True Value Hardware (TVH);** many more listed at www.truevalue.com: H & B True Value, 5329 N Milwaukee Ave, 773-631-5966; Klein TVH, 3737 N Southport Ave, 773-525-2291; Lehman's TVH, 3473 N Broadway, 773-472-4435; Tenenbaum H.A. Hardware Company, 1138 W Belmont Ave, 773-935-7374; Tipre Hardware, 229 W North Ave, 312-664-5339; Zweifel TVH, 345 W 25th Pl, 312-842-1924, and many suburban locations
- **Home Depot,** www.homedepot.com, is perfect for do-it-yourself home repair handymen as well as the professional contractor. It has an extensive garden center for spring and fall landscaping. Suburban locations include Bedford Park, Niles, Oak Lawn, Chicago Ridge, Mt. Prospect and Evanston, among others. In Chicago try: 1232 W North Ave, 773-486-9200; 2570 N Elston Ave, 773-289-4615; 2555 N Normandy, 773-745-9900; 2665 N Halsted St, 773-472-7740; 1919 N Cicero, 773-622-8860.
- **Menards,** www.menards.com; "save big money" here: 4501 W North Ave, 773-278-7534; 2601 N Clybourn St, 773-880-5954. Suburban locations include Crestwood, Hanover Park, Hillside, Mt. Prospect, Hoffman Estates, Morton Grove, Mundelein, Naperville, Palatine, Tinley Park, and Gurnee.
- Sporting Goods
- **Angler's Outlet,** www.theanglersoutlet.com; sporting goods for fishermen: 3509 W 159th St, Markham, 708-331-5711

- **Play It Again Sports,** www.playitagainsports.com; buy, sell, trade, and consignment; in the city at 3939 N Ashland Ave, 773-305-9900, and many suburban locations including Crystal Lake, Downers Grove, Hodgkins, Palatine, and Schaumburg
- **REI,** www.rei.com; 1466 N Halsted St, 312-951-6020; 888 Willow Rd, Northbrook, 847-480-1938; 17W160 22nd St, Oakbrook Terrace, 630-574-7700
- **Sports Authority,** www.thesportsauthority.com; 620 N LaSalle St, 312-337-6151; 3134 N Clark St, 773-871-8501; 1801 W Fullerton Ave, 773-935-7729, and in several suburban areas including Arlington Heights, Downers Grove, Gurnee Mills, Schaumburg, Northbrook, and Niles
- **Vertel's Chicago Running Athletics and Fitness,** 24 S Michigan Ave, 312-683-9600

## ONLINE SHOPPING SERVICES

Online shopping is the way to go if you don't like crowded malls or sitting in traffic. A couple of local web shopping sites:

- **Greater North Michigan Avenue Association,** www.themagnificentmile.com; what better way to purchase gift certificates to the stores located within the Magnificent Mile without having to actually fight the crowds? Subscribe to their newsletter to keep current on special events happening in the area.
- **Urbanstyle Shopping Guide,** www.urbanstyle.com, will get you up to speed about where to buy what in a flash. Offers a wide variety of products from Chicago boutiques for men, women, kids, pets, and the home.

## SECOND-HAND SHOPPING

There are three kinds of second-hand stores: thrift stores, where the merchandise is plentiful, cheap but not necessarily trendy; vintage stores, where the clothes are more fashionable and more expensive; and antiques stores where the merchandise may be exquisite, with prices to match. You can find a forgotten gem at thrift stores (the exciting challenge) but you may have to dig through a lot of sand along the way.

### VINTAGE STORES

- **Disgraceland,** 3338 N Clark St, 773-281-5875
- **Hubba-Hubba,** 2040 W Roscoe, 773-477-1414
- **Strange Cargo,** 3448 N Clark St, 773-327-8090
- **Wacky Cats,** 3012 N Lincoln Ave, 773-929-6701

## THRIFT STORES—CHICAGO

- **Brown Elephant Resale Shop for the Howard Brown Memorial Clinic,** 3651 N Halsted St, 773-549-5943; 5404 N Clark St, 773-271-9382; and in Oak Park at 217 Harrison St, 708-445-0612. Nicely maintained second-hand stores.
- **The Salvation Army** operates dozens of thrift shops in Chicago and suburbs. Check out 2258 N Clybourn Ave, 773-477-1771; 2941 N Central Ave, 773-283-1315 or 4315 N Broadway, 773-348-1401. For other locations, look in the Yellow Pages under "Thrift Shops."
- **Unique Thrift,** 3748 N Elston Ave, 773-279-0850; 4441 W Diversey Ave, 773-227-2282; 4445 N Sheridan Rd, 773-275-8623; huge stores with comparatively high prices but half-price Mondays and a great selection of goods. Nine other locations around the city and suburbs.
- **Village Discount Outlet,** www.villagediscountoutlet.com, has loads of stores throughout Chicago including 2032 N Milwaukee Ave, 7443 S Racine Ave, 4898 N Clark St, and 2043 W Roscoe St. Same number for all stores: 866-545-3836. Large selection and good discounts that change daily.

## SUBURBAN THRIFTS

- **Bethesda Thrift Shop,** 26 Crystal Lake Plaza, Crystal Lake, 815-455-2325
- **La Femmena,** 1022 N Blvd, Oak Park, 708-386-8830
- **Lambs Farm Thrift Shop,** 14245 W Rockland Rd, Libertyville, 847-327-9053
- **Little Mexico Thrift Shop,** 111 N Wolf Rd, Wheeling, 847-419-8935
- **Simply Sensible Shoppe,** 17010 Oak Park Ave, Tinley Park, 708-633-9180
- **Unique Thrift Shop,** 2155 W Jefferson St, Joliet, 815-730-8099; many other suburban locations. Check your local phonebook for listings.
- **Upscale Resale of Libertyville,** 330 N Milwaukee Ave, Libertyville, 847-918-9988

## ANTIQUE STORES

There are plenty of opportunities to shop for antiques around Chicago, from auctions and galleries to antique warehouses. Be sure to call and inquire about store hours before dropping in; many shops keep odd hours and some serve by appointment only. Neighborhoods that concentrate many antique stores into a single strip make for especially enjoyable antiquing. Fun antique strips to poke around include sections of Lakeview and Western Avenue in south suburban Blue Island, among others. Check the Yellow Pages under "Antiques" for listings.

## AUCTION HOUSES

Auctions can provide an entertaining and sometimes economical way to decorate your home. If you have an eye for design and know the market value, you can create a unique environment in your home by visiting auction houses. You will find announcements in the *Tribune* on Fridays and Sundays. Check the business section of the Sunday paper. Usually you will get a week's notice, but sometimes just a few days as some events are held mid-week. Try your best to get to the site before bidding starts so you can examine close up what will be on the block.

## GARAGE AND YARD SALES

As soon as the weather hints of warmer days, sale signs start popping out on lawns, beckoning drivers and passersby to yards and garages throughout city neighborhoods as well as the suburbs. Garage sales are very popular in the Chicagoland area. Some simply advertise their wares on hand-drawn signs posted at intersections near their homes; others place ads in community papers. But those who really want to draw the crowds place ads in the *Sun-Times*, *Daily Herald* or *Chicago Tribune*. Most ads are placed on Wednesdays for Friday and Saturday sales, or Fridays, for Saturday and Sunday sales. Often neighbors join forces and coordinate their sales so that you can hit two or three sales without having to get back into your car and drive down the road. Garage sales are like golfers; they linger until it's too cold to be outdoors. You may find some sales as late as November, if the weather holds out.

Some communities get together each year, sometimes under the umbrella of a local church, and host an annual garage or rummage sale. You will see signs advertising the dates and times in front of the location.

## DUMPSTER DIVING (ALLEY SHOPPING)

Many a funky Chicago apartment has been accented, or even primarily outfitted, with recycled material from alleys and dumpsters. Every neighborhood has a specific day for garbage pickup and the ideal time to go scrounging is the day or morning, before the blue Streets & Sanitation trucks cart it all away. The best times of the year to go hunting are the last weekends of April and September, when many leases expire and the alleys are piled high with whatever didn't make the cut. In areas near university campuses, where students rent housing, the end of any semester is a good time to cruise the streets for cast-offs. Another rewarding time to covet thy neighbor's trash is in springtime when people clean out their garages, basements, attics, etc. But the pickings are good at the end of any month. All in all, the alleys of Chicago offer the widest possible selection of used furniture, appliances, and household and decorative items at the lowest possible prices. Look out your back window for the one nearest you. Be warned, though: in most city neighborhoods, if you don't nab that discarded prize the moment you spot it, it will be quickly snapped up by the next treasure-seeker who happens by.

# FOOD

## GROCERY STORES

Chicago has corner grocers, vast supermarkets, specialty markets, farmers' markets, and everything in between. For big shopping trips many choose a neighborhood Dominick's or Jewel supermarket. These local chains supply everything from canned meat and deli items to laundry soap and fresh produce. Check the Yellow Pages or the web for one close to you. If you're looking for that tough-to-find cheese or pasta, you might try Treasure Island. Trader Joe's is a reasonably priced chain of specialty stores with several locations in the city and more in the suburbs. Here you will find a wide assortment of exotic frozen vegetables, terrific frozen desserts, vegetarian specialties, and great prices on staples like cheese, coffee, and wine. If you just need a few items, check your neighborhood grocers, many of which will offer a great variety of ethnic ingredients, depending on the neighborhood. If eating organic food is important to you, there are plenty of health food markets throughout the area including several Whole Foods, the formidable national chain. Bulk purchasing often appeals to those with enough pantry space; membership warehouses such as Costco or Sam's Club offer bulk foods and household items.

- **Costco** (membership fee), 2746 N Clybourn Ave, Lincoln Park, 773-360-2053, www.costco.com; suburban locations include Bedford Park, Oak Brook, Niles, and Glenview. Similar to Sam's Club, with high-quality meats, liquor department, prescription drugs, (often oversized) baked goods, and household items.
- **Dominick's**, www.dominicks.com, has many Chicago and suburban locations, including 5233 N Lincoln Ave, 773-442-1158; 3145 S Ashland Ave, 773-247-2633; 5201 N Sheridan Rd, 773-506-0558; and 6009 N Broadway Ave, 773-769-2300. The larger stores have excellent bakeries. Dominick's "Fresh Store" locations also have an extensive selection of signature deli sandwiches and soups, ready-made carryout foods, fresh-baked artisan breads, and Starbucks outlets.
- **Jewel**, www.jewelosco.com, has scores of stores in and around Chicago, including 1210 N Clark St, 312-944-6950; 4729 N Central Ave, 773-777-1142; 3531 N Broadway, 773-871-1054; 1341 N Paulina St, 773-342-3410; 3630 N Southport Ave, 773-327-2330; 438 W Madison, Oak Park, 708-383-7111. Most have decent bakeries, good deli departments, and fresh produce sections.
- **Sam's Club** (membership fee) www.samsclub.com/sams/, suburban locations in Des Plaines, Evergreen Park, Hodgkins, Addison, and Tinley Park;

online at www.samsclub.com. Warehouse-like setting, offering everything from baked goods and high-quality meats to televisions.
- **Trader Joe's**, www.traderjoes.com; in the city at 3745 N Lincoln Ave, 773-248-4920; 44 E Ontario St, 312-951-6369; and 1840 N Clybourn Ave, #200, 312-274-9733; smallish, discount supermarket that offers healthy alternative eating. Organic foods, excellent variety of frozen vegetables and fish, small liquor department with a variety of bargain-priced wines, and an interesting assortment of cheeses. Several suburban locations include: 17 W Rand Rd, Arlington Heights, 847-506-0752; 1407 Waukegan Rd, Glenview, 847-657-7821; 127 Skokie Blvd, Northbrook, 847-480-9280; 735 W Route 22, Lake Zurich, 847-550-7827; 1942 W Fabyan Pkwy, Batavia, 630-879-3234; also in Orland Park, Glen Ellyn, La Grange, Park Ridge, Downers Grove, and Naperville.
- **Treasure Island**, http://tifoods.com; 75 W Elm St, 312-440-1144; 1639 N Wells St, 312-642-1105; 680 N Lake Shore Dr, 312-664-0400; 3460 N Broadway, 773-327-3880; and 2121 N Clybourn Ave, 773-880-8880. In Wilmette at 911 Ridge Rd, 847-256-5033. Upscale supermarket offering ethnic produce, organic foods, and a wide range of cheeses, as well as more traditional foods.
- **Whole Foods**, www.wholefoods.com; health and organic foods including fresh meat and fish, deli, and baked goods. At: 3300 N Ashland Ave, 773-244-4200; 30 W Huron St, 312-932-9600; 6020 N Cicero Ave, 773-205-1100; 3640 N Halsted, 773-472-0400; 1101 S Canal St, Ste 107, 312-435-4600. In the suburbs, locations include: 760 Waukegan Rd, Deerfield, 847-444-1900; 1640 Chicago Ave, Evanston, 847-733-1600.
- **Oberweis Dairy**, www.oberweisdairy.com; located in Aurora, Oberweis delivers premium dairy products and select high-quality meats, cheeses and specialty items, including ice cream. Milk is produced at small, locally owned farms. For more information call 630-801-6100. See the website for one of their 26 store locations in the city and suburbs.

## FARMERS' MARKETS

The City of Chicago sponsors 30 farmers' markets during the summer in various locations, including Daley Plaza in the Loop. Farmers come to sell their wares mid-May through November on Tuesday, Wednesday, Thursday, Saturday, and Sunday. For example, on Saturdays it's the Lincoln Park High School's parking lot (Armitage Avenue east of Halsted Street). Farther north on Tuesday mornings, head to Lincoln Square (just south of Lawrence Avenue on Lincoln Avenue). For a list of all the markets, their locations, hours of operation, and dates, visit the city's website at www.cityofchicago.org/city/en/depts/dca/provdrs/markets_and_neighborhoodprograms.html or call 312-744-3316.

Many suburbs host farmers' markets as well. Evanston, Palatine, Park Ridge, Schaumburg, and Mt. Prospect are just a few in the northwest suburbs that hold them regularly. Check your local city hall for information about your area, or visit www.localharvest.org and search for locations nearest you.

## BYOB RESTAURANTS

Many newcomers to Chicago are pleasantly surprised by the prevalence of BYOB restaurants in the area. While restaurants with liquor licenses—especially those with well-chosen wine lists—are likely to charge hefty corkage fees for those who prefer to bring their own, Chicago is peppered with restaurants (many without liquor licenses) that don't mind at all if you bring your own. Happily for patrons who prefer to choose their own booze, this makes supplementing a meal with a lovely bottle of wine, or a few beers, a much less expensive proposition. (Some friendly restaurants will even offer to chill the remainder of your six-pack for you as you work your way through dinner!)

If you'd like to bring your own drinks to dinner, call ahead to ask the restaurant about its BYOB policy—or check out *BYOB Chicago: Your Guide to Bring-Your-Own-Bottle Restaurants and Wine & Spirits Stores in Chicago,* by Jean Iversen, www.byob-chicago.com.

## ETHNIC DISTRICTS

With all the different kinds of people that immigrate to Chicago, you would be correct in expecting it to be a land of a thousand flavors. The restaurants and eateries here reflect both the taste of the new generation of Chicagoans as well as those who helped make Chicago what it is today. While you can find ethnic food in nearly every neighborhood, some are reliable destinations for a particular type of cuisine.

South Halsted, starting around the 200 south block, constitutes Chicago's Greek Town, with Mediterranean-styled restaurants and backyard and patio seating. The Taylor Street neighborhood offers mostly Italian and French bistro-style cooking. River West offers cuisine with a Mediterranean touch as well as trendier restaurants. Lincoln Square holds on to its Middle European roots; come here for a solid selection of German/Austrian restaurants—but also take advantage of the neighborhood's several excellent Thai restaurants. Farther north along Lincoln Avenue and West Lawrence Avenue are a bumper crop of Korean restaurants. The Lakeview East area is a good destination for authentic Thai and other Asian delights. If the hearty dishes of Poland are more to your liking, look for the all-you-can-eat buffets in and around Logan Square—also here, and in Pilsen, are wonderful Mexican eateries. Albany Park, along Kedzie Avenue, offers great Middle Eastern joints. Try Wrigleyville for Ethiopian and North African dining. Of course, Chinatown offers authentic Cantonese and Mandarin fare, but between Uptown and Rogers Park, especially along Argyle

Avenue, you'll find authentic Asian cuisine, mostly Vietnamese and Thai, as well as terrific noodle shops. West Rogers Park, centered along Devon Avenue, is the main destination for Indian and Pakistani cuisine.

Middle Eastern cuisine abounds in Skokie, along with kosher delis. In the suburbs, Oak Park, Morton Grove, and Highland Park have good delis as well. Hyde Park is the place to go for southern cooking, whether it's Cajun, Creole, or barbecue. Farther south, especially in the city's southeast corner, you'll find authentic soul food, West Indian, and African joints. Most of the city's most celebrated barbecue and rib joints are located on the south side as well. The southwest corner of the city, including the neighborhoods of Beverly and Mount Greenwood, as well as nearby suburbs such as Oak Lawn and Evergreen Park, are teeming with hearty Italian and delicious Chicago-style pizza. South suburban Bridgeview and Worth host many authentic Middle Eastern restaurants and groceries, and Blue Island has authentic Mexican food.

To read reviews or to get acquainted with the restaurant offerings of any particular area, refer to *Chicago Magazine* (either hard copy or online at www.chicagomag.com), or go to www.metromix.com for the latest on local eateries. *The Chicago Reader* also offers frequent reviews and listings; its online version at www.chicagoreader.com features a handy restaurant finder that allows you to search near landmarks, movie theaters, and concert venues for cuisine of various types and in a variety of price brackets. Note that most Chicago publications give southside neighborhoods and south suburbs scant coverage. If you're living or hanging out in the city's southern regions, you may have more luck finding restaurant advice online. Helpful online venues that offer advice and comments, including information about southside eats, include **Chowhound** (http://chowhound.chow.com) and **Little Three Happiness Forum** (www.lthforum.com)—both haunts of hardcore Chicago foodies. LTH Forum also organizes frequent restaurant excursions for food enthusiasts.

If you're looking for a quintessentially Chicago meal it will probably be approved by the American High Cholesterol Society: ribs, steak, or pizza. **Twin Anchors** in Old Town or **Ribs and Bibs** in Hyde Park are good choices for ribs. Many go to **Harry Caray** or **Gibson's** for a nice steak dinner, and those looking for the deep-dish pizza that made Chicago famous usually seek out the tourist-swarmed **Pizzeria Uno, Gino's East,** and **Giordano's.** You should know however, that many Chicago natives disdain deep-dish as an aberration for tourists and consider the "real" Chicago-style pizza to boast a load of toppings atop a thin, chewy crust. (This style is generally differentiated from the New York variety by a firmer, less floppy crust, a thicker layer of toppings and cheese, and a tradition of being sliced into squares rather than pie-shaped wedges.) Examples of excellent thin-crust Chicago pizza can be found all over Chicagoland; a few particularly well-regarded places include **Nick and Vito's, Aurelio's, Chicago Pizza,** and **Sanfrantello's.**

If you are a female college graduate and enjoy tasting a variety of foods, you might consider joining the **American Association of University Women's Ethnic Dining Club**. They meet once a month, nine months of the year, each time at a different ethnic restaurant, and they post their schedule online. For more information go to www.aauw-il.org.

And finally, what is a meal without dessert? Listed here are just a few of the scrumptious **ethnic bakeries** scattered throughout the city:

- **Artopolis,** 306 S Halsted, 312-559-9000, artopolischicago.com, offers terrific Greek and French pastries.
- **Café Selmarie,** 4729 N Lincoln Ave, 773-989-5595, www.cafeselmarie.com; located in the heart of Lincoln Square, this charming café offers light food as well as a massive glass display case boasting a dazzling array of delicious French- and German-style desserts. Wedding cakes, too! Affordable for the quality, with nice art, pleasant atmosphere, and efficient service.
- **Marie Gold Bakery and Fast Food,** 5752 N California Ave, 773-561-1978; Philippine food and bakery.
- **Middle East Bakery and Grocery,** 1512 W Foster Ave, 773-561-2224, middleeastbakeryandgrocery.com; Andersonville has been traditionally known for Swedish pastries, but more recent immigrants have brought new—and equally delicious—traditions.
- **Panaderia Ayutla Bakery,** 6963 N Clark St, 773-764-9077; not much English spoken here, but if you can revive your rusty Spanish you will be rewarded.
- **Swedish Bakery,** 5348 N Clark St, 773-561-8919, www.swedishbakery.com; finely crafted European delectables, this bakery put Andersonville on the map. Everything here is mouthwatering.
- **Tahoora,** 2345 W Devon Ave, 773-743-7272, www.tahoora.com; Pakistani/Indian treats.

# CULTURAL LIFE

ONE OF THE GREAT PLEASURES OF LIVING IN CHICAGO IS THE ENORmous number and variety of events and cultural offerings. Despite inclement weather, the drive, or the lack of parking, people come into the city in droves to experience the cultural riches it has to offer. (Unless otherwise noted, all listings are in Chicago.)

So, where to start? Check with the following publications for listings of area events:

- **Chicago Magazine**, www.chicagomag.com; offers an extensive entertainment section in each monthly issue. You can also find museum exhibits, new restaurants, and art gallery openings. Occasionally it will review new clubs and new happenings in trendy neighborhoods as well.
- **Chicago Reader**, www.chicagoreader.com; comes out every Thursday. You will find this free publication in bookstores, banks, movie theatres, coffee shops, etc. The *Reader* publishes a comprehensive guide to the upcoming events of the week.
- **Metromix.com**, www.metromix.com, is an online entertainment guide from the Tribune Company. Check here for schedules of independent movies, club acts, plays, festivals, concerts, and even sports.
- Most of the traditional daily papers have a Friday/Weekend and an Arts Sunday section. Check the **Chicago Tribune**, **Chicago Sun Times**, and the **Daily Herald**.
- **Newcity**, newcity.com, is another weekly free alternative that publishes an entertainment guide.

Your neighborhood newspaper is often a source of local happenings. These weeklies can be found in most chain drugstores and convenience stores, alongside the traditional daily newspapers.

Entertainment hotlines are also popular for finding out more about area events:

- **Chicago Dance and Music Alliance Hotline**: 312-987-9296
- **Jam Concert Line**: 312-666-6667 for rock, country, blues
- **Hot Tix**: www.hottix.org, for daily listings of shows offering discounted day-of-performance tickets. These tickets are half the face value. The Hot Tix offices are at 72 E Randolph and 163 E Pearson.
- **Mayor's Office of Special Events Hotline**: 312-744-3316 or go to www.cityofchicago.org/city/en/depts/dca.html

## TICKETS

Tickets for most events and performances may be purchased at the venue box offices or through **Ticketmaster** at 800-653-8000, online at www.ticketmaster.com, or at Ticketmaster outlets. It's always a good idea to get your tickets as far in advance as possible since many shows, concerts, exhibits, and events sell out. When calling, have your credit card ready and be prepared to pay service fees. (See Hot Tix above for information about discounted day-of-performance tickets.)

## MUSIC

### PROFESSIONAL AND COMMUNITY SYMPHONIC, CHORAL, OPERA, CHAMBER

There may be more than one reason the French declared Chicago the "Paris of the Midwest"—the level of artistry here is extraordinary. Included in this section are professional groups as well as community ensembles. If you are a musician or singer, and are interested in performing, these groups are a good place to start your inquiries.

- **Artist Series at Wheaton College**, www.wheaton.edu/TicketOffice; their calendar offerings can resemble a Who's Who of the classical music world. In the past, soprano Kathleen Battle and guitarist Christopher Parkening have been included on the roster. For tickets call 630-752-5010.
- **Chamber Music Society of the North Shore**, cms-ns.org; performances are held at Evanston's Pick-Staiger Concert Hall on Northwestern University's campus. Tickets or subscriptions can be purchased by calling 847-436-0587.
- **Chicago Chamber Musicians/Chicago String Ensemble**, www.chicagochambermusic.org; Sunday performances at the Pick-Staiger Concert Hall, Evanston; Monday performances take place at the DePaul University Concert Hall. You can order tickets online or by calling 312-819-5800.

# CULTURAL LIFE

- **Chicago Sinfonietta**, www.chicagosinfonietta.org, 312-236-3681, is a small, but entertaining musical group.
- **The Chicago Symphony Orchestra (CSO)** is one of the mostly highly acclaimed orchestras in the world. When in town they perform at Orchestra Hall, 220 S Michigan Ave, from September until June. For ticket sales information: 312-294-3000 or go to www.cso.org.
- **College Church**; this Wheaton-based, non-denominational church features concerts on select Sundays, most often at 4 p.m. Offerings include organ recitals and piano trios—usually focused on sacred music. Check their website for a calendar listing: www.college-church.org, or call 630-668-0878.
- **Elgin Symphony Orchestra**, www.elginsymphony.org; nation's fastest growing orchestra with over 50 concerts annually in several locations. For tickets call the box office: 847-888-4000.
- **The Grant Park Symphony and Chorus** plays summer concerts at the Petrillo Band Shell in Grant Park (Jackson Blvd between Lake Shore and Columbus Drives). You can purchase a reserved seat or listen for free on several acres of grass (bring a blanket). For more information, call 312-742-7638 or check www.grantparkmusicfestival.com.
- **Illinois Philharmonic Orchestra,** based in Park Forest, 708-481-7774, www.ipomusic.org, offers classical, pops, family and community concerts as well as educational programs.
- **Lakeshore Symphony of Chicago**, www.lsso.org, 312-409-5670; calling itself "Chicago's Community Orchestra," this ensemble offers selections that are geared toward seniors and families, at very reasonable prices. Concerts are held at the Copernicus Center Gateway Theatre on Chicago's northwest side.
- **Network Chicago**, WTTW11 and 98.7 WFMT, is a terrific source of small, less expensive classical music programs: www.networkchicago.com.

The city also sponsors separate blues, jazz, gospel, Latin, and Celtic festivals during the summer months, as well as free ballroom dance parties accompanied by a live band. Call the mayor's office special events hotline at 312-744-3316 for more information, or go to www.cityofchicago.org/city/en/depts/dca.html.

## CHORUSES

- **Chicago Master Singers**, www.chicagomastersingers.org, in Barrington, 877-825-5267; originally known as The New Oratorio Singers, this group presents concerts in northwest suburban Chicago communities.
- **Downers Grove Choral Society**, www.dgcs.org, 630-515-0030; full spectrum of major choral works, including contemporary masterpieces and commissioned premieres.

- **Elgin Chorale Union,** www.elginchoralunion.org; Fox Valley area's oldest performing arts group. For tickets call 847-214-7225.
- **Elmhurst Choral Union** is a community chorus that performs twice a year in addition to occasional appearances with the Elmhurst Symphony Orchestra and special events. For more information visit www.elmhurstchoralunion.org, or call 630-758-1100 to purchase tickets.
- **Glen Ellyn–Wheaton Chorale,** gewchorale.org: not-for-profit, non-audition adult chorus. Information: 630-415-3066.
- **Naperville Chorus and Chamber Singers,** www.napervillechorus.org; chamber singers provide musical entertainment for intimate settings: dinners, organizational events, and community events.
- **North Shore Choral Society,** www.northshorechoral.org; community chorus for over 60 years. Information: 773-741-6727.
- **Northwest Choral Society;** located in Park Ridge, this community chorale of 50 generally performs three times a year. Visit their website at www.nwchoralsociety.org. Call 224-585-9127 for tickets.
- **Oak Park Concert Chorale,** www.oakparkconcertchorale.org; performs a variety of works, *a cappella* and with accompaniment. Call 708-383-4742.

## OPERA

The **Lyric Opera of Chicago** performs at the Civic Center for the Performing Arts (also known as the Civic Opera House), 20 North Wacker Drive in downtown Chicago. Their calendar generally runs from September through February. For information, call the box office at 312-332-2244, or visit their website at www.lyricopera.org.

## DANCE—BALLET, JAZZ, MODERN

You won't find dance, be it ballet, tap, jazz, classical or modern, in just one concert hall; it's everywhere in Chicago, showcased in art galleries, museums, and outdoor festivals. Be sure to check your local community colleges, libraries, and theaters in addition to the listings here. You can also review *Chicago Magazine's* entertainment section, which has a special section for dance performances.

- **Athenaeum Theatre,** www.athenaeumtheatre.com, 2936 N Southport, often hosts dance performances created by local choreographers. Tickets at Ticketmaster, 312-902-1500; box office information at 773-935-6875.
- **Ballet Chicago,** www.balletchicago.org, 312-251-8838; school with a studio company.
- **Giordano Jazz Dance Chicago,** giordanodance.org, 312-922-1332; founded in 1953, an international touring company, professional dance school and active educational outreach program.

- **Hubbard Street Dance Chicago** is a homegrown group that has achieved international recognition. The Hubbard Street troupe often performs in town at such venues as the **Ford Center for the Performing Arts, Harris Theater,** and the **Cadillac Palace Theatre**. You can also visit the Company's website, www.hubbardstreetdance.com, or call their office at 312-850-9744 for more information.
- **Joffrey Ballet of Chicago,** www.joffrey.com. This ballet company celebrated their 50th anniversary in 2007. They perform at 10 E. Randolph St. Call them at 312-739-0120 or check their website. Tickets available through Ticketmaster or at 312-386-8905.
- **The Dance Center**, 1306 S Michigan Ave, 312-369-8300; part of Columbia College, The Dance Center is home to one of the city's leading promoters of contemporary dance. Check their website for a schedule of events: www.colum.edu/Dance_Center.

## THEATERS

Chicago is a city of drama and it loves actors. Experimental as well as community theater abounds, and bigger productions that are working out the kinks before heading to Broadway. And don't forget the terrific ensemble theater here. Groups such as Steppenwolf work with core groups of actors, writers, directors, and invite professional actors for limited runs. The resulting work is often riveting, capturing nationwide attention. The variety and competition here means you can easily enjoy a solid performance without breaking the bank. Reduced rates are available with subscriptions or through the last-minute Hot Tix route (see above). Check the local paper, *The Chicago Reader*, and www.metromix.com for reviews and ticket information.

### PROFESSIONAL AND COMMUNITY THEATER

Provided here is a sampling of local production companies. Soon you will compile a list of your own favorites.

- **Arie Crown Theatre**, Lakeside Center/McCormick Place, 2301 S Lake Shore Dr, www.ariecrown.com, 312-791-6190 for ticket and event information
- **Bailiwick Repertory**, 1229 W Belmont, bailiwickchicago.com, 773-969-6201
- **Briar Street Theatre**, 3133 N Halsted St, 773-348-4000
- **Court Theatre**, 5535 S Ellis Ave, www.courttheatre.org, 773-753-4472
- **Eclipse Theatre Company,** 4001 N Ravenswood, www.eclipsetheatre.com, 773-325-9655
- **Ford Center for the Performing Arts, Oriental Theatre**, 24 W Randolph St, www.broadwayinchicago.com, 312-977-1700 for box office information
- **Goodman Theatre**, 170 N Dearborn, www.goodmantheatre.org, 312-443-3800

- **Lookingglass Theatre Company**; world-renowned for their innovative performances, their new home is at the Water Tower Water Works. Theatre and Box Office: 875 N Michigan Ave, 773-477-9257, lookingglasstheatre.org
- **North Shore Center for the Performing Arts**, 9501 Skokie Blvd, Skokie, www.northshorecenter.org, 847-673-6300
- **Royal George Theatre**, 1641 N Halsted St, www.theroyalgeorgetheatre.com, 312-988-9000
- **The Second City**, 1616 N Wells St, in the Old Town neighborhood, www.secondcity.com, 312-337-3992; two stages with a resident troupe at each
- **Steppenwolf Theatre Company**, 1650 N Halsted St, www.steppenwolf.org, 312-335-1650
- **The Theatre Building**, 1225 W Belmont Ave, www.theatrebuildingchicago.org, 773-327-5252
- **Victory Gardens**, 2433 N Lincoln Ave, www.victorygardens.org, 773-871-3000

Go to www.centerstagechicago.com for a comprehensive listing of theatre in and around Chicago, including profiles of theatres, scheduled performances, and links to other performing arts events.

## FILM

Chicago has a few art houses that showcase independent and art films. The Sunday section of the *Sun Times* and the *Chicago Tribune* list the (mostly) mainstream films being shown at the multiplex theaters. Occasionally art films are reviewed in those newspapers, especially in the Friday Weekend sections. You can check *Chicago Reader* and *Newcity* for film reviews and showings. In this book, check **A Chicago Year** for information regarding annual film festivals in Chicago. For commercial theaters, drive-ins, second-run cinema, and suburban locations visit www.centerstagechicago.com.

### ART FILM HOUSES

- **Beverly Arts Cinema**, 2407 W 111th St, www.beverlyartcenter.org, 773-445-3838; Wednesday evening series of art films, indies, and international films on the city's far southwest side
- **Century 12 & CineArts 6**, 1715 Maple Ave, 847-491-9751
- **Chicago Filmmakers**, 5243 N Clark St, www.chicagofilmmakers.org, 773-293-1447
- **Facets Multimedia**, 1517 W Fullerton Ave, www.facets.org, 800-331-6197
- **Gene Siskel Film Center** (located at School of the Art Institute, www.saic.edu), 164 N State St, www.siskelfilmcenter.org, Hotline: 312-846-2800
- **Lake Theatre**, 1022 Lake St, Oak Park, www.classiccinemas.com, 708-848-9088

- **Music Box Theatre**, 3733 N Southport Ave, www.musicboxtheatre.com, 773-871-6604

## COMEDY

Chicagoans laugh hard and long, so it comes as no surprise that comedians flock to Chicago and its environs, to test the waters—and their talents. Here is just a sampling of area clubs. Call for times, cover charges, drink minimums, and other up-to-the-minute details:

- **Barrels of Laughs**, 10345 S Central Ave, Oak Lawn, 708-499-2969; a little out of the way for downtowners, but this club attracts local and national talent to its stage
- **Comedy Comedy/The Comedy Shrine**, 4034 Fox Valley Ctr, Aurora, 630-585-0300
- **ComedySportz Theatre**, 929 W Belmont Ave, www.comedysportzchicago.com, 773-549-8080
- **Hog Head McDunna's**, 1505 W Fullerton St, 773-929-0944; Wednesday-night stand-up
- **iO Theater**, 3541 N Clark St, ioimprov.com/chicago, 773-880-0199
- **Lincoln Restaurant**, 4008 N Lincoln Ave, 773-248-1820; twice-weekly comedy
- **Red Pepper Masquerade**, 428 E 87th, 773-873-5700; Tuesday night comedy
- **Riddles Comedy Club**, 5055 W 111th St, Alsip, www.myriddlescomedyclub.com, 708-422-5055
- **Second City**, 1616 N Wells, www.secondcity.com, 312-337-3992, is the legendary improvisational comedy theater where aspiring John Belushis and Bill Murrays perform nightly for locals and tourists alike
- **Zanies**, www.zanies.com, 1548 N Wells St, 312-337-4027; some consider this club the best in the city. Also at Pheasant Run Resort, 4051 E Main, Saint Charles, 630-584-6342; and 5437 Park Pl, Rosemont, 847-813-0484.
- **Zella**, 1983 N Clybourn, 773-549-2910

## CONTEMPORARY MUSIC

Many newcomers are simply amazed at the music in Chicago. Enjoy...

### CONCERT FACILITIES

Chicagoland plays host to concerts big and small. Most facilities offer tickets through TicketMaster and its outlets. Check the websites listed below; most offer a diagram of the seating arrangements, which is a big help when ordering. Two questions you will want to ask are: is it partial view, and will you need binoculars? If you want more personal attention and have questions, call the venue directly.

- **Akoo Theatre (formerly the Rosemont Theatre)**, 5400 N River Rd, Rosemont, www.rosemont.com/visiting/theatre.html, 847-671-5100; with over 1,200 on-site parking spaces and over 4000 seats, this modern facility can pack 'em in. Large-scale productions include the Radio City Rockettes Christmas Spectacular. Tickets also available from Ticketmaster.
- **Allstate Arena**, 6920 N Manheim Rd, Rosemont, www.allstatearena.com; more than 150 events are hosted at the arena each year. Tickets can be purchased through Ticketmaster (800-745-3000), at the box office, or online. Parking fees range from $11 to $15 for cars. Limos and buses are extra.
- **Alpine Valley Music Center**, W2699 County Rd D, Elkhorn, WI, 262-642-4400; purchase tickets at all Chicagoland Ticketmasters or order by phone: 800-745-3000. On the day of the event you may purchase tickets at the box office.
- **Arie Crown Theatre**, 2301 S Lake Shore Dr, Chicago, 312-791-6190, www.ariecrown.com; parking costs $16, $20 for valet service. The theater is wheelchair accessible. Tickets can be purchased through Ticketmaster or from the theater's website.
- **Auditorium Theatre**, 50 E Congress Pkwy, Chicago, www.auditoriumtheatre.org; purchase tickets through Ticketmaster or in person at the box office. Historic theater located in the Roosevelt University building.
- **Bradley Center**, 1001 N 4th St, Milwaukee, WI, www.bmoharrisbradleycenter.com; Events Hotline: 414-227-0797; tickets can be purchased through Ticketmaster or at the box office. (Phone numbers vary depending on caller's location, see website for your correct number.)
- **Klipsch Music Center**, 12880 E 146 St, Noblesville, IN, 317-776-3337; tickets available at all Ticketmaster locations, by phone at 317-239-5151, online at www.livenation.com, or at the Music Center box office. A parking fee of $2.75 is added to each ticket, $4 to each ticket for festival shows. The $10 lawn ticket available for selected events includes the parking fee.
- **Marcus Amphitheater**, 100 N Harbor Dr, Milwaukee, WI, 414-273-2680; enjoyable space with a view of Lake Michigan and the Milwaukee skyline. Tickets can be purchased at Ticketmaster or at the amphitheater box office in person. Visit marcusamp.com for more information.
- **Ravinia**, Lake Cook and Green Bay Roads, Highland Park, www.ravinia.org; popular outdoor venue with a pavilion, two recital halls, terrace seating with a restaurant, and expansive lawns for picnicking while listening. Starting in mid-April, tickets can be ordered by downloading a form and faxing it to 847-266-0641, or by phone after May 25th at 847-266-5100. The box office opens in mid-May and tickets may be purchased there as well. A $7 service fee is added to all faxed, phoned, and online orders.

- **Soldier Field Concerts,** 1410 S Museum Campus Dr, Chicago; purchase tickets through Ticketmaster. Event parking prices vary widely. Stadium information is at www.soldierfield.net. You may not want to get seats on the south end as the stage is usually set up on the north end.
- **First Midwest Bank Amphitheatre (formerly the Tweeter Center),** 19100 S Ridgeland Ave, Tinley Park, 312-540-2000; tickets can be purchased through Ticketmaster. Pavilion area is handicap accessible. VIP Box or Sky Suites for private parties are available. No charge for parking.
- **UIC Pavilion,** 525 S Racine, Chicago, www.uicpavilion.com/pavilion; parking available across the street and in the parking structure next door; parking ranges from $5 to $7 depending on event. Ticket information at: 312-413-5700.
- **United Center,** 1901 W Madison St, www.unitedcenter.com, 312-455-4500 for tickets. Parking ranges from $15 to $30 for cars; $25 for limos, buses, and RVs. Wheelchair accessible. Group- and kid-friendly.

## NIGHT CLUBS

If you're a party animal, you'll be happy to know that many clubs stay open very late in Chicago, some as late as 5 a.m. Before hitting the scene, you should consider how you will be getting home at that hour. While CTA buses and trains run around the clock, night-owl service is less frequent, and some lines do not run at all late at night. You might want to call the CTA for a late night bus or 'L' schedule if you know where you are heading on a particular night out—or be prepared to hail a cab.

Take your pick for a night out from those listed here or be adventurous and find something new.

### ROCK

- **Cubby Bear,** 1059 W Addison St, www.cubbybear.com, 773-327-1662; Wrigleyville club with live music, café, and post-game parties
- **Double Door,** 1572 N Milwaukee Ave, www.doubledoor.com, 773-489-3160; Wicker Park club specializing in hard rock, alternative rock, and everything grungy
- **Empty Bottle,** 1035 N Western Ave, www.emptybottle.com, 773-276-3600; Ukrainian Village venue for eclectic live music, including indie rock, experimental, hardcore honkytonk, electronica...
- **The Metro,** 3730 N Clark St, www.metrochicago.com, 773-549-4140; 1100 capacity. All early (6–7 p.m.) shows are all ages. All shows in the adjoining Smart Bar are 21 and over. Tickets at the box office or through Ticketmaster.
- **Park West,** 322 W Armitage Ave, www.jamusa.com, 773-929-1322; intimate live venue with great views (unless there's dancing) and 1920s ambience.

- **Riviera**, 4746 N Racine Ave, corner of Broadway and Lawrence Ave, www.jamusa.com, 773-275-6800; lovely old venue with 2500 capacity and somewhat crumbling grandeur. Views are best from balcony.
- **The Vic Theatre**, 3145 N Sheffield Ave, www.jamusa.com/Venues/Vic/Concerts.aspx, 773-472-0449; well-located old theater and concert venue; performances include good musical variety; the Vic also holds second-run movies in a "Brew and View," several times weekly

### JAZZ
- **Andy's Jazz and Restaurant Club**, 11 E Hubbard St, www.andysjazzclub.com, 312-642-6805; jazz and blues near the Mag Mile
- **The Backroom**, 937 N Rush St, www.backroomchicago.com, 312-751-2433; jazz, blues, and Motown.
- **Green Dolphin Street**, 2200 N Ashland Ave, www.jazzitup.com, 773-395-0066; sophisticated dining and jazz venue. Cover ranges from $0 to $20.
- **The Green Mill**, 4802 N Broadway, greenmilljazz.com, 773-878-5552; historic Uptown venue famous for 1920s connections to Al Capone's outfit. Reasonable cover and an old-time ambience.
- **Jazz Institute of Chicago**, www.jazzinchicago.org, 312-427-1676; this nonprofit organization has sponsored the Jazz Fair for 21 years and has programmed the Chicago Jazz Festival from its inception. They commission new works, sponsor musician residencies and workshops, and collect oral histories from the greats and almost-greats. Members enjoy discounts at record stores, clubs, and on music lessons, as well as free concerts and other perks. Membership levels range from Basic ($40) to Benefactor ($1000). Their website provides a calendar of events, and a full listing of membership benefits.
- **Jazz Showcase**, 806 S Plymouth Ct, www.jazzshowcase.com, 312-360-2034
- **Velvet Lounge**, 67 E Cermak Rd, 312-794-5904; highly regarded jazz club featuring respectful audiences and musicians willing to innovate

### BLUES
You have come to the right part of the country if you like to hear live blues.

- **B.L.U.E.S.**, 2519 N Halsted, www.chicagobluesbar.com, 773-528-1012
- **Blue Chicago**, www.bluechicago.com, 536 N Clark St, 312-661-0100
- **The House of Blues**, 329 N Dearborn St, www.houseofblues.com, 312-923-2000; some blues and a little of everything else, including an award-winning southern buffet gospel brunch.
- **Buddy Guy's Legends**, 700 S Wabash Ave, www.buddyguy.com, 312-427-1190
- **Kingston Mines**, 2548 N Halsted St, kingstonmines.com, 773-477-4646; traditional blues: two bands on two stages every night of the year

## FOLK/COUNTRY/COFFEEHOUSES

- **Abbey Pub and Restaurant**, 3420 W Grace St, www.abbeypub.com, 773-478-4408
- **Old Town School of Folk Music**, 4544 N Lincoln Ave, www.oldtownschool.org, 773-728-6000; folk and world music
- **Schubas Tavern**, 3159 N Southport Ave, www.schubas.com, 773-525-2508; pleasant, small venue with adjoining bar and affiliated American restaurant, the Harmony Grill
- **University of Chicago's annual Folk Festival,** www.uofcfolk.org, takes place in February. For three days and nights, folk musicians from all over the country come and perform in various venues around Hyde Park and the U of C campus. Saturday and Sunday workshops open to the public. Call 773-702-7300 for more information.

## REGGAE

- **Exedus Lounge**, 3477 N Clark St, www.exeduslounge.com, 773-348-3998; old-school reggae club
- **The Wild Hare**, 2610 N Halsted, www.wildharemusic.com, 773-770-3511; bastion of world beat, reggae, and roots music. Cover: $7 weekdays, $10 Fridays, $15 Saturdays.

## POP

- **Funky Buddha Lounge**, 728 W Grand Ave, www.funkybuddha.com, 312-666-1695
- **Smart Bar**, 3730 N Clark St, www.smartbarchicago.com, 773-549-4140
- **Wicker Park Tavern,** 1958 W North Ave, www.wickerparktavernchicago.com, 773-278-5138; $1 burgers with drink purchase; open Sun–Fri till 4 a.m., and Saturdays till 5 a.m.

For more club-hopping information, visit www.chicago-scene.com.

## LATE NIGHT CLUBS

If you like to party into the wee hours, you'll want to head to the River North or Wicker Park sections of town. The crowds here, for the most part, are a bit younger than in the Division Street–area clubs. Many of the lounges, clubs, and trendy hangouts stay open until 4 a.m. or 5 a.m., some with late kitchens.

- **Baton Show Lounge**, 436 N Clark St, www.thebatonshowlounge.com, 312-644-5269; female impersonators.
- **Brehon Pub**, 731 N Wells St, www.bretonpub.com, 312-642-1071

- **Delilah's,** 2771 N Lincoln Ave, www.delilahschicago.com, 773-472-2771; plays great R&B, rock, punk, country—a place for music lovers with discerning taste in drink as well.
- **Excalibur,** 632 N Dearborn St, www.excaliburchicago.com, 312-266-1944; dancing and pub food in a supposedly haunted old Romanesque revival landmark.
- **Le Bar,** 20 E Chestnut St, www.sofitel-chicago.com, 312-324-4000; located in the Hotel Sofitel Chicago Water Tower, this club has a great view and a sophisticated crowd.
- **Nacional 27,** 325 W Huron St, www.n27chicago.com, 312-664-2727; modern salsa club and Latin restaurant.
- **Redhead Piano Bar,** 16 W Ontario St, www.redheadpianobar.com, 312-640-1000; old-fashioned piano bar.
- **Spy Bar,** 646 N Franklin St, www.spybarchicago.com, 312-337-2191; contemporary décor and DJs.
- **The Underground,** 56 W Illinois St, www.theundergroundchicago.com, 312-644-7600; this literally underground dance hotspot is trendy, expensive, and exclusive—a good place for celebrity sightings. $20 cover.
- **The Violet Hour,** 1520 N Damen Ave, www.thevioletthour.com, 773-252-1500; Wicker Park lounge with outstanding custom cocktails and a dim speakeasy atmosphere.
- **Vision Nightclub,** 632 N Dearborn St, www.visionnightclub.com, 312-266-3333 (days), 312-266-1944 (nights and weekends); strobe lights, VIP level, dance floor below: you know the place

## MUSEUMS

Chicago has some of the finest museums in the country, and is on most touring schedules for both national and international exhibitions. Most are closed Mondays.

### ART

- **The Art Institute of Chicago,** Michigan Ave at Adams St, 312-443-3600, www.artic.edu; incredible masters' works on display, including Picasso, Renoir, Matisse, Van Gogh, as well as ancient works from classical Greece and Rome and a noted, millennia-spanning Asian collection. The new Modern Wing is an ultra-modernist design that includes lots of glass, a metallic "flying carpet" roof, and a bridge across Monroe Avenue to Millennium Park. Touring shows often sell out, so line up early. Admission is free on Tuesdays. Memberships available.

- **Chicago Artists' Coalition**, www.caconline.org, 312-491-8888; resource for community art events. Also exhibits and sells artwork by members.
- **Illinois Arts Council**, www.arts.illinois.gov, 800-237-6994; publishes an annual art fair directory
- **David and Alfred Smart Museum of Art**, University of Chicago, 5550 S Greenwood Ave, 773-702-0200, smartmuseum.uchicago.edu
- **Intuit, The Center for Intuitive and Outsider Art**, 756 N Milwaukee Ave, www.art.org, 312-243-9088; free admission
- **Museum of Contemporary Art**, 220 E Chicago Ave, www.mcachicago.org, 312-280-2660; children 12 and under admitted free. Also free on Tuesday evenings.
- **National Museum of Mexican Fine Art**, 1852 W 19th St, www.nationalmuseumofmexicanart.org, 312-738-1503; free admission
- **National Vietnam Veterans Art Museum**, 1801 S Indiana Ave, www.nvvam.org, 312-326-0270

## GALLERIES

In recent years, especially with the rejuvenation of the River North neighborhood, Chicago's art scene has blossomed. While it has a ways to go before it can truly rival New York City's SoHo, there is a level and quality of activity here that can't be ignored. Many galleries are located between Chicago and Grand Streets, on the "Lake" Streets, i.e., Superior, Huron, and Erie. Generally, these galleries hold open evening hours on the first Thursday or Friday of the month. During that time, you can often meet artists exhibiting their work and other art lovers as well. If you want to experience the art scene up close, attend the **free Saturday gallery tours** led by local art gallery owners in the River North neighborhood. Coordinated by The Chicago Gallery News, gallery owners or directors and those interested in a tour meet each Saturday at the Starbucks located at 750 North Franklin Street. There are four different tours that go from 11 a.m. to 12:30 p.m. No reservations are required. Other art-friendly communities—still less upscale but full of artists and their studios—include Wicker Park and Pilsen.

A few galleries, almost all in the River North area, are:

- **Alan Koppel Gallery**, 806 N Dearborn Ave, www.alankoppel.com, 312-640-0730
- **Aldo Castillo Gallery**, 675 N Franklin St, www.artaldo.com, 312-337-2536
- **Ann Nathan Gallery**, 212 W Superior St, www.annnathangallery.com, 312-664-6622
- **Carl Hammer Gallery**, 740 N Wells St, www.hammergallery.com, 312-266-8512
- **Catherine Edelman Gallery**, 300 W Superior St, www.edelmangallery.com, 312-266-2350

- **Douglas Dawson Gallery**, 400 N Morgan St, www.douglasdawson.com, 312-226-7975
- **Gruen Galleries**, 226 W Superior St, www.gruengalleries.com, 312-337-6262
- **Echt Gallery**, 222 W Superior St, www.habatatchicago.com, 312-440-0288
- **Melanee Cooper Gallery**, 740 N Franklin St, www.melaneecoopergallery.com, 312-202-9305
- **Primitive Art Works**, 130 N Jefferson St, www.beprimitive.com, 312-575-9600
- **Roy Boyd Gallery**, 739 N Wells St, www.royboydgallery.com, 312-642-1606
- **Schneider Gallery**, 230 W Superior St, www.schneidergallerychicago.com, 312-988-4033; photography
- **Vale Craft Gallery**, 230 W Superior St, www.valecraftgallery.com, 312-337-3525
- **Zg Gallery**, 300 W Superior St, www.zggallery.com, 312-654-9900
- **Zhou B Art Center**, 1029 W 35th St, www.zbcenter.org, 773-523-0200
- **Zolla/Lieberman**, 325 W Huron St, zollaliebermangallery.com, 312-944-1990

## HISTORY MUSEUMS, CULTURAL CENTERS

- **Balzekas Museum of Lithuanian Culture**, 6500 S Pulaski Rd, www.balzekasmuseum.org, 773-582-6500; this museum includes exhibits on Lithuanian history and culture as well as the largest Lithuanian research center outside of Lithuania.
- **Cantigny**, Wheaton, www.cantignypark.com, 630-668-5161, www.rrmtf.org; the 500-acre former estate of Colonel Robert R. McCormick, dedicated to the history of the 1st Infantry Division from WWI to the present; historic house tours and formal gardens.
- **Charnley-Persky House Museum**, 1365 N Astor St, 312-915-0105; this house was designed by Frank Lloyd Wright while he was employed by Louis Sullivan and is now owned by the Society of Architectural Historians. Limited tours available.
- **Chicago Cultural Center**, 78 E Washington St, Randolph and Michigan Aves, 312-744-6630; the nation's first free municipal cultural center. An architectural showplace for the performing and visual arts; also houses the city's official visitor center. Hosts free exhibitions, concerts, and events.
- **Chicago History Museum**, 1601 N Clark St, 312-642-4600, www.chicagohistory.org; exhibitions, collections, and programs about Chicago, Illinois, and select periods of American history (such as the Lincoln era). Free on Mondays.
- **Cuneo Museum & Gardens**, 1350 N Milwaukee Ave, Vernon Hills, 847-362-3014; this Venetian-style mansion is home to many art collections and is surrounded by 75 acres of lakes, fountains, formal gardens, antique classical statuary, and a conservatory housing exotic plants. Closed Mondays.

- **Du Sable Museum of African American History**, 740 E 56th Pl, 773-947-0600, www.dusablemuseum.org; reasonable admission, free for those under six and for all on Sundays
- **Garfield Park Conservatory**, 300 N Central Park Ave, 312-746-5100, www.garfieldconservatory.org; six multi-faceted greenhouses, two grand exhibition halls, hands-on, interactive children's garden and demonstration garden for learning about urban gardening
- **Glessner House Museum**, 1800 S Prairie Ave, 312-326-1480, www.glessnerhouse.org; the only surviving building by architect Henry Hobson Richardson and home to the Glessner family's outstanding collection of 19th and early-20th-century furniture and decorative art objects. Wednesday is free. Tour sizes are limited and can include Clarke House, Chicago's oldest building, and/or a walking tour for an additional cost.
- **Mitchell Museum of the American Indian**, Evanston, 3001 Central St, 847-475-1030, www.mitchellmuseum.org; museum's collections range from the Paleo-Indian period through the present day. Permanent exhibitions on diverse Native American cultures. There are "touching tables" in each gallery as well as two thematic temporary exhibits. Donations suggested.
- **Museum of Contemporary Photography**, Columbia College, 600 S Michigan Ave, 312-663-5554, www.mocp.org; over 6,000 photographs and related items since 1945 as well as rotating exhibits; admission is free.
- **Naper Settlement**, Naperville, 523 S Webster St, 630-420-6010, www.napersettlement.org; a museum village where 19th-century homes, shops, public buildings, children's activities and costumed interpreters tell the story of daily life in Naperville as it changed from a frontier outpost to a bustling turn-of-the-20th-century community. Discounted admission in winter.
- **Oriental Institute**, 1155 E 58th St, 773-702-9514, www.oi.uchicago.edu; stunning collection of ancient artifacts from the cradle of civilization: Egypt, Sumer, Mesopotamia; admission is free, donations suggested.
- **Schingoethe Center for Native American Cultures**, Aurora University, 347 S Gladstone Ave, Aurora, www.aurora.edu/museum, 630-892-6431; call for information about their annual Memorial Day weekend Pow Wow.
- **Spertus Institute of Jewish Studies**, 610 S Michigan Ave, 312-322-1700, www.spertus.edu; houses a collection of over 10,000 objects, artifacts, and works of art spanning 3500 years of Jewish history, including the nation's first permanent museum exhibition on the Holocaust. Free on Friday.
- **Swedish American Museum**, 5211 N Clark St, in the Andersonville neighborhood, 773-728-8111, www.swedishamericanmuseum.org; this three-story museum includes a Children's Museum of Immigration and Swedish library, and is the place to celebrate Swedish holidays. Free on the second Tuesday of each month.

## SCIENCE

- **Adler Planetarium and Astronomy Museum**, 1300 S Lake Shore Dr, 312-922-STAR, www.adlerplanetarium.org; galleries, theaters and other exciting areas where you can learn about the stars. Admission packages come with one show; residents receive a $1 to $2 discount. Mondays and Tuesdays are free in the fall.
- **Air Classics Museum**, Sugar Grove, 630-466-0888, www.airclassicsmuseum.org; located in the Aurora Municipal Airport, the museum offers unique exhibits and educational programs for all ages, chronicling the role of aviation
- **Cernan Earth & Science Center**, River Grove, 708-456-0300, ext 3372; located at Triton College, this space-age facility has a multi-functional, 100-seat dome theatre and a Space Hall
- **The Field Museum**, 1400 S Lake Shore Dr, 312-922-9410, www.fieldmuseum.org; free Mondays and Tuesdays, September–February. $1 to $2 discounts on general admission for Chicago residents, greater discounts for special exhibits.
- **International Museum of Surgical Science**, 1524 N Lake Shore Dr, www.imss.org, 312-642-6502; housed in a landmark-status mansion are artifacts that span over 4,000 years of important developments in surgery and medicine. Free Tuesdays with a suggested donation.
- **Jurica Nature Museum**, Lisle, www.benuscience.org/museum/, 630-829-6569; small natural history museum located on the campus of Benedictine University, with many animal and bird specimens, an African savanna diorama, and many educational programs. Limited afternoon hours.
- **Museum of Science and Industry**, 57th St and Lake Shore Dr, www.msichicago.org, 773-684-1414; over 2,000 interactive units and 800 exhibits such as spacecraft, planes, trains, cars, submarine, a walk through a model of a heart, a baby-chick hatchery, and an OmniMax theater. Discounts for residents. See website for select free days.
- **Peggy Notebaert Nature Museum**, 2430 N Cannon Dr, www.naturemuseum.org, 773-755-5100; with wildflowers, trees, wildlife and animal dress-up for children, this venue has been helping urban dwellers to connect with the natural world since the 1850s; parking available at the Lincoln Park Zoo. $1 discount for residents. Thursdays free.
- **Scitech Hands On Museum**, 18 W Benton St, Aurora, scitechmuseum.org, 630-859-3434; teeming with activities that will really appeal to kids, such as a virtual reality room and outdoor science park. Discount coupon available on their website.
- **Shedd Aquarium**, 1200 S Lake Shore Dr, www.sheddaquarium.org, 312-939-2438; open since 1929, it is one of the oldest public aquariums and home to many animals and conservation efforts. Many special exhibits. Residents

get free admission on selected days of the year; check the website for more information.
- **Volo Auto Museum & Antique Mall**, 27582 Volo Village Rd, Volo, www.volocars.com, 815-385-3644, boasts over 300 classic cars, from antique to muscle (the largest collection in the world), and car stars from movies and TV—the original Batmobile!—as well as an antique mall and auto sales showroom.

## LITERARY LIFE

Chicago has a strong literary bent—from highly acclaimed authors and poets who grew up in Chicago (David Mamet, Nelson Algren, William Goldman, Michael Crichton) to those who found their inspiration here (Carl Sandburg, Saul Bellow). From area universities, vast public and private libraries, and a solid selection of chain and independent booksellers, you will come to understand that this is a reading town. Every June, thousands of booklovers from across the Midwest attend the Printers Row Book Fair held outdoors on Dearborn (Congress to Park Streets). For more information: www.chicagotribune.com/entertainment/books/printersrowlitfest/

### GENERAL INTEREST BOOKSTORES

- **Afterwords**, 23 E Illinois St, www.after-wordschicago.com, 312-464-1110; new and used titles.
- **Barbara's Bookstore**, www.barbarasbookstore.com, 1350 N Wells, 312-642-5044; 233 S Wacker Dr, 312-466-0223; 1218 S Halsted St, 312-413-2665; 111 N State St, 312-781-3033; 1100 Lake, Oak Park, 708-848-9140
- **Barnes & Noble** offers literary, reference, trade, and children's books, plus a wide selection of magazines and newspapers. Author readings and signings and other events are common. Some locations have in-store cafés and live music. Locations: Chicago, Skokie, Evanston, Orland Park, Oak Terrace, Deerfield, Downers Grove, Mount Prospect, Arlington Heights, Wheaton, Schaumburg, Naperville, and Vernon Hills. See the Yellow Pages or check www.barnesandnoble.com.
- **Sandmeyer's Bookstore**, 714 S Dearborn St, www.sandmeyersbookstore.com, 312-922-2104
- **Seminary Co-op Bookstore**, 5751 S Woodlawn Ave, www.semcoop.com, 773-752-4381.
- **57th Street Books**, 1301 E 57th St, semcoop.com/about-57th-street-books, 773-684-1300; at the Newberry Library, 312-943-9090; general interest and scholarly bookstore, also sponsoring many author readings and events.
- **Unabridged Books**, 3251 N Broadway St, www.unabridgedbookstore.com, 773-883-9119

## SPECIAL INTEREST BOOKSTORES

For academic specialty books, head to any university campus bookstore. Other specialty bookstores include:

- **Beck's Book Store**, www.becksbooks.com, several locations, including: 4520 N Broadway, 773-784-7963; 6464 N Sheridan Rd, 773-743-2281; 4000 W Lake Ave, Glenview, 847-486-4879; college textbooks.
- **Chicago Architecture Foundation**, 224 S Michigan Ave, #116, 312-922-3432, www.architecture.org
- **UIC Medical Bookstore**, 828 S Wolcott Ave #1, www.uicmedbooks.com, 312-413-5550
- **Women and Children First**, 5233 N Clark St (in Andersonville), 773-769-9299, www.womenandchildrenfirst.com; store specializing in books by women for women; also has a well-stocked children's section.

## USED BOOKSTORES/SALES

- **Friends of Arlington Heights Memorial Library**, 847-392-0100; holds "gently" used book sales in the spring and fall.
- **Friends of West Chicago Public Library**, 630-231-1552, holds an annual book sale in the fall. Contact your local library for information regarding its book sales.
- **Powell's,** 2850 N Lincoln Ave, 773-248-1444; 1218 S Halsted St, 312-243-9070; 1501 E 57th St, 773-955-7780, www.powellschicago.com; specializes in second-hand, out-of-print and collector's editions.
- **Printers Row Book Fair**. Each June, the *Chicago Tribune* sponsors two days' and seven stages' worth of literary programs for children and adults. Close to 200 booksellers set up booths, offering rare, used, old, and new books. This free and well-attended outdoor fair is held in the Printers Row neighborhood, on the blocks surrounding Dearborn and Polk Streets. For more information, go online to www.chicagotribune.com/entertainment/books/printersrowlitfest/.

## LIBRARIES

If you need to do extensive research, the libraries of the major universities in town are **DePaul**, 773-325-7863 (Lincoln Park) or 312-362-8432, **The University of Chicago**, 773-702-8740, **Northwestern**, 847-491-7658, and **Loyola**, 773-508-2632. Many universities extend library privileges to students registered in another university. Check the university library of your choice for its policy or, if you are a matriculating student, check with the university's library for policy information. If you are not a student, you may be able to use a university library but not check out materials, or, for a fee, you may be able to do both. Again, check with your local university library for details.

For public libraries, check the listings at the end of the **Neighborhood Profiles** for a branch library near you. Or visit one of these regional branch libraries:

- **Harold Washington Library Center**, 400 S State St, www.chipublib.org, call 312-747-4300 for general information. More than just a depository of books, in the ten floors that make up the Washington Library Center there are classrooms, theaters, auditoriums, video theaters, meeting rooms, typewriter rental areas, a language lab, books for the blind, computer connections, a restaurant, a winter garden and more. There are plenty of (pricey) parking lots nearby, but public transportation is so convenient to this area that, unless you are coming from the suburbs, CTA is the way to go.
- **Des Plaines Library**, 1501 Ellinwood Ave, Des Plaines, 847-827-5551, dppl. org; this new facility contains over 200,000 magazines, books, audio books, CDs, and periodicals. It offers bus tours to cultural events, seasonal reading clubs, children's programs, crafts and lectures. Conveniently located, steps away from the Metra train stop.
- **Arlington Heights Memorial Library**, 500 N Dunton, 847-392-0100, ahml. info; one of the largest libraries in the state, this facility is a great community resource offering a variety of programs for children and adults. It is well-known for its excellent book sales.
- **Evanston Public Library,** 1703 Orrington Ave, Evanston, 847-488-8600, www.epl.org
- **Oak Lawn Public Library,** 9427 S Raymond Ave, Oak Lawn, www.lib.oaklawn.il.us, 708-422-4990; one of the largest libraries in the south suburbs.

Listed below are some of the many private and public libraries in Chicago and surrounding suburbs. Please note that many of these institutions are not open to the general public. Call ahead or check the library's website for more details.

- **Art Institute of Chicago Library,** Michigan Ave at Adams St, 312-499-4260
- **Charles Deering McCormick Library of Special Collections**, www.library. northwestern.edu, 847-491-7658
- **Chicago History Museum Research Center,** 1601 N Clark St, www.chicagohs.org, 312-642-4600
- **Columbia College Library,** 624 S Michigan Ave, www.lib.colum.edu, 312-369-7900
- **DePaul University Libraries,** www.lib.depaul.edu; Lincoln Park, 2350 N Kenmore Ave, 773-325-7862; Loop Campus, 1 E Jackson Dr, 312-362-8432; Law Library, 25 E Jackson Dr, 312-362-8701
- **Dominican University/Rebecca Crown Library,** 7900 W Division St, River Forest, www.dom.edu/library, 708-524-6875

- **Garrett-Evangelical & Seabury Western Theological Seminary (The United Library)**, 2121 Sheridan Rd, www.garrett.edu/library, 847-866-3909
- **Gerber/Hart Library**, 6500 N Clark St, 773-381-8030, www.gerberhart.org; this unique library is a depository for the records of homosexuals, bisexuals, and transgendered individuals and the organizations which serve them. It is the largest library of its kind in the Midwest.
- **Government Publications and Maps**, www.library.northwestern.edu/libraries-collections/evanston-campus/government-information, 847-491-3130
- **Loyola University Libraries**; log on to libraries.luc.edu for information about the several different libraries, their locations, and their specialized collections, as well as contact info
- **National-Louis University**, www.nl.edu/library/hoursandlocations.cfm; library locations on campuses in Chicago, Elgin, Lisle, North Shore, and Wheeling
- **Newberry Library**, 60 W Walton St, www.newberry.org, 312-943-9090; a free, independent library with an emphasis on the humanities. It maintains a large, non-circulating collection of rare maps, manuscripts, and books. Anyone over the age of 16 who is conducting research is welcome to become a reader here. The Newberry also holds many events, concerts, and exhibitions for the public.
- **Northern Suburban Library System**, 125 Tower Dr, Burr Ridge, www.nsls.info, 630-734-5000
- **Northwestern University Library**, www.northwestern.edu/libraries/index.htm; several libraries in Evanston and Chicago
- **Spertus Institute of Jewish Studies/Asher Library**, 610 S Michigan Ave, www.spertus.edu/library, 312-322-1712
- **Metropolitan Library System**, www.mls.lib.il.us, provides a listing and information about 600 suburban libraries and phone numbers
- **Transportation Library**, Evanston, www.library.northwestern.edu/transportation, 847-491-5273
- **University of Chicago/Regenstein Library**, 1100 E 57th St, www.lib.uchicago.edu/e/reg, 773-702-8701
- **University of Illinois–Chicago,** 801 S Morgan St, library.uic.edu, 312-996-2716

## MISCELLANEOUS

There is a side to Chicago fun that runs a little off beat. The less traditional among you may be interested in the following less-than-traditional ways to spend a night out:

- **Beer School** at the Siebel Institute of Technology, 1777 N Clybourn Ave, 312-255-0705, www.siebelinstitute.com; forget the flavored martinis, you will soon discover that Chicago is a beer town. And now that it is both fashion-

able and legal to brew your own, consider taking a professional brewing class here. Details available on the website.
- **Nightmares Inc.**, 1945 Cornell, Melrose Park, 708-344-2084, www.dreamreapers.com; are you the kind of person whose favorite holiday is Halloween? You no longer have to wait until October to be scared out of your wits. This 14,000-square-foot haunted house, rated the best in Illinois for three years running, is staffed by professional actors and is open several times throughout the year. They are also happy to oblige corporate groups and small parties. Visit their website for more details.

## CULTURE FOR KIDS

Living in Chicago gives you the opportunity to expose your child to a rich cultural life; from bookstore events to performing arts, the Chicago child is offered a wealth of exciting opportunities. Don't overlook your local public library and park district as sources of enriching programs for your children. For information about One Book, One Chicago, visit www.chipublib.org/eventsprog/programs/onebook_onechgo.php.

### MUSIC

- **Chicago Children's Choir**, Chicago Cultural Center, 78 E Washington Ave, 5th Floor, www.ccchoir.org, 312-849-8300
- **Glen Ellyn Children's Chorus**, www.animasingers.org, 630-858-2471; this talented troupe has achieved international recognition, performing in concert with the Chicago Symphony Orchestra and at the Ravinia Festival, and touring throughout the United States, Canada, New Zealand, Brazil, and Europe. Activities include pre-choral training for the youngest children, summer workshops, an annual festival workshop and more.
- **Elgin's Children's Chorus**, elginchildrenschorus.org; over 200 children from ages eight to sixteen perform three major concerts each year, in addition to performing with the Elgin Symphony Orchestra. For tickets call 847-622-0300. For information call 847-931-SING.
- **Metropolis Youth Symphony**, www.metropolisarts.com, performs at Metropolis Performing Arts Center, 111 W Campbell St, Arlington Heights; 847-577-2121 for tickets, 847-577-5982 ext 240 for information.
- **Oak Park and River Forest Children's Chorus**, www.oprfcc.com, 708-383-1971

### MUSEUMS

- **Bronzeville Children's Museum**, 773-721-9301, www.bronzevillechildrensmuseum.com; first and only African-American children's museum in the

country, opened in the southwest suburb of Evergreen Park in 1993 and in 2008 moved to its new Chicago facility at 9301 S Stony Island Ave. It houses interactive exhibits and programs for learning in the areas of the arts, humanities, and sciences.
- **The Children's Museum in Oak Lawn**, 5100 Museum Dr, Oak Lawn, www.cmoaklawn.org, 708-423-6709; south suburban children's museum with gorgeous new facility currently under construction.
- **Chicago Children's Museum**, 700 E Grand Ave at Navy Pier, 312-527-1000, www.chicagochildrensmuseum.org; 15 permanent exhibits and programming spaces provide innovative learning experiences for families in an inviting and large building. Free Thursday evenings.
- **DuPage Children's Museum**, 301 N Washington St, Naperville, www.dupagechildrensmuseum.org, 630-637-8000; plenty of hands-on, stimulating exhibits combining science and fun. Visit their website for calendar details.
- **Kohl's Children Museum**, 2100 Patriot Blvd, Glenview, www.kohlchildrensmuseum.org, 847-832-6600; the "hands-on learning laboratory" of exhibits in this huge new facility encourage the building of strong social skills by creating situations which require children to help each other and work as a team. Children under one are free.
- **Lake County Discovery Museum**, 27277 N Forest Preserve Rd, Lakewood Forest Preserve, Rte 176 and Fairfield Rd, Wauconda, 847-968-3400, www.lcfpd.org/discovery_museum; a life-sized mastodon statue guards the entrance to this collection of hands-on interactive exhibits which introduce the history of Lake County, located on the Lakewood Forest Preserve. Discounts on Tuesdays, and for seniors after 2 p.m.
- **Scitech Hands-On Museum**; see earlier information for science museums.

## OUTDOOR

The **Forest Preserve District of Cook County** operates six nature centers. Visitors can learn about native plants and animals from the professional naturalist on staff. Group visits must be scheduled in advance. Picnicking is permitted in designated areas. Visit the Forest Preserve District's website at www.fpdcc.com, or see **Greenspaces and Beaches** for more information.

## ZOOS

- **Brookfield Zoo**, 8400 W 31 St, Brookfield, 708-688-8000, www.brookfieldzoo.org; with 200 acres of animals, this is *the* zoo in the Chicago area
- **Lincoln Park Zoo**, 2001 N Clark St, 312-742-2000, www.lpzoo.org; this small but wonderfully situated free zoo is a welcome respite for adults and fami-

lies alike. Many animals at its Pritzker Children's Zoo may be touched under supervision.

## THEATER

- **Emerald City Theatre**, 773-935-6100, www.emeraldcitytheatre.com; most performances at the **Apollo Theatre**
- **Northbrook Musical Theatre for Young Audiences**, 3323 Walters Ave, Northbrook, 847-291-2367, www.nbparks.org/Theatre-Performing-Arts/general-info.htm

## OTHER

- **Donley's Wild West Town,** 8512 S Union Rd, Union, 815-923-9000; recreated Wild West town: train rides, pony rides, and shows. Open Saturdays, Sundays, and holidays.
- **Six Flags Great America and Hurricane Harbor,** I-94 at 132 Grand East Ave, Gurnee, 847-249-4636, www.sixflags.com
- **Enchanted Castle Restaurant & Entertainment Center,** 1103 S Main St, Lombard, 630-953-7860

# SPORTS AND RECREATION

WHETHER YOU ARE A PARTICIPANT OR A FAN, CHICAGO IS A sports-crazed town. In fact, if Chicago doesn't offer the sport you're looking for—whether to play or to watch—many will doubt its existence! There's even a sport that is popular nowhere else in the United States—or the world—and that's 16-inch softball, a game that requires only a bat and a 16-inch Clincher softball.

## SPORTING RESOURCES

Chicagoans can get their daily minimum requirement of sports news from several places. Check first with the local papers: the *Chicago Tribune*, *Chicago Sun-Times*, and the *Southtown Star* all devote lots of coverage to professional sports. Chicago City Newsstand, 4018 North Cicero, 773-545-7377, and at 860 Chicago Avenue/Main Street in Evanston, 847-425-8900, claims to have the biggest and best collection of sports publications in Chicago. Visit them directly, or check their virtual newsstand at www.citynewsstand.com. Your local community paper is another good source, especially for high school and younger teams. Dozens of high school teams are highlighted at www.illinoishighschoolsports.com. For college teams, check www.cbssports.com, where each team has its own page, and you can have your sports news e-mailed to you via the website's newsletter. If you are interested in a particular professional team, check their website. Many teams have an e-mail newsletter service.

Most area colleges and universities with sports programs produce press releases and publications to keep the public aware of its activities. Here are a few:

- **University of Chicago**, Sports Information Office, 773-702-4638
- **Saint Xavier University**, Women's Basketball, Men's Basketball/Cougars; Sports Information, 773-298-3110

- **Loyola University**, Sports Information Office, 773-508-2560
- **University of Illinois**, Sports Information Office, 312-996-2695
- **DePaul University**, Sports Information Office, 773-325-7526
- **Northwestern University**, Department of Athletics, 847-491-3205

Finally, if you are interested in enrolling your youngster in a team sport, check with your local parks and recreation program, which often offers introductory lessons. Youth and adult leagues are also popular throughout the area. Many leagues work in cooperation with the park districts; the districts will offer registration for team sports through their catalogues, while the leagues will provide the coaches, gear and training.

## PROFESSIONAL AND COLLEGE SPORTS

### BASEBALL

Baseball season begins in early April and lasts until the first week in October, unless the Cubs or White Sox find themselves in post-season play. You'll find quickly that your place of residence aligns you as either a Cubs fan (North Side) or Sox fan (South Side). And you should know that the rivalry between the North Siders and the South Siders is sometimes taken to the extreme. So, don't be caught on the South Side cheering for the Cubbies!

- **Chicago Cubs** (National League), Wrigley Field, 1060 W Addison St, 60613, 773-404-2827, chicago.cubs.mlb.com; will accommodate group outings of 50 persons or more. Call 773-404-2827 for group sale information. You can purchase single game tickets at the Wrigley Field box office, at Tickets.com outlets (expect a service charge), or order by phone until two hours before game time, using American Express, Discover, MasterCard or VISA. Call Tickets.com at 800-843-2827. Phone orders will be mailed or, if time does not permit mailing, held at the special "will call" window. Tickets.com also has kiosks located in Sears full-line and hardware stores throughout the Chicago area, Wisconsin, and northwest Indiana, at select Sports Authority retail stores, and at the Chicago Tribune Tower. Log on to the Cubs' web page and follow the link for Tickets.com for specific locations. The Cubs' Box Office, 773-404-2827, is open 8 a.m. to 6 p.m., Monday–Friday, and Saturday and Sunday 9 a.m. to 4 p.m. There are wheelchair seating areas in the Field Box behind home plate and in the rear section of the Terrace Reserved section. If you need this kind of seating, make arrangements by calling 800-843-2827. Senior citizen tickets are discounted for Wednesday afternoon games in the Terrace Reserved section. MasterCard, VISA, Discover, American Express, and cash are accepted for ticket purchases at Wrigley Field.

- **Chicago White Sox** (American League), US Cellular Field (once known as Comiskey Park), 333 W 5th St, 60616, 312-674-1000, TDD 312-451-5188, chicago.whitesox.mlb.com; for season tickets, call 312-674-1000. Will accommodate group outings of 50 persons or more—call for details. All Monday night home contests are Family Night Half-Price games; Pepsi Tuesdays are also half-priced; and select Sundays are Willy Wonka days—tickets purchased at the field window that day are only $1 for kids. Other specials are listed on the website. You can purchase White Sox tickets by phone from Ticketmaster at 800-745-3000 until three hours before game time using American Express, Discover, MasterCard or VISA; at Ticketmaster outlets (locations include Carson Pirie Scott, Tower Records, Hot Tix, select Coconuts and Record Town locations); and online at the White Sox website. The post-game fireworks schedule is posted on the website. Wheelchair seating is available on each level; all levels accessible by elevators behind home plate. Wheelchair guests may make prior seating arrangements by calling 312-674-1000 or TDD 312-674-5235. For assistance during the game, or for the use of headsets, contact the guest relations booth.

## BASKETBALL

The professional basketball season begins in October, when baseball ends, and continues through April, with the NBA playoffs extending well into June.

Chicago also has several Division I men's college basketball teams, including the DePaul Blue Demons, who play at the Rosemont Horizon; the Loyola Ramblers, who play at Loyola University; and the Northwestern Wildcats, who play at McGaw Hall. Women's college basketball teams include the Chicago Blaze, who play at DePaul's Athletic Center, and the Flames, who play at the UIC Pavilion.

- **Chicago Bulls** (NBA), United Center, 1901 W Madison St, 60612, www.nba.com/bulls, 312-455-4000. Unless you're well connected, or willing to shell out big bucks to scalpers, your chances of finding last-minute tickets are slim, despite their fall from 1990s glory. Plan enough in advance, and you can purchase group and singles tickets: for individual games, tickets go on sale the last weekend of September at the United Center box office; online at www.nba.com/bulls; or through Ticketmaster outlets or at Ticketmaster.com; or call 800-4NBA-TIX. Group tickets (25 or more) go on sale through the Bulls front office in August. Purchase tickets by phone until three hours before game time with a credit card by calling Ticketmaster at 800-462-2849. Phone orders will be held at the "will call" window. There is a service charge added to the price of each ticket ordered by phone. Good luck!

## FOOTBALL

The Bears' popularity is evidenced by the approximately 60,000 die-hard Bears fans who, despite the team's less than stellar record, brave Chicago's notorious winter, a.k.a. "Bear weather," to attend home games at Soldier Field. Pre-season games start in August; the regular season ends in mid-December. The Bears began playing in their newly renovated stadium in 2003. Despite an overall consensus that the new stadium does not do justice to the classic lines of the original, which opened in 1924, the grounds surrounding Soldier Field offer 19 pleasant acres of greenspace and include an outdoor museum, a terraced garden, sledding hill, and a winter garden.

- **Chicago Bears** (NFL), Ticket Office is at 1000 Football Dr, Lake Forest, 60045, 847-295-6600, www.chicagobears.com. Bears tickets are tough to come by because season ticket holders hold most seats. If you want to get on the waiting list, go online to www.chicagobears.com and download a wait list form. It will cost you a $100 non-refundable deposit and there are only about 9,000 people ahead of you. You can purchase Bears single game tickets by mail every year by sending a self-addressed stamped envelope to the Bears ticket information office in early May. You will receive an order form, which you fill out and send back with a check on or after June 1. Any remaining tickets from the mail-order sale—and there aren't many—go to Ticketmaster for sale in July. You can (try to) purchase Bears tickets through Ticketmaster outlets or by phone with American Express, Discover, MasterCard or VISA cards by calling Ticketmaster at 800-745-3000. There is a service charge added to the price of each ticket.

## HOCKEY

Although not as high profile as the Bears, Cubs, and White Sox, the Chicago Blackhawks have a definite following, especially after they won the Stanley Cup in 2010. Like basketball, the regular NHL season runs from October until April with the Stanley Cup playoffs extending through the spring. Also in Chicago are the International Hockey League's Chicago Wolves and the US Hockey League's Chicago Steel.

- **Chicago Blackhawks** (NHL), United Center, 1901 W Madison St, 60612, 312-455-7000, http://blackhawks.nhl.com; you can purchase Blackhawks tickets at the Stadium box office, at Ticketmaster outlets or Ticketmaster phone service, 800-745-3000. With its loyal fan base of season ticket holders, tickets are difficult to get. But call and find out what's available: 312-455-7000. You can also download an order form from their website. Groups of 15 or more will get you some benefits. If you are interested in getting regular news about the Blackhawks, sign up for an e-mail newsletter at their website.

# SPORTS AND RECREATION

- **Chicago Wolves** (AHL), home games played at the Allstate Arena, 6920 N Mannheim Rd, Rosemont, 847-724-4625 or 800-THE-WOLVES, www.chicagowolves.com. Tickets are not as expensive as those for the Blackhawks games. You will see a lot more families and groups of Boy Scouts here. Ticket sales of 15 or more receive group benefits. For individual tickets, call Ticketmaster at 800-745-3000 or stop by the Allstate Arena's box office at 6920 N Mannheim Rd, 847-635-6601, 11 a.m. to 7 p.m., Monday–Friday, Saturday, noon to 5, and Sundays three hours before game time. Go to their website to order tickets, or contact the office at Chicago Wolves, 2301 Ravine Way, Glenview, IL 60025, 847-724-1652 (fax).
- **Chicago Steel** (USHL), 735 E Jefferson St, Bensenville, 60106, www.chicagosteelhockeyteam.com; home games are played out of the Edge Arena. Members of this 21-year-old and younger team are recruited by college hockey teams. The tickets for these games are the least expensive of the three teams. To buy tickets by phone, call 630-594-1161. You can also order tickets through the team's website.

## SOCCER

Although the 1994 World Cup brought international fans to town for much of the summer, temporarily increasing the sport's visibility, soccer in Chicago has remained an acquired taste. First, there was the outdoor Sting, and then the indoor Power, now the city again has an outdoor team, the Chicago Fire, a Major League expansion team. Soccer season runs from early April through late October, with twenty home games.

- **Chicago Fire** (MLS), www.chicago-fire.com; home games are played in Bridgeview at Toyota Park, an MLS regulation-sized soccer field and concert venue that opened in June 2006. For ticket information, call the Fire's general information number at 708-594-7200. Single tickets for home games go on sale in late March. To order by phone, call 888-MLS-FIRE. There is a discount for ticket sales of 15 or more, plus priority seating with advance purchase. To purchase group sales by phone, call 888-MLS-FIRE.

There are a number of strong **college soccer** teams in the area as well:

- **Augustana College**—men's and women's soccer, both NAIA, Division 1: women's link: www.augustana.edu/x1131.xml; men's link: www.augustana.edu/x1107.xml.
- **Benedictine University**—men's and women's soccer, both NAIA, Division 1: www.benueagles.com/index.aspx
- **College of St. Francis**—men's soccer, NAIA, Division 1, www.gofightingsaints.com

- **DePaul University**—men's and women's soccer, both NCAA, Division1: www.depaulbluedemons.com
- **Loyola University**—men's and women's soccer, both NCAA, Division 1: www.loyolaramblers.com
- **Northern Illinois University**—men's and women's soccer, both NCAA, Division 1: http://niuhuskies.cstv.com
- **Northwestern University**—men's and women's soccer, both NCAA, Division 1: www.northwestern.edu/campus-life/athletics/index.html
- **Saint Xavier University**—men's and women's NAIA Division: www.sxucougars.com

## DRAG RACING

- **Route 66 Raceway**, www.route66raceway.com; Chicago Speedway, 3200 S Chicago St, Joliet. Races usually take place during summer weekends. For tickets by phone: 888-629-7223, by fax: 815-727-7895; also available at the box office or online through Ticketmaster.com.

## HORSE RACING

The Chicago area offers four racetracks:

- **Balmoral Park Racetrack**, 26435 S Dixie Hwy, Crete, 708-672-1414; harness racing year-round
- **Maywood Park Race Track**, 8600 W North Ave, Melrose Park, 708-343-4800; harness racing February through May
- **Hawthorne Race Course**, 3501 S Laramie Ave, Cicero, 708-780-3700, www.hawthorneracecourse.com; thoroughbred racing and harness racing. See website for schedule.
- **Arlington Park Racetrack**, 2200 W Euclid Ave, Arlington Heights, 847-385-7500, www.arlingtonpark.com, is a beautiful, family-friendly park. Many event days throughout the season, with petting zoos, face painting for kids. Season runs May to September. Handicap accessible, general parking is free.

If you can't make it to the tracks, there's an off-track betting parlor at 233 West Jackson Boulevard, 312-427-2300.

More information on Illinois racetracks and racing schedules can be found at the Illinois Racing Board, 100 West Randolph Street, 312-814-2600.

# PARTICIPANT SPORTS AND RECREATIONAL ACTIVITIES

## PARKS, RECREATION DEPARTMENTS, AND ORGANIZATIONS

If you are looking for a neighborhood park that might offer something special—tennis courts, baseball diamond, kiddie pools, start with the Chicago Park District, www.chicagoparkdistrict.com, 312-742-PLAY. The staff is generally very knowledgeable about the facilities. If they don't know the details of your neighborhood park, they will be able to direct you to someone who can help.

Sport and social clubs also sponsor teams and leagues, in over twenty sports. Check out the Chicago Sport and Social Club, www.chicagosocial.com, or Players Sport and Social Group, www.playerssports.net.

## BICYCLING

Despite its extreme winter climate, Chicago is among the best big cities in the US for cycling. Since 1991, Chicago has established more than 100 miles of bikeways and spent millions on bike-related improvements, including over 8,000 bike racks across the city, with more in the works.

Nonetheless, the biking experience in Chicago remains decidedly urban. With the exception of the spectacular lakeshore path, the rest of the city's designated bike routes are on city streets. Some bike routes have specially marked bike lanes; others don't. If you plan on doing much biking, you should be prepared for inconsiderate—or, even worse, oblivious—motorists. Yet there are some good reasons why people choose to get around by bike.

Speed for one. During rush hour or in heavily congested areas, you'll often reach your destination faster on a bike than you will in a car. Whizzing by a quarter-mile long line of cars can be quite exhilarating. And you can forget about parking issues. You've got a guaranteed spot right outside your place of employment and it doesn't cost a dime. Last but not least, it's good for you. If you need to go farther than your legs can take you, remember bikes are allowed on the CTA trains on weekdays *except* during peak rush hours, and at any time on the weekends.

Some things to keep in mind: Get a good bike lock and use it. Bikes get stolen in Chicago all the time, and the thieves are talented and committed. Buy a U-lock and make sure you lock your bike to a fixed object (the city has recently started installing bike racks, but parking meters work well). Look out for "dummy poles" which are regular street sign poles where the bolts holding the base to the pole have been removed; the thief merely lifts up the pole and your bike is gone. More importantly, make sure you lock your frame and both wheel rims (if your wheels are of the quick-release variety) to the rack. Anything that isn't secured is fair game. Finally, buy a good bike helmet—and use it! While there is no current city or state law requiring cyclists to wear a bike helmet, your local township may have one, especially for residents under 14. Check with your local city hall for details.

A prime sign of the city's commitment to bicycle culture and the promotion of bicycle commuting: the **Millennium Park Bicycle Station,** recently re-branded as **McDonald's Cycle Center.** Located in the Loop and at the edge of Millennium Park at 239 E. Randolph, this state-of-the-art facility offers 300 free bike-parking spaces, locker rooms, mechanic services, bike rentals, and bicycle tours of downtown. By 2006, the facility had 500 members. Currently, the daily charge for use of a shower and locker space is $1. Regular users of the center would do well to purchase an annual membership ($169) or monthly pass ($30): perks include free, unlimited use of showers and lockers, as well discounts on bicycle repairs. Check www.chicagobikestation.com or 312-729-1000 for more information.

As for specific routes, the lakefront path is almost 20 miles long and runs from the northern tip of Lincoln Park to south of Hyde Park. Bicycle rentals are available in stores and at various locations along the path. Take care; the paths can get very congested on summer afternoons and weekends with foot, in-line skate, and skateboard traffic. Inland from the lake, ride on the smaller north-south and east-west streets that run parallel to the busy main drags. Avoid the heavy traffic on Ashland Avenue, Western Avenue, Addison Street, Irving Park Road, and Sheridan Road north of Hollywood.

The **Chicagoland Bicycle Federation,** www.activetrans.org, 312-427-3325, publishes a seven-county map of government-designated off-road bicycle trails in the Chicago metropolitan area as well as bicyclist-recommended roads for cycling through the Chicago area. The map is available in most bike shops as well as online. For weekend riding, check out the bike trails in various **Cook County Forest Preserves.** Call 800-870-3666 for free maps and brochures, or visit their website for downloadable maps, www.fpdcc.com. You can also visit the City of Chicago's bike page at www.cityofchicago.org; click on "Cycling" in the "Transportation" portion of the "For Residents" section for downloadable maps and other bike-related information.

Remember that on a bicycle you are subject to the same rules of the road as motor vehicles: you are expected to ride with traffic, not against it; signal your turns, do not weave in and out of traffic, and do not run red lights. In addition, it's an especially good idea to wear a helmet and bright reflective clothing when riding at night.

## BILLIARDS AND POOL

Just as Chicago has more bars and taverns per capita than any city in the United States, the ratio surely must extend to pool tables. (The film *The Color of Money* was shot in various pool halls around town.) Many pool halls are recent additions to the cityscape, but most bars in town will have a table or two in back. Here's a short list of places that are more billiards than booze:

- **Chicago Billiard Café,** 5935 W Irving Park Rd, 773-545-5102, www.chicagobilliardcafe.com; an alcohol-free café with 16 tables
- **City Pool Hall,** 640 W Hubbard St, 312-491-9690
- **G-Cue Billiards and Restaurant,** 157 N Morgan St, 312-850-3170, http://gcuechicago.com/Welcome.html
- **Marie's Golden Cue,** 3241 W Montrose Ave, 773-478-2555
- **Nick's Billiards,** 4445 N Pulaski Rd, 773-583-2011
- **Southport Lanes and Billiard** (six tables), 3325 N Southport Ave, 773-472-6600, www.southportlanes.com

## BOATING

Lake Michigan is arguably Chicago's greatest asset. During the summer, the Chicago Park District and several lakefront yacht clubs offer sailing lessons and rentals. Call the Chicago Harbors at 312-742-8520 for more information. (Classes fill by spring.) The following resources may also be helpful:

- For private lessons, try the **Chicago Sailing Club,** 773-871-7245, www.chicagosailing.com, at Belmont Harbor.
- Gillson Park hosts the **Chicago Corinthian Yacht Club** at 601 West Montrose Drive. Contact their information hotline at 773-334-9100 or visit www.corinthian.org.
- The **Chicago Yacht Club,** www.chicagoyachtclub.org, offers boating lessons; two locations: 400 East Monroe Street, 312-861-7777, and 300 West Belmont Avenue, 773-477-7575.
- The **Evanston Township High School Sailing Club** meets every Sunday afternoon from June through September.
- **Gillson Sailing Beach,** at Lake Avenue/Lake Michigan in Wilmette, offers private and group sailing lessons. Call Wilmette Park District at 847-256-6100 for information. You can also rent kayaks, Hobies, and Sunfish through the Wilmette Park District at Gillson Beach.
- The members of the **Lincoln Park Boat Club** paddle, scull, and row. Visit their website at www.lpbc.net.

If you own a boat and want to dock it in any of Chicago's 5,200 boat slips, you must lease a space through the **Chicago Park District's Marine Department,** 312-742-8520. For a mooring permit, visit www.westrec.com for an application and information about fees. There is a long waiting list for docking space, and some Chicagoans opt for an alternative—the northern suburbs or an Indiana harbor. Check with the park district offices of the lakefront suburb in which you are interested.

## BOWLING

If you placed Chicago's bowling alleys end to end, they would circle the globe. Actually, this may not be true, but it sure seems like it. There are bowling alleys in nearly every neighborhood and many that sponsor leagues. With so many bowling alleys from which to choose, here are a few recommendations:

- **Diversey/River Bowl** (36 lanes), 2211 W Diversey Ave, 773-227-5800; features a Saturday night Rock-n-Bowl. Open 24 hours on weekends.
- **Southport Lanes & Billiards** (four lanes), 3325 N Southport Ave, 773-472-6600; if you see a pair of legs standing where you've just hurled your bowling ball, you may not be drunk. Southport Lanes, a 75-year-old institution, is the last bowling alley in Chicago to use human pinsetters.
- **Timberlanes,** 1851 W Irving Park Rd, 773-549-9770
- **Waveland Bowl** (40 lanes), 3700 N Western Ave, 773-472-5900; for those who need to bowl at 3 a.m. in the middle of the week, Waveland Bowl is the place for you. Open 24/7, 365 days.

In the **northwest suburbs**, look for:

- **AMF Bowling Center**, 3245 Kirchoff Rd, Rolling Meadows, 847-259-4400
- **Arlington Lanes Bowling Alley**, 3435 N Kennicott Ave, Arlington Heights, 847-255-6373
- **Beverly Lanes**, 8 S Beverly Lane, Arlington Heights, 847-253-5238; not modern or showy, but extremely pleasant staff, and kid friendly.
- **Brunswick Deerbrook Lanes**, 10 S Waukegan Rd, Deerfield, 847-498-3575, 32 lanes
- **Brunswick Niles Bowl**, 7333 N Milwaukee Ave, Niles, 847-647-9433
- **River Rand Bowl** (21 lanes), 191 N River Rd, Des Plaines, 847-299-1001

In the **south suburbs**:

- **Burr Oak Bowl**, 3030 W 127th St, Blue Island, 708-389-2800, www.burroakbowl.com
- **Country Lanes Bowling Center**, 1009 W Laraway Rd, New Lenox, 815-485-3916
- **Eagles Bowling Lanes**, 2427 Grove St, Blue Island, 708-388-9739
- **Oak Forest Bowl**, 15240 S Cicero Ave, Oak Forest, 708-687-2000
- **Tinley Park Bowling Lanes**, 7601 183rd Street, Tinley Park, 708-532-2955

## CHESS

Whether you are 6 or 60, you will find a chess club to suit your needs here.

- **Chicago Industrial Chess League**, www.chicagochessleague.org, organizes team chess matches between downtown and suburban commercial, govern-

ment and educational organizations. The league has 21 six-member teams within its four divisions. Chess match season runs from August through April, with special festivities held in May and June.
- **Illinois Chess Association (ICA)**, http://il-chess.org, is an excellent portal for chess information beyond Chicago. Provides chess club information for suburbs and neighboring states, high school teams and tournament information, as well as links to other chess sites. You can join online or by mail: ICA Membership Secretary, Chris Merli, 1206 Waters Edge Rd, Champaign, IL 61822, or you can e-mail them at membership@il-chess.org.
- **Pick-up Games**: where do you go when you are suddenly struck with the urge to play chess and don't have a partner? Try:
- **Java Oasis**, 2240 S Michigan Ave
- **Oak Street/North Avenue Beach Chess Pavilion**.
- **Hyde Park**: 52nd and Harper Ave has concrete chess tables. In the summer, it's said chess is played here around the clock.

## DANCE

If you are interested in inexpensive dance lessons, for either yourself or your children, check with your local park district. They often have good basic dance programs for young children, and even a few hip-hop classes as well. You may also find ballroom or Latin dance classes for adults at these facilities. If you are looking for something more exacting, you might explore **Chicago Dance**, 3660 West Irving Park Road, Chicago, 773-267-3411, www.chicagodance.com. The owners, Gregory Day and Tommye Giacchino, are one time US and World Dance champions. Latin, ballroom, and swing lessons are offered. If you are looking for salsa lessons, visit www.chicagodancenews.com, for links to a variety of Latin dance programs. In some instances you can find lessons provided free of charge in area dance clubs/bars (see **Cultural Life**). **Chicago Windy City Jitterbug Club** (dance hotline: 773-467-0177) offers lessons in West Coast Swing, shag, bop and of course, the jitterbug. For lesson information call 630-231-7644, or check their website: www.jitterbugchicago.com. **Chicago Rebels Swing Dance Club** offers West Coast Swing dancing lessons, as well as hustle and motion study. They are located at The Center at North Park, 10040 West Addison Street, Franklin Park. Contact them at 847-382-0285 or get more info on the web at www.chicagorebels.net. If you are interested in dancing to live swing music, try Frankie's Blue Room, 16 West Chicago Avenue, Naperville, 630-416-3310, where there's live swing every Wednesday night. More listings for dance nights, lessons, and studios throughout Chicago—in any genre or style—can be found at www.ballroomchicago.com.

In the summer, dance aficionados would do well to check out the City of Chicago's popular Summer Dance series, 312-742-4007, held in Grant Park one to two times weekly from June to August. Set to live music of a variety of dance-friendly genres, each Summer Dance event also includes free pre-show dance lessons in the genre of the evening.

## FISHING

Fishing is popular in Chicago and you'll find plenty of places to do it. Roughly 100 lakes and ponds, 10 significant rivers, and six dams in the six-county area allow fishing—and that's in addition to the lakes and streams you will find in the forest preserves and state parks. Online, go to the **Chicago Area Paddling and Fishing Guide,** http://pages.ripco.net/~jwn, which will provide you with links to these fishing areas as well as information about water depth, the kind of fish you are most likely to find in a particular body of water, boating restrictions, and information about fishing licenses. **Chicago Fishing,** http://pages.ripco.net/~jwn/fishing.html, gives water quality information as well as lists of bodies of water and the fish therein. Also try www.ifishillinois.org and the Illinois Department of Natural Resources, which has a handy fishing link on its website: www.dnr.illinois.gov/Pages/default.aspx.

For chartered fishing try:

- **Waukegan Charterboat Association**, 847-BIG-FISH; excellent salmon and trout fishing, April through September, on Lake Michigan
- **Northpoint Charterboat Association**, Winthrop Harbor, 800-247-6727; operates out of Northpoint Marina in Winthrop Harbor. Fish Illinois and Wisconsin waters. Charters available May through October.
- **Chicago Sportfishing Association**, www.great-lakes.org/il/fish-chicago/, is a charter boat captains' organization operating out of three downtown harbors, April through October

And all Chicago residents should know about smelt fishing. Every spring millions of these finger-sized delectables head towards the lakeshore to spawn. It doesn't take any skill to smelt fish—just a dipping net. The trick? You have to do it at about 3 a.m., so bring a lantern and some warm clothes. You will find many Chicagoans lined up along the shore, chatting and laughing as they dip their nets. Many people like the area south of Navy Pier for smelting but you are almost guaranteed to get lucky standing anywhere along the shore—there are that many! This is the sort of event the local media always love to cover, so you may even find yourself 15 minutes of fame as well as a fish tale. If you find yourself shoulder to shoulder with an experienced smelter, ask him for his favorite smelt recipe; the most common way to cook smelt is to deep-fry them whole. Just add a sprinkle of salt, mmmmmm. For more details about smelt fishing, ask a local fisherman.

## FRISBEE

Another hybrid sport, Frisbee golf, or as some call it, disc golf, is actually a sport, not just a backyard game. There are bona fide courses on which to play—30 in Illinois alone—some are 18-hole courses, others nine. Some of the same rules as golf apply; there are even state championships. But unlike golf, most places do not charge, and you don't have to make reservations. Go to the **Professional Disc Golf Association** website, www.pdga.com, for more information. Area courses include:

- **West Park**, Bellevue and Wheeler Aves, Joliet, 815-725-8964
- **Koch Knolls Park**, Naperville, 630-848-5000; disc course with picnic tables and restrooms.
- **Madison Meadow**, E Wilson/S Fairfield Ave, Lombard, 630-620-7322
- **Danny Cunniff Park**, 3100 Trailway St, Highland Park, 847-831-3810; bring bug repellent!
- **Larry Fink Memorial Park**, 701 Deercreek Park, Highland Park, 847-831-3810; nine holes, beautiful setting.
- **Willow Stream Park & Twin Creeks Park**, 600 Farmington Dr, 401 Aptakisic Rd, Buffalo Grove
- **Lippold Park**, 851 W Rte 176, Crystal Lake, 815-459-0680

## GAMBLING (CASINO)

While not a sport, casino gambling is certainly a serious form of recreation for many. If playing the lottery isn't enough for you, you don't have to go far. Riverboat gambling is immediately available on the scenic Des Plaines river 15 miles south of Chicago in Joliet, or head just over the state line to Indiana for "lake boat gambling" on Lake Michigan. In Joliet, try the **Hollywood Casino**, 888-436-7737, **Harrah's**, 815-740-7800. Other Illinois establishments include **Casino Queen** in East St. Louis, 800-777-0777, **Grand Victoria Riverboat** in Elgin, 888-508-1900, **Hollywood Casino** in Aurora, 800-888-7777, and farther west, **Par-a-Dice Hotel/Casino** in East Peoria, 309-699-7711, and **Jumer's Casino** in Rock Island, 800-477-7747. In Indiana, it's the **Majestic Star Casino/Hotel**, 219-977-7777, in Gary.

## GOLF

The Chicago metropolitan area has miles and miles of fairways for your golfing pleasure. The Chicago Park District runs six public courses: **Robert A. Black** (9 holes), 2045 West Pratt Boulevard; **Columbus Park** (9 holes), 5701 West Jackson Boulevard; **Jackson Park** (18 holes), 6401 South Richards Drive; **Sydney R. Marovitz** (9 holes), 3600 North Lake Shore Drive; **Marquette Park** (9 holes),

6700 South Kedzie Avenue; and **South Shore Country Club** (9 holes), 7059 South Shore Drive. To make reservations or for more information call the Park District at 312-245-0909. In addition to golf courses, the Chicago Park District has driving ranges in Lincoln Park at Diversey and at its Jackson Park and Robert A. Black courses.

The Cook County Forest Preserve also runs a number of golf courses. They include: **Billy Caldwell** (9 holes), 6150 Caldwell Avenue, Chicago, 773-792-1930; **"Chick" Evans** (18 holes), 6145 Golf Road, Morton Grove, 847-965-5353; **Edgebrook** (18 holes), 6100 North Central Avenue, Chicago, 773-763-8320; and **Indian Boundary** (18 holes), 8600 West Forest Preserve Avenue, Chicago, 773-625-9630.

Dozens of public golf courses dot the suburbs. For a comprehensive list of Chicagoland area public courses, visit www.centerstage.net, and look for the golf link. Some of the more popular public courses include:

### NORTH
- **Bonnie Brook Golf Course** (18 holes), 2800 N Lewis Ave, Waukegan, 847-360-4730
- **Glenview Park** (18 holes), 800 Shermer Rd, Glenview, 847-724-0250
- **Midlane Country Club** (27 holes), 4555 W Yorkhouse Rd, Wadsworth, 847-360-0550
- **Pine Meadow** (18 holes), One Pine Meadow Ln, Mundelein, 847-566-4653
- **Sportsman Country Club** (18 holes), 3535 Dundee Rd, Northbrook, 847-291-2351

### NORTHWEST
- **Arlington Lakes** (18 holes), 1211 S New Wilke Rd, Arlington Heights, 847-577-3030
- **Chevy Chase** (18 holes), 1000 N Milwaukee Ave, Wheeling, 847-465-2301
- **Golf Club of Illinois** (18 holes), 1575 Edgewood Dr, Algonquin, 847-658-4400
- **Kemper Lakes**, 24000 Old McHenry Rd, Kildeer, 847-320-3450
- **Old Orchard Country Club** (18 holes), 700 W Rand Rd, Mt. Prospect, 847-255-2025
- **Villa Olivia Country Club** (18 holes), 1401 W Lake St, Bartlett, 630-289-1000
- **Wilmette** (18 holes), 3900 Fairway Dr, Wilmette, 847-256-9777

### WEST
- **Cantigny Golf** (27 holes), 27 W 270 Mack Rd, Wheaton, 630-668-8463
- **Indian Lakes Resort** (18 holes), 250 W Schick Rd, Bloomingdale, 630-529-0200

### SOUTH AND SOUTHWEST
- **Carriage Greens** (18 holes), 8700 Carriage Greens Dr, Darien, 630-985-3400

# SPORTS AND RECREATION

- **Cog Hill** (4 to 18 holes), including the infamous Dubsdread, 12294 Archer Ave, Lemont, 630-257-5872
- **Evergreen Golf Club**, (18 holes), 9140 S Western Ave, Evergreen Park, 773-238-6680
- **Gleneagles Country Club** (36 holes), 13070 McCarthy Rd, Lemont, 630-257-5466
- **Hickory Hills Country Club** (1 to 18; 1 to 9 holes), 8201 W 95th St, Hickory Hills, 708-598-5900
- **Silver Lakes** (45 holes), 147th St and 82nd Ave, Orland Park, 708-349-6940

## HORSEBACK RIDING

The **Noble Horse Theatre**, 1410 North Orleans Street, 312-266-7878, http://www.noblehorsechicago.com, is the last riding center in the City of Chicago. It holds year-round performances in its indoor riding arena and boards the performing horses here as well. Lessons for intermediate and advanced riders are also available.

In addition to the Noble Center, there are many stables in the northwest and southwest suburbs, which offer everything from equestrian to trail riding for riders of all ages and skill levels. Check the Yellow Pages under "Stables."

## IN-LINE AND ICE SKATING

During the summer, in-line skaters abound on the lakefront, so many in fact that it can be hazardous for pedestrians. If you want to participate but don't have the gear, there are rental shacks dotting the lakefront and Lincoln Park, or try **Londo Mondo**, 1100 North Dearborn Street, 312-751-2794.

If ice is your element, Chicago has outdoor skating rinks in many parks throughout the city. Downtown, try **Millennium Park Ice Skating Rink** at 55 North Michigan Avenue and the **Daley Bicentennial Plaza** at the north end of Grant Park. Navy Pier, 600 East Grand Avenue, has an indoor ice skate rink open November to January.

Head to the suburbs for **indoor ice rinks**:

- **Barrington Ice Arena**, 28206 W Commercial Ave, Lake Barrington, 847-381-4777
- **Carol Stream Ice Rink**, 540 E Gunderson Dr, Carol Stream, 630-682-4480
- **Centennial Ice Arena**, 3100 Trail Way, Highland Park, 847-432-4790
- **Center Ice of DuPage**, 1 N 450 Highland Ave, Glen Ellyn, 630-790-9696
- **Darien Sportsplex**, 451 Plainfield Rd, Darien, 630-789-6666, www.dariensportsplex.com
- **Fox Valley Ice Arena**, 1996 S Kirk Rd, Geneva, 630-262-0690
- **Glenview Indoor Ice Center**, 1851 Landwehr Rd, Glenview, 847-724-2800
- **Rocket Ice Arena**, 180 S Canterbury Lane, Bolingbrook, 630-679-1700

- **Seven Bridges Ice Arena**, 6690 IL Rte 53, Woodbridge, 630-271-4400
- **Skatium Indoor Ice Arena**, 9300 Weber Park Place, Skokie, 847-674-1500
- **Southwest Ice Arena**, 5505 W 127th St, Crestwood, www.southwesticearena.com, 708-371-1344
- **Sports Center Ice Rink**, 1730 Pfingsten Rd, Northbrook, 847-291-2993
- **Twin Rinks Ice Pavilion**, 1500 Abbott Ct, Buffalo Grove, 847-821-7465

INDOOR SUBURBAN ROLLER SKATING

- **Aurora Skate Center**, 34 W 113 Montgomery Rd, Aurora, 630-898-5830, www.skateaurora.com
- **Lombard Roller Rink**, 201 W 22nd St, Lombard, 630-953-2400
- **Mt. Prospect Park District-CCC Indoor Inline Skating Rink**, 1000 W Central Rd, Mt. Prospect, 847-255-5380
- **Orbit Skate Center**, 615 Consumers Ave, off the Northwest Highway in Palatine, 847-394-9199; indoor rink that rents in-line skates, as well as the old-fashioned roller-skate kind.

HOCKEY

If you are interested in your youngster getting involved in hockey, contact your local park district.

## RUGBY

Chicago has rugby clubs for both men and women. The season runs from late March until late May and then again in the autumn from Labor Day into November. If having your brains beaten out on the field and then drinking your brains out with your erstwhile opponents sounds like your kind of fun, call:

- **Chicago Condors Rugby Club**; practices are Tuesday and Thursday evenings at Columbus Park. Visit www.condorsrugby.com for more information.
- **Chicago Lions Rugby Club**; home games are played either at Revere Park or Schiller Woods. Clubhouse is located at Milwaukee and Addison. Visit www.chicagolions.com for more information.
- **Chicago Women's Rugby Football Club**; practices are held Mondays and Thursdays at Austin-Foster Park. Visit their website for more information: www.cwrfc.org.

## RUNNING

Chicago's lakefront provides an ideal place for running all year round, although you should be prepared for the blasting winds off the lake in the winter. In the summer you would do best to run in the morning, otherwise you'll be competing with bikers, roller bladers, and slow pedestrians. There are competitive races throughout the year, and some parks hold weekly events. Check the *Sun-Times* or the *Tribune* for schedules. It goes without saying that you should avoid running after dark in areas where there are few people.

If you're really serious about running, check out the **Chicago Area Runners Association (CARA)**, 549 West Randolph Street, 312-666-9836, www.cararuns.org, the largest association of runners in the Midwest. It organizes races and training runs and actively works for runners' rights. The group successfully lobbied a lakefront alderman to keep the Lincoln Park running paths plowed through the winter. To keep up with runners' news in the region, visit Chicago Athlete at www.mychicagoathlete.com. They also feature a magazine, *Chicago Athlete*, which you can subscribe to online.

The Chicago Marathon is held every year on a Sunday in October. It's a world-class event where you'll find the best runner in the world as well as 10,000 other runners participating.

## SOCCER

If your youngsters want to play soccer, contact the **Northern Illinois Soccer League**, 545 Consumers Avenue, Palatine, 847-398-4545, for information about outdoor and indoor leagues. Or visit their website at www.northernillinoissoccerleague.com. The outdoor season starts in April and runs through September; indoor leagues run from autumn to spring. If you have a youngster interested in the game and live in the city, check with your local park district office. Most park districts offer some soccer instruction.

**Eclipse Select**, which organizes boys and girls soccer in a variety of suburbs, has been named the number one girls' soccer club in the US based on an impressive number of national and regional championships. Visit www.eclipseselect.org for program information and contact information for the club nearest you.

Other area soccer clubs and associations include:

- **American Youth Soccer Organization**: 800-USA-AYSO, www.ayso.org/
- **Palatine Celtic Soccer Club**, www.palatinecelticsc.com
- **Illinois Soccer Association**, 312-226-7920, www.illinoissoccer.org (metro, adults)
- **Illinois Women's Soccer League**, 847-985-4975, www.iwsl.com (metro, girls, and youth)
- **Illinois Youth Soccer Association**, 847-290-1577, www.illinoisyouthsoccer.org (youth to age 19); lists many soccer programs throughout Chicago and the suburbs

## SOFTBALL

There are hundreds of softball players—16-inch, 12-inch fast- and 12-inch slow-pitch—playing in leagues across the Chicago area. Check the Chicago Park District website at www.chicagoparkdistrict.com, or your local park district for information on the park and league nearest you.

The **Chicago Metropolitan Sports Association**, the largest non-profit gay and lesbian sports organization in the Midwest, has many softball leagues. Contact them at 312-409-7932, or visit their website at www.chicagomsa.org, for more about the sports they organize. Area employers, bars, and restaurants sponsor most softball teams.

## SWIMMING

Despite its easy access, **Lake Michigan** might not be the place you want to go to swim—for many it's just too darn cold! For those hardy souls who prefer the lake to pool laps, many swim parallel to the shoreline from Ohio Street to the Oak Street curve and from Oak Street Beach to North Avenue pier. Check www.chicagoparkdistrict.com under "swim report" for a list of Chicago beaches and conditions. Also check the **Greenspaces and Beaches** chapter.

The Chicago Park District has **outdoor pools** throughout the city, but these are usually filled with screaming kids enjoying summer vacation. It's a good idea to check to see if the pools have reserved lap time. The district's **indoor pools** are one of Chicago's best-kept secrets. They are free, well maintained, and there are more than 30 scattered throughout the city. They lack the luxury and amenities of health clubs and private pools, but they'll get you in shape just as quickly. Call 312-742-7529 or check www.chicagoparkdistrict.com for the pool nearest you, or look in the White Pages under "Chicago Park District." Hours, frequency, and duration of lap swims vary from facility to facility. Here are a few you might want to investigate:

- **Austin Town Hall Park,** 5610 W Lake St, 773-287-7764; call for open swim times.
- **Blackhawk Park**, 2318 N Lavergne Ave, 312-746-4150; extensive swim times, categorized by age. Special senior swim hours on Saturday mornings and Wednesday afternoons.
- **Gill Park**, 825 W Sheridan Rd, 312-742-5807, in Wrigleyville, is the place for serious swimmers. Lap swimming is available three times a day and the pace can be blistering; if you're a novice, you'll want to stay in the slow lane.
- **Portage Park**, 4100 N Long Ave, 773-685-7189; with its Olympic size pool, this facility hosted the 1972 Olympic Swim trials in which Mark Spitz set new world records. Pool was renovated in 1998.
- **Shabbona Park**, 6935 W Addison St, 773-685-6387

# SPORTS AND RECREATION

- **Welles Park**, 2333 W Sunnyside Ave, 312-742-7515, in the Lincoln Square neighborhood, is a full-sized pool in a beautiful building with many windows and lots of natural light.

Health clubs and YMCAs throughout the city also have pools for the serious swimmer, and many high-rise apartment buildings have their own pools, but these are more for quick dips while sunning on a nearby chaise lounge than a serious workout. **Private swimming pool clubs** include:

- **Lakeshore Athletic Club—Streeterville**, 333 E Ontario St, 312-944-4546
- **South Plymouth Court Swimming Pool**, 1151 S Plymouth Court, 312-427-4950

If you are looking for a little competition, visit www.chicagomasters.com. **Chicago Masters** team members practice in the University of Illinois' Olympic-size pool in the Physical Education Building located at 901 West Roosevelt Road.

If you live in the suburbs, check with your local parks program. In the suburbs you can expect an admission fee, and many park districts support summer camps, which generally have use of the pools in the afternoons. Some allocate 15 minutes each hour to adult swims after 3 p.m. Most suburban park districts offer residents a discounted season pass if it is purchased pre-season.

## TENNIS

The Chicago Park District has nearly 700 tennis courts in parks throughout the city, but be warned: the good ones are packed and the bad ones look like the surface of the moon. The most popular public tennis courts are in Lincoln Park, between Addison Street and Irving Park Road, and at the south end of Grant Park, east of Columbus Drive.

There are also courts at some private health clubs, including the **Mid-Town Tennis Club**, 2020 West Fullerton Avenue, 773-235-2300, www.midtown.com. Many suburban park districts feature tennis courts. Check with your parks program for more information.

## WHIRLYBALL

Not exactly basketball, not quite lacrosse, but it's very cool, fast-paced, and played in electric bumper cars! You can only play whirlyball in two locations in the Chicago area, and you must make a reservation weeks in advance, but it is worth it: call WhirlyBall, 1880 West Fullerton Avenue, 773-486-7777, in Chicago or in Lombard, 800 East Roosevelt Road, 630-932-4800. For more information about "the world's only totally mechanized sport" you can go online to www.whirlyball.com.

## HEALTH CLUBS

If you're used to working out at a health club or if you want to start doing it, you're in luck: Chicago has an abundance of workout centers ranging from little more than weight and machine rooms to gigantic and luxurious mega-clubs that offer the latest fitness class, tennis courts, basketball courts, swimming pools, saunas, indoor jogging tracks, juice bars…even climbing walls.

Get a tour, and if possible a free pass or two, before signing on the dotted line—you may decide that the reality of exercising to skull-pounding music is not so healthful after all. When you're told that this week, the club you're visiting is having a "sale," take it with several grains of salt; with few fixed prices, words like "special," and "discount" are next to meaningless in the fitness business. That means the person on the treadmill next to you may have paid double or half what you paid. Ask at your place of work if they offer an employer-sponsored program. Finally, don't let yourself be pressured into signing up for a long-term commitment—unless you're *really* sure you want that multi-year membership.

- **Bally's Chicago Total Fitness Centers** are located throughout Chicago and the suburbs—check the White Pages for the one closest to you. The pulsating TV commercials notwithstanding, quality of service and equipment at Bally's varies considerably. Tour and try the place before splurging and regretting. For general information visit www.ballyfitness.com.
- **Chicago Fitness Center**, 3131 N Lincoln Ave, 773-549-8181, www.chicagofitnesscenter.com
- **Curves,** www.curves.com; the chain of women's fitness and weight loss centers has 100 locations in the greater Chicago area.
- **East Bank Club**, 500 N Kingsbury St, 312-527-5800, www.eastbankclub.com; three blocks long, this monument to fitness claims to be the largest health club in the United States.
- **Lincoln Park Athletic Club,** 1019 W Diversey Ave, 773-529-2022, chicagoathleticclubs.com
- **Metropolitan Fitness Club**, 200 W Monroe St, 312-444-1040, www.metfitclub.com

Chicago YMCAs are perfect if you're looking for no-frills health clubs. Many Ys have all the amenities of the popular health clubs at a fraction of the cost, and some of the suburban locations are very plush. Call the **YMCA of Metropolitan Chicago,** www.ymcachicago.org, 312-932-1200, for the Y nearest you. One of the most popular is the **Lakeview YMCA**, 3333 North Marshfield Avenue, 773-248-3333. In the suburbs, try **Latoff YMCA**, 300 East Northwest Highway, Des Plaines, 847-296-3376.

Finally, you might want to call your local hospital and see if they have a fitness center. An increasing number of hospitals operate non-profit fitness centers both as preventive/rehabilitative medicine and as a marketing tool. These hospital gyms can be mellower and more affordable than the commercial gyms. In the northwest suburbs, contact **Northwest Community Healthcare-Wellness Center**, 900 Central Road, Arlington Heights, 847-618-3500.

# GREENSPACES AND BEACHES

I T IS TRULY REMARKABLE THAT A CITY THE SIZE OF CHICAGO HAS BEEN able to sustain its ambitious efforts to balance nature and manmade facilities in the same space. Parks, nature centers, forest preserves, and pockets of greenery abound in Chicago. From rooftop gardens above City Hall to seating along the Chicago River, from baskets of blooming greenery on lampposts all over the city to the major accomplishment of Millennium Park—which forms a "green roof" over a massive underground parking facility in the Loop—Chicago is a green city.

## CITY PARKS

The Chicago Park District is responsible for over 7,300 acres of parkland throughout the city. From playlots to the much-beloved and well-utilized lakeshore parks that stretch almost twenty miles from Ardmore Avenue in the north to 67th Street in the south, Chicagoans are privy to a lot of greenspace. There are over 550 parks in Chicago—and that doesn't include sports fields, diamonds, field houses, county preserves, lagoons, and golf courses.

Countless bikers, in-line skaters, walkers, and runners head to the lakeshore trails for exercise. For those who like team sports, there are sports leagues and teams scattered throughout the parks. Like volleyball? Head out to North Avenue Beach. Baseball your game? Then it's the diamonds across from Waveland Avenue. Sold on soccer? Try out the lakefront fields north of Montrose Avenue. Rowers can test their might in the lagoon near Lincoln Park Zoo, while sailors head to Burnham Harbor. Golfers can tee up at the 18-hole course at Jackson Park (among others—see **Sports and Recreation** for a list of public golf courses). Whatever your outdoor needs, you can probably find a place to do it in Chicago. Call the Park District, 312-742-PLAY, or visit their website at www.chicagoparkdistrict.com for more information.

## SOME FAVORITE PARKS

- **Columbus Park**, 500 S Central Ave, 773-287-7641; now restored, the masterpiece of Jens Jensen, a landscape architect who left his stamp in many Chicago parks and neighborhoods early in the 20th century. This park pulled together many of the ideas Jensen had been developing through other projects in Chicago. Located downtown near the Congress Expressway, it features a wildflower prairie, with stepping stone paths, a meandering river, waterfalls, and an outdoor theater. Though it has lost some acreage to the Eisenhower Expressway, it is still a popular and beautiful place.
- **Douglas Park** (3000W/2100S), 1401 S Sacramento Dr, 773-762-2842; what was once a swamp was transformed into a lagoon surrounded by lawns and trees, thanks to William LeBaron Jenney and later to Jens Jensen, who added the Flower Hall and Gardens. Their work here is identified as the Prairie style of landscape architecture.
- **Garfield Park**, 100–300 N Central Park Ave, 312-746-5092; this park was originally one of three large parks that were designed with interlinking boulevards in 1869 by William LeBaron Jenney, the father of the skyscraper. When it became apparent that the plans were too ambitious to be realized at once, it was decided that Garfield Park would be developed in stages, beginning with its east lagoon. For a number of reasons, the three parks were neglected for years until Jens Jensen was named Chief Landscape Architect of the parks in 1905. Experimenting with his Prairie-style landscaping designs, he created the Garfield Park Conservatory, which opened in 1908. Today the Conservatory is still one of the jewels in the park district system; its programs and events continuously draw visitors to the Garfield Park neighborhood. Garfield Park also features the Garfield Park Formal Gardens, designed by the highly respected landscape designer, Chris Woods of the Chanticleer Gardens in Philadelphia.
- **Grant Park**, 337 E Randolph St, 312-742-7649; is perhaps the best known of all Chicago's parks. It owes its existence to the foresighted citizens who fought against development projects for the space along the shore. In 1927, the Buckingham Fountain was added. Today the park is part of the Museum Campus Project and plans are under way to add more gardens, sculptures, and performance spaces without obstructing its breathtaking views of Lake Michigan and beyond.
- **Hamilton Park**, 513 W 72nd St, 312-747-6174; Hamilton Park was the first part of a 10-park project designed to provide some recreation for those living in South Side tenements. Designed by Daniel Burnham in 1904, it included a new type of building—the field house, which included classrooms, a cafeteria, public bathing area, meeting rooms, an indoor gym, locker room, and one of the city's earliest library branches. In 1916, Chicago artist John Warner

Norton painted a series of murals in the field house's lobby, depicting scenes from American political history.

- **Jackson Park**, 6401 S Stony Island Ave, 773-256-0903; after Frederick Law Olmsted and Daniel Burnham transformed this area into the "White City" for the 1893 World's Fair, Olmsted returned the site to parkland. While his original plans were never fully realized, the results were still impressive. The city added 10 acres of landfill to create the 63rd Street Beach. The beach's Classical-style bathing pavilion was recently restored. Beyond the beach, the park maintains a golf course, and the Japanese-styled Osaka Gardens, hidden behind the Museum of Science and Industry. Its Wooded Isle attracts many migratory birds.
- **Lincoln Park**, 2045 N Lincoln Park West, 312-742-7726; what began as a lakeside cemetery for cholera and smallpox victims has long since been transformed into a 1,200-acre park/zoo/conservatory/garden landscape and more. Throughout the park's history, renowned artists have contributed to its development. The roster includes sculptor Augustus Saint-Gaudens, landscape designers Ossian Cole Simonds and Alfred Caldwell, and architects Dwight Perkins and Joseph Lyman Silsbee. The park offers many programs for adults and children, camp, and cultural events.
- **Olive Park** is a small park just north of Navy Pier. As it juts out onto Lake Michigan, it is not accessible by car, making it an especially quiet and restful area despite its urban location. Don't be surprised to find a few tired bicyclists napping on the grass.
- **Washington Park**, 5531 S King Dr (just off 55th Place); once again, Daniel Burnham was called upon to work his magic in Chicago. He designed the refectory that is now used for meetings, special community events, and locker rooms and a 1910 administrative building that has since been converted into the DuSable Museum (see **Cultural Life**). This park has an outdoor swimming pool, winding paths, the beautifully sculpted Fountain of Time, and a lovely grove of trees.

## DOG-FRIENDLY PARKS

Most parks do not allow dogs to roam without a leash, and some don't allow dogs at all. But in the parks and dog-friendly areas listed below, they are welcomed. Check with your local park district to find out your community's rules about pets and parks. In off-leash areas, for the protection of fellow pooches (as well as your conscience and your pocketbook), only allow your dog off-leash if it is a well-socialized animal. If your dog has never spent unleashed time with other dogs, start cautiously: visit off-leash areas during slow times when only a few other dogs are around so as not to overwhelm him right away, or let your dog sniff others on-leash for a few visits before allowing him or her to run free.

If you would like to give your dog an opportunity to strut his or her stuff, check into the Anti-Cruelty Society's annual "Bark in the Park" walkathon. Usually held in the spring, this 5K walk includes free doggie snacks, parades, demonstrations, and educational tips. Visit www.barkinthepark.org to learn more. For more information about dog-friendly areas in and around Chicago, visit www.tailsinc.com.

- **Challenger Playlot Park,** 1100 W Irving Park Rd (entrance on Buena Ave), 312-742-7802. Sunrise to 10 p.m.
- **Churchill Field Park,** 1825 N Damen Ave.
- **Coliseum Park,** 1466 S Wabash Ave, 312-328-0821 (S Lakeshore Dr/W 15th St); nestled among the Amtrak and Illinois Central Railroads, this park has one playground, a small recreation area, and a dog-friendly space. Off-leash area.
- **Grant Park,** Congress/Columbus Dr, 312-742-7649 (downtown Chicago); dogs are allowed but only on leashes. The Lakefront Trail Park is close by.
- **Grant Bark Park,** Michigan Ave and 11th St Pedestrian Bridge, www.southloopdogpac.org, 312-264-5630. 18,000-square-foot, fully fenced and landscaped dog-friendly area.
- **Hamlin Park,** 3035 N Hoyne St, 312-742-7785 (Hamlin Park neighborhood, Belmont/Lincoln); dogs can roam free inside the fenced-in area at Hoyne and Wellington
- **Lakefront Trail,** Lakeshore Dr, 312-742-7529; 18 miles of paved walkway accommodates cyclists, strollers, and leashed dogs. You can start your dog run at any number of points—Lakeshore Drive/Wacker is a common one. While you may be tempted to let your dog romp on the beach, resist. Except for Doggie Beach and Montrose Beach (see below), dogs are not allowed on any Chicago beaches, and police enforce the law, especially during the day. (That said, many still come to the beaches with pooches in tow on early summer mornings or late in the evening.)
- **Margate Park/Puptown,** 4921 N Marine Dr, www.puptown.org, 312-742-7522; just south of Lincoln Park, off W Castlewood Dr, 16,230 square feet of off-leash area
- **River Park,** 5100 N Francisco Ave, 312-742-7516
- **Walsh Playground Park,** 1722 N Ashland Ave, 312-742-7769 (West Town neighborhood), is a two-acre park built in memory of fireman John P. Walsh Jr., who gave his life fighting a fire in 1970
- **Wicker Park,** 1425 N Damen, 312-742-7553 (Wicker Park neighborhood); a fenced-in area where dogs can wander off-leash lies in the southeast corner of the park
- **Wiggly Field Dog Park,** 2645 N Sheffield Ave, 773-348-2832, is a park with a sense of humor! This dog-friendly area is within Grace Noethling Park in the Lincoln Park neighborhood and offers foot-and-a-half high drinking fountains, and fake mailboxes for marking territory

Chicago even has a few beaches set aside for canines:

- **Doggie Beach**, Lakeshore/Recreation drives, north end of Belmont Harbor, 312-742-DOGS; open daily during the season, sunrise–sunset. Small sandy beach for pets to romp. No facilities, and dog owners must clean up after their pets as well as providing their own cleanup tools.
- **Montrose Beach,** northwest corner of Montrose Beach, 4400 North, www.mondog.org. The only legal off-leash beach in the Chicago area: sheer canine joy! Bring your own baggies. Open sunrise to 9 p.m.

Suburbanites love their dogs, too, and Chicagoland's suburbs have the dog parks to prove it. The following suburbs (and a few others) have dog parks and parks with dog-friendly areas. See the "Animal Resources" section of www.tailsinc.com for addresses and details.

- **Northern Suburbs:** Crystal Lake, Evanston, Deerfield, Des Plaines, Highland Park, Lake Bluff, Lake Forest, Lake in the Hills, Libertyville, Park Ridge, Skokie, Wauconda, Waukegan, Wilmette, Winnetka
- **Southern Suburbs:** Homewood-Flossmoor, Orland Park
- **Western Suburbs:** Aurora, Batavia, Forest Park, Glen Ellyn, Glendale Heights, Hanover Park, Hinsdale, Naperville, Oak Brook, Oak Brook Terrace, Plainfield, Wayne

## CHICAGOLAND PARK DISTRICT TELEPHONE NUMBERS AND WEBSITES

- **Arlington Heights,** 847-577-3000, www.ahpd.org
- **Barrington,** 847-381-0687, www.barringtonparkdistrict.org
- **Blue Island,** 708-385-3304, blueislandparks.org
- **Buffalo Grove,** 847-850-2100, www.bgparkdistrict.org
- **Chicago,** 312-742-PLAY, www.chicagoparkdistrict.org
- **Deerfield,** 847-945-0650, www.deerfieldparks.org
- **Des Plaines,** 847-391-5700, www.desplainesparks.org
- **Downers Grove,** 630-963-1304, www.dgparks.org
- **Elk Grove Village,** 847-439-3900, www.parks.elkgrove.org
- **Evanston,** 847-448-4311, www.cityofevanston.org/parks-recreation/
- **Glen Ellyn,** 630-858-2462, www.gepark.org
- **Glencoe,** 847-835-3030, www.glencoeparkdistrict.com
- **Highland Park,** 847-831-3810, www.pdhp.org
- **Hinsdale,** 630-789-7000, www.villageofhinsdale.org
- **LaGrange,** 708-352-1762, www.pdlg.org
- **Lisle,** 630-964-3410, www.lisleparkdistrict.org
- **Morton Grove,** 847-965-1200, www.mortongroveparks.com
- **Mt. Prospect,** 847-255-5380, www.mppd.org

- **Naperville**, 630-848-5000, www.napervilleparks.org
- **Northbrook**, 847-291-2960, www.nbparks.org
- **Oak Lawn**, 708-857-2222, www.olparks.com
- **Oak Park**, 708-383-0002, www.pdop.org
- **Orland Park**, 708-403-7275, www.orland-park.il.us
- **Palatine**, 847-991-0333, www.palatineparkdistrict.com
- **Prospect Heights**, 847-394-2848, www.phparkdist.org
- **Rosemont**, 847-823-6685, www.rosemontparkdistrict.com
- **Skokie**, 847-674-1500, www.skokieparks.org
- **Tinley Park**, 708-342-4200, www.tinleyparkdistrict.org
- **Westmont**, 630-969-8080, www.wpd4fun.org
- **Wheaton**, 630-665-4710, www.wheatonparkdistrict.com
- **Wilmette**, 847-256-6100, www.wilmettepark.org
- **Winnetka**, 847-501-2040, www.winpark.org
- **Woodridge**, 630-353-3300, www.woodridgeparks.org

## FOUNTAINS

Few things are as refreshing on a hot summer day as sitting within view of a cool fountain.

- **Centennial Fountain**, 300 N McClurg Ct, 312-751-6633, TDD, 312-744-2947; from Memorial Day to Labor Day, seven days a week, this fountain is in action. Every 15 minutes after the hour, it shoots a powerful spray of water that reaches nearly the width of the Chicago River. There are plenty of benches and seating around Cityfront Plaza to witness the display; you'll find many office workers, lunch in hand, vying for a spot too. The popular fountain is actually only part of a winding paved river walkway that extends around the southern edge of the Streeterville neighborhood and the Chicago River. Wheelchair accessible.
- **Buckingham Fountain;** designed in 1927 and set in a Beaux-arts–styled garden in Grant Park, with a design based on the Latona Basin in the gardens of Versailles, this bronze sculpture was declared a Chicago landmark in 2000. Its four sea horses represent the four states that touch Lake Michigan. What sets this fountain apart is its innovative use of technology to create a light and water display that has become synonymous with summer in Chicago. The colored light shows are displayed hourly from 8 p.m. to 11 p.m. during the summer months. Buckingham Fountain is one of the world's largest fountains and one of the state's leading attractions.
- **Crown Fountain**; located on the southwest corner of Millennium Park (at the intersection of Monroe and Michigan aves), this playful fountain/playground has proved one of the Loop's most popular warm-weather attractions ever since it premiered in spring 2006. Designed by Spaniard Jaume Plensa, the fountain

consists of two fifty-foot glass block towers that face off over a shallow 200-foot reflecting pool. The towers display mammoth full-face videos of over 1000 Chicago residents in ultra-close-up—modern-day gargoyles. Each face mugs a little before pursing its lips to spout water. The trick is that the water is real; it spews out to fill the reflecting pool and splash anyone standing near its trajectory. When the water is on (mid-spring to mid-fall) and the weather is warm, the pool teems with shrieking playing children; benches ringing the area allow families and delighted observers alike to share in the fun.

## NATURE CENTERS

In addition to the hundreds of parks in Chicago, there are also 49 nature areas. These specially designed landscapes are all unique; some feature lagoons, others focus on recreating prairie-scapes. Here are a few:

- **Burnham Prairie Path, 47th St/Lakeshore Dr,** www.hydepark.org/parks/burnham/burnhamnatctr.htm; part of Burnham Park, near the lakefront, these winding paths lead the walker through a butterfly garden, prairie path, and a woodland area, all planted with species native to the area.
- **Columbus Woodland and Lagoon,** Central Ave and Adams St; one of the many fine examples of Jen Jensen's Prairie-style is realized here in the woodland setting. All footpaths lead to the lagoon, which was inspired by natural prairie rivers. There are also three manmade limestone waterfalls. Planted with local varieties of plants and flowers, the woodland has become home to many native birds.
- **Gompers Park Wetland Recreation,** a former oxbow in the North Branch of the Chicago River, at Foster Ave and Pulaski Rd; fed by Gompers Park Lagoon and a stretch of the North Branch of the Chicago River, the Gompers Park Wetland is now important to area flood control. Heron, butterflies, muskrat, frogs, and fish have been observed here. Nearby lies the one-acre **Gompers Park Lagoon**, a treasured fishing spot for many locals.
- **Hurley Park Savanna,** 1901 W 100th St, in the Beverly neighborhood, is one of the state's few remaining oak savannas, and the only one within the Cook County Park District's network. In 1996, a joint effort between the Park District and the Morton Arboretum restored the Savanna's understory, recreating the natural grasses, brushes, and plants that would naturally occur in such an environ.
- **Jackson Park Bobolink Meadow**; located south of the Museum of Science and Industry, Jackson Park was host to the 1893 World's Fair. Once used as a Nike missile base, then neglected and nearly abandoned, this meadow is slowly being rehabilitated to encourage the return of the bobolink, an Illinois songbird that enjoys open grasslands. Six restored acres serve as a haven for birds

and butterflies while a two-acre woodland section is still under restoration. The Park's East Lagoon has attracted turtles, muskrats, beavers, and dragonflies.
- **Lincoln Park Addison Migratory Bird Sanctuary**, 3600 N Addison, is the fenced area behind the totem pole. This is the only bird sanctuary in Chicago that denies public access. This is because many birds roost in this six-acre sanctuary several months a year, and the sanctuary has become home to a variety of animals, including an occasional fox and coyote. However, newly expanded pool areas, along with extended viewing platforms, will at least give the public a better view to the inside.
- **Lincoln Park Alfred Caldwell Lily Pool**; located on Fullerton directly north of the Lincoln Park Zoo, this extensively rehabilitated landscape was re-opened to the public in 2002. The Lily Pool is becoming a coveted spot for bird watchers.
- **Lincoln Park North Pond**, behind Peggy Notebaert Museum, is proof that you can make a silk purse out of a sow's ear. Through the efforts of the Park District and park volunteers, this pond, once a dumping ground, has become an important flyway area for over 160 species of migrating birds. It was at this pond that former Mayor Daley and the US Fish and Wildlife Service signed an Urban Conservation Treaty for Migratory Birds. In addition to the pond, 10 acres of surrounding wooded area serves as a home for a variety of animals and beneficial insects.
- **Marquette Park Ashburn Prairie** is the city's largest prairie land on the southwest side, encompassing over 300 acres. The park's field house is located at 6734 S Kedzie Ave, and the prairie, which has an unusual history, is just east of Kedzie. While some of the other prairies in Chicago needed restoration and heavy weeding, no others were transplanted as was the case with Ashburn Prairie. This prairie originally blossomed in a two-acre area near Evergreen Cemetery until encroaching development threatened its existence. In 1993, the Park District dug up several large plugs of prairie—each were at least five feet across—and brought them to the Marquette Park lagoon where the composition of the soil was similar to the prairie's original site. The prairie's continuing success is largely a measure of the volunteers who monitor, weed, and seed it.
- **Montrose Point Bird Sanctuary**, 4400 N Montrose/Lake Michigan; this lakeside bird sanctuary in Lincoln Park attracts over 300 species of migratory birds each year. East of the bathhouse is a 150-yard stretch of hedge nicknamed "The Magic Hedge" for its ability to attract an especially large number of migratory birds. This hedge is recognized internationally as a birding area.
- **Nichol's Park Wildflower Garden**, 1300 E 55th St in Hyde Park; a small blue/yellow sign signals entrance to the garden with its many native, prairie and woodland plantings. Nichol's Park Meadowlarks, a Hyde Park gardening group, contribute their energies to the maintenance of this garden.

- **Paul Douglas Nature Sanctuary in Jackson Park**; Jackson Park Lagoon is located at 6401 S Stony Island Ave. The park contains an area called Wooded Isle, which can be reached over a bridge that is within walking distance from the parking lot off of Hayes Drive. If you take the bridge on the north side of the lagoon, you will find the Osaka Japanese Gardens. The Douglas Nature Sanctuary is a favorite with birders as the area attracts as many as 250 species of birds.
- **South Shore Cultural Center Nature Sanctuary**; located on Lake Michigan, at the peninsula of the South Shore Cultural Center. The field house is located at 7059 South Shore Dr. To reach the sanctuary, you must walk south along the beach. Construction of this sanctuary began in 2001. It includes a trail that takes hikers through a sand dune, over a wetland, and into the three-acre prairie. The sanctuary has proven to be an important stopover for fall and spring migrating birds.

If you are interested in keeping up with the various programs, activities, and efforts to rehabilitate the Chicagoland area's greenspaces, visit their website at www.chicagowilderness.org.

## NATURE AND WILDLIFE GARDENS

Chicago is home to a series of six nature and wildlife gardens that demonstrate the abundant beauty of Midwestern flora and fauna. The native plant species were selected according to established criteria: providing food and shelter for wildlife, harboring beneficial insects and birds, requiring little care after initial watering, and thriving in sunny locations, wetlands, or wooded areas. All the plantings are tagged for easy identification. Gardeners may wish to take note of the designs of these gardens and type of plants used: they can be easily adapted for backyard use.

- **Bessemer Park**, 8930 S Muskegon Ave, 312-747-6023
- **Horner Park**, 2741 W Montrose Ave, 773-478-3499
- **Ogden Park**, 6500 S Racine Ave, 312-747-6572
- **Portage Park**, 4100 N Long Ave, 773-685-7235
- **Prospect Gardens Park**, 10940-11000 S Prospect Ave, 312-747-6163
- **Rutherford Sayre Park**, 6871 W Belden Ave, 312-746-5368

## OTHER CHICAGO-AREA GARDENS

- **Chicago Botanic Garden**, 1000 Lake Cook Rd, Glencoe; perhaps the most famous of all Chicago gardens, the botanical gardens comprise 385 acres of beautiful and unique cultivated gardens with over two million plants. Included in the gardens are 81 acres of waterways, 100 acres of wooded land, nine islands, six miles of shoreline, and 15 acres of prairie. Owned by the Forest

Preserve of Cook County but operated by the Chicago Horticultural Society, the Botanical Gardens feature over 20 different types of gardens, from English walled gardens to Japanese-styled gardens. The center offers a variety of programs, many hosted by internationally known experts, plant sales, horticultural classes, children's programs, an e-mail newsletter, and much more. Birders take note: over 250 species of birds have been sighted here. Admission is free with paid parking. Memberships are available. Areas in the garden can also be booked for special events such as weddings. Visit www.chicagobotanic.org for more information or call 847-835-5440. Wheelchair accessible.

- **Garfield Park Conservatory**, 300 N Central Park Ave, 312-746-5100; nation's largest public garden under glass, which also presents exhibits of art integrated with the conservatory's unique garden plantings, interior space, and grounds. (Special exhibits have featured the work of world-renowned artists such as glass-artist Dale Chihuly and sculptor Niki de Saint Phaille.) Visit www.garfield-conservatory.org.
- **Morton Arboretum**, 4100 Rte 53, Lisle, 630-968-0074; this 1,700-acre outdoor museum delights its visitors with 3,300 different kinds of plants, trees, and shrubs in woodland, prairie, wetland and garden settings. Open daily from 7 a.m. to 7 p.m. Admission discounted on Wednesdays. The Arboretum offers many programs and events, and publishes several booklets, calendars and handbooks. Visit their website at www.mortonarb.org.
- **South Shore Cultural Center Gardens**, 7059 S South Shore Dr, www.hydepark.org/parks/southshore/sscc1.html, 773-256-0149; formal gardens set in a 65-acre park against the restored 1905 Cultural Center. Grounds include the South Shore Beach.

If you are interested in learning more about Illinois wildlife, including the ongoing efforts to preserve and protect it, contact the **Illinois Audubon Society** at 217-544-2473 or visit www.illinoisaudubon.org. If you would like some information on where to look for certain species of birds, try the **Chicago Audubon Society**, 773-539-6793. For those in the northwest suburbs, local chapters are **Prairie Woods Audubon Society** in Arlington Heights, 847-485-9695; and **Lake Cook Audubon Society** in Highland Park, 847-971-1107.

## CEMETERIES

Chicago's cemeteries can provide peaceful, interesting walks. Generations ago, people often picnicked on cemetery grounds, and today cemeteries are still fascinating places to explore. Here you will find the tombs and headstones of the famous and infamous. Don't be surprised to discover the names of Chicago streets on the tombstones; street names are one way the city has honored the men and women that made Chicago what it is today. For a complete list of area

# GREENSPACES AND BEACHES

cemeteries, visit graveyards.com or buy the book *Graveyards of Chicago* by Matt Hucke and Ursula Bielski.

- **Beth-El/Ridgelawn Cemeteries**, 5736 N Pulaski Rd, 847-673-1584; small Jewish cemeteries, burials dating back to 1895.
- **Bohemian National Cemetery**, 5255 N Pulaski Rd, 773-539-8442; holds what is considered by some as the finest funerary art in the city.
- **Calvary Catholic Cemetery**, 301 Chicago Ave, 847-864-3050, on the lakefront behind Sheridan Rd, Evanston, is the oldest cemetery in the Chicago Archdiocese.
- **Forest Home**, 863 S Des Plaines Ave, Forest Park, 708-366-1900; originally the burial grounds of the Pottawattamie Indians. Of particular interest is the Druid Monument erected in 1888, and the Haymarket Monument; many anarchists, socialists and labor party movement members are buried near this monument, including Emma Goldman.
- **Graceland Cemetery**, 4001 N Clark St, 773-525-1105, is one of Chicago's best-known and most historic places of rest. The bodies exhumed from the lakefront cemetery were moved here in order to establish Lincoln Park. Among the buried here are Mies van der Rohe, Louis Henri Sullivan, Marshall Field, and Daniel Hudson Burnham.
- **Graveyards of Barrington**; Evergreen Cemetery is located at Dundee/Monument Aves, and White Cemetery on Cuba Rd. Evergreen has burials dating back to the Civil War era, and White Cemetery is said to be haunted!
- **Jewish Graceland**, 3919 N Clark St; collective name of four cemeteries adjacent to one another, but without borders. The Hebrew Benevolent Society, after which one of the four is named, was established in 1851, making it one of the oldest cemeteries in Chicago. These four cemeteries are poorly maintained and many stones are damaged beyond repair.
- **Montrose Cemetery and Crematorium**, 5400 N Pulaski Rd, 773-478-5400; several sections devoted to specific ethnic groups, such as Japanese and Serbian.
- **Mount Carmel**, Harrison/Hillside Avenue, Hillside, 708-449-8300; a final resting-place for many Italian immigrants in Chicago. Cardinal Bernardin and Al Capone are both buried here.
- **Oak Ridge/Glen Oak Cemeteries**, 4301 W Roosevelt Rd, Hillside, 708-344-5600; has several special sections: Showmen, members of the Salvation Army, Masons. Oak Ridge has a Jewish section. Blues fans will remember Howlin' Wolf, a.k.a. Chester Burnett, who is buried here.
- **Rosehill Cemetery and Mausoleum**, 5800 N Ravenswood, 773-561-5940; the largest cemetery in the city. Opened in 1859, it is also one of the oldest. A number of Chicago mayors as well as Civil War generals and soldiers are buried here.
- **St. Boniface Cemetery**, 4901 N Clark St, 773-561-2790, was dedicated in the 1860s to serve the German Catholic community.

- **St. Henry Cemetery**, Ridge Ave/Devon Ave, 847-864-3050; this small cemetery has a grave that is purported to be that of the Cracker Jack boy, from the snack box.
- **Waldheim Jewish Cemeteries**, 1400 S Des Plaines, Forest Park, 708-366-4541; over 300 cemeteries are a part of this burial ground.

## COOK COUNTY FOREST PRESERVES

Cook County is responsible for over 68,000 acres of land. Within the forest preserves, you will find picnic groves, horseback riding and hiking trails, ponds, swimming pools, model airplane flying fields, nature centers, golf courses, dog training areas, rivers, streams, and toboggan slides. The Forest Preserve website is chock-full of information about its facilities, license information, trail maps, as well as useful information for gardeners and naturalists. The Cook County Forest Preserve is always looking for volunteers. If you are interested, contact them at 800-870-3666. For more information about events and activities visit fpdcc.com.

## COOK COUNTY NATURE CENTERS

These six nature centers are free to the public and open year round (except Camp Sagawau).

- **Crabtree Nature Center**, 3 Stover Rd, Barrington, has over 1,000 acres and is the newest of the County's Nature Centers. Since its purchase by the Forest Preserve in the mid-1960s, this glacier-formed landscape is slowly being returned to its natural state. Over 263 species of birds have been identified here, with at least 89 species breeding within its boundaries. There are an exhibit building and several miles of self-guided educational trails through the center. Groups are encouraged to make a reservation by calling 847-381-6592. No bicycling, horseback riding, or cross-country skiing allowed. Picnicking is permitted only at designated areas: Deer Grove Forest Preserve, Shoe Factory Road Woods, and Barrington Road Pond. For more information, contact the Conservation Department at 800-870-3666.
- **North Park Village Nature Center**, 5801 N Pulaski Rd, 312-744-5472, is a 46-acre preserve with woodlands, prairie, pond and savannas. Offers family and adult educational programs, bird walks, owl prowls.
- **River Trails Nature Center**, 3120 Milwaukee Ave, Northbrook, walk through sugar maple woods on self-guided educational trails. There is an exhibit building, and naturalists are available to answer questions. Groups encouraged but reservations are recommended. Call 847-824-8360. For more general information, contact the Conservation Department at 800-870-3666.

- **Sand Ridge Nature Center**, 15890 Paxton Ave, South Holland; this 235-acre preserve is located near Wampum Lake Woods. It has four easy, well-marked hiking trails, none longer than two miles. Each trail leads through a different habitat: an oak savanna, marsh, ancient sand dune, and a pond. The area is especially admired for its April/May spring blossoms, summer prairie flowers, and early autumn colors. Several events are celebrated at the center throughout the year, including Earth Day, Migratory Bird Day, and Settler's Day. Free nature programs are held in the exhibit building. Guided walks are available. Contact 708-868-0606 for reservations and more information.
- **Sagawau Environment Learning Center**, 12545 W 111th St, Lemont; containing the only rock canyon in Cook County, the preserve is home to over 100 migratory birds. Opened only for scheduled programs, though over 80 family programs and hikes are presented. For more information about programs, college credit courses, and workshops, call 630-257-2045.
- **The Little Red Schoolhouse Nature Center**, 9800 Willow Springs Rd, Willow Springs; built in 1866 to replace a one-room log cabin school, this building was in use as a school until 1948. Present-day hikers can traverse trails used by former students, and fruit orchards planted in 1906 still bear fruit. Groups of 15 or more must make a reservation by calling 708-839-6897.
- **Harold Tyrell Trailside Museum**, 738 Thatcher Ave, River Forest; the museum building, built in 1874, is located in a savanna prairie. The museum building is used as a rehabilitation center for injured wildlife; once the animals are well enough to live on their own, they are released into the wild. Groups are welcome. November through February. Reservations needed. Call 708-366-6530.
- **Wampum Lake Woods**; situated between the townships of Thornton and Lansing, this 375-acre wood is host to a variety of plants not normally found in the area. Its sandy soil fosters wildflowers, trees, and shrubs. This area is considered one of the best working archaeological sites in the Chicago area (off-limits to the public). Cross-country skiing, ice fishing, and hiking are popular here, and dogs on leashes are welcomed, but boating and swimming are prohibited. Pick up a map at the Nature Center. For more information, call 800-870-3666.

# FOREST PRESERVES BEYOND COOK COUNTY

Neighboring counties also have extensive forest preserves.

## DUPAGE COUNTY FOREST PRESERVE

The DuPage County Forest Preserve covers more than 23,000 acres with 60 miles of rivers and streams, 80 miles of trails, and over 600 acres of lakes. Each year, over one million visitors come to the forest preserves of DuPage County to hike, ski, bird watch, or ride horses. You can call 630-933-7200 or visit the website www.dupageforest.com, for more information, but here are some areas you may wish to explore:

- **Egermann Woods Forest Preserve**, DuPage County Forest Preserve, Lisle; mowed turf trails follow paths originally set by Native Americans and European settlers more than 200 years ago. A great horned owl has been sighted along the Hobson Road trails. Hikers, joggers, and cross-country skiers are welcome.
- **Willowbrook Wildlife Center**, Glen Ellyn, DuPage County
- **Winfield Mounds** in DuPage County is the site of prehistoric mounds and earthworks

## WILL COUNTY FOREST PRESERVE

The Will County Forest Preserve, 815-727-8700, covers approximately 15,000 acres. At the preserve are nature programs for school groups, special events for the public, and a woodland and open grassland rehabilitation program. You can download maps, learn about new programs, and register for a newsletter at its website: www.reconnectwithnature.org.

Other Will County sites of interest are:

- **Briscoe Mounds**, Front St, Channahon (I-55 Bluff Rd exit); archeological site of prehistoric mounds and earthworks, along the Des Plaines River
- **Higginbotham Woods**, Joliet; full of mysterious and prehistoric mounds and formations
- **Lake Renwick Heron Rookery Nature Preserve**, 23144 W Renwick Rd, Plainfield; call 815-727-8700, or visit the county website, www.reconnectwithnature.org, for more information
- **Monee Reservoir**, 27341 Ridgeland Ave, Monee, 708-534-8499, is a 46-acre lake for fishing and boating. Boat rentals available April–October. Shoreline fishing, free. Ice-skating and cross-country skiing in the winter months. Visit www.reconnectwithnature.org for more information.
- **Oakwood Fischer** is the site of prehistoric mounds and earthworks
- **Plum Creek Nature Center**, 27064 S Dutton Rd, Beecher, 708-946-2216; includes family programs, night hikes, campfire programs

## LAKE COUNTY FOREST PRESERVE

A latecomer by the surrounding area standards, Lake County had no land set aside for forest preserves as late as 1957. Thanks to Ethel Untermyer's relentless efforts, a countywide referendum voted overwhelmingly for its creation. Today there are more than 23,000 acres of forest preserve lands in Lake County, with a 475-acre area named Ethel's Woods set aside in her honor. The Lake County Forest Preserve has been recognized as one of the nation's outstanding systems of parks, recreation and conservation facilities. It was awarded a Gold Medal from the National Recreation and Park Association. Go to www.lcfpd.org for more information.

Some of the facilities within the Lake County Forest Preserve include:

- **Lake County Discovery Museum**, 27277 Forest Preserve Dr, Wauconda, 847-968-3400; admission discounts on Tuesdays. Free parking. Be sure to visit the Curt Teich Postcard Archives while you are there. It's the largest public collection of post cards and related material in the world. Visit www.lakecountydiscoverymuseum.org for more information.
- **McDonald Woods Forest Preserve**, Lake County, is comprised of 304 acres of woodland in the northern portion of Lake County. There are three ponds, and trails for walking and cross-country skiing.
- **Ryerson Woods Welcome Center**; housed in a Greek Revival–style mansion, this building is listed on the National Register of Historic Places. Today it serves as the preserve's library and meeting space; the facility can be rented for special events. The visitor center is situated within the 552-acre Ryerson Conservation Area, at 21950 North Riverwoods Rd, Deerfield. Call 847-968-3320 for information about programs or visit www.lcfpd.org.

## CHICAGO BEACHES

Since 1909, the City of Chicago has operated public beaches along its shores. Initially many beaches along the lakeshore were privately owned—some as late as the 1930s. The city's struggle to take over all the lakeshore beaches within city limits was advanced by the illicit activities that often took place on private beaches.

Beach season officially begins in Chicago on Memorial Day and ends on Labor Day. Most beaches open at 9 a.m. and close at 9:30 p.m. Chicago operates 33 beaches, all free to the public. One group, mostly in Rogers Park, includes 18 **street-end beaches**. These beaches are small tracts at the end of residential streets, used mostly by nearby residents. While they all have lifeguards on duty during the season, they do not have changing facilities or restrooms. Call 312-742-7529 or visit www.chicagoparkdistrict.com for more information. Here are a few of them:

- **Hartigan Beach**, 1031 W Albion Ave
- **Jarvis Beach and Park**, 1208 W Jarvis Ave
- **Juneway Terrace Beach and Park**, 7751 N Eastlake Terrace
- **Lane Beach and Park**, 5915 N Sheridan Rd
- **Leone Park and Beach**, 1222 W Touhy Ave
- **North Shore Beach Park**, 1040 W North Shore Ave

- **Pratt Boulevard Beach and Park**, 1050 West Pratt Blvd
- **Rogers Avenue Beach and Park**, 7705 N Eastlake Terrace
- The following beaches are the best-known **Chicago area beaches**. Facilities vary, and there is lots of foot traffic.
- **57th Street Beach**, 5700 S Lake Shore Dr, 312-742-5121; used by university staff, students, and locals alike. The nearby Promontory Point serves as a vast backyard for family picnics, biking, and dog walking. Look out for flying Frisbees and up for kites.
- **Calumet Park**, 9801 S Ave G, 312-747-6039; this 198-acre park sits on Chicago's South Shore, where Illinois meets Indiana on Lake Michigan. A lakeside bicycle trail runs right along the beach. In addition to sun bathing and swimming, there are 16 tennis courts, two volleyball courts, and football, baseball, and soccer fields. In the field house, you can play basketball, work in the woodshop, or work out in the gym. The basement of the field house features a model of Chicago's East Side, circa 1940, accompanied by a model train chugging along.
- **Foster Beach**, Lakeshore/Foster Ave, 312-742-5121; open 9 a.m. to 9:30 p.m. This small beach is a nice alternative to the need-to-be-seen action at some of the other downtown beaches. Beach house offers food stands, handicap-accessible restrooms, and outdoor showers. There is a large inexpensive parking lot just south of the beach.
- **Kathy Osterman Beach**, formerly Hollywood Beach, 5800 N Lakeshore Dr, 312-742-5121. Noisy and crowded, Osterman Beach attracts families on its north end where the water is a bit shallower, while the southern part has become a popular gay spot. You can bike over on the path that hugs the shoreline or take a bus.
- **Montrose Beach**; stretching from Montrose to Wilson Avenues along Lakeshore Dr, Montrose Beach offers beach volleyball, baseball diamonds, soccer fields, and horseback riding trails, along with a clean beach. Playlot for young children, six-lane boat-launch. Restrooms are closer to Wilson Ave. Fishing is possible from the pier. Open 6 a.m. to 11 p.m. daily during the summer. Admission to the beach is free and street parking is available.
- **North Avenue Beach House**, 1600 N Lake Shore Dr, 312-742-5121; this beach is one of the most popular in the city. Its new beach house resembles an ocean liner and features restrooms, outdoor showers, concession stands, eating areas, chess pavilion, and rental offices. Some say the beach house offers one of the best views in Chicago.
- **Oak Street Beach**, 1000 N Lake Shore Drive, 312-742-5121, is the most famous of all the local beaches. It is wide, long, clean, and a favorite with locals and tourists. You can ride a bike on the path (rentals are on-site), swim, sunbathe, skate, and jog right in the shadows of the Hancock building. You will have to walk up towards the North Avenue beach for a restroom. This beach

is free to the public. There is some street parking, and lot parking too (try looking around the Palmolive Building, the Hancock Building, or the Drake Hotel). The beach is wheelchair accessible.
- **Rainbow Beach Park**, 2873 E 75th St, 312-745-1479; also offers tennis, baseball facilities, and a gym.
- **South Shore Cultural Center Beach**, 7059 S South Shore Dr, 773-256-0149; facilities in this 65-acre park include tennis courts and a golf course.

## BEACHES BEYOND CHICAGO

Many of the suburbs north of Chicago have outstanding beaches—clean, long sweeps of silky sand that are as beautiful as the mansions built along them. North Shore beaches are not free; there is an admission and sometimes a parking fee as well. Fees change periodically, so check with the park district for the latest information. The money goes to maintain the beaches, which can be quite costly, especially in years when algae bloom or bacteria threatens the quality of the water. Season passes are available or you can pay per visit. In most communities, both residents and non-residents must pay.

- **Centennial Beach**, 500 W Jackson Ave, Naperville, 630-848-5000; built from an abandoned limestone quarry alongside the DuPage River, Centennial Beach has been a family destination for Naperville-area residents since 1931. Centennial has a large sandy beach and a playground facility. Floating rafts stationed in the middle of the quarry provide places to rest. Supervised bathhouse with showers and coin-operated lockers. Free off-street parking. Season passes available. Open June–July 11 a.m. to 8 p.m., August 11 a.m. to dusk. Admission charged.
- **Centennial Park–Dog Beach**, Elder/Sheridan roads, Winnetka; dog-friendly beach, but requires membership. No swimming allowed. Off-street parking. Check with the park district office for more information, 847-501-2040.
- **Elder Lane Beach**, Elder/Sheridan roads, Winnetka; beach house with restrooms, off-street parking, and playground. Parking fee plus admission fee. Season pass can be purchased, which includes parking. For more information, call the park district at 847-501-2040.
- **Forest Park Beach**, Lake Road, Lake Forest; this 29-acre park is open year-round. You can fish off the pier, grill in sheltered areas, or walk along the woodland paths. It is also equipped with a boat launch. Handicap accessible. Contact the park district for information regarding parking and admission fees: 847-234-6702.
- **Glencoe Beach**, Hazel/Park Avenues, Glencoe; call for information about fees and parking, 847-835-1185.
- **Gillson Beach**, Wilmette, 847-256-9656; one of the biggest Lake Michigan beaches (60 acres) in the North Shore area, and the one with the most parking.

Facilities include a snack bar, dunes, main beach, and sailboat rental. Open 9 a.m. to 8 p.m. during the season. Admission charged for non-residents. Season passes are available for purchase at the Park District Administrative Offices, 847-256-6100, or through the Gillson Beach House.

- **Lloyd Park,** Winnetka; launching ramp for boats.
- **Maple Beach**, Maple/Sheridan roads, Winnetka; beach house with restrooms and off-street parking.
- **Northwestern University Beach** (also known as **Evanston North Beach**); twelve miles north of Chicago, the rocky shoreline of this beach sets it apart from the rest. Since it is owned by the university, use of the beach is restricted to NU affiliates.
- **Riviera Beach**, Wrigley Dr, Lake Geneva, WI, 262-248-3673; open May 1 to Labor Day, 9:30 a.m. to 6 p.m. Admission charged; free for kids under 7. Metered parking available. A beach literally in the middle of town is an oddity to be sure but it's also quite handy. The beach has a bathhouse with showers. Fine shopping and dining nearby.
- **Tower Beach**, Winnetka; 20 miles north of Chicago, this beach is small and a bit out of the way, so it is easy to miss from the road. It offers the most facilities of all Winnetka beaches. The parking area sits on a bluff, and you walk down toward the shore. The beach house is equipped with restrooms, showers, concession stands, and vending machines. There are a playground and two sand volleyball courts. Handicap accessible.

## STATE PARKS

For more about Illinois State Parks, contact the **Department of Natural Resources** (**DNR**), www.dnr.illinois.gov, 847-608-3100. The DNR is a good source of information about outdoor activities, state museums, campsites, and parks. Their free magazine, *Illinois State Parks*, includes information about park activities, camping facilities, lodges, beaches, and recreation areas.

- **Illinois Beach State Park**, at the lakefront, Zion, 847-662-4811; situated on Lake Michigan, this beach has over six miles of quiet sandy beaches. The park, approximately 90 minutes north of the city, includes the beach plus over 4,100 acres of dunes, woodlands, and marshes. Fishing is allowed from the beach or Sand Pond. Depending on the season, you can bike, hike, and cross-country ski here. There are 240 campsites on the south end of the park, all equipped with electricity. Make reservations several months in advance. For boaters, North Point Marina is five miles north of the Park with over 1,500 slips.
- **Starved Rock State Park**, Utica, 815-667-4726; ninety-two miles southwest of Chicago, Starved Rock State Park offers striking scenery that includes 18 canyons formed by melting glacier waters and stream erosion, along with small waterfalls in season. Enjoy horseback riding, camping, fishing, and

boating in wildlife-filled, lush vegetation. Visitor center is open daily; check for annual events schedule. Guided tours are available on weekends. A historic stone and log lodge offers luxury hotel rooms and comfortable cabins. Indoor swimming pools, sauna, and children's pool. Restaurant on premises. For lodge reservations, call 815-667-4211.

- **Chain O' Lakes,** 8916 Wilmot Rd, Spring Grove, 847-587-5512; an hour and a half northwest of Chicago, this state park is bordered by the Fox River and three lakes. Hike some of its 15-plus miles of trails and you are likely to come across deer, pheasant, and a variety of waterfowl. There are also five miles of bike trails, grasslands, meadows, and woodlands. Fishing and camping are allowed but permits and reservations are necessary. On the northern end of the trail system is a two-mile section called Nature's Way, a self-guided interpretive trail. Along the way, you can see one of the few remaining American lotus beds. The park is open May–October, 6 a.m. to 9 p.m., and from 8 a.m. to sunset in the winter. Maps are available in the park office.
- **Jubilee College State Park,** 13921 W Rte 150, Brimfield, 309-446-3758; this 3,200-acre park is a mountain biker's delight with over 40 miles of open dirt and grass trails and 10 miles of hiking and cross-country skiing trails. The park is home to 160 species of birds, including wild turkeys, plus mink, fox, and other wildlife. Although swimming is not permitted, fishing is allowed in Jubilee Creek and in the two ponds in the park, and sheltered areas equipped with electricity, water hydrants, and toilets offer picnicking opportunities. Camp facilities are open April–November, with applications downloadable from the DNR website.
- **Moraine Hill State Park,** 1510 S River Rd, 815-385-1624, McHenry; nestled in the northeast corner of the state, a little more than an hour northwest of Chicago, this park offers three easy walking trails, each set in its own landscape: hickory/oak forest, bogs and marshes, or thick vegetation. Glacier Lake Defiance is the park's centerpiece. Fishing is available at the William Stratton Dam—kids fish free, adults for a small fee, and a nature center offers weekend programs. Park hours: dawn to dusk.
- **Rock Island Trail,** 311 E Williams St, Wyoming, 309-695-2228, offers 26 miles of hiking/walking trails from Alta (Peoria County) to Toulon (Stark County). Thanks to the former rail beds that once ran alongside it, these trails are easy traversing; in fact, you will see remnants of the railroad as you walk through this tree-canopied corridor. As the rail line was abandoned, the landscape reverted to its native prairie grasses. No motorized vehicles or horses allowed on the trails. Water, parking, and pit toilets are located at access areas. The old Chicago Burlington/Quincy Depot serves as a visitor center and railroad museum. Call first if you are planning to visit as the Depot is open only as available staff permits. For more information call the DNR's Office of Public Services, 217-782-7454 or 800-720-0298.

## NATIONAL LAKESHORE

**Indiana Dunes National Lakeshore**, 1100 N Mineral Springs Rd, Porter, Indiana, 219-926-7561; fifty miles southeast of Chicago, the dunes are an easy day trip to the beach. Composed of twenty-five miles of beach on the southern shore of Lake Michigan, the park offers 45 miles of hiking and riding trails, an 18th-century French-Canadian farm house, and fishing along the lakeshore or from the Little Calumet River. West Beach is a favorite spot with its beachhouse showers, concession stands, and picnic areas. It also is one of the few beaches that has a lifeguard on duty. It can be a bit crowded so if you need some space, try the unguarded Kemil, Porter, Central Avenue, or Mt. Baldy beaches (dogs are allowed at Mt. Baldy until October). The entire park is open 8 a.m. to 4:30 p.m.; West Beach Bathhouse is open from 9 a.m. to 9 p.m. There is a user fee for West Beach. Areas of the lakeshore are wheelchair accessible, and entrance to the dunes is free.

If you prefer not to drive, the Chicago South Shore and South Bend railroads make numerous stops through the lakeshore area. For more information visit the National Park System website at www.nps.gov/indu.

## ADDITIONAL RESOURCES

For more information about the dozens and dozens of lakes and rivers in the eight-county area, visit the Chicago Area Paddling and Fishing Pages at http://pages.ripco.net/~jwn. Here you will find information not only about the neighboring lakes and their location, but what kind of fishing you can expect in each lake, maps, links to areas with whitewater rafting, sailing, canoeing, and more. Michigan's **Harbor Country** is very popular with Chicagoans. From New Buffalo to Warren Dunes State Park, it's all gorgeous. Visit their website at www.harborcountry.org. The **Great Lakes Information Network** is a great resource for outdoor recreation ideas, historical sites, shipwrecks, lake tours, and much more: www.great-lakes.net.

For more information about Chicago parks and greenspace, check the **Sports and Recreation** chapter of this book and/or the pertinent **Neighborhood Profile**.

# WEATHER AND CLIMATE

Like much of the Midwest, Chicago enjoys four distinct seasons, and though the city has a reputation for harsh winters, they are nothing like the winters in snowy Buffalo or semi-arctic Minneapolis–St. Paul. Some might argue that the sweltering summers in Chicago can be much more unpleasant, not to mention dangerous, with high temperatures and humid conditions. While the winter weather is often the product of cold Canadian air masses, the Chicago summer weather is usually brought to us courtesy of south and southwest winds—and therefore not tempered by the infamous "lake effect" that produces snow in winter. When a summer lake effect breeze does come to the rescue, neighborhoods near the lake can be cooler than their suburban neighbors by as much as 10 degrees.

The story about how Chicago became known as the "windy city" has nothing to do with the weather. Legend has it that a New York editor came up with the nickname when he was describing Chicago politicians. While hot air and politicians go hand in hand, particularly in Chicago, you won't find many Chicagoans who will deny the might of Chicago's winds. Their effect on local temperatures is significant, whether cooling lake effect winds in the summer or those chilling arctic blasts from the Canadian plains. The average annual wind speed is 10.4 mph.

## FALL/WINTER

Fall can be a great time of year for outdoor activities in Chicago. Lovely autumn colors are a pleasurable sight in this tree-filled city. Some years, autumns are dry and sunny; other years, fall can be cold and rainy. If you have out-of-town friends who want to come for a visit, fall is the perfect time. The weather is generally good, and the summer crowds are gone, making for easier shopping and sightseeing.

Dickens might have been thinking of Chicago winters when he wrote, "it was the best of times, it was the worst of times." If you aren't afraid of chilly weather, you may enjoy the Chicago winters, or at least be indifferent to them. But if you loathe cold weather, watch out! It can get downright frigid here. Temperatures in the teens and even below zero are not uncommon, and the wind chill may make that seem even colder. The winter season typically lasts from late November to late March. While winter snowstorms usually take place in January and February, long-time residents will tell you that spring snowstorms are not out of the question either. The party line on winter dress for downtown commuters is "heavy and waterproof." If you are moving to Chicago from a warmer part of the country you will want to buy a good coat (lined, windproof, and on the longish side), boots, gloves, and a good hat. Chicago receives about 38 inches of snow in a typical year.

If you have never driven in icy conditions, it can take some getting used to. Perhaps the most important caution is to drive more slowly than usual, leaving extra time for turning and braking. In extreme winter weather, tailgating is especially dangerous, and a too-fast turn can slide into a skid or spin. Experts advise leaving three times the normal amount of space between your car and the car in front of you. Also, make sure that you're familiar with your car's systems and amenities. For instance, gently pumping the brakes helps a car with standard brakes stop more smoothly on ice—but ABS brakes do this automatically, so pumping them hurts instead of helps.

Check your car's owner's manual for tips on winterizing. You'll definitely want to do a basic inspection before the winter weather hits—or pay someone else to do it. This includes checking that your battery, brakes, and all other systems are working correctly, as well as checking your fluid levels and the condition of your tires. It's a good idea, too, to keep the winter basics in your car: an ice scraper, a small shovel (for when snow piles up on top of the car or beneath your tires), a first aid kit, bottled water and non-perishable high-energy snacks (in case you're stranded), jumper cables, a flashlight with extra batteries, a blanket or sleeping bag, and a warm hat and gloves and at least one extra pair of warm socks. A cell phone, fully charged, can certainly help in case of emergencies.

If you must drive in inclement weather, or before embarking on a major winter drive, first go to www.dot.state.il.us for information about current driving conditions.

## SPRING

Springs vary in Chicago—some come in with balmy spring rains and sunny days, others are slow to come, cold, rainy, and even snowy. Generally, though, in April and May, high temperatures hover in the mid-60s, and it can be rainy.

If it is early spring and a Chinook wind has just swept down from Canada, you may experience a balmy day with dramatic downpours—an inch of rain within a few hours is not uncommon. But on average, Chicago gets nine inches of rain each spring, accompanied by thunderstorms and lighting. Snow isn't unheard of either. Though the bulk of Chicago snowfalls occur in January and February, the only two months that snow hasn't been recorded are July and August! So don't be surprised when a few sunny, warm days in mid or even late March turn fickle, bringing below-average temperatures and even a few white flakes. Typically, there won't be any more frosts after the end of April, but if you plan to set out young plants in your garden, most local nurseries will suggest you wait until May 10th, just to be on the safe side.

One consolation for Chicago's blustery spring weather is the refreshing return of green to the city. The parks and even the traffic islands in Chicago are wonderfully landscaped. The sight of flowering shrubs and trees, and colorful spring tulips and daffodils, is a welcome and soothing treat after a long winter.

Weather that produces tornadoes, particularly in the spring, does happen here, though tornadoes seldom touch the central Chicago area. However, watch it in the suburbs: the south suburbs, for example, are five times more likely to be hit by a tornado than the city.

## SUMMER

Microclimates in Chicago are not significant, except that the term "cooler near the lake" is generally true—in summer, temperatures in the northwest and southwest suburbs can vary by as much as ten degrees from the temperature downtown. Chicago summers typically offer a good couple of weeks of above-90-degree temperatures: about 15 days in the northwest suburbs; 24 in the south suburbs; and only 11 at the lakefront. July and August are when Chicagoans really pay attention to the heat index. Death from summer heat and humidity is a leading weather-related killer. According to the Centers for Disease Control, each year more people die from heat than from lightning strikes, hurricanes, flooding, and tornadoes combined! The concept of heat index was created by the National Weather Service to give people a more accurate indication of how high temperatures actually feel when high humidity is factored into the equation. Keep in mind that the heat index was developed for shady, light-winded areas. Exposure to sunlight can increase the heat index values by 15 degrees.

Over a two-week period in July 1997, Chicago temperatures ranged from 93 degrees to 104 degrees, and the heat index peaked at the city's record high of 119 degrees. In those two weeks, 465 people died from heat-related causes. In order to prevent such a tragedy from happening again, former Mayor Daley established emergency cooling centers around the city for dangerous heat index days, which are a particular concern for the elderly and disabled, many of whom live without air-conditioning. The opening of emergency cooling centers, as well as their locations, is regularly announced in area media when the heat becomes oppressive.

Pollution can create another warm weather hazard. In the summer, most urban areas are key targets for **ozone alert** days. Ozone, a powerful lung irritant, is caused when the sun cooks air-carbon-based chemicals emitted by vehicle and industry exhaust, and other pollutants. Luckily, Cook County does not have as many ozone alert days as other US metropolitan areas thanks to Chicago's offshore breezes, which help to clear out the heavy air. Several clean air initiatives initiated by an earlier mayor—promoting the planting of rooftop gardens, encouraging bicycling as an alternate means of transportation, tree-planting, installation of light-colored roofs, cleaning up industrial parks, and working closely with industry to facilitate the elimination of air pollutants—have also helped to control ozone in Chicagoland. Nonetheless, ozone may still create a problem, particularly for those with lung sensitivities. The hottest, most humid months, August especially, are most challenging. According to the Environmental Protection Agency, Chicago has been successful in meeting EPA guidelines for ozone (smog)-free days. According to a 2010 Annual Air Quality Report released by the Illinois EPA, Chicago's air quality consistently stayed within the "good to moderate" range. Cook County has at times struggled to maintain the EPA's "safe" levels for airborne carcinogens, and high-risk groups—those with asthma and other lung conditions—as in most US cities, need to be aware of particularly troublesome days.

To check the three-day (yesterday-today-tomorrow) air quality index for your area of Chicagoland, head to the Air Quality page of the Illinois EPA's website: www.epa.state.il.us/air/aqi/index.html. You can also check **current smog conditions** online at Midwest Hazecam, www.mwhazecam.net, which provides near real-time air quality data, current air pollution levels, and information to determine whether natural or manmade pollutants are causing the then-present levels of visibility impairments. Daily air quality reports are also available through the National Weather Service, www.crh.noaa.gov/lot.

If you are an **allergy sufferer**, brace yourself: in Chicago allergy season starts in the spring with the flowering of oak, elm, maple, and pine trees, followed by the summer bloom of ragweed and cottonwoods. If you live in an outlying area, agriculture-related pollen counts may also be an allergen factor. For a daily pollen and mold count in your area, check the American Academy of Allergy, Asthma & Immunology's pollen and mold report at www.aaaai.org/nab/index.cfm

# METRO CHICAGO WEATHER STATISTICAL INFORMATION

Below is a chart noting temperatures and precipitation for each month, but don't let these numbers fool you—as mentioned above, summertime temperatures can soar to the upper 90s, while winter temperatures often drop below ten degrees. The wind chill of course, dips the winter weather into the single digits on a regular basis. The National Weather Service is a good online resource for weather information and forecasts: www.crh.noaa.gov.

Weather averages, according to http://countrystudies.us/united-states/weather/illinois/chicago.htm, are:

|               | Jan | Feb | Mar | Apr | May | Jun |
|---------------|-----|-----|-----|-----|-----|-----|
| Avg. High     | 31  | 35  | 46  | 58  | 70  | 80  |
| Avg. Low      | 17  | 22  | 31  | 41  | 51  | 60  |
| Mean          | 25  | 28  | 38  | 50  | 61  | 71  |
| Avg. Precip.  | 1.9 | 1.6 | 2.9 | 3.8 | 3.6 | 4.1 |

|               | Jul | Aug | Sep | Oct | Nov | Dec |
|---------------|-----|-----|-----|-----|-----|-----|
| Avg. High     | 84  | 82  | 76  | 65  | 50  | 36  |
| Avg. Low      | 66  | 65  | 58  | 47  | 36  | 24  |
| Mean          | 75  | 74  | 68  | 56  | 44  | 30  |
| Avg. Precip.  | 3.8 | 3.9 | 3.5 | 2.4 | 3.1 | 2.8 |

(Temperatures are in degrees in Fahrenheit; precipitation is the water-equivalent in inches.)

If you'd like more information on current Chicago weather conditions, visit the **National Weather Service** website, www.crh.noaa.gov/crh, and type in your ZIP code.

# INSECTS

Chicago experiences the usual Midwestern spectrum of warm-weather pests, primarily mosquitoes, ants, bees, wasps, chiggers, fleas, mites, and ticks. While many of these insects can be annoying—especially when they bite!—only a few pose a serious risk to most people.

West Nile disease has been a problem in Illinois since the early 1990s. Though the disease remains rare, the severity of the problem varies widely by year. In 2006, statewide, 215 human cases of West Nile disease resulted in 10 deaths. By the end of summer 2007, just 28 human cases had been reported throughout Illinois, and three deaths resulted. The City of Chicago and surrounding suburbs continue to be vigilant about taking every possible public health measure to eradicate the mosquitoes that carry West Nile; however, preventative measures such as wearing repellent and protective clothing are still wise, especially at peak mosquito hours.

The American Lyme Disease Foundation (www.aldf.com) classifies the entire Chicago area as "medium risk" for tick-borne Lyme disease, which can affect dogs as well as humans. Over 100 cases have been reported yearly in Illinois since 2005. (Note that nearby Wisconsin and Minnesota generally report over ten times more yearly cases than Illinois.) Still, if you live in a heavily wooded area or if you regularly hike or camp, you should familiarize yourself with the symptoms of Lyme disease as listed at www.aldf.com. In addition, be vigilant about checking your body and your pet's body after returning from wooded areas and shores. Ticks prefer hairy areas and little crevices like the armpit, groin, behind the ear, or between fingers and toes. Never touch a tick with your bare hands; remove it with tweezers instead.

# GETTING INVOLVED

Now that you've found a place to live and settled into your new home, you may want to get involved in your community. Joining a worship group, volunteering, and meeting people with similar interests are three great ways to connect with others in your new neighborhood and city. Also see the **Sports and Recreation** chapter for more opportunities to get involved.

## PLACES OF WORSHIP

If you came from a small town, you may have gone to *the* Methodist church, *the* Catholic Church, or *the* synagogue. But here in Chicago, there are more than 2,800,000 Roman and Orthodox Catholics, 1,350,000 Protestants, 310,000 Muslims, 260,000 Jews, and 100,000 Buddhists. If you add Hindus, well, you get the idea—there are a lot of places of worship in Chicago. You'll find some of them listed by denomination in the Yellow Pages. The **National Council of Churches** (www.ncccusa.org) publishes the *Yearbook of American & Canadian Churches,* a directory listing of thousands of Christian churches. Order one for $50 at 888-870-3325. Other online directories of churches—generally limited to Christian denominations—include http://netministries.org and www.**forministry**.com. If you are interested in becoming involved in interfaith projects, you can visit the **Illinois Conference of Churches** at www.ilconfchurches.org, or the **Office of Ecumenical and Interreligious Affairs** that operates within the Catholic Archdiocese of Chicago, 312-534-5325, www.archchicago.org.

Below is a selection of religious institutions that are particularly noteworthy—maybe because of their historical significance, their physical beauty, their size, or their spirit of community. Churches, synagogues, and temples with landmark status are noted, as well as some of those known for their musicality.

# BAHÁ'Í

Bahá'í House of Worship, 100 Linden Ave, Wilmette, 847-853-2300; only one of seven temples of its kind in the world. Construction on the striking, nine-sided, bell-shaped temple began in 1920, but it took until 1953 for this now-historic temple to be completed. The Bahá'í House of Worship is open to all. See www.bahai.us/bahai-temple/ for more information.

# BUDDHIST

The Buddhist Temple of Chicago's website, www.budtempchi.org, offers links to other temples in the Chicago area.

- **Buddhist Temple of Chicago (BTC)**, 1151 W Leland Ave, www.budtempchi.org, 773-334-4661, is a non-sectarian temple. Established on Chicago's south side in 1944, it was moved to its current location in 1956. Services in English and Japanese are held separately. The temple offers its community a range of services, including religious teaching, martial arts instruction, and more.
- **Zen Buddhist Temple**, 1710 W Cornelia Ave, www.zenbuddhisttemple.org, 773-528-8685. Seminary, monastery, and temple of the Buddhist Society for Compassionate Wisdom housed in what was formerly a Freemason's temple, the Zen Buddhist Temple provides public services and meditation courses as well as retreats, lectures, and other activities.
- **Midwest Buddhist Temple**, 435 W Menomonee St, www.midwestbuddhisttemple.org, 312-943-8069, is affiliated with the Buddhist Churches of America, headquartered in San Francisco, and rooted in the Nishi Hongwanji from Kyoto, Japan, practicing Jodo Shinshu, the pure land school. In the third week of August, the Temple celebrates a Ginza holiday by bringing artisans from the Waza area of Japan to demonstrate their crafts.

# CHRISTIAN

Some of the **oldest churches** in Chicago are:

- **Old St. Patrick Catholic Church**, 700 W Adams, www.oldstpats.org, 312-648-1021 (c. 1856)
- **Episcopalian Cathedral of St. James**, 65 E Huron St, www.saintjamescathedral.org, 312-787-7360 (c. 1857)
- **Holy Family Church**, 1080 W Roosevelt Rd, 312-492-8442 (c. 1860)
- **St. Michael Catholic Church**, 1633 N Cleveland Ave, www.st-mikes.org, 312-642-2198 (c. 1869)
- **Trinity Episcopal Church**, 125 E 26th St, http://trinitychurchchicago.org, 312-842-7545 (c. 1874)

- **Holy Name Cathedral**, 730 N Wabash Ave, www.holynamecathedral.org, 312-787-8040 (c. 1875)

## BAPTIST

- **First Baptist Congregational Church**, 1613 W Washington Ave, www.fbcc-chicago.net, 312-243-8047; this church, located near the Union Park Lagoon on Chicago's west side, is often featured in historical pictures of Chicago. Today it is sometimes referred to as the Union Park Congregational Church. What is especially noteworthy about this building is its interior: a theater-like auditorium with seating that curves around the pulpit. This innovative design was very influential in church architecture. In 1869, the adjacent Carpenter's Chapel was built for the Chicago Theological Seminary. Founded in 1851 by abolitionists, it maintains its strong roots in community activism. Today, this African-American church is home to a number of choirs and hosts several community programs and schools. It achieved landmark status in 1982.
- **First Church of Deliverance**, 4315 S Wabash Ave, 773-373-7700; designed by Walter T. Bailey, Chicago's first African-American architect, in the Moderne style, this church was founded by Reverend Clarence Cobbs, who was very influential in developing gospel music and was a key figure in Christian radio broadcasting. Another architect added the twin towers in 1946. The church received landmark status in 1994.
- **Metropolitan Missionary Baptist Church**, 2151 W Washington Blvd, 773-738-0053; this church's unique design was a deliberate break with the then-current church architecture. In designing what was then the Third Church of Christ, Scientist, architect Hugh M.G. Garden combined elements of Classical and Modern influences to create a unique style that today is sometimes referred to as "Gardenesque." The church was sold to the Metropolitan Missionary Baptist congregation in 1947.
- **Pilgrim Baptist Church**, 3300 S Indiana Ave, 312-842-4417, http://rebuildpilgrim.org; originally built as a synagogue in 1890, this dramatic-looking church was the result of the collaboration of one of the premier architects of the time, Louis H. Sullivan, and the engineering skills of Dankmar Adler. The original building featured masonry and terra cotta panels, both inside and out. From 1922 to 2006, it was the home of the Pilgrim Baptist Church, a leader in developing gospel music; Mahalia Jackson and the Edwin Hawkin Singers were among its celebrated guest artists. The church received landmark status in 1981. Tragically, a fire in January 2006 almost completely destroyed the historic structure. The congregation continues to meet in a nearby building, and ambitious fundraising efforts are under way to rebuild the church.

## CHRISTIAN SCIENTIST

**Eighth Church of Christ, Scientist**, 4359 S Michigan Ave, 773-373-4126; designed by architect Leon Stanhope in 1910, and awarded landmark status in 1993, the Eighth Church of Christ is one of the country's oldest African-American Christian Scientist congregations. Built in the Classical-Revival style, it features a beautiful broad dome of a style made popular by the 1893 World's Columbian Exposition. The Church is still active, offering children's Sunday school services as well as regularly scheduled services for adults.

## ECUMENICAL

**Rockefeller Memorial Chapel**, 5850 S Woodlawn Ave, http://rockefeller.uchicago.edu, 773-702-2100 (in Hyde Park); at the request of its benefactor, John D. Rockefeller, this 1928 chapel was designed to be the central, unifying element on the University of Chicago campus. Today, the chapel hosts study groups, performances of religious music, lectures, travel/study seminars, and community service. Religious services are held each Sunday during the academic year. In 1932, Rockefeller donated the Laura Spelman Rockefeller Carillon, the second largest instrument in the world. The Carillon is played on Fridays and Sundays during the academic year, and during special events—especially during the summer months, when carilloneurs from the world over come to play the bells. A tour of the bell tower can be arranged by calling 773-702-2100. The chapel is a very popular wedding site. For wedding ceremony information, call the wedding facilitator at 773-834-8538.

## EPISCOPAL

- **All Saints Church and Rectory**, 4550 N Hermitage Ave, www.allsaintschicago.org, 773-561-0111; located in the Ravenswood section of town, All Saints is the oldest wood-frame church in the city. It was designed by John Cochrane, who is best known for designing the state Capitol in Springfield, in what became known as the Stick Style. Built in 1884, the church is considered one of the best examples of this type of architecture and was declared a Chicago landmark in 1990. All Saints attracts worshippers from all over the city with its youngish congregation and liberal bent. The church dedicates one-third of its budget to outreach programs. It feeds over 130 people every Tuesday night, hosts community dinners each month, sponsors events that encourage teens to participate in fundraisers, and hosts Sunday school for small children. All Saints is active in many social service programs throughout the area, and has many opportunities for volunteers.
- **Church of the Epiphany**, 201 S Ashland Ave, www.epiphany-chicago.org, 312-243-4242; built in 1885 in the Romanesque style, this church and

# GETTING INVOLVED

a few row houses and townhouses on the 1500 blocks of West Adams and West Jackson are all that is left of the once-fashionable Near West Side. The rough-cut stone and rounded arches are typical of a style that has its roots in Spanish and French traditions. The church and the surrounding blocks were designated as landmarks in 1976.

## EVANGELICAL

- **Wheaton Evangelical Free Church**, 520 E Roosevelt Rd, Wheaton, 630-668-6490, www.wefc.org; has an extensive outreach program for adults and children. Includes Sunday school for children and teens, bible studies for adults, youth programs, and sports activities. Sermons archived on tape and online. Sunday services are broadcast live on Wheaton College Radio.

## INDEPENDENT/INTERDENOMINATIONAL/CHRISTIAN

- **Moody Church**, 1635 N LaSalle St, 312-327-8600, www.moodychurch.org, is an evangelical non-denominational church. Facilities include a 4,000-seat auditorium that is used for the Moody Bible Institute's Founder's Week conferences, services, and multi-evening crusades. Well-known for its inspiring, upbeat services, the church influences the community through live Sunday radio broadcasts, a television network, store, and a magazine. It sponsors monthly Loop luncheons, and programs directed towards women's issues.
- **Park Community Church**, 4 locations; 312-361-0500, www.parkcommunitychurch.org. Offers an adult education program, a running club, a twenty-something group, and weekly prayer meetings.
- **Willow Creek Community Church**, 67 E Algonquin Rd, South Barrington, 847-765-5000, www.willowcreek.org; offers over 100 ministries, Sunday morning breakfasts after services, a food pantry, premarital budget workshops, and bible classes for both adults and children. Church facilities feature bookstore, café, and meeting rooms where classes are held and services geared for smaller children are conducted. Services are interdenominational and designed using multimedia, contemporary music, guest speakers and singers, mimes, full orchestras, wide screen projections, and more.

## LUTHERAN

- **Irving Park Lutheran Church**, 3938 W Belle Plaine Ave, www.iplc.org, 773-267-1667; offers adult religious education, music lessons, and youth groups including scouts, basketball, and children's choir
- **Ebenezer Lutheran Church**, 1650 W Foster Ave, http://ebenezerchurch. org, 773-561-8496; this church began as a Lutheran Synod in 1892, found-

ed by Swedish immigrants. At the height of Swedish migration to Chicago, the congregation numbered 2,000. But as Andersonville's ethnic mix began to change, so did the church. In 1988, it became a member of the Evangelical Lutheran Church in America and made changes in its mission in order to serve the changing community. The church welcomes gay and lesbian members and will even bless these unions. Swedish traditions are a focus of December services; Santa Lucia Day is observed on December 13th, and Christmas morning service is celebrated in the Swedish language. The chapel in which services are held was built in 1908.

## METHODIST

### FIRST UNITED METHODIST CHURCH
- **Chicago Temple**, 77 W Washington St, 312-236-4548, http://chicagotemple.org; this First United Methodist Church of Chicago is the oldest congregation in Chicago, dating to 1831, before the city's incorporation. Their original meeting house was a log cabin, a far cry from their current structure, which was built in the 1920s. Located in the Loop, the Chicago Temple is easily recognizable in Chicago's night sky by its massive lighted spire.

### AFRICAN METHODIST EPISCOPAL (A.M.E.)
In 1787, a disagreement between Richard Allen and the congregation of Philadelphia's St. George's Methodist Church (the first Methodist Church in the United States) forced Allen and other black Christians in this community to form their own organization. What was first called the Free African Society would grow into the first black church in America, and the first major religious movement among blacks in this country. Richard Allen would go on to become the first bishop of African Methodist Episcopal Church. The Greater Institutional A.M.E. Church has been located at its present site since 1956.

What sets the Greater Institutional A.M.E. Church apart from other congregations is that it was organized as both a settlement house and a house of worship. In its early years, the church received financial support from such figures as Robert T. Lincoln, son of Abraham Lincoln, and Mrs. George Pullman, widow of the president of the Pullman Company.

- **Greater Institutional A.M.E. Church**, 7800 S Indiana Ave, www.pgsitemaker.com/sitemaker/sites/AMEGre1/, 773-873-0880, offers its congregation a credit union, Head Start program, Boy Scout Troop, a scholarship fund, Bible study, and a nursery. It was the first church in Chicago to offer a Head Start program. In continuing its mission as a settlement house, the A.M.E. offers a variety of ministries to the community, along with support to many groups such as disaster victims, missionaries, and women's shelters.

- **Quinn Chapel**, 2401 S Wabash Ave, 312-791-1846; built in 1892, Quinn Chapel received landmark status in 1979, and is the oldest African-American congregation in Chicago. It traces its roots back to 1844 when several black Americans gathered to form a prayer circle. In 1847, it organized as an A.M.E. church. Shortly thereafter, it played an important role in the Underground Railroad. Though the original church was destroyed in the Great Chicago Fire of 1871, the congregation purchased its current site in 1890. Today the congregation continues to be active politically and socially, as well as culturally—hosting performances by Wynton Marsalis and Patti LaBelle.

## PRESBYTERIAN (USA)

- **Lincoln Park Presbyterian Church**, 600 W Fullerton Pkwy, www.lppchurch.org, 773-248-8288; a popular church, it has a choir, and offers Lenten suppers, religious studies for children and adults, and retreats. Beautiful historic organ on site.
- **Second Presbyterian Church**, 1936 S Michigan Ave, http://2ndpresbyterian.org, 312-225-4951; when it was first constructed in 1874, this city, state, and national landmark featured stained glass windows by Louis Comfort Tiffany. A fire in 1900 destroyed much of the original church, but it was reconstructed under Howard Van Doren Shaw. It received Chicago landmark status in 1977. Today, the church is very active in the South Loop community; it offers its gym facilities to a nearby charter school, feeds the poor, conducts Sunday school, and participates in several community organizations.

## ROMAN CATHOLIC

Most Catholics attend mass near their home, but a few churches, for one reason or another, attract worshipers from beyond the parish confines. One of the following may suit you. You may also call the Office of the Archdiocese of Chicago for assistance with choosing a church, 312-534-8200.

- **Holy Family Church**, 1080 W Roosevelt Rd, www.holyfamilychicago.org, 312-492-8442; Holy Family is known citywide for its extraordinary acoustics and numerous musical events.
- **Holy Name Cathedral**, 730 N Wabash St, www.holynamecathedral.org, 312-787-8040; Holy Name Cathedral is a parish and the seat of the Archdiocese of Chicago.
- **St. Michael's Church**, 1633 N Cleveland Ave, 312-642-2498, www.st-mikes.org; declared a city landmark in 1977, the original church was built on land donated by Michael Diversey, and was designed by August Waldbaum in the Romanesque style. During the Great Fire of 1871, the Church was destroyed. It was rebuilt by October 1872, and by 1886 five tower bells and the 290-foot

bell tower steeple were finished (restored in 1998). Inside are hand-carved communion rails, seven altars, German stained-glass windows, hand-carved Austrian Stations of the Cross, and commissioned frescoes. A special altar was constructed to house an icon of Our Mother of Perpetual Help; this somehow survived the fire, and retains special significance to the parish. (There is a neighborhood saying that if you can hear the bells of St. Michael's, you know you are in Old Town.) The church conducts several outreach programs, adult education classes, student groups, choirs, councils, a food pantry, and home visits, and offers many opportunities for volunteering. Sunday services are held in English or Spanish, some with a choir in attendance. Sunday evenings offer a less traditional mass. The Old Town Art Fair and St. Michael's Fest are celebrated each year on the church grounds.

- **St. Peter's in the Loop**, 110 W Madison St, www.stpetersloop.org, 312-372-5111; St. Peter's Catholic Church has been serving the downtown area for over 150 years; one million people pass through the doors each year. The Franciscan Friars built the present-day church in 1953. Programs include a broad range of services to the business and residential community: twelve-step programs, counseling for the divorced, extended hours of weekday mass and penance, and lecture series, in addition to services to the poor and homeless. Services are accompanied by a range of musical ensembles, and sometimes organ.

## RUSSIAN ORTHODOX

- **Holy Trinity Orthodox Cathedral and Rectory**, 1121 N Leavitt St, 773-486-6064; built in 1903 and designed by Louis H. Sullivan, Holy Trinity resembles a Russian provincial church. This elegant structure, built in a working-class neighborhood, was partially funded by Csar Nicholas II. It is considered one of Sullivan's best smaller works. Holy Trinity holds a vintage 1909 Louis Van Dinter & Sons organ. The Church was declared a landmark in 1979.

## UNITARIAN UNIVERSALIST

- **Lake Shore Unitarian Society**, 620 Lincoln Ave, Winnetka, http://lakeshore-unitarian.org, 847-807-5787, has made partnerships with over a half-dozen Chicagoland-area social agencies on behalf of its congregation. These include Evanston YMCA Shelter and the Christopher House. Since the year 2000, it has been a sponsor of the North Shore/Skokie CROP Walk, an interfaith fundraiser to address hunger and homelessness. The Church hosts a wide variety of clubs including a movie club, book club, investment club, and social groups for men and women.

- **Unitarian Unity Temple**, 875 Lake St, Oak Park, 708-848-6225, www.unitytemple.org; Frank Lloyd Wright was commissioned to build this church—one of his personal favorites among his designs—for the Unitarian Universalist Congregation in 1906. It contains many Cubist elements and a poured concrete frame considered very unorthodox in its time. The church is active in assisting in the preservation of this building as a work of art and is also an active member of the community. As a religious force, it hosts a concert series, does fundraising, offers assistance to the gay and lesbian community, oversees a children's religious education program, and more.

## HINDU

- **Hindu Temple of Greater Chicago**, 10915 Lemont Rd, Lemont, 630-972-0300, www.htgc.org; the temple complex offers two buildings, the Rama Temple and the smaller, Ganesha-Shiva-Gurga Temple. The Rama Temple is built in the Chola Dynasty style, a 10th-century style associated with Indian Kings, with an 80-foot tower. The Ganesha Temple is built in the tradition of the Kalinga Dynasty, known during the 1st century BC. The temple offers daily worship, grand festivals, youth activities, children's programs, and fundraising events.

## ISLAM

For a listing of mosques in Illinois, try the search function at www.islamicvalley.com.

- **Downtown Islamic Center,** 231 S State St, www.dic-chicago.org, 312-939-9095, opened in 2004 by a congregation that first came together in the 1960s; the center offers prayers, sermons, interfaith activities, and a variety of other services including Arabic language courses, Qur'an study courses, and charity initiatives.
- **Mosque Maryam**, 7351 S Stony Island Ave, www.noi.org/national_center.htm, 773-324-6000, is the national center and headquarters for the Nation of Islam. Originally built as a Greek Orthodox Church, the building was purchased in 1972 by Elijah Muhammed and the Nation of Islam. In 1988, it was repurchased and rededicated by Louis Farrakhan. The National Center, located next to the mosque, serves as a school for children ages preschool through the 12th grade. More information on the web at www.noi.org.
- **Prayer Center of Orland Park**, 16530 S 104th Ave, Orland Park, www.op-pc.org, 708-349-6592; in 2004, a heated debate surrounded the proposal to build a mosque in south suburban Orland Park which, like many of Chicago's southwest suburbs, has experienced a growing Muslim population in recent

years. However, the Orland Park Village Board unanimously approved the proposal, and the Prayer Center, clad in vibrant blue tile with a golden dome to resemble the Dome of the Rock, opened in 2006.

## JEWISH

See the **Jewish Chicago HaMacom** (http://www.jewishchicago.com/) and *Chicago Jewish News* (www.chicagojewishnews.com) for more information about Jewish congregations, events, and activities.

- **Chicago Sinai Congregation**, 15 W Delaware Pl, 312-867-7000, www.chicagosinai.org, is one of the oldest Reform congregations in the United States. Its first service was held in 1861 in what is now the financial district of the city, and then for 45 years the temple was located in the Hyde Park neighborhood. In 1997 a new structure in a more central part of the city was constructed. The new building has the distinction of being the first Reform Temple built on the Near North Side since the Civil War. The temple offers a community nursery school, religious education, classes, a library, outreach programs for interfaith couples, and meeting rooms.
- **Congregation B'nai Shalom,** 701 Apataskic Rd, Buffalo Grove, 847-415-1370, www.bnaishalom.org; B'nai Shalom was conceived in the late 1970s by a small group of Jewish families determined to find a permanent site for their new and growing congregation. Up until 1981, services were held in makeshift facilities: park district buildings, community centers, etc. Their temple now has a community center and school, as well as a gorgeous antique European ark that was custom made for the now-disbanded Albany Park Hebrew Congregation. The ark was refurbished, gold leafed, and reassembled in 1984.
- **K.A.M. Isaiah Israel**, 1100 E Hyde Park Blvd, Hyde Park, 773-924-1234, http://kamii.org; this impressive Byzantine-styled temple was founded in 1847. K.A.M. is the oldest Jewish congregation in the Midwest. It serves the Reform Jewish community through youth groups, services for families with small children, and concerts. Was designated a Chicago landmark in 1996.
- **Northbrook Congregation Ezra Habonim**, 2095 Landwehr Rd, Northbrook, 847-480-1690; a traditional congregation offering Shabbat, Torah studies, Hebrew school, Sunday morning breakfasts, and other weekly events. Call about playing Mahjong.
- **Temple Sholom**, 3480 N Lake Shore Dr, www.sholomchicago.org, 773-525-4707; founded in 1867, this Reform Temple is one of Chicago's oldest synagogues, and is well known throughout the Chicago Jewish community. It owns the Westlawn Cemetery and Mausoleum, and is equipped with a 1930 Wurlitzer organ.

## OTHER SITES OF INTEREST

- **Scottish Rite Cathedral**, 929 N Dearborn, is situated in the landmark Washington Square District, where in addition to the cathedral you will find the Newberry Library, historic row houses, and a park. Scottish Rite is not a religious sect, but a fraternal organization inviting men of different faiths and backgrounds to join in philanthropic pursuits. They are more commonly known as Masons. In 2006, the Scottish Rite sold the cathedral; while the organization no longer meets there, the historic building remains. Built in the 1870s, the cathedral has a remarkable E. & G.G. Hook & Hastings organ.

## SHRINES

- **Our Lady of the Snows**, 442 S DeMazenod Dr, Belleville, 618-397-6700, www.snows.org; operated by the Missionary Oblates of Mary Immaculate, this is one of the largest outdoor shrines in North America. Nearly one million people visit the 200+-acre grounds each year, which include nine devotional areas for all faiths and denominations, as well as a restaurant, gift shop, and hotel. More than 50 shrine events are held each year, in addition to masses and community programs. About 300 miles south of Chicago.
- **National Shrine of Mary Immaculate, Queen of Universe**, St. Pius X Church, 1025 E Madison St, Lombard, 630-627-4526
- **Shrine of St. Maximilian Kolbe, Marytown**, 1600 W Park Ave, Libertyville, 847-367-7800, www.marytown.com; offers full- and half-day guided pilgrimages of the historic complex. The chapels are decorated with marble columns, stained glass, religious relics, and mosaics. Weekend retreats available.

## ORGAN MUSIC

Some places of worship draw us to them through their music. Chicago has an abundance of houses of worship that own vintage organs. The following religious houses all own antique or vintage organs and some have outstanding choirs as well.

- **Basilica of our Lady of Sorrows**, 3121 W Jackson Blvd, www.ols-chicago.org, 773-638-0159; this church is equipped with a 1902 Lyon & Healy organ.
- **Disciples Divinity House**, 1156 E 57th St, University of Chicago, http://ddh.uchicago.edu/#, 773-643-4411; this church owns a 1930 Aeolian organ.
- **Epworth United Methodist Church**, 5253 N Kenmore Ave, www.epworthumcchicago.org, 773-561-6422, is equipped with a 1930 M.P. Moller organ.
- **First Baptist Congregational Church**, 1613 W Washington Blvd, www.fbcc-chicago.net, 312-243-8047, has a 1927 Kimball organ.

- **First Congregational Church of Evanston**, 1417 Hinman Ave, Evanston, www.firstchurchevanston.org, 847-864-8332, has a 1927 Skinner organ.
- **Good Shepherd Lutheran Church**, 4200 W 62nd St, 773-581-0096, owns an 1891 Lancashire Marshall organ.
- **Holy Family Church**, 1080 W Roosevelt Rd, www.holyfamilychicago.org, 312-492-8442, Chicago's second oldest church, has an 1879 Steinmeyer.
- **Holy Trinity Russian Orthodox Church**, 1121 N Leavitt St, 773-486-6064; this historic church has a 1909 Louis Van Dinter & Sons organ.
- **Lake View Presbyterian Church**, 716 W Addison St, www.lakeviewpresbyterian.org, 773-281-2655, owns an 1888 Johnson & Sons organ, used with a variety of the church's choirs, and in performances.
- **Lincoln Park Presbyterian Church**, 600 W Fullerton Pkwy, www.lppchurch.org, 773-248-8288; this church has a beautiful 1888 Johnson & Sons Tracker organ.
- **Pullman United Methodist Church**, 11211 S Saint Lawrence Ave, 773-785-1492, has an 1882 Steere & Turner organ.
- **St. Andrews Episcopal Church**, 48 N Hoyne Ave, 312-226-7205, has a 1905 Lyon & Healy organ.
- **St. James Catholic Church**, 2942 S Wabash, www.stjamesonwabash.com, 312-842-1919, owns an 1891 Roosevelt organ.
- **St. John Evangelical Lutheran Church**, 305 Circle Ave, Forest Park, www.stjohnforestpark.org, 708-366-3226; this church owns a 1954 Aeolian organ.
- **St. Joseph Catholic Church**, 1107 N Orleans St, 312-787-7174; owns an 1891 Hutchings organ, the only restored Hutchings in Chicago.
- **St. Luke's Episcopal Church**, 939 Hinman Ave, Evanston, www.stlukesevanston.org, 847-475-3630, owns a 1922 Skinner organ.
- **St. Mary of Perpetual Help Catholic Church**, 1039 W 32nd St, 773-927-6646, owns a 1928 Austin organ.
- **St. Paul Lutheran Church**, 5201 Galitz St, Skokie, www.stpaulskokie.org, 847-673-5030, owns a 1974 Phelps organ.
- **Temple Sholom**, 3480 N Lake Shore Dr, www.sholomchicago.org, 773-525-4707, is equipped with a 1930 Wurlitzer.
- **University Church**, 5655 S University Ave, Hyde Park, www.universitychurch-chicago.org, 773-363-8142, owns a 1928 Skinner organ.

## VOLUNTEERING

Volunteering in a new city is an excellent way to meet people who share similar interests. Whether you are skilled at building houses, caring for the elderly, tutoring underprivileged children, or canvassing neighborhoods, you can find a volunteer project that suits your interests. Chicago-area nonprofits are always in need of volunteers willing to give their time and energy. Your place of employment may even offer a corporate volunteering program; contact your human resources representative.

## VOLUNTEER PLACEMENT SERVICES

The following organizations coordinate many volunteer activities in the Chicagoland area. Call them and they will help you find a place in need of your special talents:

- If you are a student at the **University of Chicago**, contact the student-run UCSC (University of Chicago Service Center), at 773-753-GIVE, or stop by their office located in the Parking Structure office suites. Visit their website for a list of the organizations they assist: http://communityprograms.uchicago.edu/volunteer_opportunities.php.
- **Chicago North Shore Section** is a branch of the National Council of Jewish Women. Several volunteer groups assist in a number of ways, from offering a teen dating violence-awareness program to running a resale shop. Visit their website for a list of their efforts: http://ncjwcns.org/community-service/, or call 847-853-8889.
- **Community Resource Network—Chicago Volunteer**, www.chicagovolunteer.net, 866-532-0404, is a volunteer referral service. When you visit their website, you will be asked to provide your volunteer criteria (your area of interest and level of commitment), and they will provide you with a list of area opportunities in both the city and suburbs. (Outside of metropolitan Chicago, go to www.pointsoflight.org.)
- **Chicago Wilderness**, 312-580-2135, www.chicagowilderness.org/index.php; being a "wilderness" volunteer in Chicago is not as unbelievable as it sounds, and is a great way to share your outdoor expertise. There are many organizations, from zoos to gardens to parks, that appreciate the work of volunteers. Consider serving as a guide, caring for trees, working in a community garden, or organizing cleanup days. There are several affiliated groups; we have listed a few here, or you may contact the organization of your choice directly:
- **Lincoln Park Zoo**, www.lpzoo.org, 312-742-2000
- **Chicago Botanic Garden**, www.chicagobotanic.org, 847-835-5440
- **The Morton Arboretum**, www.mortonarb.org, 630-968-0074
- **Volunteer Stewardship Network**, http://nature.org/wherewework/northamerica/states/illinois, 312-580-2100
- **Openlands Project**, www.openlands.org, 312-863-6250
- **Forest Preserve District of Cook County**, http://fpdcc.com, 800-870-3666
- **Chicago Park District**, www.chicagoparkdistrict.com, 312-742-7529
- If you live in the north or northwest suburbs and would like to donate your time in your area, contact **The Volunteer Center of Northwest Suburban**

**Chicago**, 2121 S Goebbert Rd, Arlington Heights, http://volunteerinfo.net, 847-228-1320.
- The national online database, **www.volunteermatch.org**, allows you to access thousands of non-profit organizations. Provide your ZIP code, and the site will list what is available in your area, matching your interests and schedule with their database.

## AREA CAUSES

If you were involved in a volunteer effort before you moved, or if you already know the specific cause that sparks your interest, you can call the following organizations and inquire about donating your time.

### AIDS

- **Bonaventure House, Inc.**, 773-327-9921, www.bonaventurehouse.org
- **Chicago House and Social Service Agency**, 773-248-5200, www.chicagohouse.org
- **The Children's Place**, 312-733-9954, www.childrens-place.org
- **AIDS Research Alliance: Chicago**, 773-244-5800

### ALCOHOL & DRUG DEPENDENCY

- **Alcoholics Anonymous**, 312-346-1475, www.chicagoaa.org
- **Alliance Against Intoxicated Motorists (AAIM)**, www.aaim1.org, 847-240-0027
- **Mothers Against Drunk Driving (MADD)**, www.madd.org, 630-541-6099

### ANIMALS

- **Animal Welfare League**, www.animalwelfareleague.com, Chicago Ridge: 708-636-8586; Chicago: 773-667-0088
- **Anti-Cruelty Society**, www.anticruelty.org, 312-644-8338
- **Lake Shore Animal Shelter**, www.lakeshoreanimalshelter.org, 312-409-1162
- **PAWS (Pets Are Worth Saving) Chicago**, www.pawschicago.org, 773-935-PAWS, e-mail: Volunteers@pawschicago.org

### CHILDREN

Also see **Health and Hospitals** below.

- **Big Brothers/Big Sisters of Metropolitan Chicago**, www.bbbschgo.org, 312-207-5600

- **Boy Scouts of America, Chicago Area Council**, www.chicagobsa.org, 312-421-8800
- **Boys & Girls Clubs of Chicago**, www.bgcc.org, 312-235-8000
- **Girl Scouts of Chicago**, www.girlscoutsgcnwi.org, 312-416-2500
- **Shriner's Hospital**, 2211 N Oak Park Ave, www.shrinershq.org/Hospitals/Chicago/Get_Involved, 773-622-5400
- **YWCA of Metropolitan Chicago**, www.ywcachicago.org, 312-372-6600

## COMMUNITY SERVICES

Check the phonebook or search the Internet for a community service organization in your neighborhood. Almost all welcome volunteer help! Following are just a few of the active community service agencies in the Chicago area.

- **Ada S. McKinley Community Services**, www.adasmckinley.org, 312-554-0600
- **Albany Park Community Center**, http://apcc-chgo.org, 773-583-5111
- **Howard Area Community Center**, http://howardarea.org, 773-262-6622

## CRIME PREVENTION

- **Chicago Crime Commission**, www.chicagocrimecommission.org, 312-372-0101
- **CAPS (Chicago Alternative Policing Strategy)**, www.cityofchicago.org/police, 312-747-9985
- **Illinois Council Against Handgun Violence**, www.ichv.org, 312-341-0939

## DISABLED ASSISTANCE

- **Access Living of Metropolitan Chicago**, www.accessliving.org, 312-640-2100, 312-640-2102 TTY
- **America's Disabled Inc.**, http://physicianhomevisits.org
- **Association for Retarded Citizens of Illinois**, 708-206-1390
- **Blind Service Association Inc.**, www.blindserviceassociation.org, 312-236-0808
- **Chicago Association for Retarded Citizens**, http://carc.info, 312-346-6230
- **Chicago Lighthouse for the Blind**, http://chicagolighthouse.org, 312-666-1331
- **A Gift from the Heart Foundation**, 773-237-4800
- **Second Sense**, www.second-sense.org, 312-236-8569
- **Illinois Society for the Prevention of Blindness**, www.eyehealthillinois.org, 312-922-8710
- **Illinois Special Olympics**, www.ilso.org, 309-888-2551
- **Lester and Rosalie Anixter Center**, www.anixter.org, 773-973-7900

## EDUCATION

For a list of local tutoring and mentoring programs go to the **Tutor Mentor Connection** (www.tutormentorconnection.org) or contact one of the following:

- **Cabrini-Green Tutoring Program**, www.tutoringchicago.org, 312-397-9119
- **Family Start FAST Learning Centers**, www.uic.edu/educ/cfl/fast.html, 312-413-1914
- **Literacy Works**, www.litworks.org, info@litworks.org, 773-334-8255; English as a Second Language, adult basic education, and family literacy.
- **Midtown Educational Foundation**, www.midtown-metro.org, 312-738-8300
- **Tuesday's Child**, 773-282-5274; parent training program.

## ENVIRONMENT

- **Center for Neighborhood Technology (CNT)**, www.cnt.org, 773-278-4800
- **Friends of the Park**, www.fotp.org, info@fotp.org, or call 312-857-2757
- **Greenpeace USA, Inc.**, www.greenpeace.org, 800-722-6995
- **Lake Michigan Federation**, www.greatlakes.org, 312-939-0838
- **Nature Conservancy/Volunteer Stewardship Network**, www.nature.org, 800-628-6860
- **North Branch Prairie Restoration Project**, www.northbranchrestoration.org, northbranch@comcast.net
- **Open Lands Project**, www.openlands.org, 312-863-6250
- **Sierra Club**, www.sierraclub.org, 312-251-1680

## FOSTER CARE

- **Jewish Child and Family Services**, www.jcfs.org, 855-275-5237
- **Lawrence Hall Youth Services**, www.lawrencehall.org, 773-769-3500
- **Volunteers of America–Illinois**, www.voaillinois.com, 312-564-2300

## GAY AND LESBIAN

- **Gay & Lesbian Anti-Violence Project**, www.centeronhalsted.org/eva.html, 773-472-6469
- **Horizons for Youth**, www.horizons-for-youth.org, 312-627-9031
- **Parents and Friends of Lesbians and Gays** (**PFLAG**), www.pflagchicago.com, 630-415-0622

## HEALTH AND HOSPITALS

- **American Cancer Society**, www.cancer.org, 800-227-2345

# GETTING INVOLVED

- **American Diabetes Association**, www.diabetes.org, 1-800-DIABETES
- **American Heart Association Greater Midwest**, www.americanheart.org, 312-346-4675
- **American Red Cross of Chicago**, www.redcross.org/il/chicago, 312-729-6100,
- **Epilepsy Foundation of Greater Chicago**, epilepsychicago.org, 312-939-8622
- **Juvenile Diabetes Foundation**, www.jdrfillinois.org, 312-670-0313
- **Les Turner ALS Foundation** (Lou Gehrig's disease), www.lesturnerals.org, 847-679-3311
- **Leukemia Research Foundation**, www.leukemia-research.org, 847-424-0600
- **Leukemia Society of America**, www.leukemia-lymphoma.org, 312-651-7350
- **Make a Wish Foundation of Northern Illinois**, www.wishes.org, 800-978-9474
- **National Kidney Foundation of Illinois**, www.nkfi.org, 312-321-1500
- **Northwestern Memorial Hospital**, www.nmh.org/nm/volunteer, 312-926-2070
- **Respiratory Health Association of Metropolitan Chicago**, www.lungchicago.org, 312-243-2000
- **United Cerebral Palsy of Greater Chicago**, www.ucpnet.org, 708-444-8460
- **University of Chicago Children's Hospital**, www.uchicagokidshospital.org/contribute/volunteer, 773-702-4421

## HISTORIC PRESERVATION

- **Chicago Historical Society**, www.chicagohs.org/aboutus/jobsvolunteering/volunteering, 312-642-4600
- **Rogers Park/West Ridge Historical Society**, www.rpwrhs.org, 773-764-4078
- **Skokie Historical Society**, 847-673-1888

## HOMELESS

- **Chicago Coalition for the Homeless**, www.chicagohomeless.org, 312-641-4140
- **Greater Chicago Food Depository**, www.chicagosfoodbank.org, 773-247-3663
- **Heartland Alliance**, www.heartlandalliance.org, 312-660-1300
- **Inspiration Café**, www.inspirationcorp.org, 773-878-0981
- **Lakeview Pantry**, www.lakeviewpantry.org, 773-525-1777
- **Opening Doors Project**, www.homelessed.net, 800-215-6379
- **Pacific Garden Mission**, www.pgm.org, 312-492-9410
- **Voice of the People Uptown, Inc. (VOP)**, 773-769-2442
- **Windy City Habitat for Humanity Midwest**, www.windycityhabitat.org, 312-563-0296

**Note**: many religious organizations participate in **PADS programs** (Public Action to Deliver Shelter). These programs offer overnight shelter to the homeless and those in at-risk situations. Check with your local church or temple or get started by checking out the Southwest Chicago PADS website: www.swchicagopads.org.

## LEGAL

- **American Civil Liberties Union**, www.aclu-il.org, 312-201-9740
- **Chicago Lawyers Committee for Civil Rights Under Law**, www.clccrul.org, 312-630-9744
- **Lawyers for the Creative Arts**, www.law-arts.org, 312-649-4111
- **Legal Assistance Foundation of Metropolitan Chicago**, www.lafchicago.org, 312-341-1070

## LITERACY

- **Jane Addams Resource Corporation,** www.jane-addams.org/volunteer.html, 773-728-9769
- **Literacy Volunteers of Chicago**, www.literacychicago.org, 312-870-1100
- **Literacy Works**, www.litworks.org, e-mail: info@litworks.org, 773-334-8255; English as a Second Language or adult basic education.
- **Reading Is Fundamental**, www.rifinchicago.org, 708-437-2733, e-mail: info@rifinchicago.org

## POLITICS—ELECTORAL

- **US Hispanic Leadership Institute**, www.ushli.com, 312-427-8683
- **Democratic Party of Cook County,** http://cookcountydems.com, 312-263-0575
- **Illinois Green Party** (HQ in Urbana, IL), www.ilgreenparty.org, 312-252-3066
- **League of Women Voters**, http://lwvchicago.org, 312-939-5949
- **Libertarian Party**, www.il.lp.org, 312-841-7760
- **Reform Party**, http://reformpartyil.org, 312-702-0624
- **Republican Party of Cook County**, www.weareillinois.org, 312-201-9000

## POLITICS—SOCIAL

- **Amnesty International**, www.amnesty.org, 312-427-2060
- **Better Government Association**, www.bettergov.org, 312-427-8330

## SENIOR SERVICES

- **Chicago Cares**, www.chicagocares.org, 312-780-0800, offers 100 different monthly programs for volunteer opportunities, including working with the elderly.

# GETTING INVOLVED

- **H.O.M.E.: Housing Opportunities & Maintenance for the Elderly**, www.homeseniors.org, 773-921-3200
- **Little Brothers—Friends of the Elderly**, www.littlebrothers.org/chicago, 312-455-1000

## WOMEN'S SERVICES—BATTERED WOMEN'S GROUPS, SHELTERS, COUNSELING

- **Chicago Abused Women Coalition**, http://cawc.org, 773-489-9081
- **Chicago Foundation for Women**, www.cfw.org, 312-577-2801
- **Chicago Metro Battered Women's Network**, www.batteredwomensnetwork.org, 312-527-0730
- **Deborah's Place**, www.deborahsplace.org, 773-722-5080
- **Between Friends**, www.betweenfriendschicago.org, 773-274-5232
- **Sarah's Circle**, www.sarahs-circle.org, 773-728-1991, ext 300
- **Wing's**, www.wingsprogram.com, 847-519-7820
- **YWCA of Metropolitan Chicago**, www.ywca.org/chicago, 312-372-6600

## YOUTH SERVICES

- **Chicago Area Project**, http://chicagoareaproject.org, 312-663-3574; a multi-service youth agency.
- **Big Brother/Big Sister**, www.bbbschgo.org, 312-207-5600
- **Chicago Youth Centers**, www.chicagoyouthcenters.org, 312-913-1700
- **Jobs for Youth/Chicago**, www.jfychicago.org, 312-499-4778
- **National Runaway Switchboard**, www.1800runaway.org, 773-880-9860
- **Omni Youth Center**, www.omniyouth.org, 847-353-1500
- **Youth Outreach Services**, www.yos.org, 773-777-7112

## MEETING PEOPLE

In addition to volunteer groups, you might find some of these avenues an easy way to meet people:

- **Meetup.com** is an invaluable site for newcomers. Chicago is a big place, but on this site that works to your benefit. Chicago has numerous meetup groups including "The Chicago Young + New in Town Meetup" and "Chicago Girls Who Just Wanna Have Fun Meetup."
- Taking classes is another great way to meet people in Chicago. Like photography? The **Chicago Photography Center**, www.chicagophoto.org, offers a variety of classes for beginners and advanced photographers. Enjoy learning

to make new dishes? **The Chopping Block**, www.thechoppingblock.net, is Chicago's largest recreational cooking school in Chicago. With two locations, it offers convenient and varied classes for all levels. No matter what your interest is, Chicago probably offers a class in it.
- Join a **heritage club**. Because Chicago was settled by immigrants from all over the world, there is no shortage of ethnic heritage groups here. The DANK Haus German cultural center, dankhaus.com, in Lincoln Square hosts tons of events, and members of the Young Irish Fellowship Club, youngirish.com, support charities while celebrating Irish culture.
- **Sport and social clubs** offer a great way to meet people by becoming part of a team—over twenty sports are vailable. Form or join a team and join one of the leagues.Try the Chicago Sport and Social Club, www.chicagosocial.com, or Players Sport and Social Group, www.playerssports.net.
- For those of you with children, there is a club specially designed for you. The **Neighborhood Parents Network**, www.npnparents.org, connects local moms and dads for kid-centered fun activities.

# TRANSPORTATION

CHICAGOLAND ENCOMPASSES SIX COUNTIES, AND OFFERS AN EXTENsive public transportation network including the 'L,' buses, and Metra. In some situations, you may be able to get around by bicycle, but there may well be situations that will require the use of a car. See also **Getting Around in Chicago** in the **Introduction** of this book.

## GETTING AROUND

### BY CAR

Chicago has four major expressways that extend from the heart of the city like outstretched arms to the suburbs and beyond as well as one major north/south suburban tollway. During rush hour, you want to be anywhere but these thoroughfares. But of course, that may not be possible. So here are a few tips to help you survive your new town's traffic tangles.

- The **Kennedy Expressway** (Interstate 90) runs northwest to O'Hare International Airport and is reputed to be the busiest stretch of concrete in the country. Beyond O'Hare, I-90 (in Illinois called the Northwest Tollway) will take you to Rockford and on up to Madison, Wisconsin. Those looking for a fast trip to the northern suburbs should take the **Edens Expressway** (North I-94), which splits from the Kennedy just north of the Irving Park Road ramps.
- The **Eisenhower Expressway** (Interstate 290) is your gateway to the western suburbs and the East-West toll road. As you leave the Loop on the Eisenhower, you will drive right through the US Post Office (sounds scary, but don't panic, it's a tunnel). In Hillside, I-290 connects with **I-88**, which heads west to Aurora; I-290 then heads directly north to Palatine.

- The **Stevenson Expressway** (Interstate 55) is the least crowded of Chicago's interstates, although you'd never know it during rush hours. It's the route to Midway Airport, the western and southwestern suburbs, Joliet, and Springfield.
- The **Dan Ryan Expressway** (Interstate 90/94) extends straight south from the Loop and runs along the city's eastern edge. It splits at 95th Street, where one can choose between traveling southeast to Indiana on the stretch of I-94 called the **Bishop Ford Freeway** or south-southwest on **I-57** toward Kankakee, Champaign-Urbana, and, ultimately, Memphis, Tennessee. For updates on lane and ramp closings, as well as alternate routes and a project timeline, and other useful information, check www.chicagoroads.com/roads/dan-ryan/.
- The **Chicago Skyway** (a short stretch of Interstate 90) branches off the Dan Ryan Expressway south of Hyde Park near 65th Street. This 7.8-mile-long elevated tollway connects the Dan Ryan directly with the Indiana Tollway portion of I-90 by tracing a diagonal to the lakeside edge of the Indiana-Illinois border. Using the Skyway can considerably shorten travel time from downtown Chicago to certain areas of Indiana (Gary, Michigan City, and the northern end of Interstate 65, for example). However, those wishing to avoid tolls can reach the same destinations in a somewhat more roundabout fashion by continuing to follow the Dan Ryan south (see above) on Interstate 94.
- The **Tri-state Tollway** (I-294), an offshoot of I-94, runs north/south through the western suburbs. It splits from I-94 near the north suburb of Northbrook and runs all the way south through Harvey; along the way, it intersects with the Kennedy, Eisenhower, and Stevenson Expressways, as well as I-57 and I-80, before flowing back into I-94 near the Indiana border.

In a new city, a good map is indispensable. Rand McNally makes a great laminated folded map called "Chicago & Vicinity." Look in bookstores and gas stations for one. If city street information is more pertinent to you than suburb layouts, get the Rand McNally "Chicago Easy Finder"; those living north of the Loop will be particularly interested in the "Chicago North and Downtown" version of the Easy Finder, while those settling in on the south side will want the "Chicago South and Downtown" edition. For serious Chicagoland traveling, get their spiral-bound "Chicago & Vicinity 6-County Street Finder." It's not as portable as the other two but it is worthwhile having tucked into the closet for weekend trips. Many Chicago bookstores carry these and a variety of other helpful maps. Online, you can purchase maps and relocation resources from http://store.randmcnally.com or go to First Books, www.firstbooks.com, to place an order.

## TRAFFIC

Traffic congestion in Chicago is bad and getting worse. The traditional suburb-to-Chicago commute is still the granddaddy of all traffic jams, but the growing number of city-dwellers who work in the suburbs, and the even larger

# TRANSPORTATION

number of suburbanites who work in other suburbs, are changing traffic patterns. These days, roads that link suburb to suburb are competing for top spot on the list of worst congested roadways. Alas, many of the older throughways were not built to handle such heavy traffic. You might want to download a free app (e.g., Chicago Traffic Tracker by Belo, Chicago Traffic by osilabs). Alternatively, before heading out in the morning or after work, you could check on road conditions. Call 800-452-IDOT for a prerecorded message from the Department of Transportation or check any of the following websites:

- **www.traffic.com** provides frequently updated traffic information for any ZIP code you punch in
- **www.fhwa.dot.gov/trafficinfo/il.htm**; the US Department of Transportation Federal Highway Administration's Illinois traffic page
- **www.gcmtravel.com**, made available to the public through IDOT, INDOT, WisDOT, in cooperation with UIC-EECS AI Laboratory, gives real-time traffic updates for the Gary, Chicago, Milwaukee corridor.
- All the **major network channels** that provide local Chicago news also provide real-time traffic information on their websites. Try http://www.nbc5.com/traffic/index.html (Channel 5), http://chicago.cbslocal.com/traffic/ (Channel 2), the traffic page at http://abclocal.go.com/wls (Channel 7), or the traffic link from www.myfoxchicago.com (Channel 12).

On the radio, many stations give frequent traffic updates, especially during rush hour. Try 780/WBBM AM, 720/WGN AM, or 91.5/WBEZ FM.

Chicago proper has its share of traffic headaches. While Lake Shore Drive, the Kennedy Expressway, and the Tri-State Tollway can speed up north/south travel times on the city's North Side, the northern half of the city has *no* east/west expressways or freeways. This means that all cross-town traffic relies on the usually congested major avenues. Over the past decade, the continuing gentrification of much of the North Side, the resultant increase in households with two or more cars, and the blossoming of strip malls and mega-stores have made heavy traffic and the lack of parking serious problems—and it's as bad on weekends as during peak hours on weekdays. If you must drive to run errands on the North Side, you'll get around most quickly on weekdays between 10 a.m. and 2:00 p.m. For many destinations, you'll find taking a CTA train much quicker than driving. Riding the CTA bus, while rarely quicker than taking your own car, will at least give you a chance to read or decompress rather than cursing at other drivers and adding to the congestion. Better yet, walk or take a bike.

If you plan to do a lot of highway driving, you might want to consider buying a windshield-mounted **I-Pass,** which allows you to cruise at normal speed through the "Open Road Tolling" lanes of the freeway while others have to stop, roll down their windows and hand over the cash toll. Tolls are automatically deducted when you pass through the toll area. Currently, the Illinois State Tollway Authority is making I-Pass even more attractive by charging I-Pass users just half the toll amount that drivers must pay in the old-fashioned "manual" or cash lanes. The I-Pass works on the Illinois Tollway, the Chicago Skyway, the Indiana Toll Road, and throughout the East Coast E-Z Pass system. You can open an I-Pass account with a credit card or check; a $50 deposit is required to start your account. If you sign up for automatic replenishment, your account is credited for an additional sum once the account falls below $10; you can also replenish your account by check or through gift cards bought at area Jewel-Osco stores. Contact the **I-Pass Hotline** at 800-824-7200, or online at www.illinoistollway.com, for more information. I-Pass can be purchased online at www.illinoistollway.com. You can also get I-Pass and I-Pass gift cards at Jewel-Osco stores. See www.jewelosco.com for locations. Lastly, I-Pass services are available from 7:00 a.m. to 6 p.m. at all local Tollway Customer Service Centers, which are located just off the highway in the O'Hare, Lake Forest, Chicago Southland (Lincoln), Belvidere, and Des Plaines Oases.

For a pleasurable driving experience, check out the justifiably famous view from Lake Shore Drive—during non-rush hour when you can drive slowly enough to gawk. The sight of the downtown at night or shimmering in the light of dusk, not to mention sunset or sunrise over Lake Michigan, can raise goose bumps on the arms of even the most jaded Chicagoans.

## CAR RENTALS

Chicago has car rental agencies throughout the city and suburbs. Call the following phone numbers for information, reservations, and the nearest location (Many more agencies are listed in the Yellow Pages under "Automobile Rental.")

- **Ace Rent a Car,** www.acerentacar.com; O'Hare, 800-323-3221. Also in Elmhurst
- **Avis,** www.avis.com; O'Hare, 888-849-0277, as well as 23 other Chicagoland locations
- **Budget,** www.budget.com, 800-527-0700; O'Hare, 800-621-2380, as well as 12 other Chicagoland locations
- **Enterprise,** www.enterprise.com, **800-261-7331; O'Hare,** 847-928-3320, and dozens of other area locations
- **Hertz,** www.hertz.com, 800-654-3131; Midway, 773-735-7272, and over twenty other city and suburban locations
- **Rent-a-Wreck,** 1-877-877-0700, www.rentawreck.com; north, 773-637-2222; also in Hammond, Indiana (23 miles south of Chicago)

## CAR SHARING

Car sharing offers the convenience of easy access to a car without the hassle of owning a car, such as cost of insurance, maintenance and upkeep, or storage. It is recommended for those who need a car only occasionally.

## I-GO

Pay a one-time membership fee and you can reserve a slot of time (minimum one hour) and then pay only for the hours and miles used. Currently available in much of the North Side and Hyde Park. Call 773-278-4446 or go to www.igocars.org for details.

## ZIPCAR

The largest car-sharing network in the world, Zipcar offers two different basic membership plans as well as dozens of locations throughout the Chicago area. Check out their website, www.zipcar.com, to see if their service might work for you.

## TAXIS

Taxis can be found at most hotels, transportation hubs such as Union Station and O'Hare International Airport, most Metra express station stops, and cruising the city's main thoroughfares. When hiring a cab, make sure it displays the driver's photo ID and the vehicle license. There should also be information about the rates, usually posted on one of the windows. If you have any complaints or feel you have been overcharged, you can contact the Department of Consumer Services at 312-744-6060, and file a complaint. You must provide the cab number to file a complaint, and the date, time, and location of the incident. All city-licensed cabs have a silver medallion on the hood. Listed below are a few of the cab companies in the Chicagoland area. For a complete list go to www.thecityofchicago.com/taxis/index.html or check the Yellow Pages.

- **American United Cab Association**, 773-248-7600
- **Blue Ribbon Association, Inc.**, 773-279-4100
- **Checker Taxi Association, Inc.**, 312-243-2537
- **Yellow Cab**, 312-829-4222, lost and found, 312-881-3186

If you are at the airport, check the kiosk at the taxi stand for a "share-a-ride" deal. Up to four passengers can share a cab from O'Hare or Midway airports to any downtown location (between 22nd Street and Fullerton Avenue, Lake Michigan and Ashland Avenue). Rates at last check for cab sharing were:

- **O'Hare to downtown**: $19/person
- **Midway to downtown**: $14/person
- **Midway to O'Hare**: $35/person

## LIMOUSINES

Chicago has scores of limousine companies, many providing 24-hour service. While the Yellow Pages lists them all—check under "Limousines"—here are a few:

- **Crown Chauffeured Transportation**, 2440 S Wolf Rd, Des Plaines, www.cctworldwide.com, 800-960-7201, 847-803-0005
- **Five Star Limousine Service Inc.**, 20340 Torrence Ave, 877-418-6070
- **O'Hare Midway Limousine Service**, 3000 Dundee Rd, Northbrook, www.ohare-midway.com, 847-948-8050, 800-468-8989

## CARPOOLING

Carpooling is a good thing. Although, given job schedules and after-work errands, it's not a good fit for everyone, it should be seriously considered for those who can make it work. Not only does it create less wear and tear on your car, it saves money and is better for the environment. If you don't want to give up driving your car completely, but would like to do your part for the green movement at least some of the time, there are a few options. **Ride Share** will assist you in finding a carpool match in the Chicagoland area. It's free. To fill out their carpooling request form online, go to www.pacerideshare.com/en-US/. Also check with your human resources department at work. Many corporations have carpooling programs, and some offer incentives to those willing to forgo the daily drive to work. In addition, employers are sometimes willing to accommodate employees working from home a few days a week, depending on their responsibilities.

## PARK & RIDE

Park & Ride stations are CTA-owned daily parking lots that make your commute on public transportation a little more convenient. Lots are situated right next to 'L' stations, and range in size from 38 spaces to over 1,600. Parking prices run from $1/24 hours to $10.75/24 hours, depending on the station. Check with the RTA for more information by visiting www.transitchicago.com/parking/. You can also purchase monthly permits for Park & Ride lots and, in some neighborhoods, for the privilege of parking in the (usually illegal) spots beneath the El tracks. See chicago.centralparking.com/Chicago-CTA-Parking.html to buy these permits.

## BY BIKE

Former Mayor Daley not only made great attempts to promote the benefits of riding your bike to work but also implemented plans to make biking in Chicago safer. The results of the city's efforts have been so well received that in 2001 Chicago was named the best big city for cycling in the United States by *Bicycling Magazine*. Every spring there are events to promote bicycling around the city, such as Bike the Drive, and Bike to Work. There is a large section on the city's website devoted to bicycling—go to www.cityofchicago.org. The state of Illinois has joined in as well. Check the Illinois Department of Transportation's website for its special section on bicycling: http://dot.state.il.us. At this site you can purchase any of nine maps detailing regional bicycling trails. Another biking resource in Chicago is the Chicagoland Bicycle Federation; check them out at www.activetrans.org, or call them, 312-427-3325.

For more specifics on biking in the city, see the **Sports and Recreation** chapter.

## BY PUBLIC TRANSPORTATION

The **Regional Transportation Authority** (**RTA**) is the coordinator for all methods of public transportation in and around Chicago— from CTA buses and 'L' lines to suburban PACE buses and Metra trains. Call them with questions about fares, schedules, transfer options, etc., and to file complaints—they are very helpful: 312-913-3200, 312-913-3110—using any Chicagoland area code. Or visit www.rtachicago.com for more details.

The **Chicago Transportation Authority** (**CTA**) is an independent state-sponsored agency that governs all public transportation within the city limits, except Metra. Their general information number is 888-YOUR-CTA (888-CTA-TTY1 for TTY). A Chicago Transportation Authority map is an invaluable weapon in the battle against commuter confusion. You can get one at the Regional Transportation Authority Travel Information Center, 175 West Jackson; at the CTA Main Offices, 567 West Lake Street or at the Visitor Information Booths at the Chicago Cultural Center, Chicago Waterworks, or inside Sears at Madison/State. If you want information about schedules, maps, fares, or information for special needs travelers, dial 888-968-7282 or go to www.transitchicago.com. You can specifically download maps and timetables at www.transitchicago.com/travel_information/maps/default.aspx?source_quicklinks=1.

CTA Transit Cards, which can be purchased from the automatic card machines at any CTA rail station, at neighborhood currency exchanges, and at select Jewel and Dominick's supermarkets, offer both convenience and a substantial savings over paying cash fares. Transit Cards automatically keep track of how much fare credit you have and are good on CTA and PACE lines. Each time you go through one of the automatic turnstiles (or fare card machines on the bus) the fare is deducted from your total and the card returned to you. An adult fare single trip costs $2.00 (bus) or $2.25 (rail) and a transfer (to another subway line or bus route within two hours of your original trip) will set you back 25 cents. A second transfer (within the two-hour time limit) is free. If you pay cash, each ride is $2.25 and *no* transfers are available, which means that you pay full fare again for each switch you make from bus to bus, bus to rail, etc. Exact change is necessary. Drivers will not provide change.

Transit Cards can be recharged with cash at Touch-n-Go stations (machines accept change and $1, $2, $5, $10, and $20 bills) or at any CTA station. Children under seven ride free. Seniors and youths are half price, including transfers, and during the school year, students ride at a reduced rate. The CTA also sells unlimited monthly passes ($100 for an adult) and unlimited weekly passes ($33).

The Chicago Card is a sturdier plastic card that is sold online, www.chicago-card.com, or at any CTA sales office. If your Chicago Card is lost or stolen it will be replaced by CTA, and it can be shared by up to seven individuals. (To use, place it against the electronic pad; it is not swiped through the automatic turnstile.) Purchase online at www.transitchicago.com or at any CTA sales office. Go online or call 888-968-7282 for more information.

CTA rail stations are no longer staffed with cashiers; however, CTA Customer Assistants are available at all CTA rail stations to offer travel information and assistance.

## THE 'L'

The 'L' is the quickest way to get around town, if it's going your way—and it very often is. Five main lines intersect in the Loop and extend to all corners of the city. They include the **Red Line** (north/south), **Green Line** (west/south), **Blue Line** (west/northwest), **Brown Line** (north/northwest), and **Orange Line** (southwest side and Midway Airport). (If you're trying to get to either airport during rush hour, the Blue or Orange lines will be your fastest bet.) Since summer 2006, CTA has also operated a **Pink Line**, which circles the Loop then heads west and south to 54th Avenue in Cicero.

The CTA has several rider initiatives in place in order to make using the system more economically attractive to residents. Log on to www.transitchicago.com for more information about discounts for full-time students, seniors, new area residents, and those commuting by Metra train that require a connecting bus or train ride.

In addition to these city-bound lines, there also are two north suburban rapid-transit lines, the **Purple Line** and the **Yellow Line**. Both trains run from the Howard station at the north end of the Red Line. The Yellow Line runs directly west from the Howard station to the 4800 block, then continues north to just about Dempster (8800 North). The Purple Line runs north, making seven stops in Evanston and ending at Linden Avenue in Wilmette. During rush hours: 5:20 a.m. to 9:25 a.m. (southbound beginning at Linden); 3:40 p.m. to 7:10 p.m. (northbound from Clark/Lake), the Purple Line Express makes local Evanston stops and then runs express to and from the Loop—skipping stops between Howard Street and Belmont Avenue, and making all stops south of Belmont.

'L' expansions have been under discussion for years. The two major plans call for a much-needed southern extension of the Red Line and a **Circle Line**, which would start west of the Loop and connect several 'L' lines to one another as well as connecting commuter Metra train stations to the 'L'. The red line, the most heavily used of all 'L' lines, now ends at 95th Street and the Dan Ryan

Expressway, several miles short of the city's southern border; proponents want to extend it to 130th Street and connect it with the South Shore commuter rail line. The exact route for the proposed Circle Line is still in dispute.

## CTA BUSES

The CTA has bus routes running along most of Chicago's main arteries but not all lines have 24-hour service. (Lines with nighttime service are called "owl service"—look for the owl on the bus stop sign.) Exact fare of $2.00, a Transit Card, or a Chicago Card is required on buses. Drivers will not give out change. Of the 143 CTA bus routes, 126 of them are handicap accessible, and bus drivers are trained to assist with special-needs passengers. Information on which bus routes are equipped with handicap seating and stair lifts is available at www.transitchicago.com, or call 888-YOUR-CTA, using any local area code.

## PACE SUBURBAN BUS SERVICE

PACE provides bus transportation throughout Chicago's suburbs. The types of service include regular bus routes between suburban communities on a fixed route; local bus routes within a community; feeder bus routes providing morning and evening rush-hour service between residential areas and commuter train stations; and express routes providing direct service between suburbs and the Loop and between different suburbs. You can pay the exact fare of $1.75 or use a PACE transit card. (Chicago Cards are also accepted on most routes.) Transfers cost 25 cents; the second transfer within two hours is free. Bus schedules are posted in village halls, libraries, or you can get one from your bus driver, or the PACE office, 550 West Algonquin Road, Arlington Heights. They are also posted in most Metra train station waiting areas. To receive schedules by mail, call PACE at 847-364-8130, or the RTA Travel Information Center, 312-863-7000. Or visit their website at www.pacebus.com.

## TRAINS

### METRA COMMUTER RAILROAD SERVICE

Metra is the commuter railroad service that runs from the Loop to 225 suburban stations near and far. Service generally operates all day, including holidays; frequency varies by as much as three hours during non–rush hour times. Trains do not run all night. Metra's fare system is separate from the CTA, and is based on distance traveled. The following Metra lines leave from these stations:

- **Union Pacific/North Line**, Ogilvie Transportation Center
- **Union Pacific/Northwest Line**, Ogilvie Transportation Center

- **Union Pacific/West Line**, Ogilvie Transportation Center
- **Milwaukee District/North Line**, Union Station
- **Milwaukee District/West Line**, Union Station
- **North Central Service**, Union Station
- **BNSF Railway**, Union Station
- **Heritage Corridor**, Union Station
- **Southwest Service**, Union Station
- **Rock Island District**, LaSalle Street Station
- **Metra Electric District**, Millenium Station
- The station addresses and telephone numbers are:
- **Ogilvie Transportation Center**, 500 W Madison St, 312-322-6777
- **Union Station**, 210 S Canal St, 312-655-2465
- **LaSalle Street Station**, 414 S LaSalle St, 312-322-6509
- **Millennium Street Station**, 151 E Randolph St, 312-782-0676

For information regarding Metra schedules, route and fares, call 312-322-6777. For South Shore information, call 219-926-5744. Printed schedules are available at all Metra stations or you can request one to be sent in the mail by calling 312-322-6777. Visit their website for detailed station information and PACE connections: www.metrarail.com.

## AMTRAK

Amtrak, 800-USA-RAIL, www.amtrak.com, provides inter-city rail service. Trains leave Union Station, 210 South Canal Street; there are stops at the Glenview, LaGrange, and Naperville Metra stations. For affordable and efficient service to such nearby cities as Detroit, Indianapolis, Milwaukee, or St. Louis, Amtrak can't be beat. Go to their website to sign up for e-mail promotions. Buy online and you can save up to 60% on long-distance coach train tickets. Late fall and early spring are good times to look for deals on Amtrak.

## NATIONAL/REGIONAL BUS SERVICE

- **Greyhound Bus**, Chicago stations: 630 W Harrison St, 312-408-5821; 14 W 95th St, 312-408-5999; CTA Transit Building, 5800 Cumberland Ave, 773-693-2474, www.greyhound.com

There are a number of **regional bus lines** (all go to and from the airports):

- **Coach USA/United Limo**, 800-248-8747, www.coachusa.com/tristateunitedlimo/, service to and from O'Hare and Midway airports to Harvey, Matteson, and Crestwood in Illinois, and in Indiana to: Gary, Highland, Merriville, Michigan City, Mishawaka, Portage, and South Bend (Notre Dame).

- **Coach USA/Wisconsin Coach Lines**, 877-324-7767, www.coachusa.com/wisconsincoach/, service to and from Gurnee, IL, and the Wisconsin cities of: Kenosha, Racine, Mitchell Airport, Marquette University, and Waukesha.
- **Coach USA/Van Galder**, 800-747-0994, www.coachusa.com/vangalder/, service to and from O'Hare Airport and Midway Airport to Rockford, Illinois, or Janesville and Madison, Wisconsin. Bus pickup from downtown Chicago is at the Amtrak Station at Jackson/Canal.
- **Peoria Charter**, 800-448-0572, www.peoriacharter.com; service to and from O'Hare and Midway airports to: Joliet, Schaumburg, Pontiac, Peoria, Morton, Oakbrook, River Road (CTA station), and Normal, Illinois.

## AIRPORTS AND AIRLINES

### O'HARE INTERNATIONAL AIRPORT

O'Hare International Airport (773-894-9111, www.flychicago.com/About/OHare/Default.aspx); with over 70 million passengers going through O'Hare each year, it has the dubious honor of often being the busiest airport in the world. As you might expect, it can be crowded and confusing at times. O'Hare is the headquarters for United Airlines (the sparkling Terminal 1), and more than 50 other airlines have gates at one or more of O'Hare's five huge terminals. The airport is easy to get to via the 'L' or by car on the Kennedy (I-90)—if you're driving, watch it during rush hour! You can miss a flight all too easily by underestimating travel time to O'Hare. If you're coming from downtown by public transportation, the 'L' Blue Line is the fastest route—approximately 45 minutes. For drivers, there's plenty of short- and long-term parking. For those picking up passengers, the cell phone lot is an ideal place to wait for your party to let you know they've arrived. (Airport security allows absolutely no curbside waiting in arrival areas.) Call Standard Parking at O'Hare, 773-686-7530, for parking information. Those taking a taxi from downtown should expect to pay approximately $45—there are no flat rate runs to the airport—all cab rides are metered. (You can share a cab from downtown but you will have to negotiate a shared fare with the other passenger. If you are at the airport and need to go downtown, you can share a cab with other passengers. See above under **Taxis**.)

But of course, there are more ways to get to the airport than by car or the 'L.' Suburban shuttles, trains, and buses also may be options. From 6 a.m. to 11:30 p.m., **Airport Express** offers shuttle van transportation from downtown Chicago and the northern suburbs to the airport. From downtown to O'Hare, the fare is $17, and departures are scheduled every five to ten minutes. There are discounts for even small groups. Call 888-2THEVAN for more information or visit their website at www.airportexpress.com. If you would like to board a Airport Express van from the airport, go to the baggage claim level of terminals

1, 2, and 3, or outside US Customs at Terminal 5. **Omega Airport Shuttle** offers service to and from O'Hare and Midway, and between Hyde Park and O'Hare Airport. Pick-up from O'Hare Airport is at the Bus/Shuttle Center, door number four. One-way fare between airports costs $17; one-way fare to or from the South Side costs $30. Call 773-734-6688 or go to www.omegashuttle.com for more information. Regional bus lines (see above), including Owl Airport Service, 800-621-4153 (serves Lake Geneva, Lake Zurich, McHenry, Richmond, and Volo), and PACE, 847-364-7223, also offer service to and from O'Hare. The **Bus/ Shuttle Center** is located on the ground level of O'Hare's elevated parking garage. From terminals 1, 2, and 3, use the pedestrian tunnels; from Terminal 5, take the "people mover" to Terminal 3, then follow the signs.

### LOST AND FOUND

If you lose something at the airport—as opposed to losing a piece of luggage in flight—you can contact O'Hare, but you should be aware that there is no central Lost and Found at the airport. If you think you left an item at a security checkpoint, try the Transportation Security Administration at 773-377-1210. If you remember leaving your item in a washroom, near a shared terminal waiting area, or perhaps the Children's Museum, try the police non-emergency number, 773-686-2385. Many of the airport restaurants and shops have a lost and found department—try 773-686-6180. Keep in mind they eventually turn lost items over to the police. If you left your belongings on the airplane, or at the gate or ticket counter, you will need to contact that carrier. Here are a few lost and found phone numbers for three of the busier carriers at O'Hare: American: 773-686-4234, United: 773-601-3295, and Northwest: 773-686-5550.

### SOME MAJOR AIRLINES SERVING O'HARE

- **Alaska Airlines**, 800-252-7522, www.alaskaair.com
- **American Airlines**, 800-433-7300, www.aa.com/homePage.do
- **Cathay Pacific Airways**, 800-233-2742, www.cathaypacific.com/
- **Delta**, 800-221-1212, www.delta.com
- **Jet Express**, 800-538-2583, www.jetblue.com
- **United Airlines**, 800-864-8331, www.united.com

### MIDWAY AIRPORT

**Midway Airport** (773-838-9111, www.flychicago.com/About/Midway/Default. aspx) comprises one square mile on Chicago's southwest side—bounded by 55th and 63rd Streets on the north and south, and Cicero and Central Avenues on the east and west. Get there by car on the Stevenson Expressway (I-55) or by using CTA's Orange Line—the train ride from downtown is roughly 30 minutes. CTA's 55th Street/Garfield bus also ambles its way to and from Midway. Although once

Midway was easily overshadowed by O'Hare, the growth of discount airlines such as Southwest and AirTran, who use Midway, has turned this airport into a bustling commuter hub with a number of international flights as well. Though busy, Midway's bustle is a far cry from the circus of O'Hare; delays are also less frequent here. Many locals prefer to fly from Midway when fares are equal. Get there early if you need to park in the long-term lot (a shuttle bus will bring you to the terminal). Park in the garage for $23/day or in the economy lots for $10/day. (For more parking information, call 773-838-0376.) Check the shuttles mentioned in the O'Hare section for transportation options. Regional bus service to and from Midway is similar to that of O'Hare (see **Regional Bus Lines** above).

LOST AND FOUND
If you left something at one of the security checkpoints, you will need to contact the Transportation Security Administration's Lost and Found department at 773-498-1308. If you think you lost your item in the washroom, or another common area of the airport, contact the Chicago Police department at the non-emergency contact number: 773-838-3003. If your belongings were lost in the parking lot, contact Standard Parking at 773-838-0753. If you left your item at the ticket counter, on the plane, or at the gate, you must contact the airline directly. Frontier Airlines and Southwest Airlines, two of the main airlines that service Midway, both recommend calling their baggage services if you have lost something: Frontier Airlines, 773-948-6414, or Southwest Airlines, 888-202-1024.

SOME MAJOR AIRLINES SERVING MIDWAY AIRPORT
- **Air Tran**, 800-825-8538, www.airtran.com
- **Delta**, 800-221-1212, www.delta.com
- **Frontier Airlines**, 800-432-1359, www.flyfrontier.com
- **Porter Airlines**, 888-619-8622, www.flyporter.com
- **Southwest Airlines**, 800-435-9792, www.southwest.com

## ONLINE AIR TRAVEL RESOURCES

There are a number of travel-related websites all touting great deals, including **Travelocity.com**, **Expedia.com**, **Lowestfare.com**, **Cheaptickets.com**, **Priceline.com**, and **Kayak.com**; take your pick. If cost outweighs convenience, opt for inconvenient check-in or departure times. Also, many airlines post last-minute seats at a reduced rate, usually online. In fact, booking online directly with the airline of your choice often proves less expensive than what many of the so-called discount travel sites offer. Many of them also post cyber or e-savers, which are last-minute cheap fares for travel on the upcoming weekend.

To register a complaint against an airline, the Department of Transportation is the place to call or write: 202-366-4000, Aviation Consumer Protection Division, 1200 New Jersey Avenue, SE, Washington, DC 20590.

Information about flight delays can be checked online on your airline's website, or at www.fly.faa.gov. Similarly, the site www.flightarrivals.com offers real-time arrival, departure, and delay details for commercial flights.

# TEMPORARY LODGINGS

THERE ARE HUNDREDS OF HOTELS AND MOTELS IN CHICAGO, RANGING from the bare bones room-with-a-bed motel to luxurious hotel suites with breathtaking views of Lake Michigan and the Chicago skyline. When making a reservation, always remember to ask about discounts or weekend packages, as many lodgings have daily, unadvertised specials. Also keep in mind that room rates vary by the season (off-season begins January 1 and ends March 31) and by the convention (no discounts during large events like the National Restaurant Convention, which occurs each spring).

The following list of hotels and motels is by no means complete. With an eye to your pocketbook, we have shied away from most of the expensive hotels in favor of more reasonably priced accommodations in good locations. For a complete listing, check the Yellow Pages under "Hotels and Motels." Also check the Chicago Convention and Tourism Bureau's site, www.choosechicago.com/chicago-hotels/ or the Illinois Hotel & Lodging Association, www.stayillinois.com. AAA travel guides (free to members) are another good source for hotel and motel recommendations. If you need a room in a hurry, call the Chicago-based **Hot Rooms**, 773-468-7666, www.hotrooms.com, a hotel-reservation service that offers special discounted rates. **Quikbook** is a national discount room reservation service that costs nothing to join. It offers reduced room rates for many hotels. For a list of cities and hotels and information about them, visit www.quikbook.com or call 800-789-9887. Other national reservation companies include: **Hotels.com**, 800-246-3535, www.hotels.com, and **Central Reservation Services**, 800-894-0680, www.reservation-services.com.

Online travel agents, which offer room reservation services, airline tickets, and sometimes car rentals, include:

- **Expedia**, www.expedia.com.
- **Cheap Tickets**, www.cheaptickets.com
- **LowestFare.com**, www.lowestfare.com

- **Orbitz**, www.orbitz.com
- **Priceline**, travela.priceline.com
- **Tom Parsons' Best Fares**, www.bestfares.com
- **Travelocity**, www.travelocity.com

A word of advice: when making reservations through any discount site it is always wise to ask about the cancellation policy and if the rate quoted includes the **hotel tax**, which in Chicago proper is 16.4% per day. (Tax rates vary in the suburbs.) Also, some services require a full payment at the time of the reservation.

## LUXURY LODGINGS

Hotels listed in this section generally charge $300 to $600 a night, unless otherwise noted. Rates vary greatly based on season and availability.

- **Four Seasons Hotel**, 120 E Delaware Pl, 312-280-8800, www.fourseasons.com/chicagofs; room prices range from $535 to $3600 for a presidential suite. On certain weekends and holidays, rooms may cost as little as $385.
- **Omni Ambassador East**, 676 N Michigan Ave, 312-944-6664, www.omnihotels.com; special packages available.
- **Hotel Burnham**, One W Washington, 312-782-1111, www.burnhamhotel.com; only 122 rooms.
- **Hotel Indigo**, 1244 N Dearborn Pkwy, 312-787-4980, 866-521-6950, www.goldcoastchicagohotel.com; 164 rooms, recently renovated, start around $300.
- **Whitehall Hotel**, 105 E Delaware Place, 312-944-6300, www.thewhitehallhotel.com; Gold Coast location.
- **The Ritz-Carlton Chicago: A Four Seasons Hotel**, 160 E Pearson St, 312-266-1000, www.fourseasons.com/chicagorc/; this luxury property is set atop Water Tower Place, above North Michigan Avenue. It features fine furnishings and an elegant café. Standard nightly rates from $560.
- **Sofitel**, 20 E Chestnut St, 312-324-4000, www.sofitel.com; designed by renowned French architect Jean-Paul Viguier, this "Sofitel Water Tower," as it is named, offers 415 rooms (21 of them accessible for special needs) of European luxury at the corner of Chestnut and Wabash; rates often exceed $600 per night.
- **Park Hyatt Chicago**, 800 N Michigan Ave, 312-335-1234, 877-875-4658, www.parkhyattchicago.hyatt.com; elegant 202-room tower hotel, with an art gallery.
- **The Peninsula Chicago**, 108 E Superior St, 312-337-2888, http://chicago.peninsula.com; over 300 rooms, ranging from $525 to $7,500 for the luxurious Peninsula Suite.
- **The Westin/Michigan Avenue**, 909 N Michigan Ave, 312-943-7200; large hotel (over 700 rooms), recently renovated, lots of amenities.

## MIDDLE-RANGE LODGINGS

Following is a list of national hotel chains and local hotels with nightly fees ranging from about $90 to $300; suites cost more. Room rates vary by availability and type.

- **Belden-Stratford Apartments**, 2300 N Lincoln Park West, 773-880-2039, www.beldenstratford.com; apartments and hotel–styled rooms. Helpful staff, safe, secure, and clean. Near Lincoln Park.
- **Best Western**, 800-528-1234, www.bestwestern.com; 1100 S Michigan Ave, 312-922-2900; rates start at $226; **Best Western River North Hotel**, 125 W Ohio St, 312-467-0800; spacious and airy rooms start at $210, free parking, and indoor pool.
- **Days Inn Lincoln Park North**, 644 W Diversey Ave, 773-525-7010, http://daysinnchicago.net.
- **Doubletree Hotels & Guest Suites**, 312-467-0200, www.doubletreehotels.com.
- **The Drake Hotel**, 140 E Walton Pl, 312-787-2200, 800-55-DRAKE, www.thedrakehotel.com; this landmark hotel in the heart of the Gold Coast, overlooking Lake Michigan, has rates starting at $159.
- **Embassy Suites**, 800-EMBASSY, www.embassysuites.com; locations in downtown, Lombard, Deerfield, Rosemont, and Schaumburg.
- **Hampton Inn Chicago River-North**, 33 W Illinois St, 312-832-0330, www.hamptonsuiteschicago.com; also locations in the northwest and southwest suburbs.
- **Hilton Hotels**, 800-445-8667, www.hilton.com: **Palmer House Hilton**, 17 E Monroe St, 312-726-7500; this downtown hotel, a Chicago landmark, is very convenient to downtown shopping, museums, and public transportation. **Hilton Chicago & Towers**, 720 S Michigan Ave, 312-922-4400; suburban locations: Northbrook, Hoffman Estates, Evanston, Oak Brook Terrace, Lisle, Oak Lawn.
- **Holiday Inn**, 877-424-2449, www.ichotelsgroup.com: **Downtown**, 506 W Harrison St, 312-957-9100; dozens of other city and suburban locations.
- **Hyatt Hotels & Resorts**, 888-964-9288, www.hyatt.com; three downtown locations and in the suburbs: Woodfield, Deerfield, Oak Brook, Lisle.
- **Marriott Hotels**, 888-236-2427, www.marriott.com; **Chicago Marriott Downtown Magnificent Mile,** 540 N Michigan Ave, 312-836-0100; other hotel locations in the medical district near UIC, O'Hare, Schaumburg, Lombard, Elmhurst, Hoffman Estates, and Itasca.
- **Quality Inn & Suites**, 877-424-6423, www.choicehotels.com; locations near O'Hare and in other suburbs
- **Radisson**, 800-967-9033, www.radisson.com: **Downtown,** 221 N Columbus Dr, 312-565-5258; also at the O'Hare Airport

- **The Tremont Hotel**, 100 E Chestnut St, 312-751-1900, 888-627-8281, www.tremontchicago.com; small upscale hotel.
- **W Chicago Lakeshore Hotel**, 644 N Lake Shore Dr, 312-943-9200, www.wchicagolakeshore.com; located downtown on Lake Michigan.
- **Wyndham Hotels**, 800-WYNDHAM, www.wyndham.com: **Downtown**, 500 S Dearborn St, 312-986-1234; suburbs: Oak Brook, Lisle, Buffalo Grove, Naperville, Itasca, two in Schaumburg.

## INEXPENSIVE LODGINGS

Listings here include rooms with rates below $100 (also check the chains listed in the **Middle-Range Lodgings** above, some suburban locations will have rooms for under $100):

- **Days Inn**, 800-225-3297, www.daysinn.com, suburban locations: Melrose Park, Niles, Schiller Park.
- **LaQuinta Inns**, 800-753-3757, www.lq.com; in the Chicago area this hotel chain is in the northwest and southwest suburbs. Call for locations.
- **Red Roof Inns**, 162 E Ontario St, 312-787-3580, www.redroof.com; call 800-REDROOF for locations in the north and northwest suburbs.
- **Sleep Inn**, 1831 W Diehl Rd, Naperville, 630-778-5900, www.sleepinn.com

## EXTENDED-STAY HOTELS

**At Home Inn Chicago** is a reservation service that will locate furnished apartments in downtown Chicago for extended stays: 1-312-640-1050, www.athomeinnchicago.com.

Extended-stay hotels in Chicagoland include:

- **Bridgestreet Worldwide**, www.bridgestreet.com, 800-278-7338; this corporate housing firm offers units of various sizes downtown and in the suburbs. Rates downtown start at $85/night for a studio.
- **Millennium Park Plaza**, 151 N Michigan Ave, 312-616-6000, www.doralmichiganavenue.com; offers furnished apartments for a minimum 30-day stay. The lease includes cable television, kitchen amenities, health club memberships, linens, and weekly maid service. Furnished "corporate suites" start at $1,700 per month for a studio, $2,000 for a one-bedroom, $2,700 for a two-bedroom. Discounts are available for stays of three months or more. Unfurnished apartments can also be had for significantly lower rates, although a one-year lease is required.
- **Extended Stay America**, 800-804-3724, www.extendedstayhotels.com, has locations near both major airports as well as in northern and southern sub-

urbs including Rolling Meadows, Gurnee, Deerfield, Schaumburg, Hillside, Elmhurst, Burr Ridge, Downers Grove, Lansing, and Waukegan. A room with a queen-sized bed, kitchenette, utensils, and weekly maid service ranges from $300 to $700 a week (seven nights). One pet per room is allowed with a small additional deposit.

- **Flemish House of Chicago**, 68 E Cedar St, 312-664-9981, www.chicago-bandb.com; seven suites with kitchenettes; near Michigan Avenue/Oak Street Beach neighborhood. Facilities can be set up as corporate apartments for extended use.
- **Homewood Suites**, www.homewood-suites.com, 800-CALL-HOME; discounts may be available for stays five nights or more: in downtown, Orland Park, Schaumburg, and Lincolnshire.
- **Oakwood Corporate Housing**, 877-902-0832, www.oakwood.com; provides corporate housing and temporary lodgings: many downtown and city locations and dozens of properties in the suburbs as well.
- **Residence Inn by Marriott**: 888-236-2427, www.marriott.com; twelve Chicagoland locations, including River North, Magnificent Mile, and southern and northern suburbs including Lombard, Waukegan, Oak Brook, and northwest Indiana.

## BED & BREAKFASTS

For nationwide listings, including the Chicago area, go to www.bbonline.com. Or call one of the following:

- **Gold Coast Guest House Bed and Breakfast**, 113 W Elm St, Chicago, 312-337-0361, www.bbchicago.com; Victorian row house, rated AAA Three Diamond. Five-minute walk to Michigan Avenue. McCormick Place shuttles nearby. Ask about their furnished corporate studio apartments, available monthly. Recommended by *Travel & Leisure* magazine.
- **Inn on Early**, 1241 W Early Ave, www.innonearly.com; near Lake Michigan. All rooms equipped with phone and answering machine, air conditioning, and TV/VCR; daily continental breakfast.
- **Old Town Chicago Bed and Breakfast Inn**, 1442 N North Park Ave, 312-440-9268, www.oldtownchicago.com; art deco–styled mansion; four non-smoking suites, large common areas. In downtown Chicago.
- **Under the Gingko Tree Bed and Breakfast**, 300 N Kenilworth Ave, Oak Park, 708-524-2327, http://undertheginkgotreebb.com; Queen Anne Victorian inn, 20 minutes from downtown Chicago.
- **The Wheeler Mansion**, 2020 S Calumet Ave, 312-945-2020, www.wheeler-mansion.com; luxury boutique hotel. Eleven rooms/suites, each with spa bath. Decorated with 19th-century antiques. Lots of amenities including full

gourmet breakfast, down pillows, comforters, cable TV, laundry/dry cleaning, on-site bike rental, twice-daily chambermaid service, full concierge services.
- **Windy City Urban Inn**, 607 W Deming Pl, 773-248-7091, 877-897-7091; five rooms, three suites; all non-smoking. Former mansion; located in Lincoln Park.
- **Wooded Isle Suites**, 5750 S Stony Island Ave, 800-290-6844; 13 suites, non-smoking, full kitchens. Located between the Museum of Science and Industry and the University of Chicago.

## HOSTELS/CLUBS/YMCAS

- **McGaw YMCA**, 1000 Grove St, Evanston, 847-475-7400 x 214; this men's-only residence offers temporary and long-term housing. Call for rates and availability.

For a nationwide listing of hostels, including Chicago, go to **www.hostels.com**. Chicago **area hostels** include:

- **Arlington House International Hostel**, 616 W Arlington Place, 773-929-5380, 800-HOSTEL-5; dorm style ($29) or private rooms ($64–78 for up to two guests) in Lincoln Park location. Monthly stays sometimes available; speak to a staff member for details.
- **Chicago International Hostel**, 6318 N Winthrop Ave (near Loyola University), 773-262-1011; $25 for a bed in a four- to eight-bed room with showers, with a full kitchen. I.D. with a non-Chicago address required. Extended stays and private rooms available.
- **Hostelling International**, 24 E Congress Pkwy, 312-360-0300, www.hichicago.org; downtown location, 500-bunk facility, no curfew, membership not required, free breakfast and wi-fi access. 24-hour access and security, stays of longer than 30 days qualify for semi-private accommodations. Most dorm-style rooms have private baths and showers, there is access to laundry and kitchen facilities, and the hostel has two in-house restaurants; $27–33 per night per person, plus tax and a $3 fee for those who aren't members of Hostelling International. Voted hostelworld.com's "Best Large Hostel" in 2006.

## SUMMER ONLY

- **Illinois Institute of Technology**, 3241 S Wabash, 312-567-5075; three miles directly south of downtown, IIT offers its dorm rooms to travelers of all ages during summer. Private or rooms to share are available. Community bathrooms are located on each floor. Laundry and cafeteria on-site. One-time linen set-up included. Reservations accepted one week in advance with credit card guarantee.

- **Columbia College Chicago**, 731 S Plymouth Court, 312-344-6801, located in downtown Chicago in the South Loop area. From the second week of June through the last week of August, Columbia offers apartment-style housing with private bedrooms, a bathroom, living room, dining area, and a kitchen. There is a laundry facility, workout room, and meeting room/TV lounge on site as well. For individual and group stays of less than a week there is a one-time linen set offered (includes a sheet set, bath towel and face towel, but not pillows). If you need accommodations for more than a week you will need to provide your own linens. Reservations are accepted a month in advance, and the balance of your charge must be paid at least two weeks in advance of your arrival to guarantee your reservation.

## ACCESSIBLE ACCOMMODATIONS

The following national chains own hotels in Chicago and have reputations for offering many services to the disabled: **Hilton Hotels**, 800-445-8667, TTY 800-368-1133, www.hilton.com; **Hyatt Hotels**, 888-591-1234, TTY 800-228-9548, www.hyatt.com; **ITT Sheraton**, 800-325-3535, TTY 800-325-1717, www.starwood.com/sheraton; **Marriott Hotels**, 800-450-4442, TTY, 800-228-7014, www.marriott.com. However, accommodations may not be consistent from place to place, so be sure to call and talk over your specific needs in advance. Be aware that federal law requires that if a hotel guarantees reservations for its regular rooms, it must also guarantee reservations for handicapped-accessible rooms. Another issue for people with disabilities is security: some experts advise that you ask the hotel to remove the handicap sign from your door if there is one.

You may have the best luck finding fully accessible accommodations in the extended-stay facilities located outside of Chicago proper. The following hotels all claim accessibility:

- **Inn of Chicago on Magnificent Mile**, 162 E Ohio St, 312-787-3100; a moderately priced hotel one-half block east of North Michigan Avenue.
- **Days Inn Lincoln Park North**, 644 W Diversey Pkwy, 773-525-7010
- **Hilton Suites**, 198 E Delaware Place, 312-664-1100
- **The Drake Hotel**, 140 E Walton Place, 312-787-2200
- **Extended Stay America**, 800-398-7829; special rooms feature grab bars in the bathroom, fire alarms with lights, and Braille elevators.
- **Homestead Studio Suites Hotel**, 51 E State Pkwy, Schaumburg, 847-882-6900, www.homesteadhotels.com
- **The Ritz-Carlton Chicago**, 160 E Pearson St, 312-266-1194
- **Sofitel**, 20 E Chestnut St, 312-324-4000; 21 rooms available for special needs
- **W Chicago Lakeshore Hotel**, 644 N Lake Shore Dr, 312-943-9200, www.whotels.com; located downtown.

FYI, the **Society for Accessible Travel & Hospitality**, 212-447-7284, www.sath.org, offers advice and publishes a magazine for disabled travelers called *Open World*.

For more information on services for the disabled, look in the **Helpful Services** chapter of this book.

# QUICK GETAWAYS

CONTRARY TO WHAT A NEW ARRIVAL MAY BELIEVE, NOT ALL OF ILLInois is flat or filled with cornfields; in the west of the state lie rolling hills and the beautiful Mississippi River valley; in the north, wooded lake lands and, in the south, historical Native American lands and state parks.

A car makes getting to any of the following places a breeze, and railways are an option to places like Springfield or Milwaukee, and even some of the state beaches in Indiana. Most of the following locations are perfect for a long day trip, although bed and breakfasts abound for those who choose to spend the night.

Legalized gambling has sprung up on riverboat casinos along the Ohio and Mississippi Rivers as well as parts of Lake Michigan (see **Sports and Recreation**).

## ILLINOIS

For more information about area tourism, visit the **Illinois Department of Tourism** website at www.enjoyillinois.com.

## GALENA

Galena is a lovely, hilly, pre–Civil War town located on the Mississippi River three hours west of Chicago. Eighty-five percent of its buildings appear on the National Historic Register. Ulysses S. Grant was from Galena and the house presented to him by the community upon his triumphant return from the Civil War is another of the historic charms of this town. In warmer weather, you can take a walking tour through Victorian homes, explore antiques shops, brush up on your tennis or golf game, or just sit in an outdoor café and watch the world go by at a slower pace. In the winter months, Chicagoans enjoy snowmobiling and cross-country skiing in these parts. Stop into a jazz club after dinner, or one of the resorts, for some evening entertainment. The nearby Eagle Ridge resort is a golfer's paradise, set in the hills with numerous courses. Contact the Galena Tourism Information Center, www.galena.com, for more information. The official city website, www.cityofgalena.org, offers basic information and a video that can give you an idea of what kind of architecture, scenery, and commerce to expect during your visit. The main online destination for Galena tourist information is http://galena.org (or call 877-464-2536).

## SPRINGFIELD

The state capital is located about halfway to St. Louis, Missouri, on historic Route 66. Because it's a long drive (about 4.5 hours), it's best to make a weekend trip. Home of Abraham Lincoln, as well as dozens of historic buildings, the state capital also hosts the Illinois State Fair every August. Tourism centers largely around the city's proudest native son: you can visit the Abraham Lincoln Presidential Library and Museum, his former home, his one-time law office, his tomb, the old State Capitol where he famously proclaimed that "a house divided against itself cannot stand," even a reconstructed "pioneer village" called New Salem, prowled by a facsimile young Lincoln. Call the Springfield Convention and Tourism Bureau, 800-545-7300, or visit www.visit-springfieldillinois.com.

## STATE AND NATIONAL PARKS

Illinois is full of state and national parks, perfect for a one- or two-day nature excursion. Perhaps the closest park area to Chicago, just 35 miles south of the Loop, is the **Illinois and Michigan Canal Heritage Corridor**. Headquartered in Lockport, southwest of Chicago, the corridor is a network of parks, state trails, nature centers, and historical museums that mark the 97-mile canal that links the Chicago River to the Illinois River at Peru, Illinois. You can tour some of the parks by horseback, by snowmobile, or on foot. Contact the Heritage Center at 800-926-2262, or go to www.heritagecorridorcvb.com for more details on particular parks and other venues in the network.

The **Shawnee National Forest**, located in Harrisburg (about 5 hours south of Chicago), is a pristine nature site with over 200 acres available for horseback riding. The park contains privately owned areas as well as the government-owned park lands. It operates on a "leave no trace" guideline. Motorized vehicles are prohibited from traveling on off-road sites. There are extensive hiking and backpacking trails, as well as rock climbing (recommended for experienced climbers only), and fishing and hunting, for which you'll need a license. Horses can be rented from nearby vendors. For more information, check with the Saline County Chamber of Commerce, www.salinecountychamber.org;

Shawnee National Forest Headquarters can be reached at 618-253-7114 or 800-832-1355, www.fs.fed.us/r9/shawnee.

Two hours west of Chicago is **Starved Rock State Park**. The 18 canyons that make up this park include natural attractions such as waterfalls, 600 types of wildflowers, and incredible views. The area is known for its unusual rock formations, mostly St. Peter sandstone, formed in a huge inland sea more than 425 million years ago. Starved Rock State Park hosts a number of events throughout the year, and guided hikes are available on most weekends. A good spot for camping, fishing or boating, the park is also worth a visit in the winter months for viewing frozen waterfalls, ice skating, or cross-country skiing. For more information, call 815-667-4726 or check out http://starvedrockstatepark.org. Camping is possible but it's wise to plan ahead: sites fill up quickly for popular dates. The Starved Rock Lodge and Conference Center offers lodging in a rustic yet luxurious old lodge, as well as several cabins: 800-868-7625, http://starvedrocklodge.com.

The serene 385-acre **White Pines State Park**, located in the Rock River Valley less than two hours west of Chicago, offers short hiking trails, fishing, camping, and cross-country skiing all set amidst a lush pine forest. Within the park, the White Pines Inn offers lodging in log cabins with fireplaces, as well as a lodge restaurant: www.whitepinesinn.com or (815) 946-3817 for reservations and availability information. Nearby is **Lowden State Park,** nestled along the Rock River. Camping and hiking are available here as well: www.stateparks.com/lowden.html.

North of the city, near Waukegan, Illinois, Beach State Park boasts coveted beaches, including six miles of beach along the Lake Michigan shoreline in Zion, Illinois. You can camp, swim, hike, picnic, fish, and boat in the park. Camping is also available. Reservations are advisable, even on non-holiday weekends, but are accepted only from Memorial Day to Labor Day. Call the Illinois Department of Natural Resources (DNR) for more information: 815-625-2968. You can also download a reservation form from the website at www.dnr.state.il.us. If you prefer a more civilized end to your day, you can stay at the 96-room Illinois Beach Resort and Conference Center in Lake Zion. Call 847-625-7300 for reservations.

An alternative to a state park is a road trip through the **National Historic Byway Road** of Illinois. The National Roads were the precursors of America's highways. In 1806, in an effort to link the eastern states with what was then the western frontier, Congress authorized the construction of the first federally supported roads. Construction started in Cumberland, Maryland, and was to end at the Ohio River. But the road impacted the areas it passed through, bringing settlers, traders and new business to Illinois. As activity on the road increased, demand for its extension increased as well. Road construction proceeded across Ohio and through Vandalia, Illinois. Though by 1840 the increasing interest in railroads stopped further development of the National Road, it was not yet destined for obscurity. The invention of the automobile brought renewed interest in the road, which in the 1920s was renamed Route 40. It remained a major east-west roadway until the 1960s when construction of Interstate 70 replaced it. Today these old trails meander through a half a dozen states, passing by state parks, nature preserves, lakes, historic cemeteries, prehistoric archaeological sites, golf courses, quaint towns, and even a riverboat casino—the Casino Queen docked in East St. Louis. In Illinois, the Historic Road begins south of Springfield, at the Wabash River, and ends at the Mississippi. Consult the National Road Association of Illinois for maps and more information: online at www.nationalroad.org. Or get more information about attractions and historical sites along the old National Road at www.byways.org.

## BICYCLE TRIPS

For cycling enthusiasts, it's hard not to look at Illinois and think "bike trip!" The endless plains seem to have been created with a cyclist in mind, and there are several terrific areas around Chicagoland to take a spin. Here are some favorites:

- **The Great Western Trail**: 18 miles of wetlands and prairie between St. Charles and Sycamore, taking you through DeKalb and Kane Counties.
- **The Illinois Prairie Path**: a 40-mile trail through the southern suburbs, stretching from Elmhurst to Wheaton, where it splits four ways as it heads towards the Fox River. This trail welcomes horseback riders and hikers.
- If you enjoy buffalo and bird watching, you can combine both pleasures at the **Fermilab National Accelerator Laboratory**. Fermilab is located in Batavia, about 45 miles west of Chicago. While its business is high-energy physics research, its 6,800 acres of wetlands, forests, and fields offer one of the finest bird-watching areas around. You can take your bike and navigate the grounds any day of the week. Its prairie lands are home to a bison herd (numbering 25 as of 2012) established in 1969. For information, contact their Office of Communication at 630-840-3351 or online at www.fnal.gov.

## INDIANA

### INDIANA DUNES NATIONAL LAKESHORE AND STATE PARK

Forty-five minutes south of Chicago on the Indiana shore of Lake Michigan (near the cities of Porter and Michigan City) is a little bit of heaven. The sandy, lovely Indiana Dunes are a popular spot for sun worshippers. With over 2,000 acres, the state park boasts plenty of picnic spots, campgrounds (reservations must be made about six months in advance for Memorial and Labor Day weekends), long stretches of beach, and of course, gorgeous soft and silky sand dunes. For park information: contact the National Lakeshore, www.nps.gov/indu, or the

State Park, www.in.gov/dnr, 219-926-7561. Contact the Indiana Department of Tourism, call 800-677-9800 or visit www.in.gov/visitindiana for even more ideas.

## MICHIGAN CITY

If you aren't into camping after your visit to the Indiana Dunes, you'll find a wealth of hotel and bed and breakfast options in the nearby cities of Michigan City, LaPorte, and New Buffalo, Michigan; addresses and links to lodging options are available on www.michigancity.com. Shoppers will also enjoy Michigan City's designer outlet mall, Lighthouse Place Premium Outlets: www.premiumoutlets.com.

# WISCONSIN

## LAKE GENEVA

Less than two hours north, just across the Illinois/Wisconsin border, lovely Lake Geneva calls. It's been a favorite getaway for Chicagoans for generations. Stroll around part of the lake to admire the huge mansions built by wealthy vacationers in years past, listen to a concert, water-ski, take in an art fair, fish, or hunt for antiques—just a few of the ways you can spend your time. For more information, call the Wisconsin Department of Tourism, 800-432-8747, or visit their website at www.travelwisconsin.com. The official site for the Geneva Lake Area Chamber of Commerce and Lake Geneva Convention and Visitors Bureau, www.lakegenevawi.com also offers information as well as lists of lodging, attractions, and area activities.

## MADISON AND WISCONSIN DELLS

If you continue past O'Hare on I-90, in two and a half hours you'll reach Wisconsin's vibrant capital city. With hills and lakes galore, and home to the huge University of Wisconsin, **Madison** is an attractive place to visit. Its first-class schools and low crime rate also make it a great place to raise kids. Madison is just an hour south of the **Wisconsin Dells**, also along I-90; although the natural beauty of the dells and the sandstone bluffs along the Wisconsin River made the area a tourist attraction, the region's popularity with family vacationers now hinges largely on its huge collection of waterslides and "themed" entertainment. (The Wisconsin Dells website, www.wisdells.com, proclaims the area "The Waterpark Capital of the World!") If you're car-less or just don't want to drive, an easy and affordable way to get to Madison is to hop on a Coach USA/Van Galder bus at O'Hare or at the Amtrak station downtown at Jackson/Canal (see the **Transportation** chapter for more information).

## MILWAUKEE

Just two hours north of Chicago, past Gurnee, Milwaukee has been called a smaller version of Chicago. Its Central European heritage means there are plenty of taverns, restaurants, interesting neighborhoods, tempting cheeses, and of course, breweries. The Wisconsin State Fair is held in Milwaukee every summer and it is worth the trip just to see the racing piglets! More than a million visitors each year attend Milwaukee's annual Summerfest, a humongous eleven-day music festival held near the end of each June or beginning of July: www.summerfest.com. For more information, contact the Milwaukee Visitor Information Center, 800-554-1448, or visit www.milwaukee.org.

## KOHLER VILLAGE

Fifty-five miles north of Milwaukee lies Kohler, Wisconsin. More than 75 years ago, Walter Kohler began creating what was to become one of the first planned cities in America. He drew his ideas from the garden cities of Europe and worked closely with the Olmsted brothers, noted landscape designers. Today, Kohler Village still exists as a carefully planned community and home to the Kohler factory for kitchen and bathroom fixtures. Kohler Waters Spa is a first-rate spa located at the American Club Hotel, in Kohler Village. It is the Midwest's only AAA Five Diamond–rated resort. There are several museums around the resort, award-winning golf courses, such as Blackwolf Run, and guided tours of the historic American Club Hotel, the Kohler Design Center, and the Kohler Factory. The American Club resort is listed in the National Register of Historic Places. Of course, there are the usual outdoor activities—fishing, canoeing, birding, dog sledding, cross-country skiing, hiking, and much more. For more information contact the American Club by calling 855-444-2838, or visit their website at www.americanclubresort.com.

## SOUTHWEST MICHIGAN

Now that you are acquainted with Chicago and its environs due west, it's time to backtrack across the Lake to southwest Michigan. A generation ago, the area was still full of family farms and sleepy towns that evoked little interest from Chicagoans. Over the years, Chicagoans have woken up to the beauty of southern Michigan: today it's a coveted summer weekend destination. Though many local celebrities have bought large weekend homes in southwest Michigan, especially in the towns along the lakefront, the area offers a welcome respite for people of all income levels. If you are traveling without children, you might want to investigate the bed & breakfast inns, gourmet dining, and shopping outlets in New Buffalo, Union Pier, and Benton Harbor. Head farther north, with children in tow, for the lovely beach towns of Saugatuck and Grand Haven. Holland offers a glimpse of the early Dutch settlers—tulips in the spring, and lots of windmills. If you like wine tours, Paw Paw and Traverse City (five to six hours north) are good bets. Families and nature lovers should be sure to investigate the scenic and recreation-friendly areas of Sleeping Bear Dunes, St. Joseph, Mackinaw Island, Warren Dunes, and South Haven. Visit www.michigan.org for more information, or contact the Southwest Michigan Tourist Council: 269-925-6301, www.swmichigan.org.

# A CHICAGO YEAR

CHICAGOANS LOVE TO CELEBRATE. SO WHETHER YOU LIVE IN THE heart of town or in the suburbs, you will find many, many reasons and ways to make merry in and around Chicago. Join in as much as you can; it's a great way to acclimate yourself to your new surroundings. To start you on the right foot, we have put together the following incomplete list of feasts, fairs and festivals; check the newspaper for more. Also, if it's a Chicago-based event, check the city link at www.cityofchicago.org or contact the **Mayor's Office of Special Events** at 312-744-3316.

## JANUARY

- **Chicago Boat, Sports & RV Show**, McCormick Place, www.chicagoboatshow.com
- **Chicago Cubs Convention,** http://chicago.cubs.mlb.com/chc/community/com_convention.jsp
- **Chicago Winter Delights**, www.chicagotraveler.com/chicago-winter-delights
- **Ice Sculpture Festival and Ice Carving Competition**, Downers Grove, 630-725-0991
- **Monthly Skywatch Program**, Cernan Earth & Space Center at Triton College, River Grove, 708-583-3100

## FEBRUARY

- **African-American History Month**, events at the Chicago Cultural Center as well as sponsored by many other institutions at venues around the city
- **Around the Coyote Winter Arts Festival**, 312-744-2400
- **Chicago Auto Show**, 312-791-7000
- **Chicago Winter Delights**, www.winterdelights.com

- **Chinese New Year Festival**, Chinatown (Cermak Road and Wentworth Avenue), www.chicagochinatown.org
- **International Kennel Club Dog Show**, McCormick Place, www.ikcdogshow.com
- **University of Chicago Folk Festival**, Hyde Park (see **Cultural Life** for more information), www.uofcfolk.org

## MARCH

- **Bangladesh Parade**, on Devon Ave from Damen to Western
- **Big Ten Conference**, annual basketball tournament, www.bigten.org
- **Chicago Flower and Garden Show**, Navy Pier, www.chicagoflower.com
- **Chicago International Documentary Film Festival**, www.chicagodocfestival.org, 773-486-9612
- **Chicago Irish Film Festival**, Beverly Arts Center, 773-445-3838, www.chicagoirishfilmfestival.com
- **Chicago Underground Film Festival**, Wicker Park, cuff.org, info@cuff.org
- **LaSalle Bank Shamrock Shuffle**, 8K, Grant Park, www.shamrockshuffle.com
- **St. Patrick's Day Parade**, Columbus Drive, Balbo to Monroe Streets, www.chicagostpatsparade.com, 312-942-9188
- **South Side Irish Parade**, Western Ave, 103 to 113th Streets, 773-916-7747, http://southsideirishparade.org

## APRIL

- **Antique Fair,** Merchandise Mart, www.merchandisemartantiques.com/spring/
- **Assyrian New Year Parade**, Western Ave, 773-743-4027, or www.assyriancivicclub.com
- **Chicago Latino Film Festival**, 312-431-1330, chicagolatinofilmfestival.org
- **Chicago Palestine Film Festival**, palestinefilmfest.com

## MAY

- **Bike the Drive**, Lake Shore Drive, www.bikethedrive.org
- **Chicago Gaelic Park Irish Fest,** Oak Forest, www.chicagogaelicpark.org
- **Chicago Memorial Day Parade**, State St, Randolph to Van Buren, www.cityofchicago.org
- **Cinco De Mayo Parade**, Cermak Rd and Wood St
- **Comedy Festival**, last weekend in May, Vic Theater, Apollo Theater, Chicago Theatre, 847-304-6624

- **Lakeview Mayfest**, 3100 N Ashland Ave, www.starevents.com/may_fest. html, 773-665-4682
- **Chicago Kids and Kites Festival**, Montrose Harbor, 773-467-1428
- **Polish Constitution Day Parade**, Columbus Drive, Balbo to Monroe Streets, www.may3parade.org, 773-745-7999
- **St. Jude Police League March**, Michigan Ave, Chicago River to Oak Street
- **Walk & Roll Chicago**, Grant Park, www.walkroll.org, 800-227-2345

## JUNE

- **Andersonville MidSommarfest**, 500 N Clark St, www.andersonville.org, 773-728-2995
- **Backyard Bash**, 5100 W Belmont St
- **Belmont-Sheffield Music Festival** on Sheffield Ave, between Belmont/Barry Avenues
- **Bike to Work Week**, Daley Plaza, 312-427-3325; part of a week of events dedicated to encouraging people to bike to work/school
- **Chicago Blues Festival**, Grant Park, www.chicagofestivals.net/music/blues-2/blues
- **Day in the Park and 5K/2 Mile Run,** Evergreen Park, www.evergreenpark-ill.com, 708-422-1551
- **Gay & Lesbian Pride Parade**, Wrigleyville/Lakeview, 773-348-8243, www.chicagopridecalendar.org
- **Gospel Festival**, Grant Park
- **Festa Pasta Vino**, 2400 S Oakley Ave, Heart of Italy neighborhood
- **Hyde Park Art Fair**, Hyde Park, www.57thstreetartfair.org
- **Jammin' at the Zoo**, Lincoln Park, 312-742-2000, www.lpzoo.org
- **Jeff Fest**, Jefferson Park, 4850-4900 4822 Long Ave, www.jefffest.org
- **Lincoln Park Arts and Music Festival**, Lincoln Park, Racine between Webster and Fullerton, 773-880-5200
- **Maifest Chicago,** Lincoln Square, www.mayfestchicago.com
- **Old Town Art Fair**, 1763 North Park Ave, 312-337-1938, www.oldtownartfair.org
- **Pridefest**, 3656 N Halsted, www.chicagopridecalendar.org, 773-883-0500
- **Printers Row Lit Fest,** Printers Row, www.chicagotribune.com/entertainment/books/printersrowlitfest/
- **Puerto Rican Day Parade**, http://www.prpcchicago.org, 773-251-2239
- **Ribfest Chicago: Taste of North Center**, Intersection of Damen, Lincoln, and Irving Park Aves, ribfest-chicago.com *847-677-8273*
- **Run for the Zoo**, Lincoln Park Zoo, 312-742-2000
- **St. George Greek Festival,** 2701 N Sheffield, www.stgeorgechicago.net/GreekFestival/, 773-525-1793
- **St. Josaphat Summer Fest**, 2311 N Southport St, 773-426-6977

- **St. Michael's Celebration: Party in the Plaza**, Old Town, www.st-mikes.org, 312-642-2498
- **Taking it to the Streets**, Marquette Park, 773-434-4626, www.imancentral.org, bi-annual event
- **Taste of Chicago**, Grant Park, www.tasteofchicago.us
- **Taste of Randolph Street,** West Loop, tasteofrandolphstreet.com, 773-665-4682
- **Weed Street Summer Festival**, Weed Street from Kingsbury/Sheffield/Fremont, 773-868-3010
- **Wells Street Art Festival**, Wells Street, North/Division Streets, 312-951-6106

## JULY

- **African/Caribbean International Festival for Life**, 5500 S Cottage Grove Ave
- **Race to Taste**, 5K Run and 2 Mile Walk, Lakeshore Dr/Balbo, 312-744-3315
- **BenFest**, Irving Park Rd/Leavitt St, 773-588-6484
- **Chicago Children's Festival Southport,** 3700 N Southport, www.starevents.com/summ_fest.html, 773-665-4862
- **Civil War Living History Days**, Glenview, glenviewparks.org, 847-299-6096
- **DuPage County Fair**, Wheaton, 630-668-6636, www.dupagecountyfair.org
- **Fiesta del Sol**, Pilsen, fiestadelsol.org, 312-666-2663
- **Fourth of July Celebration**, Grant Park
- **Ghana Fest**, Washington Park, ghananationalcouncil1.org
- **Independence Eve Fireworks**, Grant Park, 312-742-7648
- **Irish American Heritage Festival,** 4626 N Knox, irish-american.org, 773-282-7035
- **Jammin' at the Zoo**, Lincoln Park, 312-742-2000, www.lpzoo.org
- **NBGC Family Festival**, Irving Park Road/Rockwell Ave, www.nbgc.org, 773-463-4161
- **Newberry Library Bughouse Square Debates**, Newberry Library, www.newberry.org, 312-943-9090
- **NWC Art Fair**, Naper Settlement, Naperville, napervillewomansclub.org, 630-209-1246
- **Pitchfork Music Festival,** 1501 W Randolph, pitchfork.com/festivals/chicago/2012/
- **Rock Around the Block**, 3200 N Lincoln Ave, starevents.com/events/rock-around-the-block/
- **Silent Film Festival**, www.silentfilmchicago.com, 773-205-SFSC
- **St. Andrew Greek Festival**, 5649 N Sheridan, www.standrewthodox.org, 773-334-4515
- **Summer on Southport**, 3700 N Southport, www.southportneighbors.com/sos_festival.html
- **Tall Ships**, Navy Pier, 312-451-2700

- **Taste of Chicago**, Grant Park, www.tasteofchicago.us

## AUGUST

- **Annual Port Clinton Art Fair**, Highland Park, amdurproductions.com/artfestivals/Port_Clinton_Art_Festival.html
- **Belize Day in the Park**, Washington Park, chicagobelizedayinthepark.org, 773-881-0412
- **Black Harvest International Film & Video Festival**, www.siskelfilmcenter.org, 312-846-2600
- **Bucktown Arts Fest**, Bucktown, bucktownartsfest.com
- **Bud Billiken Parade**, King Drive, http://budbillikenparade.com, 773-536-3710
- **Chicago Air and Water Show**, Grant Park, www.chicagoparkdistrict.com
- **Ginza Holiday**, Midwest Buddhist Temple, www.ginzachicago.com, 312-943-7801
- **Jammin' at the Zoo**, Lincoln Park, 312-742-2000, www.lpzoo.org
- **Jazz Festival**, Grant Park, http://www.chicagofestivals.net
- **Korean Street Festival**, 3200 W Bryn Mawr, 773-583-1700
- **Lakeshore Arts Festival**, Evanston, www.cityofevanston.org/festivals-concerts/lakeshore-arts-festival, 847-448-8260
- **Lollapalooza,** Grant Park, www.lollapalooza.com
- **North Halsted Market Days**, Halsted, Belmont/Addison, www.northalsted.com/market_days.php, 773-883-0500
- **Retro on Roscoe**, Roscoe and Damen, roscoevillage.org/event-calendar/retro-on-roscoe, 773-665-4682
- **St. Procopius Annual Kermes**, 1641 S Allport St, www.stprocopius.com, 312-226-7887
- **Tall Ships** (continued), Navy Pier
- **Taste of Greece**, 100 S Halsted, 312-665-1234
- **Taste of Polonia**, 5216 W Lawrence St, 773-777-8898
- **Ukrainian Days Festival,** 2500 W Grand, www.cityofchicago.org, 773-772-4500
- **Velika Gospa Croatian Fest**, 2823 S Princeton Ave, 312-842-1871
- **Wicker Park Fest**, Damen St, Honore/Paulina, www.wickerparkfest.com

## SEPTEMBER

- **26th Street Mexican Independence Day Parade**, 26th St from Albany to Kostner, 773-521-5387
- **African Festival of the Arts**, Labor Day weekend, Washington Park, www.africanfestivalchicago.com, 773-955-ARTS
- **Annual Septemberfest**, Schaumburg, www.ci.schaumburg.il.us/HFun/September/Pages/default.aspx, 847-923-3605

- **Chicago's Half Marathon & Kids Fest**, Museum of Science & Industry, www.chicagohalfmarathon.com, 800-596-5990
- **Chinatown Autumn Moon Festival**, www.moonfestchicago.com/index.html, 312-823-2917
- **German-American Fest**, Lincoln Square, www.lincolnsquare.org
- **Guinness Oyster Festival**, 2000 W Roscoe, Roscoe Village, www.chicagoevents.com, 773-868-3010
- **Hideout Block Party,** 1354 W Wabansia, www.hideoutchicago.com, 773-227-4433
- **Ice Cream Social & Craft Fair**, Galena, www.applecanyonlake.org, 815-492-2238
- **Jazz Festival** (continued), Grant Park, http://www.chicagofestivals.net
- **Mexican Independence Day Parade**, Columbus and Balbo Drives
- **German American Fest and Von Steuben Day Parade ,** 4800 N Lincoln, www.germanday.com, 630-653-3018
- **Park Forest Art Fair**, Park Forest, www.tallgrassarts.org, 708-748-3377
- **Riverwalk Art Fair**, Naperville, www.napervilleartleague.com, 630-355-2530
- **Windy City Wine Festival**, Buckingham Fountain

## OCTOBER

- **57th Street Children's Book Fair**, www.57cbf.org
- **Apple Festival-Long Grove**, Mount Prospect, 847-634-0888
- **Boo! at the Zoo,** weekends in October, Brookfield Zoo, www.brookfieldzoo.org
- **Chicago International Children's Film Festival**, 773-281-9075, www.cicff.org
- **Chicago International Film Festival,** chicagofilmfestival.com, 312-683-0121
- **Chicago Marathon**, 312-904-9800, www.chicagomarathon.com
- **Chicagoween**, www.cityofchicago.org
- **Columbus Day Parade**, Columbus from Balbo to Monroe, www.cityofchicago.org, 708-450-9050
- **Festival of Films from Iran**, www.siskelfilmcenter.org, 312-846-2600
- **Friends of the Grape Wine Festival,** Lincoln Square, 4920 N Claremont, **773-506-2191**
- **Halloween Happening** (parade), downtown, www.cityofchicago.org
- **St. Charles Scarecrow Festival**, www.scarecrowfest.com, 800-777-4373
- **The Berghoff Oktoberfest**, Adams/Dearborn Streets, www.theberghoff.com, 312-427-3170
- **Third Coast Audio Festival Conference,** www.thirdcoastfestival.org/happenings/conference
- **Village Scarecrow Festival**, Barrington, www.barrington-il.gov

## NOVEMBER

- **Candlelight Christmas**, www.mainstreetplainfield.org, Plainfield, 815-609-6130
- **Christkindlmarket Chicago,** Daley Plaza (50 W Washington), www.christkindlmarket.com, 312-494-2175
- **Daley Plaza Santa House**, Daley Plaza, www.cityofchicago.org, 312-744-3316
- **Gingerbread Fantasy Factory**, Chicago Children's Museum, www.chicagochildrensmuseum.org, 312-527-1000 (Nov.–Dec.)
- **Holiday Celebrations** (through first week of January), Botanic Garden, Glencoe, www.chicagobotanic.org, 847-835-5440
- **Magnificent Mile Lights Festival**, Michigan Ave, www.themagnificentmile.com
- **McDonalds Thanksgiving Parade,** State St, Congress to Randolph, www.chicagofestivals.org, 312-235-2217
- **Nouveau Wine Festival,** Galena, www.galenacellars.com, 815-777-3235
- **Old Fashioned Holiday Craft Fair,** Glenview, www.glenviewparks.org, 847-724-5670
- **Polish Film Festival in America**, pffamerica.com, 773-486-9612
- **Reeling: Chicago Lesbian & Gay International Film Festival**, reelingfilmfestival.org, 773-293-1447
- **S.O.F.A. (Sculpture Objects and Functional Art),** Navy Pier, www.sofaexpo.com
- **Tree Lighting Ceremony**, Daley Plaza, www.cityofchicago.org, 312-744-3315
- **Wheeling Festival of Lights**, Wheeling, www.wheelingil.gov, 847-459-2600

## DECEMBER

- **Annual Holiday Celebration in Many Lands**, Aurora, www.aurora-il.org, 630-265-4636
- **Annual Winter Wonderland Light Show**, Cuneo Museum, Vernon Hills, www.vernonhills.org, 847-367-3700
- **Christkindlmarket Chicago** (continued), Daley Plaza (50 W Washington), www.christkindlmarket.com, 312-644-2175
- **Christmas Around the World Holiday of Lights**, Museum of Science and Industry, www.msichicago.org, 773-684-1414
- **Christmas Tours of Frank Lloyd Wright Home and Studio**, Oak Park, www.gowright.org, 312-994-4000
- **Daley Plaza Santa House** (continued), Daley Plaza, www.cityofchicago.org, 312-744-3315
- **Holiday Magic**, weekends in December, Brookfield Zoo, www.brookfieldzoo.org

- **Julmark nad (Christmasfest)**, Swedish American Museum, www.swedishamericanmuseum.org, 773-728-8111
- **Lamb's Farm Holiday Arts & Crafts Show**, Arlington Heights, www.lambsfarm.com
- **Long Grove Countryside Christmas**, Long Grove, 847-634-9440
- **New Year's Eve Buckingham Fountain Fireworks**, Columbus Dr/Congress Pkwy, 312-744-3315
- **Toys for Tots Motorcycle Parade**, chicagolandtft.org, 708-598-4909

# A CHICAGO READING LIST

BOOKSTORES AND LIBRARIES THROUGHOUT CHICAGO WILL HAVE A regional section full of books about the Windy City. Out-of-print and otherwise hard-to-find titles can often be located in area libraries. Try searching the online catalogs offered by the Chicago Public Library or SWAN (a network of over seventy suburban libraries); the book you request can usually be sent to your local library branch. You can also find less popular titles online from **Amazon** (www.amazon.com) or from online booksellers such as **Powells** (www.powells.com) that carry used books. Here are just a few titles that may be of interest.

## ARCHITECTURE

- *And Guide Chicago: Architecture & Design,* Michelle Galindo, ed. (Te Neues Publishing)
- *Architecture in Detail Chicago,* Thomas J. O'Gorman (PRC Publishing)
- *Chicago Architecture and Design,* George A. Larson and Jay Pridmore (Harry N. Abrams)
- *Chicago Bungalow,* Dominic A. Pacyga and Charles Shanabruch, co-editors (Arcadia)
- *Chicago: A Guide to Recent Architecture,* Susanna Sirefman (Konemann)
- *Chicago Mansions* (Images of America), John Graf (Arcadia Publishing)
- *Chicago's Famous Buildings,* Franz Schulze and Kevin Harrington (University of Chicago Press)
- *Forgotten Chicago* (Images of America), Ron Gordon and John Paulett (Arcadia Publishing)
- *Frank Lloyd Wright's Chicago,* Thomas J. O'Gorman (Thunder Bay Press)
- *Louis Sullivan: Prophet of Modern Architecture,* Hugh Morrison and Timothy J. Samuelson (W.W. Norton)

- **Pocket Guide to Chicago Architecture,** Judith Paine McBrien (W.W. Norton)
- **The Sky's the Limit: A Century of Chicago's Skyscrapers,** Pauline Saliga (Rizzoli)
- **Unexpected Chicago,** Camilo Jose Vergara (New Press)
- **A View from the River: Chicago Architecture Foundation's River Cruise,** text by Jay Pridmore (Pomegranate Communications, Inc.)

## FICTION AND LITERATURE

- **The Adventures of Augie March,** Saul Bellow
- **Chicago Blues** (stories), Libby Fischer Hellman, editor (Bleak House Books)
- **Chicago: City on the Make,** Nelson Algren (University of Chicago Press)
- **Chicago Noir,** Neil Pollack, editor (Akashic Books)
- **Chicago Poems,** Carl Sandburg (Kessinger Publishing)
- **Chicago Stories,** James T. Farrell (University of Illinois Press)
- **Chicago Stories: Tales of the City,** John Miller, editor (Chronicle Books)
- **Chicago Tales,** Bill VanPatten (Outskirts Press)
- **The Chicago Way,** Michael Harvey (Knopf)
- **Childhood and Other Neighborhoods: Stories,** Stuart Dybek (University of Chicago Press)
- **The Coast of Chicago,** Stuart Dybek (Picador)
- **Hairstyles of the Damned,** Joe Meno (Punk Planet Books)
- **House on Mango Street,** Sandra Cisneros (Vintage Contemporaries)
- **Hunter and the Hunted: The Ed & Am Hunter Novels,** Frederic Brown (Stewart Masters Publishing)
- **Indemnity Only** (or any other V.I. Warshawski mystery), Sara Paretsky (Dell Books)
- **I Sailed with Magellan,** Stuart Dybek (Picador)
- **The Jungle,** Sinclair Lewis
- **A Long Way From Chicago: A Novel in Stories,** Richard Peck (Puffin Books)
- **Native Son,** Richard Wright
- **A Raisin in the Sun,** Lorraine Hansberry
- **Sister Carrie,** Theodore Dreiser
- **Spring Comes to Chicago (Poems),** Campbell McGrath (Ecco)
- **Stories of Chicago,** George Ade (University of Illinois Press)
- **Studs Lonigan,** James T. Farrell (University of Illinois Press)
- **The Logic of a Rose: Chicago Stories,** Billy Lombardo (BkMk Press)
- **The Law Review,** S. Scott Gaille (Creative Art Books)

## GETAWAYS/RECREATION

- **52 Adventures in Chicago,** Lynn Gordon (Chronicle Books)

- *Chicago Bicycle Guidebook: Great Bicycle Riding Through Chicago's Lakefront Neighborhoods*, Michael Palucki (Pastime Publications)
- *Country Walks Near Chicago*, Alan Hall Fisher (Rambler Books)
- *Kids Explore Chicago: The Very Best Kids' Activities within an Easy Drive of Chicago*, Susan Moffat (Adams Media Corp.)
- *Kids in the Loop: Chicago Adventures for Kids and their Grownups*, Ann Basye (Independent Publishers Group)
- *Off the Beaten Path Chicago*, Cliff Terry (Globe Pequot)
- *Outside Magazine's Urban Adventure: Chicago,* Lynn Schnaiberg (W.W. Norton)
- *Quick Escapes Chicago*, Bonnie Miller Rubin (Globe Pequot)
- *Somewhere Over the Dan Ryan: Day and Weekend Outings for Chicago-area Families*, Joanne Y. Cleaver (Chicago Review Press)
- *Visiting the Midwest's Historic Preservation Sites*, Majorie Grannis (Jameson Books)
- *Weekend Getaway Guide: 160 Trips to Take Within 200 Miles of Chicago*, Mike Michaelson (Rand McNally)

## HISTORICAL

- *Boss: Richard J. Daley of Chicago*, Mike Rokyo (Plume)
- *Capone: The Life and World of Al Capone*, John Kobler (Da Capo Press)
- *Chicago '68*, David Farber (University of Chicago Press)
- *Chicago Death Trap: The Iroquois Theatre Fire of 1903*, Nat Brandt (Southern Illinois University Press)
- *Chicago Dreaming: Midwesterners and the City, 1871-1919*, Timothy B. Spears (University of Chicago Press)
- *Chicago: Growth of a Metropolis*, Harold M. Mayer and Richard C. Wade (University of Chicago Press)
- *Chicago's Most Wanted: The Top Ten Book of Murderous Mobsters, Midway Monsters, and Windy City Oddities*, Laura L. Enright (Potomac Books)
- *Chicago: Then & Now*, Elizabeth McNulty (Thunder Bay Press)
- *Devil in the White City: Murder, Magic and Madness at the Fair that Changed America*, Erik Larson (Crown Publishers)
- *Doors of Redemption: The Forgotten Synagogues of Chicago*, Robb Packer (Book Surge Publishing)
- *The Great Fire*, Jim Murphy (Scholastic, Inc.)
- *How Clout and Community Built Dearborn Park*, Lois Wille (Southern Illinois University Press)
- *Jewish Chicago: A Pictorial History*, Irving Cutler (Arcadia)
- *Land of Hope: Chicago, Black Southerners, and the Great Migration*, James R. Grossman (University of Chicago Press)
- *Lost Chicago*, David Garrad Lowe (Watson-Guptill Publications)

- *Nature's Metropolis: Chicago and the Great West*, William Cronon (W.W. Norton & Co.)
- *The Outfit: The Role of Chicago's Underworld in the Shaping of Modern America*, Gus Russo (Bloomsbury U.S.A.)
- *Prairie Passage: The Illinois & Michigan Canal Corridor*, Edward Ranney (University of Illinois Press)
- *To Sleep with the Angels: The Story of a Fire*, David Cowan (Ivan R. Dee, Inc.)
- *The Windies' City: Chicago's Historical Hidden Treasures*, Greg Borzo, Suzanne Haynes, and Bernard Turner (Highlights of Chicago Press)
- *The World's Columbian Exposition: The Chicago World's Fair of 1893*, Norman Bolotin and Christine Laing (University of Illinois Press)

## NEIGHBORHOODS

- *Back of the Yards: The Making of a Local Democracy*, Robert A. Slayton (University of Chicago Press)
- *Bronzeville: Black Chicago in Pictures 1941-1943*, Maren Stange, editor (New Press)
- *Chicago's Beverly/Morgan Park Neighborhood* (Images of America), Joseph C. Oswald (Arcadia Publishing)
- *Chicago's Historic Pullman District* (Images of America), Frank Beberdick and Historic Pullman Foundation (Arcadia Publishing)
- *Chicago's Maxwell Street* (Images of America), Lore Grove, Laura Kamedulski, and Lori Grove (Arcadia Publishing)
- *Division Street*, Studs Terkel (Pantheon)
- *Lincoln Park, Chicago* (Images of America), Melanie Ann Apel (Arcadia Publishing)
- *Polish Immigrants and Industrial Chicago: Workers on the South Side, 1880-1922*, Dominic A. Pacyga (University of Chicago Press)
- *Taylor Street: Chicago's Little Italy* (Images of America), Kathy Catrambone and Ellen Shubart (Arcadia Publishing)
- *Wrigley Field: A Celebration of the Friendly Confines*, Mark Jacob (McGraw Hill)

## REFERENCE

- *B.Y.O.B. Chicago: Your Guide to Bring-Your-Own-Bottle Restaurants and Wine and Spirits Stores in Chicago*, Jean Iverson (BYOB Chicago)
- *Chicago Mountain Bike Trails Guide*, P.L. Strazz (Big Lauter Tun Books)
- *The Chicago Running Guide* (City Running Guide Series), Brenda Barrera and Eliot Wineburg (Human Kinetics Publishers)
- *The Complete Chicago Cubs: The Total Encyclopedia of the Team*, Derek Gentile (Black Dog & Leventhal)
- *A Cook's Guide to Chicago*, Marilyn Pocius (Lake Claremont Press)

- *Encyclopedia of Chicago*, James R. Grossman, Ann Durkin Keating, and Janice L. Reiff, editors (University of Chicago Press)
- *The Dog Lover's Companion to Chicago: The Inside Scoop on Where to Take Your Dog*, Margaret Littman (Avalon Travel Publishing)
- *A Field Guide to Gay and Lesbian Chicago*, Kathie Bergquist and Robert McDonald (Lake Claremont Press)
- *The Franklin Report: Chicago, An Insider's Guide to Home Services*, Elizabeth Franklin (Allgood Press)
- *Graveyards of Chicago: The People, History, Art, and Lore of Cook County Cemeteries*, Matt Huber and Ursula Bielski (Lake Claremont Press)
- *A Guide to Chicago's Murals*, Mary Lackritz Gray (University of Chicago Press)
- *Literary Chicago: A Book Lover's Tour of the Windy City*, Greg Holden (Lake Claremont Press)
- *The Streets and San Man's Guide to Chicago Eats*, Dennis Foley (Lake Claremont Press)
- *Today's Chicago Blues*, Karen Hanson (Lake Claremont Press)
- *White Sox Encyclopedia*, Richard Lindberg, Mark Fletcher (Temple University Press)
- *Zagat Chicago Restaurants*, Zagat Survey (Zagat Survey)

## REGIONAL NONFICTION

- *1001 Afternoons in Chicago*, Ben Hecht (University of Chicago Press)
- *Beer: A History of Brewing in Chicago*, Bob Skilnik (Barricade Books)
- *Black Writing from Chicago: In the World, Not of It?* Richard R. Guzman, editor (Southern Illinois University Press)
- *Chicago Blues: The City and the Music*, Mike Rowe (Westview Press)
- *Chicago Haunts: Ghostly Lore of the Windy City / More Chicago Haunts: Scenes from Myth and Memory*, Ursula Bielski (Lake Claremont Press)
- *Chicago Lives: Men and Women Who Shaped Our City*, James Janega, Editor (Triumph Books)
- *Chicago Soul* (Music in American Life), Robert Pruter (University of Illinois Press)
- *Destination Chicago Jazz*, Sandor Demlinger and John Steiner (Arcadia Publishing)
- *Eight Men Out: The Black Sox and the 1919 World Series*, Eliot Asinof, Stephen J. Gould (Henry Holt)
- *Ethnic Chicago: A Multicultural Portrait*, Melvin G. Holli and Peter D'A Jones, editors (Wm. B. Eerdman's Publishing Company)
- *Father Mac: The Life & Times of Father Ignatius D. McDermott, Co-founder of Chicago's Famed Haymarket Center*, Thomas Roeser (The McDermott Foundation)
- *The Gangs of Chicago: An Informal History of the Chicago Underworld*, Herbert Asbury (Thunder's Mouth Press)

- *Great Chicago Stories,* Tom Maday and Sam Landers (Twopress Publishing Co.)
- *My Bloody Life: The Making of a Latin King,* Reymundo Sanchez (Chicago Review Press)
- *Never a City So Real: A Walk in Chicago,* Alex Kotlowitz (Crown)
- *Our Chicago: Life & Death on the South Side of Chicago,* Lealan Jones, Lloyd Newman, David Isay (Washington Square Press)
- *Return to the Scene of the Crime: A Guide to Infamous Places in Chicago,* Richard Lindberg (Cumberland House)
- *There Are No Children Here: The Story of Two Boys Growing Up in the Other America,* Alex Kotlowitz (Anchor)
- *True Stories from Chicago's Jewish History,* Walter Roth (Academy Chicago Publishers)

## WALKING TOURS

- *Chicago on Foot: Walking Tours of Chicago's Architecture,* Ira J. Bach, Susan Wolfson, James Cornelius (Chicago Review Press)
- *Chicago In and Around the Loop, Walking Tours of Architecture and History,* Gerard R. Wolfe (McGraw-Hill Professional)
- *Chicago Street Guide to the Supernatural,* Richard T. Crowe (Carolanda Press)
- *A Guide to Oak Park's Frank Lloyd Wright and Prairie School Historic District,* Molly Wickes (University of Chicago Press)
- *University of Chicago: An Architectural Tour (The Campus Guide),* Jay Pridmore and Peter Kiar (Princeton Architectural Press)
- *A Walk Through Graceland Cemetery,* Barbara Lanctot (Chicago Architecture Foundation)

# USEFUL PHONE NUMBERS & WEBSITES

## ANIMALS

Area shelters, humane societies, and emergency animal clinics:

- **Abbott Animal Hospital**, 6721 W Archer Ave, 773-788-9000, 708-749-4200 (after hours emergencies)
- **Animal Welfare League,** 10305 Southwest Hwy, Chicago Ridge, 708-636-8586; 6224 S Wabash, 773-667-0930, www.animalwelfareleague.com
- **Anti-Cruelty Society**, 510 N LaSalle, 312-644-8338, www.anticruelty.org
- **Chicago Exotics Animal Hospital** (all animals), 3735 W Dempster, Skokie, 847-329-8709, www.exoticpetvet.com
- **City Animal Control**, 312-747-1406
- **Cook County Department of Animal Control**, 708-974-6140, www.cookcountygov.com
- **Dead Animal Removal**, dial 311
- **Dog License** (City Clerk), 312-745-1100, www.chicityclerk.com/licenses/dogs.html
- **DuPage County Animal Control**, 630-682-7197, www.dupageco.org/animalcontrol
- **Lake Shore Animal Shelter**, 312-409-1162, www.lakeshoreanimalshelter.org
- **PAWS Chicago,** 773-935-PAWS, www.pawschicago.org
- **South Suburban Humane Society**, 1103 West End Ave, Chicago Heights, 708-755-7387, www.southsuburbanhumane.org
- **To Report Animal Abuse,** 312-746-7180
- **West Suburban Humane Society**, 1901 W Ogden Ave, Downers Grove, 630-960-9600, www.wshs-dg.org

## AUTOMOBILES

- **Abandoned Vehicle Removal**, dial 311
- **Automotive Repair Bureau**, Department of Consumer Services, 312-744-4006
- **American Automobile Association (AAA)**, 800-AAA-HELP, www.aaa.com
- **State Department of Motor Vehicles**—Licenses and Registration number, www.cyberdriveillinois.com
- **Tow Lots**: To find out whether your car has been towed or impounded—and if so, where and how you can retrieve it—call 3-1-1 or check www.chicagopolice.org/vehicles.
- **Traffic Court**, Daley Center, Parking Ticket Inquiries, 312-744-PARK (7275), www.cityofchicago.org

## CHAMBERS OF COMMERCE

Please see the "Neighborhoods" and "Suburbs" sections of this book for even more Chamber of Commerce listings.

- **Chicago Southland Chamber of Commerce**, 708-957-6950, www.chicagosouthland.com
- **Chicagoland Chamber of Commerce**, 312-494-6700, www.chicagolandchamber.org
- **East Side Chamber of Commerce**, 773-721-7948
- **Edgebrook-Sauganash Chamber of Commerce**, 773-545-9300, www.sauganashchamber.org
- **Edison Park Chamber of Commerce**, 773-631-0063, www.edisonpark.com
- **Hyde Park Chamber of Commerce**, 773-288-0124, www.hydeparkchamberchicago.org
- **Illinois State Chamber of Commerce**, 312-983-7100, www.ilchamber.org
- **Jefferson Park Chamber of Commerce**, 773-736-6697, www.jeffersonpark.net
- **Lake View East Chamber of Commerce**, 773-348-8608, www.lakevieweast.com
- **Lincoln Park Chamber of Commerce**, 773-880-5200, www.lincolnparkchamber.com
- **Portage Park Chamber of Commerce**, 773-777-2020, www.portageparkchamber.org
- **Uptown Chamber of Commerce**, 773-878-1184, www.uptownbusinesspartners.com

## CONSUMER COMPLAINTS AND SERVICES

- **Attorney General Consumer Fraud Division**, 800-386-5438, www.ag.state.il.us
- **Better Business Bureau**, 312-832-0500, www.chicago.bbb.org
- **Business Affairs and Consumer Protection Department**, Chicago, 312-744-6060, TTY 312-744-1944, www.cityofchicago.org
- **Chicago Bar Association**, 312-554-2000, www.chicagobar.org
- **City Ethics Board**, 312-744-9660, www.cityofchicago.org
- **Consumer Protection Division** (Attorney Generals' Office), 800-386-5438, www.ag.state.il.us
- **County Ethics Board**, 312-603-4304, www.cookcountygov.com
- **Federal Trade Commission**, General: 877-382-4357; ID Theft: 877-ID-THEFT; www.ftc.gov
- **Illinois Department of Financial and Professional Regulation**, 312-814-4500, www.idfpr.com
- **Illinois Office of Consumer Health Insurance**, 877-527-9431
- **US Consumer Product Safety Commission**, 800-638-2772, www.cpsc.gov

## CRISIS HOTLINES

### ALCOHOL & DRUG DEPENDENCY

- **Adolescent Addiction Programs**, 800-522-3784, 800-373-1700 (Illinois only)
- **Alcohol and Drug Hotline**, 800-ALCOHOL
- **Alcoholics Anonymous**, 312-346-1475, www.chicagoaa.org
- **Narcotics Anonymous**, 708-848-4884, www.chicagona.org
- **Substance Abuse Referral Line**, 800-821-4357
- **Substance Abuse Services**, 800-962-1126

### CHILD ABUSE & FAMILY VIOLENCE

- **Abducted, Abused, Missing, and Exploited Children**, 800-248-8020
- **Girls' and Boys' Town National Hotline**, 800-448-3000
- **Child Abuse Hotline**, 800-422-4453, 800-252-2873
- **Child Social Service Agency/Protective Services Hotline**, 800-232-3798 (Illinois only)
- **National Domestic Violence Hotline**, 800-799-7233
- **Rape Crisis Hotline**, 888-293-2080
- **Suicide Prevention Hotline**, 800-SUICIDE
- **Youth Crisis Hotline**, 800-232-3798 (Illinois only)

## CRIME
- **Chicago Alternative Policing Strategy** (**CAPS**); local anti-crime/neighborhood watch program. There are over 279 police beats participating in CAPS in Chicago. To find CAPS information about your area, visit the CAPS website at portal.chicagopolice.org
- **Crime in Progress,** 911
- **Consumer Fraud Reporting Line,** Office of Attorney General of Illinois, 800-386-5438

## DISCRIMINATION
- **City/County Human Rights/Human Relations Offices,** Chicago, 312-744-4111 or 312-814-6200, TTY 312-744-1088
- **Cook County Commission on Human Rights,** 312-603-1100, www.co.cook.il.us
- **Fair Employment and Housing Department,** Illinois Department of Human Rights, 312-814-6200, www.state.il.us/dhr
- **Illinois Human Rights Commission,** 312-814-6269, www.state.il.us/ihrc
- **Women's Commission,** Illinois Governor's Office, 312-814-2121

## ELECTED OFFICIALS/GOVERNMENT

### CITY OF CHICAGO
- **City of Chicago Home Page**: www.cityofchicago.org
- **Council,** 312-744-0403
- **City Hall**: **Office of the Mayor,** 312-744-3300
- **City Ward Information,** available at www.chicityclerk.com

### COOK COUNTY
- **Cook County home page**: www.cookcountygov.org
- **Cook County Clerk,** 312-603-5656, or 847-818-2850 (northwest suburbs), www.cookcountyclerk.com
- **Clerk of the Circuit Court**; contact the Circuit Court regarding the following: child support/protection, domestic relations, traffic, probate, juvenile justice, criminal, civil, county division issues: www.cookcountyclerkofcourt.org or 312-603-5030.
- **Cook County Recorder of Deeds,** 312-603-5050, www.ccrd.info

### DUPAGE COUNTY
- **DuPage County Board,** 630-407-6500, www.co.dupage.il.us; many services can be found through the website, including the following: County Clerk, Coroner, Sheriff, County State Attorney, Auditor and Clerk of the Circuit Court.

# USEFUL PHONE NUMBERS & WEBSITES

- **County Clerk**, www.co.dupage.il.us/countyclerk, 630-407-5500

## LAKE COUNTY
- **Lake County Home Page**, www.co.lake.il.us; provides links to many government services.
- **Lake County Clerk,** 847-377-2400, www.countyclerk.lakecountyil.gov

## MCHENRY COUNTY
- **County Home Page**, www.co.mchenry.il.us, provides links to many county departments
- **Circuit Clerk**, 815-334-4310
- **County Clerk**, 815-334-4242
- **County Recorder**, 815-334-4110
- **Health Department**, 815-334-4510
- **State's Attorney**, 815-334-4159
- **Mental Health**, 815-455-2828
- **Sheriff**, 815-338-2144

## STATE
- **Governor's Office**, 217-782-0244, TTY 888-261-3336, www.state.il.us/gov
- **Illinois State Board of Elections**, www.elections.state.il.us
- **Secretary of State**, 800-252-8980, www.cyberdriveillinois.com
- **State Senate**: To view a state senator's links, records and contact information, go to www.ilga.gov/senate.
- **State Assembly**: Visit General Assembly website at www.ilga.gov/house for information on state assemblymen.
- **State of Illinois website**: www.illinois.gov
- **US House of Representatives**: The main number for the House of Representatives is 202-224-3121, or go to www.house.gov.
- **US Senate**: Call 202-224-3121 or go to http://www.senate.gov to find out information about any US senator.
- **www.statelocalgov.net**, provides links to state government, including all state departments.

## EMERGENCY
- **Fire, Police, Medical**, 911
- **FEMA Disaster Assistance Information**, 800-621-FEMA (3362), www.fema.gov

## ENTERTAINMENT

Also see the **Cultural Life** chapter.

- **Chicago Office of Tourism**, visitor information, 312-744-2400, www.explorechicago.org
- **Chicago Cultural Center Arts Hotline**, 312-346-3278, www.cityofchicago.org/Tourism/CulturalCenter
- **Jam Concert Line**, 312-666-6667, for rock, country, blues
- **Music & Theatre Information**, http://chicago.metromix.com
- **Hot Tix** (discount day-of-the-show tickets), www.hottix.org
- **Ticketmaster**, 800-745-3000 (all events), 312-902-1500 (theater and fine arts), 312-902-1400 (Broadway in Chicago), www.ticketmaster.com
- **Mayor's Office of Special Events Hotline**, 312-744-3316
- **Newspaper Entertainment Listings**: www.chicagotribune.com, www.chireader.com, www.dailyherald.com, www.dailysouthtown.com, www.chicagoreporter.com

## FEDERAL OFFICES/CENTERS

- **Federal Citizen Information Center**, 800-FED-INFO, www.publications.usa.gov, or www.info.gov
- **Social Security Administration**, 800-772-1213, TTY 800-325-0778 (both 7 a.m. to 7 p.m., Monday–Friday), www.ssa.gov

## HEALTH AND MEDICAL CARE

- **Centers for Disease Control's AIDS/STD/TB Hotline**, 800-458-5231
- **Chicago Department of Public Health**, 312-747-9884, www.cityofchicago.org/Health; care van, 312-746-6122
- **Doctor Referral Lines**; pediatric doctors: www.luriechildrens.org/findadoc. Or call your area hospital and ask for a referral for a specific specialty.
- **DuPage County Health Department**, 630-682-7400, www.dupagehealth.org
- **Illinois Department of Public Health**, 217-782-4977, www.idph.state.il.us
- **Illinois Poison Control Center**, 800-222-1222, www.illinoispoisoncenter.org
- **Kane County Health Department**, 630-208-3801, www.kanehealth.com
- **Lake County Health Department**, 847-377-8000, www.lakecountyil.gov/health
- **National Health Information Center**, US Department of Health and Human Services, 800-336-4797, www.hhs.gov
- **Nursing Home Information and Referral**, Illinois Department on Aging, 800-252-8966, www.state.il.us/aging

USEFUL PHONE NUMBERS & WEBSITES

- Office of Consumer Health Insurance, 877-527-9431, www.idfpr.com
- National Cancer Institute's Smoking Quit Line: 877-44U-QUIT, www.smokefree.gov

## HOUSING

- Chicago Rents Rights Hotline, Department of Housing, 312-742-RENT, www.cityofchicago.org/housing
- Chicago Urban League, 4510 S Michigan Ave, 773-285-5800, www.thechicagourbanleague.org
- Fair Housing Information Clearinghouse, www.hud.gov/progdesc/fhip.cfm
- Illinois Tenants Union, 4616 N Drake Ave, 773-478-1133, www.tenant.org
- Landlord and Tenant Fact Sheet from the Office of the Attorney General, www.IllinoisAttorneyGeneral.gov
- Lawyers Committee for Better Housing (Edgewater and Rogers Park), 220 S State St, #1700, 312-347-7800, www.lcbh.org
- Legal Assistance Foundation of Chicago, 312-341-1070, www.lafchicago.org
- Metropolitan Tenants Organization Hotline, 773-292-4988, www.tenants-rights.org
- US Department of Fair Housing and Equal Opportunity, 800-669-9777, www.hud.gov/offices/fheo

## LEGAL REFERRAL

- American Civil Liberties Union, 312-201-9740, www.aclu-il.org
- Illinois Attorney General Legal Assistance Referrals, www.ag.state.il.us/about/probono.html
- Legal Assistance Foundation of Chicago, 312-341-1070, www.lafchicago.org
- Public Defender Information Line, 312-603-0600

## LIBRARIES

For the local branch of your public library, check your community's resources, which follow each **Neighborhood Profile**. Also see **Literary Life** in the **Cultural Life** chapter.

- Arlington Heights Memorial Library, 500 N Dunton Ave, 847-392-0100, www.ahml.info
- Des Plaines Library, 1501 Ellinwood St, 847-827-5551, www.dppl.org

- **Harold Washington Center**, 400 S State St, 312-747-4300, www.chipublib.org
- **Metropolitan Library System**, www.mls.lib.il.us, provides a list of over 600 Chicago and suburban libraries and phone numbers
- **Naperville Library**, 200 W Jefferson St, 630-961-4100, www.naperville-lib.org
- **Newberry Library**, 60 W Walton St, 312-943-9090, www.newberry.org
- **Oak Lawn Public Library**, 708-422-4990, www.lib.oak-lawn.il.us

## PARKING

- **Booted Vehicles**, dial 311
- **City Clerk's Permit Sales Unit for residential parking permits**, 312-744-6774, www.chicityclerk.com
- **City Clerks' Offices (city stickers)**, 312-744-6774, TTY 312-744-2939
- **Parking and Compliance Violation Center**, 312-744-PARK (7275)
- **Ticket Helpline and Online Payment**, 312-744-7275, www.cityofchicago.org
- **Clerk of the Circuit Court Automated Information Line**, 312-603-2000

## PARKS AND RECREATION DEPARTMENTS

Refer to listings in the **Neighborhood Profiles**, **Sports and Recreation**, or **Greenspaces and Beaches** chapters.

## POLICE

Check the **Neighborhood Profiles** for branch stations.

- **Police Emergencies**, dial 911
- **Cook County Sheriff Department**, 708-865-4700, www.cookcountysheriff.org
- **Illinois State Police**, Des Plaines, 847-294-4400, www.isp.state.il.us
- **Non-emergency Chicago City Police Department**, dial 311

## POST OFFICE

Refer to the **Neighborhood Profiles** for post offices in your area.

- **US Postal Service**, 800-275-8777, www.usps.com

## SANITATION AND GARBAGE

- **City of Chicago Recycling Hotline**, 312-744-5702, www.cityofchicago.org

# USEFUL PHONE NUMBERS & WEBSITES

- **Chicago Department of Streets and Sanitation**, www.cityofchicago.org
- **Resource Center**, 773-821-1351, www.resourcecenterchicago.org

## SCHOOLS

Check the community resources listings following the **Neighborhood Profiles** chapter for your local school office or check the **Childcare and Education** chapter.

- **State Board of Education**, 312-814-2220, www.isbe.state.il.us
- **Chicago Public Schools**, 773-553-1000, www.cps.edu

## SENIORS

- **American Association of Retired Persons (AARP)**, 312-458-3600, www.aarp.org
- **City of Chicago Department on Aging**, 312-744-4016, www.cityofchicago.org
- **Elder Care Locator**, 800-677-1116, www.eldercare.gov
- **Illinois Department on Aging**, 800-252-8966, www.state.il.us/aging
- **National Council on Aging**, 202-479-1200, www.ncoa.org
- **Social Security and Medicare Eligibility Information**, 800-772-1213, www.ssa.gov
- **To report elder abuse**, 866-800-1409, 800-279-0400 (afterhours), TTY: 888-206-1327

## SHIPPING SERVICES

- **DHL Worldwide Express**, 800-225-5345, www.dhl-usa.com
- **FedEx**, 800-463-3339, www.fedex.com (for ground, express or air freight information)
- **Mail-Sort** (Northbrook), 847-291-4900
- **Navis Pack and Ship**, 800-334-3528, www.gonavis.com
- **Pitney Bowes**, 800-522-0020, www.pb.com
- **United Parcel Service (UPS)**, 800-742-5877, www.ups.com
- **US Postal Service Express Mail**, www.usps.com

## SPORTS

See **Sports and Recreation** chapter for full coverage of area teams.

- **Chicago Blackhawks**, www.chicagoblackhawks.com
- **Chicago Bulls**, www.chicagobulls.com
- **Chicago Cubs**, 773-404-CUBS, wwww.chicagocubs.com

- **Chicago White Sox**, 312-674-1000, www.chicagowhitesox.com
- **Professional/College Teams**, general information available from the Office of Tourism at www.cityofchicago.org
- **United Center**, 312-455-4000, www.unitedcenter.com

## STREET MAINTENANCE

- **Commissioner's Office**, 311
- **Transportation Commissioner's Office**, 312-744-3600
- **Street Cleaning and Snow Removal**, 312-745-4611
- **Traffic Signals, Sign Repair, etc.**, 311

## TAXES

### FEDERAL
- **Internal Revenue Service**, 312-566-4912, www.irs.gov

### STATE
- **State Department of Revenue Taxpayer Assistance**, 800-732-8866, www.tax.illinois.gov

### COUNTY
- **Cook County Assessor**, 312-443-7550, www.cookcountyassessor.com
- **County Treasurer**, information on getting, paying, or understanding tax bills, 312-443-5100, www.cookcountytreasurer.com

### CITY
- **Chicago**: City Comptroller's Office, 312-744-2204, www.cityofchicago.org
- **Business Call Center**, 312-747-4747, www.cityofchicago.org

## TOURISM AND TRAVEL

- **Chicago Convention and Tourism Bureau**, 877-CHICAGO, TTY 866-710-0294, www.choosechicago.com
- **Cook County Forest Preserve**, 800-870-3666, www.fpdcc.com
- **Illinois State Travel Information**, 800-2-CONNECT, www.enjoyillinois.com
- **Indiana Department of Tourism**, 888-Enjoy-IN, www.in.gov/visitindiana
- **International Assoc. for Medical Assistance to Travelers**, 716-754-4883, www.iamat.org
- **Michigan Department of Tourism**, 888-784-7328, www.michigan.org
- **Southwestern Michigan Tourist Council**, 269-925-6301, www.swmichigan.org
- **US National Park Service Information**, www.nps.gov

# USEFUL PHONE NUMBERS & WEBSITES

- **Wisconsin Department of Tourism**, 800-432-8747, www.travelwisconsin.com

## TRANSPORTATION

### AIRPORTS
- **O'Hare International Airport**, 800-832-6352, www.ohare.com
- **Midway International Airport**, 773-838-0600, www.flychicago.com
- **Gary/Chicago International Airport**, 219-949-9722, www.garychicagoairport.com
- **Chicago Executive Airport**, non-commercial airport in Wheeling, 847-537-2580, www.palwaukee.org
- **Schaumburg Regional Airport**, non-commercial, 847-985-9778, www.ci.schaumburg.il.us

### CITY OF CHICAGO PUBLIC TRANSPORTATION
- **CTA**, 888-YOUR-CTA, www.chicagotransit.com
- **RTA**, 312-836-7000, www.rtachicago.com

### NATIONAL/REGIONAL TRAIN AND BUS SERVICE
- **Amtrak**, 800-USA-RAIL, www.amtrak.com
- **Greyhound Bus**, Chicago stations: 630 W Harrison, 312-408-5821; 14 W 95th St, 312-408-5999; CTA Transit Building, 5800 Cumberland Ave, 773-693-2474, www.greyhound.com
- **I-GO**, 773-278-4446, option 2, www.igocars.org
- **Metropolitan Rail** (Metra): Union Station, 312-322-4269; Ogilvie Transportation Center, 312-496-4751; Metra general information, 312-322-6777, www.metrarail.com
- **PACE Suburban Bus Service**, 847-364-7223, www.pacebus.com
- **Regional Transportation Authority** (**RTA**), 312-836-7000, www.rtachicago.com

### WATER TAXI SERVICE
- **Shoreline Taxis**, 312-222-9328, www.shorelinesightseeing.com
- **Wendella Riverbus**, 312-337-1446, www.wendellaboats.com

## UTILITY EMERGENCIES

- **Electric**—wires down or other electrical emergencies, 800-EDISON-1, www.comed.com
- **Gas Leaks**, NICOR, 888-642-6748, www.nicor.com

- **Sewers/Water Main Leaks**, 311

## VITAL RECORDS

- **Office of the Cook County Clerk, Division of Vital Records,** www.cookcountyclerk.com: 50 W Washington St (lower concourse), Chicago, 312-603-7790
- **Rolling Meadows Courthouse,** 2121 Euclid Ave, Rolling Meadows, 847-818-2850
- **State Department of Vital Records** (Illinois Department of Public Health), www.idph.state.il.us, 217-782-4977, TTY 800-547-0466

## WEATHER

- **National Weather Service,** www.nws.noaa.gov
- **The Weather Channel Connection,** www.weather.com
- **Weather Underground:** www.wunderground.com/US/IL/Chicago.html
- **Weatherpages:** www.weatherpages.com.

## ZIP CODE INFORMATION

- **USPS ZIP Codes Request,** 800-275-8777, www.usps.com

# INDEX

**Symbols**

57th Street Beach 314
57th Street Books 269

**A**

AAA 153, 166, 177, 199, 359, 363, 372, 390
ABF U-Pack Moving 152
Accessible Accommodations 365
Address Locator, Chicago Street 15
Adler Planetarium 65, 268
African Methodist Episcopal Church 330
Afterwords 269
AIDS 200, 338, 394
Airlines 134, 164, 355-357
Air Pollution 322
Airport Noise 134
Airport Parking 355
Airports 7, 17, 99, 101-104, 118, 122, 134, 232, 268, 345, 346, 349, 352, 355-357, 361, 399
    Midway 122, 134, 346, 352, 355-357
    O'Hare 7, 10, 99, 101-105, 134, 232, 233, 345, 348-350, 354-357, 361, 371, 399
Airport Shuttles 355
Air Travel Resources, Online 357
Akoo Theatre 260
Albany Park 49
Alcohol & Drug Dependency 338, 391
Allergies 322
Allstate Arena 104, 260, 281, 401
Alpine Valley Music Center 260
American Society of Home Inspectors 146
America Online 173

Amtrak 117, 118, 123, 302, 354, 355, 371, 399
Andersonville 44
Angie's List 154
Animal Control 190, 389
Animals 138, 156, 190-192, 196, 205, 268, 274, 275, 303, 306, 311, 324, 338, 363, 389
Animal Welfare League 191, 338, 389
Annual Pride Parade 34, 206, 377
Anti-Cruelty Society 138, 191, 302, 338, 389
Antiques 44, 244, 245, 363, 367, 371, 376
Antique Stores 34, 37, 116, 119, 245
Aon Center 7
Apartment Hunting 135
Apartments
    Pet-friendly 138
Apartment Search Firms 137
Appliances, Electronics, Cameras 241
Apps 347
Arboretums 85, 117, 305, 308, 337
Archbishop of Chicago 25
Archdiocese 227, 309, 325, 331
Architecture 6, 40, 51, 52, 77, 79, 100, 237, 239, 270, 300, 327, 328, 368, 383, 384, 388
Area Causes 338
Area Codes 171
Arie Crown Theatre 257, 260
Arlington Heights 97
Arlington Park Racetrack 97, 282
Art Film Houses 258
Art Galleries 265
Art Institute of Chicago 1, 232, 264, 271
    School of the 232
Art Museums 264
Artopolis 251

ATM 161-163
AT&T 170-173
Auction Houses 246
Auditorium Theatre 260
Audubon Society 308
Au Pairs 213, 214
Aurora University 234, 267
Auto Emissions 178
Automobile Insurance 178
Automobile Registration 175, 177
Automobile Repair 199
Automobiles 179, 199, 390
Auto Pound 182
Average Annual Wind Speed 319
Average Precipitation 323
Average Temperatures 323
Aviation Consumer Protection Division 358

**B**

Babysitting 214
Bahá'í 89, 326
Bakeries 44, 45, 49, 57, 61, 87, 119, 247, 251
Ballet Chicago 1, 256
Bank Accounts 161, 163
Banking & Credit Resources 164
bankrate.com 148, 164
Banks 161-164
Bannockburn 105
Baptist Church 327, 335
Barbara's Bookstore 269
Barnes & Noble 96, 118, 269
Barrington 105
Baseball 8, 34, 35, 113, 278, 279, 283, 299, 314, 315
Basketball 104, 277, 279, 280, 295, 296, 314, 329, 376
Batavia 370
Beaches 48, 85, 93, 94, 299, 313-316
    Beyond Chicago 315
    Chicago 313
    Dog-friendly 303
    Dogs on 190
    Street-end 48, 313
Bean, The 7
Bed & Breakfasts 363
Beds and Bedding 241

Beer School 272
Beetles 134, 196, 197
Benedictine University 234, 268, 281
Bessemer Park 307
Better Business Bureau 153, 173, 199, 200, 391
Beverly 78
Beverly Arts Center 80, 376
Beverly Hills 78
Bicycle Commuting 284
Bicycle Rental 284, 364
Bicycle Trails 94, 284, 314
Bicycle Trips 370
Bicycling 283, 350
    in the City 283, 350
Billiards 284-286
Bill of Lading 156
Billy Graham Museum 114
Bishop Ford Freeway 346
Blind
    Services for the 202, 204, 339
Blommer Chocolate Company 23
Blue Island 119
Blue Island Education Center 121, 122
Blue Line 352, 355
Blues 7, 185, 262, 309, 377, 384, 387
Boating 285
Boiler Room 97
Bolingbrook 117
Bolingbrook Clow International Airport 118
Books
    Architecture 383
    Chicago Neighborhoods 386
    Getaways/Recreation 384
    Historical 385
    Reference (Chicago) 386
    Regional Nonfiction 387
    Walking Tours 388
Bookstores 45, 49, 65, 73, 138, 139, 206, 253, 269, 270, 273, 329, 346, 383
    General Interest 269
    Special Interest 270
    Used 270
Booted 7, 182, 396
Bowling 36, 286
Bradley Center 260
Breaking Your Lease 142
Bridgeport 69

# INDEX

Bridgeview 132
Broadcast and Print Media 184, 207
Bronzeville 66
Bronzeville Children's Museum 273
Brookfield 110
Brookfield Zoo 110, 274, 380, 381
Brown Line 352
Buckingham Fountain 300, 304, 380, 382
Bucktown 53
Bucktown Arts Fest 379
Buddhism 326, 379
Budget 152
Buffalo Grove 105
Bugs 134, 196, 306, 307, 323
Bundled Telecommunications 171
Burbank 122
Burnham, Daniel 3, 300, 301
Burnham Prairie Path 305
"Burnt District" 3
Buses
    CTA 353
    National/Regional 354
    PACE Suburban 353
Bus Service 353, 354, 399
Buying a Home 143
    Online Resources for 148
    Printed Resources for 149
    Strategies for 147
BYOB Restaurants 249

## C

Cable Television 171, 185
Calendar, Chicago 375
Calumet Park 132
CAPS (Chicago Alternative Policing Strategy) 193, 339, 392
Card Track 164
Car Insurance 178
Carpets and Rugs 241
Carpooling 350
Car Rentals 348
Car Sharing 348
Casinos 289, 367, 370
Catholic Schools 227
Cats 190, 191, 205
Cell Phones 172
Cellular Service Providers 172
Cemeteries 39, 306, 308-310, 334, 387, 388

Centennial Beach 116, 315
Centennial Fountain 304
Central Station 65
Chain O' Lakes 317
Chambers of Commerce 31, 36, 38, 41, 43, 45, 53, 55, 57, 71, 85, 87, 89, 93, 94, 98, 103, 111, 113, 115, 116, 118, 122, 127, 128, 130, 131, 207, 368, 371, 390
Checking/Savings Accounts 162
Chess 286, 287
Chicago
    Getting Around in 10
    Introduction to Neighborhoods 13
    Reputation of 6
Chicago Address Locator 15
Chicago Architecture Foundation 52, 270, 384, 388
Chicago Area Counties 16, 392
Chicago Bar Association 177, 200, 208, 391
Chicago Bears 8, 280
Chicago Blackhawks 280, 397
Chicago Board of Elections 183
Chicago Board of Trade 2, 65
Chicago Bulls 8, 279, 397
Chicago Cards (Transit) 352, 353
Chicago Convention and Tourism Bureau 359, 398
Chicago Cubs 181, 278, 375, 386, 397
Chicago Department of Housing 141
Chicago Fire 281, 331
Chicago Geography 4
Chicago Greeter 13, 14
Chicago Heights 58, 220, 226, 234, 240, 389
Chicago History 2, 27, 266, 271
Chicagoland 8, 16, 86, 104, 117, 118, 122, 124, 162, 166, 172, 176, 189-191, 196, 198, 199, 212, 231, 239, 242, 246, 250, 259, 260, 284, 290, 303, 307, 322, 332, 337, 346, 348, 349-351, 362, 363, 370, 390
Chicagoland Bicycle Federation 284, 351
Chicago Parent 31, 33, 36, 38, 41, 43, 45, 48, 50, 53, 56, 58, 60, 62, 66, 69, 71, 74, 76, 78, 81, 187, 215
Chicago Park District 76, 283, 285, 289, 290, 294, 295, 299, 337
Chicago Parks 299, 300, 318
Chicago Public Library 184, 204, 383

Chicago Public Schools 210, 217-219, 397
**Chicago Reading List, A** 383-388
Chicago Rents Right Hotline 141
Chicago Ridge 132
Chicago School (Architecture) 3
Chicago Skyway 346, 348
Chicago's Reputation 6
Chicago State University 127, 231
Chicago Steel 280, 281
Chicago Street Address Locator 15
Chicago Symphony Orchestra 1, 92, 255, 273
Chicago Transportation Authority (CTA) 10, 351
Chicago Urban League 69, 141, 395
Chicago Vehicle Stickers 175
Chicago White Sox 69, 279, 398
Chicago Wolves 104, 280, 281
**Chicago Year, A** 375-382
Child Abuse 210, 391
Childcare 84, 208-213, 215, 397
    General Resources for 214
**Childcare and Education** 208, 209-235, 397
Child Care Connections 214
Child Care Resource and Referral Agencies 210, 211
Children
    Culture for 273
    Moving With 158
    Volunteering With 338
Children and Family Services, Department of 210
Child Safety 214
Chinatown 69
Choruses 255
Christian 122, 185, 186, 226, 230, 231, 232, 234, 235, 325, 327-329
Christian Churches 326
Christian Scientist 328
Christmas 100, 239, 260, 330, 381, 382
Churches 26, 28, 32, 35, 37, 84, 85, 96, 226, 234, 255, 325-336
    Illinois Conference of 325
    National Council of 325
Circle Campus 58
Circle Line 352, 353
Citizens Utility Board 172, 174
City Colleges of Chicago 231

Cityfront 20
City Parks 299
City Stickers 175
Clarendon Hills 118
Classified Advertisements 136
Climate 319
Clybourn Corridor 27
Coach USA/United Limo 354
Coach USA/Van Galder 355, 371
College of DuPage 115, 234
College of Lake County 233
Colleges and Universities 1, 10, 17, 21, 23, 32, 33, 42, 43, 46-48, 57-60, 62, 65, 71-75, 81, 84, 85, 99, 101, 102, 104, 114, 115, 121, 122, 124, 127, 128, 130, 132, 135, 136, 138, 185, 189, 200, 218, 227, 231-235, 251, 254, 255, 257, 260, 263, 265, 267, 268, 270-272, 277-279, 281, 282, 295, 316, 328, 329, 335-337, 341, 355, 364, 365, 371, 375, 376, 383-388, 398
College Sports 278
Columbia College 1, 65, 185, 231, 257, 267, 271, 365
Columbian Exposition 72, 328, 386
Columbia Pointe 74
Columbus Park 289, 292, 300
Columbus Woodland and Lagoon 305
Comcast 171, 173, 185
Comedy 259, 376
Commercial Freight Carriers 152
Community Services 339
Commuter Trains 353
Complaints 134, 142, 143, 172-174, 185, 199, 200, 207, 349, 351, 391
    Consumer 174, 391
    Police 207
    Utilities 174, 200
Computer Equipment 241
Concert Facilities 259
Concordia University, 234
Condominiums 25, 42, 47, 57, 64, 65, 74, 84, 112, 135, 143-147
    Purchasing a 145
Consulates 205
Consumer Affairs 198, 200
Consumer Complaints 174, 200, 391
Consumer Protection 153, 167, 179, 185, 199, 200, 358, 391

# INDEX

Automobiles  179
Consumer Services  391
Container-Based Movers  152
Containerized Storage  157
Cook County Forest Preserves  79, 284, 310
Cook County Information  17
Cook County Nature Centers  310
Co-ops  146
Counseling  210, 218, 224, 332, 343
Credit Bureaus  145, 165, 197
Credit Cards  163
Credit Report  137, 145, 165
Credit Unions  161
Crime  13, 14, 42, 46, 47, 52, 62, 68, 72, 73, 88, 110, 115, 129, 135, 147, 192, 193, 218, 339, 371, 388, 392
Crime Prevention  339
Crisis Hotlines  391
Crown Fountain  304
CTA Transit Cards  351
Cultural Centers  266
Cultural Events Listings  253
**Cultural Life**  65, 184, 206, 253-275, 287, 301, 376, 394, 395
    for Kids  273

## D

Dance  256, 257, 287
Dan Ryan Expressway  346, 352
Daycare  209, 212
    Online Resources  212
Day Trips  318, 367
Deaf and Hearing-impaired
    Resources for the  203, 224
Dearborn Park  64
Deerfield  93
Department Stores  239, 240
    Discount  240
DePaul  32
DePaul University  32, 33, 104, 127, 138, 232, 254, 271, 278, 282
Des Plaines  102
DeVry Institute of Technology  232
Diaper Services  196
Directory Assistance  172
Disabilities  142, 177, 182, 202-204
    Services for People with  202, 366
Disabled Assistance  339

Disc Golf  289
Discount Department Stores  240
Discounts  70, 143, 175, 240, 245, 248, 268, 274, 281, 296, 357, 359, 360, 362, 394
Discrimination  142, 201, 206, 392
DNR  288, 316, 317, 369
Dog-friendly Parks  301
Doggie Beach  190, 302, 303
Dog Licenses  190
Dogs  8, 190-192, 205, 301-303, 311, 315, 318, 324, 376, 386, 387, 389
    and Beaches  190, 303, 315
Domestic Services  195
Dominican University  234, 271
Do Not Call Registry  171, 197
Door-to-Door Storage and Moving  152
Douglas  66
Douglas Park  300
Downers Grove  112
Drag Racing  282
Drinking Water  5, 23, 173, 174
Driver's Licenses  175, 176
Driving Laws  179
Driving While Intoxicated  179
Dry Cleaning Delivery  196
Dumpster Diving  246
DuPage County  17, 112, 113, 116, 166, 183, 188, 189, 204, 223, 225, 232, 311, 312, 378, 389, 392, 394
DuPage County Forest Preserve  311
DWI  179

## E

Earthlink  173
East Rogers Park  46
East Side  13, 314, 390
East Village  56
Eclipse Select  293
Ecumenical Worship  328
Edens Expressway  14, 95, 345
Edgewater  41
Education  93, 121, 122, 149, 205, 208-235, 295, 340, 397
    Volunteering in  340
Eisenhower Expressway  9, 58, 106, 300, 345
Elected Officials/Government  392
Electricity  170

Elk Grove Village  105
Elmhurst College  234
Emergency  393
Emissions Hotline  178
Emissions Test  178
Entertainment  254, 275, 394
Entertainment Hotlines  254
Entertainment Parks
  Children's  275
Environment
  Volunteering for the  340
EPA  23, 174, 197, 322
epinions.com  164
Episcopal Churches  326, 328, 330, 336
Equifax  145
Ethnic District Dining  249
Evangelical Churches  272, 329, 330, 336
Evanston  81
Evergreen Park  124, 126
Experian  145
Expressways  9, 10, 14, 23, 52, 58, 70, 95, 106, 300, 345-347, 353, 356
Exterminators  197

**F**

Fairs  1, 25, 26, 65, 71, 84, 142, 262, 269, 270, 301, 305, 332, 368, 372, 375-381, 385, 386, 392, 395
Fall  319
Fannie Mae  144, 149
Farmers' Markets  248
Federal Offices/Centers  394
Federal Trade Commission  145, 391
Fermilab National Accelerator Laboratory  370
Festivals  1, 26, 40, 61, 84, 87, 92, 93, 253, 255, 256, 258, 262, 263, 273, 333, 375-381
Fiction and Literature  384
Film  258, 376, 378-381
Film Festivals  376, 378, 380, 381
**Finding a Place to Live**  133-149]
Fines and Tickets  177, 181
Fireworks  378, 382
First Midwest Bank Amphitheatre  131, 261
Fishing  93, 288, 305, 311, 312, 314, 316-318, 368, 369, 372
Flooding  134

Food Shopping  247
Football  280, 292
Forest Preserves  2, 79, 128, 274, 284, 290, 307, 310-313, 337, 398
  Beyond Cook County  311
  Cook County  79, 284, 310
For Sale By Owner  148
Foster Care  340
Fountains  304
Fox College  234
Fraud  157, 200, 391, 392
Frisbee  289
Frisbee Golf  289
Furniture/Household Goods  242

**G**

Galena  367
Galleries  265, 266
Gallery Tours  265
Gambling  289
Gap, The  66
Garage and Yard Sales  246
Garbage  174, 175, 396
Garbage & Recycling  174
Garden(s)  20, 55, 68, 72, 80, 85, 91, 94, 96, 114, 258, 266, 300, 301, 306-308, 327, 337, 341, 376, 381
  Chicago-Area  307
  Chicago Botanic  91, 94, 307, 337, 381
  Nature  307
  Wildlife  307
Garfield Park  300
Gay and Lesbian Life  7, 26, 34, 42, 45, 188, 205-207, 294, 314, 330, 333
Geography
  of Chicago  4
Getting Around  10, 203, 345
  By Bike  350
  By Car  345
  By Public Transportation  351
**Getting Involved**  325-344
**Getting Settled**  14, 73, 169-193, 200, 207
GLBT  206, 207
Glencoe  90
Glenview  105
Gold Coast  14, 24-26, 54, 64, 73, 78, 133, 188, 212, 237, 360, 361, 363

# INDEX

Golf 20, 86, 89, 93, 98, 99, 101, 103, 110, 115, 118, 122, 127, 221, 238, 239, 289-291
Gompers Park Lagoon 305
Gompers Park Wetland Recreation 305
Government 392
Governors State University 127, 234
Grant Park 7, 10, 255, 287, 291, 295, 300, 302, 304, 376, 377-380
Great Fire 3, 26, 30, 56, 67, 331, 385
Great Lakes Information Network 318
Great Western Trail 370
Green Line 352
Greenspaces 48, 94, 190, 274, 294, 299, 396
**Greenspaces and Beaches** 48, 94, 190, 274, 294, 299-318, 396
　Resources 318
Greyhound Bus 354, 399
Grid System 15, 16
Grocery Stores 247
Groveland Park 67

## H

Habitat Company, The 138
Hamilton Park 300
Harbor Country 318
Hardware, Paints, and Wallpaper 243
Harper College 99, 102, 233
Health and Hospitals 340
Health and Medical Care 394
Health Clubs 296
Health Departments 189, 196, 393, 394
Heat Index 321
**Helpful Services** 134, 195-208, 366
Helpline
　Ticket 177, 181, 396
Heritage Clubs 344
Higher Education 208, 231
Highland Park 92
Highway Noise 135
Hindu Faith 333
Hinsdale 118
Historical Societies 30, 43, 45, 80, 81, 87, 94, 107, 341
Historic Districts 39, 42, 58, 79, 100, 388
Historic Preservation 91, 341, 385
History

　of Chicago 2
History Museums 266
Hockey 104, 280, 292
Hoffman Estates 105
Homeless 3, 332, 341
　Volunteering with the 341
Homeowner's Insurance 143, 144, 155
Homeschooling 230
Hometown 121, 126, 127, 222
Homewood Village 132
Horseback Riding 291
Horse Racing 282
Hostels 364
Hotel Reservation Companies 359, 362
Hotels
　Extended-Stay 362
　Inexpensive 362
　Luxury 360
　Middle-Range 361
Hotel Tax 360
Hotlines
　Crisis 391
　Emissions 178
　Entertainment 254
　HUD Fair Housing Complaint 142
　Non-Emergency 141
House, Condo and Co-op Hunting/Buying 143
Housing 395
Housing and Urban Development
　US Department of 144
Housing Cooperatives, National Association of 147
Housing Resource Center 141
HUD Fair Housing Complaint Hotline 142
Hurley Park Savanna 305
Hyde Park 71

## I

Ice Skating 90, 93, 291, 369
Indoor 291
Identification Card
　Military 176
　State 162, 176
I-GO 349, 399
Illinois Beach State Park 316
Illinois Commerce Commission 156, 172, 174, 203

Illinois Commerce Commission Consumer Services Division 172
Illinois Department of Commerce and Economic Opportunity 167
Illinois Department of Human Rights 142, 392
Illinois Institute of Art 23, 232
Illinois Institute of Technology 232, 364
Illinois Prairie Path 113, 115, 370
Illinois Public Schools 217
Illinois Secretary of State 176-178
Illinois State Board of Education 216, 217
Illinois State Identification Cards 175, 176
Illinois Tenants Union 142, 395
Indiana Dunes National Lakeshore 318, 370
Individual Education Plans 224, 226
Individual Family Service Plans 224
In-line Skating 291
Insects 134, 139, 196, 197, 306, 307, 323
Insurance
    Automobile 178
    Moving 155
    Renter's/Homeowners' 143
Integrys Energy Services 170
Interdenominational Worship 329
Internal Revenue Service 165, 398
International Newcomers 204
Interstate Moving 153, 154, 156
Intrastate Moving 156
**Introduction** 1-11
I-Pass 347, 348
IRS 156, 159, 165, 166, 213
Islam 333
ITT Technical Institute 130, 233

## J

Jackson Boulevard Historic District 58
Jackson Park 73-78, 289, 290, 299, 301, 305, 307
Jackson Park Bobolink Meadow 305
Jackson Park Lagoon 307
Jazz 67, 76, 92, 97, 185, 255, 256, 262, 367, 379, 380, 387
Jazz Festival 262, 379, 380
Jewish Faith/Culture 14, 49, 86, 228, 267, 272, 309, 310, 334, 337, 340, 385, 388
Jubilee College State Park 317

Junk Mail 197

## K

Kane County 17, 166, 183, 189, 224, 231, 394
Kendall College 233
Kenilworth 90
Kennedy Expressway 23, 52, 345, 347
Kenwood 71
Klipsch Music Center 260
Knowledge Systems Institute 233
Kohler Village 372

## L

'L' 10, 11, 13, 37, 47, 50, 52, 57, 84, 135, 180, 203, 261, 350-352, 355
La Grange 110
La Grange Park 110
Lake County 17, 92, 93, 169, 183, 188, 189, 211, 223, 225, 232, 233, 274, 312, 313, 393, 394
Lake County Forest Preserve 312, 313
Lake Forest College 233
Lake Geneva 234, 316, 356, 371
Lakeview 34
Landlord and Tenant Fact Sheet 142, 395
Landlords 42, 46, 133, 138, 140-143, 171, 200, 201, 395
Landlord/Tenant Rights and Responsibilities 140
Landmark Status 24, 56, 325, 327, 328, 331
LaSalle Street Station 354
Late Night Clubs 263
Lawyer Referral Service 177
Lawyers Committee for Better Housing 142
Leadership Council for Metropolitan Open Communities 142
League of Women Voters 183, 342
Leases 2, 135, 139-143, 151, 178, 181, 219, 246, 285, 362
Leash Law 190
Legal Assistance 142, 201, 342, 395
    for the Elderly 201
Legal Assistance Foundation of Chicago 142, 395
Legal Mediation/Referral Programs 200

# INDEX

Legal Referral  395
Legal Services  201
   Volunteering with  342
Lemon Law  179, 180
Lesbian and Gay Life  45, 188, 205-207, 294, 330, 333
Libraries  184, 270, 395
   Specialty  271
License Plates  177
Limousines  349
Lincoln, Abraham  67, 330, 368
Lincoln Park  301
Lincoln Park Addison Migratory Bird Sanctuary  306
Lincoln Park Alfred Caldwell Lily Pool  306
Lincoln Park (neighborhood)  29
Lincoln Park North Pond  306
Lincoln Park West  32
Lincoln Square  38
Lisle  118
Literacy  340, 342
Literary Life  65, 184, 206, 269, 395
Little Italy  58
Little Village  60
Local Lingo  7
Local Moves  156
Lodgings
   Accessible  365
   Inexpensive  362
   Luxury  360
   Middle-Range  361, 362
   Summer Only  364
Logan Square  51
Long-distance Telephone Service  171
Loop, The  6, 7, 9-11, 14, 15, 23, 26, 40, 60, 64, 65, 76, 78, 84, 88-91, 101, 102, 107, 121, 122, 124, 126, 127, 232, 248, 284, 299, 304, 330, 332, 345, 346, 352, 353, 368, 385, 388
   Explanation of  6
Lost and Found  356, 357
Lower West Side  60
Loyola University  42, 46, 48, 135, 185, 232, 272, 278, 279, 282, 364
Lutheran Churches  87, 103, 105, 228, 234, 329, 330, 336
Lyme Disease  324
Lyric Opera of Chicago  1, 256

## M

Madison, WI  371
Magnet School Programs  215, 218, 219
Magnificent Mile  1, 6, 9, 237, 244, 361, 363, 365, 381
   Explanation of  6
Mail  171, 181, 197, 198, 397
   Junk  197
Malls
   Outlet  239
   Shopping  237
Marcus Amphitheater  260
Marquette Park Ashburn Prairie  306
Mayors, Chicago  6, 8, 20, 65, 70, 104, 202, 207, 217, 254, 255, 306, 321, 322, 350, 375, 392, 394
McDonald's Cycle Center  284
McHenry County  17, 183, 211, 226, 393
Mediation  200, 201
Meeting People  343
Methodist  41, 45, 50, 234, 325, 330, 335, 336
Metra Commuter Railroad Service  353
Metropolitan Tenants Organization  142, 395
Michigan
   Southwest  372
Michigan City  239, 242, 346, 354, 370, 371
Midway Airport  122, 134, 346, 352, 355-357
Midwestern University  234
Millennium Street Station  354
Milwaukee, WI  372
**Money Matters**  161-167
Montessori Schools  230
Montrose Point Bird Sanctuary  306
Moraine Hill State Park  317
Moraine Valley Community College  121, 122, 234
Morgan Park  78
Morton Grove  105
Mount Greenwood  80, 124, 250
Mount Prospect  105
Movers  152, 153, 156, 157
   Interstate  153
   Intrastate and Local  156
Movie Theaters  21, 32, 84, 250, 258
Moving  151, 152, 157, 159, 167, 205

With Children 158
**Moving and Storage** 151-160
Moving Pets to the USA 205
MovingScam.com 154
Moving Truck Rentals 151
Moving Violations 177, 181
MSN8 173
Multiple Listing Service 148
Museums 264, 266, 273
   Art 264
   Children's 273
   History 266
   Outdoor 274
   Science 268
Music 33, 35, 40, 41, 66, 76, 254, 259, 260, 263, 273, 335, 377, 378, 387, 394
   Blues 262
   Children's 273
   Contemporary 259
   Folk/Country/Coffeehouse 263
   Jazz 262
   Organ 335
   Pop 263
   Professional and Community Symphonic, Choral, Opera, Chamber 254
   Radio 186
   Reggae 263
   Rock 261

**N**

Nannies 212, 213
Nanny Taxes 213
Naperville 115
National Council of Churches 325
National Forests 368, 369
National Historic Byway Road 369
National Lakeshore 318, 370
National Louis University 232
National Parks 368
National Register of Historic Places 34, 39, 42, 51, 77, 81, 92, 116, 313, 372
National University of Health Sciences 234
Natural Gas 169
Nature and Wildlife Gardens 307
Nature Centers 305, 310
Nature Gardens 307

Navy Pier 20, 274, 288, 291, 301, 376, 378, 379, 381
Near North 20
Near West Side 58
Neighborhood Parents Network 344
**Neighborhoods** 13-132
Neighborhood Watch 392
NetZero One 173
Newspapers and Magazines 14, 186
   Suburban 188
New Year Festivals and Parades 71, 121, 376, 382
Nichol's Park Wildflower Garden 306
NICOR 114, 170, 399
Night Clubs 261, 263
Nightlife 25, 32, 39, 181, 206
   Gay 206
Noise 134, 135
North Beverly 79
Northbrook 95
North Center 36
North Central College 234
North (Chicago Neighborhoods) 20
Northeastern Illinois University 232
Northern Illinois Gas 170
Northern Illinois University 234, 282
North & Northwest Suburbs 81
North Park University 232
North Pier 20
North Riverside 119
North Shore Gas 169
Northside Parents Network 213-216
Northwestern University 1, 21, 43, 46, 47, 81, 84, 136, 138, 185, 233, 254, 272, 278, 282, 316

**O**

Oak Forest 127
Oak Lawn 125
Oak Park 106
Oakton Community College 233
Ogilvie Transportation Center 180, 353, 354, 399
O'Hare International Airport 7, 10, 99, 101-105, 134, 232, 233, 345, 348-350, 354-357, 361, 371, 399
Old Town 26
Olive Park 301

# INDEX

Olmsted, Frederick Law  30, 301, 372
Online Banking  163
Online Resources
    Air Travel  357, 359
    Apartment Rental  137
    Banking & Credit  164
    Daycare  212
    Homebuying  148
    Moving and Relocation  159
    Travel  359
Online Service Providers
    National  173
Online Shopping  244
Online Tax Filing  166
Opera  1, 254, 256
Orange Line  352
Organs
    Antique or Vintage  335
Orland Park  129
Outdoor Concerts  114
Outdoor Shrines  335
Outlet Malls  239
Owl Service  261, 353
Ozone Alerts  322

## P

PACE Suburban Bus Service  353, 399
Palatine  105
Palos Heights  132
Palos Hills  2, 121, 126, 221, 234
Palos Park  132
Parades  1, 34, 62, 79, 206, 302, 376, 377, 379-382
Parent and Child Education and Support Society  214, 215
ParentLink  212, 214, 215
Park District Telephone Numbers and Websites  303
Park Forest  132
Parking  27, 34, 180, 181, 260, 261, 315, 337, 350, 355, 357, 390, 396
    Airport  355
    Valet  32, 55, 57
Parking Garages and Lots  180
Parking Permits
    Residential  180, 181
Parking Tickets  181
Parking Violations  177

Park & Ride  350
Park Ridge  105
Parks  283
    Chicago  299
    Chicagoland  303
    Dog-friendly  301, 303
    National  368
    State  316-318, 368-371
Parks and Recreation Departments  283, 396
Parochial Schools  227
Passports  183, 184
Paul Douglas Nature Sanctuary  307
Penske  152
Peoples Energy  169
Peoples Gas  169, 170
Peoria Charter  355
Permits
    Building  130
    Business  167
    Fishing and Camping  317
    for Dog-friendly Areas  93, 190
    Mooring  285
    Park & Ride  350
    Residential Parking  32, 35, 37, 180, 181, 396
Pest Control  196
Pet-friendly Apartments  138
Pet Insurance  192
Pet Laws & Services  190
Pet(s)  133, 138, 140, 156, 191, 192, 205, 244, 301, 303, 338
    Adoption of  191
    Lost  191
Photography  267, 343
Photo ID  176
Physician, Finding a  189
Physician Referral Services  189
picturingchicago.com  15
Pilsen  60
Pilsen East  61
Pink Line  352
PODS  152
Police  13, 182, 192, 193, 207, 357, 393, 396
Police Complaints  207
Politics
    Electoral  342
    Social  342
Pool  284

Pools 295
   Indoor 294
   Outdoor 294
   Private 295
Postal Services 153, 155, 160, 198, 396, 397
Post Offices 396
Potholes 199
Powell's 73, 270
Prairie District Homes 65
Prairie State College 234
Precipitation, Average 323
Presbyterian 331, 336
Pride Parade, Annual 34, 206, 377
Printers Row 65
Printers Row Book Fair 269, 270
Private Schools 228
Professional and College Sports 278
Property Taxes 84, 101, 103, 112, 117, 144, 166, 216
Prospect Heights 105
Public Schools
   Chicago 210, 217-219, 397
   Suburban 219
Public Transportation 107, 351, 399
Purple Line 352

## Q
Quick Getaways 367-373

## R
Radio Stations 185
RANCH 28
Ranch Triangle 27
Ravenswood 38
Ravinia Concert Facilities 260
Ravinia Festival 92, 93, 273
Real Estate Agents/Brokers 2, 134, 144, 145, 147, 148
Recycling 174, 175, 396
Red Line 352
Regional Transportation Authority 203, 351, 399
Religious Schools 228
Relocation 417
Relocation Assistance 136
Rental Agents 137

Rent Control 143
Renter's/Homeowner's Insurance 143
Residential Landlord and Tenant Ordinance 141
Resources
   Childcare 214
   Relocation and Moving 159
   School 215
   Sports 277
Restaurants 10, 20, 21, 22, 26, 28, 30, 32, 33, 35, 37, 39, 40, 42, 44, 45, 47-49, 52, 53, 55, 57-59, 61, 65, 70, 71, 77, 84, 97, 100, 104, 110, 116, 118, 119, 124, 186, 187, 188, 206, 237, 240, 249-251, 253, 260, 263, 264, 271, 294, 335, 356, 364, 369, 372
Ride Share 350
River City 65
River East 20
River North 22
Riverside 119
River West 22
Robert Morris College 130, 232
Rock Island Trail 317
Rogers Park 46
Rogers Park Community Action Network 142
Roller Skating 292
Rolling Meadows 105
Roman Catholic 331
Roommates 138
Roosevelt University 65, 101, 232, 260
Roscoe Village 36
Roselle 105
Rosemont 103
Rugby 292
Rules of the Road, Illinois 176
Running 244, 292, 386
Russian Orthodox 332, 336
Ryder 152

## S
Safe Drinking Water Hotline 174
Sailing 90, 285, 318
Saint Xavier University 122, 124, 130, 232, 277, 282
Sandmeyer's Bookstore 269
Sanitation 10, 174, 175, 246, 396, 397

# INDEX

413

Schaumburg 99
Schaumburg Woodfield Trolley 99
School Resources 215
Schools 210, 215-220, 226-228, 229-231, 397
    Catholic 227
    Chicago Public 210, 217-219, 397
    Illinois Public 217
    Parochial 227
    Private 228
    Public
        Registration 219
    Religious 228
    Suburban 219
Science Museums 268
Scottish Rite Cathedral 335
Seminary Co-op Bookstore 73, 269
Senior Services 342, 397
Shimer College 233
Shipping Services 198, 397
**Shopping** 237-251
    Online 244
    Second-hand 244
Shopping Malls 237
Shrines 335
Skiing
    Cross-country 310, 312, 313, 317, 367, 369, 372
Skokie 86
Small Schools 219
Smog 322
Soccer 281, 293
    College 281
    Youth 293
Social Security 201, 202, 394, 397
Softball 294
Soldier Field 62, 65, 76, 102, 118, 127, 261, 280
Soldier Field Concerts 261
Source Water and Assessment and Protection Program (SWAP) 173
South (Chicago Neighborhoods) 62
South Kenwood 73
South Loop 62
South Shore 76
South Shore Cultural Center 76, 78, 307, 308, 315
South Shore Cultural Center Nature Sanctuary 307

South Suburban College 127, 128, 235
South Suburban Housing Center 142
South Suburbs 119
Special Education 93, 218, 221, 224-226
Special Education Schools 226
Specialty Stores 241
Sport and Social Clubs 283, 344
Sporting Goods 243
Sports 97, 207, 244, 277, 278, 283, 292, 294, 299, 318, 325, 351, 367, 375, 396, 397
    Participant 283
    Professional and College 278
**Sports and Recreation** 97, 277-297, 299, 318, 325, 351, 367, 396, 397
Spring 320, 384
Springfield 368
Starting or Moving a Business 167
Starved Rock State Park 316, 369
State Identification Card 176
State Parks 316-318, 368-371
St. Ben's 36
Steppenwolf 1, 27, 257, 258
Stevenson Expressway 70, 346, 356
Stolen Cars 182
Storage 151, 152, 157, 158
Storage Facilities 158
St. Patrick's Day 376
Street-end Beaches 48, 313
Streeterville 20
Street Maintenance 398
Streets and Sanitation, Department of 10, 175, 397
Student Housing 85, 136
Sublets 138
Suburban Schools 219
Sullivan, Louis 3, 40, 56, 67, 266, 383
Summer 71, 127, 287, 288, 319, 321, 364, 377, 378
Supermarkets 42, 65, 119, 136, 139, 174, 247, 351
Swimming 294, 295
Synagogues 210, 325, 327, 334, 385

**T**

Taxes 127, 156, 159, 165, 166, 213, 398
    and Moving 159
    City of Chicago 166, 398

County 398
Federal 165, 398
Hotel 360
    Luxury 166
    Online Filing and Assistance 166
    Property and Sales 166
    State of Illinois 165, 398
Taxis 349, 355, 399
Taylor Street (neighborhood) 58
Telecommunications 129, 171
    Bundled 171
Telephone Service 170
Telephone Solicitations 171
Television Stations 184
Temperatures, Average 323
Temples, Buddhist 326, 379
**Temporary Lodgings** 359-366
Tenant Rights and Responsibilities 140
Tenants 25, 61, 135, 138, 140-142, 175, 395
Tennis 295
Theater 257
    Children's 275
    Professional and Community 257
Theater District 27
Thrift Stores 245
Ticket Helpline 177, 181, 396
Tickets
    Discounted 254
    Entertainment 254
Ticks 323, 324
Tinley Park 130
Title Fees 177
T-Mobile 172
Tollway Authority 347
Tornadoes 126, 321
Tourism 359, 367, 368, 371, 394, 398, 399
Towed Vehicles 182, 390
Tow Lots 390
Traffic 5, 7, 9, 17, 49, 54, 55, 99, 114, 129, 134, 177, 199, 214, 237, 239, 244, 284, 314, 321, 345, 346, 347, 390, 392, 398
Traffic Court 177, 390
Trains 353, 354
    Amtrak 354
    Metra 353
Train Service 399
Transit Cards 351, 353
**Transportation** 345-358, 399
TransUnion 145

Travel Agents
    Online 359
Trinity Christian College 122, 235
Trinity International University 233
Tri-state Tollway 346
Truck Rentals 151
TTY Phones 204

**U**

U-Haul 152, 158
UIC 10, 59, 60, 233, 261, 270, 279, 347, 361
UIC Medical Bookstore 270
UIC Pavilion 261, 279
Ukrainian Village 56
Union Station 101, 349, 354, 399
Unitarian Universalist Churches 107, 332, 333
United Center 261, 279, 280, 398
Unity Temple 106, 107, 333
University of Chicago 1, 10, 21, 71-75, 136, 185, 189, 232, 263, 265, 270, 272, 277, 328, 335, 337, 341, 364, 376, 383-388
University of Illinois-Chicago 10, 58, 60, 62, 65, 233, 272, 278, 295, 384, 386, 387
University of Illinois-Chicago
    (neighborhood) 58
University of Saint Francis 235
University Park 132
University Village 58
UofC 232
US Cellular Field 69, 118, 127, 132, 279
US Cellular One 172
US Citizen and Immigration Services 205
US Department of Housing and Urban
    Development 144
Used Bookstores/Sales 270
**Useful Phone Numbers & Websites** 389-400
US Small Business Administration Home
    Page 167
Utilities 169, 174, 200
Utility Complaints 174, 200
Utility Emergencies 399

**V**

Valet Parking 32, 55, 57
Valley Kids 215

# INDEX

Vehicle Registration 175, 177
Vehicle Stickers
    Chicago 175, 176, 180, 182
Velodrome 95
Verizon Online 173
Verizon Wireless 172
Veterinarians 192
Vintage Stores 244
Vital Records 400
Volleyball 25, 299, 314, 316
Volunteer Causes 338
Volunteering 336
Volunteer Placement Services 337
Voter Registration 182

## W

Waldorf Schools 230
Walking Tours 267, 367
Washington Park 301
Waste Management 175
Water
    Department 173
    Drinking 5, 23, 173, 174
Water Taxi Service 399
Weather 319, 321-323, 400
**Weather and Climate** 319-324
Weather Statistics 323
West (Chicago Neighborhoods) 49
Western Springs 110
Westmont 119
West Nile Disease 323
West Ridge 47
West Rogers Park 47
West Suburbs 106
West Town 51
Westwood College of Technology 233
Wheaton 113
Wheaton College 114, 234, 254, 329
Wheeling 105
Whirlyball 295
Wicker Park 53
Wildlife Gardens 307
Will County 17, 130, 211, 312
Will County Forest Preserve 312
Williams, Daniel Hale 67
Wilmette 88
Wind Speed, Average Annual 319
Winnetka 90

Winter 2, 20, 156, 169, 170, 199, 267, 271,
    280, 283, 292, 293, 312, 317, 319-321,
    323, 367, 369, 375, 381
Winterizing Your Car 199, 320
Wisconsin 8, 17, 27, 30, 44, 46, 167, 226,
    278, 288, 324, 345, 355, 371, 372, 399
Wisconsin Dells 371
Women and Children First 270
Women's Services 343
Woodlawn 74
Woodridge 119
World's Columbian Exposition 72, 328, 386
Worship
    Ecumenical 328
    Interdenominational 329
    Places of 89, 325
Wright, Frank Lloyd 3, 67, 72, 78, 90, 92, 106,
    107, 110, 116, 266, 333, 381, 383, 388
Wrigley Field 34, 35, 102, 278, 386
Wrigleyville 34

## Y

Yard Sales 246
Yellow Line 352
YMCAs 69, 96, 101-103, 107, 113, 116, 295,
    296, 332, 364
Youth Services 343

## Z

Zipcar 349
ZIP Code Information 198, 400
Zoos 30, 110, 268, 274, 275, 299, 301, 306,
    337, 377-381

## ABOUT THE AUTHOR

EILEEN MESLAR WAS BORN AND RAISED IN THE CHICAGO AREA. SHE lived in Kalamazoo, Michigan, for five years while attending Western Michigan University. After graduating with her BFA in Photography and Intermedia and a minor in Journalism from WMU, Meslar returned to her hometown and began photographing on a freelance basis. She currently holds a photography internship at the *Chicago Reader* and has contributed photos and stories to several other publications. In her spare time, she can be found at the scene of protests and marches in the city of Chicago, documenting free speech in action.

# READER RESPONSE

We would appreciate your comments regarding this sixth edition of the *Newcomer's Handbook® for Moving to and Living in Chicago*. If you've found any mistakes or omissions or if you would just like to express your opinion about the guide, please let us know. We will consider any suggestions for possible inclusion in our next edition, and if we use your comments, we'll send you a free copy of our next edition. Please e-mail us at readerresponse@firstbooks.com, or mail or fax this response form to:

**Reader Response Department**
**First Books**
**6750 SW Franklin, Suite A**
**Portland, OR 97223-2542**
**Fax: 503.968.6779**

Comments: _____

_____

_____

_____

_____

_____

_____

_____

Name: _____

Address: _____

_____

_____

Telephone: ( ) _____

Email: _____

**6750 SW Franklin, Suite A**
**Portland, OR 97223-2542**
**USA**
**P: 503.968.6777**
**www.firstbooks.com**

# RELOCATION RESOURCES

Utilizing an innovative grid and "static" reusable adhesive sticker format, *Furniture Placement and Room Planning Guide…Moving Made Easy* provides a functional and practical solution to all your space planning and furniture placement needs.

### MOVING WITH KIDS?

Look into *The Moving Book: A Kids' Survival Guide*.

Divided into three sections (before, during, and after the move), it's a handbook, a journal, and a scrapbook all in one. Includes address book, colorful change-of-address cards, and a useful section for parents.

Children's Book of the Month Club "Featured Selection"; American Bookseller's "Pick of the List"; Winner of the Family Channel's "Seal of Quality" Award

And for your younger children, ease their transition with our brand-new title just for them, *Max's Moving Adventure: A Coloring Book for Kids on the Move*. A complete story book featuring activities as well as pictures that children can color; designed to help children cope with the stresses of small or large moves.

### NEWCOMERSWEB.COM

Based on the award-winning *Newcomer's Handbooks*, NewcomersWeb.com offers the highest quality neighborhood and community information in a one-of-a-kind searchable online database. The following areas are covered: Atlanta, Austin, Boston, Chicago, Dallas–Fort Worth, Houston, Los Angeles, Minneapolis–St. Paul, New York City, Portland (Oregon), San Francisco, Seattle, Washington DC, and the USA.

### NEWCOMER'S HANDBOOKS®

Regularly revised and updated, these popular guides are now available for Atlanta, Boston, Chicago, China, Dallas–Ft. Worth, Houston, London, Los Angeles, Minneapolis–St. Paul, New York City, Portland, San Francisco Bay Area, Seattle, and Washington DC.

"Invaluable …highly recommended" – Library Journal

If you're coming from another country, don't miss the *Newcomer's Handbook® for Moving to and Living in the USA* by Mike Livingston, termed "a fascinating book for newcomers and residents alike" by the *Chicago Tribune*.

6750 SW Franklin Street
Portland, Oregon 97223-2542
Phone 503.968.6777 • Fax 503.968.6779
www.firstbooks.com